American Popular Music and Its Business in the Digital Age

American Popular Music and Its Business - The First 400 Years
Volume I - The Beginning to 1790
Volume II - From 1790 to 1900
Volume III - From 1900 to 1984
By Russell Sanjek

American Popular Music and Its Business In The Digital Age
1985 to 2020
By Rick Sanjek

For further information:
www.AmericanPopularMusicBusiness.com

American Popular Music and Its Business in the Digital Age

1985–2020

Rick Sanjek

OXFORD
UNIVERSITY PRESS

Oxford University Press is a department of the University of Oxford. It furthers
the University's objective of excellence in research, scholarship, and education
by publishing worldwide. Oxford is a registered trade mark of Oxford University
Press in the UK and certain other countries.

Published in the United States of America by Oxford University Press
198 Madison Avenue, New York, NY 10016, United States of America.

Library of Congress Cataloging-in-Publication Data
Name: Sanjek, Rick, author. |
Title: American Popular Music and Its Business in the Digital Age,
1985–2020 / Rick Sanjek.
Description: New York, NY : Oxford University Press, 2024. |
Includes bibliographical references and index.
Identifiers: LCCN 2024014982 (print) | LCCN 2024014983 (ebook) |
ISBN 9780197782897 (paperback) | ISBN 9780190653828 (hardback) |
ISBN 9780190653842 (epub) | ISBN 9780190653835 | ISBN 9780190653859
Subjects: LCSH: Sound recording industry—United States—History. |
Popular music—United States—Marketing. | Streaming audio—United States.
Classification: LCC ML3790 .S239 2024 (print) | LCC ML3790 (ebook) |
DDC 381/.45781490973—dc23/eng/20240409
LC record available at https://lccn.loc.gov/2024014982
LC ebook record available at https://lccn.loc.gov/2024014983

DOI: 10.1093/oso/9780190653828.001.0001

Paperback printed by Marquis Book Printing, Canada
Hardback printed by Bridgeport National Bindery, Inc., United States of America

FSC
www.fsc.org

MIX
Paper from
responsible sources
FSC® C103567

Contents

Illustrations

Art Direction and Photo Source Credits
Art Direction and Design by Christa Schoenbrodt
http://www.StudioHaus.net

Photo Images in Illustrations
"Music and Major Copyright Historic Highlights"
and
"The Evolution of Portable Playing Devices"
Courtesy of iStock
"About The Recording Academy®"
Courtesy of the Recording Academy®

Preface

This book is a sequel to the three-volume *American Popular Music and Its Business: The First 400 Years* written by my father, Russell Sanjek, and published by Oxford University Press in 1988. He had never before written a book but his compelling monograph *The War on Rock* published in *DownBeat* magazine in 1971 led him to Oxford editor Sheldon Meyer. In 1975 he started on what would become his life's most ambitious undertaking and final achievement.

The prologue to his first volume, *The Beginning to 1790*, opened with British privateer Sir Francis Drake's 1579 landing just north of San Francisco Bay to repair his ship, the *Golden Hind*, after raiding Spanish colonies along the Pacific Coast and before beginning its global circumnavigation. Drake was a fervent patron of the arts and a countertenor vocalist himself. His crew included performers who entertained at nightly dinners during his stop, whose audience often included Native American guests. This was the first-known performance of English-language music in North America.

The remainder of this volume then traced the development of the embryonic music business from England's Tudor dynasty forward through the colonization of the New World until the establishment of the American nation.

Volume II: From 1790 to 1900 further chronicled the evolution of the business of music in America through the events, people, and technology that defined, managed, and transformed it through to the turn of the twentieth century.

Volume III: From 1900 to 1984 picked up the narrative from that point and included discussion of the Copyright Act of 1909, which applied federal statute to the commercial use of music in the impending electronic age. It concluded in 1984, not due to any cultural allegory or historical event, but because the narrative had finally intersected with the present.

My father passed away in June 1986, though he did live long enough to read the first copyedited version of volume 1. My older brother, Roger, an urban anthropology PhD and professor/writer/editor of considerable renown, finished the editing for a 1988 publication. It was well received, winning among other accolades a Deems Taylor Award from ASCAP as one of the best music books of the year.

My younger brother, David, an English PhD and then the archives director at BMI, edited a 1992 condensed hardback version of volume 3 for Oxford University Press titled *American Popular Music Business in the Twentieth Century*. He added a brief update taking the narrative through 1991 and received a cowriter credit. He then expanded the update through 1995 for a Da Capo Press paperback version titled *Pennies from Heaven*, which contained the complete volume 3. This led him to a prodigious career as a writer on popular culture, culminating with a professorship in music at the University of Salford in Manchester, Great Britain. David was in conversation with Oxford about doing this book when he passed away in November 2011.

With encouragement from my brother Roger and the editors at Oxford University Press, I came to the realization that with my own then-over-forty year career in the music business, the experience I had within virtually all segments, and my academic degree in history, I was the person to pick up the torch and signed on in 2016 to author this volume.

The dust jacket of my father's original publication described his books as "telling the story of America's popular songs, the people who wrote them, and the business they created and sustained." This book expands upon that theme by adding the performers of those songs to the people who wrote them, as the modern music business involves well-defined streams of revenue for each category of creators. Even though often payable to the same person or group, these royalty sources remain distinctly separate as designated by copyright law and further delineated by negotiated agreements.

All revenue, whether from records, live performance, printed music, or artist merchandise emanates from consumer spending or from music licensed to movies, television, commercials, games, or other businesses that want to attract consumers to their products or services through brand association with music, whether subliminal or overt. This book compares the music business to a conduit through which this revenue flows until it reaches the creators after costs related to financing, managing, and marketing are deducted each step along the way.

Once into the project, I quickly discerned how great a role digital technology played in shaping the music business from 1985 forward. I used that realization to help structure the narrative, dividing the time frame into three parts.

The years 1985 through 1995 were dominated by the rise of the CD to almost triple consumer spending on music. Concurrently, digital technology displaced analog in recording studios and home audio systems. Administration and accounting were adapted to the ongoing advances in computer technology. In October 1994 use of the internet was extended to commercial exploitation.

From 1996 through 2006 the utilization of the MP3 by Napster for a massive wave of illicit file-sharing combined with the post-9/11 recession to reverse the consumer spending trend. Falling revenue was somewhat tempered by the 2003 debut of iTunes, which made legal downloading a viable alternative. Meanwhile Ticketmaster consolidated digital ticketing and Live Nation emerged out of the Clear Channel separation of its radio and concert divisions.

The years 2007 through 2019 saw the further decline of record industry revenue until Spotify introduced at-will on-demand legal availability to almost all the music ever recorded, leading to a rebound in consumer spending. The convenience of immediate access at a minimal cost transcended the constraints of time, place, and past industry-imposed limitations on content availability.

Eliminating the cost of accumulating a CD collection freed upper-income consumers to spend more on live music, allowing those willing to pay exorbitant prices for the best seats, and often for any seats at all, to contribute to increasing industry profits. The concert promotion behemoth created by the merger of Ticketmaster with Live Nation enabled *Pollstar*-tabulated revenue to catch up with the revitalized record business as both the recorded music and live performance sectors topped $11 billion in 2019.

Each of the book's three parts has five chapters. The first chapter outlines "The Game of Musical Thrones," tracing the growth, power structure, and leadership of the record business. Next, the "Records, Retail, Radio, and the Charts that Bind Them" chapter follows the relationship between these sectors as they set the pace for the entire industry. The third chapter examines the interrelated "Publishing, Copyright, Legislation, and Litigation" segments of the business.

Next, the fourth chapter, "The Creators of Music: Getting Paid," covers how and how much "the creators" of music get paid, and the people, companies, and developments integral to that process. The fifth chapter, "The Consumer: From Whom, How, and Where the Money Flows," focuses on "the consumers" who generate the money that fuels the music industry engine and the evolution of the technology that supports their music habit.

Over these three time periods digital innovation affected and altered the dynamics of the music business in ways never imagined. With the introduction of the internet, fans identified and interacted with artists through websites that became digital extensions of fan clubs. Social media platforms first led by

Facebook, MySpace, and YouTube; followed by SoundCloud, Bandcamp, and ReverbNation; then Twitter, Twitch, Pinterest, Instagram, Snapchat, and most recently TikTok, with undoubtedly more to come, have taken the relationship between creator and consumer to new levels of innovative synergism.

Artists were now able to produce new music and present it to the public independent of the industry's timetable. Digital technology has given consumers a greater opportunity than ever before, both passively and interactively, to influence and drive the market through data analysis of their buying habits, streaming selections, and concert attendance.

For those who haven't read my father's three volumes, I have included a prologue summarizing how the American music business developed through 1984, then continuing on to the trajectory, participants, and events of the unfurling digital age. The narrative ends in an epilogue covering 2020, a year dominated by the COVID-19 pandemic.

During one week in March the entire concert business was put on hold through the end of 2020 and beyond. The majority of the workers in the other sectors finished the year operating remotely. Even with this unexpected interruption, the consumer-creator relationship was still the economic engine that drove the music business through streaming subscriptions services; direct purchasing of physical, digital, or printed copies; buying artist merchandise online; or watching livestreamed or drive-in concerts that served as substitutes until the live performance sector returned to normal.

As of the end of the narrative, both the consumer base and creative community continue to expand as advances in technology generate new opportunities. Music is now an even greater part of people's lives, with ubiquitous access through mobile devices. The burgeoning global middle class drives the live performance industry, which is now poised to take it even higher now that we seem to be past the worst of the COVID-19 disruption. For creators, consumers, and the music business that connects them, the world grows bigger and smaller at the same time. The business has been altered, but still survives to facilitate access for consumers and maximize financial returns for creators.

Despite the transformations wrought by the digital age, the major labels remain the most effective and well-funded path for achieving universal marketing saturation. This does not, however, guarantee a hit, much less longevity, for seldom is a career built on and then sustained by one record.

This doesn't mean, however, that artists can't achieve success and enjoy a career without a major label as more than one-third of record industry revenue goes through independent or artist-owned labels, or direct to artists and songwriters through digital revenue collection agencies. There is also a vibrant live performance market that supports thousands of artists who never make the top chart listings but nonetheless make a living through their music. As always, the scope of each artist's success is based upon a unique blend of talent, luck, perseverance, aspiration, and circumstance in the ever-shifting, multidimensional matrix we have come to know as the music business.

As the world turns and as time advances without pause, the beat goes on as music remains the ever-evolving emotional tie that unites us and provides the underlying rhythm track to the lives of people around the globe.

Acknowledgments

My thirst for knowledge and infatuation with history began while still in grade school. After exhausting the Landmark series of children's history books, I discovered my father's copies of Will and Ariel Durant's *The Story of Civilization* and the Year's *Pictorial History of the World*. At the same time I was surrounded by the latest jazz, blues, Broadway show, R&B, folk, jazz, country, and rock-'n'-roll record releases my father would bring home to share with his three sons.

My immersion in history continued throughout secondary school and then at Yale, where I was particularly inspired by Professor Howard Lamar's courses on American history. As far as music, I was the guy with a stereo system in his dorm room sharing the music of Bob Dylan, The Beatles, Joan Baez, The Rolling Stones, Thelonious Monk, John Coltrane, Big Bill Broonzy, Ramblin' Jack Elliott, and so many others with anyone who would listen.

In 1971 I moved to Nashville. For the next fifteen years I worked directly with a series of five mentors, all inductees into at least one hall of fame, from whom I learned the intricacies of the relationship between the art and the business of the music industry.

First was Frances Preston at BMI, who schooled me in the rudiments of music licensing and the social etiquette of the music business. Next came Jerry Wexler, who entrusted me with opening a country music division for Atlantic Records. Our first artist was Willie Nelson, with whom I shared in the breakout of the outlaw country genre. Then three years with Sun Records legend Cowboy Jack Clement reignited my belief in the magic of music, after which Pete Drake, the "King of the Talking Steel Guitar," recruited me to manage his businesses for four years, which included securing international distribution, expanding his publishing companies, initiating a television co-production with Dick Clark, and experiencing multiple trips up the charts.

From 1986 through 1992 I rejoined Frances Preston at BMI but this time in New York as vice president of writer/publisher relations. I also served the Recording Academy as a trustee, president of the New York chapter, and member of both the awards and nominations and the New York Grammy host committees.

From 1992 forward I applied the knowledge and experience I had accumulated to work as an independent producer, publisher, artist manager, and licensing consultant. Finally, I combined all these experiences with my academic training to begin researching and writing this book in 2016.

I extend my deepest thanks and appreciation to Oxford University Press and especially Suzanne Ryan, former editor-in-chief and humanities/executive editor, music, who signed me to do this project; to my acquisitions editor, Norman Hirschy, and title manager, Rachel Ruisard, who have guided me to its completion; and to senior production editor Gwen Colvin for shepherding this project through to galley proofs and then production.

My thanks also go to my family, without whom I never would have been ready for this endeavor; to my father, who set high standards in honesty, intellectual curiosity, and appreciation of all things that are fine; to my mother, from whom I learned to never stop learning; to my late younger brother, David, whose passion for all forms of art was only exceeded by his desire to share it with others; and to my older brother, Roger, and his wife, Lani, whose love for the spirit of jazz is only matched by their social conscience and dedication to the needs of all humanity.

Roger also walked me though the initial stages of becoming an author of an academic work. I also wish to thank David's University of Salford friends and colleagues Stephen Davismoon, Kirsty Fairclough, Ben Halligan, Tim Wise, and Tom Attah, and Mark Duffett from the University of Chester, whose collective memories of David inspired me in his stead; Geoff Koch whose enthusiasm for this project motivated me at the very beginning; Laura Helper Ferris for tutoring me in the structure of academic writing; Randy Rayburn, David Bennett, Raymond Thomasson, Judge Tommy Brothers, Peter Obermeyer, and John Michael Seigenthaler, my monthly lunch round table and primary text chain; and other good friends Paris Gordon, Julia Brothers, Sara Obermeyer, Mitchell Galin, Lou Chanatry, Andy Van Roon, Mike Millius, Charlie Feldman, Mark Fried, Tim Wipperman, Al Griffin, Steve Azar, Ray Harris, Craig Oxford, Rose Drake and Sir Fred Cannon, Becky Hobbs and Duane Sciacqua, Charles and Alicia McCutcheon, Jim and Helen Stewart, and Richard and Beth Courtney who served in varying degrees as sounding boards, proofreaders, willing listeners, and constructive critics as this book transitioned from inception to completion. And to Christa Schoenbrodt who transformed my concepts for illustrations into the thirty graphics that so illuminate this book's narrative.

Industry colleagues who contributed information, encouragement, insights, and perspective include Bart Herbison, Beverly Keel, Bill Velez, Bob Emmer, Dickie Kline, Don Passman, Doug Howard, Freddie Gershon, Irv Lichtman, Jay Samit, Jim Zumwalt, Joanne Boris, Joe Mansfield, Joe Serling, John Velasco, Josh Friedlander, Marc Jacobson, Marshall Wilcoxen, Mike

Martinovich, Neil Gillis, Pat Rogers, Paul Moore, Peter Thall, Phil Graham, Randy Talmadge, Randy Wachtler, Stan Byrd, Steve Leeds, Vincent Candilora, and Willie Young.

This book is dedicated to all of the above and the thousands of others I have encountered over the course of my life for whom the love of music—from the first memory to the latest stream—has never waned.

Rick Sanjek
Nashville, TN
September 2023
AmericanPopularMusicBusiness.com

Prologue

Part One: The Roots of the Music Business

In the Beginning

Since the dawn of history, music has been a part of human society. Our voices were our first instruments. Our ancestors created music by singing, humming, whistling, clicking, and any other sound the mouth and vocal cords could create and the brain could organize into patterns of cadence and melody. Every voice is singular in its qualities of tone, timbre, pitch, and resonance, just as unique as every face and every set of fingerprints.

While some voices might sound alike, digital analysis of various vocal metrics as well as some people's ears can distinguish the difference between even the most similar voices. Some voices evoke a deeper level of passion than most others can elicit. An intense degree of both emotional and cognitive stimulation can occur when those singularly distinctive voices are coupled with unique melodies and lyrics set to a specific combination of rhythm and tempo that can result in a universally acclaimed performance.

As societies evolved, instruments were hand-crafted out of organic materials creating drums, shakers, flutes, whistles, mouth harps, and stringed instruments both bowed and plucked. With the rise of civilization, voices and instruments were utilized for both religious and secular rituals. When metal work was developed as a craft for tools, weapons, and household goods, it was adapted to musical instruments as well, creating horns, cymbals, and bells. Both state and church sponsored and supported those vocalists and musicians who could best sway the masses whether at work, war, worship, recreation, ritual, or revelry.

Music First Becomes a Business

As Western Europe advanced through the Renaissance, Reformation, and Age of Enlightenment, private commerce emerged from under the thumbs of both church and state. The recently invented movable-type printing press was taken out of exclusive church and state control and made available for the printing of secular music and verse. These first music publishers sold sheets of new lyrics called broadsides that were sung to the most popular melodies. After the typesetting of musical tablature was perfected, the sale of sheet music for both vocal and musical arrangements developed as another consumer product with music printed either alone or coupled with lyrics.

Listening to music, however, was unlike the consumption of physical goods or delivery of professional services, as music could deliver an emotional experience. Soon the commercial exploitation of music shifted into the hands of entrepreneurs who could cater to both the ruling class and the masses. Following the rise in disposable income for the wealthier members of the new mercantile society where commerce was encouraged, publishers and promoters applied a rudimentary understanding of supply and demand to the marketing of music.

The progenitors of today's concert industry built enclosed performance spaces like Shakespeare's Globe Theatre in London to control access by managing the supply of tickets, and thus monitor the flow of revenue. They calculated both the cost of presentation and the optimal price of admission to maximize both consumer demand and monetary return. Theaters emerged in other major cities including Milan's La Scala, the Walnut Street Theatre in Philadelphia, the Hôtel de Bourgogne in Paris, and the Theater an der Wien in Vienna.

Music publishing and live performance formed the foundation for the commercialization of music over the next several hundred years, led by a cadre of people willing and able to fund, promote, and manage segments of the fledgling entertainment industry. As most performers, musicians, lyricists, and composers had neither the inclination, expertise, nor resources to do so themselves, they depended on the competency, honesty, and instincts of these entertainment entrepreneurs in whom they entrusted their careers. The ability to gauge the public's interest in and its willingness to pay for tickets and printed copies became the barometer for how much, for what, in whom, and when to speculate in this high-risk but potentially high-reward industry.

This relationship is now over four hundred years old and has always been a complex one. As the music industry grew and became increasingly profitable, the need for contracts also evolved to assure exclusivity over the services of creators in order to maximize the return on investment. These contracts also defined how the money spent by consumers was divided. The music entrepreneurs initially had the upper hand as they had more experience, greater monetary resources, and multiple artists available to them. With growing popularity artists strengthened their negotiating position.

Relationships between the creators and their business partners were almost always the most successful when the initial terms were fair and respectful.

During the nineteenth century, industrial age engineering transformed the manufacture of musical instruments from a craft to a business targeting the rapidly expanding American population for whom music was the primary form of entertainment, whether at home, in social settings, or in performance venues. Just before the turn of the twentieth century, music publishers began to coalesce around what became known as Tin Pan Alley, located on Manhattan's West 28th Street between 5th and 6th Avenues. These publishers offered songs to musical theater, vaudeville, burlesque, minstrel, and other shows through employees known as song pluggers. Placement in successful shows turned into touring troupes, motivating consumers to buy sheet music and musical instruments. Song pluggers often offered financial and other incentives to the top entertainers to perform their songs, sometimes including coauthorship with a share of the resulting songwriter royalties. This practice triggered the bribery scandals of the early 1900s, the forerunner of the radio payola or pay-to-play scandals of ensuing generations.

New technology expanded the business opportunities between industry segments. The first player piano, known as an organette, debuted in the late 1860s, but widespread consumer interest in player pianos accelerated in the 1890s with a mass-produced pianola by the Aeolian Company that contained a playing mechanism with two interactive elements. A bellows blew a steady stream of air against a continuous paper roll on a spool that was propelled at an even speed through the playing device over a set of levered hammers, one for each key on the piano, onto a take-up spool. Each roll contained the musical arrangement of one song precisely notched into the paper so that as the roll passed under the air stream, the size and placement of the holes controlled the strike of the hammers to depress the appropriate piano keys to replicate what a pianist's fingers would have played. The Aeolian's bellows were manually operated by a pneumatic mechanism with foot pedals akin to an organ. The songs that would be played through this roll-playing device had to be licensed from their publishers.

Adapting to Electronic Technology

Beginning in the 1880s a determined and competitive cadre of innovative entrepreneurs inspired by the success of the telegraph in 1837, and the telephone in 1876, experimented with electronic devices that would record and transmit audio signals. Thomas Edison and Emile Berliner each filed patents for recording devices while Guglielmo Marconi, Nikola Tesla, and Lee de Forest each developed patents for radio signal technology.

In 1900 a nascent record business that sold 2.75 million units was dominated by three companies: Edison's National Phonograph Company, selling only wax cylinders; the Victor Talking Machine Company, selling only Berliner's discs; and the Columbia Phonograph Company, selling their own versions of both formats. Sales reached 27.5 million units by 1909. In 1915 Edison added his own disc to counter the declining cylinder market as the first battle of the formats was won by Berliner's shellac, flat disc and gramophone over Edison's wax cylinder and phonograph, although the term "phonograph" outlasted gramophone in the public vernacular.

Meanwhile electric motors had replaced the manual operation of pianolas. Coin-operated versions were also introduced. By 1904 the Welte-Mignon company had perfected the self-playing process so precisely that master-quality rolls were created to use for mass reproduction. Ampico, Duo-Art, and Hupfeld's Triphonola soon joined Welte-Mignon in what was to become a thriving business. The most famous pianists of the age were recruited and paid to record and often autograph the master rolls for verification as the closest possible facsimile of live performance.

In 1907 Giacomo Puccini proclaimed, "The reproducing piano renders the characteristics of the artist in the most perfect manner!"[1] Arthur Rubenstein added, "As the reproducing piano plays it, it seems that I am performing myself."[2] Other artists whose works were featured as part of this new technology included Gershwin, Stravinsky, Rachmaninoff, Saint-Saëns, Ravel, Debussy, Landowska, and Paderewski. Thousands of songs were licensed to be reproduced on rolls with millions sold to owners of reproducing pianos. By 1920 over two hundred thousand player pianos were sold annually, more than half of the total number of pianos sold.

The commercialization of electronic technology, led by the pianola and the competing phonograph and gramophone, expanded publishing revenue. Retail supply chains were established. Compensation for creators and rightsholders, however, had to be determined, including how and how much to collect, and then how to allocate the proceeds. If negotiation or application of existing statute failed to accomplish an equitable equation, the claimants could lobby for new legislation or pursue litigation. New technology could also shift power and market share, which attracted high-risk investors eager to capture market share in a business that offered glamour and the potential for high returns.

Congress passed the Copyright Act of 1909 to keep statutes governing intellectual property in step with the technological advances of the electronic age, as well as in harmony with the terms of the 1886 Berne Convention, an international intellectual property compact that granted equal protection to songs originating in other signatory nations. Most of Western Europe already conformed to the Berne standards, but the US did not. The 1909 act did not contain all of the provisions of Berne necessary to become a signatory, but it did further expand US copyright protection through several provisions that did conform to Berne standards.

The act created a statutory compulsory license rate of 2¢ per track to be paid to publishers for the mechanical reproduction of musical compositions, first applied to the thriving piano roll business and subsequently to sound recordings. Unlike Berne, however, the 1909 act did not include governmental copyright protection for the sound recordings themselves, and hence no federally legislated recourse to combat copyright infringement, which was defined as use of music for profit without a license in the recording itself. There was, however, protection in the act against infringement on the copyright in the song embedded within the recording. Recourse for infringement on recordings remained under the jurisdiction of individual state statute.

The act also established the performing right for copyright owners of musical compositions, whereby a business needed a license to use the performance of a musical composition, whether live or recorded, to make or enhance its profit. This right was a part of the bundle of rights afforded protection in Berne territories. Although the act did not set US rates for performing rights, leaving them open to negotiation between licensor and licensee, it did make infringement subject to adjudication in federal court, with statutory and punitive damages set at a high level. There were no provisions, however, for governmental prosecution of copyright infringement, leaving the burden of litigation up to those making the claim.

In 1914 a small group of composers and music publishers formed the American Society of Composers, Authors and Publishers (ASCAP), the first American performing right organization (PRO). ASCAP was modeled after European PROs such as Société des Auteurs, Compositeurs et Éditeurs de Musique (SACEM), founded in France in 1851; and Società Italiana degli Autori ed Editori (SIAE), founded in Italy in 1882. The British Performing Right Society (PRS) was also founded in 1914 under the auspices of the United Kingdom's Copyright Act 1911.

ASCAP's mission was to collect performing rights revenues and distribute the net after administration costs to its members. ASCAP also lobbied and litigated for protection and expansion of its members' rights. Famed ASCAP composer Victor Herbert had to go all the way to the US Supreme Court to validate the Copyright Act of 1909's performing rights provisions. In the

1917 ruling in *Herbert et al. v. The Shanley Company* regarding the necessity for an ASCAP license for restaurants playing music, Justice Oliver Wendall Holmes Jr. wrote, "Music is part of the total for which the public pays. . . .If music did not pay, it would be given up. If it pays, it pays out of the public's pocket. Whether it pays or not, the purpose of employing it is profit and that is enough."[3] After the ruling, ASCAP began in earnest to license theaters, dance halls, restaurants, and other entities that were using live music to enhance their business.

The Post–World War I Business Boom

During the post–World War I economic boom, the electronic technology developed during the war dramatically expanded both the public's options for consuming music and business opportunities to profit from them. After federal radio licenses were established in 1920, ASCAP added the fledgling radio industry to the other businesses from which it sought revenue.

The broadcast of music over radio not only provided a potential new source of performing rights revenue for music publishers and songwriters but also created fees for artists for their live performances negotiated by the American Federation of Musicians (AFM). It was also a new medium for stimulating sheet music, piano roll, and theater ticket sales. Almost all music on radio was performed live and remained so well into the 1930s as the radio industry continued to consider sound recordings inferior to live performance in audio fidelity, while the sound recording manufacturers maintained that playing records on radio was detrimental to sales and a violation of copyright.

By 1919 Berliner's original disc patents had expired, allowing the industry to shift almost exclusively to shellac discs. Unable to successfully compete, Edison's National Phonograph Company folded in 1929. Victor, with its iconic His Master's Voice logo featuring a terrier named Nipper listening to the horn of a gramophone, and Columbia became the original set of major labels. The entire industry surpassed $100 million in retail sales in 1920.

At first, the labels focused on artists who had become popular in Broadway theaters and national vaudeville tours, but soon they were also recording artists from the American hinterland who were unknown to urban audiences. Atlanta-based Bessie Smith was signed to Columbia by talent scout Frank Warner. New Orleans–born Louis Armstrong recorded on OKeh Records, an independent label acquired by Columbia in 1926. In 1927 in Bristol, Tennessee, Victor producer Ralph Peer and founder of the peermusic publishing company recorded both the local Carter Family and a former railroad brakeman from Meridian, Mississippi, named Jimmie Rodgers. These now legendary performers emerged from middle America to rival the established stars of vaudeville and Broadway.

In 1925, recording into recently invented condenser microphones replaced performing into audio horns, which had been standard equipment up to that point. These new electrical recordings were a monumental improvement in audio quality and frequency range over the earlier acoustic recordings. The larger electronics companies manufactured both records, as the discs were now called, and record players. Recording and playing speeds were standardized at 78.26 rpm, and the records sold to the public became known as 78s. The conformity in speed allowed for any disc to be played on a machine from any manufacturer for both home and coin-operated devices, opening the door for independent record companies not owned by player manufacturers to compete for record sales.

The 1920s were also a period of expansion for the radio industry, beginning with the issuing of federally regulated radio licenses in 1920, and the establishment of the Federal Radio Commission (FRC) in 1927, succeeded by the Federal Communications Commission (FCC) in 1934. Radio stations generated revenue by selling program sponsorships, and eventually spot advertisements, to manufacturers and service providers wanting to introduce their wares to radio's expanding audience. In 1926, NBC launched the first national radio network, and live programs were transmitted over telephone wires to local stations, who in turn broadcast them over the air. Reception benefited from the use of vacuum tube technology based on de Forest's Grid Audion triode tube, the first vacuum tube to amplify electrical signals.

In 1927 Broadway star Al Jolson performed in *The Jazz Singer* with his audio track synchronized to the film's moving images. The movie industry was quickly transformed by replacing silent movies that had been accompanied by local musicians playing the background score with sound-on-disc technology played in sync with the movie. Within a few years the more efficient sound-on-film technology, with sound and film playing through the same projector, became the industry standard. The success of talking pictures added a new stream of publishing revenue with both new songs and music scores written specifically for the movie soundtracks.

Movie studios bought Tin Pan Alley publishing firms and made it worthwhile for many successful composers, lyricists, musicians, arrangers, and conductors to move to Hollywood. Nationwide movie releases joined network radio as national platforms for the most popular entertainers. Al Jolson, Fred Astaire, Eddie Cantor, Bing Crosby, and Mae West led the transition from live performances and record success to talking pictures and network radio. Shirley Temple, Alice Faye, Gene Autry, and Judy Garland established themselves as major stars on radio and in movies before going on to recording success.

A multi-disc music player with a selector mechanism debuted in 1927 that could alternately choose a different 78 rpm disc off of one of eight spindles. A year later player piano manufacturer Seeburg introduced this device as the coin-operated Audiophone, then soon replaced it with the ten-disc Selectophone. These new machines used the same amplification technology that had improved home radio receivers and record players.

The Great Depression Slows the Tempo

With the advent of the Great Depression in late 1929, the music industry—including the record, print, musical instrument, and live performances segments—along with so many others dependent upon disposable consumer income, financially contracted. The player piano industry switched to the coin-operated, disc-playing machines that enabled speakeasies and clubs to replace the cost of live performers with revenue-generating, fully orchestrated performances with vocals rather than the solo instrumental performances offered by coin-operated pianolas. Supplying a stream of new discs sustained the record business during this time, especially the companies that distributed the favorites of the working-class listeners who patronized local clubs. By 1940 they were commonly known as jukeboxes after the juke joint drinking and dancing establishments popular throughout the South, with the term "juke" believed to have been derived from a rural African American term for rowdy or bawdy.

By 1930, the number of federally licensed radio stations had increased to over five hundred from fewer than fifty in 1920. By 1935, after fifteen years of negotiations, litigation, and legislation, ASCAP had established that radio stations were subject to the performing rights provision of the 1909 Copyright Act and entered into an agreement with the National Association of Broadcasters (NAB), acting on behalf of the radio industry. This agreement resulted in a five-year blanket license for a performing rights royalty of 5 percent of advertising revenue. ASCAP collected these fees directly from the stations and three major networks, then distributed them, after deduction for overhead, using the network programming to determine the division of royalties. This system established the use of a sample, or reduced percentage, rather than a census, or total count, method as the basis for royalty determination for radio play.

The NBC Network show *Your Hit Parade* ran on radio from 1935 through 1955, and on television from 1950 to 1959. It featured the first chart listing the relative popularity of the week's top songs. Their weekly rankings presented "an accurate, authentic tabulation of America's taste in popular music."[4] The selected songs were performed live by an in-house ensemble with the week's top song as the finale, indelibly imprinting the concept of a weekly #1 record in the rubric of the record business and, consequently, in the minds of the public. *Billboard*, the trade magazine of the entertainment business launched in 1894 and known as the "bible of the music business," introduced its own printed version of a *Hit Parade* in 1936, changing its name in 1940 to the national "Music Popularity Chart."

The music-consuming American public had become two distinct audiences. A mostly urban, middle- to upper-class segment listened to the songs featured in nationally distributed movies and network radio programs, primarily Tin Pan Alley, Broadway, and Hollywood movie compositions performed by major movie stars, network radio personalities, or big band ensembles. The big band bandleaders became well-known personalities throughout the 1920s and 1930s with top billing over their featured vocalists both on records and in live performance.

The other segment was mostly a rural or small-town, working-class audience listening to what then was termed race and hillbilly music played on jukeboxes in clubs and on local non-network radio programs, or in live performance on weekends. A few race and hillbilly artists achieved national success in movies or on network radio, but most performed on a regional basis with their records and live appearances co-promoting each other to establish, sustain, and extend their fan bases.

The ASCAP Boycott and Birth of BMI

By 1940, over 80 percent of American households had radios. Advertising on 618 FCC-licensed stations generated $215.6 million in advertising revenue. In 1939 the ASCAP agreement with radio was set to expire in eighteen months, and ASCAP proposed a raise in their rate of 5 percent of radio's advertising revenues. The NAB rejected the offer, ASCAP didn't budge, and the radio industry prepared to stay on air without ASCAP music. In anticipation of this ASCAP boycott, CBS attorney Sydney Kaye convinced the stations to organize an alternative PRO, which Kaye named Broadcast Music, Inc. (BMI), to represent the music not written or published by ASCAP members and thus available to the stations as legally licensed. Kaye then moved to BMI full time as both in-house attorney and head of operations. ASCAP, then and still a membership association, had fewer than a thousand songwriter and publisher members, primarily based in New York or Los Angeles, supplying songs for Broadway, movie, and network radio performers. Only these members received royalties from the licensing fees ASCAP collected from radio and other sources.

During the eighteen months preceding the January 1, 1941, start of the boycott, BMI assembled music from non-ASCAP publishers as well as signed a few catalogs that moved over from ASCAP. Many of them represented Latin, hillbilly, race, and other indigenous music genres as well as copyrighted arrangements of public domain songs, including Stephen Foster compositions. BMI distributed sheet music to stations for performance on live music programs once the boycott began.

ASCAP members' sheet music and record sales declined and their songs from films could not be performed on radio to coincide with their theatrical releases. In October 1941, ASCAP finally agreed to a license at a lower rate, but its repertoire was still limited to its members' catalogs. The stations maintained their licenses with BMI at a lower rate than the new ASCAP agreement to retain the music they had played during the boycott and to serve as a hedge against ASCAP boycotting at the next contract negotiation. Shortly thereafter *Billboard* established the *Harlem Hit Parade* chart, which soon became the *Race Records* chart and subsequently the *Rhythm & Blues* chart. Rural American music created by what would later be termed country performers was tracked in the new "Hillbilly Hits" record chart.

Records and Radio: Contention Turns to Cooperation

Prior to 1940, record companies had included the notice "unlicensed for public broadcasting" on record labels, still maintaining that playing records on radio damaged sales. Many stations, however, started playing records as they deemed the electronically recorded 78s, unlike their acoustically recorded predecessors, suitable for broadcast. Moreover, the discs were far cheaper than live musicians and they could be played multiple times. In 1935 New York's WNEW launched its subsequently long-running *Make Believe Ballroom*, with announcer Martin Block simulating a live theater performance. Block himself bought the records and secured the initial advertisers.

Famed columnist and radio commentator Walter Winchell coined the term "disc jockey" to categorize Block's approach to radio programming.

By 1940, playing records had become widespread enough for the record companies to file a lawsuit claiming copyright infringement, but a federal circuit court ruled against them. Then in August 1942 the AFM went on strike against the record companies, with the union refusing to allow members to play on new recordings unless the labels agreed to keep the records off the radio in an attempt to preserve member jobs playing live on radio. The stations, however, now felt legally free to play records and continued to do so. With the major labels now unable to use musicians on new recordings, they met the increased listener demand by servicing stations with older material.

This also opened the door for independent labels like Capitol Records, newly formed by songwriter/producer/vocalist Johnny Mercer; former Tin Pan Alley lyricist-turned–Paramount Pictures producer Buddy De Sylva; and Hollywood-based record store–chain owner Glenn Wallichs. Before the strike commenced, Mercer quickly stockpiled enough masters to last for over a year. Along with other independents, Capitol focused on vocalists with smaller combos rather than big bands, shipped free records to radio stations, and employed other methods of promotion to help shape the mutually beneficial relationship between radio and record companies that would last for decades.

Star billing on radio shifted away from bandleaders like Paul Whiteman, Fred Waring, Harry James, and the Dorsey Brothers to their former lead vocalists. Bing Crosby, Dick Haymes, Perry Como, Kitty Kallen, Rosemary Clooney, Peggy Lee, Kay Starr, Georgia Gibbs, Margaret Whiting, and Jo Stafford increased in popularity and would go on to dominate the charts for the next decade.

Perhaps the epitome of this shift to vocalists was the remarkable rise of former Harry James and Jimmy Dorsey vocalist Frank Sinatra, first to teen idol and then to movie star and cultural icon. The bobbysoxer craze of the early 1940s that propelled Sinatra's career wasn't that much unlike the earlier fan reaction to Al Jolson, Eddie Cantor, and other stars of vaudeville and Broadway, but was intensified by the presence of network radio and talking pictures that had not existed in that earlier era.

Without new material to sell, the major labels sought to settle with the union in September 1943. When Columbia and the renamed RCA Victor capitulated in November 1944 the strike was effectively over. With this last hurdle cleared, the end to what now seems to be an illogical animosity between radio and records was put to rest. The next year World War II ended and just as after World War I, mercantile emphasis shifted to a peacetime economy. Consumers moved from rural to urban areas, and then urban to suburban communities as a part of the postwar revitalization. For the music industry, new relationships and opportunities emerged from the ashes of five years of conflict from three different legal confrontations affecting virtually all segments of the business.

Independent labels, which had initially produced their records for jukeboxes, started to get radio play and increased sales. Records from the race and hillbilly charts began to also appear on the national popularity charts. The mingling of people from all parts of the country during World War II further exposed rural musical styles to urban and suburban audiences. Radio airplay of regional and minority musicians, singing primarily BMI-represented songs, had increased on a national scale. Music was not just a business, but also a trendsetter for social change and multicultural awareness.

The copy in a BMI ad in the January 25, 1964, issue of *Billboard* accompanying coverage of BMI's shift in leadership from retiring president Carl Haverlin to his senior vice president Robert J. Burton stated, "The expanded opportunity for new writers and publishers created by BMI has sparked a continuing process of diversification, growth and democratization of American Music since 1940, the year BMI was formed. . . .In 1939, before BMI, there were only 137 active music publishers in the United States. Today, there are many thousands of publishers in all sections of the country and more than half are affiliated with BMI. In 1939, before BMI, the music of some 1,000 American authors and composers was licensed for performance. Today many thousands of writers and composers from every state of the union share in the performance rights of their music."[5] That ad copy was written by Russell Sanjek, then BMI's director of public relations.

Prologue

Part Two: The Rise of the Modern Music Business

New Technology Drives Post–World War II Music Consumption

The postwar economic boom brought even more change to the music business as the technological innovations developed during the war years were ready for commercial exploitation. In the late 1940s, vinyl replaced shellac as the material for manufacturing records, creating a more durable product of higher fidelity. Audio tape recorders developed in wartime Germany reached the hands of American engineers, including guitar maestro Les Paul who experimented with multitrack recording. Transistor components reduced the size and cost of car radios, introduced pocket-size portable models, and delivered a greater degree of mobility and convenience to music listening.

In 1949 *Billboard* changed the names of their "Race" and "Hillbilly Music" charts, respectively, to "Rhythm & Blues" or "R&B" and eventually to "Soul," or "Urban," or "Black"; and to "Country & Western" or "C&W," and eventually to just "Country." This new and more respectful brand identification both reflected and impacted the societal changes that would sweep across both the music business and country as a whole.

The hits on the *Billboard* charts rotated in and out of hundreds of thousands of jukeboxes, which were now in family-oriented restaurants and soda shops as well as their established locations in clubs and bars. The newer jukeboxes were designed to hold forty two-sided 45 rpm seven-inch vinyl discs, known as 45s, introduced in 1949 by RCA as an improvement over the 10-inch 78 rpm shellac discs. The 12-inch 33⅓ rpm long-playing vinyl disc or LP or 33 with five to six tracks on each side had been introduced by Columbia the year before. LPs generally featured music genres that appealed to older-age demographics including classical, jazz, Broadway musicals, movie soundtracks, and the older stars of network radio who were now the stars of network television variety shows.

While 45s were directed at jukeboxes and teenagers' portable record players, LPs were manufactured for use on home record players. The higher end models were referred to as turntables, often built with the capability of changing rotation speed to play all three record formats, 78s, 45s, and 33s. Combining these turntables with power amplifiers and loudspeaker cabinets using theater-quality low-range, mid-range, and high-range horns, consumers could achieve high-fidelity sound reproduction in their home listening experience, adding the abbreviation "hi-fi" to the home audio vernacular.

Professional recording equipment also improved in quality and functionality as well as expanded availability. New independent record companies like Atlantic and Roulette in New York, Imperial and Specialty in Los Angeles, Chess in Chicago, Sun in Memphis, Hickory in Nashville, and King in Cincinnati sprang up across the country. They recorded the indigenous American music genres that were then mostly ignored by the major labels but fed the demands of local consumers and non-network radio programming.

Local and regional record distributors, known as one-stops, and vinyl pressing plants sprang up across the nation to keep the record departments in variety stores and retail record shops stocked with both 45s and LPs. They also supplied discs to the growing number of the new Top 40 jukeboxes, with product from both the major labels and rising independents alike. The ad hoc network of independents became the foundation of a national distribution system that could quickly and simultaneously supply markets across the country in response to consumer demand created by national radio play, live performance, and/or network television appearances.

In 1950 there were 2,144 licensed radio stations, of which 627 were affiliates of the three major radio networks: the American Broadcasting Company (ABC), the Columbia Broadcasting System (CBS), and the National Broadcasting Company (NBC). Collectively the radio industry generated $453 million in revenue. The fledgling television industry was already threatening radio's consumer base and advertising income. Within a decade TVs were everywhere, expanding from 9 percent of American households in 1950 having them to 64.5 percent in 1955 and 87.3 percent in 1960. The three television networks were also owned by ABC, CBS, and NBC. Most of network radio's top-rated programs—including variety shows, soap operas, dramatic presentations, and comedy features—switched to broadcasting on television. These already established consumer favorites were augmented by old movie shorts and serials. Meanwhile, their radio affiliates turned to news and talk formats, with more recorded music added to lower expenses as advertising revenue had been impacted by the expanding television industry.

Industrialization after World War II had created a wave of new manufacturing jobs, attracting rural Americans to urban areas and bringing their musical preferences along with them. By the early 1950s, R&B and country songs were invading the pop charts. The major labels scoured R&B

and country releases to create mainstream versions of the music favored by young audiences. Pee Wee King's "Tennessee Waltz" was covered by Patti Page and the Chords' "Sh-Boom" was replicated by the Crew Cuts. Pat Boone built a teen idol career covering Fats Domino and Little Richard hits. Peggy Lee created a pop classic with Little Willie John's R&B hit "Fever" while a myriad of pop artists from Tony Bennett to Jo Stafford to Ray Charles covered Hank Williams's country songs. These alternative music styles invigorated pop music and widened its audience base.

The growing economy expanded middle-class spending on many leisure items. New single-home developments were built in the suburbs to accommodate the segment of the urban population raising young families. Suburban sock hops and drag races joined soda shops and the weekend movie matinee on the teenage social calendar. Having survived the sacrifices and limitations of the Great Depression and World War II, this generation was determined to create a better life for their children. They bought their children what had been luxury items in their own youth now made affordable by ever-improving technology.

Top 40 Radio, Records, and Rock-'n'-roll

In the mid-1950s, local radio needed programming to appeal to the newly mobile and economically empowered teenage and young adult age groups highly sought after by advertisers. Radio pioneers Todd Storz, Bill Stewart, Gordon McLendon, and Bill Gavin were all involved in the development of the Top 40 format in the mid-1950s that mirrored the most popular selections on the now ubiquitous forty-disc 45 rpm jukeboxes. Almost instantly the format swept across the nation and generating huge ratings, often with two or more competing stations in the larger markets. The announcers were universally designated as disc jockeys, or abbreviated to DJs, with many achieving local fame and audience appeal equal to the artists they were playing. National Radio Hall of Fame DJs "Cousin Brucie" Morrow on WABC and "Murray the K" Kaufman on WINS provided the evening competition in the New York area during the 1960s. Los Angeles Top 40 included fellow hall of famers KRLA's Casey Kasem and KHJ's the Real Don Steele competing with KFWB's Seven Swingin' Gentlemen including Bill Ballance, B. Mitchel Reid, and Ted Quillin under the direction of legendary program director Chuck Blore.

In 1958 *Billboard* consolidated its popular sales, airplay, and jukebox charts into one entity called the Hot 100. The relationship between the radio and record businesses intensified, as the Hot 100 guided record companies in manufacturing and distributing 45s for purchase by both teenage consumers and jukebox distributors. The record companies also supplied these 45s to the stations. Soon highly competitive promotion men were mired in accusations of payola activities with influential DJs.

With a strong boost from national exposure on network television, a teen idol craze of an even larger magnitude than the 1940s obsession with Frank Sinatra swept the teenage culture. It reached a tumultuous crescendo when Elvis Presley emerged as the most popular practitioner of a fusion of R&B and country that had been dubbed rock-'n'-roll. The term was first introduced to teen audiences in 1952 by Cleveland-based Rock and Roll Hall of Fame DJ Alan Freed. Freed appropriated the sobriquet from the lexicon of blues and R&B recordings, first appearing on Trixie Smith's 1922 recording *My Man Rocks Me (With One Steady Roll)*, and reoccurred in many paraphrased incarnations over the ensuing thirty years.

Presley's dramatic emergence upon the American music scene in 1956 utilized a network television campaign to augment his live performance schedule, cross-promoted with Top 40 radio play. In the spring of 1956 he appeared on six episodes of the *Dorsey Brothers' Stage Show* on CBS, then on NBC's June 5 *The Milton Berle Show* and July 1st's *Steve Allen Show*. His September 9 appearance on CBS's *The Ed Sullivan Show* captured 82.6 percent of the national television audience. He finished the year as a national celebrity with five #1 singles, two #1 albums, and starred in his first movie. He had become the face of rock-'n'-roll and Top 40 radio. He also ended the year with the William Morris Agency (WMA) as his exclusive agent.

The teenagers of the 1950s and the not-yet-teenaged baby boomer generation the world over were influenced by his style, clothes, mannerisms, and most important his music. Most of the rock stars to emerge over the next twenty-five years followed Presley to his blues, country, gospel, and rockabilly roots on a voyage of discovery that would shape their own music. Marketing Elvis became the industry prototype for building a brand that would sustain a fan base throughout a career, and in his case, after it. Fan loyalty to Elvis was so strong that his Memphis home, Graceland, became a leading tourist attraction after his untimely death in 1977, and the vast cadre of Elvis imitators became an entertainment phenomenon in their own right.

Presley, along with other rock-'n'-roll teen idols including Jerry Lee Lewis, Buddy Holly, Ricky Nelson, the Everly Brothers, Bobby Rydell, Bobby Darin, and Frankie Avalon sparked a cultural catharsis throughout the 50s Teens generation, born 1938 through 1945, that extended into fashion, film, and other lifestyle trends. As they moved out of their teens and into college or the workforce, the baby boomers, born 1946 through

1964, extended their rebellious attitude and yearning for social libera-tion into the 1960s. They embraced the addition of R&B and the British Invasion into Top 40 playlists, strengthening the position of the inde-pendent labels that were now releasing albums to compete with the majors in the burgeoning rock market.

The Major Labels and FM Radio

There were five major labels in the early 1960s. The Columbia/CBS Record Group (CBS), (owned by the CBS broadcast group) and RCA Victor (which manufactured radios, televisions, and other electronic devices and owned both the NBC television and radio networks) still led the field. Capitol-EMI was owned by British electronics giant EMI, which had acquired the Los Angeles–based Capitol Records label in 1955. PolyGram was the result of a 1962 merger of the recording interests of Dutch Koninklijke Philips N.V. (Philips) and German Siemens AG (Siemens) electronics companies with the names of their Polydor and Phonogram label group brands consolidated to create a unified identity. MCA had been formed in 1962 by the merger of the MCA and Universal record companies, movie studios, and television produc-tion companies.

These five had deep pockets, bolstered by the profits from their exten-sive catalogs of pop hits and adult-oriented genres. Initially they weathered the loss of significant market share in both radio play and record sales cap-tured by the twin phenomena of Top 40 and rock-'n'-roll, but finally they de-cided to invest in the teen-oriented market themselves. Their deep pockets and large staffs allowed them to finance, manufacture, and distribute records more quickly and on a national scale, and thus advance local or regional hits onto the Hot 100 national chart. They began to acquire independent labels or outbid them for young talent. In 1955, RCA Victor bought Presley's contract from Sun Records. In 1958, Johnny Cash signed with Columbia when his Sun contract expired. Sam Cooke left Keen Records for RCA, and Ray Charles de-parted Atlantic for ABC-Paramount.

The 50s Teens who had driven their parents' cars in high school were now moving through college into jobs and buying their own cars. The auto industry, Lear Jet Corporation, and RCA invested in the development of the stereo 8-track tape player and accompanying cartridge, which they launched in 1965. The player was easily integrated into car sound systems giving consumers the same on-demand listening options in the car that they enjoyed with LPs at home. With this change in consumption habits the record companies began to view 45s as a marketing vehicle for the vastly more profitable albums on which the singles were included, whether on vinyl for home listening or 8-track for mobile consumption.

In the early 1960s many broadcasters set up affiliated stations on the newly created FM radio band, which had stereo broadcast capability. At first, they just simulcasted their AM signal in stereo. Then in the late 1960s, many switched their FM signal to the new album-oriented radio (AOR) format, playing longer album cuts if not entire albums. This delighted the major labels looking for an outlet to promote their growing rosters of AOR rock artists, including The Beatles and other artists from the 1960s psychedelic era. These artists created albums from which singles were released, instead of releasing an album when there were enough radio hits to fill it. They gave free promotional copies to AOR stations just as they gave 45s to the Top 40 stations. The promotional albums used for airplay were supposed to be stamped with a "not for re-sale" notification, but a new form of payola emerged as a box of cleans, that is, albums not cut or stamped, were given to DJs to resell as an alternative or supplement to the longtime practice of unmarked envelopes containing several hundred dollars in small bills.

ASCAP and BMI Battle for Radio Market Share

Radio advertising revenue in the 1960s continued its robust growth pattern reflecting the ascendency of the teenage and young adult demographic in the consumer marketplace. While radio revenue had grown less than 50 percent from $454 million in 1950 to $655 million in 1960, it nearly doubled over the course of the 1960s to $1.26 billion in 1970. In turn, stations paid proportionately higher license fees to the songwriters and publishers through the PROs. BMI's chart share increased due to the country and R&B-influenced rock artists who dominated Top 40 radio. The ASCAP Broadway and Hollywood members who were not supplying songs to these new artists lobbied Congress in the late 1950s for laws to ban rock-'n'-roll records from radio broadcasts, claiming it caused juvenile delinquency. Their efforts failed, but nonetheless gained much publicity.

In 1967 BMI songwriters had 78 percent of the year-end *Billboard* Hot 100 chart, 92 percent of the Top Country Hits, 100 percent of the Top R&B Hits, and even 48 percent of the Top Easy Listening Singles. BMI negotiated a 12.5 percent increase from radio while ASCAP begrudgingly accepted a 6.25 percent rate reduction, though its revenue was still ahead of BMI's. In 1972 ASCAP collected 63.4 percent of combined PRO revenue, leading $69.5 million to

$40 million. With a larger pot of broadcast revenue and fewer songs to divide it amongst, ASCAP initiated a concerted push to solicit R&B, country, and rock songwriters—the people who had created the music they had sought to have banned from radio a decade earlier. Two of its major acquisitions were the rights to Motown Records' Jobete Music publishing catalog and the future Rock and Roll Hall of Fame songwriting team of Jerry Leiber and Mike Stoller. ASCAP's new inclusive membership policy and its deeper pockets gradually shifted the pop and rock chart pendulum back in its favor, but BMI was able to maintain its ground on the country and R&B charts.

By the Time They Got to Woodstock . . .

FM stations' ratings and advertising revenues still lagged behind their sister AM frequencies, which were bolstered by the dominance of the Top 40 format. To increase their listener base, the FM stations co-sponsored popular bands with local clubs and concert promoters. These live shows incorporated the newest loudspeaker, multi-channel mixing boards, sound processing, and stage lighting technology. A national network of young promoters and concert sound companies extended the fan frenzy phenomenon of the teen idol era to long-haired rock bands on an even grander scale as shows expanded to larger concert venues. Record company promotions were supplemented by youth-oriented periodicals led by *Rolling Stone*, which extolled a countercultural message of "Sex, Drugs and Rock & Roll," a phrase adapted from an October 17, 1969, article in *Life* magazine that stated, "The counterculture has its sacraments in sex, drugs and rock."[1]

The zenith of this social movement occurred in August 1969 at the Woodstock Music and Art Fair in Bethel, New York, where over four hundred thousand people gathered for what was publicized as '3 Days of Peace & Music" with performances by thirty-two rock, pop, and folk acts. Although preceded by the Monterrey International Pop Festival in California in 1967 and the Isle of Wight Festival in the UK in 1968, Woodstock was on a grand scale featuring the latest audio technology in its massive speaker system custom designed to accommodate the assembled multitude. The event was forever preserved in a movie and album box set that stamped Woodstock as the apex of a golden era of love and harmony. It also demonstrated to the music business how new technology could help capitalize on the baby boomer infatuation with rock music.

New music-intensive shows on television in the 1960s that accommodated Top 40 artists included *Shindig, Hullabaloo, Where the Action Is, Hootenanny,*

The Monkees, and others that came and went. However, the Dick Clark–hosted *American Bandstand*, which had originated in 1953 on local television in Philadelphia before moving to the ABC network, outlasted them all with its final broadcast in 1989. Other shows appealed to an older demographic, including programs hosted by Perry Como, Andy Williams, Liberace, and Lawrence Welk. Johnny Cash, Glen Campbell, and Roger Miller successfully capitalized on a growing crossover appeal for country music. In 1968, the Country Music Association (CMA) annual awards were broadcast for the first time.

The social upheavals of the 1960s affected the music industry, much as it did the rest of society, as youth culture became a larger, more vocal, and even more economically empowered demographic. Seeing opportunities for increased revenues, entertainment and electronics conglomerates entered an era of acquisitions, mergers, and consolidations that would last for more than four decades. National market share of airplay and sales as chronicled by *Billboard* and other trade periodicals became the industry measuring stick for success.

By 1970, the Big Five had grown to six with the addition of the Kinney Record Group, which would become Warner-Elektra-Atlantic (WEA) in 1971, and then the Warner Music Group (WMG) after the 1989 Time Warner merger. Except for Kinney's absence from country music, all of the Big Six catalogs corresponded to the top radio formats. All aggressively competed for new acts to plug into the limited playlist spots on radio and vied for the front slots in record bins at retail outlets.

Acting independently of its partnership in PolyGram, in 1971 Philips introduced the compact cassette tape cartridge and accompanying hardware for both home and auto. Designed as an upgrade in audio quality over the 8-track, the cassette combined Dolby B-type noise reduction, an adaptation of the Dolby A-type technology used in recording studios, with a commercial-grade player mechanism from the 3M Corporation featuring two-sided storage capacity and fast-forward search. Philips licensed the technology to the entire record industry to maintain industrywide compatibility between sound carrier format and playing devices. Cassettes replaced 8-tracks in most cars over the ensuing decade to improve the listening experience in both quality and functionality. Battery-operated portable cassette boom boxes and the debut of the Sony Walkman in 1979 expanded the consumers' mobile listening options even further.

While the cassette sparked a steady rise that would double sales by the end of the 1970s, it also was perceived by the record industry as a home duplication threat. Tape companies sold the public blank cassettes of a much higher audio quality and at a lower cost than the tape used in the record labels' prerecorded cassettes. The Recording Industry Association of America (RIAA), the record industry's trade association, began a lobbying campaign for blank tape levy legislation, as they claimed to annually lose hundreds of millions, if not over a billion, dollars to what they termed illegal home duplication.

The Copyright Act of 1976

The Copyright Act of 1976 was implemented on January 1, 1978, as the first major copyright revision since 1909. The act was designed to resolve various intellectual property issues involving media created since 1909, including radio, motion pictures, jukeboxes, and television. The law was also a step toward conforming with the copyright laws of the Universal Copyright Coalition (UCC), in anticipation of the US eventually joining Berne. The act did, however, adhere to Berne standards in extending federal copyright protection to sound recordings, strengthening the record companies' legal rights in piracy infringement litigation, which, in their thinking, included home duplication.

The act also extended the copyright term for new musical compositions through the life of the last surviving creator plus fifty years, which twenty years later would be extended to seventy years. The provision with the greatest economic impact, however, was the increase in the statutory rate paid to music publishers for the mechanical reproduction of sound recordings. This rate had been set and had remained at 2¢ per track per unit sold since 1909. The new act raised the rate to 2.75¢ in 1978, and then scheduled increases every two years to 4.5¢ by 1984 and eventually to 9.1¢ in 2006, where it still remained in 2019.

Radio advertising revenues almost tripled to $3.5 billion during the 1970s. The Top 40 format of the 1960s splintered into ever more well-defined age and genre groupings for more specifically targeted audiences. In 1984, radio revenues reached $5.5 billion. That year's radio market share for the top formats were adult contemporary (AC) with 22.9 percent, contemporary hit radio (CHR) with 17.4 percent, country with 14.1 percent, beautiful music/ easy listening with 11.3 percent, AOR with 10.7 percent, black/urban with 8 percent, and news/talk/sports with 6.3 percent. The remaining 8.5 percent was divided among big band, Spanish-language, golden oldies, religious, classical, jazz, and other miscellaneous formats. While CHR radio, like its Top 40 predecessor, directly pursued the teenage and young adult demographics, the then 20 through 38-year-old baby boomers were the top target of radio advertisers, as well as the top record consumers, with their listening spread across CHR, AOR, AC, black/urban, and the more niche genres.

Music in Television and Film

The Grammy Awards presented by the Recording Academy, then officially named the National Academy of Recording Arts and Sciences (NARAS), made its live television debut on ABC in March 1971 with its 13th Annual Awards Celebration. Forty-four awards were presented in fourteen different categories, spanning the entire record industry. Simon & Garfunkel dominated the proceedings with five awards for *Bridge over Troubled Water*.

In 1973 the telecast moved to CBS, and the Dick Clark–produced *American Music Awards* replaced it on ABC. Other shows followed but along more genre-specific lines. *Soul Train* launched its thirty-five-year run in August 1971 as a syndicated program. *In Concert* on ABC, *Midnight Special* on NBC, and *Don Kirshner's Rock Concert* in syndication were directed toward listeners of the AOR and Top 40 formats. Public television first aired *Great Performances* in 1972 from WNET New York, *Sound Stage* in 1974 from WTTW Chicago, and the still-running *Austin City Limits* in 1976 from KLRU in Austin, Texas. There were also artist-hosted variety shows from Sonny & Cher, Sha Na Na, Donny and Marie, and many not-as-successful others.

The motion picture industry had long co-promoted their films with soundtrack albums, and those albums often yielded radio hits. With the success of the *Woodstock* movie, the film industry began to alter its music usage to appeal to a wider demographic range. *Shaft*, *Grease*, *Saturday Night Fever*, *The Blues Brothers*, *Honeysuckle Rose*, *Footloose*, *Urban Cowboy*, *The Jazz Singer* (Neil Diamond's new version), and *Purple Rain* were some of the most successful films to co-promote between movie, soundtrack, and singles released for radio airplay. Others like *American Graffiti*, *Car Wash*, and *Risky Business* used fairly recent pop hits as background music with the entire recording of each on the soundtrack album. Commissioned movie themes continued to help promote major movies, especially within the spectacularly produced opening credits for the James Bond films.

The 1948 *Alden-Rochelle, Inc. v. ASCAP* Supreme Court decision had long exempted motion picture exhibitors from paying performing rights royalties through ASCAP. The court ruled that since almost all film music at the time was published by ASCAP-affiliated companies owned by the movie studios, and since the exhibitors already paid 50 percent of the ticket price to those studios, then the ASCAP fee was an exorbitant surcharge in violation of anti-trust laws. The performing rights for theatrical exhibit thereafter were instead attached to the license for the right to synchronize music to moving images, commonly referred to as a sync license. BMI publishers at the time had very few film music usages, but as use of BMI repertoire in movies grew, the publishers also attached the performing rights to the sync license. All three US PROs, however, received and distributed theatrical exhibit performing rights royalties from foreign territories for their respective rightsholders, as well as for when movies initially produced for theatrical exhibit were aired on television and cable.

ASCAP, still a membership association, negotiated with all licensees under a 1941 Justice Department consent decree–mandated rate court. BMI, a C corporation still owned by its broadcaster shareholders operating on a not-for-profit basis, was also under its own 1941 consent decree, but had no rate court and had to resolve issues through arbitration, with litigation as a last recourse. The privately held SESAC had no consent decree and routinely litigated over infringement when it could not resolve licensing rates. Considering the legal cost of copyright infringement litigation, if SESAC had clear-cut evidence of infringement, even if non-willful, it was much cheaper for a station or other user to get a license than risk losing the case in court and incur legal expenses, penalties, and damages.

The cable television industry began in 1948 as an alternative for television signals to areas when over-the-air broadcast was difficult or impossible. In the 1970s, the FCC allowed expansion of cable systems to areas that had broadcast television on the condition that those with more than thirty-five hundred subscribers also carried public, educational, and government TV channels. Channels were divided into basic cable, which were part of the base subscription package fee and generated revenue from advertising; and pay cable, which charged consumers an additional fee on top of the base subscription cost but carried no advertising. Pay cable services Home Box Office (HBO) and Showtime debuted in 1972 and 1976, respectively. Ted Turner launched the first basic cable network in 1976 when he turned his Atlanta station WTBS, which carried Atlanta Braves baseball and Atlanta Hawks basketball games, into what was termed a superstation for syndicating simultaneous broadcast to cable systems across the country.

In August 1981 cable became a major media outlet for the music business with the launch of Music Television (MTV), co-owned by Warner Communications, Inc. (WCI), parent company of WEA, and American Express (AMEX). MTV was a basic cable video clip channel with a format mirroring pop radio. Its well-publicized debut featured the Buggles' "Video Killed the Radio Star." Other channels soon jumped in with video-clip programs including *Video Jukebox* on HBO in December 1981, *Night Tracks* on WTBS in June 1983, and NBC's *Friday Night Videos* in July 1983. Ted Turner launched another all-music basic cable channel with his Cable Music Channel (CMC) in 1984 but quickly sold it to MTV where it became VH1. Black Entertainment Television (BET) had been part of the programming on WCI/Amex's Nickelodeon, but then became its own basic cable channel in 1983. Both The Nashville Network (TNN) and Country Music Television (CMT) debuted in March 1983.

The pay cable industry employed a new strategy with the PROs for performing rights licenses in a per-subscriber fee rather than a percentage-of-advertising revenue model. Under this system, PRO revenue grew only with additional subscribers, with no proportional raise for increased subscription rates. The PROs then paid cable royalties quarterly on a census rather than sample basis compiling all music usages from the cue sheets of all programs listed on television channels' schedules. The then-available pool of money was divided on a pro rata basis between those listed songs and score segments and the number of airings for a particular program.

The Big Six Labels in 1984

In 1984, the Big Six major label groups were the same as they had been in 1970. CBS and WEA each had twenty-six of the top Hot 100 singles for 1984, PolyGram had fifteen, RCA and MCA both had thirteen, and EMI trailed with seven. Record sales almost doubled in dollar volume throughout the 1970s, surpassing 500 million units. Sales then contracted in the mini-recessions of the first half of the 1980s, but income stayed steady with price increases. Nonetheless, parent corporations were concerned. The sale of music videos to consumers hadn't developed as hoped, despite their exposure on cable music channels. The market for cassette sales of back catalog albums to replace 8-track copies seemed exhausted.

Furthermore, the labels were still frustrated that customers could use blank cassettes to copy their product. In addition to consumers borrowing albums from friends to copy, they were now renting LPs from record stores on a short-term basis. The RIAA claimed that this rental practice enabled home piracy of their recordings, now claiming losses of over a billion dollars in annual sales to this illegal copying. The RIAA successfully championed the Record Rental Amendment of 1984, which outlawed the commercial rental of records, but the issue of whether home copying constituted infringement would persist for the next twenty-five years.

Digital technology was already transforming the recording process. Solid-state circuitry had been integrated into recording consoles in the early 1970s. 3M's first digital audio tape recorder debuted in 1978 in the Sound 80 studio in Minneapolis, used in creating the first digitally recorded Grammy-winning album, Aaron Copland's *Appalachian Spring* by the St. Paul Chamber Orchestra. In 1979 the new 3M Digital Audio Mastering System was employed to record the first all-digital rock album, Ry Cooder's *Bop Till You Drop*, at the Warner Brothers Studio in California. In 1980 3M, Mitsubishi, Sony, and EMT Studer followed with multitrack digital recorders utilizing hard drives rather than digital tape.

In 1981 Philips unveiled a 4.724″ digital data storage optical disc dubbed the Compact Disc (CD) as the first commercial digital sound carrier. Looking like a miniature LP, the shiny disc was more consumer friendly than the cassette in both appearance and functionality with claims of greater durability. Philips enlisted Sony as a partner for the final design. The first CDs were commercially released in late 1982 in Japan with a limited number of catalog items. Billy Joel's 1978 album *52nd Street* was the first pop release on CD. CD technology was subsequently licensed to the entire industry for a royalty of 1.8¢ per unit sold to Philips and 1.2¢ to Sony along with a 2.5 percent of retail sales license fee on CD players divided in the same ratio.

There were US sales of eight hundred thousand imported CD units in 1983. In September 1984, the first US CD plant was opened in Terre Haute, Indiana, by Columbia with Bruce Springsteen's *Born in the USA* the first product off the presses. The year 1984 ended with 5.8 million US sales in a blend of imports and Terre Haute pressings. Terre Haute and the plants that followed enabled digital technology to expand rapidly in both recording studios and home entertainment centers for upper-end music consumers. The digital age was off and running.

The music industry envisioned the CD as the solution to reverse the stagnant sales they were experiencing. They justified the CD's higher price with claims of greater durability, improved audio fidelity, and capacity for a little over seventy-four minutes of music allowing for more tracks than what could be included in an LP's forty-four-plus minutes at optimal sound fidelity. The CD was also dual-purposed as it could be played both at home and in the car replacing both LP and cassette with just one sound carrier. CD components could easily be integrated into home stereo systems and in-auto CD players were designed to replace the cassette players in car dashboards. The labels expected the CD to rejuvenate back catalog sales just as cassettes had done in replacing 8-tracks. Additionally, as CDs were not then recordable, the industry viewed the new disc as a further barrier to home duplication.

WEA and CBS Lead the Big Six Pack

In 1984 all metrics, including the *Billboard* singles charts, platinum certification for over one million sales, and gold certification for over five hundred thousand sales indicated that WEA was leading the pack in market share. It was fifteen years after the publicly traded Kinney National Company, led by its president Steve Ross, purchased the recently merged Warner Bros.-Seven Arts entertainment holdings for $400 million. Kinney's previous core businesses had been funeral homes, cleaning services, car rentals, and parking lots, but had now added movie studios, record labels, and publishing companies to the corporate portfolio. Included in the purchase were Warner Bros. Records, which had started in 1958 to release soundtrack albums from its associated film division; and Atlantic Records, which was acquired in 1967 in a $17.5 million cash plus stock transaction from cofounder Ahmet Ertegun, his brother Nesuhi, and partner Jerry Wexler, who all remained in executive roles.

Warner Bros. was headed by Mo Ostin who had been label manager of Reprise Records, originally a co-venture with Frank Sinatra. Although an accountant by training, Ostin had already begun updating the roster by signing The Grateful Dead, Jimi Hendrix, Joni Mitchell, and Van Morrison. He would continue to helm the label for the next twenty-five years. In 1970 Ross added Elektra Records, opened in 1950 and still led by cofounder Jac Holzman. With Warner Bros.' rock and folk-rock roster, Atlantic's R&B and British rock, and Elektra's 1960s folk and folk-rock along with its Nonesuch Records classical and world music division, Ross was building a strong contemporary catalog to compete with his more established RCA and CBS rivals.

As a manager, Ross believed in granting autonomy to the successful record men who came along with the labels, allowing them to operate autonomously with their respective CEOs serving on the Warner/Seven Arts company board. In 1972, Kinney transferred its entertainment interests into the newly formed Warner Communications, Inc. (WCI), leaving the non-music divisions in the Kinney National Corporation. WCI next established the WEA Distribution division, acquiring or displacing the independents they had been using. Nesuhi Ertegun then set up WEA International as an integrated global distribution system with either WEA subsidiaries or established independent partners in major territories. In 1972 WEA acquired David Geffen's Asylum Records, retained Geffen at the helm, and subsequently merged Asylum with Elektra under Geffen's leadership through 1975. Jac Holzman moved up to other duties within WEA where he remained until 1986. He later returned in 2004 as a senior technology advisor.

WEA established Warner Special Products in 1973 to market and license their back catalog for all usages other than retail sales. WEA also acquired Seymour Stein's Sire Records and made distribution deals with Chris Blackwell's Island Records, Led Zeppelin's Swan Song Records, and Rolling Stones Records. WCI's other holdings included the Warner movie studios, various music publishing companies both proprietary and administrated, the Atari computer company, the Panavision film equipment company, and the Franklin Mint. In 1981, WCI cofounded MTV Networks as part of its cable television co-venture with American Express.

The record division of CBS, which in 1984 also owned both the CBS radio and television networks, originally debuted as Columbia Records in 1889 as a rival to Edison and Victor. Columbia then went through several ownership changes before being reacquired in 1938 by CBS, then and still as of 1984 under the leadership of William S. Paley. The shared Columbia name was due to a short term of common ownership before Paley acquired the radio network in 1928. The Columbia/CBS label group had a strong catalog in pop, classical, musical theater, jazz, folk, and country with two label group divisions, Columbia Records and Epic/Portrait/Associated Labels.

The record group had been headed since 1975 by Walter Yetnikoff, an in-house attorney since 1962 under then–general counsel Clive Davis. Yetnikoff had also served as president of CBS Records International from 1971 to 1975, where he had supervised the creation of the CBS/Sony Records joint venture to distribute CBS product in Japan. He was in his early forties when he assumed the top spot. Like Davis, whom he succeeded, Yetnikoff transitioned from corporate attorney to record man to best compete with the rest of the Big Six. He soon signed Michael Jackson away from then-independent Motown, enticed Paul McCartney to switch from Capitol-EMI, and brought in the Rolling Stones from Atlantic.

The two CBS record divisions also handled subsidiary imprints and distributed labels, and like the WEA labels, each had its own Artist and Repertoire (A&R), promotion, marketing, publicity, and press departments. If the two CBS labels and the three major WEA labels had stood each on its own as they did in the marketplace with their separate but parallel structures, then Columbia was actually the top individual label with seventy-eight

Billboard-charted albums in 1985. WB Records was in second place with fifty-one charted albums, including albums from Reprise and Sire.

Non-retail sales and third-party licensing were managed by the two separate Columbia House and Columbia Special Products divisions. Columbia House originated in the mid-1970s to fulfill all mail order sales of both back and current catalog, absorbing the two-decade-old Columbia Record Club. It also pressed and sold new product orders in the older formats of vinyl, 8-track, and cassette that had been discontinued at retail, as well as creating new box sets and commemorative collections. Columbia House expanded the Record Club's multimillion consumer base with ongoing subscription campaigns soliciting new members with deeply discounted multiple-album offers through monthly flyers, advertisements, and commercials. According to former Columbia House executive Marshall Wilcoxen, in some calendar quarters, the clubs could account for more than 10 percent of total industry sales.

The other division, Columbia Special Products, under the leadership of thirty-year veteran Al Shulman, developed budget line product from back catalog for retail distribution and third-party licensing. They also manufactured custom record packages for televised infomercial sales campaigns, specialty mail order fulfillment businesses, and what were called premium albums created for customers as corporate giveaways or discounted albums to be co-branded with non-music products.

RCA, MCA, EMI, and PolyGram Round Out the Big Six

In 1929, the Radio Corporation of America (RCA), then a subsidiary of General Electric, created RCA Victor Records after purchasing the Victor Talking Machine Company, then the world's largest manufacturer of phonograph records and players including the Victrola. RCA also formed the NBC radio network in 1926 and the NBC television network after World War II. By the mid-1950s, RCA and CBS were the two major competitors in the US record industry. Their affiliated radio and television divisions led their industries as well.

In 1984, RCA had four autonomous divisions within its distribution network. The flagship was the historic RCA catalog, together with the new artists signed to the RCA imprint. Arista Records was a co-venture with RCA's European distribution partner, the Bertelsmann Group of Germany, and former Columbia Records chief Clive Davis, with US distribution through RCA. Arista also controlled US distribution for Clive Calder's dance and hip hop–oriented Jive Records. Los Angeles–based A&M Records, formed in 1962 by Herb Alpert and Jerry Moss, functioned as RCA's third pop division but was actually a distribution deal that included A&M's co-venture with Miles Copeland's I.R.S. Records, home to The Police, The Go-Go's, and R.E.M.

The fourth RCA branch was the RCA Nashville country music division, which also operated with its own staff, as did all the other major label country divisions. In 1973 Jerry Bradley, the son of Hall of Fame producer/MCA executive Owen Bradley, replaced legendary guitarist/producer Chet Atkins who had headed the division since 1957. Atkins and the elder Bradley were widely credited as the developers of the crossover, cosmopolitan style of country music dubbed the Nashville Sound. In 1982, thirty-two-year-old head of marketing Joe Galante replaced Bradley to continue RCA's long run at the top of the country music record market. RCA also had its own RCA Record Club to compete with Columbia House, and RCA Special Products to do the same third-party licensing and custom manufacturing as its CBS and WEA counterparts.

MCA Records had been formed in 1962 when publicly held talent agency and television production company Music Corporation of America (MCA), then headed by Lew Wasserman with founder and majority owner Dr. Jules Stein serving as chairman of the board, merged with Universal Pictures, which also owned the long-established American Decca Records. American Decca had been created by British Decca owner Sir Edward Lewis and American Jack Kapp in 1934, but they severed their relationship in 1939. To avoid restraint of trade issues, MCA exited their original talent agency business with the 1962 merger and established Universal as a top film studio while also building the MCA Records group. During the next ten years, they augmented their Decca, Coral, and Brunswick labels with the addition of Kapp Records and other smaller labels.

In 1972 the record group was reorganized into MCA Records for the labels from the Decca merger, and Uni Records for the Kapp and other more recent acquisitions, all under the leadership of former WEA executive Mike Maitland. In 1979 MCA promoted vice president of marketing and executive vice president Bob Siner to succeed Maitland. Siner led the acquisition of the ABC Records group, which included Paramount, Dot, Brunswick, and Shelter Records. After falling behind the other label groups in market share, in 1983 Siner was replaced by artist manager Irving Azoff to steer a turnaround. Azoff's connections throughout the industry helped him make key acquisitions, including a distribution agreement with Berry Gordy's Motown

Records. He also demonstrated a firm hand in trimming staff and roster quickly leading MCA back to a competitive level.

UK-based EMI Music had roots going back to 1931 with the formation of Electric and Music Industries Limited, hence the EMI acronym. In 1971, all its historic labels, other than US-based Capitol Records, were consolidated into EMI Records Ltd. In 1978, Indian-born, longtime UK-based EMI executive Bhaskar Menon became chairman of EMI Music Worldwide, supervising operations in over forty-six countries. In 1979, EMI acquired the United Artists, Liberty, and Imperial labels, and subsequently merged with fellow British electronics conglomerate Thorn Electrical Industries to form Thorn-EMI. Its crown jewel was The Beatles catalog, including the Apple Records co-venture. Further catalog strength came from their longstanding practice of acquiring the US rights for EMI and independent product originating in other territories.

In 1972, Polydor Records, the pop division of Siemens' Deutsche Grammophon label, merged with Philips's Phonogram division, which a year earlier had itself been formed by consolidating the Philips, Fontana, Mercury, and Vertigo labels. Philips was the developer of the compact cassette and was about to co-develop the CD with Sony. The merged entity was dubbed PolyGram, a consolidation of the two names, and immediately went on an acquisition binge purchasing the MGM, Verve, British Decca, RSO, Casablanca, and Pickwick labels, as well as United Distribution Corporation, which it renamed PhonoDisc, Inc., to handle retail distribution.

By 1980, the disco wave had lifted PolyGram to a 20 percent market share, but poor supply chain management had created a huge problem with returned product. Coupled with marketing budgets based on unrealistic sales projections, the company was saddled with losses exceeding $220 million. In 1983 Philips executive Jan Timmer took over as president/CFO of the newly formed PolyGram International Ltd. After a failed 1983 merger attempt with WEA, Philips bought out 40 percent of the Siemens share, leaving their German partner with a 10 percent interest.

The Pop Concert Business Gets a Little Help from Its Friends

The bedrock of the music business has always been the performance of musical works that the public wanted to hear again whether in a live show, through electronic duplication or transmission, or performed themselves in a group setting. Since the creation of recording technology in the late 1880s and the emergence of radio in the 1920s, the artists chosen to make records and to appear live on radio, as well as the songs selected for them, were based on the popularity of their live performance of those songs.

The advances in electronic technology that boosted the broadcast and record industries also benefited the live performance sector. Before the newly developed condenser microphones and electromagnetic driven coil-cone speakers were combined in the 1920s to create public address (PA) systems, room acoustics were the major factor in determining attendance capacity. Single instrument electric amplifiers followed in the 1930s. Further advancements were made in both microphone and speaker technology over the next three decades along with the introduction of multi-input sound-mixing boards. By the mid-1960s the 50s Teen and baby boomer generations had become an economic force due to leisure dollars supplied by their parents. Their spending on music had extended beyond jukeboxes, portable 45 players, and albums by their favorite artists to the live performance industry, pushing it past $100 million in 1965.

That summer two now legendary performances dramatically exposed the need for an acoustic upgrade for large gatherings. On July 24, Bob Dylan played his controversial three-song electric set at the Newport Folk Festival accompanied by members of the Paul Butterfield Blues Band to the displeasure of several of the organizers and many of the traditional folk aficionados in attendance. Three weeks later, on August 15, the Beatles played their epic Shea Stadium concert to 55,000 screaming fans, who drowned out the stadium PA system that was normally used for announcers and organ riffs between baseball innings, but was totally inadequate for a rock-'n'-roll audience.

These incidents underscored the need for more powerful PA systems to accommodate larger facilities to fill the growing demand for rock concert tickets while providing the requisite audio quality and clarity. This drive for the ultimate auditory experience culminated in the stacked cabinet sound system with multiple theater speaker horns deployed at the Woodstock music festival, a system so substantial it could sonically envelop over four hundred thousand people. Smaller versions of this system, but still far larger and more powerful than those of the preceding decades, would allow the concert industry to expand from theaters and clubs into larger arenas, coliseums, and eventually into sports stadiums by 1984.

Since the turn of the twentieth century, *Billboard*'s sister publication *Amusement Business* (*AB*) had served as the preeminent weekly trade magazine for the business of live performance. It provided information for the bookers and promoters of performance dates for amusement parks, fairs, and theme parks, including attendance receipts organized in comparative charts, artist information and profiles, contact information for both buyers and sellers, and the latest live performance industry news. *AB* printed weekly from 1894 to 2001, and then monthly until 2006. After it ceased publishing, its reports were incorporated within *Billboard*. Competitor *Performance Magazine* published from the early 1970s until 1999 with a primary focus on artists. *Pollstar* debuted in 1981 and continues to this day as the now-leading resource for live concert and performance industry inside information.

1984 Sees Surge in Box Office Receipts

Major venue concert ticket revenues as tracked by *AB*/*Billboard* and *Pollstar* had more than tripled over the course of the 1970s to over $450 million in 1980 and reached a record-setting $700 million in 1984 highlighted by the Jacksons *Victory Tour*. Even though it was billed as a tour by the Jackson brothers, formerly known as the Jackson 5, the demand was created by Michael Jackson's *Thriller* album with its 25 million unit sales and saturated MTV video-clip play. Accordingly, *Thriller* repertoire dominated the tour set list. As a result, the promoters pursued a new ticketing and venue strategy. Unlike any previous concert tour, almost all of the twenty-one *Victory Tour* venues were sports stadiums, except for New York's Madison Square Garden, utilizing the greater seating capacity and doing multiple performances in all but one of the cities. Even with these larger venues and multiple dates, demand for the average availability of fifty thousand tickets per show exceeded supply.

The ticket price of $30 was almost twice as much as most of the previous superstar tours of the 1980s. The Rolling Stones *American Tour 1981* with an average ticket price of $17 played fifty dates to about 3 million fans in a blend of stadiums and arenas for a box office total of $52 million. The *Victory Tour* drew over 2.5 million attendees and generated over $75 million, setting the record as the top grossing tour up to that time. Bruce Springsteen's *Born in the USA Tour* was 1984's second-highest grossing tour with eighty dates at $16 average ticket prices in arenas and concert halls. The other major concert headliners that year included Neil Diamond, Kenny Rogers, Billy Joel, Willie Nelson, Luciano Pavarotti, Luther Vandross, and The Grateful Dead.

The Future's So Bright You Gotta Wear Shades

By 1984, not only were 50s Teens and baby boomers topping the charts across all genres but they were also entering the music business work force as record company staffers for sales, promotion, publicity, and A&R positions; radio DJs, engineers, and sales reps; retail sales personnel; and concert promoters, booking agents, artist managers, and their support staffs. On the creative side they became backing vocalists and musicians known as sidemen; songwriters, producers, and audio engineers; and touring personnel commonly referred to as roadies, which included drivers, security, guitar techs, stage crew, and merchandise sales personnel.

The major label groups had hedged their bets by acquiring and consolidating labels and catalogs so the profits from the hits could counter the losses from the misses on their corporate balance sheet. From their perspective, the primary industry modus operandi between radio, records, and retail was working better than ever. As a result, successful artists auctioned their services for larger cash advances and higher royalty rates. The customized tour buses that had become the favored mode of transportation gave way to private jets for the top headliners. The music video explosion on cable television not only expanded creative opportunities but also facilitated a more intimate relationship for fans with performers via the small screen long before they saw their favorite artists in live performance venues.

By the end of 1984, the American music business was poised for even greater expansion anchored by a mutually beneficial synchronicity profiting from the public's consumption of music in recorded, transmitted, printed, and live performance form. The labels, however, still stood alone in taking the lion's share of the risk on new talent. Consequentially, they also retained a greater share of the generated revenue compared to the publishers or concert promoters, but all benefited as overall consumer spending almost tripled between 1974 and 1984. With industrywide cooperation in adopting and then adapting to the advent of the digital age, the future ahead looked bright indeed.

PART ONE

1985 TO 1995

1

The Game of Musical Thrones

The CD Drives Industry Growth

Introduced in Europe and Japan in 1983, the shiny new compact digital disc (CD) had sparked an industrywide optimism that accelerated with the opening of the first domestic plant by CBS in Terre Haute, Indiana, in late 1984. CDs sold as quickly as they could be manufactured or imported while waiting for additional plant openings. Record labels expected a boost in revenue from both the CD's higher price point and an anticipated increase in back catalog sales as CDs replaced LPs and cassettes in consumer album collections. Electronic hardware manufacturers cross-promoted CD players with the labels' new discs, proclaiming superior audio quality and product durability while replacing both LPs and cassettes with just one sound carrier. The CD had a potential of seventy-four-plus minutes compared to forty-four to forty-eight minutes on an LP, allowing artists to add around thirty more minutes, resulting in both more and longer songs.

The Recording Industry Association of America (RIAA) had long kept statistics on unit shipments as supplied by its member labels to determine gold and platinum certifications. In 1973 they issued the retail value and unit amounts of industrywide shipments in what would become an annual Excel spreadsheet. The 1985 CD sales of 22.6 million units grew to 53 million in 1986 and then 102.1 million in 1987. In 1995 772.9 CDs accounted for 72.5 percent of the 997.2 million shipped album units, more than meeting the optimism expressed at the CD's launch. RIAA-reported retail revenue had almost tripled from 1985's $4.36 billion to $12.32 billion for 1995. Unit shipments, however, only grew by 88.7 percent. The higher percentage increase in value relative to unit sales was a result of the higher retail price of CDs compared to cassettes and vinyl.

Vinyl album sales dropped from 167 million to 2.2 million over the same period. CDs averaged over $17 at retail in the 1985 RIAA tally, but dropped to $15.61 by 1987, and then to $12.97 in 1995 as manufacturing became more efficient. In comparison, vinyl and cassettes together averaged $7.70 in 1985 and but rose to $8.41 in 1995 as their numbers dwindled. The record

American Popular Music and Its Business in the Digital Age. Rick Sanjek, Oxford University Press. © Frederick Sanjek 2024.
DOI: 10.1093/oso/9780190653828.003.0001

industry ascribed the increase in mechanical royalty rates paid to music publishers effectuated by the Copyright Act of 1976, the higher cost of CD manufacturing, and artists taking advantage of the increase in total time available on CDs to add more songs as justifications for the higher price for CDs.

The statutory mechanical rate, the same for all three formats, had climbed from 2¢ per song per record sold in 1977 to 4.5¢ in 1984 and was scheduled to incrementally increase to 6.6¢ by 1995, and then in 2006 to 9.1¢, where it still stood in 2019. Although just a matter of pennies, on a macro scale it became significant. On the approximately 542 million albums shipped in 1984 the labels were already paying $125 million more in mechanical royalties than they would have paid at the 1977 rate.

The Big Six label group heads were compelled to generate as much profit as possible, not just for their shareholders, but for their own remuneration and job security as well. All new artist signings, however, involved an upfront financial commitment with no guarantee of a positive return, much less profit. The people at the top of the music business pyramid were the ones who had consistently selected the artists who had produced the best returns through the steady consolidation and conglomeration of the entertainment world over the past two decades, including the acquisition of their companies by multimedia and electronics behemoths. They had led their industry through the advent of rock-'n'-roll, the transformation of hillbilly and race records into country and soul, the British invasion, Woodstock, disco, the proliferation of genre-specific radio formats, and most recently the seemingly instant omnipresence of music video.

These "record men" were from the Greatest Generation, who had served in World War II or lived through it on the home front, and the Silent Generation, also referred to as 1950s Teens, who as children had experienced the birth of both television and rock-'n'-roll. Now in their fifties or older, they had steered the industry through the development of radio formats and retail distribution, keeping the growing juggernaut on course. They referred to the marketplace as "the street" and were judged by the "street cred" they had established in balancing airplay and product flow to create both career longevity and shareholder profits. They often derisively referred to the corporate executives who were assigned to monitor them as meddlesome "suits" or "bean counters," but who were necessary for achieving their goals. On the other hand, the suits themselves often regarded their record men as secondary to the artists, just another but necessary asset they had to manage, to reward when successful, discard when not.

The longest tenured record men still standing in 1985 were Ahmet Ertegun of Atlantic; Mo Ostin at WB Records; Jac Holzman of Elektra; Clive Davis, who had helmed both CBS and Arista; Bhaskar Menon of EMI; and Joe Smith, who moved from WB Records to Elektra/Asylum, and then to Capitol, along with indie label owners Chris Blackwell of Island, Berry Gordy at Motown, Jerry Moss of A&M, Seymour Stein from Sire, and Chris Wright of Chrysalis. They had perfected the balance between corporate and creative, equally comfortable on the street or in the boardroom. By doing so they had established their companies and themselves at the top of the record industry. A new generation of baby boomers, shaped by the social upheaval of the 1960s, were working their way up the executive pecking order, poised to guide the industry into the digital age. Their ability to successfully emulate or possibly even exceed their record men role models would shape the industry over the decades to come.

The same six major label groups dominated the industry in 1985 as they had for the past decade. The Columbia/CBS Records Group (CBS) with the Columbia, CBS, and Epic/Portrait/Associated labels; Warner Elektra Atlantic (WEA) with the WB Records, Reprise, Elektra/Asylum, Atlantic, and Sire labels; RCA Victor (RCA) with the RCA, Ariola, and Arista imprints; and the MCA Records Group (MCA) were all domestically owned. Capitol/EMI and the PolyGram Record Group (PolyGram) were British and Dutch/German, respectively. They competed against one another for market share, retail shelf space, radio play, and ultimately consumer dollars in the music genres that corresponded to the major radio formats. In 1985 this included AC (adult contemporary), CHR (contemporary hit radio), AOR (album-oriented radio), country, and R&B/black/urban. Weekly charts in *Billboard* and other industry trade publications tracked and reported the shifting sales and airplay in these formats to present a weekly snapshot of the state of current national and regional market share.

The Inner Workings of the Artist Royalty System

While their parent companies had different motivations and goals tied to larger corporate strategies, record labels all operated on similarly designed business models. Their relative success and the job security of top management depended on income from already-received sales receipts, anticipated revenue from product still circulating in the distribution system, and market share on trade charts and industry analyses, but most important, on profit. The best-selling albums were not always the most profitable as profits were the difference between sales revenue and the expenses incurred in generating that revenue. A more extensive promotion campaign cost more dollars and often a larger quantity of free goods, lowering net receipts. Every album had its own unique balance between cost and profit. The most successful record executives were the ones who achieved the larger ratios of profit over cost throughout the span of their careers.

The major label groups all used similarly structured accounting systems. Each label's ledger had three distinct but interrelated sections. First were the accounts for each artist detailing expenses, and then royalty revenue. The second detailed the flow of product and cash between the labels and each of their various wholesale customers for each album. The third combined the first two into record division line items in the year-end financial statement of the overall corporate parent. Both the fixed and variable income and expense categories for both artists and customers were consolidated into single line entries summarizing the collective profit or loss but no financial pro forma on individual artists or accounts.

On each artist's ledger, the labels recouped the artist's recording costs, mutually approved marketing expenses, and cash advances against otherwise payable royalties, which in effect made artists repay the funding of their careers out of future earnings if they sold enough records to do so. If they didn't, the unrecouped share became a part of the loss column on the parent company ledger. Determining artists' precise share of revenue was complicated by varying royalty rates for different usages and multiple levels of retail prices with a myriad of conditional deductions. Between 30 and 50 percent of otherwise payable royalties were usually held in accrual as a reserve against the return of product shipped, to be liquidated over subsequent biannual accounting periods. Artists' royalties from different albums and third-party licenses were cross-collateralized against each other to maximize recoupment on each project. Essentially, the profits from artists' hits absorbed the costs from their less successful releases. For successful artists, this accounting process usually led to periodic audits of the label's books to assure that the liquidation of held-back reserves was properly administrated.

From the late 1970s forward, almost all recording contracts contained a controlled composition clause with a royalty ceiling set at ten times 75 percent of the statutory rate at the time of first release. This clause then transferred the mechanical license costs paid to publishers in excess of the controlled rate to the artist as another cost recoupable from royalties. In 1985 the statutory mechanical rate was 4.5¢, ten times that was 45¢, and 75 percent of that was 33.75¢. Artists were contractually responsible for getting publishers to agree to this rate for all tracks on the album. Any failure to do so was applied as a recoupable expense against the artist's royalties, whether emanating from additional songs or from any publishers not granting the reduced rate.

Controlled composition clauses originated prior to the introduction of the CD. Since vinyl albums could hold only twenty-two to twenty-four minutes of music on each side, ten tracks with five per side allowed for an average of around 4.5 minutes per track. At first, additional tracks on the CD version were referred to as bonus tracks, but as the LP was phased out, it became standard practice for artists to include the additional tracks. More tracks were also used to justify the higher price to the consumer. Nonetheless, the additional mechanical license costs for any amount over ten tracks or tracks over five minutes were still subject to the controlled composition clause.

If an album had twelve songs, and assuming all publishers granted the reduced rate and none of the tracks were over five minutes, the total mechanical cost at the reduced rate was 40.5¢. With the label only responsible for 33.75¢ under the controlled composition clause, the difference of 6.75¢ was applied to the artist's royalties. On a million albums, this amounted to $67,500. With the mechanical rate rising 46.7 percent to 6.6¢ per track in 1995, everything rose proportionally with the $67,500 rising to $99,000. In 1995, publishing chargebacks against artist royalties would be even higher if there were more than twelve songs on the album; if any tracks exceeded five minutes, causing an additional cost of 85¢ per minute per unit; or if any of the publishers with songs or shares of songs on the album did not comply with the controlled rate.

While some of this system may seem byzantine, draconian, and/or biased in favor of the record companies, it was the price artists were willing to pay in exchange for a record company's investment in their careers. If artists did indeed achieve the sales success needed to recoup advances and expenses, they could negotiate more favorable terms, or leave that label for another at the end of the contract.

While in today's business, labels and artists in the US collect a sizable amount of performance rights royalties through SoundExchange for digital transmissions, in 1985 the performance right was not yet included in US copyright law. This issue was rectified in 1998 for digital but not terrestrial transmissions, that is, radio, with passage of the Digital Millennium Copyright Act (DMCA). In 1985, however, this right was a tenet of international copyright law via the Berne Convention and was enjoyed by labels and artists in Berne-compliant territories. Consequentially, unlike the songwriters and their publishers who collectively received about 4 percent of radio's advertising revenue through ASCAP, BMI, and SESAC, the record companies and their artists did not receive anything from US radio despite supplying records free of cost to the over nine thousand stations that programmed music. Their consolation, of which radio was quick to remind them, was that radio exposing their music to the public was the primary stimulation for record sales, at no charge from the stations to the labels.

The Retail Shipment, Sales, and Returns Supply Chain

The product and sales ledger between the labels and their wholesale accounts tracked a constant two-way flow of shipments and then payment or return of product. Records went out on net 60-day terms, often extended with the release of additional singles anticipated to re-stimulate album sales. Return rights were 100 percent on individual albums, but by 1985 the labels had come to a general understanding with their accounts for a quarterly limit of 20 percent returns on a catalog basis accepted as credit on the next shipment. Remedies for exceeding the 20 percent limit differed from label to label. Proper management of shipping was economically beneficial to both sides, so both usually worked to adhere to this guideline. Initial shipments of hit albums generally sold out in the quarter of first release and were reordered, so seldom were they included in the 20 percent returns limit. On the other hand, albums that did not meet up to initial sales expectations could have returns that vastly surpassed the 20 percent allowance, which were balanced against the absence of returns on successful albums. Even albums that shipped gold but in industry parlance had been over-hyped could yield returns of 20 percent or more.

In 1996 Tommy Boy Records founder and chairman Tom Silverman prepared an analysis of 1995 sales data provided by SoundScan, the retail barcode scanning system introduced in 1991 (more on SoundScan in the next chapter) for the May 1996 National Association of Independent Record Distributors and Manufacturers (NAIRD) Convention. He found that only 148 out of the 26,629 albums that were released in 1995 and had their bar codes scanned at retail outlets registered over 250,000 unit sales during that year. Of these, 48 were certified as platinum or multiplatinum by the RIAA over the next two years and another twenty-five eventually certified as well. There was a total of 5,850 major label releases that sold at least one units each, while the independents released another 11,274 units exceeding that number. That left 9,505 albums that didn't break the one hundred-unit sales barrier.

Retail outlets accounted for most of the annual RIAA shipment summary, but also included within the summary were the shipment totals by the Columbia and RCA (later BMG) record clubs, divisions of CBS and

ANALYSIS OF 1995 ALBUM RELEASES & SALES

This analysis was originally created by Tom Silverman, chairman of independent Tommy Boy Records, utilizing SoundScan data in a 1996 Billboard Commentary advocating for the musical diversity that independent labels bring to the industry.

The diagram reveals that only 148 releases in 1995 sold over 250,000 copies, accounting for 116.2 million units, 56.5% of sales for 1995 releases.

The bottom row shows that, 90.5% of the year's releases sold fewer than 5,000 copies each for 6.9% of total albums scanned.

Silverman also noted that of the 17,124 albums that sold over 100 units, just over one-third were released by the Big Six but accounted for 79% of all sales. The two-thirds released by independents sold only 21% of the scanned total.

CURRENT ALBUM RELEASES TO REACH SALES LEVEL % OF ALL RELEASES	PER ALBUM SALES LEVEL	COMBINED UNIT SALES IN MILLIONS % OF ALL UNIT SALES
148 albums released **.5%** of all releases	**250,000+** units	**116.2 M** units **56.5%** of all units sold
733 albums released **2.5%** of all releases	between **249,999** and **25,000** units each	**54.5 M** units **26.5%** of all units sold
1919 albums released **6.5%** of all releases	between **24,999** and **5,000** units each	**20.8 M** units **10.1%** of all units sold
26,629 albums released **90.5%** of all releases	between **4,999** and **1** units each	**12.2 M** units **5.9%** of all units sold

Source: Tom Silverman/*Billboard*/SoundScan

Illustration 1.1 Analysis of 1995 Album Releases and Sales

RCA/BMG, respectively, although operating independently of their parent labels. These clubs offered discounts and giveaways to entice consumers into monthly continuity plans for purchase of mail-order product. In some years, club shipments could approach and even exceed 20 percent of the RIAA-listed shipment total, with 50 percent or more of the clubs' total consisting of giveaways, all of which were included in the total shipments listed in the RIAA annual report. Despite being included in the totals that determined gold and platinum sales status, artists did not receive royalties on the giveaways. These club sales, giveaways, discounted sales on front line product, and lower prices on midline and budget line releases combined to create a difference between the labels' published suggested retail list price (SRLP) and the average retail value calculated by dividing the RIAA sales totals by the number of units cited in the report.

The Label Financial Statement

Consistent with the objectives of most corporate entities, the main concern was the monetary return to shareholders and the effect of EBITDA (earnings before interest, taxes, depreciation, and amortization) on share price and dividends. The music division's financial statements were consolidated into collective line-item categories within the income and expense columns of the overall entertainment divisions. There was no itemization of individual artists' accounts or delineation of revenue items by separate identified sources. Income and expenses were divided between recorded music and publishing divisions, with revenue further subdivided between sales and licensing. Expense categories included artist and repertoire (A&R), which included recording and advances, product manufacturing, licensing, general/administrative, sales and marketing, and distribution. Further information pertaining to artist roster, gold and platinum sales certifications, Grammy awards, market share, personnel, operations, and a general industry overview were summarized elsewhere in the annual report.

The totals in the annual RIAA revenue report, however, differed from what was entered in the label financial statements as the RIAA reported the overall industry retail revenue value as what the consumers paid, not the wholesale amount the labels actually received from the distributors as income in the range of 60 percent to 70 percent of the retail price paid by consumers. Other label revenue sources absent from the RIAA reports included licensing income from sale of US product by foreign affiliates and revenue from sync licenses for use of master recordings in film, television, or other visual media.

Synch license revenue was finally added to the RIAA report as a line item · in 2009.

From the standpoint of corporate profitability, a label's misses often had more impact than their successes. For new albums designated for a full radio and videoclip marketing campaign, a label had probably invested $1.3 million or more through signing advances, recording budgets, and other marketing costs, all of which were recouped by the label from the artist's otherwise payable royalties. This $1.3 million comprised actual cash spent by the label, whether the artist ultimately sold enough records to recoup that amount against royalties or not.

The average album cost to consumers on the 1995 RIAA retail revenue summary calculated to $11.73 on 722.9 million CDs, 272.6 million cassettes, and 2.2 million vinyl albums. This netted an average wholesale price to the labels of about $8 per unit. For an album that sold a million units, the $1.3 million in upfront artist-associated costs was put on the artist ledger as recoupable against royalties, and on the company ledger as an A&R expense. There was about another $1.5 million in non-recoupable manufacturing, shipping, and product handling costs; another $495,500 in publishing royalties; and some other miscellaneous items including musicians' and vocalists' union pension fund contributions. After these costs, the label netted about $4.5 million to contribute to fixed overhead and profit. On the artist ledger, however, there was only about $900,000 in accrued royalties to apply against the $1.3 million in recoupable expenses, leaving around $400,000 unrecouped. It would take sales of about another half million units for the artist to reach a positive royalty flow whether from this album or from other albums in the artist's catalog as royalties from all albums were cross-collateralized against one another.

An album by a new artist receiving a full promotional campaign that reached the 250,000-unit level with no returns took in at best about $2 million in wholesale revenue. After adding up product manufacturing cost of about $375,000, publishing royalties of $61,875, and the $1.3 million front-end cost, there was about $264,000 left to apply to fixed overhead. At this sales plateau, however, the artist ledger recouped only about 10 percent of the front-end expenses, leaving over $1 million still in recoupable expenses before seeing any royalties. A similarly financed and promoted artist that only netted fifty thousand units sold generated about $400,000 in revenue, leaving over $1 million as losses on the company books. Too many failed albums on new artists that received a full marketing campaign quickly ate into the label profits from the successful artists as well as the revenue on catalog and niche genre sales.

New artists' initial contracts usually covered the first five to seven albums with a typical royalty rate of about 12 percent of SRLP. Veteran Los Angeles attorney Don Passman of Gang, Tyre, Ramer, Brown & Passman, whose clients included Taylor Swift, Paul Simon, Stevie Wonder, and Adele, explained artist royalty provisions in his book *All You Need to Know About the Music Business*, first published in 1991 and in its tenth edition in 2019. In addition to the controlled composition clause, provisions in most new artist contracts had long included 25 percent deductions for packaging and 15 percent for free goods/discounts, generally lowering the actual royalty base to 63.75 percent of the contractual royalty rate. Thus a 12 percent new artist contractual rate was reduced to an actual 7.65 percent, a 15 percent rate to 9.6 percent, and a superstar 20 percent rate to 12.75 percent, all calculated on the retail price. In most cases, producer royalties were about a 25 percent share of the artist rate but subject to recoupment only from the recording costs, and after recoupment, retroactively paid from the first record sold.

While this is a simplified and generalized analysis of a complex system, it does portray the variables involved in calculating profitability against income. One million is not a random figure chosen for easy math, but rather a sales milestone used for both accounting and publicity. One million units shipped on one artist was the criterion for certification as a platinum record by the RIAA. The number of platinum records achieved by each label became a major competitive barometer of relative success.

RIAA membership included all the majors and most of the larger independent labels. The RIAA estimated that they represented 90 percent of retail shipments and then adjusted the grand total to reflect the total market. Platinum and gold certifications were based on the shipping invoices provided to the RIAA by the record companies themselves. For 1985, the RIAA reported $4.36 billion in revenue value, the second year in a row it received over $4 billion following five years averaging $3.75 billion, and an amount that surpassed the previous high in 1978 of $4.13 billion.

A Hit Cures All Ills—The Measures of Success

A common industry mantra was the phrase "a hit record cures all ills," with ills being unsuccessful albums. Hits started somewhere between platinum and double platinum status. The RIAA introduced diamond record certification in 1999, signifying ten million units shipped, which was retroactively awarded to all albums ever released that had cumulatively reached the 10 million–unit plateau. Companies would go to great lengths to create a stable of flagship artists who could sell ten million units. In turn, flagship artists at the end of contracts would be in extremely favorable positions for renegotiating large advances and higher royalty rates, or in seeking competitive bidding from other labels. A single album reaching 10 million units in the pre-CD market had probably netted the label somewhere in the $40 million range. That amount almost doubled when the higher-priced CDs took over the industry.

Active artists in 1985 who would eventually earn diamond status for the CBS group were Michael Jackson, Boston, and Meatloaf on Epic; Bruce Springsteen and Aerosmith on Columbia; and Billy Joel on CBS. WEA was led by Led Zeppelin, AC/DC, and Phil Collins on Atlantic, while WB Records had Prince & the Revolution, James Taylor, Fleetwood Mac, Doobie Brothers, ZZ Top, and Van Halen. RCA had two with Whitney Houston on Arista and Carole King on Ode/A&M.

EMI also had two with Pink Floyd on Capitol and Kenny Rogers on Liberty/ EMI. MCA had only one with Lionel Richie from its distributed Motown label. PolyGram scored with two artists, Elton John and Def Leppard, as well as two soundtrack albums, *Grease* and *Saturday Night Fever*. Deceased or disbanded diamond level acts were Elvis Presley on RCA, The Beatles on Apple (EMI), Simon & Garfunkel on Columbia, the Doors on Elektra, the Eagles on Asylum, and Patsy Cline on MCA.

In label group competition for most albums certified in 1985, WEA had twenty-two platinum and thirty-eight gold certifications, CBS twelve platinum and twenty-one gold, RCA twelve platinum and twenty-nine gold, Capitol/EMI eight platinum and thirteen gold, MCA six platinum and twenty-one gold, and PolyGram five platinum and nine gold certifications. Independent Chrysalis had two gold albums. These certifications were for reaching those milestones during 1985 whether released that year or in an earlier year.

Another indication of yearly success in addition to RIAA certifications was the share of the *Billboard* charts. In 1985 WEA had 35 of the Top 100 Pop Chart artists, followed by CBS with 16. RCA and MCA (including Motown) both had 15. EMI followed with 9, PolyGram had 8, and independents came in with 4. Two artists had certified albums with two different labels accounting for the 102-album total.

In 1985 CD players were not yet capable of recording. The CD-R and CD players with a recording function were not widely available until the mid-1990s. The industry viewed this inability to make copies in the CD format as an additional level of deterrence in their battle with home duplication. While the CD's claim of greater durability was valid for both LPs and cassettes, and for cassettes as to fidelity, there was an industrywide divide over whether reproduction of sound as offered by digital technology and the CD was of higher audio quality than analog recording and vinyl discs. Although the

CD gradually replaced the LP as a consumer product except for the high-end audiophile market, the digital versus analog debate has persisted ever since among audio engineers, artists, and audiophiles.

Life at the Top of the Record Business Pyramid

Billboard and other trade paper charts were a shifting barometer of record company success and failure based on the combination of radio play and retail sales. The top industry executives who followed these charts were highly intelligent, intensely motivated, often musically talented, and super competitive. Many were as charismatic as the artists they were marketing. They conducted business like a clandestine campaign replete with military and sports metaphors. While reading and reacting to the constantly changing tea leaves, these executives were simultaneously brewing the teapot. Their ability to anticipate, design, coordinate, and, when necessary, abort marketing campaigns on a dozen or more different artists simultaneously, was a necessary skill set only acquired on the job.

They also knew that everyone in front, behind, and alongside them was also vying for the next rung up the ladder. The surface culture, however, was one of cooperation and teamwork masking the underlying machinations of intense intracompany competition. Their parent companies were constantly pushing for increased profits, expanded market share, and higher visibility through awards and press coverage, while balancing the value of their music investments against the other assets in their portfolios. This internal corporate pressure, combined with the external stress from the weekly changing charts, often pushed label executives to the edge of the risk/reward ratio to maintain their competitive balance relative to one another. While it usually took twenty years or more of juggling risks to get to the top of the record industry pyramid, one or two years of low reward could end even the highest executive's shelf life, or even send an entire label staff cascading down into oblivion.

Despite the pivotal role the top record company executives played in what music was made available to the public through radio, retail, and video clips, many had remained at arms' length from both the public and the street, the incubator where new talent and trends got their start. Contact with the street was relegated to younger staffers farther down the totem pole through the radio stations, record stores, and music clubs that served as the points of contact for consumers with the music industry. The top executives' role with artists on the label, however, was totally hands on as they decided who was signed to the label, how much money would be spent, how many records would be shipped, and which tracks would receive top priority for promotion and marketing dollars.

Industry politics, hiring, and firing were based on an ever-shifting convergence of personal relationships and obligations. The careers of both artists and label executives could heat up quickly with a hit, last for an unpredicted period, and then just as quickly go cold. The ability to manage and manipulate relationships was as crucial to success as knowing how to maximize a record's sales potential and then, when the market cooled, get out without over-shipping and thus losing profits through returned product.

The people who reached the apex of the pyramid, whether for a short interregnum or for a historic reign, knew that similar to when a #1 record left the charts, when a CEO's string of successes hit a snag, the next man up went to bat and business went on as usual, either with improved results, or the process would repeat itself with those next in line who had been as anxiously waiting for the opportunity as had their predecessors.

Only as Hot as Your Last Hit

The record business was not an equal opportunity marketplace. Artists who weren't signed by labels or the ones who had been but didn't sell enough to have their contracts renewed could not get on radio even on a local basis and had no access to national television. The new, larger venues were prohibitively expensive, or simply unavailable to these artists. Even recording new tracks was an expensive undertaking. Only thirty years prior, a musician and producer could record on a two-track machine in a radio station or storefront studio, but now to be considered professional and competitive they had to record on multitrack machines in acoustically perfected studios.

No matter how infatuated the public became with a particular artist or song, the record labels released new singles weekly by both new and established artists to compete with and eventually replace the ones already on the charts. The number one record changed on the average of every three weeks, after which the previous number one left the current radio rotation within a few weeks and then dropped from the front to the back, and then out of the retail record racks. After even the most successful singles concluded their chart runs, the artists who sang them had to start all over with a new release again competing for chart position with other artists, from both their own and rival labels. While many artists sustained long careers with multiple hits, there were far more whose careers never reached the mountaintop, or only did so once to subsequently join the ranks of what became known as "one-hit wonders."

Most artists, even ones with gold and sometimes platinum records, actually lived off their box-office income. For live performances, successful artists were paid up to 75% of the gross receipts, and this total was sometimes more for superstars. The standard industry share for an artist's professional advisors was usually in the range of between 30 percent and 35 percent of earnings with 10 percent to the agent, 15 percent to the manager, and then 5 percent to the attorney and 5 percent to the business manager if these functions were separate from management. Next, all other costs including side musicians, staging, accommodations, and transportation were deducted from artists' net income. This left artists with 30 percent to 40 percent of the box office total.

This economic equation was profitable for superstars who could draw large audiences, but new to mid-level artists, who often had to ask for additional advances from their record companies and music publishers, a request that left them in a weakened negotiating position at contract time. Labels often covered the shortfall in touring income for exciting new artists in order to get them exposure in showcase clubs or on concert tours as an opening act, but tour support was also recoupable from future royalties.

The various labels that made up each of the six major label groups—led by WB Records, Elektra, and Atlantic for WEA, and Columbia and Epic for CBS—each had separate divisions for the three radio genres that sold the most records: pop which encompassed the CHR, AOL, and AC formats; soul, rebranded from R&B in 1973 and subsequently to black/urban/R&B; and country. Each genre within each label had its own A&R, marketing, sales, publicity, and promotion staffs dedicated to maximizing record sales. Staffers usually rose through the ranks. Some A&R reps had been successful producers, songwriters, or musicians, while others came from talent or venue management companies. Personnel in sales and marketing generally had learned the ropes in record stores or at local distributors, while promotion staffers most often started in radio. As of 1985 this included the growing pool of college radio stations. Publicists usually began at fan magazines, newspapers, or local promotion companies.

Entry positions ordinarily started at the local level with the most productive advancing to regional responsibilities. By the time an even smaller number moved on to national positions, they were experienced, battle-tested, and able to immediately shift their attention from one artist to the next in rhythm with the up and down movement on the charts. It was a highly competitive, stress-laden, and elevated-risk environment. Success promised high rewards, while repeated failures meant opportunity for the next person in line. Like artists, but not to such an extreme degree, employees were only as hot as their last hit.

Creating relationships and participating in team efforts were essential in successfully weathering the misses that invariably outnumbered the hits. Close involvement with one multimillion selling artist, however, could outweigh several experiences with underachievers. As in baseball, an over .300 batting average not only kept one in the game but also garnered all-star status. Only a few would achieve the exhilaration, fame, and fortune brought by a hit record, and join a fraternal but highly competitive world of workaholics whose love for music was only matched or exceeded by their drive for success. Most stalled somewhere along the way, exiting with just memories for their efforts. An even smaller cadre reached a plateau short of the summit, but sustained a long and successful career at that level. Even fewer, however, grew old on the job, as younger, aggressive underlings were constantly seeking to displace them.

Warner/Elektra/Atlantic: The End of an Era

By 1985, WEA had long been a collection of album-centric and artist-friendly labels run independently of one another by veteran leadership, but with shared pressing and distribution. Mo Ostin was still at the top of WB Records with long-time chief lieutenants Lenny Waronker, Ted Templeman, and Russ Titelman under him. Sire Records cofounder Seymour Stein had sold the previously independent label to WB Records in 1978 and subsequently signed Madonna and the Pretenders. Cofounder and chairman Ahmet Ertegun still reigned at Atlantic Records, aided by president Doug Morris, a former songwriter and co-owner of Atlantic-distributed Big Tree Records, along with executive vice president/general manager Dave Glew. Elektra/Asylum/ Nonesuch was under the leadership of Bob Krasnow, cofounder and former president of Blue Thumb Records and veteran WB Records acquisition executive. Ahmet Ertegun's older brother and original Atlantic partner Nesuhi Ertegun was still head of Warner International.

In 1985 WEA was once again at the top of the year-end charts, led by Prince, Madonna, Phil Collins, Van Halen, Dire Straits, REM, and Fleetwood Mac, complemented by an extraordinary back catalog including Led Zeppelin and the Eagles. Long-time top management was still in place with a cadre of second-level management on the rise. In 1983, WEA had tried to merge the record division with PolyGram to strengthen the worldwide sales of its top artists, but European regulatory bodies were leery of any one record group controlling such a large share of the world market.

THE "BIG SIX" RECORD LABEL GROUPS 1985-1995

MCA MUSIC & ENTERTAINMENT GROUP 1985-1995	POLYGRAM RECORDS, INC. 1985-1991 POLYGRAM GROUP DISTRIBUTION, INC. 1991-1995	CAPITOL/EMI RECORDS 1985-1993 EMI RECORD GROUP 1993-1995	WEA (Warner Elektra Atlantic) 1985-1991 WARNER MUSIC GROUP 1991-1995	CBS RECORDS 1985-1991 SONY MUSIC 1991-1995	RCA RECORDS 1985-1986 BMG MUSIC 1986-1995

THE "BIG SIX" LABEL GROUP LEADERSHIP

Irving Azoff 1985-1989 ... Al Teller 1989-1995 ... Doug Morris 1995	Dick Asher 1985-1990 ... Alain Levy 1990-1995	Bhasker Menon 1985-1987 ... Joe Smith 1987-1993 ... Charles Koppelman 1993-1995	Bob Morgado 1985-1995 ... Michael Fuchs 1995 ... Bob Daly & Terry Semel 1995	Walter Yetnikoff 1985-1990 ... Tommy Mottola 1990-1995	Elliott Goldman 1985-1987 ... Michael Dornemann 1987-1995

CORPORATE OWNERSHIP / HEADQUARTERS / LEADERSHIP

MCA, INC. USA 1985-1990 Japan 1990-1995 Lew Wasserman 1985-1995 ... SEAGRAM Canada Edgar Bronfman, Jr. 1995	SEIMENS AG Germany & PHILIPS NV Holland 1985-1991 Wisse Dekker 1982-1986 ... Cor v.d. Klugt 1986-1990 PHILIPS NV 1991-1995 Jan Timmer 1990-1995	THORN/EMI U.K. Colin Southgate 1985-1995	WARNER COMMUNICATIONS USA Steve Ross 1985-1988 ... TIME WARNER Steve Ross 1988-1992 ... Gerald Levin 1992-1995	CBS, INC. USA Bill Paley 1985-1988 ... SONY CORP JAPAN Norio Ohga 1989-1995	RCA VICTOR GENERAL ELECTRIC USA Jack Welch 1985-1986 ... BERTELSMANN GERMANY Michael Dornemann 1987-1995

AFFILIATED RECORD LABELS

MCA Decca Uptown Geffen (after 1990) Motown (before 1991)	PolyGram Polydor Mercury Island Motown (after 1991) A&M (after 1989) Def Jam (after 1994)	Capitol EMI America Apple SBK Chrysalis Virgin Blue Note Liberty Casablanca	Warner Bros Reprise Elektra Asylum Atlantic Sire Interscope East-West Geffen (before 1990)	Columbia Epic Portrait Cleveland Int'l. Legacy Def Jam (before 1994)	RCA Arista Ariola Jive LaFace Bad Boy A&M (before 1989)

Source: *Billboard*

Illustration 1.2 The "Big Six" Record Label Groups, 1985–95

By 1988, however, parent Warner Communications, Inc. (WCI) was in debt from investing in Atari and buying American Express out of their Warner/Amex cable television co-venture. These debts had offset healthy profits from the record division and kept WCI on the lookout for a possible corporate rather than music-related realignment. In 1989 WCI finally found its dance partner in Time, Inc. after the two fought off a hostile takeover bid of Time by entertainment giant Paramount Communications. To block Paramount, Time paid WCI $14 billion in cash and acquired all WCI stock to form Time Warner Inc. While Time was a force in magazine publishing and WCI had a core strength in music, both had extensive cable television holdings. The merger was completed and WCI's Steve Ross became the CEO of the new company.

Ross then delegated the oversight of the music division to Robert Morgado, chief of staff to former New York governor Hugh Carey. Morgado had been hired by Ross in 1985 to create a more centralized structure designed to increase cost efficiency and grow record distribution for his three largely self-governing record companies. While highly efficient, Morgado was not exactly diplomatic with the record men who had created the trio of labels or who presently ran them.

In 1989 Doug Morris had Atlantic put up $20 million in funding for a joint venture with rap- and rock-oriented Interscope Records, in turn receiving a 25 percent share of the previously independent company. Interscope's founders/partners were movie producer/entrepreneur Ted Field and producer/engineer Jimmy Iovine, whose credits included studio work with U2, Bruce Springsteen, and John Lennon. They both stayed on to run the talent-friendly label, which gave creative control to artists, as well as a major voice in marketing and promotion. They attracted both rappers like Tupac Shakur and rockers like No Doubt. In 1992 Interscope signed a $10 million co-venture with pioneering rap group NWA alumnus Dr. Dre and his new partner Marion "Suge" Knight to finance and distribute independent Death Row Records, bringing them Snoop Dogg and other gangsta rappers. They then signed Nine Inch Nails and Marilyn Manson, also attracted by the artist-friendly atmosphere. By the mid-1990s Interscope was contributing close to half of Atlantic's volume and a quarter of the overall label group's sales success.

With Ross's death in 1992, chairmanship of Time Life passed to Gerald Levin, a veteran Time executive who had started at Time's HBO cable channel. Levin preferred not to replicate Ross's direct ties to the label heads and left that responsibility to Morgado as worldwide chairman and CEO of the entire WEA music group, which was renamed the Warner Music Group (WMG). Morgado openly clashed with Ostin at WB Records and Krasnow at Elektra/

Asylum. His business perspective was more in line with the corporate control ethos of Time than with Ross's laissez faire approach to which the label heads had been accustomed. This was perhaps the classic example of the cultural collision between record men and corporate suits.

Recently elevated to Atlantic cochairman as seventy-year-old Ahmet Ertegun's hand-picked designated successor, Morris fared better with Morgado than did Ostin or Krasnow. Under his leadership Atlantic had become the most productive of the three labels. In June 1994, Morgado appointed Morris president and chief operating officer of the domestic division of WMG, with Ostin and Krasnow now reporting to him. Within a week, Krasnow resigned after eleven years at the helm of Elektra/Asylum. Morris replaced him with his own longtime associate Sylvia Rhone, then president/CEO of Atlantic subsidiary East/West Records. Elektra/Asylum, East/West, and Sire Records were all merged into the Elektra Entertainment Group under her leadership. Mo Ostin's contract at WB Records was to run out at the end of the year, but rather than renegotiate, he announced his resignation in September after more than thirty years at the label. Lenny Waronker and other key executives soon followed.

In late 1994, Morris advocated for increasing the Atlantic share in Interscope, but Morgado vetoed the investment, deeming rap music's implicit lyrics and gangsta persona too controversial for Time's corporate identity. Iovine and Fields immediately began to look elsewhere for a new partner to buy out Atlantic. In response Morgado threatened to interfere with Interscope's right to negotiate with others, which only infuriated them further. When Morris unilaterally completed the increase of the Atlantic share in Interscope to 50 percent in May 1995, Morgado, as worldwide chairman over Morris, complained to Levin about the transaction. Levin took the opportunity to entice Morgado into retirement with a reportedly record-setting buyout "that would pay him between $50 million and $75 million. . . . Mr. Morgado's package includes severance payments and an undisclosed number of stock options, according to executives familiar with the details of the package. He will also receive proceeds from a profit-sharing plan for senior officials of the Warner Music Group," according to a report by Robert Landler of the *Los Angeles Times*.[1]

Levin then replaced Morgado with longtime *Time* associate Michael Fuchs, then chairman of HBO. Fuchs took on the job as an added responsibility to his duties at HBO although he had no experience in the music business. This was not, however, the end of Morris's problems with the conflict between corporate protocol and his street sense as a record man. He wanted to add independent rap label and distributor Priority Records to the WMG fold, but Fuchs objected and dismissed Morris in June 1995. In September Time Warner announced it would sell Atlantic's half interest in Interscope back to Field and Iovine for $115 million. Meanwhile Morris resurfaced at rival MCA, and in the next year so would Interscope. In November Fuchs was let go with his own severance package related to his tenure at HBO. His duties with both the record and cable divisions were reassigned to cochairmen/CEOs of Warner Pictures, Terry Semel and Robert Daly.

From CBS to Sony and Yetnikoff to Mottola

While WMG led the Big Six record label group rankings with 125 albums making it onto the Top Pop Albums chart during 1985, the CBS group was a strong #2 with one hundred of its own. Columbia Records, the larger of CBS's two label divisions, was actually the top label with 78 charted albums in 1985. The closest WMG label was WB Records (including its subsidiaries Sire and Reprise) with 51 charted albums.

By 1985 former CBS corporate attorney Walter Yetnikoff was entrenched as the flamboyant head of the CBS label group, which he had reimaged in the artist-friendly mold of the WMG family of labels. He updated the highly respected management team that Goddard Lieberson and then Clive Davis had led from 1956 through 1973 to identify top talent in all genres and maximize the market potential of multiple artists concurrently. Under Yetnikoff, Michael Jackson's *Thriller* sold over 40 million copies, Springsteen's *Born in the U.S.A.* sold over 20 million, and Billy Joel's *The Stranger* sold more than 13 million. He also oversaw the emergence of Cyndi Lauper and Gloria Estefan while extending the careers of Willie Nelson and Julio Iglesias from their respective country and Latin bases into international stardom.

CBS Records, however, like WMG, was just a part of a much larger entity where executives higher up the corporate chain could count on a successful record division to be the cash cow supporting other business endeavors. Now in his mid-eighties, founder William S. Paley had ceded control of CBS to board member and Loew's Inc. chairman Laurence Tisch, who had amassed a large share of the company's stock. CBS TV had fallen from its longstanding top spot to third place in the ratings, while foiling a Ted Turner–led takeover attempt that put CBS even deeper into debt. Yetnikoff organized and the board accepted a sale of the whole record division to his longtime Japanese associates at the Sony Corporation in late 1987 to close in 1988 for $2 billion in cash. *Rolling Stone's* Fred Goodman reported, "To retain the label's key executives, Sony offered a sizable sum—reportedly $50 million—in bonuses" with Yetnikoff's share "said to be as much as $20 million. Yetnikoff won't divulge just how much Sony paid him, but he does allow that the Japanese firm has made him a rich man."[2]

With the company heavily dependent upon its stable of established stars and in need of an infusion of new talent, Yetnikoff replaced longtime lieutenant Al Teller with artist manager Tommy Mottola, who, along with attorney Allen Grubman, were two members of Yetnikoff's tightly knit inner circle of outside advisors. After starting as a musician and singer, Mottola spent several years in publishing at Chappell & Co. From 1970 forward he built Champion Management with a roster that included Hall & Oates, John Mellencamp, and Carly Simon. Yetnikoff recognized the then-thirty-nine-year-old Mottola as having the street smarts to find new acts that would appeal to young consumers. He was also charged with hiring and overseeing a younger team of executive talent to better compete on the street with the other major labels. Mottola succeeded almost immediately, signing Mariah Carey who went on to sell over 200 million records in her career; breaking boy band New Kids on the Block, who moved over 80 million albums worldwide; and establishing Michael Bolton as a blue-eyed soul crooner who would top 75 million albums sold. Mottola also hired powerhouse promotion honcho Don Ienner away from Arista to become president of Columbia, instilling a more aggressive attitude in marketing new product.

In 1989, Yetnikoff also gained control over the recently acquired Columbia Motion Pictures, which Sony had purchased from Coca Cola for $3.4 billion. He immediately hired producers Peter Guber and Jon Peters to run the film company though they were already under contract to Time Warner, which filed suit for $1 billion. In 1990, Sony settled and kept Guber and Peters as part of an asset swap with Time Warner that included a 50 percent interest in the Columbia House Records Club mail order business. Meanwhile Yetnikoff, seemingly emboldened by his increase in power, somehow managed to alienate Bruce Springsteen and Michael Jackson and their management teams as well as former friend Grubman, who remained close to Mottola.

The final curtain fell on Yetnikoff's fifteen-year reign in early 1990, just after he signed a three-year contract extension and finished a stay in rehab, with the publication of a book titled *Hitmen* serving as a catalyst. Author Fred Dannen dramatically described record companies fraternizing with organized crime figures and chronicled Yetnikoff's often erratic behavior. A $25 million buyout was applied to what had become a public embarrassment to the decorum-conscious Sony with Mottola replacing his one-time mentor as head of the CBS Record Group.

On January 1, 1991, when the license for the CBS name expired, Sony renamed the record group Sony Music Entertainment but retained the Columbia Records and Epic Records imprints for its two labels. In 1993 Mottola's success was rewarded with the position of president and CEO of Sony Music Entertainment worldwide. In January 1994 he solidified his executive team with a flurry of promotions. Veteran business affairs executive Mel Ilberman, who had been at RCA when the Mottola-managed Hall & Oates had their major hits there, and served as president of Sony Music International since 1992, was named chairman of that division; Don Ienner became chairman of Columbia Records; David Glew, president of Epic Records since 1989 after twenty years at Atlantic, become chairman of Epic Records Group; Michele Anthony, former entertainment attorney and executive vice president of Sony Music since January 1993, was named executive vice president of Sony Music Entertainment.

From RCA to BMG as Clive Drives Resurgence

Early in 1985, RCA and privately owned German media company Bertelsmann AG, their partner in Ariola Records in Europe and Clive Davis's partner in Arista Records, announced their intention to rearrange their relationship into a new entity named RCA/Ariola International. RCA would own 75 percent of the joint venture outside of Europe with Bertelsmann owning 25 percent. European ownership would be split fifty-fifty, with Bertelsmann having managerial control. Former CBS, Arista, and WEA attorney and senior executive Elliott Goldman was brought in to reinvigorate the label group. The next year the entire RCA Corporation was acquired by General Electric for a price reported by *The New York Times* to be almost $6.3 billion. GE's primary interest was the NBC broadcasting network and it intended to sell the record division.

In December 1986 Bertelsmann closed on the purchase of GE's share of RCA/Ariola for $450 million and renamed the entire company the Bertelsmann Music Group (BMG). In September 1987 Elliot Goldman resigned and his operating responsibilities were passed to Michael Dornemann, cochairman of the BMG German division, giving a Bertelsmann insider a more hands-on involvement in the US division. Dornemann hired former artist manager Bob Buziak to lead the US operation, specifically to trim roster, hire new staff, and sign developing artists to increase market share, much like what Yetnikoff had done with Mottola.

BMG's distributed label group included Arista Records, their co-venture with Clive Davis, who had been Yetnikoff's predecessor at CBS. Arista was riding high with the 1985 debut of Whitney Houston, who would go on to sell over 200 million albums for Arista over the length of her career. In 1981 Arista had entered into a co-venture with London-based Clive Calder and Ralph Simon's Zomba Music Group. Their Jive Records label brought in the rights to British pop and dance artists while also branching out into hip hop under the A&R leadership of the streetwise Barry Weiss, son of longtime independent record man Hy Weiss of 1950s Top 40 label Old Town Records.

In 1987 Jive transferred its BMG connection from Arista to the RCA label division and brought DJ Jazzy Jeff & the Fresh Prince, The Skinny Boys, Too $hort, and Schoolly D into the RCA fold. Davis filled the void created by Jive's defection with a joint venture with LaFace Records, owned by the rising production/songwriting team of Antonio "L.A." Reid and Kenneth "Baby Face" Edmonds. The two had been the driving force behind the Cincinnati-based recording act The Deele, with chart success for Dick Griffey's Solar Records. Over the next few years, they brought TLC, Usher, Outkast, P!nk, and Toni Braxton into their venture. Davis further strengthened his position within the BMG group by opening Arista Nashville in 1989, headed by producer/songwriter/CPA Tim DuBois who struck immediate platinum success with Alan Jackson and Brooks & Dunn.

RCA Nashville had long been a major profit center for what was now BMG, as the home base for Elvis Presley and its strong roster of current country artists including Alabama, The Judds, Ronnie Milsap, and a deep, decades-old back catalog. Under the leadership of Joe Galante, RCA Nashville was *Billboard's* #1 country label for much of the 1980s. Despite his successful streamlining of the RCA pop division, Buziak's success with new product paled in comparison to that of Davis at Arista or Mottola at Sony. In 1990, BMG moved Galante to New York to replace Buziak as head of the RCA pop division.

In 1990 Davis suffered a rare setback when the music press discovered that the six million album–selling, Best New Artist Grammy Award–winning vocal duo Milli Vanilli had not sung on their own album and lip-synched in live performance. The Recording Academy revoked their Grammy while Arista dropped them from the roster, deleted their album, and complied with court-mandated rebates to consumers. Although Arista was unaware that the supposed singers were just hired actors, the damage had been done. The digital cat had been let out of the bag as the Eventide Harmonizer, the Synclavier, Fairlight CMI, Sound Designer, and other sound processing innovations that could mask vocal deficiencies by digitally tuning the vocal track were now widespread in both the recording process and live performances. *The Washington Post's* Carla Hall reported that when asked if they were just in it for the money at their initial press conference unveiling the deception, Rob Pilatus, half of the duo with Fab Morvan, shot back, "We lived in a project. We had no money. We wanted to be stars. . . . We knew if we didn't accept that [offer] we knew we would still be in Munich. I would still work at the McDonald's."[3]

But after a slight lull, Arista regained its platinum touch by 1992 with instrumentalist Kenny G, the still-booming country division, and the success of the LaFace stable of artists. The crowning touch was the worldwide success of *The Bodyguard* soundtrack album in 1993, featuring Whitney Houston's #1 single, a stirring rendition of the Dolly Parton–penned "I Will Always Love You," destined to ultimately exceed 45 million units sold worldwide. In 1993, Davis formed the Bad Boy Records joint venture with Sean "Puff Daddy" Combs, a former A&R director at Andre Harrell's Uptown Records. Combs followed with success by the Notorious B.I.G., Mase, and Faith Evans. In 1994, Arista's Swedish trio Ace of Base hit the triple crown with *Billboard*'s #1 artist, single, and album of the year.

Arista was ranked as *Billboard*'s #2 chart label in 1994, but RCA came in at #10 despite the success of the Dave Matthews Band and Lisa Loeb. Meanwhile RCA Nashville had fallen from its consistent top ranking under Galante's reign in the 1980s. Dornemann decided a change was necessary at RCA in both the pop and country divisions. In late 1994 the loyal and effective Galante agreed to return to Nashville in January 1995 in the newly created post of chairman of RCA Label Group (RLG) Nashville.

Dornemann also decided to bundle all music, movie, and interactive content under one banner, appointing Strauss Zelnick in January 1995 as president/CEO of the newly formed BMG Entertainment North America. The thirty-seven-year old Zelnick held Harvard MBA and law degrees. He already had corporate and entrepreneurial experience in film and interactive media as a digital consultant to BMG but had never been in the record business. In March 1995 Zelnick moved RCA veteran Bob Jamieson from Canada to New York to turn around the pop division. Now entering his third decade as Arista's chairman and managing partner, Davis continued to report directly to Dornemann.

MCA: Azoff to Teller to Morris as Seagram Steps In

Irving Azoff, the veteran manager of the Eagles, Steely Dan, Stevie Nicks, Heart, and others, was only thirty-five years old in 1983 when he became chairman of the floundering MCA Records. He was the first baby boomer to assume the top position at one of the six major label groups. Azoff trimmed both roster and staff, signed Motown Records for distribution in 1983, and in

1988 purchased Motown from founder Berry Gordy for $61 million in partnership with Boston Ventures. By 1985 MCA was back in the game propelled by hits from Azoff signees Glenn Frey, Tom Petty, Fine Young Cannibals, and New Edition, combined with its strong country roster and the Motown catalog. By 1988, MCA was in a revitalized fourth place among the six majors behind WMG, CBS, and BMG with 13.8 percent of the *Billboard* album and singles charts, ahead of EMI's 10.5 percent, and PolyGram's 10.2 percent. In September 1988 Azoff brought in recently exited CBS president and Harvard MBA Al Teller as president and COO of MCA Records, while Azoff remained chairman of the MCA Music Group.

In 1989 Azoff resigned to return to his own entertainment company. For the past year, MCA had been embroiled in a controversy centered around allegations of involvement with a reputed organized crime figure that included a nationwide radio payola scheme and the premature recall of recent albums, removing them from the active catalog (see next chapter). The recalled albums were then declared "deletes" for which no royalties would be due and sold at a vastly reduced price to "cutout dealers" who then profitably recirculated them in the market. Although the subject of rumors and innuendo, Azoff was never indicted or directly implicated.

When he resigned, he stated that the scandal was not the reason. Azoff told the *LA Times*, "This was basically a career decision. I wanted to be an owner again. It was (a question of) quality of life, as well as financially motivated."[4] For the past two years, he had tried to convince MCA to make a public offering for parent company MCA, Inc., which would have given him a stock ownership position, but longtime MCA Inc. chairman Lew Wasserman opposed the plan. Azoff then shopped for a home for his new label Giant Records and decided to run his distribution through WMG.

Teller was then promoted to chairman of the music group. In March 1990, MCA bought Geffen Records, the label formed in 1980 by manager and Asylum Records founder David Geffen, who received $550 million in MCA stock, giving him a 12 percent share in the company, making him the largest MCA shareholder. Geffen's catalog included Guns N' Roses, Aerosmith, Cher, Don Henley, Whitesnake, Peter Gabriel, Tesla, Rickie Lee Jones, Joni Mitchell, and Jimmy Page. The purchase shifted Geffen's product and market share from WEA to MCA's UNI distribution arm. Geffen received a five-year management contract to run the company, and upon its expiration in 1995, formed a new record label to be distributed by MCA, co-owned with Steven Spielberg and Jeffrey Katzenberg, his partners in the new DreamWorks SKG film company.

Eight months later, in November 1990, the MCA Music Group, along with MCA, Inc's other entertainment properties including movie, theme park, and television holdings, were all bought by Matsushita Electric Industrial Co. of Japan for $6.59 billion in cash and securities. Matsushita, Japan's largest electronics company and familiar to American consumers through the Panasonic, Technics, and Quasar brands, mirrored the lead of rival Sony in acquiring film and music content that could be played on its electronics hardware array of brands.

MCA continued to expand under the first two years of Teller's stewardship, especially into hard rock and rap, the two genres with the greatest appeal to the then-current fourteen-to-twenty-eight-year old demographic. Gary Gersh of Geffen brought in Nirvana, propelling the Seattle-based grunge craze to national prominence, and Andre Harrell's Uptown Records contributed Heavy D & The Boyz, Jodeci, Mary J. Blige, and Al B. Sure! Although the MCA label group was still scoring with current chart success, their loss of the Motown catalog to PolyGram weakened their market share as measured by the newly adopted SoundScan retail sales tabulation system (see next chapter), dropping them down to sixth place in scanned sales by the end of 1995.

In May 1995 Canada's Seagram, the largest distiller of alcoholic beverages in the world, bought 80 percent of Matsushita's share of MCA stock for $5.7 billion. Forty-year-old Seagram chairman Edgar Bronfman Jr. had succeeded his father the year before at the company his grandfather had acquired in 1928. He wanted to reposition Seagram as an entertainment company and sold Seagram's 24.3 percent share of DuPont stock back to DuPont for $9 billion to finance the MCA purchase. Bronfman was intent on having a hands-on role in all of MCA's holdings. When Bronfman had been a young teen his father had been a Broadway investor, started the first electronic ticketing pioneer Ticketron, and bought a large share of MGM Studios stock. The younger Bronfman had an artistic bent dabbling in film and music. When he was only seventeen, he took advantage of his father's connection to MGM to produce the Peter Sellers movie, *The Blockhouse*. He went on to cowrite *Dancing in the Dark* for Dionne Warwick and produced *The Border* with Jack Nicholson before joining the Seagram management team in 1982.

When Doug Morris, one of the most successful record man of the past decade, exited WMG in June 1995, Bronfman immediately entered into the Rising Tide Records co-venture with Morris. In November Bronfman named Morris chairman and CEO of the MCA Entertainment Group's music division hoping Morris would duplicate his WMG success at UMG. Teller exited the company at the same time. In an industry that revolves around who has the #1 spot on the charts and controls the top share of the marketplace, when an executive with Morris's track record becomes available, he does not stay that way for long. For over twenty years Teller had been a successful major label executive rising steadily through the ranks to one of the top positions, but with MCA's recent downturn and Morris's availability, there wasn't space for both in the MCA executive suite.

EMI: The Brits Hold Steady with The Beatles, Brooks, and SBK

EMI was operating two US record divisions with Capitol Records and EMI-America Records, along with a Nashville-based office handling country product for both labels. Company veterans Jim Mazza presided over EMI America Records and Don Zimmerman led Capitol Records. In 1985 the combined record group had a 16.4 percent share of the *Billboard* charts, led by Tina Turner, Duran Duran, Sheena Easton, Kenny Rogers, and Heart. Back catalog sales were driven by The Beatles catalog, the crown jewel of the entire industry, and supplemented by an extensive collection of 1960s and 1970s rock, pop, and countless country hits. In 1986 their share dropped to 14.4 percent. Anticipating a continued downward trend from their projected release schedule, chairman of EMI Music Worldwide Bhaskar Menon decided that revitalizing staff and roster was necessary to build back market share and profitability. In February 1987, former chairman of Elektra/Asylum and longtime Mo Ostin collaborator Joe Smith was installed as CEO and president of the renamed Capitol-EMI Music and its CEMA distribution arm. Mazza resigned and went on to a successful second career as partner with artist Kenny Rogers in Dreamcatcher Entertainment, while Zimmerman was reassigned to an international position.

In April 1988 Menon brought in CBS/Fox Home Video CEO Jim Fifield as president/CEO of EMI Music Worldwide to oversee all of EMI's thirty-five international divisions, including the US record and publishing arms. He would report directly to Menon, who would remain for two more years as chairman of EMI Music Worldwide and executive director of the Thorn EMI board. Although Fifield had only two years under his belt in the entertainment business as president/CEO of CBS/Fox Video, he immediately went to work to resurrect EMI from the #5 spot back to its previous success.

Fifield opened 1989 by agreeing to acquire the SBK Entertainment World publishing catalog owned by Stephen Swid, Martin Bandier, and Charles Koppelman. The deal closed that June for $310 million according to *Billboard*'s

Irv Lichtman, including "special bonuses totaling $6 million [that] went out to 250 current and former staffers—from top executives to mail room staffers—who, in the words of SBK partner Marty Bandier, 'built the best publishing company in the world' during the three years Bandier, Charlie Koppelman, and Stephen Swid ran the company."[5] SBK had acquired the bulk of their catalog in their $125 million purchase of the CBS Records publishing holdings in 1986 (see chapter 3). As part of the sale, a joint venture dubbed SBK Records was added as a third label to the EMI Music Group. Headed by Bandier and Koppelman, SBK brought new acts Technotronic, Wilson Phillips, Vanilla Ice, and Jesus Jones into the EMI fold.

Shortly thereafter, EMI purchased 50 percent of independent Chrysalis Records from cofounder Chris Wright, who had bought out cofounder Terry Ellis in 1985. The price to EMI was $73 million plus the assumption of a portion of the company's debt, and added Jethro Tull, Blondie, Spandau Ballet, Sinead O'Connor, and a back catalog dating from 1968. The purchase included an option to purchase the remaining 50 percent, which was exercised in 1991 for $30 million plus assuming $25 million more in debt. Then in 1992 EMI purchased Virgin Records from Richard Branson for $957 million, adding Janet Jackson, whom Branson had just signed away from A&M in 1991 for a $40 million advance. Also included were Phil Collins, Paula Abdul, Simple Minds, Belinda Carlisle, Boy George, Soul II Soul, UB40, Steve Winwood, and, beginning in 1992, the Rolling Stones.

The signing that had the greatest impact on EMI Worldwide over the next decade, however, was done quietly in Nashville in late 1987 when Nashville A&R vice president Lynn Shults brought Oklahoman Garth Brooks to Capitol Records. Like every other label in town, Capitol had turned Brooks down after hearing tapes and auditions in their office. But after seeing Brooks perform live at a songwriters' night at the Bluebird Cafe showcase club, Shults recognized what millions of fans would see in Brooks and would ultimately make him one of the biggest-selling solo artists and top live performance draws of all time.

Brooks would also advance the bar for recording artists' ownership of their own intellectual property. When his first contract ended, he insisted upon a provision in his new agreement providing that upon its expiration he would own all his masters from both contract terms. Over a barrel at the possibility of losing its biggest-selling act, EMI agreed to his demand. After fulfilling the term of that second contract, he left Capitol, taking his masters along with him to rerelease on his own Pearl Records. In 1993 a retiring Joe Smith was asked in an *LA Times* interview with Alan Citron, of all the artists he had dealt with, who had the keenest business sense? He replied, "Garth Brooks, without a question. He did his own negotiating. He was the guy. It was he and I, in this office for six hours one day. No manager, no agent, nobody. Then it got turned over to other people."[6]

In May 1991 EMI bought out the other 50 percent of SBK Records and established Charles Koppelman as head of the combined EMI, SBK, and Chrysalis labels operating out of New York. Martin Bandier was appointed head of EMI Music Publishing. Stephen Swid had already exited the partnership. The deal brought them an initial $35 million, with deferred payments between $100 and $400 million depending upon the performance of the acts signed to SBK over the next four years.

In January 1993, Fifield reorganized the record division, appointing Koppelman as chairman/CEO of a revamped EMI Records Group North America effective April 1, the day after Joe Smith's contract was set to expire. Koppelman would add Smith's responsibilities of overseeing Capitol Records, Liberty Records, Capitol-EMI Canada, Angel Records, Blue Note Records, Capitol-EMI Latin, the CEMA Distribution arm, and North American manufacturing to his already existing duties with EMI, SBK, and Chrysalis.

PolyGram: Buy Out—Public Offering— Spending Spree

Recovering from its losses in the early 1980s and then a failed merger attempt with WMG, in early 1985 PolyGram underwent an internal restructuring as Philips bought out 40 percent of Siemens' 50 percent share, leaving the West German electronics giant with just 10 percent, which Philips subsequently bought in 1987. Philips had been the developer of the audiocassette, and co-developer, with Sony, of the CD. With its worldwide market share at #1 in the industry, PolyGram looked to increase its catalog of American music within its extensive international distribution system. In October 1985 former deputy president at CBS and attorney Dick Asher was installed as president/CEO and brought in a new staff including vice president of A&R Dick Wingate, another CBS Records veteran, along with new promotion and marketing personnel. Over the next four years they enjoyed success with artists they had inherited including Bon Jovi, Scorpions, Deep Purple, Kiss, Tears for Fears, and Kool & The Gang, bolstering profits and market share.

With the projected growth of the CD market, Asher recognized the value of a back catalog that would sell in the new configuration to older buyers without incurring the cost of radio promotion or recording budgets inherent with new product. In 1989 PolyGram bought Chris Blackwell's Island Records, home to U2 and Bob Marley, for $272 million, taking it away from the WEA distribution system. They also purchased A&M Records from Herb Alpert and Jerry Moss for $450 million taking it away from the BMG fold, bringing along Janet Jackson, Sting, Amy Grant, Extreme, and a strong back catalog dating to the early 1960s. Then in late 1989, 20 percent of the outstanding shares of PolyGram N.V. were offered to the public on the New York and Amsterdam stock exchanges with Dutch corporate parent Philips N.V. retaining 80 percent. They expected to raise at least $512 million to help finance the acquisition spree.

In 1990 Asher left, reportedly over a dispute regarding his performance bonus, which was tied to the increase in market share and profit during his tenure but had elevated his compensation above that of the parent corporation's chairman. Head of PolyGram in Europe Alain Levy added US operations to his duties and in 1991 was named worldwide president and CEO of PolyGram N.V., overseeing all global business/entertainment operations, covering both music and film. Levy brought in former RCA Executive vice president Rick Dobbis as president of PolyGram USA and elevated Mercury A&R vice president Ed Eckstine to president of that label.

In 1991 Motown management convinced their investor Boston Ventures to exit from their MCA partnership and to move to a distribution deal with PolyGram. Motown president Jheryl Busby had led a chart revival for Motown, spearheaded by the award-winning R&B crossover group Boyz II Men. The added value of Motown's back catalog, brand, and Hollywood movie connections led PolyGram to purchase Motown in 1993 for $331 million. This figure included a budget for movies and an outstanding payment due to MCA for its 1991 release of the catalog. PolyGram did another stock offering and within a year experienced a growth in market share and profit.

In 1994 PolyGram bought Sony's 50 percent of rap label RAL/Def Jam Recordings for $33 million. Founded in 1983 by Russell Simmons and Rick Rubin, Def Jam's roster included LL Cool J., Public Enemy, Warren G, Onyx, and the Beastie Boys. Simmons and COO Lyor Cohen, signed long-term employment contracts with the company with the proviso to continue to be creatively autonomous. PolyGram's country division also contributed heavily to the company bottom line and market share during the 1990s with two major Nashville signings. Although starting as a country record, Billy Ray Cyrus's "Achy Breaky Heart" was a worldwide #1 pop record in 1992. In 1993 Shania Twain kicked off a career that would ultimately sell 85 million albums to become the greatest-selling female country artist of all time.

In late 1994, Levy dismantled the centralized PolyGram Label Group apparatus set up under Rick Dobbis, moved Dobbis to work under him in

Europe, and gave more control over marketing and promotion to the separate label heads to complement their creative autonomy, mirroring the historic WMG structure. Island remained under the chairmanship of founder Chris Blackwell, and A&M was still led by founders Herb Alpert and Jerry Moss. Former Uptown Records founder Andre Harrell was in charge at Motown, Harold Shedd remained at Mercury Nashville, and Luke Lewis helmed PolyGram Nashville.

The Independent Labels

The RIAA's top twenty members in 1985 were labels owned or distributed by the six major label groups. The RIAA attributed approximately 90 percent of its members' shipments total to these labels while the other 10 percent were attributed to independent RIAA member labels. The RIAA also adjusted its year-end total to account for sales by non-RIAA members to best estimate the retail value of the entire market. These independent labels, both RIAA members and nonmembers, rarely had recording, promotion, or marketing resources on par with the majors. They had to carefully monitor their budgets to minimize risks, and therefore had far below 10 percent of chart position or radio airplay.

Some of these independent label sales were from charted albums, but few reached the year-end Top 100, much less earned gold or platinum certification status. Most releases for independents, however, were in music genres outside of the major radio formats, including jazz, Spanish language, other foreign languages, classical, blues, world music, gospel, Christian, folk, polka, Native American, spoken word, musical theater, movie soundtracks, and some even more esoteric genres. They included new releases, reissues, and compilations ranging from budget line to full price to higher-end multi-album box sets. While the majors also released product in many of these areas, their recording and marketing budgets, unlike the albums in the top radio genres, were not high enough to preclude the independents from competing for market share.

The independents, however, performed a particularly useful function for the majors. To employ another sports analogy, the independents served as a farm system for the majors for both artists and personnel. The independents, with their ears traditionally at street level, had always been closer to the evolving taste of the music-consuming public, especially the fourteen-to-twenty-eight group that the majors considered their core sales demographic. When independents became successful enough to enter the national charts, the majors would try to sign their artists, hire their key personnel, or wholly absorb the labels themselves. They could offer a menu of different options including total purchase, joint venture, distribution, or a pressing and distribution (P&D) deal, each with a negotiable split of any profits. Each variant had further permutations depending upon the level of promotion and marketing investment contributed by each party.

In 1985 four artists signed to independent labels earned spots in *Billboard*'s Top 100 Artist rating, two of them in the Top 20. Two Chrysalis artists were regular Top 40 chart artists. Huey Lewis and the News were at #17 and a 1985 gold record recipient, while John Waite, a 1984 gold record awardee, came in at #62. In 1990, however, EMI acquired 50 percent of Chrysalis and its sales and awards totals were shifted into the EMI tally. The other half was added in 1991. The other two Top 100 acts were rap artists Priority's Run-DMC at #18 and Sutra's The Fat Boys at #64. These two were early harbingers of the widespread popularity of the rap genre to develop over the next decade.

Grass-roots consumer interaction was a major factor for successful independent labels, especially in the formative stages of the development of rap as a national phenomenon. Rap labels were gradually carving out a greater share of the independent marketplace. In 1990 three rap artists made the Top 100 album list from indie-distributed labels. Delicious Vinyl's Young MC's *Stone Cold Rhyming* led at #25, Ice Cube's Priority Records album *Amerikka's Most Wanted* came in at #82, and Ruthless Records' Michelle's self-titled album was #87. There were another five rap albums on the list from independents with major label distribution, including 2 Live Crew, Public Enemy, MC Hammer, and Digital Underground. In other niche genres instrumentalists Steve Vai and Joe Satriani, both with Relativity, also made the top 100 as did the *Ghost* soundtrack album released by soundtrack specialist Varèse Sarabande.

In 1995 ten rap albums made the Top 100 albums list. They demonstrated the extent to which the Big Six had penetrated the independent record sector with investment in new labels and establishing their own proprietary independent distribution divisions designated specifically for handling independent label product. Interscope's Tupac Shakur was the top rap artist at #34. The *Murder Was the Case* soundtrack album, released by Interscope-distributed Death Row Records, at #58 featured Snoop Doggy Dogg. The Notorious B.I.G.'s *Ready to Die* at #66 was on Sean Combs's Bad Boy Records distributed through Arista. Russell Simmons and Lyor Cohen's RAL label, a part of their Def Jam empire, was co-owned and distributed by Polygram and had three albums in the listing with Montell Jordan's *This Is How We Do It* at #67, Method Man's *Tical* at #75, and *The Show* soundtrack at #84.

Ruthless Records' Bone Thugs-N-Harmony accounted for two albums with *E. 1999 Eternal* at #35 and *Creepin on ah Come Up* at #59. Ruthless was distributed through Relativity Entertainment Distribution, then an independent but with 50 percent owned by Sony and was the progenitor to Sony's wholly owned RED independent distribution division. Scarface had *The Diary* at #98 on the Rap-A-Lot label distributed by Virgin's Noo Trybe indie rap distributor—all a part of EMI via their acquisition of Virgin. EMI also owned part of independent Priority Records, which had released the #40 *Friday* soundtrack that interspersed rap acts with funk and R&B performers. Walt Disney Records also scored heavily with two soundtracks albums. *The Lion King* was the #10 album of the year, eventually achieving diamond certification with over 12 million units sold, while the *Pocahontas* soundtrack came in at #23, selling over 3 million units.

And the Game Goes On

As 1995 closed, the Big Six label groups were divisions of larger corporations with other financial considerations that often influenced decisions affecting their music holdings. Other than the privately held Bertelsmann, they were publicly traded with shareholder obligations. Only EMI had the same corporate ownership that it had in 1985, and PolyGram had one of its 1985 co-owners still in place. MCA had been sold twice. WMG entered its merger with Time, Inc. and was the only label group remaining under American corporate ownership. Not one of them had its 1985 CEO still in charge. Baby boomers had ascended to power, including the top position at three of the label groups with Mottola at Sony, Zelnick at BMG, and Levy at PolyGram. Baby boomers had also entered the parent company corporate boardroom with Bronfman younger than both Mottola and Levy.

Despite the changes in leadership and ownership, each label group was better off from a gross revenue standpoint due to a decade of overall industry growth that saw retail revenue almost triple in value. WMG and Sony finished the decade as they had started, in first and second place in market share with PolyGram and BMG in third and fourth place, up from fifth and sixth in 1985. EMI, fourth in 1985, dropped to fifth in 1995, while MCA fell from third to sixth. Industry growth had enabled larger artist advances with increased marketing and promotion expenditures, as well as higher salaries, bonuses, and expense accounts. Executive compensation had been on a parallel if not steeper growth slope than revenue, with label staffs competing to see who could bring home a larger slice of a now-larger pie with expectations to be rewarded appropriately.

As always, however, the corporate bottom line was not derived from gross revenue or from the more easily discernible chart positions, market share statistics, number of platinum records, or Grammy nominations and awards, but rather reflected the balance between revenue and expenditure for each label group, each of their subsidiary imprints, and each artist signed to them. The management of product choice and flow, recording costs and artist advances, marketing and promotion budgets, and catalog exploitation to help fund the new acquisitions were the factors that had the greatest effect on both executive and artist retention or transition. While a hit could still cure many ills, the record men occupying the Big Six seats of power were judged not on how they looked in the press, but on how they delivered on the balance sheet.

2

Records, Retail, Radio, and the Charts that Bind Them

Marching to the Same Beat

The three-way relationship between the labels, radio, and the retail market-place established over the past four decades was still functioning smoothly. The weekly trade charts, led by *Billboard*, combined current sales and airplay data into a weekly ranking of comparative popularity. In addition to the Hot 100 singles and the Top Pop albums—which was rebranded as the *Billboard* Top 200 in March 1992—there were also separate charts for the major radio formats and several niche genres. By collecting and consolidating local data, the charts provided a weekly snapshot of the national market. The chart numbers indicated which records were going up or down in popularity, helping to manage shipments, rack space, and returns. Many of the major market stations that created their own playlists had become *Billboard*'s reporting stations that contributed to the national charts, which then helped many of the other stations determine their programming.

In 1985 the radio industry, with its nearly nine thousand stations, took in $6.56 billion as tallied by the Radio Advertising Bureau (RAB). Record companies supplied free records to the stations that played the formats charted in the trade magazines and tip sheets. Stations could choose which to play to best attract the listener demographic desired by their advertisers, albeit with constant prodding and offers of incentives from label promotion staffs. Although there was no official quid pro quo between these stations and the record companies, the labels depended on the airplay to motivate music listeners to become record buyers. While not all consumers who listened to radio also purchased records, this modus operandi still worked well enough for the labels to sustain the practice of providing the stations with free promotional copies.

Meanwhile, the labels and the retail segment still had their longstanding arrangement of goods supplied on consignment. Like the labels, retail outlets had no economic relationship with radio, but along with the labels, they were

American Popular Music and Its Business in the Digital Age. Rick Sanjek, Oxford University Press. © Frederick Sanjek 2024.
DOI: 10.1093/oso/9780190653828.003.0002

dependent on radio play to stimulate sales. Radio made its revenue from businesses who advertised their goods or services to the station's listeners. Although radio did not share its ad revenue with the record or retail sectors, it did pay approximately 4 percent of ad revenue to the PROs to be distributed as royalties to songwriters and their publishers. This relationship had been functioning smoothly for all involved for the past several decades.

Record companies manufactured and then supplied its network of distributors with millions of records into their supply chain at any given time. What records made up this inventory depended on the airplay and sales each record was projected to receive based on the artist's past history, focus group test marketing, music trade journals' reviewer reactions, or for a new artist, on the label's belief in the artist. Distributors in turn made this diversified array of records available to retail outlets including the local mom-and-pop shops, specialized record stores, truck stops, supermarkets, and the record rack sections in department and variety stores. Record companies supplied both a suggested retail list price (SRLP) for sales to consumers, and a listed wholesale price for the distributors, also known as the published price to dealers (PPD). In general, PPD was between 60 percent and 70percent of the SRLP, with the same ratio applied to any discounted product.

CDs were rapidly replacing vinyl and cassettes in sales revenue, going from $17.2 million in 1983—the year of the CD's introduction—to $930.1 million in 1986. This growth pattern inspired a new series of investor-funded record stores organized in chains that could collectively order in bulk and sell at a discounted price, undercutting both local shops and diversified retail outlets. They had no upfront costs for their on-consignment inventory, but were responsible for location, utilities, product racks, and décor. Advertising costs were partially coopted, industry jargon for "paid in cooperation," by the labels in return for favorable record bin placement.

The record store chains presented attractive investment opportunities as a quick-turnover, high-profile cash business with anticipated growth. With shipments of over 600 million units for 1986 with a $2 to $3 difference between wholesale and retail prices for cassettes and LPs, but at least two times that for CDs, there would be about $2 billion available to split between the wholesale and the retail segments, with totals growing annually.

The trade magazines and tip sheets that compiled and published weekly analysis of the record business marketplace in a chart format were the common thread that bound this alliance of radio, retail, and record companies together, even with their separate goals, competitive incentives, and financial priorities. These charts guided the labels in the weekly decisions on what to release, manufacture, and ship. For the retail outlets the charts helped determine what to order, what to feature in displays, and what and when unsold product should be returned. For the radio stations they influenced what to add, continue to air, or drop from their playlists. Moreover, high Arbitron ratings derived from measuring stations' relative market share led to greater revenue, yielding salary increases and bonuses for station staffs. Low ratings could lead to format changes and replacements for both on-air and ad sales personnel.

Billboard had been printing continuously since 1894 and as of 2019 was still the primary weekly trade magazine for the overall music industry. It has outlasted numerous tip sheets and three major competitors in *Cashbox*, which operated from 1942 to 1996; *Record World*, which was in print from 1946 to 1982; and *Radio & Records*, or *R&R*, published from 1973 to 2009. *Hits* joined the fray as a printed news and tip sheet in August 1986. Founded by independent promotion veterans Lenny Beer and Dennis Lavinthal, it added its online *Hits Daily Double* in 2000. Both print and online editions were still going strong in 2019.

In 1985 *Billboard*'s volume of information, along with high-quality reporting, was the journalistic gold standard. Each 10″ by 13″ weekly edition had around one hundred pages, depending on the amount of advertising or special sections. The first dozen pages featured the top weekly news stories with reporter bylines. After that came regular sections with featured columnists including International, Editorial (including guest columnists), Executive Turntable, Radio, Retailing, Home Video, Pro Audio/Video, Video Music, Talent, Country, Black, Dance, Canada, and Update. The Update section contained the weekly Newsline, Lifelines, and New Companies features along with a calendar of upcoming industry events. Advertisements were interspersed throughout.

The back quarter of the magazine featured the all-important charts of radio play and record sales. The first issue of 1985 included the following national sales charts for Top Albums, Rock Tracks, Country, Classical, Black, Hits of the World, Latin, Top Pop, and Bubbling Under for new releases showing their first sign of success. The radio airplay charts for Hot Singles were Hot 100 Radio Action, Hot 100 Retail Action, Adult Contemporary, Country, Country Radio Action, Country Retail Action, Black, Black Radio Action, Black Retail Action, Dance/Disco, Hits of the World, Hot 100, and Bubbling Under. Top Video/Computer ratings included Video Games, Computer Software, Videodisks, Videocassette Sales, and Videocassette Rentals. The primary feature of these charts, other than the descending numerical sequence starting at number one, was the awarding of darkened circles or stars over the chart numbers referred to as bullets and assigned to that week's largest upward movers. The phrase "number one with a bullet" became a widely used metaphor in the industry and beyond to describe extraordinary success.

In the pre-digital age, compiling chart data had been more art than science. *Billboard* had a network of hundreds of reporting stations spread across the country primarily in large and mid-sized markets, covering each airplay chart, all among the ratings leaders in both their formats and markets. Reporting stations called in or mailed their weekly chart to the *Billboard* chart department. *Billboard* collated all the information into their national listings. This process took a week, with local station charts announced on Mondays, and then the *Billboard* national charts released the following Monday afternoon. *Billboard* also had a network of store reporters, each of which reported the top sales movers of the week to collate into the national sales charts.

In 1983 *Billboard* introduced the *Billboard* Information Network (BIN) system, which used computers to collect and organize all this data, which the magazine could then sell to record companies, retailers, advertisers, and other interested parties all gathered and distributed via telephone dial-up connection. The BIN system would continue to grow as computers advanced in technology and market penetration.

The Weekly Cycle

Although the record industry operated on a perpetual weekly cycle reflected in the charts, it was only repetitive in procedure, not in the product that occupied the chart positions. The positions changed weekly, going up and then down, occasionally stalling in place but seldom for too long. By 1985 the longest a record had ever occupied the top spot was ten weeks. The span had been achieved by only two artists: Debby Boone in 1977 with "You Light Up My Life" and Olivia Newton-John in 1981 with "Physical." It would be topped five times between 1985 and 1995 by "One Sweet Day" by Mariah Carey & Boyz II Men in 1995 (sixteen weeks), both Whitney Houston in 1992 with "I Will Always Love You" and "I'll Make Love to You" by Boyz II Men in 1994 (fourteen weeks), "End of the Road" by Boyz II Men in 1992 (thirteen weeks), and "I Swear" by All-4-One in 1994 (eleven weeks).

For record companies, the first step in the ongoing weekly cycle was deciding which of its releases to promote to the stations for airplay. Stations had limited playlists, adding a limited number of new records each week. The forty-record playlists of the 1960s Top 40 format had tightened even further, prompting the change in format name to contemporary hit radio (CHR). The reporting stations had to placate each of the record companies with either a sufficient amount of new chart entries and upward movement for already charted records, or be able to explain why a given record wasn't working for the station. Stations depended upon record companies not only for the free records they played but also for advertising for local concerts, co-op dollars for in-store and print advertising, and other seasonal and special-occasion promotions.

The second step for the labels was to allocate enough records to each local market to fulfill the anticipated sales orders driven by the local radio airplay, always running the risk of returns if they overestimated. Underestimating could also be a risk. Stations might stop playing a record that their listeners couldn't buy as they felt that they were accountable to their listeners for having what they played available at retail. In the mid-1980s, some larger station chains started to program their smaller stations by having a consultant design their playlists to decrease salary overhead, a practice termed as automated programming. But in general, reporting stations' program directors controlled their own playlists with their position, salary, and longevity all depending upon how the results affected the stations' ratings.

Station market share ratings were measured by the Arbitron Company, then a division of the Control Data Corporation, one of the earliest supercomputer companies to compete with IBM in the mainframe market and one of the first to use silicon transistors to boost speed. Arbitron published quarterly reports on over three hundred media markets, noting the relative audience share of each station in each market, using proprietary sampling methodology to measure the audience size of different age groups, or demographics, across all daily time segments. These reports were designed for and sold to both advertisers to help them determine station ad buys and time slots for those ads, and to stations to set the rate for each time slot.

These ratings were a crucial business tool for the over nine thousand commercial radio stations licensed in 1985 by the FCC. Combined national Arbitron ratings ranked CHR as the top format with 17.7 percent of the national audience, adult contemporary (AC)/soft rock/oldies second with 15.9 percent, country in third place with 11.2 percent, album oriented radio (AOR) in fourth with 10.7 percent, and beautiful/EZ in fifth with 10.1 percent. News/talk stood at sixth with 9.3 percent and was outside of the records and radio relationship. Black/urban/R&B came in at seventh with 8.5 percent, middle-of-the-road (MOR)/variety at eighth with 7.0percent, nostalgia at ninth with 4.0 percent, Spanish-language at tenth with 2.3 percent, religious/gospel with 2 percent, classical with 1.4 percent, and other or unknown formats with .38 percent.

TOP 50 ARTISTS IN 1985 BASED ON YEAR-END *BILLBOARD* CHART POSITION

LABEL GROUP / ARTIST	CHART POSITION	LABEL GROUP / ARTIST	CHART POSITION
Warner/Elektra/Atlantic	#1	RCA Records (cont.)	
Madonna	1	The Pointer Sisters	10
Prince & The Revolution	3	Daryl Hall & John Oates	11
Phil Collins (also on CBS)	4	Whitney Houston	21
Don Henley	14	Sting	37
Foreigner	18	Diana Ross	41
John Fogerty	19	Rick Springfield (also on PolyGram)	44
Chicago	23	Eurythmics	45
Dire Straits	25	Capitol/EMI Records	#4
Talking Heads	26	Tina Turner	8
Julian Lennon	28	The Power Station	31
Howard Jones	36	Duran Duran	34
Motley Crue	39	Corey Hart	40
David Lee Roth	48	Sheena Easton	46
Ratt	50	George Thorogood	47
CBS Records	#2	MCA Music & Entertainment Group	#5
Bruce Springsteen	2	Lionel Richie	22
Phil Collins (also on WEA)	4	New Edition	24
Wham!	6	Stevie Wonder	27
Survivor	15	Glenn Frey	29
REO Speedwagon	16	Night Ranger	38
Billy Joel	17	Commodores	49
John Cafferty & the Beaver Brown Band	30	PolyGram Records, Inc.	#6
Debarge	32	Tears For Fears	7
Sade	33	Kool & The Gang	13
Cyndi Lauper	35	Rick Springfield (also on RCA)	44
Paul Young	43	Independent Labels	#7
RCA Records	#3	U2	12
Bryan Adams	5	Huey Lewis & The News	20
Billy Ocean	9	Run -D.M.C.	42

Source: *Billboard*

Illustration 2.1 Top 50 Artists in 1985 Based on Year-End *Billboard* Chart Positions

A July 12, 1986, *Billboard Guide to Record Company Promotion* profiled six-teen labels with a combined list of almost five hundred national, regional, and local staffers promoting their pop and black/urban rosters, which *Billboard* identified as "a complete list of promotion staff rosters as provided by the re-cord companies."[1] This list did not include secretarial and administrative per-sonnel, the promotion staffs of the country music divisions, or the staffs or any labels including many independents that did not submit staff rosters, or only used independent promoters, but were also competing for airplay. In any given week all or most of these sixteen and many other labels solicited radio stations for one or more spots that had opened in their heavy rotation, which could be from twenty to fifty records, depending on format and market, or for play as an extra that corresponded to *Billboard*'s Bubbling Under chart.

Each record company's national promotion staff, as well as regional and local reps in the top two dozen to three dozen markets, communicated with the program directors of reporting stations for the various *Billboard* charts as well as the charts of the other trade magazines and tip sheets, trying to sway them to play their records rather than their competitors' product. The six major label groups owned or distributed all of the sixteen labels listed in the *Billboard Guide* except Chrysalis, with five of the six groups having multiple labels, each with its own promotion department. WMG included Atlantic, Elektra/Asylum, Warner/Reprise/Sire, and Geffen, while CBS had Columbia, CBS, and Epic/Portrait/Associated. EMI had staffs for both Capitol and EMI-America; RCA, soon to become BMG, encompassed RCA, Arista, A&M, and I.R.S., while MCA included Motown and MCA.

Spanish-language, religious, classical, and jazz genre formats all had na-tional charts in the trades, and communicated with either independent promo men or a few multi-departmental specialists at the labels. The oldies, beautiful/EZ, and MOR/variety formats didn't have trade charts and conse-quently the labels didn't have designated promotion men for them, or regu-larly shipped promo copies to them. With an older demographic range that didn't buy albums containing current radio singles, these stations relied on their accumulated record libraries through purchase or requests to the labels.

The national pop promotion offices that oversaw the CHR, AOR, and AC stations, as well as the black/urban/R&B divisions, were located at their re-cord companies' corporate headquarters in either New York or Los Angeles. Country was the third-largest format after CHR and AOR and was oper-ated out of the label groups' Nashville offices. In 1986 the country format's share of sales closely corresponded to the format's nearly 10 percent share of radio listeners. The number of country stations, however, was about 22 per-cent of the national station total, disproportionate to their share of national airplay as many were in rural areas with smaller audiences than stations in larger markets. The country audience demographic spread trended heavier in older listeners and lighter in the fourteen-to-twenty-eight age demo target of the CHR format, coveted by the major labels as the largest record-buying age group.

The ultimate goal of a promotion staff was to spread a hit single from one format into simultaneous rotation on one or more of the others and then onto CHR stations. Notable examples of achieving this multi-format crossover success to CHR were Whitney Houston and Lionel Richie starting on black/urban/R&B, AC, and beautiful/EZ; Kenny Rogers coming from country, AC, and beautiful/EZ; Bruce Springsteen moving from AOR and college radio to CHR; and Billy Joel from AOR and CHR moving into AC. A single by one such artist could accumulate concurrent rotation on between 30 percent and 60 percent of all stations in the country, creating a huge airplay base with which to maximize record sales.

Independent Promotion: The Rise of the Network

By 1985 independent promotion men had long been established as an integral part of the record business. Combining a pre-release investment of well over a million dollars with the approximately $1.50 per unit cost to manufacture and ship, labels were highly motivated to secure the heavy radio rotation needed to stimulate sales for the new artists selected for major marketing campaigns. Shipping over five hundred thousand units to assure there was product available to fulfill demand should the record be a hit, as well as guaranteeing gold record certification, meant a label paid close to $2 million in costs up-front before seeing hoped-for sales materialize. With the intense competition for the thirty to sixty different tracks a station would play in a week, independent promotion had become a way to further bolster a label's chance at getting a share of the limited airtime that could not possibly accommodate all the records available to them.

Radio play produced income for the songwriters, who were often also the artist, and their publishers. Airplay also helped artists build their fan base for attendance at their shows. The record companies, however, did not profit directly from either airplay or live performance. They only made money from record sales, and radio play was by far the most significant driver of retail sales. Artists' managers knew their clients would never see any royalties unless they had huge sales, so they were happy for the label to allocate money recoupable from royalties to radio promotion, which would also attract concert attendees putting cash in artist and management pockets immediately. The labels either paid the promotion expense directly, or they funneled the funds through the manager. In either case, any amount unrecouped from royalties was used as a loss on the label financial statement to offset profits from more successful artists.

By 1985 the major record labels were collectively paying somewhere between $50 and $100 million annually to a coalition of independent promotion men known in the industry as The Network, either directly or through artist managers. The Network operated on an almost clandestine basis in a "don't ask, don't tell" relationship with both the labels and radio. In November 1980 *Billboard* identified a dozen members of The Network, many of whom had formerly worked for one or more of the top labels. A major reason cited for their purported effectiveness was each member's relationships with key program directors in each one's specific territory, giving them the collective ability to get records to move up and down the charts simultaneously on a national basis by coordinating the movement of the top ten spots on reporting station charts. This affected the rotation of records in the top ten on the *Billboard* Hot 100, particularly the number one spot, which in turn was a primary tool for the labels in determining record shipments. This system, however, often included the practice of paper ads, also known as phantom airplay, where play was falsely reported to create chart position. This could sometimes backfire by contributing to over-shipping to markets where the actual airplay didn't warrant the shipment size, which then resulted in excessive returns.

The Network never accounted for how they spent the money or how much they kept for themselves. They held a Svengali-like sway over the labels, who were hesitant not to use them, for if they didn't but their competitors did, they feared the risk of being shut out of the national top ten airplay rotation. Over the years prior to 1985 the cost kept mounting the more ingrained The Network became in its relationship between radio and the record companies. Mo Ostin, the accountant turned chairman of the WB label group, had tried to stop using indie promo during 1980, but after just a few months of not employing them, he begrudgingly allowed his in-house promo staff to resume the payments.

Joe Isgro, a former executive at both Motown and EMI and a Vietnam-era marine and Purple Heart recipient, was the most visible member of The Network, if not its actual head. Originally from New Jersey but operating out of Beverly Hills, he also owned several record and publishing companies. The next most visible member was Fred DiSipio, a thirty-year veteran promotion man and a decorated World War II hero. No one at the labels or radio wanted to evoke the term "payola" that had been so harmful to the industry in the previous scandals of the 1910s, 1930s, and 1950s, but almost all knew what was going on.

As Walter Yetnikoff recalled in *Howling at the Moon*, his 2004 autobiography cowritten with David Ritz, after first meeting DiSipio and telling him that CBS couldn't be involved in payola, DiSipio replied, "This is legit. If the labels had promo men who knew what they were doing, you wouldn't need me. But you do need me because I know what radio wants. Radio is hit with so much product they need to weed. Radio knows I can weed. Radio respects me. Radio listens to me. What I bring them, they play. I'm the maître d' who decides who gets in the restaurant. Give me a hit record, I'll make sure it's played. If you don't see results in a month, dump me."[2] Yetnikoff added, "I didn't. . . He and other indie promoters were the reason we were able to stay in the game. They cost a fortune. But to make a fortune, I reasoned, you had to spend a fortune. I wasn't shy about using corporate resources to gain market share. Some complained that I was killing off competitors who couldn't afford outside promoters. Bulls--t. I was looking for hits, pure and simple, and willing to pay the price."[3]

But others thought that arrangement was in fact payola that needed to be exposed. In late February 1986 NBC News aired a series of investigative reports accusing Isgro and DiSipio of being linked to payola in association with organized crime, stating that "record companies pay Mafia connected independent promoters almost $80 million a year . . . essentially to do the dirty work of the industry."[4] They claimed that Isgro and DiSipio, described as "two of the most powerful and feared men in the rock business . . . hired by every major record company to promote records,"[5] were seen in New York in January on their way to meet with the top members of the Gambino family, including family boss John Gotti.

NBC further alleged that the meeting had been arranged by Joseph Armoni, citing the FBI and NYPD as saying he had "power over millions of dollars in mob money and mob business interests . . . including a move into the two-billion-dollar rock music business."[6] Although NBC had no footage of Isgro and DiSipio with Gotti or Armoni, they did have footage of the two promo men and several suspected Gambino men walking into the same hotel. They also played footage of Isgro and DiSipio attending the first Rock and Roll Hall of Fame dinner at the Waldorf-Astoria later that evening. NBC further stated that they had interviewed dozens of music industry executives for the story, but none of them would appear on camera.

Independent Promotion: The Fall of the Network

The industry fallout was immediate. Labels dropped or substantially reduced all independent promotion whether Network-associated or not while denying any involvement in illegal activities. By July, the majors and larger independents had increased their in-house promotion staffs. The labels redirected the rest of the money they had formerly spent on indies into new promotional initiatives, including increased service of free CDs to stations, funding station concert tickets and album giveaways for listeners, supporting local listener participatory contests, supplying radio stations with short station ID recordings by top artists, and spending larger amounts on station spot ad buys for current records.

Senior promotion executive for Geffen Records Al Coury told *Billboard*'s Fred Goodman that the biggest problem his staff faced was "to reorient radio back to listening to records, to get them to start programming records without relying on a certain level of national consensus."[7] Goodman also noted that greater label involvement and direct communication seemed to have slowed the process of moving up and down the charts, expanding the air life of individual records, which also increased their shelf life at retail. Mike Bone, then VP of promotion for Elektra, commented that right after the suspension of independent promotion payments, "We had a week where we got seven [station] adds on Simply Red, and somebody from radio said to me 'That's pretty good.' Before the suspension, less than 10 or 12 adds would have meant the record was over."[8]

Meanwhile DiSipio quietly closed his forty-person operation in Cherry Hill, New Jersey. Isgro made a very public denial and filed a $25 million breach of contract suit against his former major label clients, except for the CBS group. Federal grand juries in both New York, under then-prosecutor Rudy Giuliani, and Los Angeles served major labels with subpoenas for financial records and pertinent documents. In April 1986 Senator Al Gore of Tennessee announced that the Senate Permanent Subcommittee on Investigations would be interviewing record company and radio executives, promotion men, and disc jockeys.

Over the next two years Isgro had his suit dismissed against MCA and WMG and settled the rest. In March 1988, an IRS investigation conducted by an Organized Crime Strike Force in Los Angeles resulted in indictments against four Isgro associates for cocaine and cash payola by record promoters to radio programmers. They finally plea-bargained for probation and cooperation from Isgro. In 1989 Isgro, former CBS Records executive Raymond Anderson, and another Isgro associate, were served with an indictment with over fifty counts including accusations of payola, racketeering, and kickbacks in defrauding CBS Records for actions before the Sony purchase. In 1990 the case was dismissed with prejudice, meaning it couldn't be brought back, but somehow it was revived in 1993, but dismissed again in 1996 as the Los Angeles US District Judge ruled that the federal government had violated speedy trial provisions.

Although these investigations and trials curtailed the activities of The Network, independent promotion by no means went away. The labels' preference was to leave little up to chance in the highly competitive arena of securing airplay. Jobs, bonuses, and corporate profits depended upon the successful combination of radio and record sales. Gradually indies were brought back at less cost with closer supervision, including hiring some as on-staff local reps in many of the top 20 media markets where The Network seemed to have been its most effective. Labels continued to funnel money through artists' managers, making it difficult for even label management to know just how much was now going to independent promotion. All bases were still covered whether now inhouse or still parceled out to indies, but with an added degree or two of separation from anything that could possibly be construed as impropriety.

In some cases, however, labels put less distance between themselves and the indie promoters. A *Los Angeles Times* article by Chuck Philips on March 4, 1993, revealed that Fred DiSipio had been working for EMI for the past two years as a promotion consultant. Charles Koppelman, then Chairman/CEO of EMI North America, was quoted as saying, "Fred is a wealth of knowledge and a terrific guy. I don't use him to get records played. I use him to help strategize and improve our promotion department. He knows all the players in the promotion business and who the good ones are. I brought him on board almost as a human resource player."[9] The article further cited undisclosed EMI sources saying that like most of the other major record companies, they were paying indie promoters about $5 million a year for such services.

The EMI source, however, didn't indicate whether this $5 million estimate was for each of the six label groups, or each of their individual labels. Nor did the source state whether this figure was just direct payments by the labels, or also included money going through managers. As sales and profits grew through the late 1980s and early 1990s, so did the intensity of competition for chart position, making old habits hard to break. Labels still feared being at a disadvantage if their rivals hired indies when they didn't. To paraphrase Yetnikoff, if that's the price one needs to pay for a hit, one gladly pays it.

RIAA-reported retail shipment value more than doubled, from $4.64 billion in 1986 when the indies were purportedly dismissed, to $10.09 billion in

1993 at the time of the EMI revelation about then-current independent promotion payments. The indie tab, even if still at the estimated 1986 rate of $60-plus million a year, was now proportionately less than half of its relative cost as a percentage of revenue as the industry was that much larger than it had been at the outbreak of the 1986 scandal. Salaries and bonuses had also grown commensurately, so there was a lot of internal label incentive to maximize airplay and sales by whatever means possible. The fear that others might be once again hiring independents to gain an underhanded leg up, combined with the fact that nobody from a record company had ever actually been convicted of anything, made the risk of hiring indies far outweigh the risk of not doing so in a business driven by the constant weekly battle for chart position, market share, and shelf space.

Friction between Records and Retail

At the National Association of Recording Merchandisers (NARM) convention in Los Angeles just a week after the 1986 NBC report of purported payola, MCA Music Entertainment Group Chairman Irving Azoff delivered a hard-hitting keynote speech touching on most of the issues facing the industry. Azoff was three years into his conversion from top artist manager to label group CEO and had already moved MCA's market share from the bottom to the middle of the Big Six.

Never one to pull punches or be shy in expressing himself, Azoff captured the competitive and combative nature of an industry battling both internally and externally simultaneously. He criticized radio, the Grammy Awards, the RIAA, and the labels themselves. *Billboard*'s Fred Goodman reported that while he referred to the record business as an industry under siege, he also termed it an industry poised to attack. Nonetheless he called for greater cooperation between the record labels and their retail partners on issues that negatively affected everyone's bottom line, including home taping, anti-piracy, counterfeiting, excessive returns, and parallel imports—which is shipping finished product in from overseas and thus displacing sales of domestically manufactured product and revenue to US labels and publishers. While Azoff's tirade stimulated both instant comment and some subsequent action, more significantly, he brought into the open the issues between the record and retail sectors that had been festering for years and would continue to be problems throughout the ensuing decade.

The labels believed they had been losing over a billion dollars a year in sales to home recording, in which people who would otherwise be their customers instead copied albums onto blank cassettes bought from the same retailers who sold the labels' product. Azoff facetiously asked "Why didn't you sell your customers 'Blank Tape's Greatest Hits'?"[10] The labels, including Azoff's MCA, ignored the fact that the cassettes they used in manufacturing were inferior in quality to the top blank ones. Some music consumers had discovered this and were acting accordingly. The labels also felt financially threatened by the newly affordable dual reel cassette tape recorders, which Azoff labeled as personal piracy machines for allowing consumers to copy label cassettes onto blank ones.

While Azoff did compliment retailers for improved marketing initiatives and cooperation in the ongoing shift to CDs, he was further agitated by what he viewed as an adversarial attitude. "It looks like you retailers expect labels to take all the risk. You bemoan the most minute of price increases and want an even more liberal returns policy."[11] As for hikes in SRLP, he claimed that only two of the six majors made a real profit, that "stockholders are certainly entitled to a decent profit in a free-enterprise system,"[12] and that only 20 percent of artists ever recoup the investment in their records, subsidizing the money spent on the other 80 percent.

Perhaps the one aspect of Azoff's keynote that would prove ironic was the subject of returns, as MCA would shortly be faced with federal allegations of mob-related involvement in the resale of its own returns. Returns in the record industry vernacular are the unsold records that stores send back to distributors, who in turn send back to the labels. A 20 percent cap on a company's returns to be counted as credit for new product had been agreed upon by both the labels and retailers to replace the unlimited returns policy in effect through the late 1970s. In large part this was a self-imposed restriction to avoid a repeat of the labels' own allocation excesses of the late 1970s disco era when over-shipping caused massive returns and hence losses. Returns exceeding the 20 percent cap could now trigger punitive pricing and credit policies. The retailers questioned why they should be penalized by bearing a share of the cost when the labels couldn't discipline themselves, a major cause of the animosity brought to the surface in Azoff's address.

Cutout Crisis

After an album stopped selling in the stores and exited the album chart (if it charted at all), retailers returned much of the remaining inventory to free up shelf space. The labels would then often delete the album from the active catalog. Deleted titles were eligible for sale as cutouts at a reduced price to recoup part of the label's pressing and accrued shipping and handling expenses—items that were not recoupable from artist royalties.

The term "cutout" derived from the practice of drilling, cutting, or punching a hole in the packaging, or cutting off the corner, to distinguish these records from the non-cutout full-priced ones. This marking rendered them ineligible as a return for credit after being recirculated as a cutout. Different labels had varying cutout policies and pricing. Music distributors known as cutout dealers bought them in bulk from the labels and recirculated them through truck stops, gas stations, flea markets, supermarkets, and other outlets that sold records, but only at a deep discount. They also appeared in bargain bins and discounted back catalog racks in record stores. Most artist contracts had label-imposed provisions for reduced royalty rates for albums that sold for less than SRLP, usually royalty free for albums sold for less than half the SRLP, thus making cut-outs royalty free. But as a part of the initial shipment, these cutouts were still included in the RIAA gold and platinum album calculations, which were based on the initial record shipments.

When Azoff took over a downward-spiraling MCA in 1983 with a mission to turn it around, Salvatore Pisello, whom the FBI was investigating for alleged ties to New York's Gambino crime family, somehow began handling MCA's cut-outs. Subsequent investigations and court proceedings, however, never established how or why this occurred despite interviews with various MCA executives. In negotiating purchase or distribution deals with MCA, Pisello also represented the Sugar Hill, Chess, Checker, and Cadet labels, all of which had varying financial ties to Roulette Records owner Morris Levy, who was also the subject of an FBI probe for mob-related activities. From 1983 through 1985, MCA paid Pisello hundreds of thousands of dollars for these and various other never fully defined chores.

Levy was one of the most successful and colorful holdovers from the wide-open independent music business of the 1950s still operating in the corporate culture of the 1980s. He had started as the managing partner in the Birdland nightclub. When ASCAP licensing representatives came knocking on the Birdland door for PRO license fees, Levy recognized a business opportunity and expanded his holdings into music publishing under his Big Seven Music umbrella. He subsequently cofounded Roulette Records, one of the most successful independent pop labels of the 1950s. In the 1970s he developed the Strawberries retail record chain and operated several pressing plants. From 1969 through 1983 he processed a large share of major label cutouts through his Promo Records, Inc. A 1957 article in the entertainment industry trade paper *Variety* had dubbed him The Octopus for his reach and influence into so many areas of the business. A 2016 biography by Richard Carlin was titled *Godfather of the Music Business: Morris Levy.*

In 1986 Pisello was indicted for and in 1988 convicted of tax evasion on the payments made to him from MCA. Levy was indicted for extortion in trying to collect money from Darby, Pennsylvania, cutout dealer and convicted cassette bootlegger John LaMonte, who had bought over 4 million cutouts through Pisello and Levy for $1.25 million. When LaMonte refused to pay the total bill because the best selections had been skimmed out of the shipment, Levy allegedly had him assaulted. After testifying against Levy and his accomplices, LaMonte went into the FBI witness protection program. In 1988 Levy was convicted of conspiring to extort LaMonte and was sentenced to ten years in prison and fined $200,000. His co-defendant in the case, Dominick Canterino, allegedly a member of the Genovese crime family, was sentenced to twelve years in prison and fined $50,000. Levy died in 1990 two months before he was scheduled to report to prison. He had sold his Big Seven Music publishing companies to Windswept Pacific Publishing, Roulette Records to Rhino Records for the USA and to EMI for international, and Strawberries' eighty-one stores to Trans World Entertainment to be included in a public offering roll-up of record chains.

Levy always claimed that he ran a legitimate business and was stigmatized for maintaining childhood friendships with people who went on to be portrayed as mob-connected. He told the press at the time of the indictment, "I've been on Broadway 47 years. I know some of these characters . . . . I knew Cardinal Spellman, too. That don't make me a Catholic."[13] Levy was also well known for his philanthropy. He served on the board of the Boston Opera Company and the Columbia County (NY) Hospital, was chairman emeritus of the United Jewish Appeal (Music Division) where he was Man of the Year in 1973, and helped raise millions of dollars for other charities including the New York Foundling Hospital and St. Patrick's Cathedral Choir.

Despite the drama of early 1986 with the dismantling of The Network and Azoff's rim-rattling keynote speech, business in the highly profitable three-way record-radio-retail relationship went on as usual but in a more direct and transparent way. The silver lining to emerge from under these dark clouds was that labels forged closer direct relationships with both radio and retailers. Dollars previously funneled through shady third parties were now going directly to radio or retailers in joint promotional efforts with the labels. Communication between them would be further improved and enhanced over the ensuing decades by the steady advances in computer technology.

Technology Reforms the Chart Process

By 1985 the *Billboard* Information Network (BIN) launched in 1981 was taking hold as record companies updated or installed the new generation of desktop personal computers (PCs). More efficient and less expensive PC networks supplanted mainframe computers for business functions outside of comprehensive financial accounting and royalty distribution needs. These in-house PC networks accessed the tracking information provided by BIN by way of dial-up telephone connection to help in product management and allocation. The BIN methodology, however, still depended on the reliability of the existing store-reporting system in submitting the actual biggest sales movers rather than reporting other product as favors to label representatives.

In 1991 the music industry took a great leap forward in the technology used to determine *Billboard* chart position with the introduction of the new SoundScan system, the brainchild of record industry veteran Mike Shalett and research analyst Mike Fine. SoundScan tabulated the number of album sales registered by the bar code scanners at retail outlets. Actual sales totals replaced the often-subjective store reports methodology of the past. SoundScan started as Sound Data in 1987 with reporting on music-buying habits to record companies, radio stations, and video channels as its original business model.

After a noncommittal response from the record labels following SoundScan's January 1991 demo presentation, Shalett and Fine instead entered into a co-venture with *Billboard* to use the system to determine *Billboard*'s album charts. In the debut week of May 25, 1991, for the first time the Top Pop Album chart was the result of an actual piece count of albums sold at retail, replacing the BIN top five movers reporting system. The newly constituted Top 200 album chart now included artists from *Billboard*'s country, urban, rap and rock charts, giving pop a much more inclusive definition. *Billboard* reported that over two thousand retail record outlets contributed scanned barcode data to the SoundScan debut including the Camelot, Musicland, Music Plus, National Record Mart, Record Bar, Record World, Sound Warehouse, and Trans World chains. Handleman, then the country's largest rack jobber with more than four thousand mass merchandise locations, also participated.

SoundScan first employed a weighted algorithm until their initial sample could be expanded to a more comprehensive census. Even in the initial stage, it was the most accurate picture of the national sales landscape ever published. With 65 percent of US record sales then passing through bar code scanners, and with over 90 percent of the scanner-enabled stores reporting to SoundScan, their more accurate weekly snapshot proved a success. Within a year the six major label groups subscribed. Chuck Philips of the *Los Angeles*

Times reported that the SoundScan data "would be so invaluable to record companies—who used to have to literally guess at what their records were selling each week—that the firms would pay big bucks for the information. . . . The price tag for each company: about $800,000 per year."[14]

Ten years later, *Billboard* chart director Geoff Mayfield told Marc Ferris of *The New York Times*, "We had a cataclysmic change with that first chart."[15] Mayfield added that when the SoundScan system was implemented both country and rap improved in the charts. "Rap was mostly the product of independent labels at the time, but the playing field had leveled for the smaller record companies."[16]

The next year *Billboard* launched its proprietary companion Broadcast Data Systems (BDS) to track radio airplay. It was a patented digital pattern recognition technology working on a sampling basis to compile radio play charts. The combination of SoundScan with BDS now allowed labels to use accurate sales and airplay information in pressing and shipping allocations, both on a national and regional basis. The data could also identify independent artists making a local or regional impact. Identifying where records were selling also became a useful aid in booking live shows.

A prime example of a record benefiting from this new technology was the second Nirvana album release, *Nevermind*. It was outselling product by the established Metallica in the markets where it was receiving airplay for its "Smells Like Teen Spirit" single. This prompted Geffen Records to now push the single to stations nationally that had played Metallica but not Nirvana, as well as to boost shipping allocations. This type of local breakout could easily have gone unnoticed before application of the SoundScan and BDS technology.

The six major label groups accounted for approximately 80 percent of SoundScan's tracked record sales. The majority of these sales came from either the latest release by current top-charting artists or from CD sales of the chart toppers of the past, known as legacy artists. The current releases were supported by airplay from the CHR, AOR, AC, black/urban/R&B, and country stations. These formats combined to represent about 60 percent of the cumulative national radio play. The other 20 percent of reported sales were bolstered by airplay from oldies, beautiful/EZ, Latin, classical, jazz, religious, and other genre-specific radio formats. SoundScan and BDS further solidified the decades old triangular relationship between the record, retail, and radio segments of the industry with increased efficiency and data accuracy.

Two new players were stepping into the radio arena in the late 1980s as alternatives to commercial radio. College Radio and National Public Radio both aired a lot of what was termed "alternative music." Initially outlets for independent label product, these two new options caught the attention of major labels as opportunities for airplay for promising new artists not yet ready for a CHR or AOR hit. In 1991 the Recording Academy introduced a Grammy for Best Alternative Music Album after a long internal discussion over just what "alternative" meant. The older academy leaders couldn't pinpoint a musical definition while the new guard understood the importance of this growing undercurrent of musical diversity whose recording art and science was evident but not easily pigeonholed into the existing Grammy categories. The first five winners were Sinead O'Connor, R.E.M., Tom Waits, U2, and Green Day. Other nominees in those five years included The Replacements, Elvis Costello, Nirvana, The B-52s, The Cure, The Smashing Pumpkins, Sarah McLachlan, and Nine Inch Nails.

The CD Introduces Digital Audio to the Home

The CD was a late 1970s Philips/Sony refinement of a decade-old audio/video disc technology. Their final consumer product was a 120 mm polycarbonate optical disc under a thin layer of aluminum protective lacquer film that had about 700 MB of storage, more than the standard home computer did at that time, and was designed to play seventy-four-plus minutes of 16-bit audio at a sampling rate of 44.1 kHz. The data was stored in a molded track spiraling out from the disc's center and read by a semiconductor laser through the bottom of the disc.

The CD diameter had been limited by the need for its player to be the precise size to replace the cassette mechanism in the existing audio device slot in car dashboards. In 1979 Philips asked Sony to join forces in co-developing an industrywide protocol that would avoid the development of competing standards as occurred in the Betamax-VHS rivalry in the home video business. Once the specifications were settled, CDs would be licensed to all manufacturers for both discs and players. According to the Philips website, the final dimensions were agreed upon because Norio Ohga, then in charge of Sony's team, insisted that the disc be able to hold a recording of Beethoven's longest symphony on one disc. At the agreed-upon sampling rates and physical measurements, this dictated a seventy-four-minute capacity, which required a slight enlarging of the disc from 115 mm to the final 120 mm (4.724″) diameter.

In an April 2018 article in *Nature Electronics*, Kees Immink, the Philips engineer in charge of the CD's servo-mechanics, electronics, and coding development, disputed the Beethoven 9th Symphony story. He recalled that the already-developed Philips 115 mm disc could have held seventy-four minutes' worth of music with some mathematical tweaks, but no one asked him to do so, and that the diameter change forced Philips to revise its design and release schedule. He cited a conversation with a fellow worker on the project. "In October 2017 I had a lunch conversation with my brother in arms, Sony's top engineer, Toshitada Doi, who, when I told him about my doubts about Beethoven, said, 'Of course you are right, but it was a good story, wasn't it?'"[17] Whether a nod to what many considered to be the greatest musical composition of all time, or a ploy to gain a marketing advantage in the debut of the CD player, the CD was, and is, 120 mm in diameter, can accommodate Beethoven's 9th Symphony, and the Sony CD player was the first to market in 1982.

The final specifications were the basis for the Compact Disc Digital Audio (CDDA or CD-DA) standard as defined in the 1982 Red Book, the initial entry in the series of Rainbow Books that are named for their binder colors, and which contained the technical specs for all CD formats as ratified by the International Electrotechnical Commission as the international standard for manufacturing. The Rainbow Books to follow included the Green Book in 1986 for the interactive CD-I, the Yellow Book in 1988 for the CD-ROM for read-only memory, the Orange Book 1990 for the CD-R for writable CDs, the Beige Book in 1992 for the PCD for photos, the White Book in 1993 for VCD for video on a CD, the Blue Book in 1995 for E-CD/CD+/CD Extra for enhanced content, and the Scarlet Book in 1999 for SACD for the super audio disc with master quality 24 byte sound, now known as high resolution, or Hi Res.

As the co-owners of the patents for the CD, Philips and Sony divided the 3¢ royalty per CD unit sold and 2.5 percent of the sale price royalty fee from every playing device sold on a 60/40 split in Philips's favor. Following the introduction of the CD, an ongoing series of other digital carriers designed by both firms as well as rival companies competed for a share of the growing software market for the new digital devices replacing analog tape and vinyl players. In addition to the more advanced CDs derived from other Rainbow Book specifications, other formats included digital audiotape (DAT), laser discs, and the three-inch CD for singles. Only the CD Single, DVD Audio, and Super Audio CD were able to reach a critical mass of market penetration to be included in the annual RIAA retail shipment statistics. Only the CD single regularly topped a million units sold in a single year, with the SACD achieving that feat once at 1.3 million in 2003.

Philips also developed the original packaging for the CD. A clear, slim, and hinged two-piece plastic case with a third piece that snapped into the case to hold the disc, with the album cover artwork on a paper slip under it. The lid also had interior notches to easily hold a redacted version of the album front cover artwork or a removable multi-page folded paper booklet. The Philips engineering team dubbed it a jewel case as they considered it a perfect design. The CD-containing jewel case, also referred to as a jewel box, was then placed within a 12″ by 6″ rigid paper container called the longbox that was then shrink-wrapped.

A series of competing containers were introduced by other labels over the next several years made from paper, rigid plastic, soft plastic, or biodegradable material, including Q Pack, Digisleeve, Digipak, JakeBox, Discbox Slider, Compac Plus, LP Style Slip Case, Keep Case, Snap Case, Soft Case/Green Case, ECO Pack and Lift-Lock Case, some of which are still available for custom packaging. The jewel box without the longbox shrink-wrapped on its own eventually became the dominant packaging of choice, and by 1992, the major labels collectively endorsed that decision as the standard for packaging and retail rack configuration.

The CD Reshapes the Retail Market

A myriad of economic issues accompanied the introduction of the CD. First was retail price. After the first US manufacturing plant opened in 1984, the RIAA average retail value was $17.23 per unit on 22.6 million CD sales for the year. As CD sales grew to 286.5 million units in 1990, the average value registered at $12.05, which included CDs in all price tiers, including club sales. In 1995, the average value rose 7.6 percent to $12.97. Discounts, free goods, club sales, giveaways, mid-line, and budget line all accounted for the difference between this average and the labels' SRLPs that ranged up to $19.98 for top-line releases, contributing to the ongoing four-way pricing conflict between the labels, the record clubs, distributors, and retailers.

The upswing of the economy in the mid-1990s, however, fostered the growth of disposable consumer income for spending on leisure items, including records and devices to play them. In step with the rise in CD sales was the drop in the price of home CD players. Originally introduced in 1981 at a cost of over $1,000, by 1986 low-end CD players could be bought for under $200 due to mass production and competition between manufacturers. The first in-car CD players were introduced in 1987. By 1995 they had relegated cassette players to a custom item. High-end multi-CD changers capable of shuffling tracks from different CDs, though too large for the dashboard, could be placed in trunks, glove compartments, or under the seats.

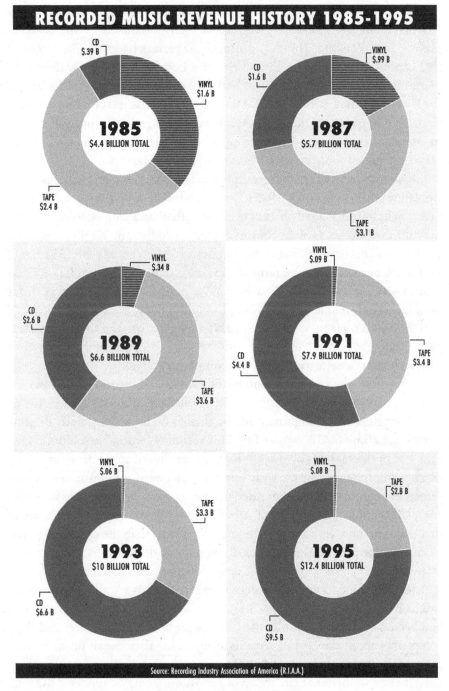

Illustration 2.2 Recorded Music Revenue History, 1985–95

In 1984 Sony debuted the Sony Discman at about $300, the first portable CD player for the mobile device market then dominated by the cassette-playing Sony Walkman. Initially portable CD players had a stability problem that caused skipping when shifted out of a horizontal plane, limiting their consumer acceptance. In the 1990s anti-skip technology was introduced and the Discman was renamed the CD Walkman. Other manufacturers joined the portable disc player market with their own models ranging from $80 to $300 for standard models and $500 and up for ones that doubled as a CD-ROM player capable of connecting to a home computer or laptop.

Initially available CD genres were primarily classical and jazz with just a few front-line pop artists, but by 1995 CD releases included all genres and all price tiers. Digitally remastered reissues of legacy artists' back catalog were available in multi-disc box set as older consumers restocked their music libraries in the CD format. This decade-long transition from a 59 percent cassette, 31 percent LP, and 10 percent CD sales ratio in 1984, to roughly 70 percent CD, 30 percent cassette, and minimal LP sales in 1995, necessitated additional costs for both labels and retailers. In addition to building new plants, the labels had to retool old ones from cassettes to CDs to keep up with the shifting marketplace. They also had to coordinate with the electronics manufacturers' rate of turnover from cassette to CD players for both car and home.

For retailers, the cost of reconfiguring racks to adjust to the CD was another contentious issue. Initially the labels offered CDs packaged in the 6″ by 12″ longbox. Two longboxes side by side could fit in the already existing album racks built for 12″ square LPs. This seemingly workable solution, however, had problems of its own as the longbox cardboard containers were easily damaged despite the shrink-wrap and were awkward for consumers accustomed to flipping through the wider, thinner racked albums. There were also complaints about the amount of paper litter involved as conservationists of that era were more concerned with preserving trees than the disposal of non-biodegradable plastic. The longbox, however, was defended by retailers concerned with shoplifting without the larger longbox acting as a deterrent.

After longbox packaging was eliminated in April 1993, all CD shipments would be in jewel cases only without the longbox. As longbox packaging had been more expensive than the CD in a jewel box, retailers revised their complaints about the cost of reconfiguring racks. They began pushing for a share of the savings from dropping the longbox to lessen their cost of remodeling their bins. Richard Harrington of *The Washington Post* reported the total cost of retail stores remodeling efforts to be an estimated $100 million nationwide. The labels countered with pledging a one-year discount at 20¢ to 25¢ to cover rack adjustment costs as well as the recently adopted radio frequency identification (RFID) source-tagging technology that would allow RFID security tags or labels to be attached to the product that would trigger alarms if unscanned product left the building.

Retail Responds to Expanding Market

Going into 1985, record sales had doubled since the introduction of the cassette in the early 1970s. Added exposure from music video channels and larger concert venues fueled hopes for even further growth. Bar codes and computerized ledgers had increased efficiency in tracking sales, ordering inventory, and managing accounting functions. Racks for videotapes and games were now competing for space traditionally reserved for music in mass merchandisers. Combo store chains selling both audio and video were the latest trend. Video also had a robust rental market, bringing in customers on a regular basis. Adding video games expanded combo stores' consumer reach to younger age groups. Trans World Entertainment of Albany, New York, and Minneapolis-based Musicland Group led the rise of publicly traded combo store chains.

Record label sales departments, however, did not deal directly with retail outlets. Instead, their regional branches shipped merchandise at wholesale price to both national and local distributors on sixty-day net terms, which ranged between 60 percent and 70 percent of SRLP, or a discounted price in the same ratio. These distributors in turn marked up their wholesale price by about 10 percent to 15 percent, and then resold to retail outlets at what was now about 70 percent to 80 percent of the SRLP. All shipments, unless discounted as one-way sales, were subject to return.

There were two types of distributors for record product. One-stops positioned throughout the country carried all major labels and select independents, with an emphasis on current releases. They were survivors from before the consolidation of independent labels into the Big Six, all of whom subsequently established their own proprietary distribution subsidiaries with regional branch offices to handle and fulfill orders from wholesalers. One-stops then sold to the chain record stores; independent retailers, including the still-surviving, nostalgically nicknamed mom-and-pop stores, and other assorted retail outlets. These retailers usually had their own buyers who would select product from the one-stop's ever-updating catalog.

By 1995 the publicly traded Alliance Entertainment Corp (AEC) had become the largest one-stop. AEC was formed in 1990 by former law professor and Lotus sports car distributor Joe Bianco. As *Billboard* senior editor

Ed Christman observed, "Bianco saw something that many of the music industry's finest financial minds had overlooked—a steady cash flow that could be marketed to Wall Street."[18] Bianco rolled up the top two East Coast one-stops, CD One Stop of Bethel, Connecticut, and Bassin Distributors of Miami, along with a string of smaller operations under the AEC banner. AEC had $720 million in 1995 sales, ranking as the largest full-service domestic distributor of music and music-related products.

Rack jobbers distributed a wide range of products, including music, to mass merchandising outlets. They focused on current chart records, managed their customers' racks, and organized their displays, eliminating the need for the retailers to have their own buyers. Rack jobbers also distributed back catalog budget product for discount bins. These genre-based compilations and greatest hits packages often used rerecordings of past hits created by budget line companies operating on small margins, usually under a dollar. K-tel was unique in owning its own library of rerecorded hits, while Madacy Entertainment, Direct Source Special Products, St. Clair, Delta Records, and others licensed tracks for their product, which usually contained ten tracks with an SRLP below $5.99. Budget line classical music specialist Naxos recorded its own masters with overseas orchestras, becoming the top-selling US label in its genre.

Handleman Company of Troy, Michigan, was the largest US rack jobber, selling to over eight thousand outlets, including Kmart, Walmart, and Woolworth. Beginning as a pharmaceutical distributor in 1934, Handleman went public on the New York Stock Exchange in 1967. In the early 1980s it started using optical scanners to order and track sales, and then added books and computer software to its product line. In 1989 Handleman did $646.7 million in entertainment products with almost 60 percent coming from audio sales. In 1991 Handleman bought and consolidated with the second-ranked rack jobber, Lieberman Enterprises of Minneapolis. In 1992 the invigorated Handleman reached $1.2 billion in record sales, about 15 percent of total industry volume.

The next year Walmart bought rack jobber Western Merchandisers of Amarillo, Texas—founded by Sam Marmaduke in 1961—and shifted 430 of its stores from Handleman to Western. In 1994 Walmart sold Western to Anderson News Corp of Plano, Texas. Anderson had already been Walmart's major book and magazine rack jobber. To compensate for the loss, Handleman purchased several small distributors, budget-line compilation company Madacy Entertainment of Montreal, and budget video manufacturer Starmaker. Rack jobbers also serviced electronics superstores including Best Buy and Circuit City, but these mass merchandisers were increasingly discounting recorded music to stimulate consumer traffic for their much higher-priced music player systems, computers, and home appliances.

Market Regroups with Recession, Retrenches for Economic Boom

In addition to one-stops and rack jobbers, there were independent distributors that managed the current and catalog product of independent labels who were not in distribution agreements with one of the major label groups. These indies rarely sold to the mass merchandisers but did sell to the chain stores that serviced the customers looking for the alternative music they heard on NPR, college radio, and stations playing niche genre formats. At the local retail shop level, music and video combo chains were replacing the mom-and-pop stores. Variety retailers were being leveraged out of business by the mass merchandisers, whose computerized tracking and accounting technology lowered costs, which in turn lowered prices to consumers.

After the introduction of the CD, both the Musicland Group and Trans World went on public offering–fueled, decade-long expansion sprees acquiring smaller chains. By 1995 Musicland with 861 stores and Trans World with 700 were established as the top chains. The Musicland chain included the Sam Goody brand, which it had acquired in 1978, 89 Media Play superstores for major markets, and OnCue stores in smaller markets. Trans World acquisitions with established brand names retained their local identity including Record Town, Tape World, Coconuts, Saturday Matinee, and Abraham/Strauss.

British market leaders WH Smith and HMV also entered the US market buying underperforming chains. As part of a 1992 worldwide joint venture, Richard Branson's Virgin Group and US video chain Blockbuster, funded by former Waste Management executives Wayne Huizenga and John Melk, opened the first Virgin Megastore on the Sunset Strip in Los Angeles. By 1995 they had twenty-three megastores in major markets. Blockbuster also acquired the Music Plus, Super Club, and Sound Warehouse chains, and was then itself acquired by Viacom in 1994. In 1995 Blockbuster was the third-largest chain with 540 stores. Supported by financing from Bahrain-based Investcorp, Camelot ranked fourth with 405 stores, while Merrill Lynch–financed fifth-ranked Wherehouse Entertainment had 348 outlets.

Russ Solomon's Sacramento-based Tower Records location grew into a 150-store international chain steered by Solomon's consumer-oriented marketing instincts featuring memorabilia displays, its own inhouse *Pulse* music magazine, in-store music programming, and label-sponsored live performance appearances. Tower stocked independent label product and major label back catalog in addition to current releases, while most chains' inventory reflected the current charts. In 1995 Tower was the first retailer to establish an online webstore.

Independent distributors carrying the product of labels not affiliated with the Big Six grew during the decade despite the continual acquisition of indie labels or their leading artists by the majors, particularly in the rap and alternative categories. In 1995 Independents had 19.2 percent of total SoundScan sales, up from 16 percent in 1994. Indies, however, had only 9.5 percent of country and 11.3 percent of R&B/rap SoundScan totals, making their share of the non-country and non-R&B/rap sales over 25 percent.

Cooperative coupling of independent distributors for more efficient economy of scale increased during the economic downturn following the 1991 Gulf War. Big State of Texas, California Record Distributors, and Malverne of New York banded together as INDI. Rounder of Boston, East Side Digital of Minneapolis, and Precision Sound of Lynnwood, Washington, formed REP, Inc. in 1993. In 1994 Rykodisc replaced Rounder and Precision in REP, while those two formed Distribution North America (DNA) with Valley Distribution of Woodland, California. Select-O-Hits of Memphis and M.S. of Elk Grove Village, Illinois, also pooled their resources in late 1994.

Relativity Entertainment Distribution (RED), founded in 1982 as Relativity Records by Barry Korbin in New York as an outlet for independent rock, expanded into rap with a distribution deal with N.W.A. founder Eazy-E's Ruthless Records. In 1990 RED entered into a partnership with Sony. LA rap label Priority Records expanded into Priority Records Distribution to service other rap labels. They also managed hard-core gangsta acts for some of the majors when the records were deemed too controversial for their label's corporate image.

The other major label groups noticed this increase in indie sales and all but Universal established an affiliated independent distributor as Sony had done with RED. EMI acquired distributor/one-stop Caroline Records when it bought Virgin Records in 1992. PolyGram took over Independent Label Services (ILS) as part of the Island Records purchase. In 1993 WMG partnered with alternative label Restless Records to open the Alternative Distribution Alliance (ADA) for alternative artists and labels, including their own Seattle-based Sub Pop, joint venture. BMG added indie distribution operation BIG.

Competition and consolidation were the driving forces at all levels of the retail sector over the course of the decade. Although dollar volume had almost doubled, tightening margins due to the cost of display, marketing, advertising, and administrative systems combined with competitive pricing to affect the bottom line. When sales slowed during the recession of the early 1990s, there were heavy industrywide losses due to overstocking. The larger distributors recovered but many smaller operations went out of business via liquidation, acquisition, or merger between survivors, including one-stops Schwartz Brothers in Lanham, Maryland, All Service One Stop in New Jersey, Vinyl Vendors in Kalamazoo, Win Records & Video in Elmhurst, New York, and Richman Bros. in Pennsauken, New Jersey. Select-O-Hits in Memphis shut down its one-stop business to focus instead on independent label distribution. Store chains that met the same fate were Douglas Stereo in Beltsville, Maryland, Ohio's Buzzard's Record Nest, Rocky Mountain Records in Boulder, Sound Future Compact Disc Centers in Dallas, and MCD Records in New York.

What a Difference a Dime Makes

By 1995 the margin between wholesale and retail prices was still the primary point of tension between the retail community and the major labels. With the RIAA reporting over 1.11 billion units shipped in 1995, just a difference of 10¢ per unit would mean over $111 million dollars going into one set of pockets rather than another. Pressure from the corporate owners of the record companies and the distribution chain of supply investors over every increment of difference between retail and wholesale prices was exacerbated by the competitive spirit inherent in a business driven by the weekly changes in the charts and shifts in record bin positioning.

   At the 1995 NARM convention Musicland CEO Jack Eugster brought the issue of pricing policies to light from the standpoint of the traditional record retailers who had to compete with lower prices available at both mass merchandising and electronics chains. He urged the labels to enforce their Minimum Advertised Price (MAP) on them, which was the lowest consumer price at which the labels would allow a retailer to offer customers and still provide that retailer with co-opted advertising. Eugster maintained that if the big-box retailers continued to advertise records at below the labels' MAP while record stores complied with the policy, there would be another round of record chain bankruptcy. Speaking for the big-box contingent, Circuit City countered with the argument that demand would gradually diminish if they had to sell albums at over $11 in actual price. The year 1995 ended without the issue being resolved. It would continue to be a matter of contention well into the ensuing decade.

Meanwhile, piracy and counterfeiting concerns went to the back burner for the labels themselves, due to increased diligence by the RIAA and its international counterpart IFPI, who inforced copyright through improved computerized tracking of bar codes and RFID tags leading to better separation of legitimate product from counterfeit copies. The claimed losses from home duplication had been partially offset by the blank tape/disc and digital device levies implemented in the 1992 Home Recording Act, while the labels continued to search for a copy code technology that could be digitally embedded into CDs. Parallel imports were more of an issue for the music publishers, so the labels let them take the lead in pursuing and litigating with transgressors through the NMPA and its international counterpart CISAC with an occasional assist from the RIAA and IFPI. Returns were still a point of contention, but management of them had continued to improve with the computerization of the ordering process and SoundScan's tracking of sales.

Motivated by the bonuses that accompanied increased revenue, the major label sales divisions were competing even more intensely for their share of retail orders. Concurrently the retailers were competing locally with one another to attract consumers to their stores. They clamored for better prices from wholesalers, who were doing the same with the record companies. The usual label response to those seeking a greater profit was to propose a price increase, but by 1995 front-line albums had already reached an SRLP of between $17.98 and $19.98 for superstars with debut artists at $15.98. Big-box electronics stores were selling records as loss leaders to attract consumers to their appliances, while record megastores like Virgin and Tower were discounting current releases to entice consumers into the stores to peruse their extensive inventory that smaller stores and retail chains didn't carry.

Retail chains insisted that lower prices would result in larger volume that would produce a greater profit, but this assertion didn't work for those that couldn't survive on a smaller margin. As stores and chains continued to fold or be assimilated, many resorted to selling used CDs, which produced a greater profit margin than selling new ones. Some even suggested that their customers join record clubs to buy new product, then resell their deeply discounted purchases to the stores.

In response, the record companies threatened to boycott stores selling used CDs. Garth Brooks, EMI's biggest-selling artist by far, endorsed the policy. NARM threatened a price-fixing class action lawsuit, but a Federal Trade Commission investigation convinced the labels to back off. Instead, MCA, Geffen, and Virgin decided to opt out of the record clubs, with PolyGram seriously considering joining them. But three of the majors owned the two primary record clubs, BMG and the now–Sony-WMG joint venture Columbia

House. With the clubs annually accounting for 10 percent to 20 percent or even more of their sales, they could not disassociate themselves.

Turn Up the Radio

Ever since Top 40 radio debuted in 1955 and expanded into other genre-based formats in the 1960s, radio and record revenues had grown in tandem. Radio expanded from $456.5 million in 1955 to $802.3 million in 1964 to $1.64 billion in 1973, while RIAA retail value rose from $227 million to $758 million and then $1.51 billion in 1973. By 1985 radio was at $6.56 billion compared to the RIAA total of $4.26 billion. In 1995 radio reached $11.47 billion, while RIAA totals were at $12.32 billion. Radio's fourteenfold income growth over thirty years combined with the low cost of programming attracted the mid-1980s' Wall Street investors who perceived greater cash flow stability and less risk in radio compared to the record business. Essentially radio was benefiting from the record sector's investment in the talent that filled its airwaves without sharing in the cost.

Digital technology had also affected the bottom line of the radio industry. By 1995 satellites expedited the simultaneous transmission of programming to multiple stations, computers allowed more stations to automate the process resulting in reduced staff, and digital discs replaced tape cartridges in station control rooms for better audio quality. The improvements in efficiency and quality were matched, if not exceeded, by the accompanying operational savings.

In 1985, Capital Cities/ABC led the top ten station groups as the result of that year's purchase of the ABC radio and TV networks, cable systems, and other newspaper and music publishing holdings by the much smaller Capital Cities Broadcasting with financial assistance from Warren Buffett. Traditional powerhouse CBS was at number two followed by number three Westinghouse Broadcasting, also known as Group W, a division of the Westinghouse electronics company. RKO General, then a division of General Tires, and *USA Today* owner Gannett rounded out the top five. NBC was at #6 and was sold the next year to Westwood One. Metropolitan Broadcasting, in the number seven spot, was then owned by John Kluge's Metromedia but would shortly go into liquidation. Independent chains Malrite Communications and Emmis Broadcasting came in at number eight and number nine with Infinity Broadcasting at number ten, led by future broadcasting Hall of Famer Mel Karmazin, who would take Infinity public to fund acquisitions and reach the number one position for 1993 through 1995.

Station revenue varied with market size and audience share as reflected in the quarterly Arbitron ratings, but a station group's revenue potential was hampered by the FCC limits on ownership to twelve AM and twelve FM stations. The duopoly rule that restricted ownership to just one AM/FM combination in a market further restricted profits. Station groups could, however, syndicate their programming to other stations in additional markets. During the post–Gulf War recession of 1991–92 radio industry revenue fell slightly compared to the $500 million annual growth of the past decade.

Starting in 1993, the Clinton Economy became the period of greatest material growth in American history. While the record industry, its retail partners, and internet entrepreneurs were enjoying a free-wheeling bull market, radio was still operating under the Communications Act of 1934, which had established the Federal Communications Commission (FCC) as the regulatory agency for all broadcasting. Despite the number of stations expanding from under a thousand in 1934 to over nine thousand in 1994, the FCC still had the same cap on station ownership that it did sixty years prior.

Many of the broadcasting groups had financed their station holdings based on the pre-recession growth pattern and found themselves in an overleveraged position. The NAB asked the FCC to relax ownership restrictions so they could reduce overhead through consolidation of administrative costs over a larger number of stations. The FCC recommended raising ownership caps to eighteen AMs and eighteen FMs, with an increase to twenty/twenty in two years, as well as lifting duopoly restrictions. Throughout 1994 and 1995 the NAB pushed for even more expansive changes to the 1934 act. A bill for comprehensive telecommunications reform was introduced into the Senate by Chairman of the Commerce Committee Larry Pressler (South Dakota-R) in March 1995 and passed in June 1995 with an eighty-one to eighteen vote. Then the House passed a similar bill in October 1995 without objection, which was sent to the joint conference committee for action in 1996.

Read the Tea Leaves or Follow the Siren's Song?

Other than changes in ownership and leadership, and a rise in revenue throughout the record, retail, and radio sectors, the most noticeable change since 1985 was the widespread adoption of the CD as the sound carrier of choice, along with the rise in price for the latest releases. In 1985 the average RIAA retail value of an album was $7.72 with sales still dominated by cassettes and LPs. In 1995 the average album price rose to $12.13 inclusive of all levels of pricing and sound carrier types, but the top artists' CD releases had a SRLP of $17.99 to $19.99.

The wild card in the business had always been the consumers. How would they decide to spend their time and money? They now had so many choices, including what stations to listen to, what records to buy, where to buy them, or whether to buy records at all as opposed to making copies at home. They could also buy concert tickets or spend their leisure dollars on non-music pursuits such as video games, movies, sports, travel, or participatory recreation.

Technological innovation had always brought new choices and distractions. First in-car tape players took listeners away from radio. Then cable television, home video, and automated recording on VCRs brought further competition for consumers' time and money. In 1985 Nintendo introduced the first home gaming console, the Apple MacIntosh was in its second year of existence, and Microsoft licensed its Windows 1.0 operating system nonexclusively to most PC manufacturers other than Apple. In 1993, the World Wide Web (WWW) protocols were adopted, leading to the commercialization of the internet in late 1994. In 1985 fewer than 15 percent of households had home computers, but by 1995 the percentage grew to almost 40 percent, primarily in homes with disposable income. Also, in 1995 Microsoft Explorer and Windows 95 debuted, close on the heels of the Netscape Navigator browser introduced in November 1994.

The teenagers of 1995 had grown up watching their parents copy tracks from vinyl, cassette, and then CD albums onto blank cassettes, whether copying them in entirety or selecting tracks to create playlists for their Walkman and other portable devices. Applying this practice to computers via the just-introduced CD-ROM drive became possible in 1990. By 1995 the price of computers with CD-ROM drives fell below $1,000. The year 1995 also saw the introduction of the WinPlay3, which could decode and play MP3 files, for Windows 3.0 and Windows 95. It would be just a few years before file-sharing and listening to MP3s on portable devices would become a disruptive threat to the stability and profitability of the entire record industry.

Nonetheless, by the end of 1995 the effects of digital technology on the music business were already quite profound. The CD now dominated retail business, accounting for about 75 percent of revenue. Overall annual record sales had almost doubled over the decade, while annual retail value had almost tripled, meaning that the consumer was listening to music more than ever but had to pay almost twice as much to purchase it. Retailers were the business sector most closely in touch with the consumer and constantly warned the record industry of the danger of this trend. The labels, however, were contently ensconced in a bubble of constant growth driven by a corporate profit ethos, rather than the read-the-street practice of the old-line record men.

As always, the next week would produce new chart numbers affecting record sales, artists' careers, and label management just as it had done the week before, and the week before that, scarcely allowing time to think about much beyond the next six months' record release schedule. Meanwhile, their core fourteen-to-twenty-eight-year-old demographic stayed closely in tune with the new technology being adapted to music consumption. While the tea leaves portended a future of even greater technological growth, the siren song of the cash registers still obscured the vision and filled the ears of those who controlled the record industry.

3

Publishing, Copyright, Legislation, and Litigation

Music Publishing in 1985

Although often treated as an adjunct to the more visible record and radio industries, music publishing preceded them both by more than three hundred years. In 1985 performing rights, mechanical reproduction rights, the right to synchronize music with moving images, and the right to print music, collectively known as the bundle of rights granted under US copyright law, were publishing's four primary revenue sources. While revenue history for recorded music was readily available from the RIAA going back to 1973, and for radio from the RAB going back to 1945, music publishing did not have a parallel industrywide revenue summary. Although performing rights revenue was traceable through the PROs and mechanicals rights could be estimated using the RIAA shipment statistics as a reference point, industrywide sync and print revenue were far more difficult to determine since license fees were negotiated with and paid directly to the individual proprietary publishers.

In 1985 the National Music Publishers Association (NMPA), established in 1917 as the Music Publishers' Protective Association, had long been the preeminent trade organization and principal voice of the music publishing industry. Most of its members were private companies that rarely revealed revenue details, not even to the NMPA. Even the publishing wings of the publicly traded members of the Big Six music conglomerates revealed little detail in their parent companies' annual reports. The Harry Fox Agency (HFA) had been the NMPA's subsidiary licensing wing since 1927, administrating both mechanical and sync licenses for many of its members. HFA maintained its own licensing database, but also rarely revealed revenue information.

In 1985, the NMPA hired its board president, Edward Murphy, away from the presidency of classical music publisher G. Schirmer, Inc., to become the full-time paid president/CEO of both the NMPA and HFA. His agenda began with an upgrade of HFA's administrative system to increase mechanical collections, achieve better results in record company audits, and improve

American Popular Music and Its Business in the Digital Age. Rick Sanjek, Oxford University Press. © Frederick Sanjek 2024.
DOI: 10.1093/oso/9780190653828.003.0003

returns from international revenue sources. He was also charged to further the harmonization of US copyright law with Berne Convention international standards. The 1985 NMPA board had eighteen members, including representatives of twelve independent publishers; the publishing divisions of entertainment conglomerates WCI, MCA, and CBS, all of which also owned both major record labels and movie studios; film studio Paramount Pictures' publishing wing; and the publishing companies associated with independent labels A&M and Motown.

Each branch of the bundle of rights had a different revenue structure. Mechanical royalties for the songs embedded in recordings were paid at a per-unit statutory rate. Print royalties were based on a contractual percentage of the retail price. Both had similar paths with several degrees of separation between the point of purchase by consumers and receipt of royalties by creators. Included within their respective retail prices, these royalties passed through retailers to wholesalers, and then for mechanicals through the record labels, and for print through print distributors. Publishers received royalties six to twelve months after the actual sale, and then accounted to songwriters forty-five days after the end of the calendar quarter of receipt. Consumers were generally unaware of the royalty process or the amounts.

Domestic performing rights revenues were collected by the three performing rights organizations (PROs)—ASCAP, BMI, and SESAC—and then divided evenly into publisher and songwriter royalty pools to be paid directly to each group in separate but parallel accountings. Sync license fees were a one-time line-item production expense for movies, television programs, advertisements, video games, home video productions, and any other media that utilized music in their productions. The length of the license could be limited or in perpetuity as negotiated. Any additional per-unit-sold sync royalties for music-clip compilations or concert videos sold in the home video market were paid by the companies that licensed the rights for manufacturing and distribution from the original producers, if not incorporated within the initial license on a royalty buyout basis.

The Mechanics of Mechanical Licensing

Mechanical rights royalties appeared to be the simplest to determine as they were based on a statutory rate for each track sold. In 1985 the rate for songs under five minutes was 4.5¢, which rose to 5¢ on January 1, 1986, as scheduled in a series of rate adjustment increases set under the 1980 and then the 1997

Mechanical Rate Adjustment Proceedings, using the Consumer Price Index (CPI) as a barometer. In 1995 the rate was at 6.6¢, a 46.7 percent cumulative increase over the 1985 rate, with the rate per minute or fraction thereof for songs over five minutes in length rising from 85¢ in 1985 to $1.25¢ for 1995.

Applying the 1985 statutory rate of 4.5¢ per track sold to an album with ten tracks and multiplying this amount by the 1985 RIAA-listed shipment totals of 528.7 million vinyl, cassette, and CD album units, then combining this with the 120.7 million singles also listed, yielded just under $250 million. Determining any year's actual total, however, had a long litany of complications. First, records shipped were not records sold, so payment for an undetermined share of any given year's shipments, if eventually sold, were accounted for in subsequent years. Additionally, records shipped in previous years but not sold until 1985 were paid at the rate in effect for the original mechanical license, as were any re-pressings done in subsequent years. As many as 10 percent of shipments were given away as free goods with no mechanicals paid, and an undisclosed amount of royalties were held back by the labels at their discretion as reserves against returns. On the other hand, in 1995 tracks that exceeded five minutes in length were paid at a per minute rate of 1.25¢, increasing the fee to 7.5¢ for records between five and six minutes long compared to 6.6¢ for those under five minutes long. Some albums contained more than ten tracks as a CD could hold a little more than seventy-four minutes compared to just above forty-four minutes for an LP; and an unknown number of sales from reserve account reconciliations or audits of previous years were included in any given year's accounting.

Further complicating mechanical license payments, almost all recording contracts signed since the passage of the Copyright Act of 1976 included controlled composition clauses that mandated rates at 75 percent of statutory for "any song in which the artist has an income or other interest. This means that, even if the artist doesn't own or control the song, if he or she wrote it or otherwise gets a piece of its earnings, it's a *controlled composition*," as explained by attorney Don Passman in his music industry primer *All You Need to Know About the Music Business*, originally published in 1991 and now in its tenth edition.[1] The controlled composition clause also made artists responsible for delivering the reduced rate for all shares of all songs on the album, whether controlled by the artist of not, and limiting the amount it would pay to 75 percent of the applicable rate for only ten tracks. This reduced the 1995 rate from 6.6¢ to 4.95¢, with ten tracks at 49.5¢. Any amount due over 49.5¢ would be deducted from the artist's royalties.

HFA administered the largest share of industry mechanical licenses due to its representation of the major publishers. Its collection fee was calculated just

MECHANICAL LICENSE RATES FOR PHYSICAL RECORDINGS

The Copyright Act of 1976 raised the statutory mechanical rate for the first time since 1909, going from 2¢ to 2.75¢ as of January 1978. Provisions were established for periodic raises supervised by a panel of Copyright Royalty Judges appointed by the Librarian of Congress.

EFFECTIVE TIME PERIOD	RATE PER TRACK IF UNDER 5 MINUTES	RATE PER MINUTE OR PART THEREOF IF OVER 5 MINUTES	AUTHORITY: COPYRIGHT ROYALTY JUDGES
1978-1980	2.75¢	.5¢	Copyright Act of 1976
1981-1982	4¢	.75¢	1980 Mechanical Rate Adjustment Proceeding
1983- Jun 1984	4.25¢	.8¢	1980 Mechanical Rate Adjustment Proceeding
Jul 1984-1985	4.5¢	.85¢	1980 Mechanical Rate Adjustment Proceeding
1986-1987	5¢	.95¢	1980 Mechanical Rate Adjustment Proceeding
1988-1989	5.25¢	1¢	Consumer Price Index from Dec 1985 to Sept 1987
1990-1991	5.7¢	1.1¢	Consumer Price Index from Sept. 1987 to Sept. 1989
1992-1993	6.25¢	1.2¢	Consumer Price Index from Sept. 1989 to Sept. 1991
1994-1995	6.6¢	1.25¢	Consumer Price Index from Sept. 1991 to Sept. 1993
1996-1997	6.95¢	1.3¢	Consumer Price Index from Sept. 1993 to Sept. 1995
1998-1999	7.1¢	1.35¢	1997 Mechanical Rate Adjustment Proceeding
2000-2001	7.55¢	1.45¢	1997 Mechanical Rate Adjustment Proceeding
2002-2003	8¢	1.55¢	1997 Mechanical Rate Adjustment Proceeding
2004-2005	8.5¢	1.65¢	1997 Mechanical Rate Adjustment Proceeding
2006-2009 *	9.1¢	1.75¢	1997 Mechanical Rate Adjustment Proceeding

* Still in effect as of Dec 31, 2020 / Source: Copyright Royalty Board

Illustration 3.1 Mechanical License Rates for Physical Recordings

to cover its overhead staying under 5 percent during this time period. Non-HFA publishers licensed directly to the labels or through smaller licensing agencies, attorneys, or business managers. *Billboard*'s Irv Lichtman, deputy editor and writer of the weekly *Words & Music* publishing column, reported that at the NMPA's June 1985 annual meeting, "Murphy, who did not reveal dollars-and-cents figures, said that results for 1984 reflected the 'happy trend' for the industry that he reported on at last year's meeting. Estimates place last year's record-setting revenues at about $100 million."[2]

In October 1990 Lichtman reported on the first annual NMPA *International Survey of Music Publishing Revenues*, stating that global music publishing in 1989 had topped $3 billion with the US share at a "nearly 35% piece of the global pie with a total of $1.056 billion. The NMPA report estimates US performance revenues at $539 million in 1989, followed by $300 million in mechanical royalties. Music print sales amounted to $167 million, while other sources of income amounted to $50 million."[3] There were no specific sources or methodologies cited to back Murphy's estimates other than referencing "a number of sources at its [NMPA's] command."[4]

Lichtman added that the NMPA report "further stated that actual [US] income could well be 15-20% higher due to the publishers who did not belong to the NMPA."[5] In the global survey for 1994 delivered at the 1995 NMPA board meeting, Murphy estimated US mechanicals at $356.1 million. In comparison, the 1995 RIAA shipments of 1.008 billion albums and 102.4 million singles at the 1994 statutory rate of 6.6¢, with all the caveats previously applied to the 1985 calculations still applicable, came to around $450 million, about 25 percent higher than the NMPA estimate, consistent with the then-generally held supposition that HFA represented 75 percent to 80 percent of mechanical license revenue.

The Evolution of Sync Licensing

Prior to 1985 most NMPA-associated publishers had used HFA as a clearinghouse for their sync licenses. The HFA sync license template had long been a single fee, worldwide, in perpetuity buyout. Most of these licenses also contained a most favored nations (MFN) clause stating that if any other similarly situated song in the same production received more favorable material terms, then those same terms would be applied to licenses containing an MFN clause, and that the rate also was on a par with the master recording sync license fee.

The introduction of sound embedded in and synchronized to the moving images on film in the late 1920s initiated the need for sync licenses. It also replaced the live musicians who played from printed scores at theaters in accompaniment to silent movies. De Wolfe Music of London had opened in 1909, and soon became the major supplier of these scores. It then successfully transitioned to providing recorded background music—also referred to as interstitial, incidental, or needle drop—to be used in films, and then in television programming and commercials. The available music came in a catalog first delivered in shellac discs, and then vinyl, audiotape, CD, and eventually digital files as each format was introduced. De Wolfe established the standard for what would become known as production music libraries with content organized according to style, tempo, mood, and instrumentation.

Both the song and master recording rights were licensed together either nonexclusively to multiple clients or customized for a single client at a higher fee, but in either case, they were less expensive than a commissioned musical score. Libraries then collected the publishing royalties from the PROs, with the composers and songwriters receiving their share separately unless they were under a work-for-hire agreement, for as long as their content was aired as part of the licensees' programs, and for the world excluding the US, as part of the box-office performing rights payments. Other libraries soon followed, led by the Boosey & Hawkes Recorded Music Library in 1937, the Chappell Music Library wing of the 130-year-old Chappell & Co. piano and publishing company in 1941, and KPM Music Group as a merger in 1959 between KP Music—with publishing ancestry going back to 1780—and Peter Maurice Music. KPM was then sold to EMI in 1969 but continued to operate independently.

As television and then cable proliferated so did the need for additional production music libraries. Pianist/composer Bob Israel opened Score Productions in 1963 to create background cues and themes exclusively for television shows including *The Price Is Right, Concentration, All My Children, ABC World News,* and the CNN main theme. *The Price Is Right* theme, "Come on Down," was written by Edd Kalehoff as a work-for-hire with no authorship credit. Kalehoff, however, went on to later success with his own library supplying music to CBS, ABC, and numerous other clients. "Come on Down" with lyrics added by artist Crystal Waters and her producer Orlando Ortiz later became the first television theme song to reach number one on a *Billboard* chart.

Other television themes to become part of the cultural consciousness included the whistled version of the *Andy Griffith Show* theme, "Fishin' Hole," cowritten by Earle Hagen and Herbert Spenser. Hagen also composed the themes for *The Dick Van Dyke Show*, *That Girl*, *I Spy*, *The Mod Squad*, and *Eight Is Enough*. There were also songs originally written and licensed for sync use in commercials that became a part of the musical mainstream. "We've Only Just Begun," written by Paul Williams and Roger Nichols was a Crocker Bank ad before becoming a hit for The Carpenters. "I'd Like to Buy the World a Coke/I'd Like to Teach the World to Sing" was originally commissioned and cowritten for the ad by McCann Erickson creative director Bill Backer and music director Billy Davis before Hall of Fame songwriters Roger Cook and Roger Greenaway adapted it to become a worldwide hit by the New Seekers.

By 1985 the use of the analog Moog and subsequent digital synthesizers integrated with live musicians, and pioneered in the library segment by Edd Kalehoff, led to the development of libraries supplying more contemporary digitally recorded content. London-based Bruton Music was opened in 1977 by former KPM executive Robin Phillips in association with ATV Music. Tom Dinoto and Robert Skomer's Network Production Music Library launched in San Diego in 1979 and Dallas-based FirstCom debuted in 1980. In 1983 Clive Calder's London-based Zomba Music and EMI Music Publishing formed Associated Production Music (APM) to both create their own catalog and distribute KPM and other foreign libraries in the US. Using library catalogs quickly became even more efficient and economical as vinyl needle drops gave way to computerized editing.

In 1988 Zomba acquired the Chappell Library from Warner Chappell after Warner's acquisition of the Chappell catalog. Zomba placed the library along with the more contemporary Bruton catalog with APM for US administration. Former BMI, EMI, and ATV executive Sam Trust opened Killer Tracks in 1989 as another library with contemporary content, sold 50 percent to BMG in 1991, and then the other 50 percent to them in 1996. Trust remained at the helm as Killer Tracks became the BMG production music division and distributor for the other BMG library acquisitions, including Atmosphere, Cezame, Koka Media, Match Music, Not Just Jingles, and Network Music.

Even with the increasing use of library music, the licensing of popular songs in films, commercials, and video games necessitated the negotiation of sync licenses specific to each situation. Wanting greater control to maximize revenue, by 1985 mainstream publishers were well into the establishment of their own in-house sync departments. MFN terms remained de rigueur applicable to both the other songs and master recordings in the production. By 1995 the NMPA reported that global sync revenue as totaled by CISAC had grown to just over $459 billion, though it didn't cite a US share.

Although information from the publishers was limited, sync licensing was expanding as referenced in the NMPA international reports, and as evident by the growth in revenue reported by the trade press and associations of the industries that used music. The publishers' sync departments tracked this growth to utilize in licensing negotiations. From 1985 to 1995, the US film box office receipts grew from $3.0 billion to $5.2 billion. Network television advertising revenue went from $7.4 billion to $10.7 billion, local and syndication advanced from $13 billion to $19.4 billion, and cable more than doubled from $4.6 billion to $10.1 billion. Revenue from foreign licensing of US programming doubled from $1.7 billion to $3.4 billion. The home video market tripled during this time period to over $5 billion. Overall, revenue for these entertainment segments grew 71.3 percent from $31.5 billion in 1985 to $53.8 billion in 1995.

Total US sync revenue was probably in excess of what conclusions could be drawn from the NMPA global surveys, considering that US television was far more commercialized than in Europe or Asia, its film industry was much larger, and both CISAC and HFA had limited if any access to data from NMPA publishers' sync departments, non-NMPA members, or production music libraries. Randy Wachtler, co-founder and former president of the Production Music Association (PMA) estimated that by combining these factors with more recent data and then extrapolating backward, a reasonable estimate for the US sync segment over this time period fell somewhere between $300 million and $750 million. Wachtler had opened the 615 Music library in 1985 and in 2010 sold it to Warner Chappell Production Music where he subsequently became president/CEO through 2017.

The Modern Print Music Market

The print market had long predated the record industry with a distribution network of rack jobbers who subsequently added records to their product offerings. Of the Big Six publishers in 1985, only Warner Bros. Publications, Inc. (WBP) still manufactured and distributed printed music. The other majors licensed their print rights to a handful of specialists led by CPP-Belwin, Inc., Hal Leonard Publishing Corp., and WBP itself. CPP-Belwin was formed by a 1988 $25 million merger financed by Boston Ventures' between Columbia Pictures Publications (CPP), which had launched in 1968, and veteran New York publisher Belwin Mills. For much of the decade it was the largest US print distributor under the leadership of CPP veteran Frank Hackinson but was challenged by Hal Leonard in the early 1990s. When WBP acquired CPP-Belwin in 1994 for $40 million, all WBP operations were moved into the CPP-Belwin facilities in Miami. The consolidated entity claimed to be the new worldwide print leader, while Hal Leonard asserted that it was still the leader in domestic sales.

Hal Leonard had been founded in 1947 by Roger Busdicker and brothers Hal and Everett (Leonard) Edstrom, the leaders of the Minneapolis-based Hal Leonard Band. After discovering they could sell their arrangements of popular songs to high school bands, they opened their eponymous retail print operation and began licensing rights for their arrangements from the songs' proprietary publishers. In the 1950s they branched out into choral music and instructional method books. In 1985 the company was sold to an employee group led by CEO Keith Mardak, who guided Hal Leonard into the top spot in print. They also managed distribution for other print manufacturers, including John Denver producer/publisher Milt Okun's New York-based Cherry Lane Music, and Music Sales Group, which included an ample collection of classical music including the G. Schirmer catalog, which dated back to 1848.

Other than WBP, the other leading print companies were privately held and seldom disclosed financial information while WBP's revenue was buried within the music publishing line-items in its parent company's annual reports. What little information that could be found appeared periodically in the trade press. In *Billboard*'s March 1987 *Spotlight on Music Publishing*, Irv Lichtman cited an Arthur Young & Co. study commissioned by the NMPA along with the Church Music Publishers Association (CMPA) and print publishing trade organization the Music Publishers Association (MPA) that estimated 1985 revenue for folios and single sheets at $275.1 million. Then for a 1991–92 twelve-month period, Lichtman reported that the NMPA claimed $334 million in print revenue for its members. If the NMPA was using its members' royalty receipts and not retail sales to consumers as the basis for its revenue claim, then its calculations were based on the standard print license royalty rate percentages of the retail price paid by distributors of 20 percent for sheet music, 10 percent to 12.5 percent for folios, 10 percent for band/choir/dance arrangements, and 5 percent to 7.5 percent for lyrics only.

A September 1994 *Billboard* article by Frank DiCostanzo cited an appraisal of the total print segment based on what consumers spent at the point of purchase. This is the same methodology historically used by the RIAA in calculating total revenue for the recorded music segment. He wrote, "The total sheet music industry is worth $3.2 billion, according to the American Music Conference [AMC]."[6] The Retail Print Music Dealers Association in its "Resources" section described the AMC as a research organization that depicted itself as dedicated to "building credibility for music and music education, and to expanding that portion of the population that enjoys and makes its own music."[7]

In addition to print sections in record shops, chains, and megastores, print sales came from the National Association of Music Manufacturers (NAMM) members, which were primarily musical instrument and equipment stores, Christian book shops, secular bookstore chains, mail-order operations, educational institutions, art centers, barbershop quartets, choral groups, and both professional and amateur performers. In addition to sheet music and song folios, products included orchestral, band, and choral arrangements, musical theatre scores, instructional books, and other music education materials.

The $3.2 billion retail valuation would have yielded $480 million at a 15 percent average royalty rate estimated by blending the differing rates for the various print usages. Reverse application of this 15 percent rate to the NMPA members' royalties of $334 million in the 1991–92 report cited by Lichtman came to just over $2.2 billion in point-of-purchase sales revenue. Assuming that print revenue was on the upswing from 1992 to 1994, an undetermined share of print music sales involved classical and liturgical works that were in the public domain and produced no publishing royalties, and there were also sales of music owned by publishers who were not HFA members, then the NMPA estimates were reasonably compatible with DiCostanzo's reporting.

Performing Rights

Performing rights revenue was the easiest of the publishing streams to calculate. The PROs' computerized databases encompassed all their administrative needs, although they were not compatible with one another. In 1985 only ASCAP revealed financial data until BMI joined them in the mid-1990s. Nonetheless, there had been enough information available to make a reasonable estimate placing performing rights revenue at about 50 percent of total publishing revenue. Businesses that used music to make or enhance their profit whether live or recorded, and whether in the foreground or background, needed PRO licenses. This included radio, television, concert promoters, music clubs, restaurants, and other areas of retail enterprise.

In 1985, total PRO revenue was estimated to be $445 million. ASCAP collected $245 million for 55 percent of that total. BMI collected about 43 percent with 2 percent going to SESAC. About 20 percent of the 1985 total came from the performance of US works collected by overseas PROs and then transmitted to the appropriate US PRO, growing to over 30 percent in 1995. Roughly 90 percent was payable to songwriters as sub-publishers in each territory collected the publisher share, kept their administrative fee, and then transmitted the balance to the original US publisher.

ASCAP was and still is a nonprofit membership association, while BMI was originally and still was as of 2020 a C corporation operating on a not-for-profit basis. At that time, SESAC was a privately held for-profit company. Both ASCAP and BMI distributed their domestic collections after deducting overhead expenses, which were in the 18 to 20 percent range of gross collections during this time period. Information on SESAC's finances was not available. The three combined to represent the US rights for virtually all the songs in the world under copyright protection until Global Music Rights (GMR) was launched in 2013. At both BMI and SESAC, songwriters and publishers were and still are referred to as affiliates, at ASCAP as members, and at GMR as clients.

Each PRO collated song and performance data with revenue collections, enabling them to create detailed quarterly domestic statements and semiannual foreign accountings for each royalty participant of all works with logged broadcast performances. PROs collected approximately 85 percent of domestic revenue through licenses with radio, television, and cable on a blanket license basis, which gave unrestricted access to all works in their respective catalogs. The other 15 percent came from non-broadcast sources under what is termed "general licenses" with rate schedules and blanket license provisions for each business category. The specific songs used under general licenses were not itemized on the premise that such a process would be cost prohibitive, and under the assumption that the songs used would closely reflect the music played on the radio. Consequently, the general license proceeds were added to the pool of money distributed based on radio play.

Grand performing rights, the term applied to music performed within the context of a theatrical production, were outside of the PROs' purview. Royalties for grand rights were usually paid at the rate of 4 percent of the box office, collectively to the composers and lyricists directly through grand rights collection agencies, with another 2 percent going to the writer of the book, as scripts were termed. According to statistics compiled by the Broadway League, the 1995 box office for Broadway and touring productions was over $900 million. At a 4 percent rate this yielded about $30 million in music royalties due to the much higher ratio for musicals compared to dramatic productions.

In 1985 both ASCAP and BMI employed a rotating sample of radio airplay to determine their domestic distributions but used different methodologies. ASCAP taped sixty thousand hours annually in six-hour blocs per station, selecting stations according to its "follow the dollar" policy, that is, monitoring larger income stations more often than smaller ones. The tapes were then analyzed by in-house music experts to identify the ASCAP songs and songwriters, with performance credits assigned for the identified airplay. At the end of the quarter, credits were tabulated and the total receipts on hand at the end of the quarter after overhead deductions were divided proportionally by the total number of credits. They were then paid out pro rata to the writers and publishers of the identified songs.

In contrast, BMI divided the music-programming US stations randomly into seventy-eight groupings covering three days each. Groupings were diverse in station income, geography, and format, creating a sample of over six hundred thousand hours out of a total of about 70 million hours of annual radio play. When requested, each designated station submitted a log of the songs played, listing title and artist, along with writer and publisher credits if available. The BMI IBM mainframe computer then matched the submitted information against songs registered on the repertoire database for the total logged performances for each song in each quarter. Logged play was then multiplied by the inverse ratio of the logged station sample to the total base of stations for that quarter to extrapolate the estimated total number of domestic radio plays. The total quarterly results counted as the number of performances to be credited on a prorated basis to the songwriters and publishers of each song.

BMI then multiplied the performances by the base rate as stated in their printed payment schedule. BMI also had four tiers of bonuses, with songs ordered according to accumulated lifetime logged performance history to determine bonus level. After the applicable bonuses were added to all qualifying songs, if any money was left in the distribution pool, it was added proportionally to all. Thus if 15 percent remained, every statement received an additional "bonus on bonus" of 15 percent. Finally, they divided each song's royalties among the song's publishers and writers according to their relative percentage splits.

The Publisher-Songwriter Revenue Relationship

Authors (more commonly known in music as lyricists) and composers (collectively referred to in pop music as songwriters) each owned their share of their works from the moment of creation unless and until they transferred ownership to a publisher through an assignment of copyright. Publishers functioned as financial supporter, exploitative agent, rights administrator, revenue collector, and royalty dispenser for their songwriters, allowing them to focus on the creative process. If performers wrote or cowrote their own songs, songwriter royalties were a distinct and separate revenue stream from their income as artists, as if paid to two different people.

The songs in the catalog of each PRO were nonexclusively contracted to them by their members/affiliates for a defined period. In this context, "non-exclusive" meant that songwriters and their publishers could withdraw the rights for a specific usage so they themselves could assign that work or works to a licensee under the grant of a direct license. It did not mean that another PRO could represent the same song or same share thereof. Songwriter contract terms were two years for BMI and three years for SESAC, both automatically renewable unless a songwriter chose to opt out. The ASCAP contract was five continuing year-to-year terms with an annual resignation option that needed to be exercised ninety days before the end of the year to be effective on the first day of the next year. Electing to terminate from any one of the three involved a detailed process that was strictly adhered to.

Publishers usually owned companies affiliated with each PRO so they could place their rights with the PRO that each of their songwriters belonged to. For instance, Sony/ATV Music had Sony/ATV Songs BMI, Sony/ATV Tunes ASCAP, and Sony/ATV Sounds SESAC. If cowriters were with different PROs, their corresponding publisher shares were divided between the PROs in the same proportion as the songwriter shares. The publisher contract term periods were five years for both BMI and ASCAP and three for SESAC. If songwriters resigned from one PRO at the contractually specified time and joined another, the songs assigned during the contract term couldn't be transferred to the new PRO until the publisher's contract renewal date because the publisher owned the songs by assignment of copyright. Then they could only be moved if the publisher wanted to switch them at its contract term date. If the publisher did not move the songs, payment remained the responsibility of the original PRO for both publisher and songwriter, but the transfer or retention of any rights depended upon the completion of all associated paperwork.

A songwriter's exclusive agreement with a publisher, or with cooperating publishers in a joint relationship known as co-publishing, had different possible variations. A songwriter could assign the copyright, grant joint ownership of copyright, or just contract for administration for a specified time period. This could cover a single song, a group of specific songs, and/or songs yet to be created. The length could range from a limited term to life of copyright. There were also certain legislated copyright recapture clauses whereby ownership of the US copyright reverts to its creator(s) during a designated period of time defined in the copyright law unless such recapture clauses were waived by the songwriter(s).

PUBLISHER-SONGWRITER ROYALTY FLOW CHART

Businesses using music to make or enhance profits pay fees to Performing Rights Organizations (PROs). The source of over 50% of publishing revenue.

▼ ▼ ▼ ▼ ▼ ▼ ▼ ▼

Paid by record companies to publishers at statutory or controlled rate – rose gradually from 4.5¢ per track in 1985 to 6.6¢ in 1995, and 9.1¢ in 2006.

▼ ▼ ▼ ▼ ▼ ▼ ▼ ▼

Performing Rights Revenue

PROs (ASCAP, BMI, SESAC, and GMR after 2017) pay royalties separately to publishers and creators. In 1985 ASCAP and BMI took approximately 18% for expenses, down to 9% by 2019.

Mechanical License Revenue

Mechanical license collection administrators include HFA, Wixen Music, lawyers, and business managers. All royalties paid through the publishers.

50% 50%

100%

CREATORS
COMPOSERS
AUTHORS
SONGWRITERS
LYRICISTS

PUBLISHERS
ALL PUBLISHERS
INCLUDING
CREATOR-OWNED
CO-PUBLISHERS

after admin fee
50%
except PRO $$

100%

100%

Synchronization Rights Revenue

Paid by television, movie, video game, and commercial producers 100% direct to publishers, individually negotiated but paid on MFN basis.

Printed Music Rights Revenue

Licensed by publishers to printed music distributors at rates from 5% to 20% depending on usage. Higher rates after 2007 for digital distribution.

PRO, mechanical, sync, and print licenses are the four major sources of revenue for publishers and songwriters as part of the "bundle of rights" granted under the U.S. Copyright Act of 1909 and as amended in 1976. Additional digital rights were granted in the Digital Millennial Copyright Act of 1996 but did not generate royalties until the following decade. Only PRO royalties are paid directly to songwriters. All the other royalties are paid through the administrating publishers.

Illustration 3.2 Publisher-Songwriter Royalty Flowchart

The administrating publisher collected 100 percent of the revenue from mechanical, print, and sync licenses on behalf of all royalty participants. Fifty percent was then paid to the songwriter(s) unless other terms were specified in the publishing agreement. If there was more than one publisher, then the publishers' 50 percent share was divided as contractually specified. If the publisher had advanced or spent money contractually recoupable against future royalties, these sums were subtracted from otherwise payable royalties, usually including any songwriter-owned co-publisher share. For songs with multiple songwriters, the writer shares, and thus royalties, were divided evenly between them, unless different percentages were agreed upon in writing prior to the date of first publication, and then the same percentages applied to the corresponding publishing shares.

Most successful artists who wrote or cowrote their own songs sought a larger share of the publishing than the traditional fifty-fifty split by retaining an ownership stake in the copyright through a co-publishing agreement. A 75 percent-25 percent split in favor of these singer-songwriters became prevalent. Many of the most successful superstars, such as Michael Jackson and Bruce Springsteen, owned all of their publishing, making limited-term administration deals at a 10 percent or 15 percent rate.

While songwriters' performing rights royalties from foreign societies came to them through their US PROs, the 50 percent songwriter share of all other royalties generated in foreign territories, as well as the songwriter-owned co-publisher share, was transmitted by the sub-publisher in that territory to the US administrating publisher for subsequent payment to the songwriter. Using incoming foreign PRO revenue along with the statistics from the 1995 NMPA global survey as the starting data points, and then extrapolating into a hypothetical but logical revenue model, there was at least another $100 million or so coming to US songwriters for revenue generated by their songs overseas from mechanical, print, and sync licenses for 1995.

The PRO Rivalry

ASCAP and BMI were rivals from the moment of BMI's birth in 1940, which ended ASCAP's hegemony over performing rights collections. By the end of the 1960s, the BMI rock/country/R&B–oriented catalog dominated the pop charts. As a membership society of older, established songwriters, ASCAP had been reluctant to embrace the creators of this new music. In 1969 ASCAP relented and adjusted its membership policies. With more income and less airplay, ASCAP aggressively pursued market share by enticing established

BMI writers to switch to ASCAP. By 1982 the revenue ratio was 59.6 percent for ASCAP at $187 million and 38.6 percent for BMI at $120 million with SESAC at about 2 percent with an estimated $7 million.

In 1985 ASCAP's advantage on the charts reached 62 percent of the Top 100 singles of the year, a reversal of the dominance in radio play BMI had enjoyed in the late 1960s. The two had competed by giving guarantees and advances until the 1981 Buffalo Broadcasting litigation before Judge Lee Gagliardi of the US Southern District Court of New York over license fees from local television threatened the stability of overall PRO revenue with growing legal fees and potential paybacks to local television stations. Although this did not directly affect royalties for radio play, the PROs were "faced with the imposition of severe economies due to the reduction of television fees ordered by Judge Gagliardi. ASCAP and BMI suspended all cash advances and guarantees to writers and publishers."[8] This created a greater focus on comparing current ASCAP and BMI payments to publishers and songwriters, particularly for songs with co-writers from each society, easily subject to a direct comparison of statements.

In 1985 BMI brought the VP of its Nashville office, Frances W. Preston, to the New York office to address their declining chart share problem. Preston had been instrumental in maintaining BMI's lead in country and R&B while BMI's share of the pop market declined. In early 1986, the BMI board dismissed incumbent president and attorney Edward Cramer after a sixteen-year tenure, replacing him with the more industry-oriented Preston, much like the record companies installing new executives with a greater street cred and promotional savvy. Preston's team analyzed the BMI distribution policy and then systematically modified the payment schedule designed to make royalties for hits competitive with ASCAP, despite having less revenue.

Simultaneously Preston wooed film and television composers in Los Angeles with guarantees and advances after the final adjudication of the Buffalo Broadcasting suit in 1984 to solidify BMI's share of music written for both cable and terrestrial television, the other half of the PRO broadcast licensing income. BMI also instituted the first survey and payment plan for music played on college radio stations. These nonprofit stations had become the proving ground for what had become known as alternative music, a role akin to the one that FM radio had played in the late 1960s and early 1970s in breaking new rock music. As the hottest alternative acts garnered major label record deals with some going on to pop success, BMI had already bolstered its share of future CHR, AOR, and AC radio play.

Preston succeeded in turning the tide with both comparative payments and market share by the end of the 1980s, a trend that would continue over the ensuing decades. BMI's share of the 1995 Top 100 singles had risen to 44 per-cent from its 38 percent share in 1985, while sustaining its greater share of the country and R&B charts, all of which strengthened its negotiating pos-ture with the Radio Music License Committee (RMLC) for upcoming negoti-ations. ASCAP still had the lead, but BMI was on the upswing.

The ASCAP-BMI acrimony was publicly expressed by the ASCAP member-ship and BMI affiliate representatives, who told highly nuanced stories of each other's respective historical origins when soliciting new songwriters or trying to persuade established songwriters to switch their representation. ASCAP reps often claimed that BMI was controlled by its broadcaster board with the motivation of depressing PRO licensing rates, while the ASCAP board was composed of songwriters and publishers. On the other hand, BMI reps pointed to ASCAP's historic repudiation of minority and ethnic music and its attempts to ban rock-'n'-roll from radio in the 1950s. They also questioned whether ASCAP's board of established publishers and writers were setting distribution policy favoring their own interests. In reality, both were ably run by management under the oversight of their boards to assure fulfillment of their fiduciary responsibilities for on-time royalty distributions and well-administered services to their respective constituencies.

By 1993, ASCAP responded to BMI's resurgence under Preston by reorgan-izing their executive team and modifying their longstanding music survey and distribution policies. In September 1993, managing director Gloria Messenger and general counsel Bernie Korman left the company after thirty-nine and forty-two years of respective service, and CFO John LoFrumento was elevated to COO. The following year board president and composer Morton Gould also stepped down and was replaced by Songwriter Hall of Fame inductee Marilyn Bergman, the first woman to serve on the ASCAP board. LoFromento was promoted to the newly created CEO position.

Over the next two years ASCAP revamped its board to better reflect current music trends, trimmed staff, more than tripled the size of its radio sample, transformed its television survey from sample to census, and lowered the overhead percentage. In 1995 ASCAP income reached an all-time high of $436 million for a 52 percent share of the total PRO collections of $838 mil-lion. Preston's aggressive leadership had elevated BMI to an estimated 46 per-cent share at $385 million with the remaining 2 percent, at about $17 million, going to SESAC.

The wave of change in performing rights also hit SESAC. Its sole owner, Alice Prager, daughter of founder Paul Heinecke, sold the PRO in late 1992 to the trio of veteran music industry lawyer and CEO/chairman of grand rights collection agency Music Theater International (MTI) Freddie Gershon,

Gershon's fellow attorney and associate at MTI Ira Smith, and former SBK partner Stephen Swid. Financial backing was provided by merchant bank Allen & Co. *Billboard* reported that the sale price was $15 million with an estimated annual revenue of $7 million.

Latin music specialist and attorney William Velez, who had prior stints at both ASCAP and BMI, was brought in to broaden SESAC's repertoire in that area. Velez then rose to COO, replacing longtime SESAC employee Vincent Candilora, who moved over to ASCAP as director and eventually executive VP of licensing. SESAC announced the computerization of its radio monitoring system beginning in 1995 by employing information from *Billboard*'s BDS airplay detection service. Its boldest move, however, came in January 1995 when SESAC enticed Bob Dylan, Neil Diamond, and their proprietary publishing companies away from ASCAP. Aside from the publicity boon, this move improved SESAC's standing with the RMLC in contract negotiations, as well as bolstered its position within the worldwide copyright community.

The Major Publisher Competition for Market Share

In 1985, five of the six conglomerates that owned the major record label groups—RCA, EMI, CBS, MCA, and WEA—also owned large publishing divisions. The sixth was the Philips-Siemens joint venture that owned PolyGram Records, still in need of recovery from losses in the disco era. In 1984 Philips-Siemens had sold Chappell-Intersong Music, then the largest music publisher in the world, for $100 million to a group headed by Freddy Bienstock, a former Chappell song plugger who had been the song screener for Elvis Presley. Bienstock was backed by investment firm Wertheim & Co. and the estate of Oscar Hammerstein in what was the largest publishing transaction up to that time.

The Chappell sale reflected the investment world's growing valuation of publishing catalogs as marketable assets bolstered by the projected growth in the two major sources of publishing revenues. Mechanical license rates were due to grow 46.7 percent between 1985 and 1995 from statutory increases, and performing rights fees were proportionately tied to the rapidly expanding revenues of the radio, television, and cable industries. Whenever entertainment conglomerates had to offset losses in other divisions or needed excess cash for asset acquisitions, or when outside investors were looking to acquire or invest in entertainment properties, publishing catalogs were becoming the most fungible commodities.

Publishers added to their catalogs in two separate ways. The more conservative and fiscally sound approach was the purchase of existing catalogs. The prospective buyer conducted a due diligence process examining the earnings history and ownership documentation to determine the net publishing share (NPS), defined as income after payment of songwriter and co-publisher shares. The average of the NPS over a three-to-five-year period, the length of which was negotiated, was then multiplied by a numeric factor mutually agreed upon by the buyer and seller, referred to in the industry as the multiple.

During this time period, the multiple normally ranged between six and twelve, but for some established and/or diversified catalogs, especially if subjected to a bidding war, the multiple could go higher. Essentially a buyer was earning back the acquisition cost of the catalog through its earnings over the same number of years as the applicable multiple. After recouping the purchase price, the buyer would profit from the earnings over the life of copyright of each song. In 1985 this was the life of the last surviving composer plus fifty years—extended to seventy years in 1998—for all songs written since 1978. For all songs written prior to 1978, the life of copyright extended seventy-five years after the year of first publication. Outside of the US, however, songs written prior to 1978 that had fallen into the public domain in the US could still be under copyright in the countries that already conformed to a life-plus-fifty, and later seventy, term of copyright.

The other acquisition scenario involved a totally speculative investment in the costs of catalog development by signing a songwriter or songwriting team to an exclusive publishing or co-publishing agreement. Money spent was recoupable from future songwriter share of licensing receipts, if any. This method had a higher immediate return than catalog purchase if the songwriter(s) quickly created hits. Then after three to five years the catalog would have established an NPS history for any sale or contract renewal negotiation. A publisher's bet in this type of acquisition was somewhat hedged if the writer(s) already had a record contract or produced artists with record contracts.

Publishers employed creative managers who worked in conjunction with label A&R staffs to develop new acts. If a label signed and invested in a new artist it believed could sell over a million albums, then creative managers competed to sign the act to a publishing contract, with an advance to help support the act through its developmental period. With the statutory mechanical rate in 1985 at 45¢ per album and then discounted to 75 percent under the controlled composition clause, a million albums would yield about $250,000 subject to recoupment against advances in a seventy-five/twenty-five co-publishing agreement. Most agreements would also contain options for extensions with further advances for each additional album.

If an unsigned act was subject to a bidding war between labels, then a parallel bidding war between publishers usually ensued. But unlike the record labels, they did not have to invest in manufacturing and distribution, so they could more easily forecast and manage profit and expenses. As most publishing financial information was confidential, the relative market success between the top publishers was gauged by chart share, number of airplay awards issued by the PROs at their annual award celebrations, and number of awards at annual industry events such as the Grammy, American Music, Country Music Association, Soul Train, and *Billboard* Awards.

In 1985 Chappell Intersong was the number one publisher on *Billboard*'s year-end pop singles chart, which reflected the most popular singles as determined by sales and airplay. Publishing companies controlled by Warner, A&M Records, the Zomba Music Group, and MCA, along with companies owned by artists Bruce Springsteen, Prince, Duran Duran, Kool & The Gang, and Tears for Fears rounded out the top ten. Chappell, Warner, A&M, and MCA had deep, diversified, and multi-genre catalogs. Springsteen had a decade of hits while Zomba had a share if not all of almost everything Jive Records released. The other four publishers were relatively new and focused on only one artist. The CBS publishing catalog was not in the top ten in the *Billboard* chart but was considered to be one of the top three publishers along with Chappell and Warner due to its extensive back catalog.

Michael Jackson Buys In: PolyGram Regroups

An unexpected buyer made the first major publishing catalog acquisition of the Digital Age when Michael Jackson purchased the ATV Music catalog in August 1985 for $47.5 million from Robert Holmes à Court, Australia's first billionaire. Holmes à Court had gained control of the television and film production parent company of ATV Music from longtime British entertainment entrepreneur Sir Lew Grade through a stock takeover in 1982. The crown jewel of the ATV catalog was Northern Songs Ltd, which contained all but a few of the songs written by John Lennon and Paul McCartney. The duo had formed Northern in 1963 with their manager, Brian Epstein, and veteran British pop publisher Dick James, who controlled the administration. After Epstein's death in 1967, James sold his share of the catalog for $1.183 million to ATV. McCartney and Lennon tried to no avail to buy the administrative rights from ATV, but then in frustration sold their shares of Northern Songs to ATV but retained their songwriter rights.

In 2016, Ben Sisario of *The New York Times* cited a 1989 interview in which Paul McCartney recalled telling Michael Jackson how lucrative it had been for the person who owned his Beatles catalog. Michael presciently replied that if the catalog came up for sale again, he would buy it. When ATV Music was put up for sale in 1984, both McCartney and Lennon's widow, Yoko Ono, passed on bidding. The other major bidder was The Entertainment Company, controlled by Martin Bandier and Charles Koppelman. Jackson's attorney, John Branca, however, quickly closed the deal, which included an appearance by Jackson for Holmes à Court on a charity telethon for the Princess Margaret Children's Hospital in Perth, Australia.

In March 1986 PolyGram re-entered the music publishing business under the direction of London-based David Hockman and purchased the remains of the Dick James Music catalog, which included songs by Elton John, Gerry & the Pacemakers, and the Hollies as part of its over twelve thousand works, for $15 million. Hockman also set up the PolyGram Publishing international network, operating under the business affairs departments of their record companies in different territories. He first focused on acquiring a share or administration of their own artists' publishing rights, including Bon Jovi, Cameo, Gwen Guthrie, and Kurtis Blow. He then purchased the Cedarwood Music catalog of country standards for $5 million in 1987, followed by the publishing holdings of bandleader/businessman Lawrence Welk in 1988 for $25 million, as reported by *Billboard*'s Nigel Hunter. Welk Music included Jerome Kern's T. B. Harms Co. catalog, the catalog built by the Nashville team of publisher Bill Hall and producer Jack Clement, Harry Von Tilzer Music Co., and Welk's own Champagne Music, Inc. Welk COO Dean Kay became president/CEO of the US PolyGram Music publishing division. In 1990 Hockman acquired the publishing interests of ABBA manager Stig Anderson's Sweden Music and Chris Blackwell's Island Records, as part of the label group's purchase of their respective record companies.

SBK Ups the Ante in the Acquisition Competition

Bandier and Koppelman were still convinced that publishing catalogs were undervalued properties. For a reported $7.5 million, they purchased Combine Music, the publishing wing of Fred Foster's bankrupt Monument Records and owner of many Kris Kristofferson, Tony Joe White, and Larry Gatlin hits and Jerry Jeff Walker's "Mr. Bojangles." This time, however, they had a new partner in Stephen Swid, a financier and former high school friend of Bandier, with whom they formed SBK Entertainment World in 1986. Their next move was to buy CBS's publishing interests for $125 million, surpassing the Bienstock purchase of Chappell as the largest publishing transaction to date. Swid's financial clout enabled them to use conventional financing rather that investment bank partners. Ironically, among the assets acquired from CBS was a publishing administration agreement with Jackson's ATV Music, which had over four years to go.

Then in early 1987 Wertheim decided to put Chappell up for sale, looking for at least $200 million. Apparently suffering seller's remorse, PolyGram wanted Chappell back and offered $175 million. MCA then offered $185 million. SBK was also interested. Warner publishing head Chuck Kaye was also doing the math, foreseeing the coming upward spike in value for music publishing. Kaye offered over $200 million in preferred stock, cash, and debt assumption a year before the Time Warner merger. The deal closed, surpassing the SBK purchase of the CBS catalog as the biggest acquisition to date. With Chappell's estimated $30 million NPS, the multiple measured at about seven, well under the twelve-plus multiples to be applied in the coming decades. Bienstock made over $30 million for his 15 percent share and continued to run his sizable stable of other publishing assets under the Carlin Music umbrella. Chuck Kaye left Warner Chappell shortly after the Time Warner merger and opened Windswept Pacific Music in partnership with attorney and longtime colleague Evan Medow, and Japan's largest media conglomerate Fujisankei Communications Group.

Meanwhile at SBK, Swid had quickly become immersed in the machinations of the music business through Bandier and Koppelman, and proved to be a fast learner, just as Bandier had anticipated. By the end of 1988 Swid concluded that to maximize publishing profits, SBK needed to control a record company as well. In a bold move, Swid put together financing and SBK offered to buy the music holdings of Thorn-EMI. Impressed with SBK's vision and aggressive style, newly appointed EMI chairman Jim Fifield instead purchased SBK Entertainment World. This set yet another milestone in publishing company valuations. As part of the deal, Bandier and Koppelman formed a partnership with EMI to create their own record label, SBK Records, totally funded by EMI. Swid exited from SBK with his share of the profit and returned to the music business a few years later with the SESAC acquisition. Koppelman and Bandier took the positions of chairman/CEO and vice chairman/COO, respectively, of both the new label and EMI Music Publishing.

With Fifield's approval, they now spearheaded the expansion of EMI publishing. In 1990, they bought London-based Filmtrax Copyright Holdings,

Inc, a catalog of ninety thousand songs gathered from various sources over the past six years. The reported purchase price was about $115 million in cash, stock, and debt, subject to completion of due diligence, calculated at about a twelve multiple on an average NPS of about $10 million. The EMI catalog was further boosted by the publishing interests acquired with the Virgin Records purchase.

In 1991, *Billboard* reported that Bandier and Koppelman sold their share of SBK Records to EMI for somewhere between $100 and $400 million, depending on earnings over the ensuing four years. They extended their contracts through 1995 and divided their duties. Bandier took over publishing and Koppelman remained with the record division. In 1988 EMI had been the number four publishing group on the year-end *Billboard* Hot 100 pop singles chart, but jumped to the number one spot in 1989, due in part to the success of the SBK artist/songwriters, and held on to that spot through 1995, with Warner Chappell consistently at number two.

Just before EMI acquired SBK in 1989, CBS decided to reenter the publishing market, buying the Nashville-based Tree International Publishing catalog for $42 million from longtime owner and former Hank Williams bass player Buddy Killen. A year later Sony appointed in-house business affairs attorney Marvin Cohn to supervise the resurrection of the publishing division. In 1993 president of Sony Publishing International and former head of the UK office Richard Rowe was upped to president worldwide with Cohn returning to business affairs.

During the remainder of the decade, the Big Six publishing divisions all prospered through a combination of acquisition of the co-publishing or administration rights of their respective recording acts; adding the publishing rights from acquisitions by their record divisions; and of course by signing new songwriters, veteran hitmakers, and artists with their first record deals. Music publishing remained the safest harbor for investment in the entertainment business with its still-steady growth pattern in both mechanical royalties and PRO revenue, as well as the long-term benefit derived from the extension of the life of the US copyright in musical compositions by the Copyright Act of 1976.

The jockeying for music publishing market share in the first decade of the digital age ended the way it began with Michael Jackson and The Beatles catalog in the spotlight. In November 1995, Jackson merged his ATV catalog, including the works of Lennon and McCartney, with Sony's music publishing holdings, creating the Sony/ATV Music publishing partnership. The new entity ended 1995 firmly entrenched in the number three position behind EMI and Warner.

Independent Publishers

New acts signed to major labels were either already with a publisher that had invested in their development, or had their representatives negotiate a publishing agreement concurrently with or directly after signing their record deal. In both cases, the publishing divisions of the major labels were better equipped financially than the independents to invest in these new acts. By all comparative measures, the major publishers had a majority share of the market, either through wholly owned, partially owned, or administered shares of songs. Nonetheless in 1995 independent publishers received 30 percent to 40 percent of mechanical licensing revenue in the range of $200 million split between the HFA-associated indies and those not with HFA.

Accordingly, the indies were well represented on both the NMPA and ASCAP boards. The 1995 NMPA board looked much like the 1985 version with five publishers owned by major-label publishing affiliates, Warner, EMI, Sony, MCA, and Polygram; Paramount Pictures' Famous Music; the required classical music publisher; and eleven other independent publishers. All the independent publishers were from the pre-1960s era except Windswept Pacific, represented by Chuck Kaye's partner Evan Medow. In contrast, the membership of the Association of Independent Music Publishers (AIMP), formed in Los Angeles in 1977 with branches in both New York and Nashville, had a younger and more broadly based membership. The AIMP, however, only performed educational and lobbying services and did not collect royalties as the NMPA did with HFA.

The non-HFA independents either collected mechanical royalties on their own, through attorneys or business managers, or through smaller administrators such as Wixen Music, Bluewater Music, Bug Music, Copyright Service Bureau, and Copyright Management. Most of these indies were not involved in competing for the publishing rights of current chart records, thus maintaining a lower overhead. Many were songwriter- or artist-owned companies. Others had what were termed evergreen copyrights, a sobriquet for songs that had decades-long earnings histories. Some maintained a profitable business from evergreens from the 1920s through the 1950s that were still played on the radio formats programmed for older demographics; used in commercials, movies, television, and traveling Broadway show revivals; and/or on vintage recordings repackaged in the new CD format. Few of these usages were reflected in the current *Billboard* charts or on industry awards shows but were an essential component in determining NPS when assessing the value of a catalog. This was evident when Michael Jackson acquired ATV, and again when EMI acquired Filmtrax, a catalog with virtually no current activity, but which maintained a consistent seven-to-eight-figure NPS from catalog revenue.

By 1995 the majors had acquired either all or a share of many publishers owned by independent record companies, allowing veteran record men including Chris Blackwell of Island, Richard Branson of Virgin, Clive Calder of Zomba, Stig Anderson of Sweden Music, Buddy Killen of Tree Publishing, and Charles Koppelman of SBK to cash out on their publishing holdings. The major publishers also entered into co-publishing deals with major artists, as Warner Chappell did with Madonna for Maverick Music and Sony/ATV's partnership with Michael Jackson, to both acquire catalog and sign new artists.

Perhaps the most anomalous publisher of the decade was Diane Warren's Realsongs, named the number one *Billboard* Pop Publisher of the Year in 1990, topping all the publishers controlled by the Big Six music conglomerates. Realsongs was wholly owned by Warren, who usually wrote alone, was not a recording artist, and did not publish other songwriters' works. Warren and Realsongs landed forty-five top ten singles over the decade. ASCAP hailed Warren as its Pop Songwriter of the Year for 1990, 1991, and 1993.

Developments in Copyright and Legislation

Each country in the worldwide copyright community had its own laws governing intellectual property within its own borders, whether originating domestically or coming from another territory. Most countries had one copyright society, or one for performing rights and one for mechanical and other rights. Many were quasi-governmental or heavily regulated with strong protection for copyright owners. The US, however, had no limit on organizations representing copyright claimants, hence its three primary PROs in 1985 and an abundance of collection agents for mechanical license revenue. United States copyright law defined the terms of infringement but placed the financial burden for pursuing and defending copyright infringement claims on the litigants whereas most territories in the copyright community had strong governmental enforcement incorporated within their legal framework.

CISAC had over two hundred member societies in 123 countries representing audiovisual, dramatic, literary, and visual arts creators as well as music. CISAC was dedicated to improving and protecting the rights of these creators, and seeking harmonization, or uniformity, in copyright law on a worldwide basis. Ever since the US Copyright Act of 1909, differences between US and CISAC regulations have been problematic since many

European societies would not share their domestic license revenue with US rights holders for rights that American law did not protect. This had historically cost US songwriters and copyright owners income from overseas that they would have earned under harmonization.

In 1988, the US Congress passed the Berne Convention Implementation Act of 1988, finally enabling the US to join the 1886 Berne agreement. The 1976 Copyright Act had paved the way by establishing a US copyright in master recordings and extending the term of US copyright for musical compositions to life of the last surviving creator plus fifty years. This replaced the antiquated twenty-eight-year initial term of copyright and twenty-eight-year renewal term, which had several extensions added while waiting for the long-anticipated Copyright Act of 1976. For the songs written prior to 1978, the renewal term was extended from twenty-eight to forty-seven years for a total of seventy-five years for the two terms.

Historically, European copyright had its basis in the intrinsic artistic and moral rights of the creator, while US copyright's constitutional basis emanated from commercial concerns. It was finally these commercial concerns that overturned the longstanding iconoclastic attitude of the US toward intellectual property. Music had long been a major contributor to the positive balance of US trade, but as digital technology pushed computer software to the front of the intellectual property marketplace, Berne's worldwide protection of US intellectual property became an even more important concern. The music industry had long lobbied Congress for harmonization, but now thanks in large part to the lobbying efforts of the digital intellectual property community, further Berne compliance was on the horizon.

The next step forward was the Copyright Renewal Act of 1992, which eliminated the requirement that copyright holders file a renewal registration for songs written prior to 1978 before the expiration of the first twenty-eight-year term. Songs would no longer fall into the public domain in the US just because of the failure to file this paperwork. This scenario had happened to several well-known songs including Jimmy Thomas's "Rockin' Robin," popularized by Bobby Day; Dion's signature recording "The Wanderer," written by Ernie Maresca; and Sonny Curtis's "Walk Right Back," recorded by the Everly Brothers. The 1992 Copyright Renewal Act ensured that this could no longer happen, in a major step toward compliance with the Berne Convention.

The federal Audio Home Recording Act of 1992 (AHRA) added "Chapter 10, Digital Audio Recording Devices and Media" to the US copyright statute. Both the record and publisher sectors were concerned that digital recording devices and media would allow consumers to make perfect digital copies, or clones, of music that would replace sales and thus depress the market. They had lobbied Congress for years to pass legislation implementing both copy protection technology and royalties from the manufacturers of home recording hardware and software. The AHRA was the first governmental mandate linking digital technology to intellectual property rights in music. It also imposed a royalty on consumer purchase of digital recording devices. Opponents to the provision dubbed this royalty a tax.

The AHRA also mandated that the music industry set up a Serial Copy Management System (SCMS), and that the royalties collected under it would be distributed by the Copyright Office through its Digital Audio Recording Technologies Fund (DART). It did not, however, completely satisfy the record companies' complaints about what they termed illegal home recording, as the AHRA exempted devices not sold primarily as recording devices. This included computers and ultimately smartphones, exempting them from AHRA jurisdiction and DART collections.

DART royalties were generated by a 2 percent surcharge on digital audio recorders and 3 percent on blank digital formats including tape, CD, DAT, DCC, and Mini Disc. One-third of the royalties collected under the AHRA went into the Musical Works Fund, to be split 50 percent to writers via ASCAP, BMI, and SESAC; and 50 percent to publishers via HFA. The other two-thirds went to the Sound Recordings Fund (SRF). Four percent of this amount was paid to the union musicians and vocalists who accompanied the artists on the records as contracted sidemen through the American Federation of Musicians (AFM) and the American Federation of Television and Radio Artists (AFTRA). The remaining 96 percent of the SRF went to the Alliance of Artists and Recording Companies (AARC), which was further split into a 60 percent share to the owners of the master recordings and 40 percent to the featured performers on the recordings.

In 1994 the Uruguay Round Agreements Act (URAA) implemented the 124-nation Marrakech Agreement. The URAA was the eighth round in twelve years of multilateral trade negotiations that transformed the General Agreement on Tariffs and Trade (GATT) into the World Trade Organization (WTO). Included in the URAA was each country's adherence to the jurisdiction of the WTO through The Agreement on Trade-Related Aspects of Intellectual Property Rights (TRIPS) regarding trade rules and regulations for intellectual property. The primary application in US copyright law was to extend copyright to some foreign works that had previously been in the public domain in the United States due to the lack of harmonization in the US with the provisions of the Berne Convention.

The final legislative action of the 1985–95 decade involving copyright came with the Digital Performance Right in Sound Recordings Act of 1995

(DPRA), which extended the Copyright Act of 1976 protection to cover sound recordings. Specifically, it granted copyright owners the exclusive right to per-form the copyrighted work publicly by means of a digital audio transmission. This was dubbed the performance right applicable to recordings parallel to the performing right already vested in musical compositions. The performing right would proactively apply to digital as well as analog transmissions, but the performance right for sound recordings was limited to digital transmissions, and hence not applicable to the analog transmissions of terrestrial radio. This exclusion was a concession to the lobbying efforts of the radio industry for its support of the bill's other provisions, the price the copyright community had to pay to enact the DPRA.

Copyright Infringement: Piracy, Plagiarism, and Parallel Imports

Before the onset of digital technology, three forms of copyright infringe-ment had been of major concern. The most prevalent was the illegal dupli-cation and sale of both vinyl and cassette sound recordings known as record piracy. Record and publishing companies prosecuted piracy on a worldwide basis under the authority of the copyright laws in the territory in which the infringement occurred. The RIAA and NMPA led the pursuit in the US and the International Federation of the Phonographic Industry (IFPI) and CISAC did so internationally with the support of the International Criminal Police Organization (INTERPOL).

Another form of infringement known as parallel imports involved bringing records that had been legally pressed and purchased in other counties into the US for resale. The importation of these records without licenses from the US owners of the copyrights in both the musical composition and the sound recording specifically violated US copyright law and TRIPS provisions. Importation of goods and commodities in this matter was generally referred to in business as gray market sales. Although gray market sales were allowed for many businesses under the aegis of the World Intellectual Property Organization (WIPO) to promote open trade, prohibition of parallel imports remained in effect for intellectual property.

Parallel imports that did manage to escape notice and were successfully sold in the US were deemed to have replaced the sale of what would otherwise have been domestically manufactured. Even if the imported records came from a foreign subsidiary of a US company, which then paid a share of revenue to its US affiliate, the amount paid was far less than what would have been netted from the sale of domestically manufactured units. Artists also received reduced royalties as their contracts stipulated lower rates from foreign sales. It could also take an additional year or more for the eventual payment, if any, to reach them from an overseas licensee. Further complicating the issue, if the imported records were sold through cutout dealers, there probably would be no payment at all. Similarly, parallel imports replaced music publishers' income from domestic sales. They ultimately, if at all, received delayed and reduced payment from their sub-publisher in the territory of manufacture, which in turn also delayed and reduced payment to the songwriters. Nonetheless, Tower Records and other major outlets and distributors regularly sold these illegally imported records.

The parallel import issue came to a head in 1985 as the major labels pushed back using the power of economic persuasion in the form of threatening to block access to current hits for both the domestic distributors and international licensees who were complicit in parallel import sales. This approach proved successful in getting the problem under control for the major labels, but for the independent record companies without current hits, and the publishers whose songs were in the imported independent product, the problem was more difficult to combat. Most of the parallel imports were sold without the fanfare or publicity of radio play and chart position. The NMPA continued to prosecute and publicize intermittent victories against infringing importers throughout the decade. These cases were usually settled for payment to the affected publishers of domestic mechanicals for the imports since cases that went to litigation could result in statutory and compensatory damage penalties in excess of the standard penalty of $100,000 per willful infringement.

The third form of infringement was plagiarism, in which a song is claimed to be a new and original work, but the copyright owners of a preexisting musical composition deem it to be sufficiently similar to or the same as theirs. If unable to reach a settlement with the alleged infringer(s), the claimant(s) could then initiate a copyright infringement suit in federal court. Occurrences of plagiarism litigation, especially when a major artist was involved, usually generated a lot of publicity, and could have major economic consequences. Successful pursuit of this type of infringement under the Copyright Act of 1976 hinges on two primary criteria: sufficient similarity and establishment of access to the purportedly infringed-upon song by the alleged infringer(s).

Although the damages defined in the Copyright Act are federal statute, the cost of both prosecution and defense falls upon the litigants, with the final costs for both usually borne by the losing party. Many defendants whose hit song was cited for supposed infringement of a previously existing but unknown song settled these cases to avoid the high cost of defending them, while the claimants' attorneys often worked on a contingency basis. Accused parties who considered themselves innocent regarded these actions as nuisance lawsuits and an unwelcomed but unfortunately unavoidable part of doing business. Some settled when the contention seemed plausible whether intentional or coincidental, and the settlement was the best economical and public relations decision. Some, however, went all the way to jury trial with varying results.

Perils of an Infringement Showdown: The Isley Brothers vs. Michael Bolton

A suit by R&B legends The Isley Brothers against the 1991 Michael Bolton single *Love Is a Wonderful Thing*, cowritten by Bolton with Andy Goldmark, demonstrated the potential perils of copyright infringement accusations if the sides didn't settle and instead went to trial. The single reached number four on the Hot 100 and was included in Bolton's album, *Time, Love & Tenderness*, which sold 16 million units. The Isleys sued Bolton, Goldmark, their publishing companies, and Bolton's record company, Sony Music, for supposedly infringing upon their 1966 single of the same name, released on United Artists Records. That record only reached number 110 on *Billboard's Bubbling Under: The Hot 100* singles chart.

The track was never released on an album until the 1991 *The Isley Brothers: The Complete UA Sessions*, which came out after Bolton and Goldmark wrote their song. The Isleys' suit claimed that Bolton had access to the song at the time of its release as a single and produced playlists from Bolton's hometown R&B station with the song listed on them. They argued that even though its play in the market lasted for only a few weeks, and although Bolton was only thirteen years old at the time, he nonetheless must have heard their song on the radio and, as an aspiring singer, noticed it. Bolton maintained he had never heard the song and any similarity was coincidental. If true, there was no basis for infringement as there would be no proof of access.

The case went to trial in Los Angeles and in 1994 a jury ruled in favor of the Isleys, ordering that over $5 million in profits from the sales of Bolton's recording be turned over to them. At the time, this was the largest amount ever awarded for music plagiarism. The Isley Brothers were granted 66 percent of the song's earnings and 28 percent of the profits from the album *Time, Love & Tenderness*. Bolton et al. challenged the ruling all the way to the US Supreme

Court, which declined to hear an appeal. The Isleys' were to be awarded the total amount with $4.2 million from Sony Music; $932,924 from Bolton; $220,785 from Goldmark; and the balance from Bolton and Goldmark's music publishing companies.

Had the defendants worked out a settlement with the Isleys as cowriters with a 66 percent share, or even granted them the rights to the entire song, the outcome would have been quite different. With 16 million albums sold, and assuming another one million in singles sales, at the 5.7¢ mechanical royalty rate applicable at the time of the record's release, 17 million sales of the song would have equaled $969,000. If performing rights royalties over the life of the song reached $1.5 million for all songwriter and publishers, then the total earned would have been roughly $2.5 million, with 66 percent of that equaling $1.67 million—less than one-third of the final adjudication.

Two aspects of the award that warranted notice were that Bolton and Goldmark were cowriters, but Bolton was dunned over four times as much as Goldmark, and that Sony Music Entertainment, which was the record company but had no interest in the publishing, was even subject to the suit, much less the award. If Bolton were being charged more than Goldmark because he was the artist, had a settlement on the song been made, no share of artist royalties would have been paid to the Isleys since the alleged infringement only involved the copyright in the musical composition. Furthermore, Sony would not have been subject to paying a record royalty to the Isleys as their form of compensation should have been only a share of the publisher/songwriter royalties. This case was a prime example of the inherent risk-reward variables involved when an infringement lawsuit goes to a jury trial, a situation that would arise again over the ensuing decades, often with significant consequences for more than just the litigants involved, and possibly setting industrywide case law precedent.

A Sampling of Music Sampling Litigation

Digital technology in the form of sampling introduced not only a new methodology for creating musical sounds and thus records but also greatly expanded the ways in which one could infringe other persons' musical works. Sampling of preexisting music was not infringement in and of itself, but the failure to obtain a license for use of that sample in a commercially exploited new work was subject to infringement claims for both the musical composition and the sound recording.

Sampling originated when club deejays used drum machines, analog tape loops, or manipulated vinyl discs to create a beat that was the basic pulse or time signature maintained throughout a musical work. This technique became an underlying element in disco, different electronic music genres, and eventually a cornerstone for rap. The process became digital with the introduction of computer-based sampling synthesizers such as the Computer Music Melodian in 1976, the Fairlight CMI in 1979, and the E-mu SP-1200 percussive sampler in 1987. Korg, Akai, and Yamaha subsequently introduced even more sophisticated models to expand sampling capabilities.

As digital technology replaced analog in studio recording, artists found sounds, beats, and riffs on other peoples' recordings that they could digitally isolate as samples. They could then extract and incorporate these samples within their own newly created tracks. Although a creative process in and of itself, sampling of copyrighted works necessitated the appropriate licensing to avoid any resulting legal action. It took several years for the industry as a whole to define licensing procedures for sampling. During this period, several major infringement cases with a range of rulings illustrated the complexity of the issues arising from seemingly simple acts of creative sampling.

In 1990, veteran R&B performer/songwriter Rick James sued breakout rap artist MC Hammer. Without permission, Hammer had sampled James's 1981 single "Super Freak" in the number one international hit and double Grammy Award–winning track "U Can't Touch This," which was on Hammer's album *Please Hammer Don't Hurt 'Em*, which sold 18 million units. The parties settled out of court, giving a 50 percent share of credits and royalties to James, his cowriter Alonzo Miller, and their publishers. It's unclear why Hammer did not get permission ahead of time. He had at least half a dozen other samples on the album, crediting Prince, Marvin Gaye, James Brown, Barry White, and Faith No More as cowriters.

In 1991 Howard Kaylan and Mark Volman of the 1960s rock group the Turtles sued rap innovators De La Soul for using a looped twelve-second sample of their recording "You Showed Me" in the De La Soul track "Transmitting Live from Mars" on the 1989 platinum album *3 Feet High and Rising*. De La Soul had made the album with producer/DJ Prince Paul for $13,000, using just a Casio RZ-1 drum machine/sampler and an Eventide harmonizer. Like many of the early rap artists, they did not clear samples in advance, leaving that task to their label, Tommy Boy Records. Label owner Tom Silverman told authors/filmmakers Kembrew McLeod and Peter DiCola in their documentary *Copyright Criminals* and their book *Creative License* that he indeed did clear the samples that he was made aware of. "It's a lot of accounting work," Silverman recalled. "You have to pay out on 60 different people on one album. It's quite a nightmare actually."[9] And it continued to be one. As of 2019 the album had never been released for legal downloads or streaming due to sample licensing issues.

According to published reports in *The New York Times* and *Rolling Stone* the Turtles' suit was settled for a reported $1.7 million although De La Soul claimed it was much less. Songwriters Roger McGuinn and Gene Clark—who wrote "You Showed Me" when they were members of the band Jet Set before they found fame as members of The Byrds—were not credited, nor did they sue since the four-bar segment was an instrumental rhythmic pattern not related to the melody and they were not members of The Turtles. Only nine of the twenty-four tracks on *3 Feet High and Rising* credit songwriters other than the members of De La Soul and/or their producer, while almost all the tracks credited the artists on samples from recordings. Only the parties involved know if other infringement claims were made and settled, or if "You Showed Me" was the only sample to evade Tommy Boy's post-production licensing effort. The purported size of that one settlement, however, was sufficient to alert the entire rap community to the perils of unlicensed samples, even when only twelve-second segments not including either lyrics or melody.

Also in 1991, Rock icons Queen and David Bowie sued rapper Vanilla Ice for using the bass line from their 1981 hit "Under Pressure" throughout the global number one single "Ice, Ice, Baby" from the album *To the Extreme*, which sold 15 million copies. A settlement was reached that gave cowriting credits and royalties to Bowie and the members of Queen, with corresponding shares to their publishers.

In 1992, English alternative band Radiohead released their breakout single "Creep." They were promptly sued for infringing "The Air That I Breathe" by songwriters Mike Hazelwood and Albert Hammond. Hammond first recorded it in 1973 and it hit the charts before becoming a worldwide hit for the Hollies in 1974. Hazelwood and Hammond claimed that "Creep" plagiarized their chord progression and melody. They settled for half of the songwriting and publishing credit and royalties.

A protracted infringement case concluded with a Supreme Court ruling in 1994 involving "Pretty Woman" as recorded and released by 2 Live Crew and "Oh, Pretty Woman" written by Roy Orbison and Bill Dees and a huge hit single for Orbison in 1964. Producer/label owner/group leader Luther Campbell's 2 Live Crew had made a raucous and off-color album titled *As Nasty as They Wanna Be*, which was ruled to be obscene by a Florida federal court and was to be withdrawn from public circulation. Campbell edited and remixed the album and re-released it with the title *As Clean as They*

Wanna Be, adding his version of "Pretty Woman" as an additional track with the group rapping over a sample of the original Orbison recording.

Publisher Acuff Rose Music had denied permission to use the song when Campbell sought a license, but Campbell released the track anyway as part of the new, sanitized album. Ultimately the Supreme Court ruled that the track was a parody and therefore legitimate, remanding the case to settlement between the parties. This reversed an appeals court decision favorable to Acuff-Rose, which had reversed the original district court ruling in Campbell's favor concluding that the track was a parody and as such was fair use of the song under copyright law. Under the parody determination and settlement between the parties, Orbison and Dees were credited as the only writers and Acuff Rose the sole publisher. They received the appropriate royalties with no other penalty to Campbell et.al.

Perhaps the most far-reaching court ruling came in the *Grand Upright Music, Ltd. v. Warner Bros. Records Inc.* litigation. Grand Upright on behalf of Gilbert O'Sullivan sued for use of an unauthorized sample of "Alone Again (Naturally)" on the track "Alone Again" on rapper Biz Markie's *I Need a Haircut* album, released in August 1991 by Markie's Chillin' label and distributed by WB Records. Because Markie had requested a license but was denied, the US District Court for the Southern District of New York issued an injunction forcing the company to recall the albums and pull the offending track. This ruling established the case law precedent that all samples of sound recordings must be cleared before release as dictated by the Copyright Act of 1976, or possibly face the consequences of willful infringement.

The cases cited above are not the totality of disputes involving the various permutations of copyright infringement, but rather a few samples from the gamut of conclusions reached both in and out of court. The Bolton case exemplified the hazards of a jury trial, while the Hammer case demonstrated the wisdom and fairness of settlement. The "Pretty Woman" case revealed how differently separate courts could rule in their decisions. The De La Soul case reinforced how costly it could be to miss just one twelve-second sample of a master recording, even one that did not involve the song itself.

As a result of these and other contemporaneous cases, negotiated terms for samples became the industry norm. Agreements ranged from a lump sum buyout to agreed-upon splits applied to both master recording and publishing. Careful monitoring by labels' business affairs departments for unlicensed samples became necessary to keep the labels and their artists out of legal proceedings that could stall or halt record releases or result in onerous penalties. Sampling emanated from deliberate actions, with the chosen samples based on creative decisions. While the clearance of multiple samples was costly and time consuming, failure to do so had proven to be far more troublesome. By 1995, advances in studio and synthesizer technology offered alternatives to digitally lifting samples from other artists' tracks. In place of using existing tracks to create the underlying beat or rhythmic pattern, artists could create their own beats and riffs instead, avoiding costly clearance issues and retaining a larger share of the royalty pie for themselves.

4

The Creators of Music: Getting Paid

It All Begins with a Song

Matching the right song with the right performer to capture the heart and soul of the listening public has been the key to success in the music industry since its earliest days. From "Greensleeves" to "Over the Rainbow," from "White Christmas" to "Heartbreak Hotel," from "Yesterday" to "I Will Always Love You," great songs have been the foundation of the music industry's relationship with its audience. Some are forever associated with one artist, while others are recorded over and over with different approaches or interpretations, finding new audiences with successive generations.

When the Nashville Songwriters Association International (NSAI) first organized in 1967 as the Nashville Songwriters Association (NSA) to initiate a campaign to get songwriters' names credited on the label and in the packaging of record releases, it adopted "It All Begins with a Song" as its motto and mantra. In the four years it took to achieve its goal, the NSA laid the groundwork for the leadership role it would play over the next half century in advocating for the rights of the songwriter community. While "It All Begins with a Song" originated with the NSA, it succinctly expressed the pivotal role songs have played as the creative foundation supporting the entire infrastructure of the music industry.

Since its birth just before the turn of the twentieth century, the record business selected artists and songs based on their popularity with live audiences. Then when radio emerged as a commercial industry in the early 1920s, music was broadcast in live performances for radio's first two decades. After the breach between radio and records was put to rest in the 1940s, radio developed Top 40 and other popular formats that revolved around a constant stream of new songs in order to build a cadre of stars in each genre. After a few hits, labels released albums featuring them accompanied by two or three more projected singles. In the 1960s teenage singles buyers were transformed by FM radio into album-consuming young adults who attended concerts to hear favorite artists perform entire albums. As

American Popular Music and Its Business in the Digital Age. Rick Sanjek, Oxford University Press. © Frederick Sanjek 2024.
DOI: 10.1093/oso/9780190653828.003.0004

record sales and radio ad revenue trended upward, so did royalties for artists and songwriters.

Just as *Billboard* had tracked the evolution of recorded music, its sister publication *Amusement Business* (*AB*) had served as the weekly chronicle for live performance. From its start, *AB* provided information on fairs, theme parks, and amusement attractions, including attendance receipts organized in comparative charts, artist information and profiles, contact information for both buyers and sellers, and the latest news on all aspects of the industry. *AB* printed weekly from 1894 to 2001 and monthly until 2006 when it was absorbed by *Billboard*, by then the primary trade journal for all sectors of the music business.

As the concert industry grew from about $100 million a year in 1965 when The Beatles played Shea Stadium, to around $700 million in 1984, *AB* tracked its expansion, sharing its findings with *Billboard* in a weekly top box-office chart. Competitor *Performance Magazine* published from the early 1970s until 1999, covering the music business with a primary focus on the artists. *Pollstar* debuted in 1981 and continues to this day as the leading resource for performance industry information.

Advances in electronic technology affected live performance just as it had done in the broadcast and record sectors. Historically, room acoustics had limited the size of facilities until electronic sound amplification systems combined condenser microphones with electromagnetic-driven coil-cone loudspeakers in the 1920s, providing amplification for larger facilities. Single instrument electric amplifiers followed in the 1930s. Advancements were made in speaker technology over the next three decades that miniaturized theater speaker horns and saw the introduction of multitrack sound-mixing boards. Through the mid-1960s live performance was still largely limited to clubs, dance halls, theaters, and tents with the quality of sound reception due more to room dimensions and acoustics than capacity of the sound system.

When Bob Dylan played three songs with amplified instruments at the 1965 Newport Folk Festival, he dramatically exposed the need to improve acoustics for large gatherings. The incident indirectly inspired the stacked cabinet sound system with multiple theater speaker horns for the Woodstock festival, a system so substantial it could acoustically envelop the entire outdoor assemblage of what Joni Mitchell described as half a million strong in her post-festival "Woodstock" paean. Smaller versions of this system, but still far larger than those of the preceding decades, would allow music performance to expand into larger arenas and eventually into open-air and domed sports stadiums.

Ascending the Talent Pyramid

As in previous decades, artists who reached the top of the charts began the same way as the ones who never advanced beyond small gatherings on the front porch, by honing their craft through hours of practice. Next came the transition from amateur to professional by charging admission. As their audience widened and their peer group narrowed, artists ascended further with assistance from family, friends, and, for some, financial backers who believed in them. House parties and playing for the door transcended to clubs and dance halls with contracts and guarantees, and then for some, to concerts and festivals. By this stage artists usually had fulfilled the demand for a record that their fans could buy at their gigs or, in the early years of the new millennium, online.

Each year thousands of records were created, either self-financed or backed by investors, self-released, or sold through independent distributors. The next step was to sign with a booking agency and/or an independent label followed by managers and publishers eager to guide promising artists to a major-label contract. Then came record label A&R staffers eager to hitch their own careers to artists who could continue up the ladder and reach the pages of *Billboard* and *Pollstar*. Those few hundred who sustained a successful career for several decades joined the ranks of legacy artists with a fan base that had been on the journey with them; still bought tickets, records, and merchandise; and who would like, add, and request their records on digital services.

The industry's upper-echelon power brokers were and still are laser-focused on those who generate sizable amounts of revenue, and are constantly on watch for those who appeared to have the requisite attributes to rise to the top. Investment of time and money was often the same for those who succeeded as for those who didn't, but only the few who maintained their success beyond one or two records would achieve financial reward and, hopefully, artistic fulfillment. The most fortunate of the others found a niche at varying levels of the industry pyramid where they were still able to make a living from music, whether through their creative talents or on the business side. The vast majority, however, fell behind the ever-alluring beat of the industry drum, hopefully with the memories of their journey intact, but more often than not, becoming just a memory themselves.

William Morris, MCA, and the Modern Booking Business

Vaudeville agent William Morris, born Zelman Moses in Germany, organized the William Morris Agency in New York in 1898, later adding his son William Morris Jr. and Abe Lastfogel as partners. By the time in the mid-1920s that the radio, record, and movie industries were emerging as national entertainment powerhouses, WMA was the dominant booking agency for stage performance. It quickly adapted to these new electronic media, guiding top vaudeville stars Amos 'n' Andy, Martha Raye, and George Burns and Gracie Allen to radio success, and Charlie Chaplin and the Marx Brothers to film stardom.

WMA coasted through the Great Depression on the back of Mae West's radio and movie success, ran USO tours during World War II, and embraced the postwar television boom by expanding into program packaging for the new medium. After opening a Beverly Hills office in 1938, WMA quickly grew into a $15 million-a-year business. True to its advertising slogan, "Our Small Act of Today Is Our Big Act of Tomorrow," WMA nurtured new talent through its stage and nightclub departments. The agency originated the partner-ownership model that became the standard for the booking business, and created a mail room intern program that became the entry-level platform for many industry leaders of the future including David Geffen, Barry Diller, and Michael Ovitz.

In 1962, WMA's major competitor was Music Corporation of America (MCA), started by Dr. Jules Stein in Chicago in 1924 as a talent agency booking bands into clubs and speakeasies. It soon relocated to Los Angeles and diversified into records, films, and television under the leadership of Lew Wasserman and Sid Sheinberg. In 1962 MCA merged with Decca Records and its affiliate Universal Pictures forcing it to dissolve its booking division to comply with antitrust laws. Agents and artists both scurried to find new homes. Some joined other established agencies, including General Artist Corporation (GAC), which had opened in New York in 1939 under chairman Tom Rockwell, who led the agency until his death in 1958. With headline artists including Bing Crosby, Johnny Mathis, Duke Ellington, Fletcher Henderson, and the Dorsey Brothers, GAC also operated offices in Los Angeles, Chicago, and Las Vegas.

Associated Booking Corporation (ABC), formed in New York in 1940 by Louis Armstrong and his manager, Joe Glaser, was another option for the former MCA agents, as was WMA. Some agents opened their own smaller agencies or banded together to create a diversified agency based on the MCA model. The longest lasting has been the Agency for the Performing Arts (APA), opened in New York in 1962 by former MCA agents David Baumgarten,

Roger Vorce, and Harvey Litwin, with offices in Chicago, Hollywood, and Miami Beach. Their new agency included former MCA clients Rowan & Martin, Victor Borge, Johnny Cash, Rosemary Clooney, Liberace, and Harry Belafonte.

Bernstein, Barsalona, The Beatles, and the Birth of the Rock Concert

In 1964, Sid Bernstein of GAC brought both The Beatles and The Rolling Stones to America with concert tours and appearances on *The Ed Sullivan Show* that ushered in the rock concert era. He was assisted by twenty-six-year-old Frank Barsalona, who left GAC that year and opened the Premier Talent Agency to specialize in booking rock tours. After experiencing the reaction of teenage crowds to The Beatles and The Rolling Stones, he believed that rock-'n'-roll was more than a passing fad, and that live shows would be rock's biggest revenue generator. Barsalona's career contributions were honored in 2005 when he became the first booking agent inducted into the Rock & Roll Hall of Fame. "You cannot exaggerate the role Frank played in creating the infrastructure of the rock 'n' roll world as we know it today," E Street Band guitarist Steven Van Zandt stated in Barsalona's *New York Times* obituary. "It was his unique vision that rock 'n' roll was here to stay, and that it wasn't just going to be about records, but about how good a band plays live."[1]

While building Premier, Barsalona encountered and encouraged a network of enthusiastic 1950s Teens and baby boomer promoters who shared his vision and helped create the rock concert business. Many of these future impresarios began as college campus booking agents. They survived the competition to become dominant in their local markets, progressing from frat parties to clubs and theaters. Next, they raised the guarantees needed for star talent to play in arenas. Many became partners in or owners of the leading local venues. Then the most successful moved up to organizing arena and then stadium tours.

The arrangement between the agent who booked the show on behalf of the act with the promoter who took the financial risk began with negotiating a guaranteed fee for the appearance, paying 50 percent up-front and the other 50 percent just before showtime. Negotiations centered on facility capacity and ticket prices, then extended to define what share of overage above guarantee would be paid to the act; could the agent secure a share of concessions, parking, and merchandise; and what scope of market exclusivity would the promoter impose upon the act. Because repeat business and long-term relationships depended on maintaining a high level of efficiency, honesty, and communication, Premier's Barsalona insisted promoters pay 75 percent of the gross receipts to the artists with transparent accounting. This was in contrast to the then-prevalent practice of paying as small a fee as possible to the artist so the promoter could net the bulk of the profit. Premier established its booking commission at 10 percent of the artists' gross compensation.

Over the next ten years sound systems improved, stage lighting became more sophisticated, and rock tours grew larger and more frequent, as Barsalona had envisioned. The listening habits of young consumers advanced from singles to albums, creating greater revenues for the record companies, and hence the artists. The labels increased their cooperation with rock concert promoters on advertising and tour support. The music business was collectively coalescing around this youth market as its radio, record, and live performance sectors all more than doubled their revenue.

The same post-Elvis influx of 1950s Teens and baby boomers that supplied the core of new artists, record executives, and local promoters was about to invade the booking agency sector as well. Of the 153 agencies listed in the 1974 year-end *Billboard* "Talent in Action Spotlight" section, only nine had offices in both New York and Los Angeles. They were ABC, APA, American Talent International (ATI), Creative Management Associates (CMA), Hurok Concerts, Inc., International Famous Agency (IFA), Magna Artists Corp., Queen Booking Corp. (QBC), and WMA. Only WMA also had a Nashville office. Most of the others—including Barsalona's Premier, the Jim Halsey Agency of Tulsa, Buddy Lee Attractions in Nashville, Howard Rose Agency in Beverly Hills, Phil Walden's Paragon Agency in Macon, Georgia, and Variety Artists in Minneapolis—were smaller and focused primarily on music.

CAA, Monterey, ICM, and ITG Join the Competition

In 1975 five junior agents at WMA—Mike Rosenfeld, Michael Ovitz, Ron Meyer, Bill Haber, and Rowland Perkins—decided to leave and establish the Creative Artists Agency (CAA) with a $35,000 line of credit and a $21,000 bank loan. They first found success with television series and films, and then expanded into music. By 1985 *Pollstar* named them Booking Agency of the Year, a feat they repeated four times over the following ten years. Although they had planned to be a medium-sized full-service agency sharing proceeds equally, by 1989 Ovitz owned 55 percent of the agency, with Haber and Meyer owning the rest after having purchased other agents' partner shares. With estimated commissions at around $90 million, however, there still was ample revenue to pay senior agents very handsomely. Following WMA's lead, they also initiated their own internship program.

International Creative Management, Inc. (ICM) also debuted in 1975 created when manager and entrepreneur Marvin Josephson's publicly traded Josephson International, Inc. merged Creative Management Associates (CMA)—which had previously acquired GAC—and the International Famous Agency (IFA). Josephson already owned the Ashley Famous Agency which it had purchased in 1968 from Kinney National when it bought Warner Brothers and had to divest itself of its booking agency business. Legendary CMA agent Sam Cohn remained on board as executive vice president. Hurok Concerts, Inc. was added in 1977.

Monterey Peninsula Artists also launched in 1975 during the IFA/CMA merger when leading IFA music agents Dan Weiner and Fred Bohlander exited to focus on rock acts. They named the agency after their very non-Hollywood, serene location a hundred miles south of San Francisco where the famed music festival was staged. They brought Chicago, the Doobie Brothers, David Gates, Jesse Colin Young, and Leo Kottke with them.

In 1981, WMA music agents Wayne Forte and Michael Farrell formed International Talent Group (ITG) to specialize in pop and rock with a core of new British acts. Within a year, Duran Duran, Joe Jackson, The Clash, The Vapors, The Cure, Depeche Mode, Adam and The Ants, David Bowie, Peter Gabriel, Genesis, King Crimson, and Billy Idol were on their roster.

In 1985 *Pollstar* listed ICM as the top pop-rock booking agency followed by CAA, ITG, Monterey Peninsula, and Premier. The *Pollstar*-tracked live concert revenue that year was about $600 million, 10 percent of which went to the booking agencies. The 1985 revenue was down from the all-time high of about $700 million achieved in 1984, which had been driven by The Jacksons' *Victory Tour*. *Pollstar*'s 1985 top music booking agent was Fred Bohlander of Monterey followed by Barry Bell of Premier, Bill Elson of ICM, Mike Farrell and Wayne Forte of ITG, and Rob Light and Tom Ross of CAA.

Over the next five years, *Pollstar*'s reported revenue increased to over $1.1 billion in 1990 as higher-capacity stadium tours increased, with ticket prices rising between 50 percent and 75 percent. *Pollstar*'s total hovered around $1 billion through the recession of the early 1990s, then shot up to about $1.4 billion in 1994 on the backs of the Pink Floyd, Rolling Stones, and Eagles tours, which grossed over $700 million just between the three of them.

The same top-five agencies of 1985 continued to dominate the decade with the addition of Triad Artists and Famous Artist Agency, and—after their 1992 acquisition of Triad—a rebounding WMA. Agents with recurring Agent of the Year nominations included Rob Light (five-time recipient), Bobby Brooks (two times), Carole Kinzel, Kevin Gasser, Tom Ross, and Mark Pirinian at CAA; Alex Kochan, Bill Elson, Martha Vlasic, and Terry Rhodes at ICM; Fred Bohlander (three times), Chip Hooper, and Dan Weiner at Monterey Peninsula; Barry Bell and Jane Geraghty at Premier; Michael Farrell and Wayne Forte at ITG; Don Muller and Marc Geiger at Triad/William Morris; Jerry Ade at Famous Artists; and Tony Conway at Nashville-based, country-centric Buddy Lee Attractions. After 1990, the *Pollstar* Agent of the Year award was renamed the Bobby Brooks Award for the much-beloved and well-respected CAA agent who tragically died at age thirty-four in the August 27, 1990, helicopter crash that also took the life of his client, the legendary guitarist Stevie Ray Vaughan.

The Top Agencies Expand to Nashville as Competition Grows in All Genres

The move to larger venues also rocked the country market, motivating the agency sector to join the major labels and publishers in opening Nashville branches to be in closer touch with the country music industry. Triad's Rick Shipp moved there in 1984, and Monterey Peninsula opened subsidiary Monterey Artists in 1986 with agents Bobby Cudd and Steve Dahl. CAA opened in the Music City in 1991 with Ron Baird focused on country and John Huie working both country and the growing Christian music market. Rod Essig joined them in 1993, moving from Variety Artists in Minneapolis.

Starting in 1990, *Pollstar* initiated a separate Third Coast Agent of the Year award category for Nashville-based agents. Despite the gradual transfer of new label signees to the larger agencies, the Buddy Lee Agency continued to be a major player with agents Tony Conway, Paul Lohr, and Sol Safian consistently on the top-agent list. Veteran Buddy Lee agent Joe Harris signed Garth Brooks in 1988 at the very start of his career. Working with experienced managers like Alabama's Dale Morris and George Strait's Erv Woolsey, the Nashville agents expanded touring through the 1980s beyond the traditional fairs, clubs, dance halls, and theaters to arenas and outdoor facilities. The magnitude of the sound systems, touring logistics, and box-office receipts grew correspondingly. Then the meteoric rise of Brooks led them all into stadiums and coliseums as well as pushed country record sales toward a 20 percent market share.

Triad Artists formed in 1984 as the merger of three successful small agencies with different service bases. Peter Grosslight and Richard Rosenberg had opened Regency Artists in 1974 as an MOR-oriented agency and gradually expanded into pop with Joan Baez, Tina Turner, and Olivia Newton-John, and then into country and rock. New York–based Adams, Ray & Rosenberg had specialized in literary clients and TV/film packaging since 1964. David, Hunter, Kimble, Parseghian & Rifkin of Los Angeles had a roster of motion picture, television, and stage clients. They had just launched two years earlier in a merger of the Jeff Hunter Agency, formed in 1953; Arnold Rifkin and Nicole David's Rifkin-David Agency, formed in Los Angeles in 1982; and the Kimble-Parseghian Agency, founded in 1978 by John Kimble and Gene Parseghian in New York.

The newly consolidated agency retained offices in both cities with a Nashville presence headed by Regency veteran Rick Shipp. Looking to improve its competitive position, in 1992 WMA acquired Triad, whose partners settled in at the WMA divisions of their various specialties in both New York and Beverly Hills. Shipp joined WMA veteran Paul Moore as co-head of the now combined Nashville office. This merger, along with the 1989 acquisition of top country independent The Jim Halsey Company, helped sustain WMA's recovery from its mid-1980s slump to propel it back into top-five status.

Famous Artist Agency was formed in 1988 when Jerry Ade bought out his General Talent Agency (GTA) partners Norby Walters and Sal Michaels. GTA had been a major agency for top Black talent including Kool & The Gang, Patti LaBelle, Janet Jackson, and Gloria Gaynor, but Walters opened a sports department for graduating college football players with NFL aspirations and got indicted in an illegal payments scandal. He withdrew from the business with a plea bargain after a colorful thirty-year career spanning big bands to doo-wop to disco to rap. Ade brought in new acts including Milli Vanilli, Tone Loc, and New Kids on the Block while diversifying into sponsorships and television.

Changes were also happening at ICM. In 1988 cochairmen Jeffrey Berg and Guy McElwaine, along with president Jim Wiatt, took the company private with a $70 million management buyout financed by Chase Manhattan. In 1992 ICM acquired British rock agency Fair Warning with a roster replete in heavy metal, including Metallica. In 1994 they added another rock agency, Wasted Talent, who represented U2 and R.E.M. ICM reimaged as ICM International, which was named *Pollstar*'s International Booking Agency of the Year in 1994 and landed in the top five for 1995.

CAA Changes Top Management but Continues to Lead

The year 1995 represented the greatest upheaval for talent booking since the five young agents bolted from WMA to form CAA twenty years earlier. The remaining three of the five original CAA partners exited when Michael Ovitz became president of Disney under chairman Michael Eisner, Ron Meyer became president/COO of Universal Studios under Edgar Bronfman Jr., and Bill Haber retired from the business to join nonprofit Save the Children. Michael Rosenfeld had exited in the early 1980s and Rowland Perkins left in 1993.

The future of CAA now laid in the hands of Jay Moloney, Richard Lovett, David (Doc) O'Connor, Kevin Huvane, and Bryan Lourd—an alliance of thirty-something, ultra-competitive agents. They had been groomed by Ovitz and Meyer and were referred to as the Young Turks. The five were slated to share ownership of CAA with three senior colleagues now serving as cochairmen: motion picture department heads Rick Nicita and Jack Rapke, and TV department head Lee Gabler. Lovett was named president. Their two biggest collective tasks would be to finance the buyout of Ovitz, Meyer, and Haber, and to divvy up the departing founders' clients and accounts.

The Big Three of the talent agency business—CAA, ICM, and William Morris—now covered the entire spectrum of the entertainment business, including sports. They made lucrative deals with top consumer products like Coca-Cola, Visa, and General Motors to co-brand with their entertainment clients. They were also serving as marketing consultants and deal makers. CAA had brokered both the sale of MCA to Matsushita in 1990 and the resale five years later to Seagram, as well as helped banker Le Crédit Lyonnais dispose of Metro-Goldwyn-Mayer assets.

As private companies, the agencies' actual income was not public information, but WMA's revenue in 1997 was estimated by the St. James Press *International Directory of Company Histories* to be $150 million, while CAA in 1999 was estimated at $200 million. Live concert revenue as reported by *Pollstar* averaged approximately $1.5 billion annually during this time. Assuming a 75 percent artist share of the total gate on those shows at $1.125 billion, commissions from them were $112.5 million including all agencies whether Big Three or boutique. This was about 20 percent to 25 percent of total agency revenue from all sources. The Big Three's multitiered connections were a tremendous attraction to music stars interested in film, television, and corporate tour sponsorships.

The Growth of Live Performance

By 1985 the top concert promoters in the country included two in the metropolitan New York area in John Scher of Monarch Entertainment Bureau and Ron Delsener of Ron Delsener Enterprises, Don Law of the Don

Law Company in Boston, Larry Magid of Electric Factory Concerts in Philadelphia, Jack Boyle of Cellar Door Productions in Washington, D.C., Michael Cohl and Bill Ballard of Concert Productions International in Toronto, Mike Belkin and Jules Belkin of Belkin Productions in Cleveland, Arnie Granat and Jerry Mickelson of Jam Productions in Chicago, Alex Cooley of Concert Promotions in Atlanta, Jon Stoll of Fantasma Productions in West Palm Beach, Louis Messina of Pace Concerts in Houston, Barry Fey of Feyline Presentations in Denver, Larry Vallon of MCA Concerts in Los Angeles, and of course the legendary Bill Graham of San Francisco.

These promoters were handling a sizable share of the dates for the major superstars' tours in addition to smaller shows in the clubs and theaters they controlled in their home markets. Always on the outlook for new talent, some expanded into artist management, others added sports promotion to their portfolio, many acquired or managed concert facilities, and almost all engaged in merchandise sales.

As mentioned earlier, 1984 had been a watershed year for concert promotion. The Jacksons' *Victory Tour* set new standards in both venue size and ticket prices. *Victory Tour* tickets were the highest ever at $30, considerably more than the $17 charged by Bruce Springsteen's concurrent *Born in The USA Tour*. The Jacksons also broke the record for highest-grossing tour in history at $75 million, topping the $50 million from The Rolling Stones *American Tour* in 1981. Although Springsteen's tour would eventually top the Jacksons to earn $85 million, it took The Boss one hundred more concert dates and another year to do so.

The *Victory Tour*'s average of $1.36 million per show remained the highest ever for almost a decade until topped by Madonna's *The Girlie Show Tour* in 1993 at $1.79 million per show. She was quickly bettered by Pink Floyd's *The Division Bell Tour* in 1994 at $2.3 million and then The Rolling Stones at $2.6 million for their *Voodoo Lounge Tour*. The *Victory Tour* was also the first with most of its shows in outdoor facilities, with only ten of the fifty-five in arenas or domed stadiums. Although billed as a tour to support the Jacksons' *Victory* album, it actually rode on the incredible success of the *Thriller* album and its accompanying video exposure.

The tour had its downside as well, as there was an associated ticket lottery scam supported by Michael's brothers and promoter Don King. Michael canceled their planned European leg and cut off future dealings with both King and his brothers. King's co-promoter was Billy Sullivan, scion of the family that owned the New England Patriots football team, who set up twenty-six tour dates at seventeen NFL stadiums at very favorable rates. This was Sullivan's first attempt at concert promotion, and his last. He was no match for the wily King or the extravagant Jackson clan. He wound up selling both the Patriots and Foxboro Stadium to avoid bankruptcy. King had also secured a $5 million sponsorship from Pepsi in exchange for a television commercial co-branding with the tour.

Industrywide concert box office totals had been climbing in steady increments from the 1975 level of about $250 million to over $700 million in 1984. After a slight fall back in 1985, receipts jumped to over $750 million in 1987, then to over $1 billion in 1988 and 1989, reaching about $1.4 billion in 1990. Once again Michael Jackson led the way with his fifteen-country, 123-concert *Bad Tour*, once again sponsored by Pepsi, but this time for $10 million, and without his brothers or Don King. Former CBS Records executive Frank DiLeo joined Michael as his personal manager, veteran business management firm Gelfand, Rennert & Feldman handled finances, and John Branca of Ziffren Brittenham LLP did the legal work. Among the 132-person entourage was a young Sheryl Crow, performing as one of the backup singers. Commencing in Tokyo on September 12, 1987, and concluding on January 27, 1989, in Los Angeles, Jackson did fifty-four North American dates in mostly indoor facilities with the international legs adding another sixty-nine concerts, mostly in outdoor stadiums. The entire tour played before 4,498,300 fans and grossed over $125 million.

Pink Floyd, The Rolling Stones, and Other Top Tours of the Late 1980s

Starting at about the same time as the *Bad Tour* in September 1987, Pink Floyd began the first segment of their seven-leg *Momentary Lapse of Reason Tour* to support their new album of the same name. One hundred ninety-seven concerts later the tour concluded in July 1989 in Marseilles. They eclipsed Jackson's *Bad Tour* box office record by $10 million with $135 million in ticket sales, but it took seventy-four more shows to get there. While their average ticket was a few dollars higher, their average attendance was 21,250 compared to Jackson's 36,291. They played a larger percentage of indoor facilities than Jackson, but three of their more diverse outdoor locations were Olympic Stadium in Moscow, the Grand Canal in Venice, and the Palace at Versailles.

Pink Floyd hadn't performed since their 1981–82 *The Wall Tour*. They had gone through internal problems of their own as original bassist and primary lyricist Roger Waters had left the band in 1985. He threatened to sue if they went back on the road, but all was settled privately. They resumed the high-tech staging that had put them in the forefront of progressive rock for the past two decades. With Waters's absence, *The Wall* coproducer Bob Ezrin worked in the control room with Dave Gilmour who tripled as lead vocalist, lead guitarist, and primary songwriter. The new album, however, didn't quite match *The Wall* in critical praise or consumer success. There were two number one singles on AOR radio and a number five on the *Billboard* Rock Tracks chart, but nothing entered the CHR Top Singles Chart. Nonetheless, the album sold over five million copies worldwide while their total tour attendance was reported at 4.25 million. *Pollstar* named Pink Floyd the 1987 comeback artist of the year, number one major tour production of 1988, and the tour itself as the most creative staging for both 1987 and 1988.

The other top-grossing tours of the late 1980s included David Bowie's *Glass Spider Tour*; U2's *The Joshua Tree Tour* in 1987; and The Rolling Stones' *Steel Wheels Tour* in 1989–90. Veteran art rocker Bowie's eighty-six-date tour with opening act Duran Duran matched the *Victory Tour* in scope and pricing with an average ticket price of $28, attendance at thirty-five thousand, and average gross of $1 million. U2 had been touring for ten years, since its formation, going from clubs to theaters to arenas, building fans and album sales without the benefit of a hit CHR single. Now two number one singles with MTV video play from the *Joshua Tree* album attracted over 3.1 million attendees at a cautious $18 average ticket price for their 109 shows.

Pollstar named the 1989 Rolling Stones' *Steel Wheels Tour* as the most creative production, major tour of the year, and concert industry event of the year. Over twenty-five years of touring had transformed the veteran rockers, especially Mick Jagger, into savvy businessmen, following the advice of Prince Rupert Lowenstein, their longtime aristocratic business manager. Canadian Michael Cohl outbid longtime Stones' promoter Bill Graham with a $65 million guarantee for the entire tour and merchandising rights. Cohl's financial backing came from the BCL Group, his new partnership with brewery LaBatt Brewing Company,. Ltd., and Concert Productions International (CPI) partner Bill Ballard, whose family owned the Maple Leaf Gardens and Toronto Maple Leafs hockey team.

For the *Steel Wheels Tour*, Cohl sold a December 19, 1989, Atlantic City Convention Center concert as a three-hour pay-per-view at $24.99 per household. BCL claimed over $300 million in gross revenue from tickets, merchandise, TV rights, sponsorships, and other ancillary rights for the entire 115-date world tour. The *Steel Wheels Tour* was the prototype for Cohl's international promoter/producer model. He subsequently bought all tour dates and merchandising rights for future tours with The Rolling Stones, U2, David Bowie, Pink Floyd, Barbra Streisand, and many others, with accounting usually handled by New York City–based business manager Rascoff/Zysblat. This

HIGHEST GROSSING TOURS - 1980-1999

The Jacksons' *Victory Tour* in 1984 was the first to play primarily in stadiums and have tickets reach $30. *Pollstar's* 1985 major concert tour total grew from $600 million to $1.7 billion in 1999. The average ticket price for 1999's top 100 tours was $36.84.

ARTIST / TOUR NAME / YEAR(S)	SHOWS/ TICKETS	BOX OFFICE RECEIPTS (in millions)
Rolling Stones -*Voodoo Lounge Tour* - 1994-95	124 / 6.3 m	$320 m
Rolling Stones - *Bridges to Babylon Tour* - 1997-98	108 / 4.4 m	$274 m
Pink Floyd -*The Division Bell Tour* - 1994	120 / 6 m	$250 m
Eagles - *Hell Freezes Over Tour* - 1994-95	not available	$200 m (est.)
U2 - *PopMart Tour* - 1997-98	93 / 3.9 m	$172 m
Michael Jackson - *HIStory World Tour* - 1996-97	83 / 4.5 m	$165 m
U2 - *Zoo TV Tour* - 1992-93	157 / 5.4 m	$151 m
Pink Floyd - *A Momentary Lapse of Reason Tour* - 1987-89	199 / 4.3 m	$135 m
Michael Jackson - *Bad Tour* - 1987-89	123 / 4.5 m	$126 m
Garth Brooks - *World Tour* - 1996-98	220 / 5.5 m	$105 m
Rolling Stones - *Steel Wheels Tour* - 1989-90	115 / 3.3 m	$98 m
David Bowie - *Glass Spider Tour* - 1987	86 / 3 m	$86 m
Bruce Springsteen - *Born in the U.S.A. Tour* - 1984-85	156 / 3.9 m	$85 m
The Jacksons - *Victory Tour* - 1984	55 / 2.75 m	$75 m
New Kids on the Block - *The Magic Summer Tour* - 1990	152 / 3.29 m	$74 m
Tina Turner - *Foreign Affair: The Farewell Tour* - 1990	121 / 3 m	$70 m
Madonna - *The Girlie Show* - 1993	39 / 1.37 m	$70 m
Janet Jackson - *Rhythm Nation 1814* - 1990	117 / 2 m	$65 m
Madonna - *Blond Ambition World Tour* - 1990	57 / .89 m	$63 m
U2 - *The Joshua Tree Tour* - 1987	109 / 3.9 m	$56 m

Source: *Billboard / Pollstar* / artist websites

Illustration 4.1 Highest Grossing Tours: 1980–99

formula turned Cohl into a major force in concert promotion for the next 20 years while financially benefiting all involved.

While Jackson, Springsteen, Pink Floyd, Bowie, U2, and The Stones set new standards in ticket pricing, attendance numbers, tour longevity, and gross receipts, they also raised the bar in stage design, acoustic quality, lighting, pyrotechnics, and video screens. Other acts whose tours were at the top of the rankings were Bryan Adams, Dire Straits, and Prince in 1985; Genesis, Bob Dylan with Tom Petty, Bob Seger, John Mellencamp, Journey with Glass Tiger, Neil Diamond, Van Halen, and ZZ Top in 1986; Neil Diamond, Paul Simon with his Graceland package of South African artists, Bob Dylan with The Grateful Dead, Billy Joel, and Genesis in 1987; Van Halen's Monsters of Rock, Def Leppard, George Michael, Aerosmith with Guns N' Roses, Elton John, and The Grateful Dead in 1988; and The Who, Neil Diamond, The Grateful Dead, Metallica, and Bon Jovi in 1989.

McCartney Highlights the Early 1990s

Perhaps the highlight of 1990 was the *Paul McCartney World Tour* with the former Beatle in his first appearance in America since the *Wings over America Tour* of 1976 and the first time he publicly performed Beatles songs on his own. After playing indoor arenas in November and December of 1989 in six cities and seven more in February, he returned in spring and summer for twenty stadium dates in fourteen different cities. His forty-seven US concerts averaged almost fifty thousand people at an average $30 ticket price for an estimated $70 million, with another fifty-six dates outside the US. His August 21 show in Rio de Janeiro played to 184,368 attendees, then a world record for a stadium rock concert. McCartney's box office competition that summer included the final legs of The Stones' *Steel Wheels Tour*, The Grateful Dead, Billy Joel, and Madonna's *Blond Ambition Tour*, along with newcomers Janet Jackson, with her *Rhythm Nation 1914 Tour*, and New Kids on the Block's first concert outing, *The Magic Summer Tour*.

Concert touring revenue for 1991–93 fell back from the 1990 record high of over $1.4 billion to hover around $1 billion as a minor recession hit the US after the First Gulf War. The leading tour was U2's 1992–93 157-show *Zoo TV Tour*, stretching over twenty-two months doing both arenas and stadiums, averaging 34,080 attendees with $151 million at the box office. Veteran multiplatinum acts Springsteen, Genesis, Elton John, and Billy Joel were also out during this period, but their tours were not on as grand a scale.

Other acts doing well at the box office included Liza Minelli, who nearly sold out fifteen straight dates at Radio City Music Hall; Frank Sinatra & Shirley McLaine doing the same for eleven dates; and the perennially popular Grateful Dead, New Kids on the Block, Dire Straits, Neil Diamond, MC Hammer, ZZ Top, Yes, Paul Abdul, Gloria Estefan & The Miami Sound Machine, and Tom Petty. Riding along with the Garth Brooks–triggered explosion of country music in concert attendance were George Strait, Brooks & Dunn, Clint Black, Mary Chapin Carpenter, Wynonna, Tricia Yearwood, Mark Chesnutt, Alan Jackson, Randy Travis, Reba McEntire, and the two worldwide country-pop crossover phenomena Billy Ray Cyrus and Shania Twain.

Pollstar named Garth Brooks's 1991–92 *Ropin' the Wind Tour*, his first outing as a headliner, as the number one tour for 1992 over runners-up U2, the Metallica & Guns N' Roses dual billing, and Lollapalooza II. Brooks's managers Bob Doyle and Pam Lewis received the 1992 Managers of the Year award. At the end of the year his first three albums had sold over 22 million units combined. His 1992 album *The Chase* shipped over 5 million in two months. He repeated in 1993 as the year's top tour with *The Garth Brooks World Tour* over Bette Midler, The Grateful Dead, Jimmy Buffett, and Peter Gabriel. Brooks's ninety-seven-date schedule extended into 1994 covering ten countries.

Playing stadiums, arenas, civic centers, and rodeos, Brooks extensively employed pyrotechnics and elevating risers with rain and thunder effects. In the show encore, he flew about the venue in a specially modified trapeze harness. All this staging was new to the country market. He also taped an NBC network concert special early in the schedule, as he had done on his previous tour. He bucked the rising ticket pricing trend by keeping the average cost below $20 while almost every other tour exceeded $30. Brooks's sudden rise was even more phenomenal considering that he only received country airplay and country chart action without the extensive CHR, AOR, and/or AC airplay that had propelled previous country crossover stars like Willie Nelson, Kenny Rogers, Olivia Newton-John, or Dolly Parton.

Music Venues from Club to Coliseum

Other than outdoor locations that could be adapted for massive crowds by adding portable stages, crowd-control barriers, seating, bathrooms, concession stands, and other amenities, the largest available permanent structures were sports stadiums or coliseums, whether open air or domed. There were nine in the US that could accommodate over one hundred thousand attendees, another seventy-one with a capacity ranging down to sixty thousand, and forty more above forty thousand. It usually took multi-platinum album success and multiple hit singles for artists to join the select group of acts that could stage a national tour utilizing these facilities. Networks of facilities with smaller audience capacities also existed in the top one hundred designated market areas (DMA)—Nielsen terminology for local media markets—and even into the next one hundred DMAs.

Next in capacity came the indoor arenas, civic centers, or outdoor amphitheaters with eight thousand to thirty thousand seats. At the $30 ticket plateau that had become the norm by 1990, this would produce $240,000 to $900,000 sellout potentials per night. Top fifty markets usually had two or three such venues with even more in top twenty-five markets. Some acts would do multiple shows in these facilities, like The Grateful Dead's six-show sellout run at the Boston Garden in September 1991. Tickets at the 14,466-seat configuration went for $23.50 each for a six-day box-office tally of $2.04 million. The Dead exemplified the ability to build a dedicated following over years of live performance but minimal radio success, creating a consumer base for album, ticket, and merchandise sales. Other acts who performed in facilities of this size included both artists on their way up to multi-platinum album sales and stadium success on future tours, as well as those coming down from that plateau.

The next capacity level were theaters, some of which dated back to vaudeville, together with music halls, community arts centers, outdoor amphitheaters, and college auditoriums with capacities from twelve hundred to eight thousand, with corresponding box-office potential of $36,000 to $240,000 at the $30 level. Top facilities like Radio City Music Hall in New York or the Universal Amphitheater in Los Angeles usually sold tickets from $50 down to $20. The Barry Manilow run of forty-four shows over four weeks, with matinees most days, at New York's Gershwin Theatre in April and May of 1989 drew 77,079 attendees with a gross box office of $3.18 million.

For artists just starting out and receiving both radio promotion and tour support from their record companies, as well as acts without label support but with local or regional followings, there were nightclubs of all sizes catering to differing demographics and genres, including the House of Blues locations, Billy Bob's Texas in Ft. Worth, Gilley's in the Houston suburb of Pasadena, Cowboy's in Dallas, Irving Plaza and the Ritz in New York, the Metro and the Cubby Bear Lounge in Chicago, the Fillmore and Slim's in San Francisco, the Grizzly Rose in Denver, the Electric Factory in Philadelphia, the Empire Club in Cleveland, the Avalon in Boston, and the Crazy Horse Saloon in Santa Ana, California. These clubs ranged in size from several hundred to several thousand.

Local clubs and bars were the incubators for new bands or songwriters playing original music. Often the compensation was merely the door receipts, often at $5 to $10 a head. Many superstars who eventually reached the top started on the local club scene. A 1977 *Rolling Stone* article by David McGee stated, "In 1971 Bruce Springsteen was playing clubs in Asbury Park, New Jersey. . . . His career was at a low ebb; in five years as a professional musician he'd never even made $5,000 in a year."[2] The Boss had just turned twenty-two and was still two years away from his first album release and four years away from *Born to Run*.

The Logistics of Touring

Touring revenue at each facility level had an accompanying economy of scale determining stage production, means of transportation, and hotel accommodations, if any. An artist had to pay the band and their expenses, any sound or road crew, and all travel costs from gate receipts, as well as commissions to booking agents and managers if they yet had them, or unless their agreement called for commissions not to kick in until a higher income level. All this before personally netting out anything.

For artists with tour support, the label would make up the shortfall when promoting a new record, but after that initial support, they were on their own. An act without tour support at all, playing fifty weekends a year in clubs averaging three hundred seats for one hundred dates with an average door of $10 a head, would gross $300,000, but between musicians, roadies, meals, and travel expense, the money would quickly be gone, as Springsteen had experienced.

Enthusiastic crowd support at multiple locations was what A&R staffers were looking for, but it could take several years to build a fan base and develop a repertoire of suitable songs. The process of signing, recording, and scheduling a record release would take another year or two. After that initial release, only 10 percent to 30 percent of artists would get the chance to make another record and have it promoted. The rest would either settle into being a club or bar band, prepare for a second chance wiser for the experience, or just give up the dream for a day job, perhaps on the business or artist-support side of the music industry.

At every level, artists usually developed supplemental sources of revenue including T-shirts, posters, records, and other items at their shows. All this merchandise, however, had a manufacturing cost that artists had to pay themselves or through family and friends. Once an initial supply was produced and sold, ongoing sales financed new inventory. An initial run of five hundred albums, whether recorded live or in a studio, could be manufactured for $2 each and sold for $10 or more. T-shirts had a comparable pricing structure.

The rule of thumb for merchandising for top touring acts, according to Ray Waddell, then still at *AB*, was approximately $10 to $15 per attendee, so a thirty thousand-person audience could yield another $300,000 to $450,000 on top of the box office. This would necessitate one or more semi-trucks just for the merchandise, portable sales setup, and personnel. The top artists had several options other than their own organization for managing their merchandise, including delegating the task to their record company or their promoter with a cash advance against their share. There were also third-party merchandise companies—including Bravado, Winterland Productions, and Cinderblock—who would often advance a large sum against a 25 percent share of gross sales. Competition in this market sector would grow with increasing concert attendance.

The Creative Community Steps Up for Charity with Live Aid

The industry had a long history of supporting charitable causes with annual fundraising events including the T.J. Martell Foundation, the United Jewish Appeal, the American Cancer Society, the City of Hope, St. Jude Children's Research Hospital, and other favorites of the top record and publishing executives. Their annual dinners normally had an honoree from the very highest rung on the industry ladder whose company led that year's fundraising by selling high-dollar dinner tickets, supplying the night's entertainment, and soliciting ad buys in the dinner program and a *Billboard* supplement. Hundreds of millions of dollars have been raised for charity in this manner.

Artists also have a history of charitable events but of a much more spontaneous nature in reaction to a calamity or crisis in which the artists donate their services with all proceeds going to the supported cause. In 1971 George Harrison and Ravi Shankar set the standard with the Concert for Bangladesh, which spawned a live album, movie, and eventually a DVD. Over the next thirteen years a who's who list of top acts banded together in concerts supported by albums, movies, and television shows for charities Amnesty International, UNICEF, and Musicians United for Safe Energy (MUSE), an anti–nuclear energy advocate.

In late 1984, the power of rock star charity reached a higher level than ever before starting with a Christmas recording created by Irish rocker Bob Geldof and Scottish collaborator Midge Ure. "Do They Know It's Christmas?" was inspired by a BBC telecast on the famine in Ethiopia. Phil Collins, Boy George, Paul McCartney, David Bowie, Paul Young, George Michael, and members of U2, Duran Duran, Kool & The Gang, Spandau Ballet, and Bananarama were among the forty-three artists performing on the record under the group name Band Aid. The record stayed at number one in the UK for five weeks during the Christmas season and sold over 3 million copies by January, becoming both the fastest- and biggest-selling single in UK chart history. Another estimated 2.5 million copies sold in the US. In its first year the record raised over $9 million.

After hearing "Do They Know It's Christmas?" artist/activist Harry Belafonte contacted Ken Kragen about doing a similar American project. Kragen was then manager of Kenny Rogers and Lionel Richie and known to Belafonte for his work with the late Harry Chapin on anti-hunger activism. On January 21, 1985, Kragen got Richie together with Michael Jackson to write a song, then brought in Quincy Jones to produce, and on January 28 they began recording "We Are the World." In order of appearance, Lionel Richie, Stevie Wonder, Paul Simon, Kenny Rogers, James Ingram, Tina Turner, Billy Joel, Michael Jackson, Diana Ross, Dionne Warwick, Willie Nelson, Al Jarreau, Bruce Springsteen, Kenny Loggins, Steve Perry, Daryl Hall, Huey Lewis, Cyndi Lauper, Kim Carnes, Bob Dylan, and Ray Charles all sang on lead lines. Another twenty-eight vocalists and musicians including Belafonte and Jones joined in, all under the group name USA for Africa.

"We Are the World" reached number one in America, stayed there for five weeks, and topped the charts in another ten countries. It sold over 20 million units worldwide, making it the biggest-selling single of all time. The single was accompanied by a studio performance video clip, a home video on *The Making Of . . .* , T-shirts, additional merchandise, and a *Life* magazine special edition. On Good Friday, 1985, over eight thousand radio stations around the globe participated in a simultaneous worldwide radio broadcast. In the first year after the single's release, $44.5 million was raised for African hunger relief, to eventually total over $63 million.

Geldof and Ure then organized the July 13, 1985, televised Live Aid concert performance, held simultaneously before a crowd of seventy thousand at Wembley Stadium in London with production handled by Harvey Goldsmith, the producer of the Prince's Trust Fund concerts, and one hundred thousand at Philadelphia's JFK Stadium with production under the supervision of Bill Graham. Performances at each venue were shown live on giant video screens in the other. More than seventy-five acts performed, including Elton John, Madonna, Santana, Run-DMC, Sade, Sting, Bryan Adams, The Beach Boys,

Mick Jagger, David Bowie, Queen, Duran Duran, U2, The Who, Tom Petty, Neil Young, and Eric Clapton.

Satellites transmitted the live broadcast to more than 1 billion viewers in 110 countries, with 40 of them holding telethons for African famine relief during the broadcast. Phil Collins flew by Concorde after his London performance to New York and helicoptered to Philadelphia to perform again, this time as drummer for a reunion of the surviving members of Led Zeppelin. Crosby, Stills, Nash & Young reunited for the show. Queen's twenty-one-minute set was hailed by all with none other than Elton John, who preceded Queen that day, telling Queen's Freddie Mercury, "Well, nobody needn't go on now Freddie, you've just completely and utterly swept the board."[3] At the end of the London segment Paul McCartney and Pete Townsend held Bob Geldof on their shoulders to lead a closing performance of "Do They Know It's Christmas?" while the Philadelphia show ended with an ensemble version of "We Are The World." It was one of the most awe-inspiring events in the history of the music business.

Live Aid eventually raised $127 million for African famine relief and created enough attention and action from the world community to supply surplus grain to end the then-current hunger crisis. A year later Geldof was knighted for his efforts. Twenty years later in 2005 Ure received his belated knighthood as well. With all the 1950s Teens inspired by Elvis now over forty, and the baby boomers due to start following them the next year, rock-'n'-roll had symbolically come of age, demonstrating its social conscience and cultural relevancy on a massive scale.

Willie Nelson Follows with Farm Aid

During his Live Aid performance, Bob Dylan quipped, "I hope that some of the money . . . maybe they can just take a little bit of it, one or two million, maybe—and use it, say, to pay the mortgages on some of the farms and, the farmers here, owe to the banks."[4] While the Live Aid organizers were reportedly miffed by his comment, Willie Nelson, who was somewhere on the road watching from his tour bus, was inspired. He had been a groundbreaker for outdoor festivals with his annual Willie Nelson & Family 4th of July Picnic that began in 1973 at rural Dripping Springs, Texas, and went on to draw as many as three hundred thousand people to other locations in subsequent years. Next Nelson enlisted John Mellencamp and Neil Young to help him establish a new charity concert they dubbed Farm Aid.

On September 22, just seventy-two days after *Live Aid*, the trio led an ensemble of fifty-two artists before eighty thousand people at the University of Illinois's Memorial Stadium in the first Farm Aid Benefit Concert. Bob Dylan was there, along with Billy Joel, B. B. King, Roy Orbison, Bon Jovi, Foreigner, Huey Lewis, Carole King, Joni Mitchell, John Denver, The Beach Boys, Tom Petty, Bonnie Raitt, and over a dozen of Willie's country superstar friends, including fellow Highwaymen Johnny Cash, Kris Kristofferson, and Waylon Jennings. Nelson then postponed his picnic for the next ten years in favor of restaging Farm Aid, later reviving the picnic on a smaller scale in 1995.

The first Farm Aid raised over $9 million for America's family farmers. Nelson and Mellencamp then brought a contingent of farmers to testify in Congress about the plight of small farmers, spurring the passage of the Agricultural Credit Act of 1987 to help save family farms from bank foreclosure. Thirty-four Farm Aid concerts later, the nonprofit organization operating out of Cambridge, Massachusetts, had raised over $57 million and operated a hotline and emergency fund for threatened family farms. In 2001 Dave Matthews became the fourth board director.

Live Aid and Farm Aid were by no means the only charitable endeavors by the music industry's creative community, though none could compare with Live Aid's one-time impact or Farm Aid's effective longevity. In June 1986, the six-city *Conspiracy of Hope US Tour* was staged for Amnesty International, featuring U2, Sting, Joan Baez, Lou Reed, Jackson Browne, The Neville Brothers, and a reunion of The Police for the final three concerts. In September and October 1988, the *Human Rights Now! World Tour* of twenty rock concerts in sixteen countries, also for Amnesty, featured Bruce Springsteen and the E Street Band, Sting, Peter Gabriel, Tracy Chapman, and Youssou N'Dour, plus local guest artists. Their goal was to increase awareness for both the Universal Declaration of Human Rights on its fortieth anniversary and the work of Amnesty. The Reebok Foundation sponsored the tour and at each location human rights activists and former prisoners of conscience addressed the gathering, handed out copies of the Universal Declaration, and signed up new members for Amnesty.

In 1989 Randy Owen of the group Alabama and a handful of other country artists and radio stations organized the Country Cares for Kids annual radiothon, which has raised more than $70 million over the ensuing years for St. Jude Children's Research Hospital in Memphis.

Charitable efforts were also made for environmental causes. In 1990 The Eagles' Don Henley founded the Walden Woods Project to preserve the land around Walden Pond in Concord, Massachusetts, where Henry David

Thoreau wrote many of his works, from commercial development. The Project acquired ninety-six acres through a series of benefit concerts spearheaded by Henley and included Elton John, Aerosmith, Melissa Etheridge, Sting, Jimmy Buffett, John Fogerty, Neil Young, and Roger Waters. In 1992, Henley organized the recording of a charity album titled *Common Thread: The Songs of The Eagles*. The album was released on Giant Records, owned by Henley's manager, Irving Azoff, and featured contemporary country artists including Tanya Tucker, Alan Jackson, Suzy Bogguss, Brooks & Dunn, Trisha Yearwood, and Travis Tritt performing Eagles hits. In all, the project has raised over $22 million and established Walden.org as a major voice in environmental conservation.

Superstar Tours Drive the Live Performance Industry

The success of the *Common Threads* album inspired the Eagles to end their fifteen-year sabbatical by reuniting for both an album and a tour, both titled *Hell Freezes Over*. The album contained fifteen tracks comprising four studio cuts of new songs and eleven live versions of past hits taken from the audio tracks of a television special done for MTV. Only one single made it to the Hot 100 as "Get Over It" reached number thirty-one, but they fared better at AC with "Love Will Keep Us Alive" reaching number one, and with "Get Over It" going to number four on the Mainstream Rock Tracks chart. Nonetheless, the album drove ticket sales and vice versa. The album reached number one in the US, selling over 9 million units, and more than another million worldwide. The companion video also sold over a million copies. The tour covered 121 dates in North America and another 33 overseas between May 1994 and August 1996. Although full tour accounting is not available, it has been estimated that the US and international dates together brought in over $200 million.

The tour covered both stadiums and arenas and for the first time, ticket prices to a rock concert topped $100 while most others at that time peaked at $40 to $50. Irving Azoff, the Eagles manager for their entire career, years later told *Billboard*'s Ray Waddell, "Tickets should be priced at what the fans are willing to pay to see the performer,"[5] as demand after a fourteen-year hiatus was sky high. He added, "It wasn't just about making more money. . . . It was also about sending the message that The Eagles were America's biggest band, and perhaps one of the biggest in the world—charging like it influenced both fans and media that we were the biggest ever."[6]

Two other superstar bands helped drive the 1994 *Pollstar* box office tally to an all-time high of about $1.7 billion, an amount not to be topped for another five years. Pink Floyd's *The Division Bell Tour* and The Rolling Stones' *Voodoo Lounge Tour* were both presented by concert impresario Michael Cohl. Both were sponsored in part by Volkswagen, and both successively became the highest-grossing tour in rock music history up to that date. Cohl's costing model utilized the same crew for the entire tour to maximize efficiency, which he had calculated by comparing the transportation costs for the traveling crew to that of locals crews and discovering that utilizing the traveling crew to be more profitable than hiring locals who didn't need hotels and transportation but were less familiar with setup and breakdown, and thus more expensive on the bottom line.

Both tours played mostly in stadiums and coliseums around the world with both tours selling over 6 million tickets. Pink Floyd averaged forty-five thousand attendees per show and The Stones drew an average of fifty-one thousand. The average ticket prices were $41.67 for Pink Floyd and $50.50 for The Stones, averaging $2.3 million and $2.6 million per concert, respectively, both topping Madonna's record average of $1.79 million per show in her 1993 *Blond Ambition World Tour*. Neither had much chart success from radio play but sold over 4 million albums each.

This was the second Pink Floyd tour without Roger Waters, and the final of fourteen total tours for the band. Their production was bigger than ever, with special effects including two custom-designed airships. They did 120 shows in 213 days, with multiple days in twenty-one cities, culminating with fourteen shows in London. The tour required a fleet of fifty-three trucks and a total of 161 people, with staging cost of almost $30 million.

The *Voodoo Lounge Tour* was The Stones' first tour without Bill Wyman on bass, but it was business as usual as just one of their forty-six tours between 1963 and 2019, and the second-highest-grossing tour of their fabled career. Even then there were comments about their age as both Mick Jagger and Keith Richards had just passed fifty. Mick told Rich Cohen of *Rolling Stone*, "There were lots of hacks out there who said we couldn't do it anymore, but maybe what they meant was *they* couldn't do it anymore. Anyway, once we started playing, all that died down. You can talk about it and talk about it, but once we're onstage, the question is answered."[7] They did, however, proceed at a slightly slower pace than Pink Floyd, stretching 124 shows over 386 days.

With the *Hell Freezes Over Tour* doing over $200 million, *Division Bell* taking in over $250 million, and *Voodoo Lounge* grossing over $320 million, these three tours alone did more business than the entire live concert revenue of 1984, the year of the then-groundbreaking *Victory Tour* by the Jacksons.

Ticket prices had more than doubled, staging had become more spectacular, merchandise was selling better than ever, and concert attendance had become a giant social networking experience for the audience.

Diamond, Platinum, and Gold

For a business driven by competition for radio play and chart numbers, it seems only natural that awards and industry recognition above and beyond press coverage and fan adulation would be front and center. First were the RIAA certification of album shipments with a gold (five hundred thousand), platinum (1 million), or diamond (10 million) level. Then there was the nomination for and winning of one or more of the annual Grammy Awards. While both are among the top benchmarks of success, they differ in derivation. The certification reflected the number of records shipped by the artist's label while the Grammy Awards are voted on by members of the National Academy of Recording Arts and Sciences (NARAS), since 2005 known as the Recording Academy.

The RIAA had been formed in 1951 as a trade organization for record labels and in 1958 issued its first gold single and album awards. In 1975 it changed its criteria for gold from $1 million in sales to 500,000 units shipped, and in 1976 added the platinum category for 1 million units. Shipping information was submitted by the labels and confirmed by RIAA audit. Actual records painted gold or platinum with an RIAA seal on a plaque were engraved, framed, and presented, at the label's expense, to artists, producers, songwriters, executives, or anybody else the artist and/or label considered to have made a meaningful contribution to the success of the album, including key D.J.s, managers, session musicians, and so forth.

Artists with albums released between 1985 and 1995 that eventually went Diamond were *Billy Joel's Greatest Hits*, Creedence Clearwater Revival's *Chronicle: The 20 Greatest Hits*, Phil Collins' *No Jacket Required*, the Doors *Greatest Hits*, and *Whitney Houston* in 1985; the Beastie Boys's *Licensed To Ill*, Bon Jovi for *Slippery When Wet*, and *Bruce Springsteen & the E Street Band (Live)* in 1986; U2 for *The Joshua Tree*, Def Leppard's *Hysteria*, George Michael for *Faith*, Guns N' Roses *Appetite For Destruction*, Michael Jackson's *Bad*, and the *Dirty Dancing* soundtrack in 1987; Journey's *Greatest Hits* in 1988; *Garth Brooks* in 1989; Garth Brooks for *No Fences*, Madonna's *Greatest Hits*, MC Hammer's Please *Hammer, Don't Hurt 'Em*, and the Led Zeppelin complete box set in 1990; Metallica's *Metallica (The Black Album)*, Nirvan for *Never Mind*, and Pearl Jam's *Ten* in 1991; Eric Clapton's *Unplugged*, Kenny G

TOP 25 *BILLBOARD* HOT 100 ARTISTS & TOP POP ALBUMS OF THE 1980s

The 1980s were pre-SoundScan/BDS with the national charts compiled from local radio and store reports. The decade's top 25 Hot 100 artists were determined by collating the top ten chart positions for each year in the decade. Platinum certifications came from reports submitted by the labels to the R.I.A.A. The differences between radio play and platinum certifications reflect the uniqueness of each artist's path to success.

TOP 25 HOT 100 ARTISTS

HOT 100 RANK	ARTIST	ARTISTS' LABEL / LABEL GROUP	ARTIST'S TOP-SELLING 1980S ALBUM	US PLATINUM CERTIFICATION
1	Michael Jackson	Epic / CBS	*Thriller*	34 million
2	Whitney Houston	Arista / BMG	*Whitney Houston*	14 million
3	Madonna	Sire / WMG	*Like A Virgin*	10 million
4	Prince	Paisley Park / WMG	*Purple Rain*	13 million
5	Kenny Rogers	Liberty / EMI	*The Gambler*	5 million
6	Bon Jovi	Mercury / PolyGram	*Slippery When Wet*	12 million
7	Pat Benatar	Chrysalis / Indie	*Crimes of Passion*	4 million
8	Def Leppard	Mercury / PolyGram	*Hysteria*	12 million
9	The Police	A&M / BMG	*Synchronicity*	8 million
10	Duran Duran	Capitol / EMI	*Rio*	2 million
11	Guns N' Roses	Geffen / WMG	*Appetite For Destruction*	18 million
12	Bruce Springsteen	Columbia / CBS	*Born in the USA*	17 million
13	John Cougar Mellencamp	Riva / Polygram	*American Fool & Scarecrow*	5 million
14	Lionel Richie	Motown / Indie	*Can't Slow Down*	10 million
15	Phil Collins	Atlantic / WMG	*No Jacket Required*	12 million
16	Billy Idol	Chrysalis / Indie	*Rebel Yell*	2 million
17	Hall & Oates	RCA / BMG	*H2O & Big Bam Boom*	2 million
18	George Michael	Columbia / CBS	*Faith*	10 million
19	Huey Lewis/the News	Chrysalis / Indie	*Sports*	7 million
20	Journey	Columbia / CBS	*Greatest Hits*	18 million
21	New Kids on the Block	Columbia / CBS	*Hangin' Tough*	8 million
22	R.E.O. Speedwagon	Epic / CBS	*Hi Infidelity*	10 million
23	The Rolling Stones	Rolling Stones / WMG/CBS	*Tattoo You*	4 million
24	The Go-Go's	I.R.S. / BMG	*Beauty and the Beat*	2 million
25	U2	Island / Indie	*The Joshua Tree*	10 million

Source: *Billboard* / R.I.A.A.

Illustration 4.2   Top 25 Billboard Hot 100 Artists & Top Pop Albums of the 1980s

for *Breathless*, and Whitney Houston's *Bodyguard* soundtrack in 1992; Mariah Carey for *Music Box*, and Tom Petty & the Heartbreakers' *Greatest Hits* in 1993; Boyz II Men for *II*, Garth Brooks' *In Pieces*, Green Day for *Dokkie*, Hootie and the Blowfish's *Cracked Rear View*, the *Forrest Gump* soundtrack, *The Lion King* soundtrack, and TLC's *CrazySexyCool* in 1994; Alanis Morissette's *Jagged Little Pill*, Jewel for *Pieces of You*, Mariah Carey's *Daydream*, No Doubt for *Tragic Kingdom*, Shania Twain's *The Woman In Me*, and the Smashing Pumpkins for *Mellon Collie and the Smashing Sadness* in 1995.

This array of artists reflected the wide spectrum of consumer tastes and trends for the decade. There were 1960s and 1970s artists who added to their initial sales totals on vinyl and cassette as catalogs resold to their baby boomer fans in the new CD format; a new generation of MTV rockers to achieve market dominance; soundtracks that confirmed the marketing power of cross-promotion between film and music; Garth Brooks and Shania Twain leading the country music revival; the teen rebellion and angst of Gen X expressed in the rap, metal, and grunge genres; and the instrumentalist who was the exception to the rule that records need a lyrical message to reach mass appeal.

The Recording Academy and the Grammy Awards

The Recording Academy had been organized in 1957 as the music industry's equivalent to the Academy of Motion Picture Arts and Sciences, now known as the Motion Picture Academy, which was founded in 1927. In 1959 NARAS presented the first Grammy Awards for records released in 1958, their equivalent to the Oscars, in two separate ceremonies in New York and Los Angeles. The major winners were *Nel blu, dipinto di blu (Volare)* by Domenico Modugno for Record of the Year and Song of the Year, *The Music from Peter Gunn* by Henry Mancini for Album of the Year, and Bobby Darin for the Best New Artist. The runners-up included Perry Como, Peggy Lee, David Seville and The Chipmunks, Frank Sinatra, Van Cliburn, and Ella Fitzgerald.

The Academy had two levels of membership, voting and nonvoting. A voting member needed to have a credit on a minimum of six recorded and released tracks as a performer, producer, musician, songwriter, engineer, arranger, or liner note writer, in other words, eligible for a Grammy oneself. The criteria for nonvoting status was to be a professional in the music business, whether on salary or self-employed. This relegated record company executives, publishers, promotion men, disc jockeys, managers, agents, and lawyers to nonvoting status unless they happened to also have the required creative or technical credits. While they all could receive duplicate thank-you copies of gold or platinum records at the request of the record company, they could not vote for the Grammy Awards nor receive duplicates of the award.

Academy members and accredited members of the press submitted nominees for records released from October 1 through September 30 for the awards ceremony held the next January or February. Nominee eligibility was screened, and then a comprehensive first-round ballot was sent out early to voting members to narrow down to five nominees in each of the four general categories of Album of the Year, Record of the Year (single track), Song of the Year, and Best New Artist. They could also vote in nine other categories of their choice. Starting in 1989, a final screening was conducted by the Awards and Nominations Committee before the final nominees were announced. This committee was also the arbiter of any post-nomination or award-eligibility disputes. They were called upon the next year to vote, and the Academy acted, to strip Fab Morvan and Rob Pilatus of Milli Vanilli of their 1990 Best New Artist Grammy Awards when it was revealed that they did not sing on their own record.

Voting membership, once established, was for life as long as one continued to pay annual dues or had paid extra for a lifetime membership. This led to a membership older in average age than the fourteen-to-twenty-eight demographic range that was the core target of the record companies, and probably also older than the average age of the A&R, promotion, and marketing staffs involved in the records. This often led to a more conservative slate of nominees than what the music press or record companies would have preferred. Elvis didn't win a Grammy until the 1970s and then it was for his gospel recordings. Grammy Awards for a rock music category weren't initiated until 1980. Before then rock records were eligible only in the general and pop categories. The Beatles did, however, win the Grammy for the best new artist in 1964, but it took another decade for rock artists to establish a meaningful presence in the nomination process.

In 1985 there were seven NARAS chapters located in New York, Los Angeles, Nashville, Memphis, Atlanta, Chicago, and San Francisco. The Academy was governed by a board of trustees divided among the chapters in proportion to voting membership. At its annual June 1985 board meeting, Atlanta trustee Mike Greene was elected national president, a non-compensatory part-time position, along with a national vice president from each chapter. After going through negotiations with the record labels for a Grammy sticker program for award-winning albums, in 1986 the board decided that to better represent its constituency in intra-industry relations, television contract negotiations, and legislative issues, they needed to hire a full-time paid president with industry experience. Former Elektra/Asylum chairman Joe Smith was selected, but after only six weeks on the job, Smith resigned to become chairman of Capitol Records. Fearing a similar result with any other top record industry veteran, in 1988 the board moved Greene into the position.

Under Greene's watch the Academy added metal and rap categories in 1989 and a best alternative album category in 1991 to better reflect the fast-moving trends of the public's music consumption. Greene also established the Academy's political advocacy initiatives on issues such as intellectual property rights, First Amendment protection, music and arts education, funding for the national arts agencies, and the archiving and preservation of America's musical legacy. The Academy also initiated the Grammy in the Schools educational outreach, the Grammy Foundation, and the MusiCares Foundation that helped musicians and other industry professionals with substance abuse and healthcare crises. Although relations with the press and record companies' top management remained strained, affected by exclusion from the voting process, the cooperation between the awards show and the labels improved with Grammy nominee compilations and an improved sticker program. With the advent of SoundScan demonstrating the real impact that the awards had on the sales of artists performing on the show, the value of the Grammy Awards grew in the eyes of the labels, leading to a more cooperative relationship.

Honoring the Creative Icons of the Past: The Artists

The Country Music Hall of Fame and Museum (CMHOF) debuted in 1967 in Nashville with a location at the northern end of the section of 16th Avenue South that is now known as Music Square East. By 1985 the facility had already gone through three expansions and had twenty-five inductees from Hank Williams and Jimmie Rodgers, through Patsy Cline and Johnny Cash to Marty Robbins and legendary publisher/producer Ralph Peer who discovered The Carter Family and Jimmie Rodgers. Bill Ivey led the CMHOF as director from 1971 through 1998 while also serving twice as chairman of the Recording Academy and became the executive director of the National Endowment for the Arts (NEA) from 1998 through 2001. Assistant director Kyle Young succeeded Ivey and supervised the relocation of an expanded CMHOF to downtown Nashville a few blocks away from the Lower Broadway honky-tonk district and the historic Ryman Auditorium.

In 1983 a group of music industry veterans in New York led by Ahmet Ertegun and attorney Suzan Evans decided that it was time for rock-'n'-roll to have a museum of its own. They enlisted the aid of Walter Yetnikoff of CBS Records, Seymour Stein of Sire/Warner, *Rolling Stone* publisher Jann Wenner, Springsteen manager Jon Landau, attorney Alan Grubman, and PolyGram attorney David Braun, to found and spearhead the initial funding for the Rock and Roll Hall of Fame Foundation.

A nominating committee was formed including Ertegun, Stein, Wenner, Bob Krasnow of Electra/Asylum, *Los Angeles Times* music editor Robert Hilburn, *Rolling Stone* writer Kurt Loder, musicologist Norm N. Nite, Columbia's legendary A&R man John Hammond, producer/musician Nile Rodgers, and former Atlantic partner Jerry Wexler. Their initial ballot then went to a carefully selected list of more than a hundred performers, journalists, songwriters, producers, D.J.s, and label executives to choose the first class of inductees. Chuck Berry, James Brown, Ray Charles, Sam Cooke, Fats Domino, the Everly Brothers, Buddy Holly, Jerry Lee Lewis, Little Richard, and Elvis Presley were inducted in the Performer category; Jimmy Yancey, Jimmie Rodgers, and Robert Johnson in the Early Influences category; Alan Freed and Sam Phillips in the Non-Performer category; and John Hammond honored with the Ahmet Ertegun Award.

The first induction ceremony was held in the ballroom of the Waldorf Astoria in January 1986. Later that year Cleveland, with a $65 million local commitment, was awarded the museum over bids from New York, San Francisco, Chicago, and the sentimental favorite Memphis. Cleveland's major claim to the honor was that WJW D.J. Alan Freed is credited as the first radio personality to use the term rock-'n'-roll on radio and at station-sponsored shows in 1952 in lieu of rhythm and blues to attract a teenage white audience. In 1954 Freed moved on to WINS in New York and then in 1957 to a dance party on the ABC television network. A few years later he was indicted and pled guilty to payola charges, ending his career in radio. He died penniless at age forty-three in 1964, asserting to the end that he never played a record he didn't believe was a hit.

The groundbreaking for the Cleveland Rock Hall, as it was also called, was on June 7, 1993, with Pete Townshend, Chuck Berry, Billy Joel, Sun Records founder Sam Phillips, and R&B pioneer Ruth Brown in attendance along with many of the founding committee. Museum doors were opened to the public on September 2, 1995, accompanied by a benefit concert at Cleveland Municipal Stadium. Chuck Berry played with Bruce Springsteen & The E Street Band. Other performers included James Brown, Bob Dylan, Jerry Lee Lewis, Aretha Franklin, Johnny Cash, and Booker T. & The MGs. Since its opening, more than 10 million visitors have been there, with an estimated economic impact of more than $2 billion. In 2019, 563,000 visitors created an economic impact of $200 million on the Cleveland community.

Other organizations have also honored the creative pioneers of the music business but not on as grand a scale. The Rhythm & Blues Foundation was established in 1987, again under the aegis of Ahmet Ertegun, with prodding from Ruth Brown, Stax guitarist/producer/songwriter Steve Cropper, attorney Howell Begle, and other early Atlantic artists after they collectively questioned back royalty payments from Atlantic's independent label days. Ertegun persuaded WMG to make the initial $1.5 million donation, with other labels joining in to launch the foundation in 1988 to provide financial support, medical assistance, and educational outreach to support the R&B artists of the past. Along with the founders, Bonnie Raitt, Ray Benson of Asleep at the Wheel, and producer/songwriter/musicians and owners of Philadelphia International Records Kenneth Gamble and Leon Huff have been instrumental from the start in keeping the foundation going.

Honoring the Creative Icons of the Past: The Songwriters

Songwriters also have traditionally celebrated their creative predecessors, and once again Nashville led the way. In 1967 songwriters Eddie Miller, Buddy Mize, and Bill Brock enlisted thirty-eight others as fellow founding members of the NSA, including Kris Kristofferson, Marijohn Wilkin, Liz and Casey Anderson, Felice and Boudleaux Bryant, Jerry Chestnut, Danny Dill, and Ted Harris. Publishing administrator Maggie Cavender came on board as executive director, a position she held for the next twenty-two years.

In addition to their lobbying initiatives, the NSA inducted the first twenty-one members of its Hall of Fame in the fall of 1970 at an awards ceremony during Nashville's annual country music week celebrations. This event has continued since then to become a yearly staple along with the CMA TV show and the ASCAP, BMI, and SESAC awards dinners. In 1988, Pat Rogers of Tree Publishing succeeded Cavender and led the renamed Nashville Songwriters Association International (NSAI) in creating dozens of local chapters and regional workshop programs. The NSAI increased its advocacy work in Washington, D.C., and in 1993, launched the Tin Pan South songwriter festival as an annual weekly homage to and celebration of the songwriting profession. In 1997 Bart Herbison took over as executive director. With ten years of experience on Capitol Hill as an assistant to Tennessee congressman Bob

Clement, Herbison expanded the NSAI's presence and effectiveness in its Washington lobbying efforts.

In 1969, songwriter Johnny Mercer and publishers Abe Olman and Howie Richmond founded the Songwriters Hall of Fame (SHOF) in New York to honor the creators of the works contained in what is respectfully known to as The Great American Songbook. One hundred fourteen songwriters were inducted in the first ceremony in 1970 including Stephen Foster, Francis Scott Key, George M. Cohan, Victor Herbert, Irving Berlin, Scott Joplin, George Gershwin, W. C. Handy, Rodgers & Hammerstein, Jerome Kern, Cole Porter, Fats Waller, Jimmie Rodgers, Hank Williams, Lead Belly, and Woody Guthrie.

Each year additional songwriters were inducted to eventually surpass four hundred. Other awards acknowledging the contributions of prominent industry professionals were presented at a gala banquet in New York. President Sammy Cahn, Oscar-winning lyricist for "Three Coins in a Fountain," "All the Way," "High Hopes," and "Call Me Irresponsible," ably led the organization from 1973 to 1993, followed from 1993 to 1999 by Bobby Weinstein, BMI executive and cowriter of "I Think I'm Going Out of My Head," "Hurts So Bad," and "I'm on the Outside Looking In." The SHOF also maintained a series of endowed scholarships, conducted workshops for promising songwriters, and advocated in Washington for increased benefits to songwriters and improvements in copyright law. WMG veteran executive Linda Moran has led the SHOF as president since 2001, adding CEO to her title in 2011.

Industry Growth Benefits the Creators

The creative community finished 1995 on better financial footing than they had been in 1985. The economy boomed as digital technology proliferated. Since the internet opened to commercial pursuits in late 1994, artists were already closer to their fans through websites and email. With the record industry almost tripling in revenue since 1985, the artist royalty pool had expanded accordingly. Faster recoupment of recording costs put artists into a positive royalty flow more quickly. More money from increased profits was also available to use as advances for both renegotiating existing contracts and signing new talent.

For songwriters, revenue from mechanical licenses had more than doubled due to the rise in record sales compounded by the 46.6 percent increase in the mechanical statutory rate between 1985 and 1995. Their performing rights revenue from ASCAP, BMI, and SESAC had almost doubled due to the growth in radio, television, and cable advertising revenue. Sync and print revenue were on the upswing. SoundScan and BDS tracking benefited both artists and songwriters with more accurate accounting.

Concert revenue had almost doubled. Performers were now firmly ensconced at a standard 75 percent or sometimes higher share of box-office receipts. The charts and rankings, however, were limited to the several hundred highest-earning tours staged primarily by the top booking agencies and concert promoters. This relationship between trade press and concert industry was as synergistically bonded as the labels were with their own trade journals. Both sectors benefited from radio airplay and MTV as the primary promotional tools for sales of both tickets and albums. Consequently, the artists with the top tours usually mirrored the ones who were fixtures in the Hot 100 singles and Top 200 albums charts. Together both sectors financially supported the trade journals as a marketing tool with ad buys, subscriptions, and attendance and advertising at trade shows and awards events.

There were no accurate metrics, statistics, charts, or rankings, however, for the acts that performed on the club and bar circuits who had only record product they had manufactured themselves or the finished product they purchased from their labels to sell at their gigs. Industry leaders were focused on the artists who showed an immediate and sizable return or they believed had the potential to do so. Nonetheless, the lure of making the charts, playing arenas, or just the love of music motivated artists to keep chasing their dreams. Aspiring novices and seasoned veterans seeking another shot both hoped to benefit from the increased number of slots on label rosters and the opportunities provided by the promoters who supported the small venues. They also benefited from the advances in digital technology that made the home recording process more affordable, enabled a higher level of sonic quality, and provided a new and wider circle of interactivity through the internet.

Access to these resources also anchored a surge in independent labels. Whether survivors of the conglomeration of the industry or startups ready to compete on the street for rising talent, these indies were capturing the attention of both young consumers eager to discover new music and adults keeping up with the favorites of their own youth that no longer had new releases from the majors. Whether at the top or the charts sustaining their careers, at the base of the pyramid seeking a quantum leap upward, and at levels and niches in between, the 1990s were a good time to be making music.

5

The Consumer: From Whom, How, and Where the Money Flows

The State of Music Consumption in 1985

Among the several common ways the verb *consume* is used in the American vernacular, aside from the obvious "to use as a customer," are the more visceral "to become engaged in fully," "to enjoy avidly," and "to devour." The consumption of music in all of these connotations had been an ingrained element in human interaction for thousands of years through family, ceremony, civic socialization, and peer group influence as either an active participant or member of an audience. Without consumers spending time and money on music in a recorded, printed, or live performance context there would be no music business to sell music to them.

By 1985 recorded music had become omnipresent from birth in nurseries, in schools, in places of worship, on the radio, in films, on television, in the background in businesses, on elevators, in shopping malls, in restaurants, and between the action at sporting events. Even though the relationship between consumer and music in many of these instances was passive in nature, specific melodies, lyrics, genres, and artists were imprinted in both individuals' memory banks and the collective consciousness of the public as a whole. Although consumers did not directly pay for most of this subliminal presence of music, the advertisers and businesses that courted them to buy products and services licensed music to set or enhance ambience by paying license fees to the owners of both the recorded music they used and the publishers of the songs or musical scores embedded within those recordings.

While over 95 percent of the public in 1985 listened to the radio as a part of their music consumption, not all radio listeners spent money on records or tickets. Some were content to hear whatever was playing while others reveled in the repetitive rotation of current Top 40, CHR, or AC radio hits. Others preferred listening to niche genres, the favorites of their youth on oldies stations, or the latest trend on AOR. For many of those on the lower economic rungs, buying music for on-demand access rather than listening to radio was

American Popular Music and Its Business in the Digital Age. Rick Sanjek, Oxford University Press. © Frederick Sanjek 2024.
DOI: 10.1093/oso/9780190653828.003.0005

a luxury item not in their budgets, but their enthusiasm for music was equal to anyone else.

For those who did spend money on music, they too had started by listening for free on the radio or watching music videos. Fan magazines were also an influential element. Reviews in *Rolling Stone*, *Crawdaddy*, *Creem*, or *The Village Voice* could make or break an artist's career. Those who became lifelong buyers of recorded music usually started as teenagers buying singles at the local music store, absorbed in the culture associated with their favorite music genres. In 1985 there were 35.8 million Americans between ten and nineteen accounting for 15.5 percent of the population. In addition, 120.7 million vinyl singles were bought in 1985 for 18.6 percent of total units sold and most probably purchased by these teenagers or sold to the jukeboxes that were catering to them.

The US Bureau of Labor Statistics reported that in 1985, consumers spent $91.6 billion on all forms of entertainment combined, including fees and admission charges, television, radio, sound systems, and other entertainment-related supplies and equipment. Music-specific spending identified by the industry itself included the estimated $4.6 billion on records as reported in the RIAA annual retail value report, several hundred million more in royalties from printed music acknowledged by the NMPA, and $600 million on major-venue concerts as tracked by *Pollstar*'s annual box office recap. This doesn't include the money generated by acts not in major venues, secondary ticketing market markup, or other associated costs including ticket handling fees, concessions, and parking; the difference between what consumers paid for sheet music and the royalties received by NMPA members; the money spent for audio equipment; music related merchandise; fan magazines; or the approximate $400 million the RIAA claimed was spent on blank tapes used in what it termed home duplication. Adding in these factors increased the estimated spending on music to over 7percent of total consumer entertainment spending.

In comparison, consumers spent about $3.75 billion in 1985 at the US movie box office, $3.3 billion in home video sales, and $4.69 billion in the video game market. The home electronics hardware industry, including both audio and video devices, accounted for about $17 billion and musical instruments were around $3 billion. This left about $53.5 billion for other forms of entertainment, including both participatory and spectator sporting events; family events including theme parks, circuses, ice capades, and other nonmusical events, but nonetheless often utilized music in the background; outdoor recreation; and various home recreation goods and supplies.

The state of consumer technology in 1985 was quite different from what we now take for granted as a major part of our daily lives. The largest television screens in mass distribution were 26" or 27" diagonally with cathode ray tube (CRT) screens that extended backward behind the monitor. Larger rear-projection screens had just entered the market at a cost of about $1,500 and up. Flat-screen televisions wouldn't be introduced until 1997, and then at a minimum cost of $15,000. Video gaming was just beginning to recover after a retail crash in 1983 ignited by market oversaturation. The revival was sparked by the 1985 release of NES's Nintendo third-generation home console that contributed to the transformation of gaming from an arcade to a home industry. PlayStation and Xbox were still ten and sixteen years in the future, respectively.

Mobile telephones didn't reach 1 percent market penetration until the late 1980s and only 12.67 percent by 1995. The ones that did exist in 1985 had an extremely short battery life, took what seemed like an even longer time to recharge, and were extremely expensive. More streamlined phones with longer battery life were introduced in the early 1990s. Display windows and full QWERTY keyboards weren't introduced until 1996. The first Macintosh home computer had been introduced in 1984 and the Windows 1.0 operating system in 1985. The first .com domain name registration, systematics.com, occurred in 1985. The internet had about nineteen thousand US users in 1985—mostly academic, scientific, and military. By 1987, less than 15 percent of Americans had home computers.

The relationship between records, radio, and retail in 1985 supplied what at the time was regarded as close to instant gratification as possible for music consumers as records were available at retail only a car ride away as soon as they were heard on radio, or their corresponding video clips appeared on television. This mass availability, however, was restricted to the titles chosen for release by the major labels and their degree of efficiency in restocking depleted inventories. Consumers bought records at locally owned retail outlets nostalgically termed mom-and-pop stores, specialty record shops, the record departments of larger variety stores, and at the ever-increasing number of regional record chains such as Tower, Musicland, Strawberries, Record Bar, and Camelot. As the rock concert business grew in scope, concert promoters tracked sales, airplay, and television success to select the artists for tours.

The Battle for Electronic Ticketing Supremacy—
Round 1: Ticketron vs. Computicket

In 1985 fans could order the best available seat or general admission concert tickets over the telephone, buy them at their local record store, purchase them from one of the new electronic ticketing kiosks, or visit the venue ticket window. Tickets for live events as a receipt for the consumer and a record-keeping method for the promoter had long existed in the entertainment business. As payment to artists shifted from flat fee to guarantee plus a percentage of revenue above the guarantee and after deduction of mutually agreed upon costs, the box-office ticket records became one of the major determinants in calculating and settling up the post-show split of the night's profit between promoter, venue, and artist.

The seeds of electronic ticketing were sowed in 1965 when Seagram chairman Edgar Bronfman Sr.'s CEMP Investment family trust funded Ticket Reservation Systems (TRS) in New York to accommodate consumers who bought tickets for sporting events and Broadway shows—areas in which Bronfman was already an investor. TRS contracted with Control Data Corporation (CDC), the computer manufacturer ranked number two behind IBM, for a customized and simplified model CDC-1700 as the central database connected by telephone lines to teletype latch key printers in sales outlets to both place and print the ticket orders. The TRS sales terminal did not have a CRT screen, making the process much faster than competing systems equipped with viewing monitors that required greater bandwidth, and thus more time to complete the transaction.

Outlets paid monthly rental fees for their terminals, with service fees charged to the consumer, the contracted venue, and the show promoter or sports team. Key ticket providers were hesitant, however, to commit their entire ticket inventory to the new system, so TRS established its model with only 30 percent to 40 percent of an event's available tickets. Abraham & Straus department stores, Grand Union groceries, and American Express travel agencies were among the first outlets. The historic Herald Square Gimbel's department store in Manhattan was the most visible and highly promoted location. The system debuted in 1967 with tickets for Robert Merrick's Broadway production *I Do! I Do!*, off-Broadway show *Drum in the Night* at the Greenwich Village Circle in the Square Theater, and the New York Generals soccer team. All were seeking a needed boost in sales. In 1969, CDC came in as a 51 percent partner and the name was changed from TRS to Ticketron.

Meanwhile rival Computicket opened in 1967. Owned by Computer Sciences Corporation (CSC), a Los Angeles-based software company that also owned the proprietary tax preparation program Computax. CSC also provided software for IBM, Honeywell, GE, NASA, and other government agencies. Computicket software ran simultaneously on two IBM 360/50 mainframe computers to assure backup. CRT monitors were connected to a mainframe by telephone lines, enabling them to see the available inventory at point of purchase. Computicket began operation with LA-based Ralph's Markets and Bullock's department stores as outlets and mirrored the Ticketron model of charging commissions to both the promoter/venue and the consumer.

As soon as these two nascent ticketing services became aware of each other, a battle ensued between them for signing up venues and outlets. Bronfman's deeper pockets, however, gave the advantage to Ticketron, which set up a lavish outlet in the Beverly Hills Hotel right in Computicket's back yard, and contracted exclusivity with the Los Angeles Forum. In turn, Computicket invaded Ticketron's New York home base with a contract to develop a network of betting terminals for New York City's Off Track Betting Corporation (OTBC). By the end of 1970 Computicket was $12.7 million in developmental debt, couldn't fulfill the OTBC contract, and shut down, forcing parent CSC to sell its profitable Computax business in 1971 to cover the losses. In 1973, CDC bought out the rest of the Bronfman share of Ticketron and continued to build the business.

Additional companies entered the electronic ticketing market, including Select-A-Seat in Arizona in 1972, which merged with Arizona Cattle Company but went out of business in 1977. Bay Area Seating Service opened in the San Francisco area in 1974, got into a software lawsuit with Arizona Cattle Company, and went bankrupt itself in 1979. In 1978 the Fotomat Corporation, which had over four thousand drive-up photo development kiosks, decided to expand into ticket sales. They took the ticketing model one step further, insisting on access to 100 percent of the tickets for an event, rather than the 30 percent to 40 percent Ticketron received. The company, however, was hampered by financial reversals emanating from its videocassette rentals, and then from the invention of the one-hour photo lab, which decimated their core film development business. This resulted in their shutting down the ticketing venture and eventually selling the company to Konica in 1981.

The Battle for Electronic Ticketing Supremacy—Round 2: Ticketron vs. Ticketmaster

The one company to survive and become a real rival for Ticketron was the embryonic Ticketmaster, formed in 1975 by Arizona State graduates Albert Leffler, Gordon Gunn, and Peter Gawda. They were about the same age as Bill Gates and Paul Allen, who were developing Microsoft, and Steve Jobs and Steve Wozniak, then creating Apple. In 1978, they finalized a proprietary program for a network of computer terminals that could buy and print tickets from the home database via telephone lines, posting transactions in real time. In 1981 Ticketmaster sold about $1 million in tickets, but that was only about 1 percent of market leader Ticketron's total of close to $100 million.

In 1982 Hyatt Hotel chain owner Jay Pritzker bought Ticketmaster for $4 million. He brought in attorney Fred Rosen to run the company. They believed that the future of the electronic ticketing industry had a far greater potential with music concert sales, which had a large percentage of impulse buys, than for sporting events, which were dominated by perennial season ticket holders buying directly from the team venue with one purchase for an entire season. Rosen had also observed the giant lines that would form at box offices for rock concerts, evidence that the demand for tickets driven by saturation radio play often exceeded supply.

Concurrently, trends in the music business were forming a perfect storm for the ascendance of Ticketmaster's computerized ticketing model over the technologically outdated Ticketron system. The concert industry had grown from about $150 million in 1970 to over $700 million in 1984 and would grow to over $1 billion by 1990. Venues for superstars had shifted to arenas and stadiums. The greater size, scope, and resulting expense of sound systems, visual enhancements, staging, and transportation were motivating artists to seek larger venues and greater guarantees. By necessity, the promoters and venue operators, together with the agents and managers who represented the artists, were all looking for improved technology to manage logistics and the nightly reconciliation of the box-office receipts, with each side intent on maximizing their profit margins.

A cagey and hardnosed negotiator, Rosen designed his strategy for Ticketmaster to achieve dominance of the market by recognizing and exploiting the changing industry landscape. His technology, which utilized real-time accounting and the ability to sell specific seats on the spot, proved to be more consumer friendly than Ticketron's best-seat available methodology. His demand that 100 percent of tickets, rather than Ticketron's lower percentage, be available on the Ticketmaster system turned out to be a convenience for all involved. Consumers got access to tickets as soon as they went on sale at Ticketmaster outlets or by telephone. Rosen eliminated charges to promoters and venues, instead offering them both advances for ticket-handling exclusivity and a share of the ticketing surcharges paid by consumers.

He also increased these charges, labeling them convenience fees, which Ticketmaster's detractors claimed could be as high as 45 percent. Consumers, however, generally accepted if not welcomed the fee as a trade-off for being assured of a ticket and specific seat without having to stand in line at the venue box-office window. Ticketmaster could sell out a show in a few hours or quicker, reducing promoters' costs for box-office labor and advertising while whipping up fear among fans of missing out. This also opened the door to the secondary market of ticket scalpers who bought tickets and resold them at a higher cost to fans who had missed out on the initial sale. For the concert promoters and artists' representatives, the Ticketmaster system's computer readout also improved the efficiency of the post-show revenue accounting.

In 1985 Ticketmaster sold over $200 million worth of tickets, compared to Ticketron's estimated $600 million. Rosen then bought out smaller regional competitors to increase his market share, including Ticket World USA in 1985, Capital Automated Ticketing and Dayton's Ticketing in 1989, and Atlanta's SEATS and Denver's Datatix/Select-A-Seat in 1990. By 1988, Ticketmaster had pulled even with Ticketron, each selling just under $400 million worth of tickets including a large share of *Pollstar*'s $1 billion in top concert tours' ticket sales.

This reversal of fortune resulted in CDC selling Ticketron in 1989 for $16 million to a group led by Washington, DC, pro sports team owner Abe Pollin, but his group could not resuscitate the floundering company. Pollin sold the operation to Ticketmaster in 1992 for $11 million, giving Rosen close to a 90 percent share of the concert ticket business. To pass muster under US antitrust law, Ticketron separated out the New York Broadway theater ticket market, selling its system and accounts there to the long-established Shubert Organization theater ownership group, which rebranded the system as Telecharge.

The Battle for Electronic Ticketing Supremacy— Round 3: Ticketmaster Takes Command

In 1993, the now-combined Ticketmaster and Ticketron were on course to repeat the more than 52 million tickets sold and $1.1 billion in face value totaled in 1992. The service, convenience, printing, and/or mailing fees were somewhere between 15 percent and 55 percent depending on the ticket price, location, and performer, as reported in a 1990 survey by the New York State Consumer Protection Board. These fees were in addition to the face value printed on the ticket, which also included any applicable taxes. The additional charges were noted on the sales receipt, but not on the ticket itself.

Entrepreneur and Microsoft cofounder Paul Allen agreed in November 1993 to buy the majority stake of Ticketmaster from Pritzker for more than $300 million, according to *Bloomberg Business News*. Fred Rosen stayed on as CEO, receiving a large bonus and a small share of the company. Allen planned to integrate Ticketmaster operations, including its computer systems, consumer mailing list, retail outlets, and phone bank with four thousand operators, with his other technology holdings, which included a 25 percent stake in the America Online (AOL) internet service. Allen told *Bloomberg*, "Ticketmaster is an important vehicle for the informational and technological highway of the future and complements my existing suite of technology companies. . . . The company's consumer base as well as its reputation for being on the cutting edge of entertainment and marketing make it a key part of my plans for the future."[1]

The Ticketron acquisition, however, had created negative public relations for Ticketmaster, as reports continued to circulate about increased service fees, not only above the fees that Ticketron had been charging, but even above the Ticketmaster fees prior to the acquisition. This maelstrom came to a head in 1994 when Pearl Jam told Ticketmaster that it wanted to price its tickets at $18 and limit service charges to a $1.80 fee that would be clearly listed on the ticket. The two couldn't come to an agreement and the band could not find any suitable venues that did not have a Ticketmaster-exclusive ticketing agreement. Pearl Jam canceled its tour.

With Justice Department prodding, Pearl Jam filed an antitrust complaint, followed by a June congressional subcommittee hearing to examine the ticketing industry. Pearl Jam's Jeff Ament and R.E.M.'s attorney and co-manager Bertis Downs testified against Ticketmaster. Rosen testified for them, claiming that the average ticket fees were $3.15, and that after sharing fees with venues and promoters, and after paying expenses including credit card and phone company bills, their profit was just 10 ¢ per ticket.

In response to all the testimony, Congress proposed a bill requiring ticket companies to list service fees on all tickets. But it was defeated, largely due to the efforts of a team of five Ticketmaster-employed DC lobbying firms led by Black, Manafort & Stone. The Justice Department conducted a year-long investigation, interviewing artist managers, tour professionals, Ticketmaster competitors, and venue box-office staffers to determine if the Ticketmaster-exclusive contracts violated antitrust laws. Then, in a two-sentence statement on July 5, 1995, the Justice Department declared the case closed with no further comment.

In May 1995, *Billboard* uncovered a document that contradicted Rosen's sworn testimony to Congress. Prepared by investment banking firm Lazard Frères for use in the 1993 sale to Paul Allen, it said that Ticketmaster projected a profit of 70 ¢ per ticket. Ticketmaster representatives did not respond to *Billboard*'s inquiry on the discrepancy between Rosen's sworn statement and the securities filing.

Billboard's Eric Boehlert spoke with a venue manager familiar with both Ticketmaster and Ticketron who questioned Rosen's claim of making only 10 ¢ a ticket. A manager at a small regional ticketing company told Boehlert that they could currently net 50 ¢ a ticket at their level of service charges, which were below Ticketmaster's. "To be honest with you, their business is much more lucrative than ours because in the ticketing business, the absolute cream of the crop are the concerts where you advertise in the media that [a show's] coming, then your phones light up and the tickets are gone in a few hours or a day. That's a low-service, high-margin type of business."[2]

Boehlert also reported that the Lazard Frères document further stated, "Company revenues are driven largely by demand for tickets to concerts and, to a lesser extent, sporting, and family entertainment events. . . . Popular music concerts account for approximately 55 percent of the Company's ticket sales, and a higher proportion of revenues."[3] Since the entire music concert industry knew that Ticketmaster's convenience fees usually exceeded $3.15, the above statement might explain the apparent difference between Rosen's contention and the Lazard Frères document. In Congress, it is likely that Rosen had referred to all tickets, including circuses, ice skating shows, sports, and other family events in the not-as-profitable non-concert revenue estimated to account for 45 percent of its sales, although the hearings focused on concert ticket charges. No one asked Rosen or any other witness to clarify the different charges for different types of events.

Undaunted, Pearl Jam decided to avoid Ticketmaster for its 1995 tour, using the just-opened ticketing service ETM Entertainment Network. Founded by ticketing veteran Peter Schniedermeier and touring pro David Cooper, ETM planned to deploy a fully automated, operator-free phone system with a five thousand–call capacity; place five hundred freestanding kiosks at to-be-announced retailers; and run a marketing campaign on the newly commercialized internet. The best intentions and latest technological updates, however, could not overcome Ticketmaster's exclusive contracts with 63.2 percent of the major concert venues, or its exclusive handling of the ticketing for many major tours that played at the venues that were not exclusive with them.

Pearl Jam was able to book the first leg of its tour in venues west of the Mississippi, but many were sub-par in security and/or logistics. They were unable to book anywhere in Los Angeles and found few if any available venues east of the Mississippi capable of accommodating their needs. They stopped trying to find an alternative and worked out a deal with Ticketmaster for the remainder of the tour. EMT ended the year $4.4 million in debt, shifted its focus to sports and other non-music events, and prepared for a $25 million public offering in 1996 to complete its kiosk marketing plan.

Ticketmaster ended 1995 in a stronger position than ever, having defeated Pearl Jam's insurgency, and then welcomed the prodigal band back into the fold. They also created their own online ticketing initiative. Many top rock acts had followed the Eagles' lead in raising ticket prices over $100, which raised Ticketmaster's fees proportionally, even though it took the same effort to sell a $20 ticket as it did for the $100 ones. The baby boomer demographic, which was the audience for the Eagles, Pink Floyd, Rod Stewart, Elton John, Billy Joel, The Rolling Stones, and other legacy acts, didn't seem to mind the pricing, as many of these artists didn't tour that often, so for the consumer, the surety of having tickets more than outweighed the extra cost.

In contrast, younger audiences did not have pockets as deep, and would not pay as high a ticket price for the younger artists that toured more often. Most of these artists, including Pearl Jam, Green Day, Stone Temple Pilots, Soul Asylum, Hootie and the Blowfish, and most country performers, were aware of the total cost to consumers. Anxious for repeat business on the next tour, they kept their tickets at more reasonable prices. Nonetheless, Ticketmaster fees and charges were typically much higher than the $3.15 Fred Rosen had claimed. While concerned about the total cost to their fans for their tickets, these artists were just as diligent as the ones with $100 tickets in trying to negotiate a share of concessions, parking, and merchandise.

The Secondary Ticketing Market

Whatever the tour or its ticket prices, all but a handful of consumers had to deal with the growing problem of the added costs associated with the secondary ticketing market, historically known as ticket scalping. A scalper is generally defined as a person who buys tickets for concerts, sports events, and so forth, and then sells them to other people at a higher price.

In his 2007 book *Ticket Scalping: An American History, 1850–2005*, cultural historian Kerry Segrave traced the practice back to the 1850s when P. T. Barnum was promoting the American tour of Jenny Lind, the famed Swedish Nightingale. Segrave recounted that at that time, the resale of tickets was termed "speculating" with "scalping" reserved for the railroad ticket resale market. The earliest application of "scalping" to live performance occurred in *The New York Times* in 1887 and by the turn of the century had replaced "speculating" in the entertainment business vernacular. As the entertainment industry, including sports and other non-musical categories, grew in popularity so did the practice of ticket scalping driven by supply, demand, and American ingenuity. From the very onset, a large share of scalping was driven by insiders who could obtain tickets, and often the best seats, before they went on sale to the public. They then sold them to an increasingly sophisticated class of scalpers who were as in tune with the technology of ticketing as were the industry leaders.

For much of the twentieth century, scalpers referred to as sidewalk men bought tickets through their hirelings who got on the box office line, or they had a deal with a ticket supply insider. They then stood outside the event on show nights hawking their supply for a profit. In metropolitan areas ticket brokers advertised in newspapers. Some had brokerage booths in hotels and upscale retail establishments for resale of tickets to sold-out shows. By 1985, the secondary market had developed on a comparable scale with the growth in attendance, ticket prices, and electronic ticketing of the overall concert business. Segrave cited several prominent attempts to control scalping. In 1965 the New York Licensing Commissioner called in the police to help combat scalpers at the fourteen thousand-seat Forest Hills Stadium for a sold-out Frank Sinatra concert. In 1972 and again in 1981, The Rolling Stones initiated a lottery system for their Madison Square Garden performances. Somehow scalpers were still able to get a supply of tickets, which they offered through newspaper ads offering a pair of tickets that brought in bids starting from $250 to $500.

Differing and sometimes contradictory laws on both state and local levels complicated the scalping problem, which was further exacerbated by inconsistent enforcement. In May 1979 rock concert promoter Jim Rissmiller and manager David Krebs announced the formation of a statewide committee to place an anti-scalping proposition on California's June 1980 ballot. KMET, the highest-rated FM rock radio station in Los Angeles, also joined in the committee's formation. California's state law then prohibited scalping on the premises of an event, but the only effect was that speculators worked just outside the event's defined perimeter.

Artists had responses of their own. At a fall 1980 show at the Inglewood Forum, Bruce Springsteen told his audience, "If you've gotta pay $200 to buy a ticket that's marked $12.50, it's not right and you shouldn't stand for it. Tickets should go to the fans not the scalpers."[4] His booking agent, Barry Bell, responded to scalpers controlling front-row blocks of tickets for every show, by stating that obviously "you can't do that by mailing in requests."[5] The Boss himself recorded a radio spot urging fans to support the anti-scalping bill. California State assemblyman Meldon Levine, however, remarked, "The scalpers lobby is one of the strongest in the state. When I introduced my first anti-scalping bill, in 1977, colleagues came up to me saying 'that bill of yours hurts my friends.' Unless we get support from the entertainment industry, we'll never overcome that."[6]

Despite the efforts, *Rolling Stone*'s Michael Goldberg reported that on a certain Sunday in 1988 twenty-five brokers, including Good Time Tickets and Front Row Center, had ads in the *LA Times* advertising tickets for sale with markups of 100 percent to 500 percent on tickets for sold-out shows. In another *Rolling Stone* article in 1990, Goldberg reported that an unnamed LA broker told him that scalping was now potentially more profitable than the ticket sales themselves. For example, one thousand Forum seats, which was about 5 percent of capacity, at $70 per ticket would yield $70,000, more than twice the Forum's net from the original sale. These insider-group transactions were often disguised as concert clubs or season-ticket programs but were actually done by ticket brokers. Goldberg concluded that the computerized ticketing systems developed over the past decade had actually made insider dealing easier to accomplish and harder to trace.

Despite legal action, attempts at legislation, lottery and ID voucher plans, artist protestations, and purges of employees when caught, the secondary market continued to thrive, and the internet was about to expand that success exponentially. ICM agent Troy Blakely added, "The scalpers are getting tickets from at least one of three sources; the promoter, the building or the ticket agency. And they're probably getting them from one, two or all three sources in just about every market."[7] Washington, DC–based promoter Seth Hurwitz concurred. "This business about brokers claiming they had people standing in line is horse manure. They've got deals with people in ticket agencies, they've got deals with promoters, sources in the box office."[8]

While almost everybody in the concert sector admitted to the existence of scalping, few led a sustained charge to make it go away. Irving Azoff's introduction of the $100-and-up ticket price for the 1995 Eagles tour was recognition that the market would bear a higher price without objections from enough of the public to hurt business. The surety of tickets in hand, even at the increased face value, still outweighed the high cost. The higher face value, however, only drove the secondary market even higher. While the 1995 *Pollstar* summary of the total ticket value of top concert tours was over a billion dollars, it actually cost the public as much as twice that in real expense due to the surcharges and markup extracted from them by secondary ticket-market brokers.

Consumer Listening Trends

By 1985 the relationship between consumers and the radio/record/retail alliance hadn't changed much since the late 1950s, but it had grown in dollar volume and available technology. CHR had replaced Top 40 as the leading radio format, but instead of gathering around jukeboxes to hear the latest singles, 1985 consumers watched video clips on MTV. This audience was primarily upper middle class, the economic group with the most disposable income. Former 1950s Teen and now over-forty baby boomer parents had stereo hi-fi systems at home, and sometimes upgraded the speakers in their cars to replace the factory-issued models. Their children had access to these systems, if not their own smaller versions, as well as on-demand portable access to their favorite music via Walkman cassette players or boom boxes, the upper end of which had dual cassette reels for making duplicate copies.

From 1955 to 1985 radio income had surged almost 1,000 percent from $456.5 million in 1955 to $4.376 billion in 1985, while the population increased just 43 percent from 165.9 million to 237.9 million, and the number of radio stations jumped from about thirty-five hundred to over nine thousand, a nearly 250 percent increase. Over this thirty-year span, radio formats evolved into specific repertoire for different demographic groups, dictated primarily by age but with ethnicity and other cultural considerations also as factors. These demographics guided advertisers on where to place their spots and for which products. They also directed record companies on what records to promote to which stations, and retail outlets on what to stock. The spike in radio advertising income derived from subliminally co-branding music with other consumer products worked well for all involved.

Teens and young adults were still the primary targets for the record companies to break new acts as they had been since the advent of Top 40 radio. The labels sought to bond a steadfast group of consumers to a specific cadre of artists who would maintain this fan base throughout their careers, sustaining record sales without the labels having to spend additional annual marketing dollars. Sinatra, Elvis, Streisand, The Beatles, Madonna, The Stones, Billy Joel, James Taylor, Elton John, Pink Floyd, and other artists had achieved this status with their dedicated core of consumers.

CHR was the largest format in 1985 in Arbitron-measured listeners with 17.74 percent of the radio market, and had the youngest core demographic, ranging from fourteen to twenty-eight, covering teens, college students, and young adults. The AC format, which included the various oldies formats in its station count, was the second largest with a 15.91 percent market share. AC played artists well established with middle-aged listeners who were the parents of the CHR audience and who bought both the new releases and back catalog in the new CD format of the artists to whom they had become attached as teens.

AOR, the third-largest pop format, was directed at suburban middle-class teens and young adults. AOR was the direct descendant of the free-form

FM stations of the 1960s and held a 10.71 percent market share in 1985. The format, however, was far more standardized than the freewheeling programming of the 1960s FM rock stations in order to meet the demands of their advertisers for playlist uniformity. The major labels also maintained promotion and marketing staffs for the country and black/urban/R&B formats. Country was fourth in 1985 with 11.19 percent, while black/urban/R&B was seventh at 9.53 percent.

Over the course of the decade, as in the previous decades, the station formats maintained the same age range, but as both artists and listeners aged, they often moved together to a station with a format and advertisements directed at their current age group. The baby boomers who were the Top 40 audience of the 1960s and 1970s grew into the AC audience of the 1980s and 1990s. They continued to support the surviving hitmakers of their youth who had matured into album sellers and concert ticket attractions. These artists had also moved on radio along with their fan base from CHR and AOR to AC and oldies, but still occasionally had CHR hits. AOR showed the greatest growth, moving into the top spot in 1995 with 14.62 percent. AC/oldies maintained the second spot and CHR dropped to fifth at 8.95 percent behind country at 13.3 percent and black/urban at 10.19 percent.

Country radio was in a world of its own, as were the country divisions of the major labels. The country audience core demo was a mid-twenties to low-thirties female, an older age than the other two major singles-oriented genres, CHR and black/urban. Country had the largest number of stations with over two thousand, but as they were more prevalent in smaller markets, the total listeners market share was half the percentage of the total number of stations. As a prime example, between 1987 and 1996, the New York City DMA didn't have a single country station. During this time, country artists rarely crossed over to CHR, although Billy Ray Cyrus's "Achy Breaky Heart" and three Shania Twain singles were the exceptions to prove this rule with top ten pop radio play. Four country artists made the *Billboard* Top 50 Pop artists chart for 1995 with Garth Brooks at number twelve, Tim McGraw at number twenty-two, John Michael Montgomery at number thirty-one, and Shania Twain at number thirty-eight.

The black/urban/R&B format differed from country with far fewer stations concentrated in larger media markets. New York had five black/urban/R&B stations in 1985, including number two and number six overall, and was number one with teens. The top black/urban/R&B artists often crossed over to CHR and AC, especially with ballads, resulting in eleven of the *Billboard* Top 50 Pop artists of 1985, fourteen in 1990, and eighteen in 1995. In 1985 only one of these was from the newly emerging rap category, which included hip hop and hip hop/soul: with Run-DMC coming in at number forty-two. In 1990 three rap artists made the Top 50 Pop list, MC Hammer at number six, Luke featuring the 2 Live Crew at number twenty-seven, and Young MC at number thirty-seven. In 1995, there were five with the Notorious B.I.G. at number nine, Montell Jordan at number sixteen, Bone Thugs-N-Harmony at number nineteen, Tupac Shakur at number twenty-nine, and Shaggy at number forty-nine.

The teens who came of age in the 1980s and 1990s were the children of parents who had grown up during the emergence of rock. They had been influenced by the social upheaval of the 1960s exemplified by Haight-Ashbury and Woodstock. The 8-track and then the cassette, combined with the spread of stereo FM radio, enabled these young baby boomers to turn from singles to album consumers. Like their parents, the teens and young adults of the 1980s and 1990s expressed their own social rebellion in the music they embraced while the record companies competed to find new artists to supply this demand. The technology at the disposal of these young consumers allowed them to isolate, duplicate, and couple their favorite songs together to play on their mobile cassette devices. Together with a saturation of single track video clips on music television channels, this teen demographic shifted its consumption focus back to single tracks.

As baby boomer consumers moved along the path from teens in the 1960s to young adults in the 1970s and then to parents in the 1980s and 1990s, more singer/songwriters with societal messages and deeper emotional context like James Taylor, Carole King, and Crosby, Stills, Nash & Young inundated CHR. Heavy metal rockers with hedonistic personas, soaring guitar solos, and driving rhythm sections fed the growth of AOR. The surviving Top 40 stars of the 1950s and 1960s became the album sellers of AC. The Motown roster of artists and the Philly Sound created by Kenneth Gamble and Leon Huff of Philadelphia International Records reflected the social advances of the civil rights movement to gain multi-format acceptance for black/urban/R&B artists. The outlaw movement led by Willie Nelson, Waylon Jennings, and Kris Kristofferson brought a more literate and sexually implicit tone to the already lyrics-oriented country format.

This clearer association of societal demographics with music formats further solidified the co-branding opportunities between advertisers and music. Manufacturers of top-selling products increasingly looked to sponsor the concert tours of the top-selling performers, as Pepsi did with Michael Jackson on the *Victory* and *Thriller* tours and Budweiser accomplished with The Rolling Stones on their *Steel Wheels Tour*.

MTV Adds Visual Context to Listening Experience

Artists' physical appearance and stage charisma, so visibly apparent in live performance, have always supplemented their music in the public's attraction to them. Artists as diverse as Bruce Springsteen, Elton John, Madonna, U2, Willie Nelson, Prince, Jimmy Buffett, Tina Turner, Pink Floyd, Dolly Parton, Talking Heads, and Garth Brooks solidified their careers through their live persona and stylistic panache reinforcing their radio success. This innate star quality has always affected both audiences and record executives. Live performances gave tremendous boosts to the careers of many artists, from Judy Garland and Bing Crosby in movies in the 1930s, through Elvis Presley in the 1950s on *The Ed Sullivan Show*, and then The Beatles in the 1960s on television, in their movies, and at their transformative Shea Stadium appearance.

Memorable moments on live television could also establish or elevate a career, including Michael Jackson's 1983 moonwalk, Tina Turner's career-resuscitating "What's Love Got to Do with It" in 1985, Whitney Houston's regal "One Moment in Time" in 1989, and Mariah Carey's career-making "Vision of Love" in 1991. In 1990 on the CMA awards show, Mary Chapin Carpenter's out-of-left-field performance of the tongue in cheek "Opening Act," which was not even on her album much less a single, clinched the transformation of her public persona from East Coast folk singer to two-time CMA female vocalist of the year.

The launch of the Warner-Amex Satellite Entertainment music cable channel venture Music Television (MTV) and subsequent video channels introduced visual impact to what had previously been the audio-only first impressions of new artists or new songs offered by radio. Now tens of thousands of viewers could simultaneously get a first look at professionally produced video clips of new artists who didn't yet merit a live booking on a televised show, rather than waiting six months or more down the road until the artist appeared on tour in their town.

John A. Lack was charged with transforming the MTV concept into a bona fide music television channel. He assembled a staff led by former radio programmer Bob Pittman, who viewed MTV as a video version of radio and organized it like an edgy, irreverent AOR station. He also selected a group of young, unknown, stylish presenters termed VJs to be the on-air face of the channel and used recording artists as guest VJs. Because the UK had entered the music video age several years earlier, there was an existing library of British rock and dance videos, so the MTV debut had a Second British Invasion feel to it. The first video played on the August 1, 1981, launch was the Buggles' "Video Killed the Radio Star," which followed an opening clip of the

Apollo 11 launch countdown and landing with Lack's voice-over proclaiming, "Ladies and Gentlemen, Rock & Roll!"[9] backed by the newly created MTV theme music as an MTV logo was superimposed over the American flag Neil Armstrong planted on the moon. Lack left MTV in 1983 in the hands of his assembled staff of cofounders.

MTV debuted an annual New Year's Eve show in Times Square in 1981 and the annual MTV Music Video Awards in 1984. By 1985, partially in response to charges of exclusionary programming that led to public criticism, MTV had altered its AOR-oriented playlist to more closely resemble a CHR format, incorporating crossover black artists like Prince, Whitney Houston, Lionel Richie, and Tina Turner. Michael Jackson was credited with breaking the MTV color barrier with "Billie Jean" in 1983. Pittman and his team, however, defended their initial programming, insisting that it had just been genre-based with the same music and racial mix as its AOR radio equivalents.

In October 1984 MTV agreed to buy Ted Turner's Cable Music Video channel for $1 million and $500,000 in advertising time buys on other Turner channels. On January 1, 1985, MTV relaunched the Turner channel as Video Hits One, soon to be condensed to the acronym VH1. Programming on VH1 had a softer sound than MTV, with a mix of AC, classic rock, and R&B/soul crossover, directed toward a twenty-eight-to-fifty-four demographic in contrast to MTV's fourteen-to-twenty-eight age target. They started with experienced New York–area radio personalities including Don Imus, then of WNBC; Frankie Crocker, program director and DJ for urban/AC WBLS; and Scott Shannon from CHR giant Z-100, along with artists Jon Bauman (Bowzer from the oldies revival group Sha Na Na), and Rita Coolidge.

In 1984 Warner-Amex decided to spin off and sell their jointly held cable channels, allowing WCI to buy Amex out of their co-owned cable subscriber system. The new programming entity was renamed MTV Networks, Inc., which also encompassed the Nickelodeon children's channel and WCI's half of the pay-TV service Showtime/The Movie Channel, which was a co-venture with cable conglomerate Viacom International. In August of 1985 Viacom agreed to the $667.5 million purchase price for the two-thirds of MTV Networks owned by Warner/Amex (the other third was publicly held) and WCI's half of Showtime/The Movie Channel. Viacom outbid an attempted management takeover by Pittman and his cohorts aided by Forstmann Little & Co. WCI then used $450 million to buy Amex out of their cable system. By then MTV had expanded to about 26 million cable subscribers, VH1 had grown from Turner's 400,000 to 8 million, and Nickelodeon had reached 25 million.

The sale of MTV was the end of the honeymoon for Pittman and his team. Much like the Time Warner merger's effect on WEA, the paternal support of WCI chairman Steve Ross was replaced by Viacom corporate financial managers. The culture changed from a music-centric independent to a buttoned-down subsidiary. Pittman and original programming head, Les Garland, left in 1986 to form a joint venture music television production company with MCA. Co-founder John Sykes also left in 1986, first for the agency business with CAA, then to Tommy Mottola's Champion Management when Mottola went to work for CBS Records, followed by a span at Chrysalis Records, and afterward to EMI Music Publishing. Eventually he returned to Viacom in 1994 as president of VH1.

Two other co-founders stayed on. Tom Freston became Viacom co-president, president/CEO of MTV, and eventually CEO of Viacom itself. He had coined the ubiquitous "I want my MTV" slogan, ran the related MTV branding campaign, and oversaw MTV's international expansion. Judy McGrath served as president/CEO of MTV Networks from 2004 through 2011. With the Viacom takeover, MTV moved away from its successive video-clip format into theme-based, music-oriented lifestyle programming including the *MTV Spring Break* week from Daytona in 1986, *Dial MTV* also in 1986, *Yo! MTV Raps* in 1988, and the *MTV Unplugged* specials in 1991. In the 1990s, MTV branched into reality shows, news programming, comedy, and game shows that did not play video clips but related to a music-centric lifestyle.

Taking It to the Streets

By 1985, teens and young adult were still the core demographic for CHR and the record companies sought artists who could appeal to their Gen X zeitgeist. The technology that helped shape this generation were the Sony Walkman with its set of miniaturized hi-fi headphones, both arcade and home video games, the family computer, and cable music channels led by MTV. The children of record-buying parents could easily plug a cassette recording component into the family home entertainment center to make copies of selected tracks. Overall, almost 50 percent of homes had cable TV and over 90 percent of US consumers still listened to the radio, especially in the car. Despite the corporate consolidation of the music industry, the remaining record men of the past and the young A&R staffers who were their eyes and ears continued to look to the street to stay in front of the music trends that were attracting young record buyers.

The street was an allegorical composite of different places where new talent debuted before the most dedicated fans and cultural trendsetters whose reactions to the music signaled a metaphorical thumbs up or thumbs down. This included the play-for-the-door circuit of small clubs that featured new artists with original material, dance clubs with D.J.s spinning records and new mix tapes, and house and block parties that featured new artists with their self-recorded tracks. There were also the showcase rooms in the major music centers like CBGB in New York, the Troubadour in Los Angeles, the Continental Club in Austin, and Nashville's Exit/In. There were also industry conventions with sponsored showcases including South by Southwest in Austin, both the New Music Seminar and the *College Music Journal* Music Marathon festival in New York, and the Midwest Music Convention in Chicago. Collectively these locations and events were the cutting edge of the latest musical trends, the street where the A&R community sought their next signings.

With smart phones and texting still in the future and email in its infancy, word-of-mouth networking spread the buzz about new artists. Growing crowds for repeat performances became the barometer in the search for the stars of the future. The next task was to fan the flame of consumer reaction into industry enthusiasm with press coverage, marketing plans, and genre/repertoire determination. In their talent quest the A&R reps received leads from and were often accompanied by a coterie of personal and professional acquaintances including music publishing creative directors, entertainment attorneys, freelance record producers, local D.J.s, music press stringers, PRO writer relations representatives, talent agents, and sometimes just superfans they knew from the neighborhood. Their collective analysis of the public reaction to the ever-overflowing pool of new talent determined who would get a multimillion dollar shot at the path to stardom.

Nonetheless, as Irving Azoff had stated in his keynote address at the 1986 NARM convention, "It's a fact that 80% of all the artists out there never recoup what is spent on their product. The other 20% are subsidizing our entire industry."[10] A&R reps seeking a better-than-average result in their signings to advance their careers needed to be confident that an artist who could consistently excite two hundred consumers in a small club would be able to also connect with twenty thousand people in an arena, and then transform that collective excitement into record sales.

Just as in previous decades, the teens and young adults of the mid-1980s were attracted to new artists closer to their age who reinvigorated the industry with next-generation appeal. Bon Jovi and Guns N' Roses epitomized the evolution of glam rock and heavy metal into anthem pop with sing-along choruses. Metallica, Megadeth, and Anthrax transmuted heavy metal into thrash. Nirvana and Soundgarden transformed the message and sound of punk rock into grunge. They all achieved tremendous commercial success without losing their musical intensity and anti-establishment leanings. R&B survived the disco era to integrate dance elements into both the pop cross-over mainstream and the emerging hip hop culture. In country music, new traditionalists George Strait, Randy Travis, and Alan Jackson led a youthful roots revival after successive waves of outlaws and urban cowboys. Alabama, Brooks & Dunn, the Judds, Vince Gill, and Reba McEntire added a more contemporary sound without deserting country for pop.

Rap Rises from Street Corner to Voice of Gen X Angst

Rap, however, stands out as perhaps the most significant new genre to emerge from and appeal to the teens and young adults of the 1980s and thereafter. Rap began as a performance art on the streets of the inner cities of the 1970s. Its D.J. and MC elements were a part of hip hop culture, which also included graffiti, break dancing, and fashion as other means of artistic expression. Street and house party DJs created dance mixes by jiggling vinyl records under a turntable stylus to produce rhythmic beats integrated through a small mixer with other tracks or live vocals.

Next came the introduction of original lyrics. MCs would recite their words in the rhythmic cadence of the beats produced by their partner D.J.s. Soon D.J.s and MCs were making tape copies of their performances and selling them to attendees and other consumers on a word-of-mouth basis. Success on the street with consumers caught the attention of record labels. The first rap record to gain national chart success was the 1979 *Rapper's Delight* by the Sugarhill Gang on Joe and Sylvia Robinson's Sugar Hill Records, based in Englewood, New Jersey. Rap developed primarily within the purview of independent record companies and soon divided into two major subgenres, East Coast centered in New York, and West Coast based in South Central Los Angeles. Other cities across the country also had rap communities, but New York and L.A. had the advantage with their proximity to the major labels.

Clive Calder's independent Jive Records was distributed through BMG via Arista but ran its own A&R and promotion departments, with recent college grad Barry Weiss, son of 1950s label Old Town Records owner Hy Weiss, on the street looking for new talent. Jive's first East Coast rap success was Whodini's 1984 album *Escape*, which became the first platinum-certified rap album. They followed with more platinum by DJ Jazzy Jeff & The Fresh Prince, acquired from Philadelphia indie Word Up Records.

In 1985 CBS Records bought into Rick Rubin and Russell Simmons' Def Jam Recordings, which had enjoyed platinum chart success with LL Cool J, Run-DMC, and the Beastie Boys, who were an all-white rap group. Def Jam had insinuated rap into the MTV rotation and CHR chart with high-quality singles and infectious music videos. Run-DMC climbed the pop chart with the 1986 US number one and international top-ten cover of Aerosmith's "Walk This Way." The Boston rockers guested on the recording and in the video. The Beastie Boys exploded into teen pop culture in 1987 with the diamond-certified *Licensed to Ill* album and its CHR number seven single *(You Gotta) Fight for Your Right (To Party!)*.

Meanwhile, West Coast rap developed organically on the street level in the Compton neighborhood of South Central L.A., focused around a more polit-icized and profane style that became known as gangsta rap. Alonzo Williams formed the World Class Wreckin' Cru, which included Dr. Dre and DJ Yella, operating from a studio behind his Eve After Dark night club. Shortly there-after, drug dealer and rapper Eazy-E formed Ruthless Records with music management veteran Jerry Heller and distribution by indie Priority Records. Eazy-E recruited Dr. Dre, Ice Cube, DJ Yella, The D.O.C., DJ Ren, and the Arabian Prince to join him in creating the N.W.A. (N****z Wit Attitudes) album *Straight Outta Compton* with its controversial tracks "F**k tha Police," "Gangsta Gangsta," "Parental Discretion Iz Advised," and "Express Yourself."

The album's explicit lyrics, drug references, radical political tone, and gen-erous use of the N-word made it a sensation. *Rolling Stone* gave it a five-star review and the RIAA insisted on a newly introduced lyric content warning label, both of which Ruthless and Priority gladly embraced as marketing tools. *Straight Outta Compton* went on to sell over 3 million units and positioned gangsta rap as a dominant cultural force throughout the 1990s and beyond. Priority reported that over 80 percent of gangsta rap album sales were made to suburban outlets, demonstrating the penetration rap had achieved into the predominantly white, middle-class teenage audience.

WMG's Atlantic Records noticed the success that BMG and Sony were having with the CHR listeners also embracing this mushrooming music genre. Atlantic head Doug Morris invested $10 million into Ted Field's and Jimmy Iovine's Interscope Records. A scion of the Field Department Store family turned movie producer and now record company owner, Field insisted Interscope would be a label run by record men. In 1991, they released Marky Mark and the Funky Bunch's *Music for the People*, which included the number one single "Good Vibrations," and Tupac Shakur's debut album *2Pacalypse*

Now. In 1992 Interscope made a $10 million deal of their own by financing Death Row Records, bringing them Dr. Dre's *The Chronic* and Snoop Doggy Dogg's *Doggystyle* albums. Interscope's baby boomer A&R team led by Field, Iovine, Tom Whalley, and John McClain noticed that many white suburban teenagers and young adults embraced new forms of alternative rock as well as rap. They signed Nine Inch Nails, No Doubt, Bush, and Marilyn Manson. These signings combined with Interscope's rap roster made the label one of the hottest in the business.

Interscope's fellow WMG division Geffen Records shifted to MCA in 1990, bringing with it Guns N' Roses, Tesla, Sonic Youth, and the rejuvenated Aerosmith. The label was in lockstep with Interscope in recognizing the mass appeal of alternative rock to the teenage and young-adult demographic. Geffen's equally street savvy A&R team of Ed Rosenblatt, Gary Gersh, John David Kalodner, and Tom Zutaut, created a second imprint label, DGC Records, to focus on more progressive subgenres. Gersh found multiplatinum success for DGC with the grunge band Nirvana, led by vocalist/guitarist Kurt Cobain. The band's 1991 *Nevermind* album included the hypnotic single "Smells Like Teen Spirit" accompanied by its transcendental video clip featuring the band in a simulated basement club playing to a crowd of teens ranging from stoners to cheerleaders all freaking out together. The charismatic but shy Cobain became the rock idol counterpart to rapper Tupac Shakur in the musical expression of the emotional angst and social rebellion of Gen X, parallel to the "Sex, Drugs and Rock & Roll" attitude of their parents' baby boomer generation.

Following in the steps of Elvis, Jimi Hendrix, Janis Joplin, Brian Jones of The Stones, Jim Morrison of the Doors, and John Bonham of Led Zeppelin, both Cobain and Shakur flamed brightly and died prematurely. Cobain committed suicide in Seattle at age twenty-seven in 1994 with only three Nirvana studio albums ever released. Shakur was gunned down in Las Vegas at age twenty-five in 1996 in a suspected gang-related or even East Coast/West Coast rap rivalry shooting, with only four albums released prior to his death.

As a genre rooted in live performance, clothing style, lyrical storytelling, and social impact, rap was ideal for music video. In 1987, MTV expanded its programming of the burgeoning genre by launching its *Yo! MTV Raps* on MTV Europe and in 1988 in the US. Its acceptance by the record industry as a new genre rather than just a fad was further evidenced in 1988 when the Recording Academy added a Best Rap Performance category to its Grammy Awards for 1989. The first statuette went to "Parents Just Don't Understand" by DJ Jazzy Jeff & The Fresh Prince, which reached number twelve on the *Billboard* Hot 100, over other nominees J.J. Fad, Kool Moe Dee, LL Cool J, and

Salt-N-Pepa. In 1990 the award went to "Bust a Move," which reached number seven on the Hot 100, by Young MC, over De La Soul, DJ Jazzy Jeff & The Fresh Prince, Public Enemy, and Tone Loc.

In 1991 the Academy divided the rap category into separate awards for solo artist and for group, giving the Grammy to MC Hammer for solo and to Quincy Jones, Big Daddy Kane, Ice-T, Tevin Campbell, Kool Moe Dee, and Melle Mel & Quincy Jones III for their work as a group on the multiple-Grammy-winning album *Back on the Block*. In 1992 the awards went to LL Cool J for solo and DJ Jazzy Jeff & The Fresh Prince for group, in 1993 to Sir Mix-a-Lot and Arrested Development, in 1994 to Dr. Dre and Digable Planets, and in 1995 to Queen Latifah and Salt-N-Pepa.

Explicit Lyrics vs. Free Speech = Parental Advisory Stickers

While rap was gaining acceptance from the record industry on the corporate level and from consumers at retail, it was also gaining the attention of the Parents Music Resource Center (PMRC) and its explicit lyrics sticker. In 1985 Tipper Gore, wife of then-Tennessee Senator Al Gore, had organized the PMRC with three other Washington Wives, as they were called in the press, that eventually grew to a total of twenty-two.

The catalyst was a lyric from Prince's track "Darling Nikki" on the *Purple Rain* album, which referred to masturbation and was included in a list the PMRC dubbed the Filthy Fifteen. The list also included Madonna's "Dress You Up," Sheena Easton's "Sugar Walls," and Cyndi Lauper's "She Bop," as well as tracks by Def Leppard, AC/DC, Judas Priest, Mötley Crüe, Black Sabbath, and Twisted Sister. The PMRC called for a lyrics rating system, akin to what the Motion Picture Association of America (MPAA) applied to movies, with categories X for profane or sexually explicit lyrics, O for occult references, D/A for lyrics about drugs and alcohol, and V for violent content.

In August 1985, the RIAA compromised with the PMRC to affix a *Parental Guidance: Explicit Lyrics* label on albums designated by the RIAA to qualify for the explicit lyric categorization. The US Senate, however, had already agreed to hold a hearing. It began on September 19, with testimony from members of the PMRC, Senator Gore, and consumer advocate Senator Paula Hawkins of Florida all supporting labeling. Artists Dee Snider of Twisted Sister, Frank Zappa, and John Denver denounced labeling as censorship and anti–free speech, expressing concern that some retail outlets wouldn't carry stickered albums.

On November 1 in the midst of the hearing, the RIAA introduced Parental Advisory labels for a few selected albums that stated "WARNING: Tone of this record unsuitable for minors." The artists' fear of exclusion from the bins came true as family-oriented Walmart, Sears, and J.C. Penney would not stock the stickered albums. But other outlets where teenagers were more likely to shop carried them. Filthy Fifteen designee Mötley Crüe's lead singer, Vince Neil, commented, "Once you put that sticker on, that parental-warning sticker, that album took off. Those kids wanted it even more."[11] Jon Wiederhorn of MTV News concurred in 2002, adding, "Ever since 'explicit lyrics' warning stickers were introduced in 1985, artists have been only too happy to have their albums labeled, figuring kids who want graphic material will see the sticker as incentive to buy the disc."[12]

The PMRC accepted its partial victory and reduced its profile but reignited the crusade in October 1987 at a symposium in Washington, D.C. Then-current surgeon general, Dr. C. Everett Koop, warned that what they considered explicit sexual and violent imagery might lead to substance and alcohol abuse, Satanism, or even suicide. Dr. Koop said many videos "are a combination of senseless violence and senseless pornography to the beat of rock music."[13] MTV senior VP Marshall Cohen replied that MTV already had stringent standards in place. "Rock-and-roll has always been somewhat rebellious and on the edge, [but] if they make it through [our] standards, they should be on MTV."[14]

Tipper Gore rejoined the conversation at a meeting in February 1988 organized by Irving Azoff, Norman Lear, and Don Henley with a group of potential Hollywood supporters for her husband's pending presidential campaign. This time she also targeted music videos, but with a somewhat modified stance. Her then-new book, *Raising PG Kids in an X-Rated Society*, discussed the negative influence of music videos and television programming on children, especially from heavy metal videos. While she maintained that the proposed ratings system for records had been mistaken as a call for censorship, she still wanted some sort of system to minimize children's exposure to these videos. Gold Mountain Records president Danny Goldberg, who had attended the meeting told *The New York Times*, "The Gores sought to put the most moderate and benign face on her activities, but it didn't sway anybody. . . . Their attempt to scare the living daylights out of parents has reached a dead end."[15]

In 1990, the now-standard black-and-white warning label design reading "Parental Advisory: Explicit Lyrics" was introduced by the RIAA to replace the previously released label and placed on the bottom-righthand section of the album cover. The first album to bear this new identifier was the 2 Live Crew's 1990 *Banned in the USA*. By May 1992, approximately 225 records had been labeled and the sticker appeared to be standard packaging for gangsta rap albums. Other than keeping product out of Walmart and other family-oriented stores, the sticker's effect seemed minimal as ninety-four rap albums were certified platinum or multi-platinum between 1985 and 1995.

Consumer Spending on Music and Technology

Advances in both computer hardware and software technology between 1985 and 1995 enabled the music business, like much of American industry, to better measure and collate statistics on consumer behavior at a decreased cost, and hence to better manage its data and finances. Mainframes with multiple terminals had given way to networked PCs or Macs. The SoundScan system implemented by *Billboard* for tracking real sales by totaling bar code scans enabled both labels and retail outlets to manage inventory more efficiently and profitably. The Broadcast Data System (BDS) introduced in 1992 for tracking airplay modernized radio promotion. Arbitron followed suit with improved measurement of radio audiences. Ticketmaster had taken over the concert ticket business with a superior computer program as consumers accepted the convenience fee surcharges as a time saver and surety about both tickets and specific seats.

Although SoundScan tabulations had been available for several years, in 1995 the RIAA still used their member labels' shipment totals as the industry's retail revenue value. They also employed Chilton Research Services to compile other metrics for their annual *Consumer Profile Report* with a stated "+ /-1.7% at a 95% confidence level."[16] The 1995 report noted that 52 percent of consumers preferred to purchase records at either chain or local record stores, and 28.2 percent favored larger outlets with discounted prices for a total of 80.2 percent of the public preferring some form of retail outlet. Additionally, 14.3 percent favored record clubs and 4 percent were partial to some other form of mail order including informercials selling customized compilations.

The report further revealed that rock was the most popular genre with 33.5 percent of the surveyed consumers, country came in at 16.7 percent, R&B scored with 11.3 percent, pop had 10.1 percent, rap was at 6.7 percent, and then gospel with 3.1 percent, jazz at 3 percent, classical with 2.9 percent, and oldies at 1 percent. The remaining 9.1% included soundtracks, new age, children's, and other unspecified genres, all of which were under1 percent each.

The report also cited 1.11 billion units shipped in 1995, with $12.32 billion reported as gross retail revenue. These statistics were also broken down by age

CONSUMER SPENDING ON MUSIC IN 1995

In 1995 data collection, collation, and analysis was just beginning, but there were sufficient statistics and evidence to estimate music-related consumer spending.

CDs had supplanted vinyl discs for at-home, on-demand listening while also offering improved audio quality in the car, but at twice the price of either cassette or LP.

Most publishers had delegated print rights to distributors for an average royalty rate of about 15% of the retail price. The NMPA estimated yearly print royalties at $335 million in 1992-93, calculating to $2.2 billion in retail sales at that rate.

Another study cited $3.2 billion in yearly print purchases covering all genres and markets. The chart below averages the two studies at $2.7 billion for 1995.

Pollstar reported 1995 major concerts at $950 million. Smaller venues including fairs, nightclubs, dance halls, and music theaters took in a similar amount. Taxes, handling, and processing costs accounted for another 20%, then another 20% for concessions and parking, and 15% more for artist merchandise, are all grouped together in the chart as "Other Costs".

Ticket aggregators and scalpers cost consumers an estimated 50% above ticket prices for major concert tickets bought through the secondary ticketing market.

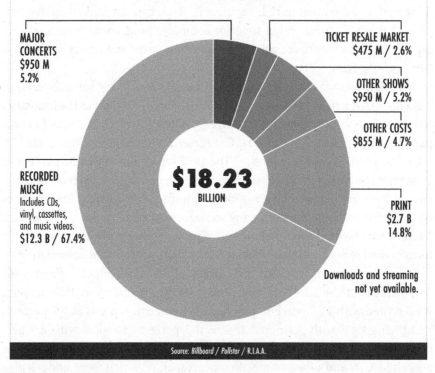

MAJOR CONCERTS $950 M 5.2%

TICKET RESALE MARKET $475 M / 2.6%

OTHER SHOWS $950 M / 5.2%

OTHER COSTS $855 M / 4.7%

RECORDED MUSIC Includes CDs, vinyl, cassettes, and music videos. $12.3 B / 67.4%

$18.23 BILLION

PRINT $2.7 B 14.8%

Downloads and streaming not yet available.

Source: *Billboard / Pollstar / R.I.A.A.*

Illustration 5.1 Consumer Spending on Music in 1995

demographics into five-year groupings, except for the 45+ demo, which had no age cap. The age group with the largest percentage of sales was fifteen to nineteen at 17.1 percent, followed by ages forty-five+ with 16.1 percent, ages twenty to twenty-four with 15.3 percent, ages twenty-five to twenty-nine at 12.3 percent, ages thirty to thirty-four with 12.1 percent, ages thirty-five to thirty-nine at 10.8 percent, ages ten to fourteen with 8 percent, and ages forty to forty-four at 7.5 percent.

The pre-teen, teen, and young adult demos together covering ages ten to twenty-nine, who were the primary target of record label marketing as well as the prime listenership of CHR radio programming, represented a consolidated 52.7 percent of total buyers. The baby boomer generation born between 1946 and 1965 were aged thirty to forty-nine in 1995. Added together, the 1950s Teens, born prior to 1946, and all seniors over age sixty-five accounted for 47.3 percent.

Pollstar-tracked concert ticket spending increased from about $600 million in 1985 to $1.1 billion in 1995. The national median income more than doubled from $22,259 in 1985 to $45,770 in 1995. The population increased by 10.8 percent from 240 million to 266 million. The GNP rose 34 percent from $7.59 trillion to $10.18 trillion. All were signs of a booming economy.

The traditional forms of home entertainment in 1995 were television and radio. Both remained above 90 percent market penetration, with an average of 5.3 radios and 2.3 televisions per household. Cable television rose · from 35.4 million subscribers in 1985 to 60.9 million in 1995, a 63.4 percent market penetration. Eighty-one percent of households in 1995 had videotape players and/or recorders, and consumers spend $7.4 billion on home video purchases, up from $3.3 billion in 1985. They spent another $2.4 billion on video rental, $708 million more on blank video cassettes, and $2.82 billion on video equipment. Consumers also spent $6.15 billion on home and mobile audio equipment.

The movie theater box office had grown to $5.49 billion in 1995, a 47 percent increase over 1985, and the video gaming business more than doubled to $10.82 billion. In summary, consumers had more money and were spending more on all forms of entertainment from 1993 forward until 9/11, as these years were the longest period of sustained economic growth in American history. The economic boom had kept all boats afloat on a rising monetary tide bolstered by technological advances in both hardware and software.

The introduction of the Apple Macintosh in 1984 and the Windows 1.0 operating system in 1985 had ignited the growth of computer use and sales in both business and homes. The Internet Protocol was universally adopted in

1990 and the World Wide Web went online in 1992, opening the information superhighway with commercial exploitation restrictions eliminated in the fall of 1994. By 1995, almost a quarter of US households had computers, with about one-eighth of them laptops. Memory was generally limited to eight megabytes without external storage. Only about half of those computer owners were connected to the internet with email as their primary use, and about one in five surfed the web. Access was almost strictly telephone dial-up.

CompuServe, AOL, and Prodigy had emerged as the major providers and Netscape Navigator as the primary browser. American industry, including the record business, realized that e-commerce was inevitable and embraced that possibility. In 1995 home personal computer prices ranged from $1,600 and up depending on capacity of hard drive, amount of memory, monitor size, and whether it had a Pentium processor and/or CD-ROM drive. Packard Bell Electronics, Compaq Computer, Apple, Gateway, IBM, and Hewlett-Packard were the leading manufacturers. All were offering the new Windows 95 operating system, except for Apple, which had its own proprietary macOS operating system.

Following the 1985 introduction of NES's Nintendo third-generation home console, the video game business revitalized as it gradually transformed from an arcade to a home consumption base. It was further bolstered by the introduction in 1993 of fifth-generation video games using 32-bit, 64-bit, and 3D technology led by the Sony PlayStation, the Nintendo 64, and the Sega Saturn. With 43 percent of households in 1995 having video games and 24 percent with computers, the children of families with disposable income had become quite dexterous in navigating digital technology.

With the growth in consumer spending on recorded music, live music, video games, and computers as the internet was opened for commercial exploitation, the initial response of the music business, as with most businesses engaged in selling products to the public, was to apply the new technology to both communication and enhancement of established sales methodology. Domain names were registered, web pages were designed, email addresses assigned, and encrypted payment programs developed. Use of the internet was also quickly integrated into the existing direct-mail and advertising methods already employed, as well as serving an adjunct to the kiosks and terminal outlets in retail establishments for the ticketing business.

The same was true for the radio industry seeking both additional listeners and outlets other than terrestrial broadcast for their signals. The first live multicast concert on the internet by a major act was The Rolling Stones from the Dallas Cotton Bowl in November 1994. Also in November, WXYC-FM, the college station of the University of North Carolina in Chapel Hill, became the first radio station to transmit music on the internet in simulcast with its terrestrial signal. In November 1995, Minneapolis radio personality Scott Bourne launched the first internet radio station, NetRadio, streaming its music via RealAudio 1.0, developed by RealNetworks, which had been founded in 1994 by former Microsoft executive Rob Glaser. Bourne sold online banner advertising, reached listeners as far as Australia, and obtained the first PRO internet license from ASCAP.

A Disruptive Innovation in the Making

In 1995 Harvard professor Clayton M. Christensen and his colleague Joseph Bower published an article in the *Harvard Business Journal (HBJ)* titled "Disruptive Technologies: Catching the Wave." In a summary for the *HBJ* website they wrote, "One of the most consistent patterns in business is the failure of leading companies to stay at the top of their industries when technologies or markets change. Why is it that established companies invest aggressively—and successfully—in the technologies necessary to retain their current customers but then fail to make the technological investments that customers of the future will demand?"[17] Christensen went on to expound upon this theory of disruptive innovation in his 1997 book *The Innovator's Dilemma*, hailed by both *Forbes* and *The Economist* as one of most influential business theories of the past fifty years.

In hindsight, the rollout of the MP3 looked like a textbook example of Christensen's hypothesis. Both the industry and its core fourteen to twenty-nine age demographic were ready for a new digital sound carrier and the MP3 appeared to be right for that role. The industry, however, tried to squash digital downloading and develop next-generation physical discs for retail sales instead, investing in the technology of the past rather than that of the future.

The genesis of the MP3 occurred in 1982. Seeking a way to transmit music over digital connections of suitable quality for use in personal computer operating systems, German electrical engineering doctoral student Karlheinz Brandenburg and his colleagues separated digital sound into three sections, or layers, which could be preserved or discarded according to their importance to the overall sound. This allowed reduction in file size, referred to as compression, by eliminating sounds obscured by a sound more important to the listener's perception, a psycho-acoustic phenomenon known as auditory masking. This process produced smaller compressed files that retained an acceptable level of the sonic quality of the original file for listening over headphones or small speakers with a limited dynamic range.

The Motion Picture Experts Group (MPEG) was formed in 1988 to develop worldwide standards in digital audio recording under the auspices of two long-established engineering bodies, the International Electronical Commission (IEC), which had begun in 1906 to set standards for units of measurement; and the International Organization for Standardization (ISO), a United Nations–sanctioned standard-setting organization founded in 1947. MPEG adopted Brandenburg's work for which he subsequently received his PhD. His thesis outlined and quantified Layers I, II, and III, with III producing the highest quality at low-bit rates. "Bit" is an abbreviated term for binary digit, which is defined in the Internet Protocol as the smallest unit of measurement used to quantify computer data containing a single binary value of 0. According to techterms.com, a byte comprises eight bits.

MPEG-1 Audio Layer III—dubbed MP3—was finalized in 1991. Brandenburg then went to work for the German research organization The Fraunhofer Society, which released the first software MP3 encoder called L3enc in July 1994. In September 1995, they established the file extension .mp3. They subsequently released the first real-time MP3 player, dubbed the Fraunhofer WinPlay3, a proprietary freeware to play MP3 files on personal computers with the then-existent Windows 3.0 or the new Windows 95 operating systems.

In 1995, teenagers and young adults were still the core demo targeted by the record business, MTV, and the CHR and AOR radio formats. They bought over 50 percent of recorded music and had watched MTV with its 60 percent penetration of American households since their teens. Only 8.1 percent of record sales were singles while over 90 percent of product sold was in the various album configurations, with over 75 percent in the CD format. The record industry had made a concerted effort to decrease consumer availability of singles as they were far less profitable than albums. This general unavailability of singles made it difficult, if not impossible, to buy audio copies of a popular video clip or track in regular radio rotation without buying the entire album, a $10 to $18 proposition depending on where one shopped.

This age group, however, was experienced in making copies from LP or CD tracks on cassette recorders interfaced with home audio systems or on dual reel cassette players. This home duplication process also allowed them to bunch together tracks from different albums onto one cassette, enabling them to create their own playlists for listening on their Walkman. Headphones or headsets had become the standard listening experience for this generation.

These conditions combined with the introduction of the freeware MP3 player technology to sow the seeds for the market disruption to come.

The record industry, however, was comfortably ensconced in year eleven of what would be a fifteen-year term of constant income growth buoyed by the period of greatest economic expansion in American history. Their answer to problems related to market fluctuations was to raise prices while they searched to create some form of copy code protection for the over fifteen-year-old CD technology. Over the preceding four decades, the record industry had given consumers a new sound carrier technology virtually every decade with improved audio quality, increased functionality, and/or extended portability. From shellac to vinyl to 8-track to cassette to CD, the industry had progressively enhanced the consumer listening experience. In the first half of the 1990s, however, the record industry seemed to have neither plan for nor knowledge of the digital file technology under development, a more than suitable successor to the innovations of the past.

A perfect storm was brewing within a young generation of consumers whose computer skills were further developed through video gaming than their parents, much less the upper echelons of the record business. These young consumers next transferred their skill set to email and web surfing. Over the impending decade, the barely birthed theory of disruptive technology was about to be substantiated in real time when downloading and file sharing were added to the arsenal of computer skills accumulated by what would be termed the millennial generation.

Early in the development of the MP3, an English entrepreneur, after contemplating the possible effects of Brandenburg's work, asked him if he knew that the MP3 would destroy the record business. He had no answer as his work had been intended to enhance the music industry, not to harm it. If the MP3 was indeed a disruptive technology, it was because the record companies kept investing resources in trying to maintain the CD as an album-only physical format sold through the existing retail supply chain, ignoring the growing demand from their core customer base for convenient access to single tracks via digital transmission. Combined with their fixation on copying restrictions for digital files while no such device, mechanism, or process was in place for the existing physical sound carriers put them totally out of sync with the consumption habits of their most sought-after customer demographic.

While the MP3 didn't destroy the record business or cause what damage did occur on its own, it became the symbol for the disruptive role that digital technology played in reordering the industry's business, financial, and distribution structure as well as altered its relationship with its consumer base of the future. Revenue streams and power centers shifted to those who could better read the street, now a digital highway with data traveling at not quite the speed of light, but definitely way faster than the speed of sound. Meanwhile consumers still listened to and spent money on music, but their habits and choices would be increasingly directed by forces outside of the established hierarchy of the music business.

PART TWO
1996–2006

6

From Big Six to Big Four

The Six Major Labels Circa 1996

As of the beginning of 1996, ownership at five of the Big Six majors' label groups had changed since 1985, with both MCA and BMG doing so twice. Together the six sold 78.8 percent of the SoundScan-tabulated 1996 retail sales. The other 21.2 percent was sold by independent labels, which if grouped collectively as a seventh listing, would have ranked first, just .1 percent ahead of WMG. On the year-end *Billboard* Top 200 album chart, however, the independents had only five of the top 100 artists, putting them behind all of the majors. This disparity between sales and charts reflected the power of the Big Six's marketing and promotional budgets in maximizing both artists' sales and airplay.

WMG was the leader by far in SoundScan market share with 21.1 percent, compared to second-place Sony with 14.7 percent. In *Billboard*'s Top 100 artists WMG had twenty-seven, with MCA next at eighteen. The veteran record men who had built and sustained WMG were all gone except for Ahmet Ertegun, who remained as chairman emeritus as well as a major shareholder. As of the beginning of 1996, supervision of the entire record group had just passed into the hands of Warner film division co-heads Terry Semel and Bob Daly, neither of whom had experience in the music business, but were still reaping the benefits of the ousted Doug Morris's regime.

Sony ranked second among the Big Six in SoundScan sales with a 14.7 percent share, third on the Top 100 chart with sixteen, and was the second-largest international distributor. Tommy Mottola was firmly ensconced as president and CEO worldwide. Under his watch Sony had developed Celine Dion, Michael Bolton, the Backstreet Boys, and Mariah Carey into multi-platinum status, while sustaining the success of established stars Michael Jackson, Bruce Springsteen, Barbra Streisand, and Billy Joel.

Polygram had 13.1 percent of SoundScan sales for third place but was fifth on the *Billboard* album artist list with thirteen. Their ownership change occurred when Philips bought out its longtime partner Siemens. Under worldwide CEO Alain Levy, PolyGram was the number one international

American Popular Music and Its Business in the Digital Age. Rick Sanjek, Oxford University Press. © Frederick Sanjek 2024.
DOI: 10.1093/oso/9780190653828.003.0006

MAJOR LABEL GROUP LEADERSHIP 1996-2006

THE "BIG SIX" 1996-1999

MCA	POLYGRAM	EMI	WMG	SONY	BMG
Doug Morris 1996-1999	Alain Levy 1996-1999	Charles Koppelman 1996-1997 ... Ken Berry 1997-1999	Bob Daly & Terry Semel 1996-1999	Tommy Mottola 1996-1999	Michael Dornemann 1996-1999

CORPORATE OWNERSHIP / HEADQUARTERS / LEADERSHIP

| SEAGRAM Canada Edgar Bronfman, Jr. 1996-1999 | PHILIPS N.V. Holland Cor Boonstra 1997-1999 | EMI GROUP PLC U.K. Colin Southgate 1996-1999 | TIME WARNER USA Gerald Levin 1996-1999 | SONY Japan Norio Ohga 1996-1998 ... Akio Morita 1998-1999 | BERTELSMANN Germany Mark Wössner 1996-1998 |

THE "BIG FIVE" 1999-2004

UMG	EMI	WMG	SONY	BMG
Doug Morris 1999-2004	Ken Berry 1999-2001 ... Alain Levy 2001-2004	Roger Ames 1999-2004 ... Lyor Cohen 2004	Tommy Mottola 1999-2003 ... Andy Lack 2003-2004	Michael Dornemann 1999-2001 ... Rolf Schmidt-Holtz 2001-2004

CORPORATE OWNERSHIP / HEADQUARTERS / LEADERSHIP

UMG	EMI	WMG	SONY	BMG
SEAGRAM Canada 1999-2000 Edgar Bronfman, Jr. VIVENDI UNIVERSAL France Jean-Marie Messier 2000-2002 ... Jean-René Fourtou 2002-2004	EMI GROUP PLC UK 1999-2004 Colin Southgate 1999-2001 ... Eric Nicoli 2001-2004	TIME WARNER USA 1999-2001 AOL TIME WARNER 2001-2003 TIME WARNER 2003-2004 Gerald Levin 1999-2002 ... Richard Parsons 2002-2004	SONY CORP Japan Norio Ohga 1999 ... Akio Morita 1999-2004	BERTELSMANN MUSIC GROUP Germany Thomas Middelhoff 1998-2002 ... Gunter Thielen 2002-2004

THE "BIG FOUR" 2004-2006

UMG	EMI	WMG	Sony BMG
Doug Morris 2004-2006	Alain Levy 2004-2006	Lyor Cohen 2004-2006	Rolf Schmidt-Holtz 2004-2006

CORPORATE OWNERSHIP / HEADQUARTERS / LEADERSHIP

UMG	EMI	WMG	Sony BMG
UNIVERSAL VIVENDI France Jean-René Fourtou 2004-2006	EMI GROUP PLC UK Eric Nicoli 2004-2006	WARNER MUSIC GROUP USA Edgar Bronfman, Jr. 2004-2006	SONY/BERTELSMANN J-V Japan / Germany Sir Howard Stringer 2004-2006

Source: *Billboard*

Illustration 6.1 The "Big Six" Leadership, 1996–2006

distribution system. Levy delegated responsibility for the US to his label heads while he focused on the international side, as well as expanding PolyGram's film interests.

German-owned BMG, fourth in both SoundScan sales with 10.7 percent and in the Top 100 album artist listing with fourteen, continued to ride Clive Davis's decade-long run of success at Arista while the other BMG labels under recently appointed Strauss Zelnick floundered in comparison. Davis's contribution was most evident with Arista being named *Billboard*'s top singles label for the year with eighteen charted singles of its own and another twenty-eight from its distributed LaFace, Bad Boy, and Jive imprints. RCA Nashville, with Joe Galante back in charge after his five-year hiatus in New York, continued to flourish in the country format.

MCA, which had just been acquired by Seagram from Matsushita in mid-1995, had the greatest disparity between sales market share and chart artists. It was in second place on the Hot 100 chart with eighteen artists, but fifth in sales at 10.6 percent. MCA had been mired in last or next-to-last place in sales among the Big Six since 1993. Bronfman hoped Morris would work the same magic with MCA that he had performed building Atlantic Records into the number one label and then WMG into the number one label group. Just one year into his new role at the end of 1996, Morris's presence was reflected in the year's performance on the singles charts, but not long enough to yet affect overall SoundScan album sales.

EMI, the only one of the Big Six not to change ownership, registered in last place in both the Top 100 with seven artists in the rankings, and in SoundScan sales at 8.7 percent. At the start of 1996, the entire US record group, including Virgin Records and Capitol Records, was still in the hands of Charles Koppelman under the watchful eye of worldwide EMI Music chairman Jim Fifield. EMI had alternated between last and next-to-last in both SoundScan and chart share for much of the 1990s, despite the massive success of Garth Brooks and the longevity of The Beatles catalog.

Successful Big Six executives had become commodities in their own right, often with competing bids for their services when their contracts were up. They used the same entertainment attorneys who represented the top artists to negotiate their employment contracts, which included bonuses, incentives, expenses, and other perks. The game of musical thrones had intensified for all involved.

Other than the label ownership and leadership changes, the most noticeable change over the decade was the emergence of the CD as the sound carrier of consumer choice growing to 72.5 percent of shipments. Album unit sales had almost doubled, while RIAA revenue value from shipments had almost tripled from $4.64 billion in 1985 to $12.32 billion in 1995. This discrepancy in units and revenue was created by the rise in average album price. The combined average of CDs, cassettes, and LPs went from $7.71 in 1985 to $11.73 in 1995 due to the higher priced CDs. The price for new CDs by the top-charting artists had suggested retail list prices (SRLP) as high as $19.99. The average sales price from the RIAA year-end report, however, for all sales combined, including majors and independents, million-sellers, back catalog, budget line, non-charting artists, niche genres, and record club sales averaged $12.97.

Bronfman and Morris Reshape MCA

Doug Morris, just turned fifty-seven when he took over at MCA, had started as a songwriter with the Chiffons' "Sweet Talkin' Guy" in 1966 but soon moved into label management with Laurie Records. He then opened the Atlantic-distributed Big Tree Records with partner Dick Vanderbilt in 1970. After success with Lobo, England Dan & John Ford Coley, Brownsville Station, Johnny Rivers, April Wine, and Hot Chocolate, they sold Big Tree to Atlantic in 1978 and Morris joined the Atlantic executive team as an understudy to and eventually cochairman with founder Ahmet Ertegun. In 1994 he landed in the top spot of the entire music group. Like Ertegun, Morris balanced his expertise in corporate politics with his street smarts. He had wisely fused the two in bankrolling Interscope Records in 1990, which became a major component of Atlantic's success with its West Coast rap and edgy rock roster.

Upon arriving at MCA at the end of 1995, Morris found a label group that had gradually drifted into last place among the Big Six. Morris's first move was to rename the Rising Tide Records co-venture he had just formed with MCA as Universal Records, to be located in New York. He brought in longtime Atlantic and WMG associate Mel Lewinter as his label chairman and former Chrysalis, SBK, and EMI executive Daniel Glass as label president. The addition of Universal Records to the already existing MCA and Geffen/DGC labels now gave the MCA Music Entertainment Group three separately staffed, full-service record companies, much like the WMG setup.

Morris retained Los Angeles–based veteran MCA attorney Zach Horowitz as president of the record group, with oversight over international, publishing, and distribution, which he had been doing since 1986 throughout the Mitsubishi and Seagram transitions as global senior VP of business and legal affairs. Also based in Los Angeles, Jay Boberg, the incumbent president of MCA Music Publishing and former partner with Miles Copeland in

I.R.S. Records, was moved to president of MCA Records, where he immediately cleared out the A&R staff. At I.R.S., Boberg had worked with R.E.M., The Go-Go's, The Bangles, Berlin, and Fine Young Cannibals. Morris charged him with the task of developing a roster with an emphasis on alternative rock.

The country division under MCA Nashville chairman Bruce Hinton and top producer Tony Brown, however, was already one of MCA's bright spots, with a number two ranking and 17.5 percent share of country sales in 1995, coming off the number one spot in 1994 at 20.1 percent. The Nashville roster included perennial platinum artists George Strait, Reba McEntire, and Vince Gill. Morris had no changes in mind other than to open a Rising Tide country imprint.

Morris's next move was the January agreement for MCA to acquire the 50 percent of Interscope that WMG had just sold back to the label's founders Ted Field and Jimmy Iovine for $115 million. Time Warner's CEO Gerald Levin insisted that WMG disassociate itself from the explicit lyrics of Interscope's rap acts. This time Morris had corporate backing from Bronfman, who helped negotiate the purchase. Interscope got $200 million, with an option for MCA to buy the other half in five years based on performance over that period. Field and Iovine also maintained creative control over products, including lyric content. EMI and PolyGram had also made bids, but with the constant rumors that both were up for sale, combined with their longtime relationship with Morris, MCA seemed the more stable choice.

The lyrics of gangsta rap stars Snoop Doggy Dogg and Dr. Dre had garnered Interscope the most attention, due to the anti-explicit lyric advocacy led by Republican GOP presidential front-runner Bob Dole and C. Delores Tucker, civil rights activist and chair of the National Congress of Black Women. The label, however, was also strong in rock with Nine Inch Nails, No Doubt, and Bush. Just like the already-MCA-owned Geffen/DGC Records, Interscope had elevated alternative and rap artists to platinum status while transforming them into video stars through top-notch video clips and marketing campaigns. Interscope's album market share helped MCA climb from 1996's 10.6 percent to 12.1 percent by the end of 1997, but the label group then fell back to 10.5 percent, coming in last in 1998 by losing ground to both PolyGram and EMI.

By the end of 1998 Bronfman was under pressure from Seagram shareholders, both family and investors, for moving half of the company's assets from their long-held DuPont stock to the music business. Despite assembling a top A&R team, the addition of Interscope's catalog, and making the label group profitable, MCA was still in last place in Big Six market share. The entire Universal Entertainment Group parent company—including film, television, music publishing and theme parks—had generated $6.5 billion in revenues for fiscal 1997, but only yielded $242 million for a 3.7 percent profit. Meanwhile, the discarded DuPont shares had more than doubled in value.

Bronfman believed, however, that the music industry would continue to grow as it learned to harness the internet as a sales vehicle and thus was a better long-term option and far more interesting than passive interests in other industries. He decided to sell MCA's controlling share of its television assets including the USA Network to Barry Diller's HSN Inc. for $4 billion. He then went shopping for a merger partner on the supposition that consolidated back office, manufacturing, and distribution services would yield a larger profit on a larger market share. He focused on two primary targets: PolyGram and EMI. Both were more often than not in the bottom half of the Big Six in the US annual market share rankings, but both had excellent international distribution networks, the lack of which was MCA's greatest weakness.

The Thorn EMI De-Merger and Re-Structure

In February 1996 at their annual board meeting, Thorn EMI shareholders voted to divide their electronics and music divisions into separate companies. As of June, the EMI Group would continue to be listed on the London Stock Exchange with the record and publishing divisions, the HMV retail music chain, and the UK Dillon's retail book chain as its major assets. Chairman Sir Colin Southgate remained in place at the helm of each of the now-separated divisions, acknowledging that a prime responsibility would be to present any viable offer for either to its shareholders. Thorn Electronics was eventually sold in 1998 to Future Rentals, a subsidiary of Japanese financial holdings company Nomura Group. As to any potential buyer for the music group, Southgate told *Billboard*'s Jeff Clark-Meads, "As I've said many times before, they're going to have to pay maxi-, maxi-dollar."[1]

EMI had declined from 11.8 percent of SoundScan sales in 1993 to 8.2 percent in 1996, equating to a decrease of about $396 million in EMI's share of RIAA shipment value while the industry grew from $10.05 billion to $12.51 billion. This 2.6 percent drop in EMI's market share of the 1.1 billion albums shipped in 1996 represented over 26 million albums despite having Garth Brooks, Bonnie Raitt, and the Beastie Boys on Capitol; the Spice Girls who debuted in 1996, Janet Jackson, and The Rolling Stones on Virgin; and Pink Floyd outside of the US; and being bolstered by a diversified back catalog led by The Beatles. Such a decline in revenue during a period of overall industry growth usually resulted from not having enough new acts achieving sales expectations to absorb their initial marketing budgets. In EMI's case, this was compounded by managers and attorneys who were hesitant to commit their best new acts to a label perennially rumored to be for sale.

Southgate decided to shake up the management team in an attempt to bolster market share. In May 1997, Koppelman received a $50 million buyout on the remaining four years of his contract as chairman/CEO of EMI-Capitol Records Group North America. Since his entry into the business in 1960 as group member and producer of the Ivy Three's top-ten single "Yogi," Koppelman had executive tenures at both CBS Records and EMI. He also co-masterminded two of the biggest music deals of the 1980s as part of SBK's purchase of the CBS publishing catalogs, and then its subsequent sale along with SBK Records to EMI.

Ken Berry, the head of EMI Music International and ten years younger than Koppelman, took over in the newly created post of president of EMI Recorded Music, to be based in Los Angeles. Berry had started at Virgin as an accounting clerk in 1973, rose through the ranks and received a bonus of over $30 million when he negotiated the deal for Richard Branson to sell Virgin to EMI in 1992. Berry, however, came as a package deal with his even younger wife and vice chairwoman Nancy, who had started at Virgin as his secretary in 1978. She specialized in artist relations with top stars and was dubbed the "Platinum Amex woman"[2] by Mick Jagger for her lavish use of the company credit card. The British tabloids referred to her as the Queen of Rock and Roll. Despite gossip about her personal relationships with artists, she was actually the top A&R person at Virgin for sixteen years, and was instrumental in signing The Stones, George Michael, Janet Jackson, and the Spice Girls.

Berry shuttered the EMI America label, dismissing president Davitt Sigerson and 120 other staffers. Artists were shifted to the Virgin or Capitol labels. Berry next ousted five-year president and CEO of Virgin Records America Phil Quartararo, a marketing wiz who had developed Smashing Pumpkins, Lenny Kravitz, Paula Abdul, and Ben Harper, as well as heading the US marketing blitz for the Spice Girls. He was replaced by EMI Records UK veterans Ray Cooper and Ashley Newton as Virgin co-presidents.

Richard Cottrell, another EMI Records UK transfer, took over at EMI Music Distribution (EMD), replacing the well-respected Russ Bach, who had just supervised the restructuring of CEMA Distribution—an acronym for the Capitol, EMI, Manhattan, and Angel record labels—into the streamlined and computerized EMD. Many in the business were baffled that Berry replaced a thirty-seven-year veteran with someone who had never worked in the US, and who was self-admittedly not a music man. Tower Records/Video president Russ Solomon said, "It was a shock. For my money, Bach is one of the best managers of all."[3] Another retail chairman added, "To have someone come in who is unfamiliar with the U.S. market is a mistake. . . . Bach did a good job and I can't figure out why they fired him, other than to cut expenses."[4]

Capitol cornerstone Garth Brooks was especially concerned about the marketing of his upcoming new album *Sevens*. He postponed its release, despite his already-scheduled August Central Park show, which was designed to be a nationally televised launch party for the album. His first six releases and a greatest hits collection combined had already sold over 65 million units in the US, and he wanted assurances on the sales strategy for this new one. With prodding from Brooks and his manager, "Major Bob" Doyle, the team at Capitol Nashville was shuffled. Their main marketing contact executive VP/GM Pat Quigley replaced production veteran Scott Hendricks as president/CEO. Finally released in November, *Sevens* sold 3.3 million units by year's end, and quickly thereafter joined his six previous releases in reaching Diamond sales status.

EMI closed 1997 with 12.6 percent of SoundScan sales, up 54 percent over 1996's 8.2 percent share, or roughly $350 million in increased revenue. At the February 1998 EMI board meeting, Fifield made a play to be named as Southgate's eventual successor as chairman, but the board rejected his bid. Fifield described this to *Billboard* as a vote of no confidence. Within weeks he was gone with an $18 million buyout. Berry absorbed his responsibilities. Berry then outbid Arista for its nineteen-year veteran and Clive Davis's top lieutenant Roy Lott to become the number-two executive just under Berry himself, expanding Lott's responsibilities from just domestic oversight at Arista to worldwide command at EMI. The restructuring was termed complete as cost reduction combined with a 13 percent market share in 1998 to give the publicly traded EMI an $8 billion cap evaluation. Meanwhile Southgate was holding discussions with both Seagram and Disney for the sale of EMI but reportedly wouldn't budge below a $9 billion asking price.

PolyGram Comes into Play

Royal Philips Electronics owned 75 percent of the stock in the PolyGram N.V. record company. The other 25 percent had been sold in the 1989 and 1990 public offerings. Cor Boonstra was named chairman of Philips in October 1996, replacing the retiring Jan Timmer. He had joined the Philips board in 1994 after a twenty-year stint at the Sara Lee food company and was regarded as a marketing expert. In 1995 PolyGram had accounted for $4.7 billion of Philips worldwide revenues of $37 billion. Philips overall, however, had lost $313 million and Boonstra was charged with making the lethargic electronics behemoth profitable by reducing the workforce and disposing of the most unprofitable segments of its more than thirty divisions. Philips also announced that it would "embrace any strategic option to maximize value to shareholders" for its 75 percent stake in PolyGram.[5]

Since the acquisition flurry that brought Island, A&M, and Motown into the fold, PolyGram had consistently ranked in fourth place in market share among the Big Six in the US, and first internationally. Although ably managed and profitable under Alain Levy and his team, it had produced only a few consistent multi-platinum artists, most notably Sheryl Crow and Shania Twain, with catalog sales outperforming new releases. Boonstra's mandated cost-cutting played a role in the departure of Island Records founder Chris Blackwell from both the label and the PolyGram board. Andre Harwell departed from Motown. Both Blackwell and Harwell were replaced by less-experienced executives with less-expensive contracts.

When MCA's Edgar Bronfman was rebuffed in his pursuit of EMI, he turned his attention to PolyGram. In May 1998, Philips agreed to a combined $10.6 billion in cash for both Philips's 75 percent and the other 25 percent publicly owned shares, as well as a seat on the board for Boonstra. To help finance the deal, Bronfman had already sold more than half of Seagram's roughly 5 percent share of Time Warner stock in February for $966 million and sold the rest in May for an additional $900 million. He also sold Seagram's Tropicana juice division to Pepsico in July for another $3.3 billion. After board approval by both companies, passing both US and European regulatory muster, and acceptance by the requisite number of shareholders, the deal closed in December 1998 at $10.4 billion, adjusted for PolyGram's third-quarter downturn.

The combined record company would operate as the Universal Music Group (UMG) and have a worldwide market share of 23 percent and revenue of $6.1 billion. The US market share would be a slightly larger percentage as the MCA component was much stronger domestically than it was internationally. The need to expand the international business was a major motivator for Bronfman since two-thirds of UMG's revenue came from North America, while three-fourths of PolyGram's came from outside North America, making them a good fit.

The domestic distribution systems, label operations, and administrative functions of the formerly separate companies would be consolidated to achieve an estimated annual savings of $300 million within two years, a task Bronfman assigned to Doug Morris and his team. These income and savings projections did not include the film, television, publishing, home video, or venue divisions of the two newly merged entities. Before Morris could begin his analysis, Alain Levy, who had not been consulted by Boonstra about the deal, resigned in June. He threatened a breach of contract lawsuit and received a $10 million settlement, according to Chuck Philips and Claudia Eller of the *Los Angeles Times*. Otherwise, business at PolyGram continued as usual with personnel on all levels hoping to make a good impression and survive the coming staff reductions.

Morris's executive team included Bruce Hack, former CFO of Universal Studios and before that vice chairman at Tropicana, Zach Horowitz as president/COO, and twenty-year Sony International veteran Jorgen Larsen as chairman/CEO of Universal Music International. Morris in turn reported directly to Bronfman. "This acquisition is his vision," Morris told *Billboard*'s Don Jeffrey. "He will be involved in all major management decisions and strategy. But day to day, the four of us will run the company."[6]

By November 1999, the executive team was ready to announce the structure of the merged company. There would now be four pop/rock/R&B/rap label groups with two on each Coast. In New York, Mercury, Island, and Def Jam were combined into the Island Def Jam Music Group, to be chaired by Jim Caparro, former president/CEO of PolyGram Group Distribution, with former Def Jam president Lyor Cohen to serve as label president under Caparro. PolyGram had bought out Sony's 50 percent share of Def Jam in 1994 and another 10 percent from Def Jam founder Russell Simmons in 1996, bringing Method Man, Jay-Z, DMX, Ja Rule, Ludacris, Kanye West, and label deals with Roc-A-Fella, Murder Inc., Ruff Ryders, and Disturbing tha Peace into the PolyGram fold.

The other New York faction was the Universal Records Group, combining Universal Records, Polydor, and Motown under chairman Mel Lewinter. Jean Riggins stayed on as president of black music while senior VP of Universal Records Kedar Massenburg moved to Motown, bringing artists Erykah Badu and Chico DeBarge with him. Although a part of the label group, Motown continued to operate as a fully staffed autonomous label.

On the West Coast, MCA Records remained intact under incumbent president Jay Boberg. Interscope, Geffen, and A&M were combined as the other LA-based label group under the leadership of Interscope founders Jimmy Iovine and Ted Fields as co-chairmen, with Interscope president and WB Records A&R veteran Tom Whalley tapped to manage the entire label group. With Interscope's West Coast rap roster and distributed labels combined with Def Jam's East Coast parallel, UMG now had the best of the rap genre under its umbrella. UMG then bought out the remaining Iovine/Field half interest in Interscope for an undisclosed sum, and the outstanding Russell Simmons/ Lyor Cohen 40 percent of Def Jam for $130 million.

The Nashville operations of the two record companies remained autonomous, with incumbents Luke Lewis as chairman of Mercury Nashville, and chairman Bruce Hinton and president Tony Brown at MCA Nashville. PolyGram's Verve and Universal's GRP jazz divisions were combined under veteran producer Tommy LiPuma. In the classical field where PolyGram had been historically strong and Universal severely lacking, PolyGram Classics & Jazz veteran Chris Roberts was installed as head of Universal Classics.

The US UMG sales and distribution system continued under incumbent president Henry Droz, executive VP/GM (audio) Jim Urie, and executive VP/GM (video) Craig Kornblau, but absorbed many PolyGram field veterans. The PolyGram international distribution system was retained. UMG product sales outside of the US were transferred from former distributor BMG to its now-proprietary network, moving what was formerly BMG's handling fees to the new UMG's balance sheet.

Over two hundred recording acts were dropped, and about three thousand staffers out of an estimated fifteen thousand combined employees were terminated, including the entire A&M staff, about 80 percent of the Geffen staff, and five hundred from other UMG labels. Long-term executives with contracts were presented with buyouts and lower-level staffers with severance packages. Notable departures included chairman/CEO of Mercury Records Group Danny Goldberg, Island Records chairman Davitt Sigerson, president/CEO of Motown George Jackson, chairman/CEO of A&M Al Cafaro, and Ed Rosenblatt, longtime chairman/CEO of Geffen.

Records Sales Reach Their All-Time Peak in 1999

The year 1999 marked the first year of the Big Five and the fifteenth year of an upward growth pattern for the record industry. It ended with the newly unified UMG on top with 25.4 percent of SoundScan sales, followed by Sony with 16.3 percent, closely trailed by BMG and the independent segment both with 16.1 percent, and then WMG with 15.8 percent. Trailing in the rear was EMI at 9.5 percent.

BMG, however, led the field with 31.4 percent of platinum album sales. Jive acts the Backstreet Boys and Britney Spears led the way with 9.4 million and 8.4 million units, respectively. UMG came in second at 29.8 percent with Shania Twain their top seller at 5.8 million, followed by Limp Bizkit with 5 million. Sony was third at 23.7 percent led by 6 million units for Ricky Martin. WMG was in fourth at 12.5 percent led by Kid Rock's 4.3 million units. EMI also held up the rear in this category at only 5.3 percent, with

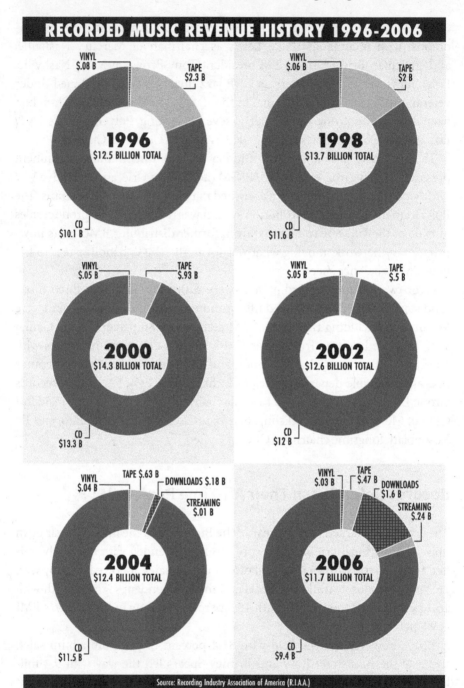

RECORDED MUSIC REVENUE HISTORY 1996-2006

1996
$12.5 BILLION TOTAL
VINYL $.08 B
TAPE $2.3 B
CD $10.1 B

1998
$13.7 BILLION TOTAL
VINYL $.06 B
TAPE $2 B
CD $11.6 B

2000
$14.3 BILLION TOTAL
VINYL $.05 B
TAPE $.93 B
CD $13.3 B

2002
$12.6 BILLION TOTAL
VINYL $.05 B
TAPE $.5 B
CD $12 B

2004
$12.4 BILLION TOTAL
VINYL $.04 B
TAPE $.63 B
DOWNLOADS $.18 B
STREAMING $.01 B
CD $11.5 B

2006
$11.7 BILLION TOTAL
VINYL $.03 B
TAPE $.47 B
DOWNLOADS $1.6 B
STREAMING $.24 B
CD $9.4 B

Source: Recording Industry Association of America (R.I.A.A.)

Illustration 6.2 Recorded Music Revenue History, 1996–2006

only five platinum and no multi-platinum albums. Indies had only two plat-inum albums, Disney's *Tarzan* soundtrack and Koch Entertainment's *Rock & Wrestling*.

By 1999 RIAA shipment values had more than tripled to $14.32 billion from 1985's $4.36 billion. RIAA-certified unit shipments had almost doubled from 617 million to 1.16 billion. The disparity in percentage between revenue expansion and unit growth was due to the almost total displacement of the LP and cassette by the much higher-priced CD as the dominant format of con-sumer choice.

WMG Prepares for the Millennium

The 1995 decision by Time Warner to disassociate itself from WMG-distributed Interscope Records may have seemed politically correct, but its cost became apparent over the next few years. In addition to losing the serv-ices of one of the top record executives of the digital age in Doug Morris, its market share of SoundScan sales fell from 21.9 percent in 1995 to15.8 percent in 1999 under the Semel-Daly regime. The attrition was even more drastic in market share on current product, which fell from 22.6 percent to 13.7 percent. Meanwhile, Interscope became the leading label for UMG while the WMG labels were failing to find enough new acts that were as productive.

In July 1999 Semel and Daly, who were the last remaining Time Warner senior executive holdovers from the Steve Ross era, announced that they were not renewing their contracts, which were due to expire at the end of the year. Although overseeing WMG for only four years, they had led the Warner film division since 1980, accumulating over $300 million each in WMG stock on top of their annual $20 million compensation packages.

They were replaced by former PolyGram president Roger Ames, who had been hired six months earlier as president of Warner Music International. Ames's appointment was applauded by the three WMG incumbent label heads, chairman/CEO and twenty-year WMG veteran Russ Thyret, and the two Doug Morris protégés Val Azzoli, co-chairman/co-CEO with Ahmet Ertegun at Atlantic, and Sylvia Rhone of Elektra. The record industry in ge-neral concurred with Island Records Founder Chris Blackwell, who had worked with Ames during his PolyGram tenure, when he opined, "He's one of the few people around who really has a grasp of the overall business structure as well as someone who can judge records and hear hits."[7]

Time Warner chairman Gerald Levin commented to *The New York Times* that it was the first time in about two decades that WMG would be led by someone from the music business, rather than a general corporate executive. While this aptly referred to Morgado, Fuchs, Semel, and Daly, it disrespectfully marginalized Doug Morris's albeit-brief tenure in that top post. This perhaps best epitomizes the disconnect between the Time corporate mindset of Levin and the modus operandi of Steve Ross, who emphasized creative decision-making without sacrificing financial accountability, a management style widely emulated throughout the music business. Despite the high regard for Ames throughout the industry, WMG remained mired in the 15 percent to 16 percent market share range though 2004, and remained consistently lower in current product.

Directly following the WMG leadership transition, in January 2000 Levin stunned the entire business community by announcing that Time Warner was merging with web portal and service provider AOL to unify their content and cable access with AOL's online presence and millions of subscribers. Implemented at the height of the dot.com investment euphoria, the move was ostensibly designed to position Time Warner as the industry leader in the transition to digital commerce. They had been searching since 1994 for a way to use the digital highway to their advantage, but the economy of scale needed to justify the costs had so far eluded them. Levin's move was hailed at the time as a transformative first marriage between old and new media. Seth Sutel of ABC News reported at the time of the announcement, "The deal marks a major turning point in the media industry, highlighting the massive power and value that Internet companies like AOL have built up in a relatively short time. . . . In combining the leading Internet company with the leading traditional media company, the deal also shows that new media and old media need each other more than ever before."[8]

At the time of the $150 billion merger announcement, AOL market capitalization was twice that of Time Warner, bolstered by investors' enthusiasm for the internet with analysts' valuations for new media companies based on multiples far in excess of those used for old media businesses. Although referred to as a merger, AOL shareholders received 55 percent of the new Time Warner AOL stock issue and Time Warner shareholders got the remaining 45 percent. AOL's Steve Case was named chairman with Levin as CEO.

Less than a month after the January 2000 Time Warner/AOL announcement, in a deal that had been in discussion since the previous summer, months before the inception of the negotiations with AOL, WMG and EMI announced that they would merge their music interests in a fifty-fifty joint venture to be called Warner EMI Music, which would have a $20 billion valuation. They proposed that WMG would pay $1.3 billion in addition to stock to be distributed to EMI shareholders.

Since this would also be a transaction between publicly traded companies—Time Warner on the New York Stock Exchange (NYSE) and EMI on the London Exchange—the merger was subject to approval by regulatory agencies in both the US and the EU. While the combined record companies would represent only 25 percent of the world record market, a few percentage points smaller than the UMG/PolyGram merger, both sets of regulators were concerned that the combined publishing interests would approach a 50 percent share of the worldwide publishing market. The EU Commission was also concerned that the combination would reduce the number of global music companies from five to four, a move they had consistently opposed since the UMG/PolyGram merger.

In October 2000, just weeks before rulings were due, the Warner/EMI merger applicants withdrew their request under the pretense that they needed more time to work on a plan that would be acceptable to both regulatory bodies. The Big Five remained intact, at least for the time being. The EU Commission then quickly approved the Time Warner/AOL merger followed by the US Federal Trade Commission. The merger was finalized on January 11, 2001. The Time Warner/AOL coupling intensified industry awareness of the potential for digital commerce and the need to devise a strategy before outside digital interlopers insinuated themselves into the market to the detriment of the established music business hierarchy.

BMG Shuffles Its Own Deck

In July 1997, forty-four-year-old Thomas Middelhoff was designated to become CEO/chairman of the board of Bertelsmann AG, parent company of BMG Entertainment, in November 1998 when fourteen-year incumbent Mark Wössner, who had chaired Bertelsmann through the RCA acquisition, reached the mandatory retirement age of sixty. Middelhoff, who had a doctorate in marketing, had joined the Bertelsmann graphics division in 1986 and joined the board of directors in 1990. An early believer in the potential of the internet, he led Bertelsmann into buying a 5 percent share of AOL and then into a 50 percent joint venture position in AOL Europe.

When Middelhoff assumed the top role, Wössner protégé Michael Dornemann was in his fifteenth year as chairman of BMG Entertainment, operating out of Bertelsmann headquarters in Germany. His hand-picked CEO of BMG North America Strauss Zelnick was in his fourth year. From 1994 through 1998, BMG fell out of the top half of the Big Six in overall SoundScan sales, but consistently placed third or current product sales. The success with current releases was due primarily to Arista under Clive Davis, which included the product released through Arista co-ventures with Antonio "L.A." Reid and Kenneth "Babyface" Edmonds's LaFace Records, and Sean "Puff Daddy" Combs's Bad Boy Records. The distribution deal with Clive Calder's Jive Records also fell under the Arista banner. From 1996 through 2000, the Arista-controlled group of labels had 70 percent of BMG's platinum and multi-platinum albums, leading BMG back into an overall second place in the now–Big Five in 1999. Dornemann pointed out that had Universal and PolyGram not merged, BMG would be in first place.

With Davis's contract due to expire in June 2000, he was looking for an extension and raise in his compensation, reported by Doreen Carvajal of *The New York Times* to have been in the range of $50 million per annum. Despite Arista's success, however, friction had grown between Davis and the Dornemann-Strauss alliance. For the past fifteen years Davis operated Arista independently, reporting directly to Dornemann, and still did so, circumventing Zelnick who was twenty-five years his junior and had only four years of experience in the music business compared to Davis's thirty-eight.

Davis was seven years past BMG's generally adhered-to age sixty retirement requirement, which became the rationale offered by Dornemann and Strauss to end contract talks with Davis. Dornemann and Strauss then initiated discussions with LaFace's Reid to replace Davis as Arista CEO. As an alternative role for Davis, they suggested a joint venture label deal with him. In May, Zelnick named Reid as Davis's successor at Arista, concurrently buying the 50 percent of LaFace not already owned by BMG for $100 million from Reid and his partner, Edmonds. At the same time, the Arista Nashville office was folded into the independently operating RCA Label Group Nashville under veteran Joe Galante with the Arista staff all terminated.

After shrewdly shopping his talents to the other majors as a negotiating chip, Davis pressured BMG to commit somewhere over $150 million to launch J Records in September as a fifty-fifty joint venture between Davis and BMG. Several developing BMG artists were transferred to J, the most significant of which turned out to be Alicia Keys. Davis also retained production duties with Arista acts Whitney Houston and Carlos Santana. Joining him at J were Arista veterans Charles Goldstuck as president/COO, Richard Palmese as senior VP of promotion, Tom Corson as senior VP of worldwide marketing, Julie Swidler as senior VP of business and legal affairs, Keith Naftaly as senior VP of A&R, Peter Edge and Hosh Gureli as VPs of A&R, and Alan Newham as senior VP of finance and administration.

Zelnick's problems didn't stop with Davis. Head of BMG International Rudi Gassner had resigned in January 2000, protesting in writing about the way both Zelnick and Dornemann were treating Davis in trying to force him out of Arista. He also criticized Zelnick's dealings with Clive Calder, founder and still 80 percent owner of Jive Records. Jive was then providing over 30 percent of BMG's market share with its R&B acts and teen idols Backstreet Boys and Britney Spears. In 1999 Calder had signed NSYNC to Jive when the band successfully sued to get out of its contract with their manager Lou Pearlman's Trans Continental Records.

Pearlman had licensed the band's first album to BMG's Ariola Records in Europe and RCA in the US. The suit with Pearlman also got the group out of its record contract, making them free agents. The band then signed directly with Jive rather than re-up with RCA, which had sold over 7 million units in the US of their first album. The group felt that Zelnick had publicly denigrated their talent on several occasions. Calder then licensed the band for international distribution to EMI and his close friend Ken Berry rather than putting them with BMG, a move designed to further distance them from Zelnick. The album sold over 15 million units worldwide earning EMI over $50 million in profit, a windfall that would have belonged to BMG had Calder licensed the international rights to them.

Meanwhile, Middelhoff, while watching the Davis-Zelnick affair play out from afar, told the Bertelsmann board that he would elevate BMG into first place in the current market while leading the industry into e-commerce. He predicted that 13 percent of content-related goods would be sold via the internet within four years, and then reach 33 percent by 2014. In June 2000, he announced that BMG's internet initiative would start with the opening of the new Bertelsmann eCommerce Group to be headed by Andreas Schmidt, former managing director of AOL Europe. He planned to shift the BMG Record Club and all new media sales initiatives from the record division to this new department.

The following month, July 2000, the RIAA's lawsuit against rogue file-sharing platform Napster, which included BMG as one of the plaintiffs, produced a ruling to shut Napster down if it couldn't comply with the suit's demand to cease the file-sharing of RIAA-members' recordings. Napster, however, received a stay allowing it to attempt to meet the labels' demands (covered more extensively in the following chapters). Then in August 2000, in his keynote speech at the German music industry convention PopKomm, Middelhoff commented on Napster's potential as a sales alternative rather than its legal shortcomings that seemingly contradicted the industry's position toward Napster: "For all the reservations we have, Napster is cool, a fantastic music brand with the following characteristics: high quality, free music; easy to use; global selection for all labels' repertoire; prompt service; and free choice. I ask you: Which one of you—and I expressly include Bertelsmann here—is able to offer music fans a comparable service?"[9]

Conflict Continues at BMG with Davis the Last Man Standing

With his query receiving no replies, on Halloween 2000 Middelhoff startled the entire industry with the announcement of an agreement with Napster, in which BMG would pull out of the industry-wide lawsuit as soon as Napster developed and implemented a subscription version that compensated copyright holders. In the deal Bertelsmann's eCommerce Group would also loan tens of millions of dollars for technology development in exchange for options on as much as 58 percent of Napster stock. The deal came without the knowledge or participation of either Zelnick or Dornemann, much less UMG, WMG, Sony, or EMI, BMG's co-plaintiffs in the litigation.

Zelnick exited within a week, claiming that he had resigned. Middelhoff immediately rehired Gassner, who would return to BMG to take Zelnick's position on January 1, 2001, and then replace Dornemann as chairman when his contract expired in June. The fifty-eight-year-old Gassner, however, suddenly died on December 23 from a heart attack while jogging. The death of the former pro soccer player and fitness buff was a huge blow to BMG, and he was mourned throughout the industry. He was immediately replaced by Rolf Schmidt-Holtz, who had been reporting directly to Middelhoff as the Bertelsmann chief creative officer.

Concurrent with his dalliance with Napster as a part of the answer to the digital riddle of the future and development of the BMG eCommerce group, Middelhoff pursued the acquisition of EMI after WMG ended its courtship but encountered the same regulatory roadblocks that had stymied WGM's attempts. In June 2001, with its court stay expired, Napster suspended operations of its platform to concentrate, with BMG's financial backing, on transition into a subscription service. By May 2002, BMG had loaned close to $100 million to Napster and agreed to a total acquisition as part of a June Napster bankruptcy filing. During this same period, Middelhoff had spent additional hundreds of millions on other music-related internet ventures that had failed to generate returns, including $100 million to online retailer CDNow and several times that in a joint venture between barnesandnoble.com and Bertelsmann European webstore BOL.com.

Then in June 2002, Clive Calder decided to exercise a put he had established when he sold the 20 percent stake of Jive to BMG in 1996. The put gave him the option to demand that BMG purchase both his 80 percent share of Jive and the 75 percent of his Zomba Music Publishing that he had retained in a separate 1992 publishing agreement. Coming off a string of incredibly profitable years for Jive, the terms of the put established the acquisition cost at about $2.8 billion. Most industry observers and analysts felt this number was way too high, but the put was on solid legal ground and would undoubtedly stand if BMG disputed it.

Calder had begun in his native South Africa in the early 1970s producing cover records of pop hits that the major labels wouldn't ship to South Africa due to the anti-apartheid boycotts. In 1975 he moved to London, along with partners Mutt Lange and Ralph Simon. Their first success came with the UK publishing rights for the Village People. Lange moved on to become a top producer and songwriter, including work with Def Leppard and Shania Twain. In 1990 Calder bought out Simon, who became a leader of the nascent mobile market and is often referred to as the Father of the Ringtone. In 2015 the *Music Revolution* blog declared the private and independent Calder "the single richest man the music business has ever produced,"[10] while *Forbes* stated his net worth at over $4 billion.

At the time of Calder's put call, Middelhoff was advocating a plan to use the share of the privately held Bertelsmann not owned by the founding Mohn family as the anchor for a public offering by 2005 that would fund the acquisition of additional music assets to put BMG on a competitive footing with UMG, but the bigger picture was not in Middelhoff's favor. The record industry finished 2002 with a 13.5 percent decline in RIAA-reported revenue from its 1999 peak and an 11.3 percent drop in SoundScan-tabulated retail album sales. Bertelsmann's board and shareholders, like the other members of the Big Five, were more interested in cutting costs in the present than spending on theoretical synergies for the future, especially when faced with an unbudgeted $2.8 billion due to Calder. In July 2002, Middelhoff was replaced as chairman of the Bertelsmann board by Gunter Thielen, who had been the head of Arvato, the Bertelsmann business and computer services support division. He scuttled the Napster plan, and rolled the other BMG internet initiatives, printing, and manufacturing services into Arvato.

With the other key BMG music executives of the 1990s all gone, in November 2002 Thielen turned to Clive Davis who had been with BMG for twenty-eight years, since Arista's 1974 founding, despite Davis being over Bertelsmann's mandatory retirement age. After Davis sold his 50 percent interest in J Records to BMG for a reported $20 million, he was appointed chairman of the newly named RCA Music Group with a five-year contract, overseeing both RCA Records and J Records. The restructuring would consolidate back-office services for four freestanding labels to cut costs. Jive would focus on its teenage pop roster under Calder protégé Barry Weiss, Arista would concentrate on urban music under L. A. Reid, and Joe Galante would continue at the helm in Nashville. Under Davis's umbrella were the RCA label led by holdover Richard Sanders doing mainstream pop, and J Records under longtime Davis lieutenant Charles Goldstuck with a larger focus on R&B. The well-regarded Bob Jamieson and much of his RCA team were casualties of the restructuring with their duties reassigned to the retained J Records staff. Davis, Weiss, Reid, and Galante would all independently report to BMG chairman/CEO Rolf Schmidt-Holtz, who in turn reported to Thielen.

Universal Doubles Down

Thomas Middelhoff and Gerald Levin were not the only executives in the Big Five who sought a new alliance from outside the music business to succeed in the digital future. Seagram's Edgar Bronfman Jr. believed that to expand the profitability of his UMG holdings, both audio and visual, he needed to control the digital delivery looming in the future. After exploring possibilities with Disney, News Corp., USA Networks, and Bertelsmann, he found his dance partner in Jean-Marie Messier, the chairman of the French media, telecom, and utility conglomerate Vivendi SA. Messier's stated vision was to create a company that "will be the world's preferred creator and provider of personalized information, entertainment and services to consumers anywhere, at any time and across all distribution platforms and devices,"[11] reported Mark Coatney in *Time* magazine.

While both men were in their mid-forties, their paths to success had been quite different. Bronfman had parlayed his family's multi-billion-dollar interest in whiskey into one of the world's leading content owners, while Messier manipulated the 150-year-old French water utility Compagnie générale des eaux, which he renamed Vivendi SA in 1998, into a $51 billion global media giant with interest in both cable TV and mobile carriers throughout Europe. In June 2000 Bronfman and Messier forged a three-way stock-swap merger. Seagram shareholders received $34 billion in shares of the Paris-based Vivendi, which assumed $6.6 billion in Seagram debt. The shareholders of third-party and leading French cable TV provider Canal+ received $10.9 billion in stock for the 49 percent of the company that Vivendi hadn't acquired in an earlier purchase.

Messier became chairman of the newly christened Vivendi Universal with Bronfman as vice chairman with responsibility for content. The Bronfman family trust became the largest shareholder in the new entity. Many wondered if Bronfman would be content being number two to Messier, but he avoided the issue as he commented to *Billboard*, "Control is only valuable if it can create value. As we looked at the opportunities for Seagram and remaining independent, we felt that while we would continue to grow, it would not be the best way to optimize the assets that we have."[12] In December 2001, however, Bronfman resigned from his operational duties, but remained on the board as vice chairman, leaving the record company in the hands of Doug Morris.

At the same time, Vivendi Universal was losing value and piling up debt after Messier's buying spree. By June 2002, the stock had lost 70 percent of its merger price. Audits revealed discrepancies in valuation and write-off practices, resulting in Messier's forced resignation in July. Board member Jean-René Fourtou, former chairman of the French chemical giant Rhône-Poulenc, replaced Messier, with Bronfman remaining vice chair. The board deemed it necessary to sell assets in order to climb out of the trench Messier had dug. Messier himself, however, won a mediation hearing a year later awarding him a $26 million severance package.

In October 2002, Vivendi Universal sold 80 percent of its US non-music holdings (Matsushita still owned 20 percent) to General Electric in a cash and stock deal valued at $3.8 billion. Included in the purchase were Universal Studios, the USA Network, the Sci-Fi Channel, the five Universal theme parks, and 50 percent of Canal+. In 2006, Vivendi Universal bought out the remaining 20 percent share of music assets still owned by Matsushita (which shortly thereafter renamed itself Panasonic.

The sale of these assets, however, was too late to turn the tide. Although UMG had been one of Vivendi's profitable divisions, Morris nonetheless had to join the corporate-wide downsizing in 2003 by terminating 11 percent of his over twelve thousand-person worldwide workforce to add an annual $200 million to the overall expense reduction. In 2004 MCA Records was closed, with Jay Boberg departing the company, and merged into the Jimmy Iovine–led Interscope/Geffen/A&M label group. Lyor Cohen departed for WMG, and Morris brought in L.A. Reid, released by BMG, to replace Cohen. Morris's former Atlantic cohort Sylvia Rhone, who had also exited BMG, came in to assume the reins at Motown. Morris maintained UMG's number one position in the US music market, averaging over 30 percent total and 31 percent of current chart product through 2006.

EMI Restructures . . . Again

The success of the Spice Girls had swept Ken Berry into the top post at EMI and the label group from last place in market share in 1996 to fourth in 1998. That success, however, went from sweet to sour in 1999, sending the label group back to last, and last again in 2000. In 1999 only five EMI albums sold over a million units, but not one exceeded 2 million. In 2000, seven releases sold over a million, led by The Beatles' *One*, the *Romeo Must Die* soundtrack, and two *Now That's What I Call Music* multi-label compilations. Compounding the losses from the lack of current artists breaking the platinum barrier was the signing of Mariah Carey to Virgin Records with a four-album deal for a reported $100 million total. The first album, the soundtrack for Carey's movie *Glitter*, failed to register a million SoundScan sales compared to her nine albums with Columbia that had averaged over 15 million units each. The movie itself also did poorly at the box office. Carey decided to refrain from releasing albums for the immediate future.

Berry's tenure at EMI came to an end in October 2001 after the company posted a $2.8 million pre-tax loss for the first half of 2001 compared to an $85 million profit in 2000. Berry received a $10 million buyout package, and his now-estranged wife, Nancy, exited a week afterward with a $3 million severance of her own. Berry was replaced by former PolyGram CEO Alain Levy, who brought former PolyGram associate David Munns with him as vice chairman. Under Levy's leadership from 1989 until the Seagram purchase ten years later, PolyGram had achieved a 13 percent compounded annual growth that tripled its share value, greatly contributing to the $10 billion purchase price paid by UMG. EMI was hoping for similar results.

By the end of February 2002, the company's transformation was underway in both name and substance. The EMI acronym was retired as a label name, replaced worldwide by resurrecting the Capitol Records brand. Future use of the EMI designation would be limited to corporate identification and music publishing. Carey was released with a $28 million contract buyout. Between that and the money already spent on her *Glitter* album, Virgin suffered a loss of over $50 million. Most Berry-appointed Virgin executives were terminated or reassigned, and the label was moved to New York. Levy named Munns chairman/CEO of EMI Recorded Music North America in addition to his global number two position. Matchbox Twenty producer Matt Serletic took over as Virgin Records America chairman/CEO to work with holdover president/COO Roy Lott. Back-office functions for Virgin and Capitol were consolidated to help achieve mandated cost-cutting and increase efficiency. By the end of the year over eighteen hundred positions, about 20 percent of the EMI global work force, had been eliminated.

AOL Time Warner Unravels

Much like Middelhoff's internet strategy for BMG, the AOL Time Warner merger proved that being early out of the starting gate does not guarantee a finish in the money. The dot.com bubble that had driven tech stock valuations began to deflate and online advertising began to slow. Like so many others caught up in the frenzy, AOL couldn't meet its financial forecasts. High-speed internet access began to replace the dial-up service that was a major component of AOL's business model. Telecoms and cable companies offered their own web access packaged with cable TV and/or telephone service.

In 2002 *The Washington Post's* Alec Klein broke the news that AOL had been improperly inflating its advertising revenue prior to the merger. In a *New York Times* 2010 retrospective on the ten-year anniversary of the merger, Tim Arrango wrote that Klein's "stories that were published in 2002 prompted investigations by the S.E.C. and the Department of Justice. Eventually the company paid hefty fines and was forced to restate past earnings. The accounting scandal became a rallying cry for the Time Warner side."[13] Levin announced his May 2002 retirement in December 2001, just before Klein's findings were publicly revealed. In January 2003 AOL Time Warner reported a loss of $98.7 billion for 2002. At the time, this was the largest corporate loss ever reported, and was essentially the supposed value of AOL at the time of the merger. Steve Case subsequently stepped down as chairman as the stock took a severe beating. The AOL acronym was dropped from the corporate name.

Several theories were floated about the underlying cause for the unraveling of the merger, including overpaying for an over-hyped property, underestimating the time and logistics needed for the internet to reach commercial potential, falling victim to the bursting of the dot-com bubble itself with the resulting loss of confidence and market value, and perpetrating actual deceit and fraudulent bookkeeping. Perhaps in hindsight, some mixture of all of the above is the best explanation. Whatever the reason, Time Warner was now looking to sell assets to pare down debt.

Arrango further reported that the combined value of the companies in 2010, which by then had been totally separated, was about one-seventh of their worth on the day of the merger. Fifteen years after the fact in 2015, Rita Gunther McGrath of *Fortune* reported that the coupling was generally "described as the worst merger of all time."[14] One of the biggest losers was

Ted Turner, whose Turner Broadcasting was acquired by Time Life for stock in 1996. In the 2010 retrospective, he told the *Times* that he had lost $8 billion due to the decline in stock value, which was over 75 percent of his wealth. At the same time, Tim Bond quoted Levin in *The Hollywood Reporter* from his mea culpa appearance on CNBC's *Squawk Box*, "I presided over the worst deal of the century, apparently . . . I have been obviously reflecting on it. I was the CEO. I was in charge. I'm really very sorry about the pain and suffering and loss that was caused."[15]

Further Merger Mania—Sony and BMG Unite

An overall bear market began in 2000 for the US financial sector, following the extended bull market of the 1990s just as the AOL Time Warner merger was closing. This market reversal opened with accounting scandals, the dot-com bubble burst, and then the stock market crash directly after the 9/11 terrorist attack. Overall, the Dow Jones index dropped 27.4 percent from January 2001 to September 2002. These events affected the finances of the conglomerates that owned the Big Five label groups to a far greater effect than the problems arising from digital downloading. SoundScan sales were up by 4 percent in 2000 over 1999, and then went down 2.3 percent in 2001 and another 9.1 percent in 2002. The labels jointly pinned the decline on the illicit file-sharing craze, pointing to Napster as the primary culprit.

As always, the parent companies looked to their valuable music assets to make up for the recession-associated losses in other divisions by squeezing out higher returns from record sales. The entire record industry responded through 2002 by trimming staff, consolidating back-office services, and improving inventory management to lessen the amount of free goods and record returns. The 9.1 percent sales decline in 2002, however, was exacerbated by the expenses of preparing for the anticipated shift to the internet that had yet to show any return on investment. Declining sales and the cost associated with e-commerce acclimation drove merger and sale discussions throughout 2003.

Still reeling from the AOL fiasco, Time Warner spent 2003 in discussions first with BMG about buying the music division, and then with EMI, but terms satisfactory to both parties could never be worked out. At a dead end with Time Warner, BMG changed tack and in early November 2003 announced a 50-50 joint venture with Sony. The agreement excluded the companies' publishing and manufacturing operations, making it easier to pass muster with regulatory agencies, which it did in July 2004. Sony BMG Music

Entertainment would be number one worldwide, slightly ahead of Vivendi Universal, but slightly behind them in US market share. Annual savings of $350 to $400 million were predicted and the worldwide workforce, now combined, would be reduced from a pre-venture total around 13,500 in 2002 to about 8,000 by 2006.

In the spirit of the 50-50 joint venture, the new company divided duties between holdover executives from each company with BMG's Rolf Schmidt-Holtz as chairman. Sony Music's Andy Lack, who had replaced sixteen-year veteran Tommy Mottola in January 2003 as Sony chairman/CEO, was named CEO of the venture. Incumbent BMG CEO Michael Smellie became COO and Sony's Michele Anthony was named executive VP. Label operations, however, were kept separate with Columbia's Don Ienner as president/CEO on the Sony side and Clive Davis as chairman/CEO of all BMG labels.

Despite the hoped-for synergy, the consolidated management team at Sony BMG was on fractious footing trying to blend two vastly different corporate cultures into an effective unit as joint market share fell behind what the sum of the two parts had been individually. Lack's leadership came under fire from BMG board members led by what they considered an excessive $110 million contract extension for Bruce Springsteen. This was compounded by a $10 million fine from New York State in a payola suit settlement paid by Epic Records for gifts to D.J.s for playing Jessica Simpson and a few lesser-known artists. In February 2006 Sony Corp. chairman Sir Howard Stringer agreed to mollify the Bertelsmann board members impatient with falling revenue by shifting positions between his top two executives. Schmidt-Holtz moved from chairman to CEO giving him hands-on control over the music division while Lack assumed the more corporate role of music division chairman and head of Sony BMG Films. Sony veteran Tim Bowen was upped to COO, replacing BMG veteran Michael Smellie who had retired at the end of 2005.

Then in June 2006, Don Ienner and Michele Anthony, the two highest-ranking incumbents from the Mottola executive team, left under pressure from Schmidt-Holtz. Sir Howard's younger brother Rob Stringer, Sony BMG Music UK chairman/CEO, moved to New York to take over Ienner's slot as president of the Sony Music Label Group in September 2006. Stringer's resume and connections went way beyond his fraternal tie as he was the key executive in the Sony Music relationship with the *American Idol* producer Simon Fuller of 19 Entertainment. In December, Sony urban music president Lisa Ellis was named executive VP of the Sony record group, directly under Stringer, as urban music was rolled into the pop division. Ellis had been instrumental in the careers of Beyoncé and John Legend. Stringer said in announcing her promotion that she would "be involved in all aspects of the

Sony Music Label Group's activities, with particular emphasis on broadening our growth as an entertainment company in the digital era."[16]

Bronfman Back in the Ballgame with WMG Acquisition

In a November 20, 2003, board meeting, Time Warner executives expressed uneasiness about whether regulators would push back against the proposed EMI acquisition of their music interests on the heels of the Sony-BMG announcement. They also wondered how long they could pursue that deal without guarantee of approval. They decided to consider offers from other parties, as there was interest from a private equity group led by Edgar Bronfman in acquiring the music group. Time Warner rightly believed a sale would face far less regulatory opposition than a merger. Such a purchase would prevent further shrinkage of the industry to a Big Three on the heels of the shift from Big Five to Big Four pending in the Sony/BMG pairing.

Bronfman's bid of $2.6 million for both record and publishing companies included $250 million of his own money; over a billion dollars from Wall Street investors Thomas H. Lee Partners, Bain Capital, and Providence Equity Partners; and an undisclosed amount from Haim Saban, the man behind the *Power Rangers* TV show and partner with News Corp in Fox Family Worldwide. The rest would be in debt financing. Bronfman was actually better known and of higher regard on Wall Street than he had been in the entertainment world. He was able to parlay his corporate success prior to the Vivendi disaster into this investment coalition to buy WMG at what was considered a good price. He planned to create profit with better management of expenses and staffing coupled with a return to an A&R-driven operational philosophy. His blueprint also included prospective exit alternatives through a public stock offering, a merger, or an outright sale. The deal closed in February 2004.

Bronfman immediately installed Lyor Cohen, who had gone through the Universal-PolyGram merger with him, as the North America chairman/CEO, blending reasonable salary with performance bonus stock. Cohen promptly consolidated Elektra into Atlantic, cutting staff from both labels to achieve the projected cost reduction. He brought his longtime Def Jam protégé Julie Greenwald in as co-president of Atlantic with incumbent Craig Kallman in April 2004. In July he also added former Def Jam executive Kevin Liles to expand the WMG share of the rap and R&B markets. Incumbent WMG CEO Roger Ames departed in June for a consulting agreement with his former employer Time Warner.

In May 2005 WMG joined the other three majors as a publicly traded stock with an IPO offering. Its plan for the proceeds included buying out Time Warner warrants, cashing out some of the investors, and investing working capital in marketing. The $554.2 million offering proceeds fell about 20 percent short. Apparently not enough investors shared Bronfman's optimistic vision of how fast the industry would turn over to digital distribution for a sales rebound, or at least not as enthusiastically as Bronfman had hoped.

The company had undertaken $250 million in annual overhead reductions in preparation for the IPO, but this left some major acts unhappy with the diminished pool of marketing dollars while WMG was raising money based on their success. Multi-platinum rock band Linkin Park demanded a share of the IPO proceeds. Their first two albums had already combined for sales of over 14 million units on their way to an eventual 50 million worldwide. Claiming to be an integral part of WMG's financial valuation, they delayed their new album to pressure WMG into meeting their demand. In December 2005 they settled for a $15 million advance and a boost in royalty rate to the upper-echelon 20 percent-plus range, which would yield about $3 per album.

Independent Labels Make Their Mark

The introduction of the SoundScan sales tabulation via album bar code methodology in 1991 revealed actual sales numbers, including the market share of independent labels handled by the independent distribution system. Prior to SoundScan it was difficult to measure the size of the indie market since most of these labels didn't publicly reveal their financial information. While the majors still dominated both the *Billboard* charts and platinum album certifications from 1996 through 2006, independent distribution maintained an average of 15.1 percent of all SoundScan-tabulated sales for a total of 103.8 million albums per year. The high was 21.2 percent in 1996. Sales then averaged 16.7 percent from 1997 to 2004 before dropping to 13.2 percent in 2005 and 12.6 percent in 2006. The decline had been affected by the majors opening distribution branches catering to independents, with the sales from them then included in the major labels' overall market share percentage.

The analysis of 1995 SoundScan annual total sales prepared by Tom Silverman of WMG-affiliated indie Tommy Boy Records, for presentation at the May 1996 National Association of Independent Record Distributors (NAIRD) Convention, revealed that just 17,124 of the 26,629 albums released in 1995 scanned over one hundred copies. Of those, 5,850 had been released by the major labels, and 11,274 had been released by independents. The major label releases, however, accounted for 78.8 percent of all sales, averaging 9,134 units per album, while the indie releases averaged 1,363 units per release. Only 336 albums scanned more than 250,000 units during that year, and 298 of these were on major labels while only 38 were released by independents.

The 1995 statistical breakdown between majors and independents was relatively typical of the years between 1985 and 2006. Successful independents, although selling far fewer units per album than the majors, were more likely to make a profit on their releases. Without a parent conglomerate's balance sheet to absorb losses, they more carefully budgeted their manufacturing, marketing, and promotional costs.

Given the size of the independent market as revealed by SoundScan statistics, the majors decided to build subsidiary distribution divisions that would operate apart from their existing systems to help finance and service independent labels in competition with the existing independent distributors. In 1993 Sony bought 50 percent of RED—originally Relativity Entertainment Distribution, created in 1989 by alternative-rock company Relativity Records to service other labels—and then bough the other half in 1995.

WMG opened the Alternative Distribution Alliance (ADA) also in 1993. EMI had acquired Caroline Distribution in 1992 as part of its purchase of independent Virgin Records. PolyGram operated its Independent Label Sales (ILS) prior to the UMG merger. In 2004 UMG further expanded its Indie distribution business by opening Fontana Distribution, using the name and logo of the historic 1950s Philips-owned Fontana pop label.

In addition to feeding additional manufacturing through parent company pressing plants, these major-owned indie distributors took a handling fee of about 20 percent of gross receipts in a pressing and distribution (P&D) arrangement, after deducting the manufacturing and shipping costs. The handling fee varied according to the perceived strength of the catalog and extent to which any additional services or financing were included. The distributed label was responsible for all marketing and promotion costs unless defined otherwise in the agreement. An established company like Disney could drive the distribution charge as low as possible, and a new company with current radio play could merit advances to pay out-of-pocket promotion expenses.

From 1996 through 2006, only about 5 percent of the over eight hundred albums that scanned more than 1 million units sold in a single year had been released by independents. These included Bone Thugs-N-Harmony on Ruthless Records, distributed by Relativity; Master P on No Limit Records, distributed by Priority; Moby on Richard Branson's V2 Records; The White Stripes on Jack White's Third Man Records, distributed by V2; The Baha Men on Curve Records, distributed by Danny Goldberg and Daniel Glass's

Artemis Records; Mannheim Steamroller on its own American Gramaphone label; Ray Charles on his own Hear Records, distributed by Concord Records through Starbucks; and Alison Krauss on Rounder Records.

Independent Ruthless Records had been the focal point of West Coast rap since its success with N.W.A. Group member and label founder Eazy-E continued to run the label after the group's break-up in 1991 until his death in 1995. The label struck platinum again in 1996 with Bone Thug- N-Harmony eventually selling more than a combined 10 million albums on the group's five Ruthless albums. According to No Limits owner and principal artist Percy "Master P" Miller, the label had sold over 75 million albums, primarily between 1991 and 2004, when it filed for reorganization. No Limits was known for having up to twenty tracks on albums, multiple rappers on each album in both featured and cameo performances, and its unique 3D cover designs termed pen and pixel.

With financing from investment banker Morgan Stanley, V2 was Sir Richard Branson's second foray into the record business after selling Virgin to EMI in 1992 and waiting out his five-year non-compete agreement. In 2006 the American division of V2 was acquired for $15 million by Sheridan Square Entertainment, founded by former Alliance Entertainment founders Joe Bianco and Anil Narang with funding from former Bain Capital director Joe Pretlow and private equity firm The Stephens Group. Sheridan Square also acquired Glass and Goldberg's Artemis in 2006, catalog company Compendia Records and Gospel label Light Records of Nashville, distributor Musicrama, and other catalog items from Tone-Cool Records, Triloka, Ropeadope Records, and Vanguard Classical. Sheridan Square released both Moby and The White Stripes from their V2 contracts but kept their back catalogs, deciding to move the company into a content management direction, emphasizing digital distribution and sync licensing.

American Gramaphone was formed in 1975 by Omaha-based producer/composer Chip Davis, who had created the 1976 number one Country hit "Convoy" during the citizens' band (CB) radio craze as an outgrowth of a character he had developed for an advertising campaign. Unable to find a distributor for his neoclassical New Age music group Mannheim Steamroller, Davis opened his own company to handle his Fresh Aire series followed by his multi-platinum first two Mannheim Steamroller Christmas albums, which went on to sell over 6 million copies each. Their ten studio albums, compilation reissues, and live versions have together sold over 28 million units.

In 1999 television producer Norman Lear and his partner Hal Gaba purchased the twenty-six-year-old Concord Jazz label and moved it from Northern California to Beverly Hills to be the anchor of their Concord Music

Group. In 2004 they acquired the Fantasy, Inc. group of labels from longtime owner and movie producer Saul Zaentz, which included Fantasy Records, home to the Credence Clearwater Revival, as well as the Prestige, Milestone, Riverside, and Specialty imprints, along with the post-Atlantic Stax catalog. They then partnered with Starbucks to release Ray Charles's final album, *Genius Loves Company*, featuring duets with Natalie Cole, Elton John, James Taylor, Norah Jones, B. B. King, Gladys Knight, Diana Krall, Van Morrison, Willie Nelson, and Bonnie Raitt. The album won eight Grammy Awards for 2004 and sold over 4 million albums worldwide. In 2005, Concord acquired digital audio engineering pioneer Telarc International and in 2006 reactivated Stax, re-signing original Stax legend Isaac Hayes.

Rounder Records was founded in 1970 in Boston by Ken Irwin, Bill Nowlin, and Marian Leighton-Levy, three college friends with no experience in the music business, as an outlet for their favorite folk, blues, bluegrass, and other roots music. Rounder's first big success came with blues-rockers George Thorogood and The Destroyers in 1978 selling over a half million of their self-titled debut album. Rounder was awarded the first of their more than fifty Grammy Awards with blues guitarist Clarence "Gatemouth" Brown in 1983. Alison Krauss followed with twenty-two Grammy Awards for her solo recordings as well as her work with Union Station, the Cox Family, and Robert Plant. Other Grammy recipients included Bela Fleck, Steve Martin, Ricky Skaggs, Professor Longhair, Irma Thomas, reissues of Jelly Roll Morton, and reggae group Burning Spear.

Walt Disney Records—including its Buena Vista, Hollywood, and Lyric Street imprints—considered itself an independent although it had P&D agreements with majors both domestically and overseas. Elektra had been its US distributor prior to its switch to UMG in 2005. In both arrangements, Disney maintained fully staffed marketing, promotion, and A&R departments. Disney had a long history of releasing soundtrack albums and records by performers from its movies and television shows. Hollywood Records, however, was opened in 1989 to acquire other products, most notably the US rights to the Queen catalog in 1991.

In 1998 Disney brought in former Earth, Wind & Fire and Prince manager Bob Cavallo as chairman of the music group. They sold over 5 million albums with *Lizzie McGuire* star Hillary Duff and launched the recording career of Miley Cyrus with the multi-platinum first *Hannah Montana* soundtrack album. Country vocal trio Rascal Flatts also achieved multi-platinum status on its first four albums on country division Lyric Street Records from 2000 to 2006 under the direction of president Randy Goodman, a former BMG top executive under Joe Galante, and senior VP of A&R Doug Howard. Disney also scored platinum success during this period with the *Tarzan*, *Mission Impossible 2*, *Save the Last Dance*, and *The Lizzy McGuire Movie* soundtrack albums.

Curb Records owner Mike Curb was one of the youngest and longest-surviving independent record men of the 1960s, as well as a songwriter, producer, and film score composer. His Sideways Records had scored hits in the 1960s with the Stone Ponies featuring Linda Ronstadt, the Electric Flag featuring Mike Bloomfield and Buddy Miles, and the Mike Curb Congregation. He then parlayed this early success into the presidency and 20 percent ownership of MGM Records in 1969 at the age of twenty-four, where he continued his success with Sammy Davis Jr., the Osmonds, and Lou Rawls. After leaving MGM in 1974, he had hits on his Warner/Curb joint venture with The Bellamy Brothers, the Four Seasons, Exile, Shaun Cassidy, Hank Williams Jr., and Debby Boone's "You Light Up My Life," the biggest-selling single of the 1970s.

In the 1980s, after a term as lieutenant governor of California under Ronald Reagan, Curb enjoyed success in country music with joint ventures with the Judds on RCA/Curb, Lyle Lovett on MCA/Curb, and Hank Williams Jr. on Warner/Curb. In the early 1990s he himself moved to Nashville and opened Curb Records as an independent label. In 2002 he acquired 20 percent and management of WMG-owned leading Christian label and distributor Word Records. Between 1996 and 2006, Curb artists Leann Rimes and Tim McGraw each sold over 30 million albums. Rimes was nominated for seven Grammy Awards and won two; McGraw was nominated for thirteen, won three, and was named the Country Music Association Entertainer of the Year in 2001. Curb's philanthropy included donations to endow the Mike Curb College of Entertainment and Music Business of Belmont University, one of the nation's top music business programs.

Digital Sales Debut in Industry Revenue Accounting

The year 2004 was the first year that Sales of Downloads were entered as a line item on the RIAA year-end shipment and sales report. That year, 139.4 million single-track downloads and 4.6 million downloaded albums totaling $185.3 million in retail value were reported, only 1.5 percent of the industry total. Apple's iTunes had actually debuted in April 2003, registering about $30 million in sales for that year, and there were sales from other webstores as well, but there were no line items on the 2003 RIAA report for digital revenue. Also in 2004, the RIAA introduced a line item for Performance Rights Revenue in the amount of $6.9 million collected by SoundExchange from digital radio and internet transmissions on behalf of recording artists and their record companies as the owners of the copyright in master recordings. (More on iTunes and SoundExchange in ensuing chapters.)

In 2005 the RIAA added new line items for Kiosk, Download Music Video, Ringtones & Ringbacks, and Paid Subscriptions to its year-end report to accommodate the revenue generated by these new digital sources. An On-Demand Streaming (Ad-Supported) line item wouldn't be added until 2011 when Spotify entered the US market. In 2006 download and streaming revenue combined to account for $1.89 billion, which was 16.1 percent of the RIAA-tabulated industry retail revenue value of $11.76 billion. The digital future had finally arrived in monetized form, but from outside of the traditional channels of industry commerce.

With the alliance between Sony and BMG in 2004, the Big Five became the Big Four. UMG continued its run in first place in market share through 2006, growing from 26.4 percent in 1999, the first year of the MCA/PolyGram merger, to 31.6 percent in 2006. The Sony/BMG venture immediately advanced into the second spot in 2004, but its 27.4 percent share in 2006 was down from the 30.6 percent the two labels' separate shares achieved in 2003, if added together. WMG had been in the top spot in 1996 with a 21.1 percent market share but fell to a low of 14.7 percent and fourth in the Big Five during the Time-Warner-AOL turmoil. Under the Bronfman regime, however, WMG rebounded to 18.1 percent and third place behind its two bundled competitors. EMI consistently held up the rear, hovering around a 10 percent market share.

Independents, as tabulated by SoundScan, lost the most over the decade, falling from 21.2 percent to 12.5 percent in 2006, a 41 percent loss of their market share. This SoundScan share for independents, however, consisted only of the records sold by independent distributors, and didn't include the product distributed by the RED, ADA, Fontana, and Caroline major label–owned distribution wings that serviced independent labels. The sales by this quintet ranged somewhere between 10 percent and 20 percent of their parent label groups' market share.

Most significantly, however, the RIAA market total in 2006 was 621.3 million physical album units reported as shipped with another 27.6 million album downloads sold. This was down from the 1.1 billion albums, all physical, in the peak year of 1999. In dollar terms, industry revenue started the time frame of this chapter at $12.5 billion in 1996, then peaked at $14.6 billion in 1999 before receding to $11.8 billion in 2006, a decline of 23.7 percent from its 1999 height and 5.9 percent below 1996. Although digital commerce was hailed as the path of the future, it hadn't yet solved the problems of the present.

7

Digital Technology Rocks the Record/ Radio/Retail Relationships

Disruption Lurks Inside the Economic Boom

By 1996, the record industry's preoccupation with weekly charts and product shipments had long made it difficult to plan too far beyond the upcoming release schedule. Going into the fourteenth year of upward growth since the first CD imports entered the country, record industry revenue expanded from $3.76 billion in 1983 to $12.3 billion in 1996. This momentum would continue as revenue climbed to $14.6 billion in 1999 before external forces began to undermine the control of the records/radio/retail alliance. Over the next decade these forces coalesced to undermine the revenue growth, supply chain, and power structure of the record industry. By 2006 the euphoria born of constant growth had morphed into a come-from-behind uncertainty while trying to reassume control over the present, much less the future.

The year 1996 was in the midst of not only the greatest period of economic growth the US had experienced, but also at the center of what had been termed the Information Age, as technology accelerated the transition from paper transaction to digital connection. The effect of this economy-wide trend was as fundamental to the record industry's future as any of their policies or decisions. As household income surged, so did the disposable share for entertainment. While all bull markets eventually turn bear and spending slows, this time the burst of the dot-com bubble combined with the attacks of 9/11 to shake consumer confidence and spending way beyond the normal economic downturn.

The World Wide Web (web) had opened to commercial purposes with its first paid advertisements in late 1994. A product of scientific and academic research and development conducted by a team under Englishman Tim Berners-Lee in the late 1980s, the web was a system by which information was transmitted as electronic signals between computers. During the early 1990s, while the protocol for the web was being finalized, a core of digital

American Popular Music and Its Business in the Digital Age. Rick Sanjek, Oxford University Press. © Frederick Sanjek 2024.
DOI: 10.1093/oso/9780190653828.003.0007

entrepreneurs worked on an infrastructure that could supply the services needed to support the anticipated level of online commerce.

Meanwhile, a smaller and younger cadre of business novices who were also experienced coders and hackers were designing a digital future for music focused on the needs of consumers rather than the dictates of the record labels. They believed that if they built a system to facilitate online access to music, the industry would embrace it as an integral element of both sales and promotion. Then investors would follow, possibly the record labels themselves. Creators, consumers, and the music business connecting them would all benefit as digital technology facilitated an on-demand, real-time experience whenever music couldn't be enjoyed in live performance.

Utilizing the web for marketing, information, advertising, and mail order potential while setting up websites and email accounts had become as integral to the music industry as to the rest of society. The CD dominated retail sales, digital equipment supplanted analog in recording studios, and radio programming became digitally automated. Royalty tracking and accounting were compiled and collated for computerized delivery. The economy percolated as the digital lines of communication dubbed the internet developed its structure and capacity. The younger Gen-Xers and oldest millennials were honing their computer skills through gaming, social networking, and searching for new music. Their digital IQ and dexterity had developed to a far greater degree than that of their baby boomer predecessors who were now entrenched in the upper echelon of industry executives.

Since the 1950s, the labels had debuted and marketed a new sound carrier every decade, each enthusiastically embraced by teens and adults alike. In 1996, however, the music industry was not involved in developing the MP3 file, hardly aware of digital file sharing, and definitely unprepared for its impact. Instead, they planned to replace the 16-bit CD with 24-bit discs, which were also termed high-resolution (Hi-Res), the file size used in the digital recording process. Sony.com explains the difference in file formats as follows, "High-Resolution Audio's bitrate (9216 kbps) is nearly seven times higher than that of CDs (1411 kbps) and almost 29 times higher than that of MP3s (320 kbps). And the higher the bitrate, the more accurately the signal is measured."[1]

The Hi-Res DVD Audio (DVD-A) was released in 2001 and the Super Audio CD (SACD) in 2003. While the CD had served all age groups, these two Hi-Res discs appealed only to upper-income consumers as both the discs and their players were even more expensive than CDs. At the other end of the spectrum, teens and young adults listened to both portable devices and their computers on headphones, headsets, or ear buds, which didn't have the dynamic range necessary for high–bit-rate files. The MP3 file was easy to transmit over the internet for file sharing, and sufficient for listening through the small speakers used in headgear or built into desktop computers.

The Art and the Science of the Music Business

By 1996 SoundScan and BDS had transformed the synergy between airplay, retail sales, and chart positions into a far more orderly process than it had been in the pre-digital days. The actual number of plays on radio and sales in stores were now measurable metrics collected and collated into metadata spreadsheets. This information was utilized to help determine record release dates, product shipping orders, where to spend marketing dollars, and most of all, make the weekly charts a more accurate reflection of the marketplace. Not to say that all ways to game the system had been eliminated, but the ones that persisted had become far more sophisticated and subtle.

The artistic process of creating records, however, remained in full bloom. Having the ability and instincts, commonly referred to as the "ears," to anticipate which artists would capture the public's favor was of the most paramount importance. Next came the ability to formulate the marketing campaigns needed to stimulate sales, solicit airplay, and select the co-branding opportunities needed to indelibly embed a new artist into a critical mass of consumer consciousness to influence them to buy or request that artist's latest release.

The label heads who had assembled the A&R staffs that best listened, learned, and fulfilled these tasks were the record men of their generation. Their protégés were in line to become the label heads of the future. Only a few percentage points usually separated the second through fifth-place label groups in market share, so the art of creating hit records was extremely competitive. With the RIAA-stated value of $12.53 billion in 1996 on 1.14 billion units, one percentage point of market share was $125 million on 11.4 million albums. Even those with the best ears, however, were not always right, and the records with the most airplay didn't necessarily go platinum. Some top-ten records never sold enough to recoup their costs and some that sold millions didn't fare well on radio. Each release by each artist had its own unique trajectory, reaffirming that the art of the music business could never truly become a science, no matter how methodically applied. It was a necessity, however, for the science of the business to be artfully employed to maximize sales.

While radio audience measurement had long been a science, during the decades leading up to the digital era, D.J.s had maintained a voice, or more metaphorically, an ear, in determining their own playlists. By 1996, however, the art of radio programming had begun taking a back seat to the data collected by BDS and subjected to automated playlist curation by consultants. Revenues continued to grow but consumer involvement and loyalty waned as digital technology provided new and far more interactive listening alternatives than commercial radio.

A Street-Level Look Behind and Between the Numbers

Although SoundScan was used in 1996 to gauge the market and guide shipments, the RIAA year-end report represented the official industry financial statement issued to the press and used as part of the IFPI worldwide summary. It had become evident, however, that there was a discrepancy between the SoundScan and RIAA album sales numbers. In 1996 the RIAA reported 951.1 million albums shipped net of returns, while SoundScan tabulated 646.8 million albums at retail, which was only 68 percent of RIAA shipments.

Simple math also revealed that the average retail price in the RIAA report was $12.49, but top-line new albums had an SRLP ranging between $15.99 and $19.99. Other than the year-end market share summary of total sales appearing in *Billboard*, more complete SoundScan information including title, price, time, and location of sales was limited to paying subscribers. Robert G. Woletz of *The New York Times* had reported in January 1992, after one year of operation, that "according to one source, major record companies pay as much as $750,000 each a year for Soundscan's data."[2] Just where these unaccounted-for 300 million-plus albums that constituted the difference between the RIAA and SoundScan's totals went to was subject to conjecture, whether resulting from free goods, club and mail order sales, inaccurate reporting on returns, and/or padded shipping invoices to help generate gold- or platinum-record certifications.

This discrepancy led to questioning the information the labels provided to the RIAA which, if not explained, could cause problems with upper management, corporate regulators, and/or shareholders. The 1998 RIAA report added line items for Total Retail Units and Total Retail Value alongside Total Units and Value. Analyzing the difference revealed that retail units were 73.3 percent of the total, leaving 274.3 million albums outside of the retail supply chain. The difference calculated to $1.56 billion for non-retail sales at a $5.64 average per album. The lower unit price could possibly be explained by the giveaways and low-price policies of the record clubs.

WHEN A CONSUMER BOUGHT A CD, WHERE DID THE MONEY GO?

In July 1995 then *New York Times* music critic and *The Pop Life* columnist Neil Strauss researched and authored an article titled "Pennies That Add Up to $16.98: Why CD's Cost So Much" outlining how the retail list price for a CD was divided. The then new Rod Stewart CD *A Spanner in the Works* was used as his research model.

He cited Michael Bolton's *Timeless: The Classics* in 1992 as the first album to raise its SRLP from $15.98 to $16.98. This upswing continued in 1993 led by Frank Sinatra's *Duets* at $17.98, and then with *Page & Plant* and *The Three Tenors* in 1994 at $19.98.

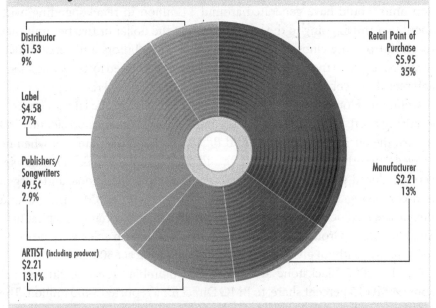

Distributor
$1.53
9%

Label
$4.58
27%

Publishers/
Songwriters
49.5¢
2.9%

ARTIST (including producer)
$2.21
13.1%

Retail Point of
Purchase
$5.95
35%

Manufacturer
$2.21
13%

NOTES

- As Strauss didn't list publisher/songwriter royalties in his article, this analysis has assumed that he included them in the Artist's share, and therefore has created a separate listing at 49.5¢ per album, the then maximum payable under controlled composition clauses.

- Rod Stewart probably had a legacy artist royalty rate in the 20% range, but contractual deductions reduced it to a 13.1% range.

- *A Spanner In The Works* was certified Gold for at least 500,000 units shipped. If all were sold at SRLP, the wholesale to the label would have been $4.75 million, netting $2.29 million after royalty and manufacturing expenses.

- At an actual artist rate of 13.1%, an artist would earn about $1.1 million on 500,000 albums, from which all advances and agreed upon expenses were recouped.

- U.S. publisher/songwriter royalties on 500,000 units would have been at least $247,500.

Source: *New York Times* / *All You Need To Know About The Music Business* / R.I.A.A.

Illustration 7.1 When a Consumer Bought a CD, Where Did the Money Go?

These 274.3 million units accounted for 92.1 percent of the 297.9 million-unit discrepancy between the SoundScan and RIAA totals, making the difference in reports a moot point. Nonetheless, the report reignited the labels' longstanding concern that the clubs were eating into their sales. The BMG Record Club and Columbia House, co-owned by Sony and WMG, operated independently of the labels but were a competing intracompany source of product for consumers. Had these units been sold through retail outlets at around a $15 combined average SRLP for all price levels, then the 274.3 million units would have generated around $4 billion in retail spending, with about two-thirds going to the labels instead of the dollar or two per unit they received from the clubs. The combination of distributors and retail outlets would have gotten the other third. At this level of perceived lost revenue, labels and retail both considered the clubs just short of organized record piracy.

Columbia House finally reacted in September 1999 to the labels' concerns by hiring Scott Flanders from book publisher MacMillan as president/CEO to turn the business around. He told *Billboard*'s Ed Christman that when he arrived, "two-thirds of CDs were free and one-third were sold."[3] Flanders severely reduced giveaways, eliminated membership solicitations, and purged non-complying members. After Flanders flirted with a BMG merger and then a sale to Blockbuster, in 2001 he sold 85 percent to venture capital firm The Blackstone Group for $410 million. By 2003 album sales were down to $250 million without giveaways, and DVD sales were at $500 million.

In May 2005 Blackstone agreed to sell Columbia House, including the Sony/WMG 15 percent share, to BMG Direct for a reported $400 million. The purchase combined Columbia House's $800 million annual revenue, stronger in video, with BMG's $700 million, stronger in records. The RIAA listing of non-retail shipments in 2006 was down to 13.9 percent of total physical units with a $599 million value on 89.3 million albums for an average of $6.71 per unit, still undercutting the labels' retail prices but on a smaller scale, and still a good deal for consumers.

Although consumers were turning to online sources for music, the trend wasn't keeping pace with the decline in retail sales. In 2006 the RIAA-reported $11.51 billion total revenue was down 21 percent from the peak year of 1999 and even 8.2 percent below 1996. Cassettes generated only $3.7 million on seven hundred thousand units in 2006. Vinyl formats did 2.4 million units (LPs and singles combined) for $24.6 million. The Hi-Res formats yielded only $17.9 million. Only 3.2 million physical singles were sold compared to 586.4 million downloaded single tracks.

Getting a Handle on the Digital Future

Although the commercialization of the internet was not yet a factor in record sales in 1996, the entire industry understood it soon could be. Aside from the marketing possibilities, the retail supply chain believed that the most feasible and imminent probability was a shift of physical product to mail-order fulfillment through record webstores. The specter of downloads had not yet entered the discussion.

E-commerce was a major topic at the 1997 NARM Fall Conference. Tower Records, Camelot Music, Walmart, Borders, and other major retailers had opened websites for direct-mail ordering. The labels were including their own website addresses on the packaging of albums sold in stores, alarming the retailers. Capitol and WMG were the most active online, with Sony Music and PolyGram (pre-UMG merger) right behind them. Capitol's webstore was limited to singles and linked to retailers' websites for album sales, while PolyGram insisted that their upcoming online efforts would focus on titles unavailable in stores. Nonetheless the retail segment remained understandably leery.

Research group Jupiter Communications presented a comprehensive study in June 1997 predicting that by 2002 worldwide online physical sales would grow to $2.8 billion, with the US share in the billion-dollar range, further fueling the apprehension of a retail sector already up in arms about being undercut by the record clubs. While the Jupiter prediction about 2002 turned out to be fairly accurate, the growth in online sales was caused by more of a shift from club sales to online stores, than from retail to online, as reflected in the RIAA consumer preference reports.

The Jupiter report also mentioned sales of downloaded files, which had only recently caught the attention of the industry due to the first RIAA lawsuits against what it termed internet music archive sites. *Billboard's* Brett Atwood reported that Jupiter predicted that "digitally delivered music will represent less than 1% of the market by 2002, according to the study. The sales growth of digitally delivered music is restricted by limited hard drive space, ongoing copyright challenges, bandwidth limitations, and a low proliferation of CD-R drives."[4] At the time of the NARM convention, Capitol had just made Duran Duran's *Electric Barbarella* the first-ever major-label download to be sold on the internet. Jupiter's forecast for downloads, however, was a bit optimistic. In 2002 download sales were under the RIAA radar, as were iTunes' 30 million sales in 2003, which would have constituted .24 percent had they been included. The first listing of downloads by the RIAA came in 2004 at $183.5 million in sales value, which was 1.49 percent of total RIAA revenue.

Both the RIAA file-sharing lawsuits and the Jupiter study were first reported in the same June 21, 1997, issue of *Billboard*, the first time that the term "MP3" itself ever appeared there. Use of MPEG files, of which MP3 is the third layer, in digital video players had been covered since the February 2, 1991, issue, but not in relation to audio-only portable devices or files. Although the labels themselves seemed oblivious to the upcoming MP3 maelstrom, the lawsuits were evidence that the RIAA was paying attention.

One of the so-termed internet music archive sites had asked users to upload tracks in return for the downloads. While these sites didn't generate revenue, the RIA argued and won based on the premise that "there's still commercial harm to the industry,"[5] as RIAA CEO Hilary Rosen told *Billboard*'s Don Jeffrey. The RIAA equated file sharing to record piracy, but of a digital rather than physical nature thus making it difficult to substantiate its exact extent. The term "MP3" appeared in *Billboard* articles two more times in 1997, jumped to 37 appearances in 1998, and then to 264 times in 1999 when Napster and fellow file-sharing sites made it front-page news.

The First DRM-Compliant Wave of Digital Innovation

Although both labels and retailers knew they needed to incorporate the internet into their business beyond viewing it as just a tool for mail-order sales, they didn't quite know how. They did want, however, some form of digital rights management (DRM) encryption to prohibit copying. The RIAA regarded home duplication as piracy, but with the potential for far more monetary damage than physical record piracy. Opponents of DRM favored an open-format file that could be used within an unencrypted marketplace based on a blend of nominal subscription fees and advertising revenue. They believed that convenience and quality would convert the file-sharing offenders into dutiful subscribers, while freeing them from possible infringement prosecution. They also pointed out that there was no such encryption on CDs. Although record piracy had to be constantly battled, it had never been put out of business.

The first wave of digital innovators emerged from the tech industry with proprietary codecs, a blended word for the code and decode process, for compressing and decompressing music files. This made the files easier to transfer via the then-limited amount of available internet bandwidth without skipping, stalling, or buffering. By 1997 RealNetworks and Liquid Audio were the industry-leading DRM-compliant suppliers of internet-related services and devices.

The team of former Microsoft executive Rob Glaser, software developer Phil Barrett, economist Andy Sharpless, and entrepreneur MBA Stephen Buerkle opened what would become RealNetworks in 1994 as Progressive Networks. Their technology included the RealAudio file format and the RealPlayer originally designed for internet broadcasts of progressive social, political, and cultural content. After observing the commotion surrounding file-sharing, they sensed opportunity in the music business and became RealNetworks in September 1997 and debuted the RealPlayer. In November 1997, they raised over $350 million in an initial public offering (IPO) with the stock jumping in value 55 percent in the first day. Their business model centered on licensing their RealPlayer and then selling software applications (apps) to users. Windows 98 incorporated RealNetwork's technology, making RealAudio the leading file format for DRM-compliant websites, especially for live broadcasts intended to reach multiple users while maintaining transmission integrity.

Liquid Audio launched in 1996 as a B2B technology provider led by former percussionist and digital workstation developer Gerry Kearby, Child's Play bassist and electrical engineer Phil Wiser, and venture capitalist Robert Flynn. They developed proprietary, watermarked digital files with Dolby encoding designed "to enable secure online preview and purchase of CD-quality music."[6] Also a DRM advocate, Liquid Audio pioneered copy-restricted media distribution that properly licensed from all rightsholders. By 1998 Liquid Audio was supplying watermarked song clips for free previews on *Billboard*'s online audio library. Other products included an integrated bundle of tools for encoding, serving, and playing their files. The Liquid Player could display album graphics, lyrics, credits, and could be updated with news, announcements, and tour dates as well as play MP3 files imported to the player.

Former senior Sony and PolyGram executive Dick Wingate joined Liquid Audio in 1997 to secure licenses with the major labels and publishers. With $2 million in venture capital seed money, they floated an IPO in 1999, raising $63 million. Wingate told Robert Conlin of *E-Commerce*, "Liquid Audio's turn-key distribution and e-commerce services are enabling scores of brick-and-mortar and Internet retailers to offer major label and independent music in their online stores. These new music sales and promotions demonstrate that Liquid Audio is building the label and retail relationships it needs to succeed as an Internet music distributor."[7]

In June 1998 RealNetworks and Liquid Audio led the founding of the Digital Media Association (DiMA) as a Washington, D.C.–based industry trade association. By 2000 Liquid Audio's secure downloading menu and RealNetworks' streaming services appeared to be the leading solutions for the expansion of the music industry into a DRM-managed digital future.

Open File Advocates Enter the Digital Arena

While second-generation Silicon Valley tech companies pursued DRM-encrypted technology, a grassroots cadre of self-funded entrepreneurs and coders developed download websites not long after Karlheinz Brandenburg unveiled his MP3 technology. San Diego–based Creative Fulfillment, Inc. mail-order business owner and attorney Mark Chasan joined forces with Kent Kiefer of Nordic Music in Napa after Kiefer had developed a proprietary codec for duplicating and transmitting MP3 files. Under Chasan's eMusic.com brand they become the first digital download retailer as well as the first to sell MP3 players over the internet using Kiefer's proprietary codec. eMusic also sold the first mass-produced portable solid state digital MP3 player MPMan, a South Korean import.

They employed veteran L.A.-based music executive Don Blocker, whose career went back to signing The Ventures to Liberty Records in the late 1950s, to license a catalog of more than six thousand masters for legal downloads from independent labels with artists including Jimi Hendrix, Ray Charles, Chuck Berry, Billie Holiday, and a lot of big band, jazz, and niche ethnic genres. They also launched the first online radio network, LoudRadio, to simulcast over a terrestrial radio station via KLOD-FM in Flagstaff, Arizona.

In December 1997 San Diego–based Michael Robertson launched MP3.com. Two months earlier Robertson and associate Greg Flores were operating their Z Company, which brokered and administered click-through ad placements with no connection to music. When Flores found a high number of incoming searches for MP3, Robertson sought an appropriate domain name, found MP3.com, and purchased it for $1,000. The owner, Martin Paul, had used his initials and the number 3, since MP, MP1, and MP2 were already taken. Paul was also unaware of the new digital music file. Robertson then purchased the Dutch website MP3 Shopping Mall, which listed software programs but not music files, paying the previous owner $2,500 for the website and offering him $500 a month to stay on as webmaster. He then transferred the MP3.com IP address to the existing MP3 Shopping Mall and launched the MP3.com website to exploit the high level of MP3 search traffic they were receiving. On its first day MP3.com had over eighteen thousand unique visitors and received its first advertising purchase inquiry, causing Robertson to re-evaluate the potential for MP3.com and thus switch its focus to music.

Meanwhile Robertson, who didn't even have a home CD library, much less a collection of vinyl records, immersed himself in learning the music business. As part of his crash course in early July 1998 he co-hosted an unprecedented MP3 Summit at the University of San Diego. The approximately one hundred attendees were treated to demonstrations of new products from MP3 player manufacturers and service providers, including eMusic, Winamp, Sonique, FreeAMP, AMP, GoodNoise, MusicMusicMusic, XING, MPMan, MPlayer3, and Remote DJ. Speakers and panelists included MP3 developer Brandenburg, digital rights attorneys Bob Kohn and Ken Hertz, Steve Marks of the RIAA, DiMA counsel Seth Greenstein, Jim Griffen of Geffen Records, Todd Steinman of WB Records, Congressman Brian Bilbray of San Diego, and Xing CEO Hassan Miah, cosponsor of the confab along with MP3.com and the university.

Discussions were dominated by the philosophical and economic dichotomy between the proponents of DRM and those favoring open-format files with unsecured conveyance, that is, no DRM. The labels were determined to avoid repeating what they considered in hindsight to be their major mistake with the CD, that is, not including copy-prevention encryption at its initial launch. Despite the recent RIAA legal action against file-sharing, the attending industry representatives still viewed downloading as a means to drive retail sales. They were more concerned about the internet displacing traditional retail commerce via mail-order fulfillment, if they were concerned at all. The 1997 RIAA Consumer Profile report had added internet as a sales outlet line item to its survey of habits and preferences for buying records. It measured at .3 percent. Internet sales combined with the Record Clubs and Mail-Order line items to total 14.3 percent in consumer preference for shopping alternatives to the retail supply chain.

The Dot-Com Bubble Engulfs Music Tech

Although most labels and retailers still had digital commerce on the backburner in 1997, there were several early advocates hoping to benefit from a ground-floor position. Avant-garde Jazz label N2K—owned by Grammy Award–winners Phil Ramone, Larry Rosen, and Dave Grusin—opened MusicBlvd.com in July 1997 using Liquid Audio files. CDNow, owned by brothers Jason and Matthew Olim, had opened as an online retailer in 1994 using Valley Record Distributors for fulfillment. After doing sales of $17.4 million in 1997, they raised $65.6 million in a February 1998 IPO. In March 1999 CDNow acquired N2K, including MusicBlvd.com, for $522 million. The transaction made CDNow the largest music-only e-tailer, and third overall behind Amazon.com, which had added music to its online book business in June 1998 as part of the Jeff Bezos expansion blueprint.

Overall retail sales growth continued as the total RIAA retail shipment value passed $13 billion in 1998 for the first time, with preference for retail stores registered at 85.2 percent, the highest level since 1991. Internet shopping preference measured at 1.1 percent. Mail order came in at 2.9 percent, a downward trend over the past seven years from 4 percent in 1991. Record clubs were at 9 percent, also a downward trend, which pleased the labels' retail divisions. Nonetheless, other than a few business development executives and recently hired tech consultants, the labels were far too busy meeting the weekly demands of the ever-shifting charts while luxuriating in the gold and platinum glow of accelerating revenue to be too concerned about the digital future.

The MP3 Summit had exposed the potential of the digital file format as the next-generation sound carrier to a wide array of both Silicon Valley and Wall Street venture capitalists. Between 1997 and 2000 an investment frenzy known as the dot-com bubble put billions of dollars into tech companies in hope of cashing in on the commercial expansion of the internet. Home computers were approaching 50 percent market penetration and widespread broadband access was on the near horizon. Music was poised to become a part of the digital gold rush.

While RealNetworks, Liquid Audio, and a host of competitors looked to capture the attention and business of the major labels with their DRM-compliant technology, Robertson's MP3.com, eMusic, and other small operators sought to find ways to legally sell MP3 downloads without DRM constrictions. In early 1998 GoodNoise Records was organized by twenty-four-year-old Gene Hoffman, a North Carolina State graduate then working for the Pretty Good Privacy (PGP) encryption company; then-PGP attorney Bob Kohn, son of longtime WMG publishing executive Al Kohn, with whom he had coauthored *Kohn on Music Licensing*; and veteran entertainment attorney Gary Culpepper, who had worked at both Sony and Paramount Pictures. Hoffman had assembled a roster of undiscovered bands with visions of using the internet to launch a record label.

In October 1998 GoodNoise agreed to merge with eMusic. The deal was finalized in February 1999 using private financing, which gave Chasan and Kiefer $2 million in cash, $10 million in restricted stock, and executive positions. The newly combined assets would be under the eMusic.com banner. Within a year both Chasan and Kiefer exited, leaving Hoffman in control of operations. Blocker continued to license download rights from independent catalogs, now in exchange for cash advances, while Hoffman still pursued unknown bands. Their goal was to build the catalog to the critical mass of fifty thousand tracks that the new eMusic management team felt was necessary for a public offering. They also decided to continue using an open-format file that could be played on any device, aligning their future with the 20 percent market share independent of the major labels, at least until the majors reversed their DRM position.

In 1999 dot-com investors with high hopes and deep pockets put up more than $1.5 billion in public equity and debt financing for music-related tech companies. MP3.com led the way with a $350 million IPO, with seed investment from radio chain Cox Communications. Liquid Audio gathered in $72 million with investors including broadcasters Media One and Metromedia, tech behemoth Intel, and Vulcan Ventures, owned by Microsoft cofounder Paul Allen. Amazon.com, TowerRecords.com, and barnesandnoble.com were three of the e-tailers already using Liquid Audio on their websites to play digital samples for prospective buyers of physical copies.

eMusic raised $92 million in September 1999 and acquired the Internet Underground Music Archive, Cductive, and Tunes.com, which managed Rollingstone.com and DownBeatJazz.com. Launch Media, one of RealNetworks' streaming audio/video competitors, scored with a $75 million IPO. Net Radio received $35 million from investors. Barnesandnoble.com raised $450 million with an investment from BMG, topping MP3.com's $350 million haul. The IPO of digital rights management specialist Intertrust Technologies raised $117 million in October, followed by another $92 million in April 2000.

The major labels also jumped into the digital derby. UMG debuted its new artist site Farmclub.com. BMG invested in another new artist website, Riffage.com. EMI Music participated in the $117 million IPO for Musicmaker.com, which produced custom-order compilation CDs. EMI then took the investment frenzy to the next level, selling $500 million in ten-year bonds with an 8.375 percent yield for its US subsidiary Capitol Records, earmarked primarily to invest in internet properties. In April UMG and BMG announced their joint e-tail initiative, Get Music, designed to launch online music channels with click-through capability to purchase CDs through mail-order fulfillment. CEOs Edgar Bronfman Jr. at UMG and Thomas Middelhoff of BMG were the two most bullish advocates for the future of e-commerce.

Enter the Napster

Just as the dot-com bubble was reaching its zenith in July 1999, two nineteen-year-old coder/hackers, Shawn Fanning and Sean Parker, launched the peer-to-peer (P2P) MP3 file-sharing platform Napster. It started in Boston-area colleges, where students had broadband access through their school email addresses. Most of them had grown up using gaming consoles, home computers, dual cassette decks, CD-to-cassette recorders, and/or record-able CD drives to make compilations for listening in the car or on portable audio devices. Now they had an even more convenient and extensive source of tracks.

Evolving out of the web bulletin board networking community, the Napster platform housed a directory of users who connected through it, providing a path between their IP addresses to share MP3 files with each other. The code for Napster was written by Northeastern University freshman dropout Fanning on a minimalist basis with no extraneous capabilities to bog it down. With an initial $50,000 provided by Parker through his own internet earnings, over the next year the duo raised addi-tional capital to move to Silicon Valley and sustain operations. Eventually they attracted as many as 80 million active users, constantly expanded the infrastructure to service them, made the cover of *Time* magazine, and got sued by the RIAA.

Although no files were ever stored on the Napster platform, nor did it manage any financial transactions, Napster's phenomenal and sudden market penetration catapulted the MP3 into a major concern for the record industry. P2P file-sharing had grown from a nuisance into a real and present danger. The RIAA suit prevailed in July 2000, was affirmed in an appeals court in February 2001, and in June forced Napster to cease operations (more on Napster's rise and fall in the following chapters). Over Napster's two-year tenure, billions of files were shared among its user base. After those two years, virtually every record ever released by the major labels was now stored on the computers of former Napster users and still available for file-sharing through Napster's cur-rent and future clones and competitors.

The dot-com bubble continued through early 2000, with the NASDAQ index, home to most new technology stocks, peaking at 5,132.52 points that March. Then the bubble burst began. An eighteen-month decline ensued, further intensified by the events and aftermath of 9/11. The NASDAQ finally settled at under 2,000 in early 2002 to stay there through 2004. The cyber-euphoria waned as many overvalued internet companies folded or merged. The record companies cut back on their digital initiatives after several years of spending hundreds of millions of dollars in preparation for a digital fu-ture that failed to materialize, falling far short of the predictions of Jupiter and other prognosticators.

Meanwhile Back on the Street: The Ups and Downs of the Retail Market

Despite all the attention paid to and investment made in the future of e-commerce before, during, and after Napster's two-year reign of disruption, brick-and-mortar sales remained the bread and butter of the music industry. The string of fourteen years with continually rising CD sales was briefly interrupted in 1997 with a 3 percent decline to 753.1 million units from 1996's 778.9 million. Then the upward trajectory resumed in 1998 to reach an all-time high of 942.5 million CDs in 2000. During the same period, cassette shipments fell by 52 percent from 158.5 million units to 76 million while vinyl album sales averaged a steady but paltry 2.8 million units per year. The combined results lifted RIAA shipment value from $12.2 billion to a high of $14.6 billion as total album shipments topped a billion units in all three years.

Then in 2001 the downward spirals on both Wall Street and Main Street combined to affect consumer confidence and spending in all areas of the economy, including the record business. RIAA-reported retail value in 2001 finished 4.2 percent below that of 2000, followed by an 8.2 percent drop in 2002, and then another 6 percent in 2003. The economy stabilized and produced a 2.5 percent rise in 2004 to accompany the boost from the iTunes launch resulting in a 4.1 percent overall gain for 2004 over 2003.

This uptick, however, proved to be an anomaly. Revenue fell from $12.2 billion in 2004 to $11.2 in 2005, a drop of 8.3 percent. The decline continued with another 13.6 percent drop in 2006 to $9.1 billion. Digital revenue sources—including downloads, subscriptions, and mobile usages—grew to $1.6 billion in 2006, making up for about half the retail loss. On a comparative note, in 2006 *Pollstar* reported $3.6 billion in major concert ticket sales, twice what they had been in 2001 and 28.6 percent over what they had been in 2004. Consumers were spending money on music again, but not in the ways the retail and record sectors wanted and needed.

In 1996 and 1997, customers migrating from record stores to big-box outlets combined with a 2 percent drop in total sales to lead to Chapter 11 bankruptcy filings by record chains Camelot, Peaches, Nobody Beats The Wiz, Strawberries, Wherehouse Entertainment, Tower, and Kemp Mill Music. Top one-stop Alliance Entertainment Corporation (AEC) also filed for reorganization, costing founder Joe Bianco his CEO position. While some of these companies subsequently reorganized, others were forced to fold, or were acquired by their more successful competitors.

TOP 25 *BILLBOARD* ALBUMS & SINGLES OF THE 1990s

By 1999, 977 million CDs provided 87.94% of the industry's all-time revenue high of $14.6 billion, almost double 1990 revenue. Sales revenue and radio play data were now digitally collected by SoundScan and BDS. Meanwhile, home duplication through Napster and other file-sharing platforms had just begun.

	TOP ALBUMS OF THE DECADE			TOP SINGLES OF THE DECADE	
	ALBUM	ARTIST		SINGLE	ARTIST
1	Jagged Little Pill	Alanis Morissette	1	"One Sweet Day"	Mariah Carey/ Boyz II Men
2	The Bodyguard	Whitney Houston	2	"Macarena"	Los Del Rio
3	Come On Over	Shania Twain	3	"Come On Over"	Shania Twain
4	No Fences	Garth Brooks	4	"Un-Break My Heart"	Toni Braxton
5	Titanic	Soundtrack	5	"Candle In The Wind 1997"	Elton John
6	Falling Into You	Celine Dion	6	"End Of The Road"	Boyz II Men
7	Cracked Rear View	Hootie & The Blowfish	7	"I Will Always Love You"	Whitney Houston
8	Metallica	Metallica	8	"The Boy Is Mine"	Brandy & Monica
9	Please Hammer Don't Hurt 'Em	M.C. Hammer	9	"I Swear"	All-4-One
10	Backstreet Boys	Backstreet Boys	10	"I'll Be Missing You"	Puff Daddy/Faith Evans
11	Let's Talk About Love	Celine Dion	11	"The Sign"	Ace of Base
12	Ropin' The Wind	Garth Brooks	12	"How Do I Live"	Leann Rimes
13	II	Boyz 11 Men	13	"Gangsta's Paradise"	Coolio
14	Ten	Pearl Jam	14	"On Bended Knee"	Boyz II Men
15	Breathless	Kenny G	15	"Fantasy"	Mariah Carey
16	Millennium	Backstreet Boys	16	"Too Close"	Next
17	'N Sync	'N Sync	17	"That's The Way Love Goes"	Janet Jackson
18	Daydream	Mariah Cary	18	"Because You Loved Me"	Celine Dion
19	Spice	Spice Girls	19	"Waterfalls"	TLC
20	To The Extreme	Vanilla Ice	20	"Dreamlover"	Mariah Cary
21	The Lion King	Soundtrack	21	"Creep"	TLC
22	Tragic Kingdom	No Doubt	22	"Can't Help Falling In Love"	UB40
23	Some Gave All	Billy Ray Cyrus	23	"Jump"	Kris Kross
24	The Hits	Garth Brooks	24	"Take A Bow"	Madonna
25	Crazysexycool	TLC	25	"Tha Crossroads"	Bone Thugs-N-Harmony

Source: Billboard

Illustration 7.2 Top 25 *Billboard* Hot 100 Artists and Top Pop Albums of the 1990s

The labels were affected as well. Rack-jobbers sought discounts from them to absorb the lower wholesale price demanded by the big-box retailers. As records were not their primary business, these mass merchandisers used pricing as a negotiating tool. Circuit City suggested that if albums went above a certain wholesale price, other products would be more profitable to sell in place of them. At the 1997 NARM convention, Sony Music Distribution president Danny Yarbrough spoke for the Big Six label groups when he said, "It is our opinion that music is being devalued. . . . We don't think the consumer has the right idea about the value of music. We will continue to work with our marketing department to correct that."[8]

Sony subsequently raised its Minimum Advertised Price (MAP), the lowest price it would allow for advertising its product, by a dollar for front-line CDs. The other majors followed in varying degrees. Then the labels cut off their coopted advertising with the big-box retailers that continued to sell below MAP, moving their ad dollars to the retail chains trying to preserve the public perception of the value of music in their print ads. Despite the complaints by the big-boxes, the average MAP and SRLP increased over the next three years by another 10 percent.

In May 2000, the Federal Trade Commission (FTC) announced a five-year consent decree against the major labels, ruling that MAP policies constituted illegal price-fixing, which overcharged consumers by about $500 million from 1997 through 2000. Although they weren't fined, the labels agreed to end MAP and not initiate any similar industrywide marketing agreements. FTC chairman Robert Pitofsky believed that the market would now freely regulate itself. Savings to consumers were estimated to reach $17 million a month, or from $2 to $5 on top-selling albums. Meanwhile forty-one state attorneys general concurred with Pitofsky's assessment of damage to consumers. In 2002 they settled their own price-fixing investigations against retailers, including Trans World, Musicland, and Tower Records. Fines reached $3 million. Nonetheless, the average SRLP continued to rise from $13.59 in 2000 to $14.68 in 2002, and reached $15.12 by 2006.

The Demise of the Physical Single

Ever since the rise of the CD, with its much higher profit margins, the labels and especially their corporate parents had regarded the 45 RPM single to be unprofitable but a key element of the radio/retail equation that was essential to their sales operations. The RIAA had reported average annual shipments of over 107 million units between 1985 and 1997. The average $3.49 SRLP in 1997 had a wholesale price of around $2.35, with the average cost for manufacturing, publishing, handling, and shipping at around $1.90. This left a net of about 19 percent for the label to contribute to overhead, including the cost of promotional copies sent free to radio, far below both the net return on CDs and corporate financial targets. There were still about 250,000 jukeboxes in the mid-1980s, but CD-playing models were introduced in 1989 followed by internet-connected MP3 versions in 1998, gradually eliminating the need for physical singles for jukeboxes.

Radio's need for singles had also diminished as labels were providing full CDs in hopes of more than one hit from an album. In 1998 the labels launched a new digital delivery system that electronically transmitted CD-quality files to the stations that had upgraded to digital equipment with broadband connection. Meanwhile retail stores were battling the big-box discounters for customers. They wanted to use singles as a loss leader of their own, selling them at prices ranging from 49¢ to $2.99 to attract and retain the ten to eighteen age group, which had historically bought around 25 percent of all records sold. The stores wanted the labels to absorb or at lease share in these discounted prices, which would necessitate free goods or a discounted wholesale price.

Then the final blow to the single's survival came when *Billboard* adjusted how it determined the Hot 100 Chart, starting with the December 5, 1998, issue. Previously, records were required to be available as singles at retail, but going forward *Billboard* would chart album tracks receiving airplay. At the same time, the weighting formula point structure for the Hot 100 was altered from a mix of 60 percent for radio and 40 percent for retail to 75 percent for radio and 25 percent for retail, lessening the role of sales in determining chart position.

All these factors combined to reinforce the labels' decision to cut back on releasing and distributing physical singles despite the still existing consumer demand for them. Because this was six months before Napster's debut, the issue of P2P file sharing was not yet front of mind. Although selling single-track downloads to promote new albums was being contemplated, the labels still lacked a pricing plan, a clear definition of who would control digital sales, and the desired DRM system to ensure the protection against illegal duplication that they so fervently demanded be encoded in any new sound carrier technology.

As a result of these market changes, singles' share of total revenue dropped from 5 percent in 1997 to 3.4 percent in 1998 to 2.8 percent in 1999, the year in which Napster bowed. The revenue decline continued to 1.6 percent in 2000 and .9 percent in 2001. Even though Napster shut down in July 2001, singles revenue further declined to .4 percent in 2002. Then the Apple iTunes Store debuted in March 2003. By 2006 sale of physical singles had continued to decline to a floor of .16 percent of total RIAA shipment value, while downloaded single tracks had increased to 5.2 percent of total revenue with 586.4 million tracks sold, fulfilling the still existing consumer desire for acquiring their latest favorite song for on-demand listening without having to buy an album.

Seeking a Solution to the Digital Riddle

In late 1998, over two hundred leaders from the information technology, consumer electronics, security technology, and internet service provider (ISP) sectors met with music industry representatives to establish the Secure Digital Music Initiative (SDMI). Their purpose was to find a process by which legal MP3 files could be differentiated from illicit ones. According to the SDMI website, the goal was to develop "technology specifications that protect the playing, storing, and distributing of digital music such that a new market for digital music may emerge."[9]

Dr. Leonardo Chiariglione was appointed president. He also headed the Moving Picture Experts Group (MPEG), which supervised the worldwide standards for digital video compression and transmission, including the MP3. Two and a half years later, in May 2001, the SDMI was suspended. Chiariglione reported in an open email that "unfortunately it turned out that none of the technologies submitted could satisfy the requirements set out at the beginning. . . . SDMI decided to . . . wait for progress in technology."[10]

While the SDMI was conducting what would be its unsuccessful mission, the record labels were pursuing their own strategy. In February 1999, just two months after the SDMI first convened, the Big Five label groups launched the Madison Project to test IBM's newly developed Electronic Music Management System (EMMS) designed to handle downloading, DRM, playback, and clearinghouse functions. The project equipped a thousand cable households in San Diego, the most advanced broadband-access DMA in the country, with the hardware and product needed for a year of operation. A thousand different major-label albums and hundreds of singles were made available for downloading. In late 2000, the labels declared the test a success.

WMG executive VP Paul Vidich, who oversaw the project, cautioned that EMMS was just one of seven different technologies that labels were considering as "a commercial industrial-strength"[11] system for selling digital downloads. In December 2001, the major labels finally debuted their download platforms, five months after the Napster shutdown. But rather than utilizing an industrywide approach as the Madison Project had been, there were two separate services offering two different, noncompatible systems. Neither one utilized IBM's EMMS.

On December 4, 2001, MusicNet launched with WMG, EMI, and BMG as the majority owners and The Box cable channel developer Alan McGlade as the managing partner. RealNetwork's new hybrid jukebox/media player/web browser dubbed the RealOne Player offered one hundred thousand tracks from ten thousand artists in two subscription levels. Their $9.95 per month tier allowed selection of 100 downloads per month and one hundred tracks available for on-demand streaming. The $19.95 per month alternative dubbed RealOne Gold upped the offering to 125 downloads and 125 streams, and added streamed video content from ABC, CBS, CNN, E! Networks, Fox Sports, and others, along with forty-eight advertising-free, programmed radio channels. All content was in DRM-encoded Real files that could only be imported to RealOne players housed on computers, but not on portable devices.

Originally announced as Duet the previous March, the competing PressPlay was released on December 15, 2001. This system was also computer-based only, for $15 a month. PressPlay offered five hundred audio streams in DRM-protected Windows Media Audio WAV files along with fifty song downloads. Subscribers could burn ten songs to CD and build and store playlists. PressPlay also had its own set of limitations. Not every song could be downloaded, users could not burn more than two tracks from the same artist to CD, downloads expired after thirty days, and songs could not be transferred to a portable player.

In a November 24, 2001, article *Billboard* associate editor of merchants and marketing/new media Brian Garrity wrote a laundry list of deficiencies and problems shared by the two services including "tenuous consumer demand, undefined economic models, unknown costs, as well as a lack of compelling content selection, clearance from all interested rights holders, an understanding of how to market the new services, a relationship with traditional retail, and despite hundreds of millions of dollars of collective development spending, sustained support from the labels and their parent companies themselves."[12]

With over $500 million already spent in development, the recession deepening, and the litany of difficulties recited by Garrity, insiders and analysts agreed that there would be at least several more years before possible profitability, if at all, as continuing digital innovation on other projects might well outpace the efficacy of the two platforms. Even more important, neither PressPlay nor MusicNet was able to establish a sales base. A Jupiter survey found that consumers deemed portability and copying capability their two top needs in a subscription service, but neither system filled those requirements. Another problem was that even though EMI was the only major to license product to both services despite its proprietary interest in MusicNet, neither offered product from all labels. EMI president of digital distribution Jay Samit had told Forbes' Penelope Patsuris in October 2001, "My job is to make buying music easier than stealing it. . . . These services will fail if they don't have the music that coumers expect them to. You can't have a top-40 channel with only 22 of the top 40 songs."[13]

There was also a divide between the two label groups over how to structure pricing. PressPlay allowed the labels to set the rates while MusicNet set their own pricing structure. Billboard's Garrity reported that RealNetworks' Rob Glaser defended the MusicNet pricing policy, arguing that the digital music industry needs "to develop in an independent fashion vs. something 100% controlled by the rightsholders."[14] UMG's Bronfman, as part of the PressPlay alliance, responded to the differences and their impediment to a uniform business model, stating that the PressPlay plan "protects the music industry from a company with a very different business model using the MusicNet model at the expense of the industry."[15] There were also concerns that one unified, all-label sales platform dictating pricing would be ruled in restraint of trade as the label's MAP policy had just been rendered.

Five months into the PressPlay/MusicNet era, the situation seemed even more dire than Samit's foreboding prognostication. In the May 4, 2002, issue of Billboard, Garrity cited a recent report from Redshift Research titled Fighting the File-Sharing Dragon, "Subscription services MusicNet, PressPlay, and Rhapsody on average contain only 10% of the top 100 U.S. singles and only 9% of the top 100 albums."[16] Redshift president Matt Bailey added, "Subscription services are not being given the popular music needed to compete against widely used free file sharing networks."[17] Jupiter senior analyst Aram Sinnreich metaphorically summarized the situation to Garrity, "Digital music subscriptions are, as yet little more than a pipe dream with a press release."[18]

For an industry desperate to counter P2P file sharing, the major labels' long-awaited first foray into digital commerce appeared to be more of a failed test market initiative than a serious attempt at a viable infrastructure to facilitate the emergence of a new digital marketplace. Further complicating the issue, their tech partners, Microsoft and RealNetworks, were in a bitter battle for the internet's music-streaming space as a whole, which resulted several years later in a $761 million legal settlement from Microsoft to RealNetworks and subsequent reconciliation. In 2001, however, they were not inclined toward cooperation.

The aforementioned Rhapsody also debuted in December 2001. Its founder, Silicon Valley entrepreneur and author Rob Reid, had launched Listen.com in 1998 as a legal online file-sharing music directory. Reid then expanded into internet radio by acquiring content-streaming websites WiredPlanet in September 2000 and TuneTo.com in May 2001. Rhapsody let customers stream an unlimited amount of music for $9.99 a month. Starting with independent labels, including classical budget line Naxos, Rhapsody subsequently secured licenses from all five major labels by July 2002, giving them a streaming reper-toire of over 175,000 tracks, more than either MusicNet or PressPlay. In April 2003, RealNetworks announced it would acquire Rhapsody for $17.3 million and 3 percent of RealNetworks stock, then valued at $18.7 million. The deal was concluded in August. By the end of 2003, Rhapsody claimed that it had enrolled over one hundred thousand subscribers who were listening to over a million streams a day.

By the end of 2002, the recession had turned around, but the record busi-ness was down for the year by about $2 billion from its height in 1999. Record labels' depleted coffers were exacerbated by the failure of either PressPlay or MusicNet to gain any traction with the public. The stock of music tech compa-nies that lacked corporate parents funding them had lost their luster as well as value. Left out of the major-label download initiative, Liquid Audio liquidated itself, selling its patent portfolio to Microsoft. The download licenses for its 2.5 million tracks were acquired by Anderson Merchandisers, primary music supplier to Walmart. Anderson named their new asset Liquid Digital Media to use as the foundation for the Walmart download store that would open in March 2004 using Windows Media files.

E-commerce giant Amazon bought CDNow in 2002 to be integrated into its already-existing music department. Amazon then let customers down-load tracks for free as teasers for album sales, with the tracks expiring after thirty days. These downloads were available in WAV, Liquid Audio, and MP3 along with free downloading apps. Amazon also sold portable players for all three file formats. They also assumed mail order product fulfillment responsibilities for Target and other retailers who didn't have adequate re-sources of their own but had a growing base of music buyers who were shop-ping on their websites.

At the end of 2002, a year and a half after Napster's shutdown, all prop-erly licensed downloading services combined failed to generate enough sales to cause the RIAA to add Downloads as a revenue line item in its year-end report. Meanwhile, consumers continued to share files through unauthor-ized P2P websites like KaZaA, The Pirate Bay, Music City, Aimster, Gnutella, LimeWire, Morpheus, and Audiogalaxy. There were even far more audacious acts of willful piracy than those of the hackers who pioneered file-sharing, or the consumers sued by the RIAA (more on this in later chapters).

In his 2015 book *How Music Got Free: The End of an Industry, the Turn of the Century, and the Patient Zero of Piracy*, Stephen Witt tells the story of Dell Glover, a shrink-wrap machine operator in a North Carolina CD pressing plant. In 1999 Glover started taking home new CDs before their release, then funneling them to the internet pirating group Rabid Neurosis (RNS).

Witt wrote, "RNS had leaked over 20,000 albums over the course of eleven years, numbers independently sourced to the FBI investigations [and] the RIAA's internal tracking database. . . . The group's key asset was Glover. . . . He was a primary source of contact for hundreds of millions of duplicated MP3 files—perhaps even billions. There was scarcely a person under the age of 30 who couldn't trace music on their iPod back to him. He was the scourge of the industry. . . . He was the greatest music pirate of all time."[19] Witt estimated that Glover participated in providing RNS with over twenty thousand pre-release CDs.

Apple Assumes Control of the Digital Assault

By 2003 it was apparent that three trends had converged to cause alarm for the record industry. First was the downward slide of CD sales, second was the file-sharing epidemic, and third was another downward trend revealed in an analysis of music-buying habits in the annual RIAA Consumer Profile. For the decade leading up to 1996, the ten-to-twenty-four-year-old demographic had purchased over 40 percent of records sold, with a high of 52.1 percent in 1989. In 1997 the percentage was at 39.5 percent before dipping to 34 percent in 2001, the year Napster was closed down, and would finish 2003 at 30 percent. This age group was the one most likely to have used Napster and then switched to other file-sharing sources after Napster's demise. Unless the labels could lure these consumers back into the retail music ecosystem, the MP3 indeed looked to be a prime example of disruptive innovation.

From out of the ether into the void stepped Apple's Steve Jobs with the iTunes store selling tracks that could be downloaded to Apple's two-year-old iPod player as well as to iMac computers. In addition to iTunes being far more consumer friendly, less complicated, and better audio quality than P2P file-sharing, Apple also had the corporate resources to finance both the music licensing and the iTunes launch. For much of 2002 Jobs personally wooed the Big Five to cooperate. He finally agreed to use DRM, which he deemed ill-conceived, but only in Apple's proprietary FairPlay encryption system that utilized Apple's Advanced Audio Coding (AAC) file format, an MPEG-4 next-generation successor to MP3. iTunes was limited to downloads only, with no streaming available since Jobs ardently believed that consumers wanted to own their music, not "rent" it, which is how he referred to streaming. (More on Apple in chapter 10.)

The parties agreed to charge 99¢ per track with 70 percent of earnings going to the labels, who would pay the publishers, and 30 percent retained by Apple, approximating the wholesale-retail ratio of physical sales, but without distribution middlemen. At first only available for use on Apple devices, iTunes sold over a million downloads in its first week after its April 2003 opening and over 25 million by the end of the year. With the approval of the labels, Apple made an iTunes version for Windows available in October, expanding its reach to the far larger share of the public using Microsoft technology. iTunes sold 100 million downloads by July 11, 2004, and 1 billion by February 23, 2006, capturing a dominating 70 percent share of the download market.

The iPod's slick styling combined with iTunes' ease of navigation in creating playlists and multi-file format storage capability helped seal the demise of PressPlay and MusicNet, which fared no better with the tech world than it had with the public. In May 2006, *PC Magazine* named PressPlay and MusicNet collectively as the ninth of the twenty-five worst tech products introduced up to that time. In May 2003, the PressPlay assets were acquired by Lucasfilm audio division Sonic Solutions, which had already bought digital device manufacturer Roxio as well as the Napster name, technology, and trademarks to use as the base for a music service under the Napster brand. When RealNetworks closed on Rhapsody that August, it shuttered MusicNet and integrated its download service into Rhapsody, initiating a pricing competition with iTunes, but even its 79¢ per track couldn't counter Apple's marketing clout or overcome the consumer appeal and superior functionality of the iPod.

The iTunes-Rhapsody competition sparked the addition of download sales to the RIAA 2004 revenue summary. The total grew from 2004's $183.5 million to $503.7 million in 2005 and $878.1 million in 2006. Together with ringtones, downloads cushioned but did not totally offset the drop in retail sales. Record chain and independent stores maintained their consumer base at about 35 percent of total sales value, but the big boxes and mass merchandisers dropped from 53.8 percent in 2004 to 32.7 percent in 2006. Online sales in 2006 accounted for 22 percent of physical product through the clubs, e-tailers, television infomercials, and print ads, while 6.8 percent of consumers preferred buying downloads. Two percent bought albums from merchandise booths at concerts. Altogether the RIAA value of all industry revenue was $11.76 billion in 2006, it was down 19.5 percent from the peak year of 1999 and about even with 1996 revenue, with retail sales at only 68.1 percent of all revenue.

While most of the download sites sold only DRM-encoded files from the major labels, eMusic continued to sell uncoded files from the independent labels more concerned about reaching the consumer than the perils of potential file-sharing. UMG bought eMusic in April 2001 for a reported $23 million as part of the Jean-Marie Messier spending spree, but let it remain a standalone unit. Fifteen months after Messier's July 2002 ouster, eMusic was sold to Dimensional Associates, funded by private equity firm JDS Capital Management. Dimensional also bought fellow independent subscription download service The Orchard, which had been started by Sire Records co-founder Richard Gottehrer in 1997. Together the two had about five hundred thousand tracks from independent labels offered to consumers on an unlimited basis for a $9.99 monthly subscription fee.

Radio Has a Transformation of Its Own

The Telecommunications Act of 1996 went into effect on February 8, 1996. The act was comprehensive in nature affecting radio and other media "to provide for a pro-competitive, de-regulatory national policy framework designed to accelerate rapidly private sector deployment of advanced information technologies and services to all Americans by opening all telecommunications markets to competition."[20] The 63.3 percent growth in radio ad revenue between 1986 and 1995 had spawned a plethora of capital investors waiting for passage. Over the next four years the larger radio groups grew exponentially through mergers and acquisitions focused on major market stations, while local ownership survived primarily in smaller markets.

The top-fifteen transactions in 1996 involved 292 stations changing ownership for a total of $10.41 billion. The $3.7 billion Westinghouse merger of the top-two radio groups CBS and Infinity into the CBS Radio Group was the top deal. In 1997, another 2,138 stations exchanged hands in transactions totaling $17.8 billion, and in 1998, 1,695 more stations were involved in deals totaling $13 billion. Then in 1999 Westinghouse sold the CBS radio group to Viacom along with the other CBS broadcast properties.

By 2000 Clear Channel Communications (CCC) was the top radio chain in both income and station count with 1,224 stations producing $3.79 billion in revenue, 19.1 percent of the $19.84 billion total. Two of its biggest acquisitions were $4.4 billion for Jacor Communications, which itself had acquired Citicasters, Regent, and Noble; and AMFM Inc., the company created by the Chancellor-Capstar merger in 1999, in a $23.5 billion transaction. The 82 stations in SFX Entertainment had been one of Capstar's purchases for $2.1 billion in 1997. Together with Texas radio veteran Steven Hicks, Robert F. X. Sillerman had expanded SFX from 18 to 82 stations by 1997, simultaneously acquiring concert promotors and facilities in a grand scheme to create an entertainment empire exploiting the cross-promotional and operational synergies between radio and pop concerts. Hicks left SFX in 1996, formed Capstar, and then purchased the SFX stations from Sillerman, who continued to amass live performance assets and outdoor advertising, which he sold to CCC in 2000 for $4.4 billion. The plan, an expansion of Sillerman's SFX model, was to cross-promote music through these three revenue-producing divisions to attract corporate sponsors to increase ancillary revenues and consolidate expenses. (more on Sillerman and CCC in chapter 9).

Second-place CBS had 184 stations with $2.5 billion in 1999 revenue for a 12.6 percent market share. The high average revenue per station indicated a concentrated presence in major markets. In third place, Cox Radio took in $482 million from 83 stations, 2.4 percent of the total. Only two other chains had more than 100 stations, sixth-place Citadel Communications with 204 stations producing $368 million, and eleventh-place Cumulus Media with $235 million coming from 227 stations.

This was a far cry from 1995, the year before the Telecommunications Act was passed, when number-one Infinity had 22 stations with $360 million in revenue, just 3.1 percent of the $11.47 billion national total. That year Clear Channel had been in seventh place with $133 million from 30 stations, the highest number of stations for any chain. In the first five years under the 1996 Act, industry revenue grew 73 percent. In 1995, the top-ten radio groups had 198 stations with $2.05 billion in revenue, 17.9 percent of the industry total. In 2000, the top-ten groups had 1,980 stations with $9.06 billion in revenue, 45.7 percent of total national revenue.

The flurry of mergers and acquisitions were fueled by the same late-1990s investment mania that drove venture capital investment and public offerings. Radio revenue in 2000 as reported by the Radio Advertising Bureau (RAB) was at an all-time high of $19.85 billion, $2.17 billion over 1999 revenue for a 10.9 percent increase. But then in 2001, revenue dropped $1.49 billion to $18.37 billion, a 7.5 percent loss. It started to bounce back in 2002, finally surpassing 2000's peak in 2004.

In 2003 the RAB added an Off-Air line item to their annual revenue summary, defined as "revenue generated from and related to gate receipts, signage, concessions, sponsorships, merchandising and print activities."[21] That first year, off-air was listed at $1.26 billion and grew to $1.52 billion in 2006. The emergence of this revenue stream was a by-product of the CCC acquisition of the SFX concert-promotion holdings.

A pay-for-play policy, whereby record promoters bought on-air slots to play their records, became another revenue source for stations. While looking like a new form of payola, it was a legal practice as long as the airplay was accompanied by a stated disclosure that the spin was a paid advertisement. This practice perturbed independent labels, who feared that the rechristened Clear Channel Entertainment (CCE) could pay for airplay on their stations for acts performing in their venues, limiting access for other acts. Cries of restraint of trade garnered FCC attention.

Radio Goes Online

By 1999 almost fifteen hundred stations were webcasting their signals, but the majority of the industry hadn't yet deciphered how to use the internet as an additional revenue source. They quickly became concerned, however, when XM Satellite Radio launched on September 25, 2001, with programming directed by Lee Abrams, one of the prime architects of the AOR format and a future Rock Radio Hall of Fame inductee. Sirius Satellite Radio followed on July 1, 2002. Both created competition for radio in the car with a menu of mostly commercial-free programming with a blend of diverse genre-specific offerings combined with talk, sports, and news including cable channel audio feeds. Both XM and Sirius were launched with capitalization sufficient to maintain operations as the subscription base developed. At the same time radio revenue was faltering due to the economic downturn, making it difficult for stations to subsidize the fixed costs of their internet transmissions. The same decline in ad buys affected many internet-only platforms hoping to compete with terrestrial radio, causing BroadcastAMERICA.com, Monster Media, SoundsBig.com, and Audiohighway.com to be among the webcasters to sign off.

Bolstered by the growing source of off-air revenue and the recovering economy, radio revenue rebounded by 2004, going past $21 billion. Broadcasters' complacency, however, was shattered in October 2004 by the announcement that shock jock Howard Stern would be moving to Sirius from syndication by Infinity due to new FCC regulations designed to censor his content. Although Stern did not broadcast music, his huge national audience was sure to move with him, introducing them to Sirius's diverse slate of programming. Stern's move indicated that satellite radio was here to stay, prompting terrestrial radio to revisit the additional revenue sources that the internet and other digital technology could bring them.

In December 2005, on the eve of Stern's Sirius debut, eight major broadcast groups announced a high-definition radio initiative under the HD Radio Alliance. Long in development, its multicasting digital technology allowed broadcasters to run simultaneous digital feeds through a station's licensed frequency. The larger chains, including CCC, Cox, and CBS Radio, promoted web simulcasts as well as alternative content on terrestrial radio. Programming consultant Jeff Pollack noted that European broadcasters, such as France's Skyrock FM, were getting up to 20 percent of their revenues from licensing their signal to cell phones, personal digital assistants, and other mobile devices. "Broadcasters who are not embracing new media," he opined to *Billboard*, "cannot grow their business."[22] Similarly, new NAB president/CEO David Rehr told the 2006 Consumer Electronics Show in Las Vegas that radio's survival "hinges on our ability to exploit every new technology. Our future is a broadcast signal on every gadget."[23]

The genres and formats of radio in 2006 closely mirrored 1996 but with more spot ads per hour and a few changes in format market share. Spanish-language programming made the greatest leap from a combined 2.9 percent share in 1996 to 11.1 percent in 2006, jumping from tenth place to fourth. News/Talk/Sports expanded from fourth place at 12.6 percent in 1996 to first place in 2006 with 17.3 percent. Smooth Jazz emerged with 2.8 percent and the combined black/urban subgenres grew from sixth place with 7.8 percent in 1996 to fifth place in 2006 with 10.1 percent. The biggest loser was Country music, which was in first place in 1996 with 16.3 percent but sixth in 2006 with 9.5 percent.

The year 2006 ended with the two biggest broadcasting dealmakers of the decade once again in the headlines. CCE, ensconced as the most powerful conglomerate in radio and possibly in the entire music industry, had spun off the live entertainment division into a separate entity in late 2005. CCC retained the Clear Channel Outdoor advertising division while Live Nation was created to be the successor to CCE's live events division. The family of Lowry Mays, cofounder of CCC in 1972 with Red McCombs, remained in executive control of both public companies with sons Mark at CCC and Randall at Live Nation. In 2006 CCC decided to go private in a stock buyback led by private equity firms Thomas H. Lee and Bain Capital for $18.7 billion, then the fourth-largest stock buyback offer to date in any field of commerce.

The other major headline-maker, Viacom, controlled by Sumner Redstone, had owned MTV Networks since 1984; acquired Paramount Pictures in 1993,

CBS Broadcasting in 1999, BET in 2002, and the share of Comedy Central it didn't already own in 2003. In January 2006 Redstone decided to split the publicly traded company in a tax-free spin-off into two separate public companies, hoping that once separated they would reap greater profits than they were producing as one.

MTV cofounder and then-Viacom co-president Tom Freston took over Viacom's cable properties including MTV, Nickelodeon, and Showtime as well as Paramount Pictures and Simon & Schuster book publishing. The other incumbent co-president, Les Moonves, would lead the CBS television and radio networks, the CBS owned-and-operated stations, Paramount Television productions, and the outdoor advertising division. The plan had mixed results. CBS under Moonves thrived immediately, but the Viacom stock faltered under Freston, and he departed in September 2006 after a twenty-seven-year tenure.

Back on the Street: The Shifting Sands of the Retail Landscape

By 2000 the retail segment had grown increasingly attractive to venture capitalists, who felt it was a less risky investment than record companies. Product came on consignment on a 100 percent return basis for individual titles, but with a 20 percent cap on combined catalog for returning unsold goods before adjusting credits would be applied. Product flow was determined through a combination of industry experience and market analysis through SoundScan. The retail segment share was the nearly 30 percent margin between the wholesale cost from the labels and retail price paid by the consumer. At the RIAA retail shipment value of $14.6 billion in 1999, this came to somewhere around $4.3 billion. Leading distributor AEC and top rack jobber Handleman were publicly traded as were chains Trans World, Wherehouse, and Musicland, with other leading chains and superstores financed through private venture capital investment.

Competition within the retail segment for consumer dollars was as intense as it was between the record labels. As in the previous decade, at the transaction level from label to wholesale, and then wholesale to retail, a dime's difference one way or the other, multiplied by millions of units, was a serious incentive to capture a larger market share. With all distributors offering essentially the same product, a retailer could negotiate a more favorable price, or switch to a different distributor. The label-wholesale relationship had a wholly different dynamic. Each piece of product had only one source, but the label could sell it to multiple wholesalers. Whenever labels upped wholesale prices, the wholesalers had to accept the increase or forgo the opportunity to sell through to retailers, so they usually passed the increase along to the retailers, who then passed it along to consumers.

For example, at a $15 retail price, a label received about $10 with expenses of between $3 and $5 depending on manufacturing, royalty rate, and marketing expense. This $5 to $7 margin was many dimes greater than what the wholesalers and retailers netted, making the SRLP the greatest point of contention. The most fluid factor within the entire ecosystem, however, was at the point of purchase, where consumers could usually buy the same product from any retailer. Comparative shopping by consumers pushed prices down, and thus profits for all parties in the supply chain.

By 1996 many independent mom-and-pop stores had given way to record chains that could offer a better price to consumers while still offering a wide variety of independent music, esoteric genres, and back catalog. These chains were now competing, however, with mass merchandisers like Walmart and Target, which only carried the hits but at an even lower price, settling for a lower profit margin. Then to further undermine the record chains, electronics giants like Best Buy and Circuit City were offering even lower prices, sometimes as a loss leader, to entice buyers into their stores in hopes of selling them higher-priced items as well.

The most successful retail chains sought purchasing power and improved margins in consolidation, taking advantage of the investment frenzy of the late 1990s. Trans World acquired Strawberry's and Camelot Music while Wherehouse Entertainment bought Blockbuster Music from Viacom, positioning them as the two largest retail chains. Together with other retailers—including National Record Mart, Musicland, CD Warehouse, HMV, Virgin Entertainment, Barnes & Noble, Hastings Entertainment, and J&R Music World—they hired web marketeers to drive traffic to their sites.

In 1999, leading one-stop AEC emerged from Chapter 11 bankruptcy. Yucaipa Companies, owned by leveraged buyout specialist Ron Burkle, pounced on AEC with plans to expand its digital business. Burkle formed Checkout.com with former CAA head Michael Ovitz and then bought Digital OnDemand, which had developed in-store kiosks where consumers could buy and burn multi-artist compilation CDs. In December, Wherehouse bought 50 percent of CheckOut.com and merged online divisions with AEC.

Retail consolidations continued through 2000 and into 2001, with business leaders hoping that a larger economy of scale would reduce operating costs. Best Buy acquired Musicland's 1,300 stores, including Sam Goody's, Suncoast, and MediaPlay; Trans World acquired the 230 WaxWorks stores; Music

Network added 63 Wherehouse stores; and 111 other Wherehouse units went to Trans World. Then with the economic downturn after the events of 9/11, conditions worsened for the smaller record store chains and the distributors that serviced them. Five major distributors shut down. California's Valley Media had $800 million in sales in 2000, but filed for the largest bankruptcy liquidation in music business history in 2001. The declining sales trend intensified through 2003 as independent and chain stores continued to lose customers to mass merchandisers, and to mail-order sales through clubs and internet fulfillment.

Despite a 1.9 percent upswing in CD sales and the introduction of download sales due to the iTunes launch, the 2004 total was only 4.1 percent over 2003. Then in 2005 and 2006 the record industry resumed its downward trajectory. Retail and mail order combined for a 7.9 percent drop in 2005 physical sales, and then another 13.8 percent drop in 2006. Although digital sales cushioned the overall losses in 2005 to keep the rate at just .6 percent, 2006 showed industrywide decline of 6.2 percent despite a 74.4 percent increase in digital revenues.

Distributors and retail outlets were all affected. Using its relationship with Walmart outlets as a wedge, Anderson Merchandisers in 2005 pushed for a $7.50 wholesale price from the labels in order to sell CDs for under $10 or else threatened to discontinue selling them altogether. In 2005 AEC agreed to merge with Source Interlink, which published sporting and automotive magazines, each to expand their product lines into the other's outlets to replace declining sales in their own specialties. The number of record stores continued to contract, including the closure and sell-off of the one thousand-unit Musicland chain in 2006. Mass merchandisers including Best Buy and Circuit City, as well as book chains Borders and Barnes & Noble transferred CD shelf space to other products. In 2006 rack jobber Handleman acquired videogame software, hardware, and accessories distributor Crave Entertainment Group to compensate for its decline in revenue from diminishing CD sales.

But perhaps the most poignant symbol of the decline of retail was the liquidation of the Tower Records chain of eighty-nine superstores. After several years of flirting with bankruptcy while still reaping accolades as retailer of the year, Tower ceased operations on December 22, 2006. Ever since Russ Solomon opened the first store in Sacramento in 1960, Tower was the epitome of the record-buying experience, blending a wide array of product, accessories, and merchandise with listening booths, hip décor, and an abundance of atmosphere. It even had its own music magazine. Elton John reminisced about Tower with Ton Hanks's son Colin in Hanks's 2015 film documentary about the beloved record chain. "Tuesday mornings, I would be at Tower

Records. . . . And it was a ritual, and it was a ritual I loved. I mean, Tower Records had everything. Those people knew their stuff. They were really on the ball. I mean, they just weren't employees that happened to work at a music store. They were devotees of music."[24]

Mike Dreese, CEO of the Tower competitor Newbury Comics chain, added, "It's not the loss of the account per se, but its closing will come to be marked as the day that physical music died."[25] In 1995 Tower had been the first retailer to open its own website for online sales. In 2019 it existed only as a music webstore operating out of Ireland and a cherished memory for generations of music lovers.

With Retail Disrupted, the Labels Adapt for the Digital Future

The 2006 RIAA income summary reflected just how much the digital age had affected the record business. In 1985 it had been a $4.36 billion industry, 90 percent dependent on retail outlets with the remaining percentage coming through club and mail-order sales. Sales were 91.1 percent tape and vinyl analog product with the other 8.9 percent digital CDs. Two decades later, only 57 percent of its $11.29 billion in revenue came from traditional retail, 93.6 percent of that in CDs. Another 22.1 percent was from mail-order sales of physical product. The other 20.9 percent of revenue came from digital files delivered either as downloaded tracks, streaming music royalties, or the use of snippets of songs as ringtones or ringbacks on mobile telephones.

The 2004 Sony/BMG merger was primarily due to budgeting ramifications from declining sales. That same year WEA Distribution downsized its own branch warehouse system to save costs. Attempting to capture a piece of the growing independent label sector, the majors all ramped up their own indie distribution divisions. UMG opened its Fontana division in 2004. Also in 2004 newly installed WMG chief Lyor Cohen funded two new incubator indie labels to be distributed through its ADA division. In 2006 WMG acquired Ryko Distribution to merge with ADA, EMI reinvested in its Caroline indie label distribution, while Sony/BMG's RED Distribution continued to lead the indie sector.

In 2006 UMG's Doug Morris decided to take the lead in a more aggressive tack with tech entrepreneurs. In addition to content license fees, Morris negotiated an add-on royalty for each Microsoft Zune digital media player sold in Microsoft's short-lived bid to compete with iTunes and the iPod. He also threatened YouTube with copyright infringement on the eve of its $1.6

billion acquisition by Google, walking away with an equity share on top of content licenses, a ploy then replicated by the other majors. UMG also filed suit against MySpace, then the largest social media networking platform with over 100 million users, for copyright infringement by some of the site's users, with similar action against smaller social-networking websites bolt.com and grouper.com.

Billboard's Brian Garrity covered Morris's actions in his 2006 year-end "The Music Industry Big Ten" column as the #1 story of the year. "While critics in tech circles have decried UMG for bullying startups and new, untested services into paying 'label taxes,' credit Morris for reaping big and potentially precedent-setting dividends from the strategy. As Morris publicly stated at the time of the Zune deal: 'Any business that's built on the bedrock of music, we should share in.'"[26]

As retail contracted, the record industry reacted as best it could to the transfer of consumer preference from brick-and-mortar to digital commerce by consolidating from six major labels to four, improved management of their inventory, downsized staff, trimmed rosters, and tried in different ways to resuscitate or reinvent the connectivity with consumers that had sustained the industry for decades. With none of their initiatives succeeding, the opportunity opened for the Apple-led download wave to take over. The labels, however, were still trying to maintain the sale of music, whether physical or digital, in the album format, while the preference of younger consumers had shifted to single tracks on portable devices sequenced in playlists far less homogenously programmed than traditional radio.

Meanwhile in a small cabin outside of Stockholm, a guitar-playing twenty-three-year-old computer programmer and a music-loving thirty-six-year-old internet marketing specialist, each of whom had made his first millions through web advertising innovations, were trying to design the music industry's answer to the P2P piracy problem. Like Napster's Fanning and Parker before them, Daniel Ek and Martin Lorentzon had no music business experience and oriented their model toward consumers' tastes, habits, and tendencies. But unlike the Napster duo who disrupted a behemoth at its all-time zenith, they were about to present their concept to a declining industry in need of a digital rescue.

8

Publishing, Copyright, Legislation and Litigation

Publishing Prepares for the Digital Future

As the music industry entered 1996, the commercialization of the internet was just beginning. Far more data was being collected, collated, analyzed, and organized than ever before and applied to maximize revenue from traditional outlets and new media alike. Despite this increase in metadata aggregation, the music publishing sector still lacked an industrywide summary of publishing revenue. Data existed to construct fairly accurate valuations for performing and mechanical rights. Assessing revenue for the print and sync segments was still problematic, necessitating approximations. Resources that were available included reports and surveys from the NMPA, HFA, and the PROs; the few publicly traded music companies' SEC Form K-10 reports; RIAA and SoundScan summaries; *Billboard*, *Variety*, and other trade periodical information; and a wide array of news outlets, academic studies, and other research sources.

The consensus indicated that the PROs were still providing about 50 percent of revenue throughout the period. Mechanical licenses brought in an estimated 25 percent but fell to about 15 percent by 2006 with the decline in physical sales. They were kept from falling further by the scheduled mechanical rate increases and the addition of mechanical licenses for digital sales. Sync licenses and print sales provided the majority of the remaining 25 percent in 1996 and 35 percent in 2006, but there were few disclosed details other than an occasion mention by the NMPA to the trade press, leaving determination of revenue totals still up to educated estimates based on available data.

Performing Rights

By 1996 BMI had joined ASCAP in publicly disclosing its annual report with collection totals itemized by licensing categories. Total 1996 PRO revenue

American Popular Music and Its Business in the Digital Age. Rick Sanjek, Oxford University Press. © Frederick Sanjek 2024.
DOI: 10.1093/oso/9780190653828.003.0008

was about $893 million. ASCAP received about 52.8 percent of the total at $483 million, BMI had roughly 45 percent at $411 million, and SESAC was estimated to be about $20 million for 2.2 percent. By 2006, BMI's $779.4 million had almost drawn even with ASCAP's $785.5 million in a 48 percent to 48.3 percent split. SESAC's share had grown to an estimated $60 million in 2006 for a 3.7 percent share. Both ASCAP and BMI had reduced their overhead from the 18 percent to 20 percent range in 1986 to 11 percent to 12 percent for 2006, mostly due to growth in revenue without proportionate increases in overhead.

Incoming PRO revenue from copyright societies in other countries for the US songs performed there fluctuated annually between 26 percent and 33 percent of total revenue. One hundred percent of the writer share generated in each territory was remitted directly to each writer's US PRO, but most of the publishers' shares were collected by sub-publishers at source who then paid directly to US original publishers after subtracting their administrative percentage. The actual songwriter/publisher split of the incoming PRO foreign funds was not publicly disclosed, but generally believed to be around 90 percent due to songwriters and film/television score composers.

Despite the 2001 economic crisis and gradual migration of music consumers to digital alternatives, radio remained the top medium for access to music. Radio advertising revenue reached an all-time high of $21.7 billion in 2006, a gain of 74.6 percent over 1996, which was reflected, in turn, in rising PRO radio license fees. As digital alternatives—including satellite radio, webcasting, ringtones/ringbacks, mobile telephones, and subscription streaming services—gained ground, the PROs were quick to license them. Radio, television, and cable, however, remained the primary revenue sources, accounting for over 80 percent of PRO domestic collections in 2006 with general licensing providing another 15 percent or more. Revenue from digital media sources was under 5 percent.

In the mid-2000s all three PROs began collecting the set lists from the *Pollstar* Top 200 concert tours, and then collated the songs performed with the license fees collected to create a Live Performance line item on distribution statements, replacing the longstanding practice of adding these revenues to the radio distribution pool. The improved functionality of the PRO computer systems allowed for more efficient administration of the growing pools of information, revenue, and new licensees without altering the dependability of quarterly royalty distributions to tens of thousands of payees.

Perhaps the most significant event for performing rights during this period was the 2004 retirement of BMI's Frances Preston, after a forty-six-year tenure that began with the opening of BMI's Nashville office in 1958. Her myriad of accomplishments included testifying before Congress as a champion of intellectual property rights; cofounding the Country Music Association and its Hall of Fame; serving as a member of the Rock and Roll Hall of Fame executive committee, Peabody Awards elector, chairman of CISAC; receiving a Grammy Trustees award; and funding the Frances Williams Preston Research Laboratories at Vanderbilt University as part of the T.J. Martell Foundation mission on cancer, leukemia, and AIDS research. She was also inducted into the Country Music, Gospel Music, Broadcasting, and Cable Television Halls of Fame. When her retirement was announced *Variety* dubbed her "the highest-ranking woman in the music business."[1]

One of her final accomplishments and culmination of BMI's successful eighteen-year push for parity with ASCAP was to initiate a ten-year agreement with the industrywide Radio Music License Committee (RMLC) in August 2003. This new pact altered the license format to a guaranteed-fee basis rather than the percentage methodology of the past, in hopes of lowering expenses and stabilizing economic forecasts for all parties. The agreement was retroactive to 1997 ending a six-year period of interim rates, and would remain in effect until 2006. Preston left the president/CEO chair to senior VP of performing rights Del R. Bryant, a thirty-two-year BMI veteran who had moved from Nashville to New York with her in 1985. She also left an established executive team including COO John Cody and general counsel Marvin Berenson with senior VPs Fred Cannon in governmental affairs, Ron Solleveld in international, Bob Barone in IT, John Shaker in licensing, and senior VP of writer/publisher relations Phil Graham, who then replaced Bryant as senior VP of performing rights.

ASCAP management remained stable through 2006 following the 1994 installation of Marilyn Bergman as president/chairman of the board and elevation of John LoFrumento from CFO to CEO. The rest of the team included Todd Brabec as worldwide director of membership, Vincent Candilora as VP of licensing, COO Al Wallace, senior VP of industry affairs Karen Sherry, and hall of fame songwriter Roger Greenaway running the London office. In 2004 ASCAP followed BMI with a ten-year radio agreement similar to BMI's. Although still competitors for market share, this new parity shifted emphasis to common technological and global challenges including a shared North American cue sheet database with SESAC and Society of Composers, Authors and Music Publishers of Canada (SOCAN), which standardized North American song identification numbering for improved flow of worldwide PRO revenue from video and film productions.

SESAC's ownership troika of Stephen Swid, Freddie Gershon, and Ira Smith led revenue expansion from 2 percent to almost 4 percent of total PRO revenue following the 1995 signings of Bob Dylan and Neil Diamond. Their content strategy over the ensuing decade was to maintain a select group of songwriters to have a small but essential market share in each radio format to necessitate licenses, but not to the extent that royalties would reduce profit margin. Former ASCAP licensing executive Pat Collins replaced Bill Velez in 2004 as president/COO. Former NSAI executive director Pat Rogers joined in 1996 as senior VP of membership and remained throughout the period. Veteran London publisher Wayne Bickerton served as chairman of SESAC International.

Digital Sources and Rising Statutory Rate Bolster Mechanical Revenue

Matching 1996's RIAA shipment totals of 1.003 billion albums and 113.2 million singles to the then-current statutory rate of 6.95¢, and then applying the same litany of conditional criteria as in the preceding decade remained the most effective way to calculate mechanical royalties for an estimated $575 million. As there were no ringtones or downloads in 1996, all mechanicals came from physical sales.

By 2006 RIAA album shipments had fallen by 35.2 percent to 650 million with over 95 percent in physical formats, while there were 592.8 single tracks sold, 97.1 percent in downloads. The statutory rate had settled at 9.1¢. The estimated mechanical revenue tally for tracks came to $515.5 million, with another $76 million on 315 million ringtones at 24¢ each for a total mechanical revenue of $591.5 million. This was 2.9 percent over 1996 thanks to the rising statutory rate and digital alternatives that countered the plummeting sales of physical product.

At HFA, new president/CEO Gary Churgin had been hired from Citibank in 2001 to update HFA's systems and licensing processes, reducing Murphy's responsibilities to just NMPA business. After David Israelite took over from Murphy at the beginning of 2005, Churgin revealed HFA collection totals for the first time in the year-end issue of its *Soundcheck* newsletter, reporting 2006 HFA license collections were anticipated to be above $379 million but didn't differentiate between records and ringtones. If still applying the approximate 80 percent assumption for HFA's market share, then the HFA estimated total for the entire industry expanded to around $474 million. There was a 20 percent difference, however, between the HFA and RIAA methodologies.

Perhaps 80 percent market share was too high an estimate for HFA, or the mitigating conditions in the RIAA calculation were greater than assumed. Or a combination thereof. Splitting the difference would put the 2006 mechanical revenue estimate somewhere in the $532 million range.

Digital Technology Expands Print Revenues

As 1996 began, most mainstream publishers still licensed print rights through either Hal Leonard or Warner Bros. Publications (WBP). Both distributed sheet music, song folios, and other forms of print music culled from their clients' catalogs and their own proprietary content. Hal Leonard, however, was also very involved in marketing to the instructional, educational, and religious markets; licensing scores and arrangements for schools and arts centers; and exploiting public domain material. EMI and Warner Chappell were distributed through WBP. UMPG, Sony/ATV, and BMG went through Hal Leonard, as did the next two largest print specialists, Cherry Lane and Music Sales Corp.

As in the past, neither Hal Leonard nor WBP revealed specific financial details, and the NMPA only did so sporadically. In 1996 the NMPA *International Survey of Music Publishing Revenues* stated that CISAC members' worldwide print royalties were coupled together with revenue from CD rentals and referred to collectively as distribution income at 10 percent of the CISAC total of $6.22 billion in royalty payments, or $622 million. The survey, derived from the CISAC annual report, also stated that 1996 worldwide collections were just .3 percent over 1995, which had been 6.4 percent over 1994. It did not specify the US share of world collections.

From 1996 through 2006, digital delivery took over a growing share of the print music market starting with SheetMusicPlus.com in 1995, Hal Leonard's SheetMusicDirect.com in 1997, and MusicNotes.com in 1998. They gradually expanded into digitally delivered sheet music, folios, and interactive guitar and piano tablature. Ad-supported websites offering free song lyric downloads soon followed, including AZLyrics.com in 2000, Lyrics.com in 2001, and MetroLyrics.com in 2004.

In late 2005 Edgar Bronfman Jr. decided to sell WBP to Alfred Music, an instructional and educational print operation that didn't have any content from the contemporary music business. The 2005 WMG Annual Report revealed that despite $35 million in revenue through WBP, there was only a $1 million net after royalty payments and expenses. The sale also included a twenty-year exclusive license with Alfred for the Warner Chappell catalog. WMG expected that Alfred would expand the catalog into educational, religious, and instructional markets that had been beyond its reach and make print rights more profitable than when they had been in-house. With the sale to Alfred, the major publishers had totally farmed out print rights, the original foundation of music publishing, to third-party purveyors.

Billboard's Irv Lichtman retired in 2000 after a forty-five-year career in music trade journalism. He was followed by Jim Bessman, Susan Butler, and Ed Christman, who covered the publishing sector (including the print sector) when information was available. In early 2007 Butler reported that a National Association of Music Merchants (NAMM) study pegged 2006 print retail revenue at $532 million through its member retail outlets used to supplement their primary business of musical instruments and equipment sales.

Determining the extent of consumer spending on print music was still a daunting task due to the limited amount of available data. Similar to the record business, spending on print at retail, online, by mail order, and through licensing to civic, secular, or education organizations passed through the music industry funnel from the point of purchase to the music's creators. Consumers paid retailers, who paid distributors, who paid the rights holders, who then accounted to the songwriters. Every dollar spent at retail or mail order on print music became between 5¢ and 15¢ to the songwriter(s), depending on the product configuration and co-publishing situation. Digital print revenue at its higher royalty base was closer to 25¢ to 37¢ per sale.

By analyzing and understanding the relationship between royalties received and retail prices paid by consumers, point of purchase spending in the US on print music might well have approached the $3 billion threshold as deducted by *Billboard's* Frank DiCostanzo in 1994 and outlined in the previous publishing chapter. There were major differences, however, between the print and record segments that kept print from suffering a digitally triggered revenue decline similar to what had happened with records. Although both derived their revenue from sales, print had a more diversified range of products and customers. Moreover, the purchase of a physical or digital print copy couldn't be replaced by just listening to a recording except for the most musically gifted. Finally, unlike the record business, print didn't have a Napster-like disruption driving their consumers to unauthorized file-sharing.

Sync Revenue Boosted by Box Office and Home Video

By 2002 HFA had stopped administrating sync rights, putting the entire segment in the publishers' hands for direct negotiation with each licensee. HFA's

Churgin later told *Billboard*'s Butler that sync rights had become "a very labor intensive, inefficient and a costly configuration to license."[2] In 2006 Butler polled a panel of twelve industry veterans about sync license market share. The consensus agreed that licenses negotiated one at a time at different rates for each usage meant specific terms are usually not revealed. Butler concluded that there is no accurate method or measure for determining sync license market value.

During this time, however, there was accurate accounting on the revenue of sync licensee clientele. Film and television industry trade associations and press had built comprehensive databases to track the dollar flow in their respective sectors. This information helped publishers better negotiate license fees commensurate with the growing revenue of their clients. According to Box Office Mojo, an offshoot of film industry data aggregator Internet Movie Database (IMDb), movie box-office receipts expanded by 63 percent from $5.7 billion in 1996 to $9.2 billion in 2006 while theatrical releases increased from 306 in 1996 to 746 in 2006, signifying more than twice as many opportunities for opening and ending theme sync licenses as well as in context feature and background usages.

A July 2013 study by Rachel Soloveichik of the Bureau of Economic Analysis of the US Department of Commerce outlined network television advertising revenue growth of 53 percent from $11.3 billion in 1996 to $17.3 billion in 2006 while local and syndicated television added 41 percent from $10.5 billion to reach $14.8 billion. Cable revenues were a combination of subscriptions and advertising that more than tripled in volume from $11.5 billion to $36.4 billion. Foreign licensing fees doubled from just over $3.6 billion to almost $7.2 billion. Collated data from *Screen Digest*, *Forbes*, and CNBC.com tracked the growth of the home video market from about $5 billion in VHS sales and rentals in 1996 to over $16.8 billion in 2001 with the then-recently introduced DVD at 27.3 percent of the total. By 2006 DVDs had more than 90 percent of sales and rentals, with totals surpassing $25 billion.

The collective revenue for these business sectors more than doubled from $47.7 billion in 1996 to $109.9 billion in 2006 and was more than three and a half times the 1985 total. All used music to varying degrees. As an alternative to known songs licensed through traditional publishers or scores composed and produced for higher-budget theatrical release, production music libraries presented clients with a varied and adaptable array of options. In 1997 a proposed PRO cap on production music royalties inspired the formation of the Production Music Association (PMA) as an industrywide trade group and lobbyist, drawing from both independent and major publisher-owned libraries.

Both major and independent publishers recognized the value of libraries with their wide range of appeal to all consumer demographics and availability for varying licensee budgets. In addition to its partnership with EMI in APM, Zomba opened Zomba Production Music in 1996 to house the Bruton, Chappell, and FirstCom libraries under one roof. In 1997 Extreme Music emerged out of the punk rock world to fill the need for cutting-edge content. In 2003 Zomba became BMG/Zomba Production Music as part of BMG's purchase of the remaining part of Zomba it didn't already own. Killer Tracks continued to operate autonomously. In August 2005 Viacom bought Extreme for $45.1 million leaving the operation intact under founder Russell Emmanuel.

In 1998 *Billboard*'s Irv Lichtman reported that the NMPA international survey for 1997 cited a global increase in sync revenue by 30.9 percent to $864.17 million driven by the growing cable and film industries, and was expected to continue well into the new millennium. Applying the same suppositions assumed in the first section to the growth in sync client revenue, Randy Wachtler's US estimate of between $300 million and $750 million for 1995 grew to between $500 million and $900 million in 2006.

Shifting Market Share for Major Publishers

In 1996, as in the previous decade, the parent conglomerates of the major label groups still also owned a large majority of the music publishing industry, maintaining their control throughout the ensuing decade. The top-five ranked publishers on the *Billboard* Hot 100 Singles year-end chart for 1996 controlled 77.1 percent of the year's top singles with Warner Chappell at 27.6 percent, EMI with 24.8 percent, Sony/ATV with 9.1 percent, Zomba (25 percent owned by BMG but independently administered) with 8.2 percent, and MCA with 7.4 percent.

In 2001 the top-five publishers' share grew a point to 78.1 percent. EMI moved to first with 26.5 percent as Warner Chappell dropped to second with 19.2 percent. The Universal Music Publishing Group (UMPG) took over the third position with 14.2 percent, consolidating the former MCA and PolyGram companies. Sony/ATV was fourth with 7.8 percent, and Zomba came in fifth at 6.9 percent. The other BMG publishing interests had another 4.1 percent.

By 2006 the top-five music conglomerates still owned the top-five publishing slots in the top singles chart, with a slight rearrangement in order. EMI pulled further ahead in first place with 29.8 percent. UMPG and Warner

Chappell flipped the next two spots with UMPG at 17.4 percent and Warner Chappell with 16.5 percent. Sony/ATV grew to 12 percent to capture fourth place while the now-combined BMG and Zomba catalog was just behind in fifth place at 11.7 percent. This totaled an increase to 87.4 percent for the Big Five. Although the Sony and BMG record groups had formed a joint venture merger in 2004, the publishing companies remained separate.

The two main takeaways from this analysis of chart position were that over the decade EMI had established itself as the clear-cut publishing leader, and that the majors effectively dominated the market for hit records. Their larger economies of scale and income from catalog enabled them to make greater investment in the publishing rights for both new acts and established artists and producers.

Bandier Builds EMI Powerhouse

During Martin Bandier's eighteen-year tenure, EMI advanced from fourth amongt the Big Five in 1989, when it put him in charge, to first when he exited as chairman/CEO and president in 2006. One of his major accomplishments was the three-stage acquisition of the Jobete Music catalog, which contained the publishing rights to the majority of the Motown Records catalog, both founded by Berry Gordy in Detroit in 1959. In 1997 EMI bought 50 percent of Jobete and its administration rights for $132 million with the net publisher share (NPS) multiplier estimated to be at a factor of about twenty. EMI added another 30 percent in 2003 for $109.3 million, and the final 20 percent in 2005 for $80 million.

For $200 million EMI then added more than forty thousand songs from Windswept Pacific including the classic rock Big Seven Music catalog, the publishing arm of Morris Levy's Roulette Records. Adding Windswept and Jobete to The Beatles catalog and the Don Kirchner/Al Nevins's Aldon Music—which included Carole King, Gerry Goffin, Barry Mann, Cynthia Weil, Jeff Barry, Ellie Greenwich, and Neil Sedaka—gave EMI a treasure trove of golden oldies for movie and advertising sync licenses.

Bandier also assembled a top administrative staff anchored by his SBK team. Tracking licenses and collecting sync fees had helped propel the increase in the NPS value of the SBK catalog bought from CBS in 1986 for $125 million and sold to EMI three years later for around $310 million. Executive VP of music services Joanne Boris, who had been with Bandier since the beginning of his partnership with Charles Koppelman, organized and then computerized the EMI catalog, which had been cobbled together from a myriad of acquisitions with different administrative systems. Just as her team had done at SBK, new sync licenses were negotiated and handled internally rather than through HFA, leading to increased fees, administrative efficiency, and roy- alty payments. Direct contact with clients allowed the EMI licensing team to foster relationships and participate in creative decisions with licensees.

Bandier's creative team rejuvenated EMI's chart share by nurturing new songwriters and bringing established artists and producers into co-publishing partnerships or administrative agreements. Jody Gerson had gone from tape copy room to West Coast office head while signing teenager Alicia Keys, as well as Enrique Iglesias and Nora Jones. "Big Jon" Platt was a former club D.J. turned talent scout and eventually an EMI senior VP who brought in Jay-Z, Beyoncé, Kanye West, Usher, Pharrell Williams, and Snoop Dogg. On the East Coast Evan Lamberg also rose through the ranks from his start as a scout for new bands to executive VP of creative for North America. Former Alan Jackson manager Gary Overton took over the Nashville office in 1995.

In 2005 Bandier announced his intention to transition out, moving twelve-year EMI veteran and then-CFO Roger Faxon to co-president in prepara- tion for his ascent to chairman/CEO in 2007. In a *Billboard* salutary article, John Eastman, attorney for Paul McCartney and Billy Joel, who were both represented by EMI, lauded Bandier as "an old fashioned creative publisher." Berry Gordy added, "It isn't about his ego or company politics, it's about getting the product right and working with creative people." Top music at- torney Allen Grubman stated, "Marty is the finest music publisher of the last quarter of a century."[3]

Bider Guides Warner Chappell from Ross to Bronfman

Les Bider joined Warner Music as CFO in 1981 and replaced Chuck Kaye as CEO when WCI merged with Time Life in 1988. His accounting back- ground was a better fit with the new Time Life corporate mindset than Kaye's more creative record man style. Bider retained longtime Warner executive and ASCAP and NMPA board member Jay Morgenstern as overall GM and CEO of WBP, and veteran song plugger and Frank Sinatra associate Frank Military. Still riding the momentum of the 1987 Chappell acquisition, Warner Chappell finished 1996 at number one with a slight lead over EMI but slowly lost ground on the pop charts, finishing 2006 in a clear-cut second position.

Under Bider's leadership Warner Chappell emphasized administrative efficiency with increased revenue for syncs under licensing VP Pat Woods, and for print revenue under Morgenstern. President Rick Shoemaker on the West Coast oversaw creative services, working with senior VP John Titta in New York and executive VP Tim Wipperman in Nashville. Among Warner Chappell chart performer/songwriters during this period were Green Day, Sheryl Crow, Nickelback, Dr. Dre, Van Halen, Missy Elliott, Kid Rock, Collective Soul, india.arie, and Gavin DeGraw.

After Bronfman's group bought WMG from the floundering AOL Time Warner in 2004, he revamped Warner Chappell's executive team. He replaced Bider with attorney Richard Blackstone, who had worked his way up the Zomba Publishing hierarchy to president in 1989. Also departing were Shoemaker, Titta, and Wipperman, as Blackstone reshaped the creative team with his own appointees.

During Bider's twenty-five-year tenure he transitioned through the Chappell purchase, the merger with *Time*, and then with AOL. He supervised integration of the Warner business model with Chappell's business and accounting services, absorbed the Atlantic and Elektra-owned publishing companies, grew the Warner print division with the acquisition of CCP/Belwin, expanded co-publishing and administration agreements, and solidified the Warner Chappell worldwide publishing network. From the time Bider joined as CFO in 1981 until his departure in 2005, annual publishing collections grew from about $50 million to over $500 million.

Sony/ATV Partnership Builds New Catalog

The integration of the Sony and Michael Jackson–owned ATV publishing catalogs after their November 1995 merger agreement occupied much of Sony president Richard Rowe and his staff's time in 1996. The purchase had a special significance for Rowe since his father, legendary London-based Decca A&R man Dick Rowe, had been known as the man who turned down The Beatles before they signed with rival EMI rather than his many positive accomplishments. Now the younger Rowe was himself working with Paul McCartney and Yoko Ono. In early 2000 the Sony Tree division acquired Atlanta-based Lowery Music containing Joe South's string of hits for $20 million followed by the $157 million purchase of venerable Acuff-Rose Music in 2002 with its library of standards by Hank Williams Sr., Felice and Boudleaux Bryant, Roy Orbison, John D. Loudermilk, and many other country music hall of famers.

In 2004 David Hockman, former head of PolyGram publishing from 1986 until its sale to MCA in 1998, replaced Rowe. Hockman added Danny Strick, former president of BMG Music from 1989 to 2000, as president of Sony/ATV. Strick was charged with revitalizing creative acquisitions to complement the back catalog amassed over the past ten years. In Nashville Acuff-Rose veteran Troy Tomlinson replaced the retiring Donna Hilley in 2005 after her thirty-one-year tenure, which began at Tree as an administrator, transitioned to partner, and then to president/CEO of Sony/ATV Nashville. Top Sony/ATV–affiliated writers included Babyface, Bobby Braddock, Oasis, Brooks & Dunn, Mariah Carey, and John Mayer.

Firth Pilots BMG through Two Decades

BMG Music Publishing's chairman/CEO Nicholas Firth had grown up in the music business, beginning in 1964 after college with his grandfather Louis Dreyfus's Chappell & Co. He became president after PolyGram bought Chappell in 1968 until its sale to Freddy Bienstock's investment group in 1984. Three years later he took over the top spot at BMG. Although BMG was one of the top-three publishers internationally with strong classical and European pop catalogs, the US division had never reached the top five of the annual *Billboard* publisher rankings. Working under Firth as president were Danny Strick from 1996 to 2000 and Scott Francis from 2000 to 2006. Karen Conrad led the Nashville office from 1993 through 2006. Top BMG songwriters included Coldplay, Nelly, Jason Mraz, and Seal.

In 1992 BMG purchased 25 percent of the publishing wing of Zomba Music, then the incumbent #5 top publisher. Zomba continued to operate independently. In 1996 BMG bought 20 percent of Zomba's record division, with a proviso to buy the rest of the company, both publishing and records, by the end of 2002 at a preagreed multiple of the-then current NPS. After massive success with Britney Spears, R. Kelly, INXS, and the Backstreet Boys, Zomba founder Clive Calder exercised the purchase option, which calculated to $2.74 billion for his shares.

BMG finally reached *Billboard*'s top-five publisher listing following the Zomba addition. Zomba also included the contemporary Christian Provident Music Group and the traditional Christian Benson Music Group, both based in Nashville. Many analysts felt the price was almost twice as much as Calder's share of Zomba's real market value, but the terms of the purchase set in the 1996 agreement were deemed legally ironclad. Calder became one of the wealthiest single individuals in the music business with no obligation beyond a short-term consultancy agreement.

Renzer Leads UMPG Expansion

In 1996 Doug Morris appointed thirty-five-year-old David Renzer as worldwide president of MCA Music. Renzer came from Zomba publishing where in ten years he rose from junior creative director to president. Morris was comfortable putting UMPG in the hands of a streetwise executive to push the creative growth mandated by Edgar Bronfman Jr. Renzer brought in Betsy Anthony-Brodey from the Epic A&R staff as VP, talent acquisitions.

After the 1998 PolyGram merger, Renzer consolidated publishing divisions in over forty territories as well as three US offices, combining the best from each company as Morris was doing with the record division. Veteran Pat Higdon was brought in to oversee the Nashville office. PolyGram had been one of the top international publishers, but it had been weak in the US, while MCA was weak internationally but stronger than PolyGram domestically. The unified assets, however, combined to achieve the number-three spot in the 1999 *Billboard* ranking.

In addition to securing the publishing or administration rights for many artists signed to the UMG labels, UMPG made a major acquisition in 2000, buying the Rondor Music catalog from owners Herb Alpert and Jerry Moss. Chuck Philips of the *Los Angeles Times* reported a price tag of $400 million primarily in stock at a twenty multiple of NPS. Rondor not only included the publishing rights for songs owned by A&M Records, which had been sold to PolyGram in 1989, but also the East/West Music catalog that contained almost all the hits from the seminal Memphis soul label Stax Records. Longtime Rondor head Lance Freed, son of the legendary D.J. Alan Freed, was retained as part of the deal.

In 2006, UMPG won the bidding for the BMG publishing catalog, including the Zomba companies. Sony, EMI, and WMG were all also interested, as were private equity and hedge funds ready to back both Charles Koppelman and Les Bider. Firth had grown the BMG NPS to $218 million in 2005, overcoming the cost of the Zomba purchase. In September UMPG and BMG agreed to a reported $2 billion sale pending regulatory approval and final accounting, which would set the multiple of NPS around nine. The acquisition was designed to propel UMPG into a post-purchase first- or second-place slot in what would become the Big Four publisher rankings. UMPG-represented writers included 3 Doors Down, Adam Levine, Glen Ballard, Justin Timberlake, Shania Twain, John Popper of Blues Traveler, 50 Cent, and Ludacris.

The Top Independent Publishers

The dominance in the *Billboard* charts by the Big Five publishing groups reflected their share of pop, country, and black/urban/R&B radio play as well as mechanicals from record sales. In the 2006 year-end rankings of the Hot 100 singles, the Big Five had 79.5 percent of the chart entries for the top-ten publishers. In overall publisher rankings, however, their share was not quite as high. According to the *Financial Times*, the global publishing industry generated around $8 billion. The Big Five generated about 70 percent of the global total. Several established independent publishers had sufficient funds from back catalog revenue to compete with the majors for the publishing rights for new artists signed to major labels and were often in the sixth through tenth slots in the *Billboard* year-end top ten.

Peermusic was led by CEO Ralph Peer II and president/COO Kathy Spanberger. Peer's legendary father had started the catalog in the 1920s by acquiring the publishing rights from artists he signed as an RCA Records A&R man, including Jimmy Rodgers and the Carter Family. By the late 1990s, the younger Peer had expanded his father's inroads into the European and Latin American markets by signing smaller US companies for international representation.

Carlin Music America contained the catalogs Freddy Bienstock retained after his sale of Chappell & Co. to Warner in 1988. By 1996 his children, Caroline and Ron, had assumed much of the operational responsibility. The elder Bienstock had built his company through initiating savvy acquisitions and establishing his own international network. Carlin was now approaching the value of the Chappell catalog he had sold to Warner for $200 million, but this time Bienstock himself had the primary ownership stake.

Famous Music, the publishing wing of Paramount Pictures, which had been owned by Viacom since 1994, was ably run by veteran attorney Irwin Z. Robinson, who had previously been president of both Chappell Music and EMI Music, was then chairman of the NMPA board, and vice chairman of the ASCAP board. Supported by a catalog of movie music going back to 1928, Famous was empowered by Viacom to compete on a financial level with the majors for new talent under the creative leadership of president Ira Jaffe.

Chrysalis Music, retained by Chris Wright after he sold Chrysalis Records to EMI, became a regular presence in *Billboard*'s yearly list of top-ten publishers after veteran Warner Chappell creative director Kenny MacPherson came on board as president in 2002.

Windswept Holdings, still under the leadership of Evan Medow after the sale of its Big Seven Music catalog to EMI in 1999, acquired Jerry Leiber and Mike Stoller's Trio Music/Quartet Music catalog of rock hits, excluding the ones they wrote themselves, which they retained in Leiber-Stoller Music, supervised by veteran in-house catalog administrator Randy Poe. The transaction was reported to be in the mid-eight figures by *Variety*'s Justin Oppelaar. Windswept reached *Billboard*'s top-ten Hot 100 chart publishers from 2002 through 2006, settling in at #6 in the last two years. Windswept also acquired Affiliated Publishers Inc. from veteran Nashville songwriters/producers/managers Johnny Slate, Danny Morrison, and Tony Harley, which included multiple top-ten hits by their management clients Tim McGraw and Joe Diffie.

Right alongside Windswept and Chrysalis in the year-end top ten was Cherry Lane Music, the folk music and print specialist opened by producer Milt Okun in 1960. Originally the conductor and arranger for Harry Belafonte, Okun produced and/or arranged for Peter, Paul and Mary, The Chad Mitchell Trio, The Brothers Four, John Denver, and Miriam Makeba. Son-in-law Peter Primont joined Okun in 1986 and built the Cherry Hill contemporary catalog into its top-ten status.

Continuing her string of success from the previous decade, Realsongs' owner and only songwriter Diane Warren won her fourth and fifth ASCAP Songwriter of the Year awards in 1998 and 1999, and Country Songwriter of the Year in 2000 with Realsongs ranking in *Billboard*'s top-ten publishers list each of those years as well. Realsongs handled its own administration with international sub-publishing through EMI Music.

The Rise of Independent Administrators and Catalog Aggregators

The increased size of the publishing market and growing emphasis on metadata management created a heightened demand for independent publishing administrators. This led to a growing cadre of companies working on a percentage basis ranging between 10 percent and 20 percent just to perform the requisite administrative services. While some remained small operations with just a few clients or were handled in-house by artists' business managers or attorneys, others grew to become multimillion-dollar operations, moving up in the ranks of the independent publishing community.

Dan Bourgoise opened Bug Music in 1975 to administrate the songs of his management client, 1950s pop star Del Shannon. His brother Fred joined the company and over the next twenty years they added songs by artists including

Johnny Cash, Willie Dixon, Muddy Waters, Stevie Ray Vaughan, Iggy Pop, Wilco, the Foo Fighters, and a plethora of Los Angeles punk bands, to grow into a $15 million business by 1996, then to $30 million by 2006. Their business model was based on a 10 percent administration fee with another 10 percent fee charged for overseeing sub-publishing in other territories.

In 1978 Randall Wixen opened Wixen Music Publishing, Inc. as an administrator and advocate for the rights of independent songwriters, publishers, and recording artists. Wixen had graduated from UCLA with a degree in economics and became music editor of the *Daily Bruin*. Similar to Bug, Wixen operated on 10 percent of net receipts and made sub-publishing administration agreements for another 10 percent through its worldwide network of over forty independent sub-publishing administrators. Wixen administered all licenses for its clients, bypassing HFA for mechanicals, and structured its contracts on a yearly renewal basis. Wixen himself·was also a producer, soundtrack consultant, member of the Recording Academy, and author of *The Plain and Simple Guide to Music Publishing* (4th ed., 2020) published by Hal Leonard. The company's clients have included Neil Young, the Doobie Brothers, John Prine, Tom Petty, John Lee Hooker, Janis Joplin, George Harrison, The Doors, Richard Marx, and many other songwriters, artists, and bands.

Former BMI executive Mark Fried launched Spirit Music Group in 1995. At BMI Fried had organized and implemented the first PRO survey and direct accounting for college radio, expanding BMI's royalty distribution to countless alternative music acts. Fried employed his computer skills to develop Spirit's then-revolutionary transparent royalty database featuring customized client services and interactive support. Spirit was among the first publishers to digitize its entire catalog; initiate licenses for ringtones, video games, and mobile apps; and establish relationships with new download, streaming, and video services. John Phillips, Henry Mancini, Charles Mingus, Brian Wilson, Lou Reed, T. Rex, Chaka Khan, Boz Scaggs, and Bob Marley were some of the legendary artists signing with Spirit as well as the seminal rock catalogs Cameo Parkway, Brunswick, and Laurie Records. Spirit was also active with alternative music artists such as Scissor Sisters, MGMT, and Justice.

Another area in need of specialized administration came from older songwriters or their estates for renewal and recapture rights. For songs created prior to 1978, copyright would revert to songwriters or their estates after the expiration of the first twenty-eight-year term of copyright, due to the absence of renewal rights in the original contract, or death of a songwriter during the first term of copyright. These were standard features of the agreement recommended by the Songwriters Guild of America (SGA). For songs written in 1978 and after, there was a period of copyright recapture rights that began thirty-five years from the date of creation, with notification of intent allowed over the preceding ten-year period, thus commencing in 2003 for the songs created in 1978.

The venture capital sector of the financial industry had long viewed music publishing as a more stable investment than record companies were. While success in the record industry depended upon the weekly decisions of current label executives and were further subject to the whims of radio programmers, publishing profits were anchored by established earnings trends and management of overhead. With the rate of growth of the publishing sector in the early 2000s accelerating due to new licensing opportunities created by digital technology while record industry revenue declined, investors were eyeing small, established publishing companies that were profitable with just a few long-established copyrights, referred to as evergreens, earning revenue from syncs, print, and back catalog record releases with minimal expenses, thus yielding a high NPS.

If an established catalog that was bought on an eight multiple of a $10 million NPS for $80 million should continue to earn at that $10 million NPS over the next year eight years, then the investment would be recouped, other than interest, and the catalog would still be worth $80 million at the same multiple. If the NPS increased by successfully working the catalog to produce higher annual return or by reducing overhead, then the value would go up with the multiple also applied to the incremental revenue increase. Aggregating small catalogs under a common administrator became the prevailing modus operandi for investors in publishing. Every dollar saved by pooling overhead costs became another dollar of profit included in the NPS.

The young Swedish tech entrepreneur Willard Ahdritz founded the Kobalt Music Group in London in 2000 with financing from tech investor Spark Ventures. He believed digital technology could foster a more efficient and transparent industry that better served content creators and copyright owners through a global licensing management system linking them to PROs, sub-publishers, and other copyright administrators around the world. With a second round of investment in 2005, Ahdritz unveiled software that allowed clients to track and manage their own catalogs. Trent Reznor of Nine Inch Nails, Gwen Stefani, Nick Cave, Dr. Luke, and Sanctuary Music Publishing all came on board. Kobalt only administered and did not compete with its clients in copyright ownership. The Kobalt website stated that its mission was "to build a future where all songwriters, artists and creators get paid fairly and trust the music industry,"[4] and Ahdritz's business mantra has always been "transparency and accountability."[5]

In 2005 Joel Katz, then-chairman of the music and entertainment division of the Greenberg Traurig law firm, partnered with veteran publishing administrator Richard Perna and former Miramax Music VP David Schulhof to launch Evergreen Copyrights with $150 million in backing from Lehman Brothers Merchant Banking. Their initial catalog contained Warlock Music (Nick Drake), the Teddy Riley catalog, Audigram (J. J. Cale), Bill Monroe Music, the Matt Slocum (Sixpence None the Richer) catalog, and Rykomusic, which had a publishing partnership with Rough Trade Music encompassing works by the Violent Femmes, Rocket from the Crypt, and the John Spencer Blues Explosion. "We looked at publishing assets that were underserved and undermarketed that were owned by people we have dealt with in the past,"[6] stated Schulhof.

In early 2006 private equity investors Crossroads Media, led by former Viacom COO Tom McGrath, and Spectrum Equity Investors of Boston brought in former Windswept CFO John Rudolph as Bug Music CEO. Rudolph had formed Music Analytics consulting company in 2001 after he left Windswept. He had been involved in the Trio/Quartet sale to Windswept, the Bronfman-led acquisition of WMG, the sale of DreamWorks Music Publishing to Dimensional Associates funded by JDS Capital, and the Compendia Music sale to Sheridan Square/Artemis, helmed by former Alliance Entertainment CEO and founder Joe Bianco. Rudolph's goals at Bug were to consolidate, acquire more assets, and prepare to sell for a profit.

The Digital Millennium Copyright Act

In 1974 the World Intellectual Property Organization (WIPO), a part of the Berne Convention, became one of the fifteen specialized agencies of the UN dealing with commerce, health, and/or other international concerns specifically charged "to encourage creative activity, to promote the protection of intellectual property throughout the World."[7] In 1996 WIPO initiated the two new treaties—the WIPO Copyright Treaty (WCT) and the WIPO Performances and Phonograms Treaty (WPPT)—to incorporate specific language extending and/or defining copyright protection provisions for digital technology related to the commercialization of the internet.

The Digital Millennium Copyright Act (DMCA) was introduced in July 1997 to amend the Copyright Act of 1976 in order to implement these two WIPO acts in the US. The act was signed into law by President Bill Clinton in October 1998. While dealing with many aspects and classes of intellectual property, the two provisions with the greatest effect on the music business

MUSIC & MAJOR COPYRIGHT HISTORIC HIGHLIGHTS

1789	The U.S. Constitution, Art. I, Section 8 stated "Congress shall have the Power... To promote the Progress of Science and useful Arts, by securing for limited Times to Authors and Inventors the exclusive Right to their respective Writings and Discoveries."
1790	Modeled on the British *Statute of Ann, the Copyright Act of 1789* had a 14 year term with a 14 year renewal option.
1870	The Library of Congress was opened in Washington DC to handle all aspects of copyright, with the Copyright Office then added to it in 1897.
1879	A general revision of the copyright law added musical compositions to protected works, and increased the first term to 28 years, but kept the 14 year renewal.
1897	The Copyright Amendment Act of 1897 codified the right to license public performance of music under copyright law.
1909	The Copyright Act of 1909 granted protection to all works published with a valid copyright notice on them, without which they would enter the public domain. The renewal was extended to match the 28-year term. The act also included a compulsory mechanical license, allowing a work to be used after first publication without consent provided royalties were properly paid.
1912	Under the Act of 1909, protection was extended to motion pictures. This led to sync licenses for the soundtracks and songs embedded in "talking pictures".
1962	Congress passed the first in a series of term extensions for works with expiring renewals until a revised copyright law could be enacted.
1972	Copyright protection was extended to future sound recordings. Pre-1972 releases remained under state law with no federal protection.
1976	The Copyright Act of 1976 superseded the 1909 Act as of January 1, 1978. The term of copyright for new works became life of the last surviving author plus 50 years, later extended to 70 years by the 2002 Sonny Bono Copyright Term Extension Act.
1998	The Digital Millennium Copyright Act provided an economic framework for the monetization of music in digital media and protection from unauthorized access and online infringement. It also created a "safe harbor" for online service providers as long as they cooperated in protecting the rights of intellectual property owners.
2018	The Orrin G. Hatch-Bob Goodlatte Music Modernization Act, authorized the Copyright Office to designate a Mechanical Licensing Collective to administrate a performance rights royalty to artists and record labels from digital transmissions. The Act also covered protection for certain master recordings created before 1972.

Source: U.S. Copyright Office: copyright.gov/timeline / Photo credit: iStock

Illustration 8.1 Music and Major Copyright Historic Highlights

were that "no person shall circumvent a technological measure that effectively controls access to a work protected under this title" and "no person shall manufacture, import, offer to the public, provide, or otherwise traffic in any technology, product, service, device, component, or part thereof, that . . . is primarily designed or produced for the purpose of circumventing protection afforded by a technological measure that effectively protects a right of a copyright owner under this title in a work or a portion thereof."[8]

These provisions were designed to support the incorporation of Digital Rights Management (DRM) encoding into the downloading process to prevent illegal duplication. The record industry hoped that such encoding would reduce digital home piracy, which they claimed by then had increased to billions of dollars annually. As a concession to the internet service provider (ISP) category of web platforms, which then included AOL, Yahoo, CompuServe, Earthlink, Prodigy, GTE, and Microsoft's MSN, the Online Copyright Infringement Liability Limitation Act (OCILLA) was passed as part of the DMCA, granting ISPs and other internet intermediary companies safe harbor status, which allowed them to make their own copies as well as provided protection from any secondary liability for infringement perpetrated by their users.

While hearings on the DMCA were being held in the US House of Representatives, the Copyright Term Extension Act of 1998 (CTEA) was introduced in the US Senate by Orrin Hatch, a musician and songwriter himself with ninety-seven songs in his ASCAP catalog. CTEA was also known as the Sonny Bono Copyright Term Extension Act in honor of the former producer, songwriter, and half of Sonny and Cher. Bono represented the 44th congressional district of California from 1995 until his death in a skiing accident in January 1998. Signed the day before the DCMA, CTEA extended the life of copyright in the US for songs written in 1978 and after from fifty to seventy years after the death of the last surviving author. The term for works written before 1978 that had not already fallen in the public domain was extended from seventy-five years to ninety-five years, putting the US in harmony with the CISAC standards.

Another provision of CTEA pertained to copyrights of corporate authorship, which were extended to 120 years after creation or 95 years after first publication, whichever came first. This clause led to the informal dubbing of CTEA as the Mickey Mouse Protection Act. The Disney character had debuted in 1928, so its copyright protection was extended until 2024. Much to the dismay of music publishers, however, was the attachment of HR 739, the Fairness in Music Licensing Act, to CTEA during the House debate, which exempted restaurants and bars under 3,500 square feet from needing PRO licenses. This provision was rationalized as a trade-off for agreeing to the copyright extension windfall.

The No Electronic Theft Act and Cybersquatting

A third act concerning digital copyright infringement was introduced by Rep. Bob Goodlatte (R-VA) in July 1997 within days of DMCA and CTEA. The No Electronic Theft Act (NET Act) closed a loophole in the definition of criminal copyright infringement, expanding it to include "the receipt, or expectation of value, including the receipt of other copyrighted works."[9] Prior to the NET Act, transmitting digital files of copyrighted works for no financial gain could not be criminally prosecuted. Peter H. Lewis of *The New York Times* covered the 1994 case *US vs LaMacchia* in which Massachusetts Institute of Technology (MIT) student David LaMacchia had used the university computers to create an encrypted digital bulletin board folder dubbed Cynosure to accept and transmit what was described as being software applications and games. During its operational run between November 1993 and when MIT shut it down in January 1994, Cynosure purportedly transmitted over a million dollars' worth of software.

Lewis reported, "Prosecutors said that while Mr. LaMacchia apparently did not profit from the trading, his operation was one of the largest hubs in a worldwide electronic black market that traded billions of dollars' worth of illegally copied software each year."[10] Federal district court judge Richard Stearns dismissed the case in December 1994, ruling that the federal wire fraud statutes under which the case was prosecuted were not applicable to LaMacchia's actions. He suggested that new legislation should be passed to deal with willful infringement of copyrighted software when there was no monetary gain. The NET Act was crafted to be that legislation.

The practice of cybersquatting had become endemic by 1999. Senator Hatch told his colleagues, "For the net-savvy, what we are talking about is 'cybersquatting,' of the deliberation, bad-faith, and abusive registration of Internet domain names in violation of the rights of trademark owners."[11] These cybersquatters would either attempt to extort payment from the rightful owners or cause consumer confusion by using the appropriated name to direct them to the cybersquatter's main site. Hatch further added, "Imagine logging on to what you think is your favorite online retailer only to find out later that the site was not that retailer at all, but rather a facade for an unscrupulous individual who is collecting your credit card and other personal information for unknown and possibly nefarious purposes."[12]

At that time, the only option to avoid a protracted and expensive legal action complicated by foreign trademark and domain name registrations had often been to pay the purported infringers their price for transfer of the domain name. In court, brand name owners depended upon the 1995 Federal Trademark Dilution Act (FTDA) in seeking legal recourse, which could be cumbersome and expensive at best, and sometimes inconclusive. In September 1998, the Commerce Department's National Telecommunications and Information Administration (NTIA) contracted with the nonprofit Internet Corporation for Assigned Names and Numbers (ICANN) to oversee the database of domain name registrations.

Just prior to that in May 1998, the domain name Madonna.com was registered with domain name administrator Network Solutions based on a trademark subsequently registered in Tunisia in June 1998 by Dan Parisi, who initially linked Madonna.com to an adult entertainment website. The US trademark for Madonna, however, had been owned and in use by recording artist Madonna for entertainment services and related goods since 1979. Madonna filed in October 1999 under the ICANN Uniform Domain Name Dispute Resolution Policy.

Madonna's case went to the WIPO Arbitration and Mediation Center in July 2000 before a three-person panel. As the proceeding was civil, the panel judged on a preponderance of the evidence, not on the reasonable doubt standard found in criminal cases. The panel ruled on October 12, 2000, that under the policy, "The disputed domain name is identical or confusingly similar to a trademark in which Complainant [Madonna] has rights; Respondent [Parisi] lacks rights or legitimate interests in the domain name; and the domain name has been registered and used in bad faith. Therefore, we decide that the disputed domain name 'madonna.com' should be transferred to the Complainant"[13] by the ICANN-compliant Network Solutions.

Although this course of action took a year, it was probably more expeditious and less expensive than a federal suit brought under US Trademark Law. Other artists who went to WIPO arbitration rather than buy a domain name at an unreasonable price or resort to a federal infringement suit included Paul McCartney, Eminem, Bruce Springsteen, Sting, The Rolling Stones, and Mick Jagger individually. In November 1999, while Madonna's suit was under WIPO deliberation, the US Congress passed the Anticybersquatting Consumer Protection Act (ACPA), which protected both the public and owners from false representation of familiar brand names.

Fine-tuning the DMCA

The Satellite Home Viewer Improvement Act of 1999 (SHVIA) also passed. It included a provision intended to amend the Copyright Act of 1976 by adding sound recordings to the list of intellectual property that could be registered with the Copyright Office as work made for hire, and as such, would be ineligible for copyright recapture by recording artists. This provision was presented to the House Subcommittee on Courts and Intellectual Property as a technical correction, but the creative community viewed it as a substantive change detrimental to their best interests.

Don Henley, who had cofounded the Recording Artists Coalition (RAC) with Sheryl Crow, told *Billboard*'s Bill Holland: "For a record company to claim, simply because it gives an artist an advance and puts up a little marketing money, that it then owns that artist's work or that copyright in perpetuity is preposterous and outrageous."[14] When the problem was brought to the attention of ranking subcommittee member Howard Berman, known as a champion of creators' rights, the subcommittee encouraged the RIAA and the RAC to come to an accord. Henley and Crow brought in veteran music attorney Jay Cooper, with additional backing by the Recording Academy, ASCAP, BMI, the American Federation of Television and Radio Artists (AFTRA), the AFM, the NSAI, and a bevy of managers, lawyers, and copyright law professors.

Echoing Henley in the same *Billboard* article, Cooper made it clear that the RIAA had to pivot and reverse their position. "The labels face . . . a disastrous situation. They are going to need artists to help on these other issues, such as online piracy, where the views of artists and the companies come together. They just won't get them otherwise."[15] The Work Made for Hire and Copyright Corrections Act of 2000 passed in October 2000, negating the inserted work-for-hire provision of SHVIA.

SoundExchange, then a division of the RIAA, had been accepted by the Copyright Arbitration Royalty Panel (CARP) as the authorized receiving agent under the auspices of the DMCA to enter into agreements on behalf of recorded music copyright owners and performers for distributing performance royalties. Attorney, former touring musician, songwriter, former Mary Chapin Carpenter manager, and longtime advocate for the DMCA and other copyright reforms John Simson was named as the founding SoundExchange executive director in 2000. In 2003 SoundExchange separated from the RIAA to become the sole authorized digital performance rights collection organization operating on a nonprofit basis with a board comprising representatives from all parties involved in the performance rights flow of revenue.

Independent and noncommercial webcasters, however, had contended through their Voice of Webcasters advocacy group that the rates established by the DMCA had been designed for larger corporate media companies, were onerous and excessive for the small independent operator, and would force many of them out of business. The Small Webcaster Settlement Act of 2002 (SWSA) was passed to specifically authorize SoundExchange to establish a more palatable alternative for these small webcasters to the royalty rates set by CARP for large commercial websites.

Infringement Spawns Copyright Litigation

Music industry legal action triggered by digital infringement began in June 1997. The RIAA filed suit in New York, Texas, and California federal courts against three MP3 file-sharing sites, shutting them down with restraining orders that resulted in permanent injunctions six months later. None of the three had charged customers for downloads, but one asked for uploaded files in return. Nonetheless, the RIAA contended that these downloads represented lost sales and if allowed to continue, could add to what would be almost $2 billion annually in lost worldwide sales, with over $300 million of that in the US. At the estimated $12.50 average suggested retail price, this represented 24 million albums in the US, and hundreds of millions worldwide, most of which were quite likely copies of albums by US superstars. Although the industry had not yet ascertained how to profit from the new digital file technology, they certainly didn't want anyone else doing so, much less displace their sales with free music. There were two more suits against infringing MP3 file-sharing websites in 1998 that also resulted in permanent injunctions, but this time were accompanied by monetary damage awards and mandated community service.

In October 1998, just prior to the passage of the DMCA, the RIAA applied to the Central District Court of California under the auspices of the Audio Home Recording Act (AHRA) of 1992 for a temporary restraining order against the Diamond Multimedia Systems' Rio digital MP3 player, a pocket-sized, battery-operated portable device that could hold up to an hour of MP3 music files transferred from a computer. The order was initially approved, but quickly rescinded. That reversal was upheld in June 1999 by the US Court of Appeals for the Ninth Circuit, which affirmed that the Rio was not a recording device used for downloading, but rather a device used for the noncommercial copying of already downloaded digital files for personal use, allowable under the AHRA.

The court ruled that to space shift files from a computer to the Rio was fair use just as the time shift of television programming onto a videotape was ruled not to be infringement in the *1984 Sony Corp. of America v. Universal City Studios, Inc.*, commonly known as the Betamax case. Rather than take the Rio case to the US Supreme Court, the RIAA and Diamond Multimedia came to a confidential settlement and Diamond joined the Secure Digital Music Initiative (SDMI) in seeking a DRM-protected system for MP3 files. The Rio stayed on the market to become the first MP3 player to sell over two hundred thousand units. In 2000 Diamond and its 1999 merger partner, S3, Incorporated, changed the company's name to SONICblue, but then went bankrupt in early 2003. They sold the Rio to Japanese-based D&M Holdings, the parent company of Denon and Marantz, which subsequently stopped producing MP3 players in 2005.

The Battle Against Napster

In December 1999, the RIAA sued the peer-to-peer (P2P) file sharing platform Napster for massive copyright infringement six months after its June launch. The case epitomized the clash between the major-label determination to repress what it considered home piracy and young tech entrepreneurs trying to supply the market demand created by digital-age consumers. Rap artist/producer/entrepreneur Dr. Dre and heavy metal mega-group Metallica filed suits of their own. Napster founders Shawn Fanning and Sean Parker, both nineteen years old, intended to create a better system for accessing music that proved beneficial to consumer and industry alike (covered in more depth in chapter 10). They believed that the legalities would be worked out and were more than willing to continue within a framework acceptable to the record industry.

The labels, however, were well into the Madison Project, testing the IBM digital downloading product and participating in the SDMI, which was still seeking practical copy prevention encoding for MP3 files. Although Napster had close to 80 million users at its peak, it had no plan for monetizing the business, making it difficult to compete with established tech giants like IBM or well-funded digital entrepreneurs such as RealNetworks, all of whom were complying with DRM provisions. The legal battle played out over the next eighteen months. Napster received a court order to shut down in July 2000, appealed, and was granted a temporary stay. It brought in venture capital investors willing to gamble on reaching an accord with the industry and continued to negotiate.

In October 2000 BMG's Thomas Middelhoff agreed to invest in Napster and in early February 2001 the Napster-BMG alliance offered the other labels $1 billion to settle the suit and turn Napster into a properly licensed platform, but the other labels wouldn't comply. Middelhoff was also facing internal opposition at BMG. On February 12, 2001, a three-judge panel of the Ninth District Court overruled the stay and ordered Napster to take down all existing files of copyrighted works. Fulfilling this task as mandated by the order was impossible without shutting down the entire platform, forcing Napster to cease operation on July 1, 2001. At that point Napster still had over 50 million users. An unknown multiple of billions of files had been downloaded during its two years of operation. Meanwhile the majors were preparing for the December launch of their own competing proprietary platforms, Sony-UMG's PressPlay and BMG-EMI-WMG's MusicNet.

In March 2002, a lawsuit by the other majors and the NMPA resulted in a ruling against the BMG investment in Napster, forcing its final shutdown and bankruptcy. Napster's assets were sold to CD-burning software maker Roxio, which would eventually relaunch Napster in 2006 as a subscription service. Middelhoff was forced out of BMG in July 2002. His digital technology initiative had created far more debt than revenue and was assigned to another BMG division out of the purview of the record group division. Forrester Research analyst Josh Bernoff succinctly summarized Napster's effect, "It energized consumers to the idea they could be getting access to media over the Internet, it turned MP3 into a standard, it scared the hell out of Hollywood. It really did change everything forever."[16]

The Case Against MP3.com

Directly on the heels of the Napster filing, the RIAA initiated another suit in US District Court for the Southern District of New York on January 21, 2000, against MP3.com, claiming that its newly launched platforms Instant Listening Service and Beam-it infringed as many as 45,000 commercial CDs. MP3.com allowed consumers to create their own storage lockers of tracks that could be listened to from any internet connection. If they bought CDs from any of MP3.com's webstore partners they could instantly listen through MP3.com as soon as they forwarded a purchase receipt from the webstore. The flaw in their procedure was that MP3.com already had a database of tracks without licenses, which they transferred into the lockers rather than have consumers actually upload their purchased tracks into their lockers. What was perceived by MP3.com as a matter of customer convenience was considered by the labels to be infringement and hence subject to litigation.

On January 21, 2000, RIAA president/CEO Hilary Rosen wrote in an open letter to MP3.com CEO Michael Robertson, "Simply put, it is not legal to compile a vast database of our member's sound recordings with no permission and no license. And whatever the individual's right to use their own music, you cannot exploit that for your company's commercial gain."[17] In an open letter of his own, Robertson termed the lawsuit an action "against consumers' rights, against new technologies, and against expansion of artists' revenues."[18] Unlike Napster, which was operating on a shoestring budget, MP3.com was well financed from its $350 million IPO funding. On February 7, 2000, MP3.com filed its own lawsuit in the US Superior Court in San Diego, claiming that the RIAA and Rosen specifically had "been engaged in a pattern of actions with agents and have put pressure on advertisers to interfere with our business in any way they can."[19] Robertson further proclaimed, "We have a huge mountain of evidence to prove this."[20]

Forrester Research analyst Dan O'Brien told *Billboard*'s Eileen Fitzpatrick, "It would be much better if record companies and the RIAA would work with companies like MP3.com, since they have demonstrated they don't have the gene for the Internet and are locked into a business model they've had for 30 to 40 years."[21] Greenberg Traurig attorney Bobby Rosenbloum sagely added, "What the RIAA should really be concerned with is technology that makes it easier and less expensive to get music. What they're doing is attacking a business model. The RIAA could win the battle but lose the war."[22]

Taking its cash reserve in hand, MP3.com negotiated settlements with BMG, EMI, Sony, and WMG. *The New York Times* reported that analysts estimated the proposed payments to be about $20 million each, leaving UMG as the sole remaining plaintiff. MP3.com also came to terms with the NMPA in March 2000 to settle the separate infringement litigation with the publishing industry. MP3.com agreed to pay $30 million to the NMPA publishers collectively for past-due license fees and advances on a three-year license. The terms included one-quarter cent each time a song was streamed from the company locker to a customer.

Nonetheless, MP3.com had to shut down its service in April 2000 after a ruling from the US District Court for the Southern District of New York on the litigation with UMG. The sides continued to negotiate and produced a $53.4 million settlement. Further discussion led to the purchase of MP3.com by UMG in May 2001 for approximately $372 million in cash and stock. The other labels, however, rejected the licensing proposals on the now-UMG-owned MP3.com. Then the economic downturn following 9/11 with its 10 percent drop in record sales put a damper on the industry's ability to sustain their investments in digital sales initiatives. UMG was especially overextended, forcing Jean-Marie Messier to resign as CEO of Universal Vivendi in July 2002 and the sale of both the MP3.com URL and logo to CNET in 2003.

The RIAA Continues the Battle

Having now dismantled what it perceived to be the two leading digital threats to its members' hegemony over recorded music, the RIAA continued to pursue other offenders like Aimster, Grokster, Audiogalaxy, PureTunes, iMesh, and KaZaA. None of them, however, could match the public impact of Napster, or MP3.com's deep pockets capable of actually making a deal had the labels been willing.

Motivated by studies that showed a gap in consumer awareness as to the illegality and ramifications of unauthorized downloading, the RIAA initiated the Music United for Strong Internet Copyright (MUSIC) coalition to wean consumers away from illegal downloading through an aggressive multimedia campaign. The wide and diverse collection of supporters included the Recording Academy, the AFM, AFTRA, ASCAP, BMI, SESAC, the NSAI, the SGA, the CMA, the Christian Music Trade Association, the Gospel Music Association, the Hip Hop Music Action Network, the Jazz Alliance International, the Music Managers Forum-US, the Recording Industries Music Performance Trust Funds, and SoundExchange.

MUSIC's initial theme was "Who Really Cares About Illegal Downloading?" Madonna, the [then Dixie] Chicks, Sheryl Crow, Eminem, Elton John, Sting, Phil Collins, Luciano Pavarotti, Brian Wilson, Natalie Cole, Trisha Yearwood, and more than fifty other major acts, songwriters, and indie artists produced personalized messages. MUSIC also wanted to correlate lost sales due to illegal downloads with lost income at all levels, from artists and songwriters to studio engineers and record shop clerks. The campaign launched in September 2002, utilizing print, radio, television, and the internet. Full-page ads were placed in *the New York Times*, the *Los Angeles Times*, and the Capitol Hill publication *Roll Call* as well as other newspapers throughout the country. The television commercials were also shown at an overview hearing on P2P file-sharing services before the House Subcommittee on Courts, the Internet, and Intellectual Property.

By the fall of 2003, an RIAA-commissioned study showed a declining trend in illegal downloads, but retail sales were still suffering. The RIAA decided to accelerate litigation of individual infringers. By 2006 they had sued thousands of consumers. Jeff Leeds of *The New York Times* estimated from his investigations that the number was over thirty thousand, creating greater awareness of the perils in home piracy, but also garnering negative publicity for their sometimes heavy-handed approach with litigation against single mothers and unemployed students.

In a further attempt to limit home copying from CDs, the Sony/BMG partnership inserted copy protection software onto certain CDs, first in Europe in 2001 and then on over 22 million CDs in the US in 2005. The software, however, created vulnerabilities in both Microsoft and Apple operating systems, corrupting computers on which the CDs had been played. After tech research blogger Mark Russinovich blew the whistle and the US Department of Homeland Security issued a security advisory on the software, Sony/BMG offered a recall and exchange for DRM-free CDs. The attorney general of Texas filed a suit while class-action proceedings commenced in New York and California. At the beginning of January 2006, the courts accepted an overall settlement proposal whereby Sony/BMG paid $7.50 along with a free album download, or three album downloads for each contaminated CD. For those with damage to their computers, they could continue to litigate or accept a software patch from Sony/BMG. The primary outcome of the case, however, was that it put an end to the labels' attempts to imbed copy prevention codes in commercial CDs.

From Ledger to Metadata: Tech Transforms Music Administration

Publishing administration has always centered around the management of information related to record sales, airplay, print music sales, and revenue from other licensed usages kept in ledgers with the computation and distribution of royalties the primary function. After World War II, computerized files gradually replaced paper documents in the overall world of business, including the music industry. Information became data, defined in the *Oxford Dictionary* as "facts and statistics collected together for reference or analysis."

BMI had installed an IBM 704 mainframe in the mid-1950s for collating airplay totals and license fee collections to create its royalty distributions. Major publishing and record companies followed suit in computerizing their accounting functions but not on as grand a scale, relying on smaller systems from IBM or one of its competitors. In 1960 Charles W. Bachman designed the Integrated Database System (IDS) for GE, the first Database Management System (DBMS), as a process to organize a collection of data for easy management and access. IBM and the other computer companies quickly followed with their own DBMS designs.

In his 1968 treatise *Extension of Programming Language Concepts* written for the Air Force Office of Aerospace Research, Phillip R. Bagley suggested, "As important as being able to combine data elements to make composite data elements is the ability to associate explicitly with a data element a second data element which represents data about the first data element. This second data element we might term a 'metadata element.' "[23]

Database and metadata were now embedded as new terms within the music industry lexicon as prime elements in the transformation of publishing administration from hand-kept general ledger rows and columns to digitally managed spreadsheets. With the introduction of personal computers (PC) in the 1970s, compatible spreadsheet programs followed, including VisiCalc in 1979 for the Apple II, SuperCalc in 1980, and the Microsoft Multiplan in 1981, most of which gave way to the Lotus 1-2-3 after its January 1983 launch. After dominating the spreadsheet market for the next decade, Lotus in turn yielded to Microsoft Excel, which subsequently became the market leader when it was also included within the Windows 95 suite of software.

The International Standard Recording Code (ISRC) was introduced in Japan in 1988, as an identifier for sound recordings. IFPI put it into worldwide use in 1992 as the official numbering system to determine the correct owner and hence royalty recipient of records when sold or played. A unique ten-digit ISRC number was assigned and encoded into the digital master of each recorded track and hence every duplicated digital copy of that track thereafter. Separate recordings of the same song by the same artist, however—whether live version, studio version, rerecorded, or unplugged—had their own unique ISRC numbers.

The major publishers pursued CISAC to develop and implement a numbering system parallel to ISRC for the songs performed on recordings throughout its membership network. The goal was to expedite royalty flow and lower the differing collection fees imposed by each society to the 6 percent rate charged by the UK's Mechanical Copyright Protection Society (MCPS). *Billboard*'s Jeff Clark-Meads reported that Martin Bandier had two major complaints about the European societies. "Primarily, he argues that they have been too ready to cut publishers' incomes in order to give rebates to record companies when competing for the labels' business. Second, he has been unhappy about the level of social and cultural deductions the continental societies have taken from the sums to be distributed to publishers."[24]

In response, CISAC initiated its Common Information System (CIS) in 1994, but a year went by with no action, spurring Bandier to set up EMI's own collecting organization, Music Rights Society Europe. In 1996 MCPS and PolyGram began direct distributions to publishers, bypassing the continental societies. CISAC responded by adopting the International Standard Musical Work Code (ISWC) as its unique nine-digit identifier for musical works. Like the ISRC, the ISWC was authorized by the International Organization for Standardization (ISO) under the auspices of the United Nations Economic and Social Council. CIS then assigned the first ISWC number, 000000001 to Abba's "Dancing Queen" with all related information posted on its newly formed, internationally accessed metadata network, WorksNet.

The further implementation of CIS was put on the agenda for the April 1997 CISAC annual meeting in Paris. Planning director at the UK's Performing Right Society (PRS) Terri Anderson told Clark-Meads that accessing the data from STIM would clear each society from keypunching the data itself. It would also remove confusion between songs with the same title. Noting that the UK's National Discography contained 117 songs titled "The Power of Love," she stated, "What the Paris conference will be talking about is digitally and indelibly marking every work so that it is traceable through its every use; thereby you eliminate one of the problems that has bedeviled the distribution of royalties worldwide."[25]

Prior to the CISAC meeting at the January 1997 Midem Convention in Cannes, the publishing community and CISAC societies agreed to the Cannes Accord, in which the continental societies would lower commissions to 6 percent and speed distributions, the publishers agreed to drop their own collection initiatives that had bypassed the societies, and all agreed to work together on the full implementation of CIS. Ralph Peer II stated, "It's good for us and good for everyone. It's in the interests of all the European societies, who have had a significant wake up call to the fact that the single European market is going to mean a different structure to what they have been used to for decades past."[26]

CISAC, however, moved slower than the pace of digital development. Not until the September 1998 conference did CISAC designate ASCAP COO Al Wallace as chairman of the working group for implementing the ISWC numbering system. Cees Vervoord, chief executive of Dutch society BUMA/STEMRA, rationalized to *Billboard* that CIS wasn't behind schedule as no schedule had ever been set, but conceded that "if we see the speed of the development of the online environment, we understand that we must move forward with CIS."[27]

At the September 2000 CISAC Word Congress BMI, PRS, BUMA/STEMRA, Germany's GEMA, and France's SACEM seized the initiative and announced the formation of FastTrack as a new alliance to develop the software needed to implement CIS. They also agreed to let each PRO issue licenses to cover one another's territory for online music performance. But perhaps the clearest message to the CISAC Congress was delivered by BMI's Frances Preston, who articulated, "This is definitely a new era. . . . For us, this cannot be a time just for talk. We must act now, act quickly, act accordingly, and act efficiently. And the two key dynamics in this new era will be new technology and new alliances."[28] By 2002 the PROs in Spain, Italy, Austria, Belgium, and Switzerland had also joined FastTrack.

The ISRC and ISWC numbers joined the already-existing Compositeur Auteur Editeur (CAE) number identifying each composer, lyricist, and publisher. The CAE database had been created in 1968 by the Swiss PRO SUISA as a universal identifying tool. SUISA general manager Dr. Ulrich Uchtenhagen was quoted in the1976 *Billboard Spotlight* special celebrating CISAC's fiftieth anniversary, "The high cost of labor here meant constantly rising costs for the relatively small community of composers, lyricists and publishers in Switzerland. It was vital that we found a more efficient and up to date system at a time when such a development wasn't so important to most other societies."[29] The CAE database was first codified on microfilm. By 1976 it had grown to include CAE numbers for all composers, authors, and publishers from around the world, with 810,000 entries. Updated copies were distributed on microfiche for a small fee to copyright societies six times a year. In 2001 the CAE directory and its assigned numbers were incorporated into the newly christened IPI/CAE number as a basic component of FastTrack and WorksNet. IPI was the acronym code for Interested Parties Information.

Finally, at its February 2004 Congress, CISAC announced the launch of CIS-Net, its FastTrack-powered digital copyright network expected to connect all 209 CISAC member societies within the next few years. All societies were invited to register their indigenous works. "This is the practical implementation of a vision outlined 10 years ago," CISAC secretary general Eric Baptiste effused, calling the CIS-Net launch a "landmark agreement" that will expedite "the increasingly global diffusion" of music.[30] FastTrack managing director Chris van Houten added that CIS-Net's transparency and efficiency "offers the additional promise of accelerating the distribution of royalties to authors throughout the world. All of CISAC's member societies should be connected through the system in two to five years."[31]

By 2006, both Microsoft Office 2003 and Apple Mac OS 10.4—when combined with the improved capacity, functions, and stability of the latest generation Excel V-11 spreadsheet files—enabled music publishers to operate their own databases. Many publishers licensed administration software programs, including market-leading Counterpoint Systems, founded in 1987 by London-based Robert Katovsky. Others created their own proprietary customized systems. The publishers' already-assigned in-house catalog numbers served as digital contact points with CIS-Net, the systems of the publishers' local societies, and their record company licensees to direct the flow of data and payments. Both the publishers themselves and their copyright societies worldwide were now equipped with the first round of tools for the digital future of the music business.

The weakest link in this database collection system, however, would prove to be the US mechanical rights collections community. Many CISAC territories had one society that collected and distributed royalties for its entire indigenous publishing industry. The NMPA's licensing branch HFA, however, was one of only two US mechanical rights societies associated with CISAC and represented about 80 percent of the US market. The other CISAC member, the American Mechanical Rights Association (AMRA) had been set up by German society GEMA in 1961 and by 2006 had a negligible market share. With no other US mechanical rights administrators associated with CISAC, CISAC mechanical rights members looked primarily to HFA as a conduit for the mechanical rights royalties for US-originated works that were not collected through sub-publishers. This would lead to future difficulties for all involved, not only for the non-HFA US publishers collecting royalties emanating from the subscription streaming tsunami looming just beyond the horizon but also the streaming services that depended on HFA to distribute to those publishers, as well as for HFA itself.

9

The Creators' Side of the Money Equation

Artist and Songwriter Royalties Reflect Industry Revenue

The creators' share of revenue has always been subject to the applicable contracts and governance for that specific industry sector. Recorded music sales, publishing royalties, live performance, merchandise sales, and sponsorship fees all had general industrywide contract templates, but the monetary terms pertinent to each agreement were negotiated on an individual basis, including the relevant royalty percentages, revenue splits, length of term, territory, and other applicable conditions. PRO agreements, mechanical licenses, and booking contracts had perhaps the most standardized templates, but even then, there still were individualized customizations for royalty rates, percentage splits, advances, and guarantees.

By 1996 artist earnings from record sales had almost tripled over the previous decade in tandem with the dramatic rise in industry revenue. New artists were getting larger advances and bigger budgets than ever before, and if successful, selling more product. Catalog artists had seen a sales resurgence in the CD format. For many artists from the 1950s, 1960s, and 1970s, original contracts had to be modified since there were no provisions in them for CDs. The definition of a sound carrier varied according to the year the contract was signed and the company involved, sometimes putting into question whether the label had rights under the contract to rerelease the album in a digital format. In such instances, artist advances were sometimes necessary to modify the terminology in order to secure the right to sell digital sound carriers.

Don Passman explained in his *All You Need to Know about The Music Business* that by the 1970s most new contracts contained a modification to the grant of rights that clarified the language defining a record as both an audio recording and audiovisual recording and "any other device *now or hereafter known.*"[1] Then after the introduction of downloads another modification was

American Popular Music and Its Business in the Digital Age. Rick Sanjek, Oxford University Press. © Frederick Sanjek 2024.
DOI: 10.1093/oso/9780190653828.003.0009

added defining "'records' to mean *any kind of delivery of your performance for consumer use*. This language is designed to ensure that the company has rights to mobile, Internet, and whatever else comes down the pike."[2]

Artists that sold platinum or better, won Grammy Awards, and consistently topped the charts were regarded as franchise acts. Labels were happy to pay them exorbitant advances against future royalties rather than lose their sales to a rival. Artists benefited from the application of SoundScan, BDS, and the technological upgrades in royalty accounting systems and data management. Cash advances remained the primary currency in artist-label negotiations, but artists' access to accurate sales accounting helped to maximize both advances and long-term earnings.

The royalty total for recording artists took the same roller-coaster ride as the industry shipments that were tracked in the annual RIAA report, as outlined in the previous chapters. They rose steadily upward until 1999, then fell in 2001, revived slightly though 2004, and then fell even more precipitously in 2006. Songwriters' royalties, however, benefited from their publishers' success in identifying, licensing, and collecting from new digital usages as US publishing revenue more than doubled over the course of the decade. They also benefited from the increased statutory mechanical rate that began at 6.95¢ in 1996 and settled at 9.1¢ for 2006, a 30.9 percent increase. Successful songwriters, especially the ones who were artists who wrote their own repertoire, either negotiated a co-publishing arrangement after their original agreement expired, usually with a large advance, or retained ownership of their works with a 10 percent to 15 percent administration charge. Meanwhile the PROs pursued the opportunities presented by the growing trove of new technology, unlike the record labels that sought to impose an ill-conceived and inconvenient set of restrictions on the emerging digital marketplace that only succeeded in alienating the younger consumer base.

Live Performance Revenue in a Growth Pattern of Its Own

Led by Frank Barsalona and other booking agents who had grown up with rock music, by 1996 the pop music concert circuit had firmly established a 75 percent of box-office net after agreed-upon shared expenses as the standard live performance formula. The venues that booked the top tours as tracked by *Pollstar* and the *Amusement Business (AB)/Billboard* tandem were mostly heavily concentrated in the Top 50 Designated Market Areas (DMAs). DMAs were ranked according to the population of the market's mass media reach and used in comparative market analysis by Nielsen, Arbitron, and other ratings services.

Some of the larger markets had more than one major promoter, but in almost all cases, the successful ones were independent operators who had staved off competition over the past twenty-five years to become dominant in their markets. They had to use their own money or solicit investors to buy the talent at 50 percent down and the other 50 percent on show night. The artists' booking agents planned the tour and negotiated separately with each promoter to finalize initial fees, share of any box-office overage, promoter/venue's merchandise override, any share of ancillary house revenues, and the provisions of the artists' tour rider. The rider listed the specific terms and conditions defining the show day schedule, including arrival and soundcheck, backstage catering, fan interaction windows, any pre-show date promotion or press, complementary ticket allocation for the artist, and any other provisions or demands specific to the artist or that location.

From *Pollstar*'s 1981 debut through 2006, the Top 100 box-office tours were used to gauge the year-to-year relative strength of the concert music business in its year-end "Business Analysis." Like the rest of the music industry and US business as a whole, the data they used and the means to manage them expanded as computer technology progressed from mainframes to networked PCs and Macs, through generations of Windows and macOS operating systems, from simplistic spreadsheets through Lotus 1-2-3 to constantly improving generations of Excel, and from dial-up to broadband internet access.

Pollstar's Top 100 tours averaged $1.03 billion between 1990 and 1995 with a high of $1.4 billion in 1994 and low of $830 million in 1991. The Top 100 in 1996 totaled $1.05 billion with an average ticket price of $25.81. In 2001 the total grew to $1.51 billion at an average of $43.86 per ticket. The total for 2006 expanded to $3.6 billion with a $61.58 average ticket price.

During this period, live performance became a more important element of artist income not only due to the growth in box-office totals and the high net percentage of ticket revenue but also because of the immediacy of its receipt. Artists earned money from the first to last ticket with real-time final accounting but had to wait for record royalties until after recoupment of the cost of recording and promotion, and even then, royalty accounting to them was only twice a year. Publishing also had a favorable split of revenue in the favor of successful songwriters, but depended on record sales to generate mechanical payments and on radio airplay for PRO royalties. Both royalty streams were accounted for quarterly and delivered six to twelve months after the fact. Print and sync revenue skewed toward the most popular songs by the top artists.

Songwriter royalties, however, had very few related business costs while performing artists had to pay their touring expenses—including musicians, road crews, equipment, stage production, and travel—out of their share of the box office. They also had to pay their business team, usually consisting of a manager in the 10 percent to 20 percent range, a business manager at another 5 percent if the manager wasn't handling these duties, an attorney at 5 percent to 10 percent or on hourly billing, and the 10 percent booking agency commission.

Platinum Albums Spearhead Record Sales and Artist Royalties

In 1996, fifty-seven albums each registered over a million units sold on the SoundScan system, totaling 109.5 million units among them. *Jagged Little Pill* by Alanis Morissette topped the list with 7.4 million US sales and eventually sold 16 million units domestically and another 17 million worldwide. Celine Dion's *Falling into You* moved 6 million units in 1996, going on to 11 million domestically with another 21 million worldwide. *Fresh Horses* by Garth Brooks did 5.8 million in 1996 and eventually topped 10 million domestically and another million in international sales. No Doubt's *Tragic Kingdom* registered 4.4 million sales and went on to tally over 8 million in the US and over 2 million more foreign sales.

Of the remaining fifty-three albums, twelve were multi-platinum, including triple platinum albums by Metallica, Tupac Shakur, and Mariah Carey. Double platinum certifications included works by Toni Braxton, the Dave Matthews Band, Tracy Chapman, Keith Sweat, Hootie & the Blowfish on two separate albums, Bush, Shania Twain, LeAnn Rimes, and Bone Thugs-n-Harmony, and the *Waiting to Exhale* soundtrack. Some of these albums had been released in 1995 with part of their sales in that year. All had additional sales going forward. Very few albums tabulated over a million sales in successive years, but there were superstars like Brooks, Morissette, Dion, and Hootie & the Blowfish who actually accomplished that feat.

In 2000, the peak year for SoundScan album sales, eighty-eight topped 1 million units, selling a collective 196.9 million. NSYNC's *No Strings Attached* sold 9.9 million units with 2.4 million of those in the first week, eventually reaching total worldwide sales of over 11 million. Both Britney Spears's

Oops! . . . I Did It Again and Eminem's *The Marshall Mathers LP* sold 7.9 million units during 2000 on their way to over 14 million and another 15 million worldwide. Creed followed with 6.6 million, Santana with 5.9 million, and The Beatles *One* anthology with 5.1 million. The Backstreet Boys and Dr. Dre scored with quadruple platinum while Christina Aguilera, Destiny's Child, the Dixie Chicks, 3 Doors Down, Limp Bizkit, DMX, Sisqó, Faith Hill, and *Now That's What I Call Music Volume 5* achieved triple platinum with another twelve albums tallying double platinum. Forty-one other albums garnered single-platinum status.

RIAA reported physical retail shipments of over a billion units in 2000, but then declined to 621.3 million in 2006 with only fifty-two albums scanning over a million units and only three of those exceeding 3 million. The top seller was the *High School Musical* soundtrack, accounting for just over 3.7 million units. Rascal Flatts' *Me and My Gang* followed with over 3.4 million, and 2005 *American Idol* winner Carrie Underwood did just over 3 million on her debut album *Some Hearts*. Just four albums garnered double platinum with Nickelback's *All the Right Reasons* at 2.7 million, Justin Timberlake's *Futuresex/Lovesounds* came in just under 2.4 million, James Blunt's *Back to Bedlam* scored just over 2.1 million, while Beyoncé's *B'day*, released in September, did 2 million in 2006 on its way to reaching over 6 million units worldwide.

The ten top-selling albums of 2006 added up to only 23 million sales, compared to 60.5 million for the top ten in 2000 and 39.2 million in 1996. The downward trend in sales following 2000 resulted in a shrinking pool of royalty income. Labels reduced costs by trimming rosters and releasing fewer albums but did not scale back on radio promotion budgets on a per-album basis. With platinum albums now composing a dwindling pool, artists' live performance earnings and PRO royalties for those who wrote their own songs became even more important than ever.

SFX to Clear Channel: Creating a Concert Promotion Behemoth

From 1997 forward, the rise in box-office receipt revenue for performers was greatly impacted by Robert F. X. Sillerman's scheme to use his SFX Broadcasting—as outlined in chapter 7—as the anchor of a roll-up of more radio stations, top concert promoters, and large venues in major markets in a synergistic vision of generating greater profits.

In October 1996 SFX agreed to buy New York–based Delsener/Slater Enterprises to kick off the promoter roll-up aspect of the plan. One of the top concert promotion organizations in the northeast, Delsener/Slater staged 268 events in 1996. It operated an 11,000-seat amphitheater at Jones Beach on Long Island and also promoted shows in Providence, Rhode Island, Albany, New York, Springfield, Massachusetts, and Hartford, Connecticut, all markets where SFX already owned radio stations. The price was a purported $20 million and executive positions for principals Ron Delsener, who had started the company in 1966, and Mitch Slater, who had become a partner in 1992. Slater told *Billboard*'s Chuck Taylor and Melinda Newman, "There have been opportunities we wanted to invest in that we couldn't take advantage of because of limited capital resources. Now we can."[3] Indiana-based Sunshine Promotions Inc., which owned two amphitheaters, an indoor theater, and leases on several other facilities, was quickly added for another $55 million.

In August 1997 Sillerman reunited with Steven Hicks, who agreed to have Capstar acquire SFX, but the deal was delayed by regulatory scrutiny. In the interim, SFX issued $350 million in bonds and arranged for $300 million in credit to continue its pursuit of concert promotors. In December SFX added Bill Graham Presents in San Francisco for approximately $65 million, Contemporary Group in St. Louis for about $90 million, and Concert/Southern Promotions in Atlanta for $15 million. A few weeks later it added Houston-based Pace Entertainment, the largest Texas concert promoter as well as the leading producer of theatrical tours outside of New York, a major presenter of motorsport events, and managing partner of Pavilion Partners' eleven amphitheaters. SFX then bought the outstanding ownership share of Pavilion from Viacom and Sony.

The sale of SFX's stations to Capstar was completed in late 1997 for $2.1 billion in cash, stock, and assumption of $1.1 billion in SFX debt. Sillerman retained the concert division under the SFX Entertainment banner and continued on his frenzy of acquisitions. In May 1998 he announced the $80 million purchase of the Boston-based Don Law Company and retention of Law in an executive position. The major concert promoter in New England, Law brought along his computerized ticket service Next Ticketing, the twenty thousand-seat Great Woods Amphitheatre in Mansfield, Massachusetts, and operating agreements with Boston's Harbor Lights Pavilion and the Orpheum Theater. SFX then added Southern California promoter Avalon Attractions for $27 million, and the forty-eight hundred–seat Oakdale Theater in Wallingford, Connecticut for $12 million.

SFX further diversified by acquiring an 80 percent interest in Event Merchandising Inc. (EMI) and its merchandise agreements with over two dozen amphitheaters for $8 million from Howard Kaufman, Irving Azoff's partner in Frontline Management. SFX also paid $70 million for Network

Magazine Group and SJS Entertainment, adding research, programming, and production services, including the Album Network tip sheet. Stepping outside of the music arena, Sillerman added sports agency Falk Associates Management Enterprises (FAME) for $100 million, netting tennis star Andre Agassi, basketball's Michael Jordan with his Air Jordan Nike deal, and many other top-line sports clients.

Going into the 1998 tour season, SFX either owned or exclusively operated forty-six major concert venues in twenty-two of the top fifty markets, including twelve amphitheaters in seven of the top ten markets. Its EMI subsidiary had long-term merchandise agreements with twenty-six North American amphitheaters, including the Metro New York–based *PNC Bank Arts Center in Holmdel, New Jersey and the Jones Beach Amphitheatre, as well as the Hollywood Bowl and the Irvine Meadows Amphitheatre in the Los Angeles area. There were eleven SFX-promoted major venue tours in 1998 including Ozzy Osbourne's Ozzfest, the George Strait Country Music Festival, Michael Crawford of *Phantom of the Opera* fame, Wynonna opening for Michael Bolton, Stevie Nicks paired with Boz Scaggs, Rod Stewart, Chicago co-billed with Hall & Oates, and the H.O.R.D.E. Festival.

In August 1998 SFX added another major component by purchasing Fort Lauderdale–based Cellar Door Productions from founder Jack Boyle for $104 million with $78 million in cash, and the rest in stock, stock options, and debt assumption, along with the board chairmanship of the concert division. Boyle had started in the business moonlighting from a government job as a bartender at the legendary Cellar Door folk and jazz listening room in Washington, D.C. He then bought the club to anchor what became a $100 million-a-year enterprise operating from Washington to Florida.

Although SFX acquired two ticketing systems, Ticketmaster handled 60 percent to 70 percent of the approximately 30 million SFX tickets sold in 1998. These sales accounted for about 28 percent of Ticketmaster's music total. Sillerman clashed with Barry Diller, who had just bought Ticketmaster parent company USA Networks from Universal to add to his Home Shopping Network empire, but both saw the greater good in working out a mutually beneficial relationship. In November 1998 they agreed to a seven-year pact for Ticketmaster to become the exclusive SFX ticket handler, while existing contracts with other ticketers would segue to Ticketmaster when they expired, and SFX would roll its two proprietary systems into Ticketmaster. With rebates on all tickets to SFX, Sillerman retained an income stream while eliminating operational expense.

In early 1999 SFX paid $100 million for Las Vegas–based MagicWorks, which counted David Copperfield as one of its clients. Leading Pittsburgh promoter DiCesare-Engler, and The Next Adventure (TNA), the Bermuda-based successor to Michael Cohl and Bill Ballard's Concert Promotions International (CPI), were also acquired for undisclosed amounts. Cohl and Ballard had exclusively handled The Rolling Stones for the past ten years for all tour dates, merchandise rights, and other ancillary income streams on a worldwide basis. They also worked with U2, Pink Floyd, David Bowie, and Crosby, Stills, Nash & Young. In 1998 TNA did $238 million in ticket sales from 105 shows.

Cohl told *Billboard*'s Ray Waddell that the appeal in joining SFX included being a part of the industry leader with a huge pool of capital, which eliminated the need to raise money on a tour by tour basis, access to SFX's venues, and being allowed to operate the business independently. Unstated but most certainly a major part of the attraction for not only Cohl, but for all of the very independent-minded promoters who joined the SFX roll-up, was the financial golden parachute after decades in the high-risk concert promotion business.

By the end of 1999 SFX had transformed twelve of the major independent promotion companies into regional corporate divisions. This group represented a healthy percentage of the veteran concert promoters who had followed Frank Barsalona's blueprint as laid out in the 1960s. Included in the acquisitions were ownership of or management agreements for eighty-two concert venues in twenty-eight of the country's Top fifty markets, including forty-two concert amphitheaters. SFX's twenty-three major tours in 1999 included The Rolling Stones, Billy Joel, 'NSYNC, Bob Dylan/Paul Simon, Tom Petty, Chicago/the Doobie Brothers, Cher, and repeat tours of Ozzfest and the George Strait Country Fest. And Sillerman was still shopping.

In 1999 SFX totaled $747 million in concert ticket sales out of the *Pollstar* total of $1.3 billion for the Top 100 grossing tours. It also had additional revenue of several hundred million dollars from the concessions, parking, and merchandise sales at its facilities, as well as a share of handling fees. These additional income streams gave SFX an economic advantage over independent promoters, allowing it to raise artist guarantees from the customary 75 percent of gate receipts to as high as 85 percent.

SFX's national tours also created sponsorship and advertising opportunities for businesses wanting to get their products before the eyes of consumers through event banner signage, coopted national and local advertising in print and electronic media, and on the internet in both banner and pop-up ad formats. Sharing these additional income sources with headlining artists also became a negotiating chip in SFX's favor over the competition.

The Competition Responds to the SFX Roll-Up

The promoters not within the SFX fold were apprehensive about Sillerman's master plan. Jerry Mickelson of Chicago-based Jam Productions told *Billboard*'s Los Angeles bureau chief Melinda Newman, "I honestly believe SFX's intention is to leverage their position—with all the money that they've got, with all the deals they can offer artists, with their corporate sponsorships, and with their holdings, such as Album Network—to put all of us out of business."[4] Seth Hurwitz, owner of Washington D.C.-based I.M.P. Concerts added, "This is all about a stock play for SFX. It's not about the day in/day out concert business. God bless Bob Sillerman; that's his prerogative. But let's agree that that's the game."[5]

In the face of SFX's consolidation, eleven of its competitors formed the Independent Promoters Organization (IPO) to serve as a nationwide alternative to SFX. The IPO itself would not book tours leaving that to the individual members, but rather serve as a marketing and information sharing vehicle. The members of the IPO were Mike and Jules Belkin's Belkin Productions based in Cleveland; Jack Utsick's Entertainment Group Fund Inc. of Miami; Evening Star Productions from Phoenix run by Danny Zelisko; John Stoll's Fantasma Productions of Ft. Lauderdale; Hurwitz's IMP Concerts of Washington/Baltimore; Jam Productions of Chicago led by Mickelson; Metropolitan Entertainment Group serving New York and New Jersey headed by Jon Scher; Bill Reid's Rising Tide Productions serving the Virginia Tidewater and the Carolinas; Stone City Attractions of San Antonio helmed by Jack Orbin; Mark Lee's 462 Inc. of Dallas/Ft. Worth; and Universal Concerts, the club and concert division of the Universal Music Group headed by president Jay Marciano and veteran VPs Alex Hodges, Larry Vallon, and Melissa Miller. Chicago's Mickelson was tapped as CEO.

The 11 members had collectively accounted for more than $500 million in touring grosses in 1998, compared to SFX's $600 million. According to *AB*, four of the IPO members were among the ten top-grossing promoters of 1998. Collectively as experienced and successful as the SFX team, the IPO members ramped up their control of competing facilities. They also expanded into smaller surrounding markets where theaters were the largest venue and thus not a part of the SFX model. Nonetheless, SFX dominated the concert industry trade news from 1997 through 1999, while the business community at large was still immersed in the dot.com bubble financial frenzy. Investors took note of Sillerman's success with both broadcast and concert promotion roll-ups.

Meanwhile two new challengers emerged as competition for both SFX and the IPO members for national tours. The House of Blues (HOB) was launched in 1992 by Hard Rock Café co-founder Isaac Tigrett and actor/Blues Brother Dan Ackroyd. Its first location was a 180-seat club in Harvard Square. In addition to Tigrett and Ackroyd, investors included some of the Aerosmith band members, Paul Shaffer, River Phoenix, James Belushi, and Harvard University itself. By 1999 HOB had evolved into a chain of live music and restaurant venues with larger locations in West Hollywood, New Orleans, Chicago, Orlando, Atlanta, Myrtle Beach and Las Vegas averaging 1,917 in seating capacity. They were also an early internet presence with live online concerts, established their own radio network, produced a nation television program, and were praised for their Sunday Gospel Brunch shows.

In August 1999 HOB acquired Universal Concerts from Seagram's Universal Music Group. Chase Capital, J.H. Whitney & Co., and Kit Goldsbury's Silver Ventures of San Antonio provided $190 million in private equity funding. The combination of Universal's 20 concert venues with three more amphitheaters and additional smaller theaters in development with HOB's existing facilities and plans for a half dozen more would create a second national promoter. Marciano and his team were retained to run the entire operation from club tours to arenas, with their larger venues competitive with SFX. They would also manage the Hollywood Bowl, ownership of which Universal retained.

The surging concert promotion business also caught the attention of Philip Anschutz, a multi-billionaire and philanthropist with holdings in energy, railroads, real estate, newspapers, movies, and most recently sports teams, including six Major League Soccer (MLS) franchises. He became co-owner of the LA Kings hockey team in 1995. In 1997 he began plans for what became the Staples Center in downtown Los Angeles for the new home for the Kings and the Lakers NBA team as well as the anchor for his billion dollar L.A. Live entertainment complex and real estate development. Anschutz believed a key to success was to control and/or manage the facility in which his teams played. Concerts and other events on days when the teams didn't play added to his profit. Staples opened in October 1999 with a Bruce Springsteen concert.

Anschutz then enticed Tim Leiweke away from the presidency of the Denver Nuggets to become the CEO of his Anschutz Entertainment Group (AEG). Leiweke was empowered to expand AEG into entertainment promotion by acquiring companies that could fill open nights in AEG facilities, as well as at the arenas and stadiums of other sports owners, essentially to build a competitor to SFX and HOB.

By 1999 the total for the Top 100 tours was at $1.5 billion with 75 percent or more going to the artists. There was an additional undocumented amount for the smaller tours playing clubs, theaters, and other small venues, as well as the tours in large venues with fewer shows that didn't have the total box-office gross to make the Top 100.

Clear Channel Buys into the SFX Vision

While Leiweke was exploring his opportunities, SFX announced in March 2000 that it would be purchased by Clear Channel Communications (CCC). CCC was the broadcasting behemoth created by Sillerman's former partner Steven Hicks and his brother Tom's Dallas-based Hicks Muse Tate & Furst venture capital firm. The family of Lowry Mays, the original CCC owner, was the principal investor. CCC consolidated 1,224 radio stations including the CapStar, Chancellor, and Clear Channel chains under the CCC brand by the end of 2000. CCC also corralled a group of signage vendors to create the largest purveyor in the world of outdoor advertising with over 500,000 billboards and other display locations.

Sillerman kept up his own acquisitions splurge right to the closing of the transaction with CCC, finishing with ownership or management of 120 live entertainment venues in 31 of the top fifty US markets with 16 amphitheaters in the top 10 along with merchandising, marketing, touring Broadway shows, motorsports, and a sports marketing/management division. The deal finally closed in August 2000 as a stock exchange of $3.3 billion in CCC stock going to the SFX shareholders. CCC also assumed $1.1 billion of debt. Sillerman and Ferrel were the only SFX shareholders to get preferred voting stock while all others received non-voting common shares.

With the departures of Sillerman and Ferrel, former Pace principal Brian Becker was named CEO of CCC's new concert production division rebranded as Clear Channel Entertainment (CCE). Becker appointed former Cellar Door owner Jack Boyle as chairman of the music division; Irv Zuckerman formerly of Contemporary Productions of St Louis and Pace's Rodney Eckerman were named co-CEOs; and former head of global touring for Toronto's TNA Arthur Fogel would continue in the same role for CCE assisted by the Magic Works' team of Bruce Kapp and Brad Wavra along with Pace veteran Louis Messina. Michael Cohl remained as a senior consultant, while also retaining his exclusive representation of the Rolling Stones through his CPI with CCE as a profit participant.

Becker and Boyle set out to turn CCE into a more organized and disciplined structure than what Sillerman had built at SFX. They established eight regional management teams with divided responsibilities for booking and operations. Boston veteran Don Law with Dominic Roncace would handle the Northeast; former Electric Factory of Philadelphia co-owners Larry Magid and Wilson Rogers were named for the Mid-Atlantic region; Cellar Door alumni Wilson Howard and Joe Nieman in the Southeast; veteran promoter Rick Franks from Detroit and Mark Campana, hired away from the Nederlander Organization for the North Central division; Dave Lucas, formerly of Sunshine Productions in Indianapolis and Patrick Leahy from the Polaris Amphitheater in Columbus OH would lead the Central division; Pace veterans Bob Roux and Fran MacFerran would direct the Southwest; former Bill Graham Presents executives Gregg Perloff and David Mayeri would lead the West; and Canada would be managed by Steve Herman, co-founder of Toronto's Core Audience Entertainment, which had been acquired by SFX just before the closing of the sale to CCE.

Becker and Boyle's organizational chart was a more efficient version of Sillerman's vision of a diversified media giant, integrated both vertically and horizontally and capable of serving the musical tastes of all age demographics. This configuration was even more threatening than SFX had been to the still largely self-financed members of the IPO. CCE, however, still faced several major hurdles as SFX's intense acquisition mode had produced a heavy debt load spawned by its focus on building an infrastructure rather than managing the bottom line.

John Scher, whose Metropolitan Entertainment was the major SFX competition in New York and who had turned down a $17 million buy-out and job offer from Sillerman, told *Billboard's* Waddell that he understood the SFX play from an investor standpoint. "They were losing a huge amount of money, but it was successful because they flipped the business to someone who must think it can be profitable."[6] Scher, however, remained optimistic about the future under Clear Channel. "It appears that Bob Sillerman's original team didn't want to operate the business—it was a roll-up. The new people are bottom line people."[7]

The new CCE music team was equally positive. Jack Boyle responded to Waddell about the company's status, "If we were a mature business, we'd see nice, substantial profits. Our losses are not from running the company— they're from expenses, like any other start-up company."[8] Expectations for the next three years included 15 percent annual earnings growth from maximizing facility occupancy by booking more dates and selling more tickets, increasing sponsorships revenue, licensing venue naming rights, and selling more entertainment-related advertising. They would also benefit from being part of a larger whole, as only 12 percent of overall CCC income was projected to be from CCE and sports promotion, with 60 percent coming from radio, and 23 percent from outdoor advertising. The profit from these two more or-ganized divisions would lessen the pressure on CCE through its formative period.

Some of the IPO membership owners, concerned that the CCC acquisition of SFX would make it even more difficult to compete, were not able to resist the CCE allure of a combined multimillion dollar buy-out, CCC stock, and sala-ried executive position. Both Evening Star and Belkin Productions accepted offers from CCE in 2001. The Belkin brothers and Zelisko joined CCE's execu-tive team. Former SFX executive Mitch Slater had bought Metropolitan from Jon Scher in March 2002 and in turn sold it to CCE the following December.

Radio income was expected to quickly absorb the cost of the SFX pur-chase, as the annual revenue growth of the radio industry had averaged $1.29 billion a year from 1996 through 2000. But with the 2001 downturn of the economy, national radio revenue dropped by $1.48 billion from $19.85 billion in 2000 to $18.37 in 2001. Moreover, the vision of synergy between live performance, radio, and outdoor advertising as touted by Sillerman and appropriated by CCC, never quite materialized. Closer cor-porate oversight of the previously independent concert promoters created a cultural clash reminiscent of the dichotomy between the record men and the suits of the record sector. This combination of circumstances resulted in a gradual exodus of top executives who had come with their compa-nies in the roll-up and had stayed in position through the sale. This in-cluded Jack Boyle from Cellar Door, Tim Orchard from the Entertainment Group, Steve Schankman of Contemporary Productions, Louis Messina and Rodney Eckerman of Pace Concerts, Mitch Slater from Delsener-Slater Presents, Irv Zuckerman of Contemporary Productions, Gregg Perloff and Sherry Wasserman from Bill Graham Presents, and Steve Sybesma of Sunshine Productions.

Others thrived in the new structure, especially thirty-five-year-old head of European operations Michael Rapino, the other cofounder of Core Audience. Prior to Core, he had a corporate background with Toronto-based beer giant Labatt, where he coordinated tour sponsorships with TNA's Michael Cohl and Arthur Fogel. With better financial results in his European division than CCE had in the US, Rapino was upped to president of global music in August 2004 and moved to Los Angeles. His assignment was to right the high-grossing but low-producing US music division, replacing Dave Lucas, who had been in the post the past two concert seasons. Don Law, however, remained as a mentor from his chairman position. Rapino then set out to implement a series of changes to reinvigorate what had become a ponderous organization with declining goodwill with both artists and consumers.

Rapino restored the original identities of many of the formerly independent operations that had built the concert business and established local goodwill prior to the national consolidation, including Electric Factory Concerts in Philadelphia, Bill Graham Presents in San Francisco, Pace Concerts in Texas, Cellar Door in D.C., and Evening Star in Phoenix, pleasing the remaining original owners who were now key executives and regional managers. He then upgraded facilities and reduced handling and service fees that weren't printed on the tickets but showed up on the credit card receipts, and reduced prices for general admission and balcony sections. Then, turning to artist relations, Rapino introduced a plan to modify the then–85 percent-15 percent box-office split by giving 100 percent of the net back-end to the artists in exchange for a lower guarantee. In return, CCE would retain all the revenue from concessions, sponsorships, parking, and other ancillary sources. Rapino told *Billboard*'s Ray Waddell, "We believe in the end we will sell more tickets, and [artists] will easily make up for any of the reduction in guarantees they have been living off in the past."[9]

In late April 2005, after failing to sell the concert division for a $2 billion asking price, CCC announced that CCE would become a separate publicly traded company at the end of the year. The Mays family and their other shareholders felt that the underperforming music division was holding down the CCC share value. Although it had already written down the SFX purchase, CCC had concluded that the hoped for synergy between the concert and radio divisions hadn't and wouldn't materialize. Seth Hurwitz told Waddell, "Based on what they paid, everyone knew that [CCC] bought the Brooklyn Bridge and it was just a matter of time before they figured it out."[10]

In December 2005, the spin-off was completed under the new name of Live Nation with shares allocated in the same ratio as CCC shares. CCE CEO Brian Becker and other veteran executives exited, leaving the division in Rapino's hands with Law remaining as chairman; Miles Wilkin, formerly of Pace Concerts, as COO; and Arthur Fogel still in charge of International.

AEG Emerges as the Primary Rival

While the SFX/CCE/Live Nation drama played out, Phil Anschutz and Tim Leiweke were building the base for their own concert promotion network. With Anschutz's deep pockets and his membership in the sports facility owners' fraternity, Leiweke looked to build the AEG model on arenas and stadiums, leaving CCE atop the outdoor amphitheater market, also referred to as sheds, and the leadership in clubs and theaters to HOB. In addition to the Staples Center, AEG also owned L.A.'s Great Western Forum, the London Arena, and ownership shares in or management agreements with many other facilities.

In December 2000, four months after the close of the SFX sale, AEG announced the purchase of Los Angeles-based Concerts West. Founders Paul Gongaware and John Meglen agreed to stay on board as co-CEOs with equity positions. The price was estimated to be between $50 million and $80 million. Irving Azoff assisted Leiweke in identifying them as the right fit for AEG's expansion plans due to their combination of experience with nationwide tours and strength in their home market. Concerts West's national tours in 2000 had included Andrea Bocelli, Mariah Carey, and a third of the Dixie Chicks dates. Azoff believed they only needed capitalization to become a major international force. He demonstrated his confidence in the plan by agreeing to come on board as cochairman with Leiweke, who told *Billboard*'s Waddell, "We hope next year alone these guys do at least a dozen tours. . . . We want to jump in and be a major player very quickly."[11] Azoff added, "I'm not running the day to day operations. As a veteran of 30 years in the business, I will keep the ship from hitting icebergs."[12]

In March 2002, AEG formed AEG Concerts, a new wing to oversee live events, television projects, internet broadcasts, and a new artist-in-residency concept for Las Vegas. At Azoff's suggestion, AEG hired former Rod Stewart, Toni Braxton, and Usher co-manager Randy Phillips as AEG executive VP and CEO of AEG Concerts. Meglen and Gongaware were now under Phillips, but still operating Concerts West independently. Celine Dion and the four thousand-seat Colosseum at Caesars Palace showroom were selected for the first Las Vegas residency. Her ninety-minute *A New Day . . .* show was directed by Cirque du Soleil veteran Franco Dragone and opened in March 2003. The five-year run grossed over $385 million with Dion on a 50 percent of net agreement. Elton John followed, eventually doing 450 shows through 2018. Other artist residencies have included Dion (again), Rod Stewart, Cher, Bette Midler, Shania Twain, Mariah Carey, and Reba McEntire with Brooks & Dunn, as well as single-night or weekend appearances by two dozen other *Pollstar* Top 100 artists.

In July 2003 Azoff resigned from AEG Live to concentrate on his management interests. He remained as a consultant for the parent AEG, which reacquired his accumulated stock interest. Leiweke remained as chairman. According to *Billboard* Boxscore, AEG Concerts, including Concerts West, had grown from $30.5 million on 72 shows in 2001 to $145.9 million on 181 shows in 2002 including the Eagles, Britney Spears, Paul McCartney, Neil Diamond, and Barry Manilow. Although AEG's 2002 total revenue gross was behind Live Nation and HOB, it was a very respectable $806,077 per show. HOB was just ahead at $164.6 million on just under 1,000 shows, down from $173.8 million in 2001 on over 1,200 shows. Their average of $162,500 per show reflected their predominance of smaller venues compared to AEG's focus on arenas and stadiums.

Live Nation Leads the Upswing in Live Performance Revenue

Pollstar's estimates for the revenue from North American major concert tours grew from $2.1 billion in 2001 to $3.6 billion in 2006 in annual increments ranging between $300 million and $500 million. In 2006 the recently christened Live Nation sold $1.325 billion in tickets on 6,192 shows with over 27 million attendees, having steadily grown from $979 million in 2001. AEG expanded to $342 million in 2003 and then to $417 million in 2005 on 1,125 shows with over 6 million tickets sold. HOB grew to $245 million in gross volume in 2005, just over half the money that AEG produced, but did it on three times as many shows in its smaller venues.

Several independents also flourished during this time period. Jack Utsick Presents of Southern Florida grew from over $50 million in 2003 to over $100 million in 2005. Other promoters doing over $50 million in a year during this time included Chicago's Jam Productions in 2003 and 2005, Mexican-based OCESA Presents in 2003, The Messina Group of Houston in 2003, The Nederlander Organization in 2002 and 2004, Atlanta Worldwide Touring in 2004, and 3A Entertainment in 2005 with its growing festival business. In the years in which The Rolling Stones toured, Michael Cohl's CPI ranked in the top three as it did in 2003 with $299 million, and again in 2006 with $425.1 million. Although Cohl had been affiliated with CCE since his 2000 sale to SFX, he had maintained independent control of The Stones tours through CPI with CCE as a profit participant, and thus The Stones tallies through CPI were listed independent of the CCE or successor Live Nation's totals.

In July 2006 Live Nation purchased HOB for $350 million, acquiring its ten clubs, eight amphitheaters and exclusive booking rights to another five locations. The purchase boosted their total owned and/or managed facilities to 176 venues, ranging from clubs to colosseums. *Pollstar's* editor-in-chief Gary Bongiovanni observed to Charles Duhigg of the *Los Angeles Times* that the purchase would, "allow artists to work with one promoter to set up a national tour."[13] Gwen Stefani and Nine Inch Nails manager Jim Guerinot commented, "This deal gives Live Nation the mass heft it needs to challenge

Ticketmaster, T-shirt merchandisers, all sorts of ancillary businesses. By becoming this big, Live Nation can become a company that participates in every part of the live music economy."[14] Rival AEG's Phillips less enthusiastically added, "This marks the end of all of the small, independent promoters who have been the entrepreneurs of this industry."[15]

While both *Pollstar* and *Billboard* continued to track US performances for their year-end US tallies, both also started to report on worldwide concert statistics reflecting the now-global scope of the industry. *Billboard*'s 2006 worldwide year-end total for Live Nation, now including the former HOB venues, in its Top 25 Promoter listing was $2.37 billion on 38.3 million tickets to 9,367 shows. Of this, 20.4 percent came from coproductions with independents, primarily in foreign markets. The remaining $1.8 billion came from their wholly controlled productions. Live Nation's gross was over four times AEG's total of $543 million. AEG was the sole promoter on only 54 percent of their 1,347 shows, selling 8.3 million tickets. Their percentage of sell-outs, however, was 51.9 percent compared to Live Nation's 35 percent.

Michael Cohl's CPI was in third place in 2006 doing $533.7 million. The Rolling Stones tour brought in $425.1 million on 3.7 million tickets. In New York, they sold out the 5,800-seat Radio City Music Hall at a $1,500 face value per ticket for a one-night haul of $8.7 million. Barbra Streisand generated another $76.1 million from 265,224 tickets, primarily in arenas at a price tier ranging from $750 down to $100.

In 2006, the other twenty-two of the *Billboard* Top 25 promoters did $1.1 billion in their independently controlled promotions. This was just slightly more than the $1.05 billion total top concert market of 1996. They also often served as co-promoters for the top three, especially the ones who were local leaders in international markets. In total, the world market for *Billboard*'s Top 25 promoters was approximately $4.44 billion.

Only six outside of the top three did more than $30 million in total business, their share of coproductions with the top three and sole productions combined. OCESA Presents took in $57.1 million, primarily in Mexico and 60 percent sole promotions; Chicago's Jam Productions was at $51.3 million with 73 percent sole promotions; Montreal-based Gillett Entertainment did $40.8 million mostly in copromotions; Nashville's Outback Concerts grossed $37.9 million with 53 percent sole productions; and both Nederlander with 68 percent sole productions and San Francisco's Another Planet Entertainment at 82 percent sole productions were just above $30 million. Nine more did in the $20 million range with the 21st through 25th ranging down from $19.3 million to $17.6 million.

As trade magazines, both *Pollstar* and *Billboard* were oriented toward upper-echelon members of the industry who could afford to be subscribers and, more important, advertisers. They both tabulated major concert tour information provided to a large degree by the same venues, promoters, and agencies but they differed in the depth of their coverage on year-end details. *Pollstar* estimated the 2006 top-facility concert industry at $3.6 billion while *Billboard* cited $3.4 billion. *Pollstar's* principal year-end ranking was its Top 200 North American Tours.

Billboard's tour coverage was now under the direction of former *AB* mainstay Ray Waddell as executive director of content and programming for touring and live entertainment. He focused "The Year in Music & Touring" year-end analysis on the top end of the market with Top 25 rankings for concert promoters, top-grossing tours, and individual-event box scores. There was another set of top ten listings for various types of venues including stadiums, amphitheaters, festivals, and four sets of indoor venues grouped by audience capacity. All rankings were based on gross revenues as tabulated over the year by *Billboard's* weekly "Boxscore" chart designed to give "a snapshot of the current week's top box-office statistics"[16] as chart manager Bob Allen explained in his "How We Compile The Boxscore Charts" addendum.

Neither system, however, gave a complete picture of the entire amount of money consumers spent on live performance because they were based on the face value of the tickets of only the top tours. Absent were the service charges collected by Ticketmaster or other ticket handlers. Nor did they measure the secondary ticketing market of both scalpers and legitimate online ticket brokers. None of these add-on charges paid by consumers were shared with the artists. This secondary market is more deeply examined in chapter 15.

Superstars Lead the Concert Market

The 1995 Rolling Stones *Voodoo Lounge Tour* set the box-office single-tour record at $320 million, passing the $250 million earned by Pink Floyd on their *Division Bell Tour*, which turned out to be their final outing. U2's *Vertigo Tour* of 2005–6 took in $389 million and held the all-time top-grossing tour record for just a little under a year until The Stones reset the record in 2005–7 with the *Bigger Bang Tour* taking in $558 million worldwide. Both tours drew over 4.6 million attendees. U2 had thirteen fewer shows but drew about three thousand more per show, while The Stones averaged $3.8 million per show to U2's $2.96 million. The Stones' audience demographic skewed deeper into the wealthy baby boomer and 1950s Teens age groups, more accepting of higher ticket prices. Both tours were promoted by Michael Cohl, who offered large advances to his acts to buy all associated rights, and then supplemented the box-office take with DVD, pay-per-view, and merchandising revenue. He also negotiated a share of concessions and parking whenever possible.

The venerable British rockers, along with the younger Irish quartet nipping at their heels for the top rock band crown, were not the only acts benefiting from rising box-office revenues and competition between CCE/Live Nation, AEG, and the still-thriving alliance of independents. Prior to 1996, Michael Jackson, Pink Floyd, and the reunited Eagles had joined U2 and The Stones with tours grossing over $100 million. Then between 1996 and 2006, U2 and The Stones did three tours each. The three-tour total for the boys from Dublin was about $700 million, while Mick, Keith, and crew took in over $1 billion. Also during that time another eight artists joined the group of artists earning over $100 million on a tour.

Michael Jackson's 1996–97 *HIStory World Tour* encompassed eighty-three performances—mostly in stadiums, domes, and outside park—averaging 54,878 tickets totaling over 4.5 million attendees. Only two shows were performed in the US, both in Hawaii. The tour grossed more than $165 million with an average ticket price of $37. *HIStory* turned out to be his last set of live performances other than five charity events and his multi-artist 30th Anniversary Celebration in 2001. He died in 2009 while preparing for his fifty-show *This Is It Tour*. Aside from his appearances as part of the Jackson 5, which ended in 1984 with the *Victory Tour*, Michael Jackson only did three extensive solo tours in his career, *Bad, Dangerous, and HIStory*, covering 274 concerts, primarily in sold-out stadiums and domes for a three-tour total of $390 million, averaging $1.42 million and 47,100 tickets per show.

At the same time as Jackson's *HIStory Tour*, Tina Turner took in $130 million on her *Wildest Dreams Tour* covering Asia, Africa, Europe, and North America in 255 dates. Country superstar Garth Brooks's 1996–98 *World Tour* took in $105 million on 220 dates, playing to 5.5 million fans with an average attendance over twenty-five thousand and ticket prices around $20, which was consistent with his concern about affordable pricing for his fans. Although termed a world tour, only thirty-eight shows were outside of the US with twenty-nine in Canada, eight in Ireland, and one in Brazil. After he concluded the 106-week tour in November 1998, he retired from the road to be with his children through high school, but did do nine shows in 2007 in Kansas City, five shows in Los Angeles in 2008, and a Las Vegas one-man residency sometimes accompanied by wife Trisha Yearwood at the Wynn Encore

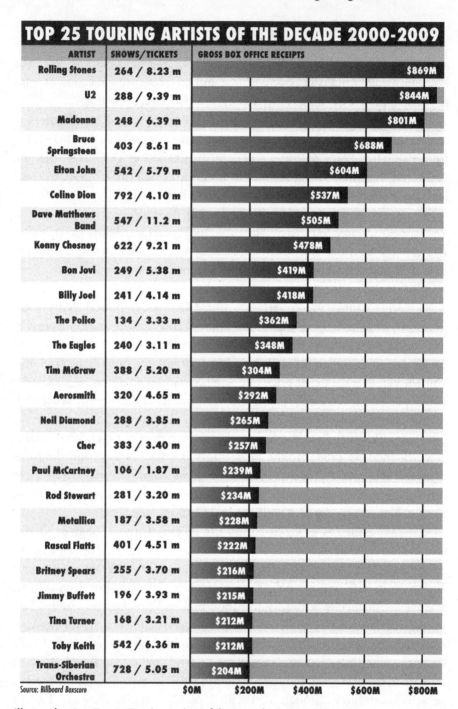

TOP 25 TOURING ARTISTS OF THE DECADE 2000-2009

ARTIST	SHOWS/TICKETS	GROSS BOX OFFICE RECEIPTS
Rolling Stones	264 / 8.23 m	$869M
U2	288 / 9.39 m	$844M
Madonna	248 / 6.39 m	$801M
Bruce Springsteen	403 / 8.61 m	$688M
Elton John	542 / 5.79 m	$604M
Celine Dion	792 / 4.10 m	$537M
Dave Matthews Band	547 / 11.2 m	$505M
Kenny Chesney	622 / 9.21 m	$478M
Bon Jovi	249 / 5.38 m	$419M
Billy Joel	241 / 4.14 m	$418M
The Police	134 / 3.33 m	$362M
The Eagles	240 / 3.11 m	$348M
Tim McGraw	388 / 5.20 m	$304M
Aerosmith	320 / 4.65 m	$292M
Neil Diamond	288 / 3.85 m	$265M
Cher	383 / 3.40 m	$257M
Paul McCartney	106 / 1.87 m	$239M
Rod Stewart	281 / 3.20 m	$234M
Metallica	187 / 3.58 m	$228M
Rascal Flatts	401 / 4.51 m	$222M
Britney Spears	255 / 3.70 m	$216M
Jimmy Buffett	196 / 3.93 m	$215M
Tina Turner	168 / 3.21 m	$212M
Toby Keith	542 / 6.36 m	$212M
Trans-Siberian Orchestra	728 / 5.05 m	$204M

Source: *Billboard Boxscore*

$0M $200M $400M $600M $800M

Illustration 9.1 Top 25 Touring Artists of the Decade, 2000–2009

Theater with 186 shows between 2009 and 2014 before reviving his *World Tour* in 2014.

In 2002 Paul McCartney returned to the road after a nine-year hiatus on his fifty-eight-date *Driving World Tour*, primarily playing in arenas, with a seventeen thousand average attendance, for a total of over 980,000 tickets. At an average ticket price of $128, he grossed $126.2 million. That same year Cher embarked on her three-year, 326-show *Living Proof: The Farewell Tour*, playing mostly arenas and large halls. Her average attendance was 10,800, totaling 3.5 million attendees and taking in $250 million with an average ticket price of $71. Bruce Springsteen & The E Street Band were also out again in support of their *The Rising* album, doing 120 shows in arenas, large halls, and several multi-date stadium appearances in his Northeast home territory and overseas. The fifteen-month tour grossed $221.5 million with a $68.50 average ticket price.

Bon Jovi started their *Have a Nice Day Tour* in November 2005, selling out fifty-six arena shows in North America by early March with multiple shows in New York, New Jersey, Boston, Chicago, Detroit, Philadelphia, Tampa, Toronto, and Montreal. They then played six dome dates in Japan and seventeen stadiums in Europe, finishing with nine more US dates in May 2006, all but one in stadiums. The entire tour took in $131.4 million with a $72 ticket average, playing to 1.82 million fans. Madonna reinforced her superstar status in 2006 on her *Confessions Tour* by averaging $161 per ticket on sixty shows. The North American leg sold out thirty-four shows in fifteen cities, with six shows in both the Los Angeles area and at Madison Square Garden in New York. All but one of her twenty-two European shows were sellouts, including eight dates in London's Wembley Arena, following by four domed sellouts in Japan.

Both the Tim McGraw and Faith Hill *Soul2Soul II* and Barbra Streisand's *Streisand* tours started in 2006 doing $88.8 million and $76.1 million, respectively, by the end of the year. They continued into 2007 finishing with a $141 million tour total for the country couple and $119.5 million for the legendary diva. Tim and Faith played 117 shows at an average ticket price of $84, a top-ticket average for a country tour. Streisand performed just twenty shows in North America and nine in Europe. Her shows included a fifty-six-piece orchestra, and averaged close to $300 a ticket, setting house sales records at all but two of her North American locations.

Only two acts grossed between $50 and $100 million in 1999: Bruce Springsteen & The E Street Band at $61.4 million and NSYNC taking in $51.5 million. In 2000 there were three: NSYNC with $76.4 million, KISS at $62.7 million, and Tina Turner generating $80.2 million. The total increased to five tours in 2001: the Backstreet Boys at $82.1 million, the Billy Joel and Elton John *Face to Face Tour* with a shared $57.2 million, the Dave Matthews Band at $60.5 million, NSYNC with $56.8 million, and Madonna gathering in $54.7 million.

Business slowed to just three tours between $50 million and $100 million in 2002 as Cher did $73.6 million, the Dave Matthews Band at $68.2 million, and the *Face to Face Tour* of piano men Billy and Sir Elton with $65.5 million. The industry rebounded in 2003 as eight tours earned in the $50 to $100 million range. The dual bill of Aerosmith and KISS grossed $64 million, the *Face to Face Tour* collected $50.9 million, Cher gathered in $68.2 million, the Dixie Chicks took in $60.5 million, the Eagles did $69.3 million, Fleetwood Mac generated $69 million, Metallica garnered $68.8 million, and the Simon & Garfunkel reunion grossed $64.5 million.

In 2004 another seven tours topped $50 million. Prince led the way with $87.4 million followed by Madonna at $79.5 million, and the Eagles totaling $78.4 million. Elton John going solo without piano partner Billy Joel took in $65.8 million, Metallica grossed $60.5 million, Bette Midler did $59.4 million, the Dave Matthews Band made $57 million, and Van Halen came in at $54.3 million. Kenny Chesney and Sting both just topped $50 million, with $50.8 million and $50.1 million, respectively.

In 2005 U2 grossed $260.1 million at an $85 ticket average while the Eagles did $116.9 million with a $113 average. Only three other tours fell between $50 and $100 million. Neil Diamond led the way with $71.3 million at $67 a ticket followed Kenny Chesney at $61.8 million with a then-reasonable $53 per ticket. Paul McCartney, however, took in $59.7 million in twenty-nine shows, charging a superstar average price of $132 per ticket.

The growing trend of superstar tours with superstar prices continued in 2006 as The Stones scored their $425.1 million haul at a $121 average ticket price while Madonna grossed $194.8 million with an average $164 ticket price. Bon Jovi earned $131.4 million with a more consumer friendly $72 average price. On the second year of their *Vertigo Tour*, U2 took in $95.9 million, followed by the first half of Tim and Faith's *Soul2Soul* outing, and Streisand's box-office record-setting tour de force. Kenny Chesney collected $66 million, Dave Matthews did $58 million, and veteran rockers Aerosmith took in $57.9 million.

Booking Agents and Concert Promoters

Accompanying the artists and concert promoters on the live music bandwagon were the booking agencies. Unlike promoters, whose profit was determined on how wisely they bought and how well they promoted talent, the agencies were on a straight commission, traditionally at 10 percent, which paid both agents and overhead. Although agencies didn't receive commissions from record or songwriting royalties, they did supplement their live performance commissions with fees for setting up product endorsements, obtaining tour sponsorships, and booking television appearances and movie roles. William Morris (WMA) and CAA were the two leading booking agencies with film, television, sponsorship, and literary divisions. Agents in these divisions shared their commissions for anything they procured for music artists with the artists' responsible agents.

By 2006 the practice of granting total control over both national and world-wide tours to one promoter, pioneered by Michael Cohl and emulated by both Live Nation and AEG, was cutting into the historic role of booking agents for the top-grossing acts. According to Ray Waddell, Rich Barnet, and Jake Berry in their 2007 book, *This Business of Concert Promotion and Touring: A Practical Guide to Creating, Selling, Organizing, and Staging Concerts*, in 2006 six of the top ten tours did not use a booking agent at all. Instead, touring contracts were negotiated directly with the promoter, saving the 10 percent that would have gone to agents.

Cohl's CPI dealt directly with The Rolling Stones management, saving the band the over $40 million that would have been due in agency commissions. Although Cohl had sold TNA to Live Nation's predecessor SFX, he still managed Live Nation's interests in dealing with both Madonna and U2. Live Nation itself exclusively represented the Cirque du Soleil's *Delirium Tour*. The Messina Group and AEG Live took over tour promotion for Kenny Chesney but worked directly with Chesney's manager, Clint Higham, at Dale Morris & Associates rather than go through an agency. Morris himself had pioneered arena and stadium tours for country artists with the Hall of Fame band Alabama during the 1980s and 1990s, introducing larger sets, video screens, and computerized lighting packages into country music.

Although this practice of bypassing agents theoretically took over $90 million out of the booking agents' 10 percent commission pool on major concerts in 2006, there was still over $270 million in that pool from just *Pollstar*-tracked tours to sustain the agency sector. There were also commissions from smaller venues and tours that didn't make the annual top tour list. Nonetheless, in response to the loss of what had been commission revenue in the past, booking agencies actively pursued additional revenue sources.

A year after he succeeded the retiring Tom Ross in 1998, CAA music division managing partner Rob Light initiated a diversification plan. He opened an internal marketing wing to compensate for labels' reduction in artist development budgets. He also opened a private events and corporate bookings department that would grow from $6 million to over $180 million over the next two decades. In 2002 he added a sponsorships department, later renamed music brand partnerships.

In a January 2019 interview with *Billboard*'s Melinda Newman, marking his thirty-fifth anniversary at CAA, Light expounded on artists' need for booking agents. "When you're a promoter, you're making a big bet. Your first job is to cover that bet. You're somewhat impeded by all the other tours you have to book; all the relationships you have with venues, with Ticketmaster. I have one goal: The only person who pays me is the artist. When I [saw] Twenty One Pilots, I [wrote] a letter to 50 to 60 festival buyers and said, 'I've just seen one of the great live bands, and they're playing a showcase in their hometown, Columbus [Ohio]. I'm going to pay for you to come. That's how sure I am that they should be on your festival.' They got into every festival that summer. That's what an agent does. No promoter can do that."[17]

The Waddell, Barnet, and Berry book recounted that in 2006 seventy of the Top 100 *Billboard* Boxscore tours were represented by eight agencies. CAA and WMA shepherded more than fifty of the tours, with the rest handled by Artists Group International (AGI), Monterey Peninsula Artists, The Agency Group, Agency for The Performing Arts (APA), the Howard Rose Agency, or the Marsha Vlasic Organization. Agents from these companies also dominated the nominations for *Pollstar*'s annual Bobby Brooks Agent of the Year and Third Coast Agent of the Year, which was exclusively for the Nashville booking community.

Rob Light, who had been Brooks's closest friend, won the award in 2001 and 2003, while fellow CAA agents Tom Ross won in 1998 and Rod Essig in 1999. Chris Hooper of Monterey Peninsula Artists won in 1996, 2002, and 2004. Other winners were Marty Diamond of Little Big Man Booking in 1997, David Zedneck of Evolution Talent Agency in 2000, Tom Chauncey of Partisan Arts in 2005, and Marc Geiger of WMA in 2006. Total nominees from 1996 through 2006 included twenty-two CAA agents, ten from WMA, ten from Monterey, with Little Big Man's Marty Diamond nominated five out of the eleven years.

Agency of the Year went to Monterey from 1996 through 1999, CAA in 2000, back to Monterrey in 2001, then back to CAA from 2002 through 2006. While CAA and WMA were the music divisions of large agencies replete with an array of other revenue-producing divisions, Monterey was a boutique music agency with niche market artists who did clubs, halls, and festivals. They were acquired in 2005 by the Paradigm Talent Agency in the midst of a roll-up to become a full-service agency competing with CAA and WMA.

In 2006 Paradigm also acquired Marty Diamond's Little Big Man Booking whose roster included Coldplay, Sarah McLachlan, Barenaked Ladies, Dido, and Avril Lavigne.

The Expanding Festival Factor

In 1997 *Pollstar* added a Music Festival of the Year category to its annual awards, a sure sign that managers and booking agents now regarded festivals as a growing revenue source for their music clients. Prior to the mid-1970s most multi-day music festivals had been annual events with municipal support that included other arts and crafts along with music performance, an urban parallel to the traditional state fair. There were also niche genre-specific events like the Newport Folk and Jazz Festivals. Woodstock, Monterey, and Altamont in the late 1960s were one-time happenings designed to attract FM radio listeners. They also were the blueprint for music festivals of the future with powerful audio systems for the teenage and young-adult audiences, dozens of artists performing all day and into the night over three-day weekends, and tens if not hundreds of thousands of fans in attendance.

In 1970 New Orleans staged its first Jazz & Heritage Festival. In June 1972, the country music industry organized its first Fan Fair in Nashville as an annual multi-day fan appreciation event with most major-label country artists participating. In 1973 Willie Nelson staged his first Fourth of July Picnic in Dripping Springs, Texas, where he had headlined a similar event the previous year. Other festivals followed, both urban and rural, gradually growing in attendance and amenities piquing the interest of the booking agencies. Then the festival market took an even larger leap with the establishment of the *Pollstar* festival award category and the emergence of SFX/CCE and AEG.

At the 1997 *Pollstar* Awards, the first Festival of the Year award went to the Jazz & Heritage Festival over runners up Bumbershoot in Seattle, Fleadh in New York, Music Midtown in Atlanta, and Milwaukee's Summerfest, which held the *Guinness Book of Records* nod as largest music festival with over a million attendees. In 1999 the inaugural Coachella Festival was staged at the Empire Polo Club in the Coachella Valley desert community of Indio, California, by independent promoter Goldenvoice, headed by Paul Tollett and Rick Van Santen. Despite losing money, it drew almost forty thousand fans to hear alternative rock acts and was named *Pollstar*'s Festival of the Year. Seeing the potential in such festivals, AEG acquired Goldenvoice and funded the April 2001 return of Coachella, which was again named *Pollstar*'s Music Festival of the Year in 2003, 2004, and 2006.

The Bonnaroo Festival on a farm in Manchester, Tennessee, sixty-five miles southeast of Nashville, debuted in June 2002. Organized by Knoxville, Tennessee, promoter Ashley Capps of AC Entertainment and Kerry Black, Rick Farman, Richard Goodstone, and Jonathan Mayers of Superfly Productions of New Orleans, Bonnaroo also was named the *Pollstar* Festival of the Year in its debut year. Bonnaroo, which is Creole slang for a really good time, was modeled as a combination of several predecessors including Coachella, the English Glastonbury Festival, and the jam band outdoor performance tradition of The Grateful Dead, Phish, the Allman Brothers, Widespread Panic, Dave Matthews Band, and the Charlie Daniels Band.

The Austin City Limits Music Festival, inspired by the public television show of the same name, also debuted in 2002, organized by Charlie Jones and Charles Attal, founders of Austin's C3 Presents. It was named Festival of the Year in 2005. That same year C3 Presents partnered with WMA to transform the traveling Lollapalooza Festival, run from 1991 to 1997 and in 2003 and 2004 by Jane's Addiction vocalist Perry Farrell, into a permanent event in Chicago's Grant Park. In 2006, Austin City Limits, Bonnaroo, and Lollapalooza all joined #1 Coachella in the *Pollstar* top-four festival rankings.

In 2006 both Bonnaroo and Austin City Limits were listed by *Billboard* as two of the top twenty-five–grossing box-office events of the year. Bonnaroo was in sixth place with $14.7 million in gate receipts from 80,681 attendees over its three-day weekend. Tickets were $169.50 and $184.50. The promoters also had a monopoly on concessions and a percentage of merchandising. With a bare minimum of motels in Manchester, attendees stayed in tents and campers with the festival providing water, showers, toilets, and food and beverage concessions. Austin City Limits came in at twenty-fifth with $8.1 million on a combination of $115 three-day passes and $50 one-day passes. Three-day attendance averaged 75,276. With an urban locale and a huge university in town, Austin didn't present the infrastructure challenges presented by the very rural Manchester.

The only 2006 events exceeding the Bonnaroo haul were Madonna's eight-day stand at London's Wembley Arena, which grossed $22.1 million with 86,061 in attendance; Mexican superstar Luis Miguel's thirty-show run at the Auditorio Nacional in Mexico City, which played to 267,528 aficionados with a $19.3 million gross; Billy Joel's twelve sellouts at Madison Square Garden, grossing $19.2 million from 226,038 fans; U2 with opening act Kanye West, drawing 206,568 Aussies to Sydney's Teistra Stadium over three days, taking in $18.5 million; and Madonna's six-day run at Madison Square Garden with a box-office of $16.5 million from tickets ranging in cost from $60 to $350 with three sellouts.

Outreach, Unrest, and Diversity at the Recording Academy

The Recording Academy and its Grammy Awards continued to prosper under what some viewed as the autocratic control of President/CEO Mike Greene. In 1997, with the able assistance of the Greenburg Traurig law firm entertainment division head Joel Katz, who served the Academy over the years as Atlanta chapter president, national trustee, chairman, and general counsel, Greene negotiated a five-year contract with CBS for $20 million a year and renewed in 2001 for another five years. The average audience for the Grammys was 22.8 million viewers during this time frame.

Greene also led the creation of the Grammy in the Schools program, the MusicCares charity for needy Academy members, and the Latin Recording Academy, with its separate awards program. During Greene's tenure from 1987 to 2002 the Academy saw its membership grow from 3,500 to 17,000, and its capital assets increased from $4.9 million to $50 million. Awards categories were added for rap and alternative, and new chapters were established in Philadelphia, Seattle (Pacific Northwest Chapter), Washington, D.C., Texas, and Florida, joining the seven existing chapters in New York, Los Angeles, Chicago, Nashville, Memphis, San Francisco, and Atlanta.

On the flip side of this sterling record, however, *Billboard*'s Melinda Newman reported that in late April 2002 Greene resigned during an emergency board meeting concerning the findings of a sexual harassment investigation and payment of $650,000 Greene paid to a former staffer who had accused Greene of sexual abuse. Board chair Garth Fundis was charged with leading the search for Greene's replacement. Newman further reported that "Greene denied the allegations, as well as two other sexual abuse accusations by former employees. According to a subsequent statement by Nashville-based record producer Fundis, the investigation 'revealed no sexual harassment, no sex discrimination, and no hostile work environment at the Recording Academy.'"[18]

There were other uncomfortable issues involving Greene including the solicitation of a recording contract from the major labels for his own album, viewed by many Academy insiders as a blatant abuse of his position. Of even more consequence, Greene was sued by Dick Clark's *American Music Awards* for threatening to keep artists from appearing on the Grammy telecast if they appeared on Clark's award show. By September the search committee recommended Neil Portnow, a longtime Academy trustee and officer, and senior executive at the Zomba Group, as Greene's replacement. He assumed the president/CEO position in December 2002.

Despite the backstage drama, from 1996 to 2006 the four major Grammy awards—Record of the Year, Album of the Year, Song of the Year, and Best New Artist—continued to reflect the breadth and diversity of the major music genres that drove both radio programming and retail sales. The progressive music press, however, often criticized the Academy for having what they considered to be a more conservative slant due to membership demographics, specifically the disproportionate share of older members from engineering, liner notes, and other nonperforming categories, as well as classical, jazz, and other niche genres with older fan bases.

Over the time period, however, younger acts, including rap and alternative artists, were receiving a large number of finalist nominations and were even winners. Both Lauryn Hill for 1998 and Norah Jones for 2002 captured both the New Artist and the Album of the Year awards. Rappers Outkast scored an Album of the Year award in 2003. Other newer and/or more progressive acts to receive Album of the Year nominations during this time period included The Fugees and Smashing Pumpkins for 1996; New Artist award winner Paula Cole and Radiohead in 1997; the Backstreet Boys and Dixie Chicks for 1999; Eminem and Radiohead again in 2000; India.Arie and Outkast for 2001; Eminem again and Nelly in 2003; Missy Elliott, New Artist award winner Evanescence, Justin Timberlake, and The White Stripes for 2003; Usher and Kanye West in 2004; Kanye West again in 2005; and in 2006 Gnarls Barkley, John Mayer, and Justin Timberlake again.

From 1996 through 2006, these younger artists accounted for twenty-five of fifty-five, or 45.5 percent, of the nominations in the Album of the Year category. In Record of the Year, which went to the top single track, the percentage of young artists in their first three years of eligibility was even higher at 63.6 percent, reflecting the programming of the CHR and AOR radio formats. Older artists appealing to the baby boomer generation and AC and Classic Rock radio also garnered their share of golden gramophones, including Eric Clapton, Santana, U2, Ray Charles, Luther Vandross, Bob Dylan, and Steely Dan.

Perhaps the most surprising outlier to win a major Grammy Award was the 8 million–selling *O Brother, Where Art Thou?* soundtrack collecting the 2002 Album of the Year award in addition to awards for Best Male Country Vocal Performance for "O Death" by Ralph Stanley; and the Best Country Collaboration with Vocals for "I Am a Man of Constant Sorrow" for the trio of Union Station's Dan Tyminski, songwriter Harley Allen, and the Nashville Bluegrass Band's Pat Enright. In the movie George Clooney and his fellow members of the fictitious Soggy Bottom Boys lip-synced to the track's three-part harmony. Equally anomalous for this bluegrass/Americana album was its over twenty weeks on the *Billboard* Top Country Chart. It also won the Album of the Year Award and Single of the Year Award at the Country Music Association Awards, and Album of the Year Award from the Academy of Country Music.

Eligible Academy voters comprised current members who had qualified to vote by having creative or technical credits on at least six commercially released tracks or their equivalent at some point in their career. Record company executives—including CEOs and other officers, A&R personnel, and any other staff member who did not have these qualifications—could not vote. Although there were continuing accusations of pervasive bloc voting by the record companies, this practice was subject to voter disqualification if detected. With membership approaching twenty thousand in the first decade of the new millennium, it would be hard to imagine that there could be enough employees at any one of the majors who were both qualified to vote and willing to compromise their creative credentials for their employers' ballot-stuffing machinations.

Nonetheless, in a business known to push the envelope to sell records, it is possible that in such an intensely competitive atmosphere such schemes did exist. Only seventy-two Grammys were awarded from just under four hundred final nominations, culled by ballot from the over twenty thousand initial submissions. With the positive effect that a Grammy could have on the winner's career and record sales, it is also believable that there would be a degree of dissatisfaction from the industry professionals whose artists made the final cut but didn't win. Their salaries, bonuses, and jobs often depended more on commercial success than on the artistic merit and audio craft that were the twin criteria for the Grammy Awards.

Despite the Fall in Retail, It Was a Good Decade for Artists

While the decline in retail sales was clearly reflected in artists' royalties, new digital forms of music consumption cushioned the fall as well as offered great promise for the future. In addition, for those artists who wrote their own songs, royalties were far more than just icing on the cake. As a whole, songwriter royalties had almost doubled over the decade thanks to their publishers licensing new digital revenue streams, increased PRO royalties stemming from the growth in radio and television advertising revenue, and the mechanical royalty rising from 6.95¢ in 1996 to 9.1¢ for 2006.

Concert performance and its ancillary add-ons of merchandise sales and sponsorships, the other major sources of performers' earnings, had more than tripled over the decade, led by *Pollstar*'s year-end tally rising from $1.05 billion in 1996 to $3.6 billion in 2006 without including the ancillary sources adding more than 20 percent on top of the box-office receipts. What's more, remuneration for their services was immediate with 50 percent of the fee for each performance deposited into the agent's escrow account upon execution of the booking contract, and the other 50 percent paid before going on stage the night of the show.

Billboard instituted a ranking of the 40 Top Moneymakers in 2005 that analyzed revenue and expenses, concluding that the take-home from live performances came to an average of about 34 percent of overall box-office receipts after all expenses were paid. Applying this supposition to *Pollstar*'s 2006 total of $3.6 billion yielded $1.22 billion in net earnings. Artists' share of merchandise and sponsorship revenue brought their take-home before taxes to over $1.5 billion, roughly three times the 1996 total. This didn't include, however, the artists whose tours, solo engagements, or club appearances were not tracked by *Pollstar* or *Billboard*.

Although the 2006 RIAA retail record value of $11.8 billion was much higher than the box-office total, the percentage paid to the artists was much lower. Actual royalty rates after applicable deductions ranged between 7.65 percent of SRLP for new artists who were on a 12 percent contractual royalty rate, and 12.75 percent for top stars with a 20 percent royalty rate. For all artists, however, the costs of making and marketing records had to be recouped from otherwise payable royalties before the artists saw anything beyond their advances, which of course also had to be recouped. Then if artists sold enough records to go beyond recoupment and into royalties, 15 percent to 25 percent usually went to manager/attorney/business manager commissions.

While there wasn't verifiable information to ascertain the details of individual artists' royalty accounts, or at what point they finished recoupment, it can be estimated that artists at the top rate generated over $2.1 million in royalties for each million albums sold with an SRLP of $16.98 or higher. New artists on a lower royalty rate generated about $1.3 million on the first million units, sometimes enough to recoup the initial investment spent on advances, recording, videos, promotion, and tour support. The labels, however, received in the range of $11 million in wholesales receipts on each million units sold at an SRLP of $16.98, and even more at higher SRLPs.

What the record and live performance sectors did have in common, however, was a similar demographic spread among the artists in the year-end

Billboard charts and *Pollstar* rankings to appeal to all age groups. Consumers tended to remain fans of the artists they first encountered during their teen and college years who continued to record and perform over the ensuing decades. Ten out of the 2006 top twenty-five tour earners were considered legacy acts who were twenty-five years or more into their careers and either in or eligible for one or more Halls of Fame. The Rolling Stones, Barbra Streisand, the Who, and Crosby, Stills, Nash & Young had been stars since the 1960s, while U2, Madonna, Aerosmith, Billy Joel, Elton John, and both Def Leppard and Journey—who toured together in 2006—all began their climb to fame in the 1970s. Although not yet Hall of Fame eligible, Bon Jovi already had twenty years as a headliner. Mariah Carey, Tim McGraw, Faith Hill, Kenny Chesney, Dave Matthews Band, Pearl Jam, Nickelback, Coldplay, Take That, Brad Paisley, and Trans-Siberian Orchestra all began their careers in the 1990s, while Rascal Flatts, RBD, Cirque Du Soleil, and the American Idols Season Live! Tour emerged in the early years of the new millennium.

The average 2006 ticket price for the Top 25 tours was $81.72, over $20 more than the average of the Top 100 tours. They appealed to every age group from affluent baby boomers who might be seeing the idols of their youth for the last time, to their millennial children supporting the latest radio sensations like Nickelback or Coldplay, often through the largesse of their parents. There were die-hard country fans who wanted to hear ten years of their favorite artist's radio hits in one show, and successful Gen X'ers reliving the music of their own teen years from Madonna, Bon Jovi, or Mariah Carey. Fans of television phenomenon *American Idol* saw all the contestants live on one stage, and those who couldn't get to Vegas for Cirque du Soleil had Vegas come to them. The orchestral rock-'n'-roll Christmas show of Trans-Siberian Orchestra was there to make the season jolly.

While the powers at the top of both the concert and record industries were focused on the several hundred artists who were in the *Pollstar*-tracked tours and *Billboard*'s Top 200 albums from year to year, there were thousands of other artists with album releases by both majors and indies that didn't crack the Top 200 but still made their living on the road. The consumer shift to spending money on tickets rather than purchase albums didn't stop at the Top 200 tours. By 2006 there were more clubs, theaters, and other smaller venues with many owned, operated, or supported by the major promoters, enabling a larger number of artists to perform live.

The internet, advanced computer programs, and broadband access further expanded the avenues for self-promotion and home recording to an even wider array of artists. Social media platforms were just beginning to establish themselves as online communities for direct connection to a wider array of artists than ever existed in the now-fading brick-and-mortar marketplace. Even the major label groups recognized this trend with their expansion into independent distribution divisions to service product thar could thrive without commercial radio and traditional retail distribution.

The decade ended on a positive note for the creative community with the promising potential of iTunes, Pandora, smartphones, college radio, NPR, the upcoming Sirius-XM merger, and YouTube. Many other digital innovations that would become the building blocks of the digital future were still in their incubation stages, and all signs pointed to even more to emerge in the decade ahead.

10

The Emergence of the Digital Consumer

The State of Consumption: 1996

Bob Pittman had been the driving force behind the success of MTV and later the transformation of Clear Channel into the iHeartRadio internet platform. He began his career in local radio in the 1960s. In 2011 he told Andrew Hampp of *Ad Age* what he had learned from his early on-air days about the relationship between radio and its listeners, and the listeners themselves. "We have a social connection, which adds a whole other layer. Radio really does have a tribe that wants to talk to each other."[1] Radio advertisers wanted to subliminally implant their products in the minds of as large a share of that tribe as possible, counting on their uniformity in music choice to extend to those products.

Although consumers were selective in what they bought, that selectivity often reflected the tribal tendencies within their peer group. Tastemakers that shaped musical trends existed long before the emergence of P2P internet communities and what are now termed "influencers" on TikTok and other social media platforms. This tribal tendency has been evident going back to the bobbysoxers craze of the 1940s followed by the teen idol obsession of the 1950s. Beatlemania, the British invasion, and psychedelic rock in the 1960s were followed by the singer/songwriters, outlaw country, and disco eras of the 1970s. Michael Jackson, album rock, and urban cowboys of the 1980s gave way to rap, grunge, and Garth Brooks in the 1990s. With the turn of the twentieth century came boy bands, EDM, and *American Idol*. All of these trends had their own distinct elements of tribalism.

Tom Silverman's analysis of 1995 SoundScan data revealed that only 148 out of the 26,629 albums introduced that year sold over 250,000 copies, supplying almost 60 percent of 1995 sales. With one-third of all albums released by the major labels, there were hundreds if not thousands of albums other than those 148 with comparable budgets that never sold out their initial shipment or made it into regular radio rotation. The fact that so few found favor on a mass scale was another indication of peer group uniformity in choosing music. The results of this consumer-driven culling process not only shaped radio play but

American Popular Music and Its Business in the Digital Age. Rick Sanjek, Oxford University Press. © Frederick Sanjek 2024.
DOI: 10.1093/oso/9780190653828.003.0010

also influenced concert promoters when deciding which artists to put on tour, the venue size, and the price of tickets.

In its two-year run from 1999 through 2001 Napster became the then-ultimate expression of tribalism in music consumption independent of the record/radio/retail troika. The complacency the industry developed toward the voice of its consumer base was a major contributor to, if not the cause of, its loss of control over the evolution of sound carrier technology to outside digital development. Napster was an online bulletin board listing files that could be exchanged directly between users' computers, but the files themselves were never stored there. As its community expanded to 80 million or more, its users enjoyed an unprecedented file-sharing access to almost all music ever recorded, further distancing the Napster tribe from the grip of the record industry.

By the time Napster was shut down in June 2001, billions of MP3 files had been shared and subsequently stored on computers and portable devices around the world. Although Napster was gone, dozens of other file-sharing platforms were still operational. The introduction of the BitTorrent protocol in 2001 then took the file-sharing process to another level of interaction as higher bit rates and increased broadband speed enabled faster P2P exchange, especially when sharing whole albums, DVDs, or even movies.

Prior to the 2003 iTunes launch, legal download sales were severely limited by DRM and repertoire availability constraints. The labels chose to fight new technology if they couldn't control it rather than adapt their business model to the changing consumer trends as they had done so well in the past. In the process they surrendered control of the narrative.

Since 1989 the RIAA's annual Consumer Music Profile, separate but complementary to its year-end retail value report, was based on a monthly national telephone survey of over three thousand interviewees. The surveys tracked age and gender as well as consumer purchasing preferences for genre, sound carrier format, and point of purchase. The 1989 profile revealed that 12 percent of consumers favored non-retail purchases, 7.9 percent of which were through record clubs and 4.1 percent by other mail-order sources. This preference then peaked at 18.7 percent in 1995 and bottomed out at 6 percent in 2002. The profile first introduced internet sales of physical copies as a purchasing preference in 1997 registering .3 percent of total sales, growing to 3.4 percent in 2002.

Non-retail purchases of music registered about 14 percent of the 2006 total of $11.53 billion. These consumer dollars went to digital products including both singles and album downloads, ringtones, and streams for a total of $1.65 billion. There were no true measurables, however, on the volume of P2P file-sharing, and thus no accurate accounting as to what extent the tribal element engrossed in home duplication actually affected the industry. But as Bob Dylan stated in "Subterranean Homesick Blues," "You don't need to be a weatherman to know which way the wind blows."[2]

Expanded Options for Consumer Spending

Throughout the 1990s the record business was competing with itself as its club operations were undercutting retail sales, while the retail sector was having its own price war as outlined in the preceding chapters, giving consumers an abundance of comparative shopping opportunities. Mass merchandisers offered lower prices, often at 60 percent or less of SRLP while record clubs gave away a sizeable share of their shipments as membership incentives. The ten-to-twenty-nine age groups were still the primary target of the labels since they accounted for 52.6 percent of sales. The oldest of this grouping had been twelve years old when the Walkman cassette player debuted in 1979, fourteen when MTV was launched in 1981, and seventeen when CDs began the climb to market dominance.

In 1996, just two years after the opening of the internet to commercial exploitation, about one-third of households had computers. At an average 1996 cost of around $2,000, home computers with detached keyboard and desktop monitor were owned predominantly by upper-income consumers. This same group was likely to also own a home audio system, have cable television access, buy video game consoles for their children, use a VCR for taping shows, and spend disposable income on both records and video games. Most home computer purchases from 1996 forward also had an internal CD-R drive. In 1997 the re-writable CD (CD-RW) was introduced, but was initially limited to higher-end computers. Given their introduction to video games and other new technology at an early age, the ten-to-twenty-nine age demos were far more computer literate than their parents, and more adept at adapting to the exponential growth of the digital toolkit.

More powerful web browsers, increased chip storage capacity, and more sophisticated operating systems proliferated as higher-speed internet access via cable, dubbed broadband, supplanted dial-up at tech-savvy households, businesses, and universities in the late 1990s. Students at the upper-end colleges were given their own email addresses on the school's powerful computer systems, something very few had enjoyed at home. In 1999 the home cable industry added a new layer to its Data Over Cable Service Interface Specification (DOCSIS) that enabled cable systems to provide broadband delivery over their existing coaxial cable networks. By 2006 broadband had replaced dial-up for over 50 percent of American households.

In the early 1980s home duplication by the younger age groups was limited to those whose families had cassette recorders integrated with their home audio components. Then in the mid-1980s the dual reel cassette deck that Irving Azoff had so aptly dubbed a personal piracy machine became available at accessible prices, as well as on some portable boom boxes. The ability to make inexpensive copies on high-bias blank cassettes, which had less distortion than the label's pre-recorded cassettes, improved home copying quality despite the generational loss inherent in analog tape replication. In the mid-1990s the CD-R drive transferred copying capability from cassette to CD, but the instability of the CD Walkman and other portable CD players when running or walking helped keep them from unseating cassette players as consumers' portable device of choice.

By the late 1990s retailers were concerned about the decline of the single, which had historically served as the introduction to the record-buying experience for many teenagers. Record labels, however, viewed singles as a promotional vehicle and unprofitable at retail. They further claimed that buying singles cannibalized album sales since consumers who had the single might not buy the album. From the consumer perspective, around 90 percent of singles sales were in the CD format, costing an average of over $4 for two tracks, one of which was the B side, which they would probably never hear on radio. By the time Napster debuted in 1999, the labels had basically discontinued distributing singles, but with the broadband access students then had at college, Napster became the way to access music without radio play or retail availability.

Consumers and the record industry seemed at loggerheads. For decades, the record-buying public had readily but selectively acquired what they heard on radio as singles, and then bought the albums. The labels, however, were intent on preserving the dominance of the album format and the profits from them. Discontinuing the sale of singles was part of that plan. If the declining supply of singles couldn't meet the demand, the labels expected fans to buy albums costing over $10, and as high as $19, to get the one track they wanted, an unintended invitation to home duplication.

As tech sector entrepreneurs competed in the second half of the 1990s to develop a compressed digital file that met the labels' DRM requirements, consumers eagerly awaited the availability of the latest music in such a convenient and hopefully affordable format. By 1998 it had become apparent that the MP3 could fit the bill, but the labels preferred to leave the consumer demand unfilled until they could find and control its distribution with DRM copy restriction.

Despite the shutdown of both Napster and MP3.com, consumers still had their accumulated libraries of MP3 files and their portable devices for listening to them. They could not be transferred, however, to either the PressPlay or MusicNet alternatives offered by the record industry, whether they were legally replicated by making MP3 copies of the CDs they had purchased; had been legally purchased through DRM-free webstores like EMusic; or they were surreptitiously acquired through P2P file-sharing. Even more, PressPlay and MusicNet were only computer compliant and could not be installed on any portable devices.

Instead of making a deal with either Napster or MP3.com to utilize their consumer base, technology, and goodwill with the public while transitioning to a legal digital market, the labels left consumers with no acceptable, legitimate alternative for acquiring single digital tracks. As the industry stewed in its own self-made muddle between the 2001 demise of Napster and MP3.com, and the 2003 debut of iTunes, young consumers continued to flock to the growing throng of illicit sources that had replaced the two now-defunct upstart file-sharing platforms.

While the digital tide was rolling over the recorded music sector, other forms of entertainment were also competing for consumers' leisure dollars. The US Bureau of Labor Statistics cited a 1996 total consumer entertainment expenditure of $191.1 billion. The record industry's $12.5 billion was just 6.6 percent of that total. By 2006 total entertainment spending had increased 47.7 percent over 1996 to $282.4 billion, but recorded music declined to $11.8 billion, dropping to just 4.2 percent of consumer spending on entertainment.

The bureau also reported that average household spending on entertainment increased from $1,834 in 1996 to $2,376 in 2006, a rise of 29.6 percent. The average expenditure on recorded music, however, was down to $96.85 in 2006 from $127.27 in 1996, a decline of 31.4 percent. Other entertainment categories fared much better. The video game market grew from $3.3 billion in 1996 to $12.5 billion in 2006. Home video sales/rentals went from $5.6 billion in 1996 to $21.5 billion in 2006. The motion picture box office grew from $5.71 billion to $9.21 billion. The public was spending more money per capita on entertainment, with all forms other than recorded music in an upward growth pattern.

Consumer Demographic Differences

The annual RIAA Consumer Profile between 1996 and 2006 continued to reflect the public's shifting preferences in music consumption habits. Each year's profile was divided into seven five-year age groups, going from ten to fourteen, fifteen to nineteen, twenty to twenty-four, twenty-five to twenty-nine, thirty to thirty-four, thirty-five to thirty-nine, and forty to forty-four, along with forty-five and over as an eighth grouping. The three youngest age groups bunched together covered middle schoolers, high school teens, college students, and young adults up to age twenty-four. In 1996 this blend of the youngest Gen X'ers and oldest millennials was the most computer and video game savvy, had the most free time, wase exploring the internet, and was poised to become the core component of the surge in MP3 file-sharing. This demographic grouping used computers and the internet primarily for entertainment and social networking.

The next three groups in the RIAA profile covered ages twenty-five to thirty-nine. In 1996 they were in the work force or creating businesses, and raising families. They had the least free time, and added business and home management chores to their computer usage. They had grown up through the cassette to CD transformation, the emergence of the rock concert business, the birth of MTV, the explosion of rap and grunge as expressions of societal rebellion, and if they were serious music fans, probably had a Sony Walkman.

Pairing together the forty-to-forty-five and forty-five-plus groupings created a demographic encompassing the oldest Gen Xer's, baby boomers, 1950s Teens, and the World War II generation. They grew up with Frank Sinatra, Elvis, The Beatles, vinyl albums, rock-'n'-roll, and Woodstock, and lived through the transformation of FM radio into AOR, which then overtook the singles-oriented Top 40 format and its successor, CHR, in popularity.

According to the RIAA 1996 Consumer Profile, the ten-to-twenty-four group bought 40.1 percent of the records sold for a total value of $5.03 billion. The twenty-five-to-forty demo accounted for 35 percent, at a $4.39 billion value, and the forty and over grouping purchased 24.2 percent for a $3.03 billion value.

In 2001 these comparative consumption totals started to shift. Overall, the 2001 totals were about 10 percent higher than in 1996, up from $12.53 billion to $13.74 billion. The ten-to-twenty-four and forty-plus groups tied at 34 percent of the total, each with $4.62 billion. The twenty-five-to-thirty-nine demo was just slightly behind at 32 percent for $4.32 billion.

Total consumption in 2006, now including digital, was down 19.4 percent in total value from 2001, a decline of $2.23 billion. The ten-to-twenty-four demo had fallen to 30.2 percent of total value, spending $1.12 billion less than they did in 2001 and $1.47 billion less than they did in 1996. The twenty-five-to-thirty-nine grouping declined $376 million from 2001 to $3.94 billion in 2006, accounting for 33.5 percent of total value. The forty-plus demo

CONSUMER SPENDING ON MUSIC IN 2006

In 2006 consumer spending on physical product was down 32.2% from a high of $14.6 billion in 1999, the year of Napster's debut, to $9.9 billion. The R.I.A.A. began tracking downloads in 2004, followed by ringtones and streaming in 2005.

Consumer spending on digital products totaled $1.8 billion in 2006 but made up for only 45% of the decline in money spent on physical sales.

The value of major concerts tickets as reported by *Pollstar* more than tripled from $1.05 billion in 1996 to $3.6 billion in 2006. The secondary ticket re-sale market, handing and processing fees, parking, concessions, and merchandise sales grew accordingly, as did the volume of shows at smaller venues not tracked by the trade journals.

Printed music entered the digital age shortly after the internet opened for commercial enterprise in late 1994. New online start-ups sold directly to consumers at better prices with a digital portfolio of sheet music, interactive tablature, and method books.

At the end of 2006, the transfer of digital consumption from desktop to smartphone was already underway. A generation of computer-savvy teens and young adults were already experiencing digital interactivity through web-based streaming services and the Pandora algorithm. Convenience and timely access at a minimal cost were far better than the legal pitfalls and time-consuming process of P2P file-sharing.

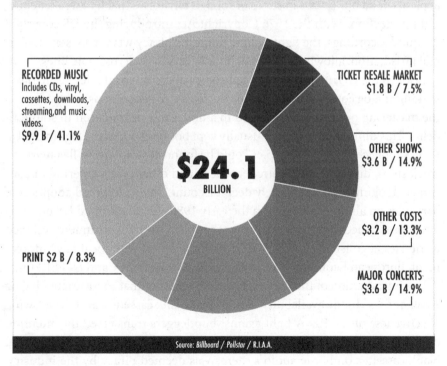

RECORDED MUSIC
Includes CDs, vinyl, cassettes, downloads, streaming,and music videos.
$9.9 B / 41.1%

PRINT $2 B / 8.3%

$24.1 BILLION

TICKET RESALE MARKET
$1.8 B / 7.5%

OTHER SHOWS
$3.6 B / 14.9%

OTHER COSTS
$3.2 B / 13.3%

MAJOR CONCERTS
$3.6 B / 14.9%

Source: *Billboard* / *Pollstar* / R.I.A.A.

Illustration 10.1 Consumer Spending on Music in 2006

accounted for 35.1 percent of the 2006 total, falling $545 million from 2001, but was up $1.09 billion over 1996.

These data seem to confirm that the ten-to-twenty-four age group that had traditionally driven retail record sales, record label marketing budgets, and CHR radio playlists, was now turning its attention and dollars to other forms of entertainment in addition to the free file-sharing of tracks rather than buying them. Their decrease in spending on recorded music probably contributed to the $9.2 billion increase in spending on video games between 1996 and 2006.

Digital Record Piracy

Digital technology added an entirely new element to the anti–record piracy crusade, shifting the labels' focus from illegally manufactured copies to consumer file-sharing. Historically, record piracy had involved duplication of finished product from the LP, 8-track, and then cassette formats by bootleggers at plants or ad hoc setups in states or foreign territories that had weaker copyright protection. With the 1976 Copyright Act introducing the US copyright in sound recordings, the fight against domestic piracy went from state to federal jurisdiction, allowing pursuit of bootleggers to go across state lines.

Prior to the CD, illegally produced copies of commercial releases involved making analog copies of analog copies, at least two generations removed from the mastering process. This resulted in a noticeable degradation in sound fidelity. This difference in quality usually kept bootlegs out of the legitimate US retail supply chain. Pirated copies could be found at swap meets, flea markets, truck stops, discount stores, street corners, and other places catering to consumers looking for an extremely deep discount. The widespread adoption of bar codes on album packaging in the early 1980s further limited US bootlegging. It remained, however, a persistent problem overseas in underdeveloped territories, a constant battle for IFPI in conjunction with local law enforcement, European Economic Community (EEC) authorities, and INTERPOL.

The introduction of the dual reel cassette recorder that so infuriated Irving Azoff, the rise in the availability of high-bias blank cassettes, and the growing effectiveness of the RIAA fight against bootleggers transferred the attention of anti-piracy advocates to home duplication. Making copies at home from blank cassettes on home audio systems was deemed piracy by the industry. Consumer advocates, however, claimed the public had the right to make copies of previously purchased records for use within a playlist designed for mobile listening on a Walkman or car tape deck as it was parallel to legally taping a television show for later viewing.

As consumers embraced the CD from the mid-1980s forward so did bootleggers. CD copies were clones of whatever was copied onto them. This made cassettes replicated from CDs far superior to cassette-to-cassette copies. When CD-Rs were introduced, bootleggers adopted them as well. In the eyes of the RIAA, the CD-R extended illegal CD-to-CD duplication into the home. The industry finally achieved a small victory with the levy on sales of blank digital tape, digital discs, and digital recording devices as legislated by the 1992 Audio Home Recording Act (AHRA).

In 1987, chairman of WEA International and president of IFPI Nesuhi Ertegun estimated the illegal worldwide market at over 500 million albums, which were sold for over $1.2 billion. He told *Billboard*'s Mike Hennessey that "one in every four cassettes sold throughout the world is a pirate. For the most successful artists the ratio is even more alarming. For every two Madonna or Springsteen records and tapes we sell, there is a pirate copy on the market somewhere in the world."[3] In 2001, ten years after the introduction of CD-R technology, IFPI reported their yearly estimate at 950 million pirated units, at a value of $4.3 billion. CD-Rs made up almost half the total at 450 million units. With online file-sharing also considered piracy, the RIAA claimed that more than 2.6 billion monthly illegal downloads were also a part of the piracy problem.

Consumers' computers, however, were exempt under the AHRA from being considered audio recording devices. The act defined a digital audio recording device as "any machine or device of a type commonly distributed to individuals for use by individuals, whether or not included with or as part of some other machine or device, the digital recording function of which is designed or marketed for the primary purpose of, and that is capable of, making a digital audio copied recording for private use."[4] It further defined digital audio recording media as "any material object in a form commonly distributed for use by individuals, that is primarily marketed or most commonly used by consumers for the purpose of making digital audio copied recordings by use of a digital audio recording device."[5]

These definitions were the basis of the 1999 court ruling in the 1998 RIAA lawsuit against the Diamond Rio MP3 player. The court found that the Rio was not a recording device, but a copying device that did a space shift, that is, made a copy of a file already in a user's possession on a personal computer. The AHRA had previously established that audio recording was not a PC's primary purpose, which exempted the transferal of digital files from a home computer, no matter how the file had been obtained, from prosecution by the RIAA as illegal home duplication. Although somewhat set back by the ruling, the RIAA shifted its campaign against home duplication to the burgeoning problem of P2P file-sharing.

File-sharing was, and is, an integral element of digital communication and not inherently illegal when not sharing copyrighted material without permission. It originated with the 1971 IBM 8″ floppy disc with 80 kilobytes of memory to which information could be copied and transferred to another computer. The next significant file-sharing development was the 1978 creation of the first bulletin board file transfer protocol by Ward Christiansen of IBM and fellow computer hobbyist Randy Suess. Their Computerized Bulletin Board System (CBBS) allowed binary files to be transferred between modems over a dial-up telephone connection.

In 1985 the File Transfer Protocol (FTP), which is still used today, was designed to operate through the Transmission Control Protocol and the Internet Protocol (collectively TCP/IP) and was funded by the Department of Defense through the Defense Advanced Research Projects Agency (DARPA). The internet is the worldwide network of computers that are connected via TCP/IP.

Then in 1991 the World Wide Web (WWW), also referred to as "the web," was released to the public after two years of development by English scientist Sir Tim Berners-Lee—knighted in 2004 for his digital pioneering—and his team at Conseil européen pour la Recherche nucléaire (CERN), a United Nations–affiliated research organization. His browser allowed web pages to be connected through hypertext links that allow information written in Hypertext Markup Language (HTML), along with image, video, and/or audio data, to be transmitted over the internet between web locations identified by their Uniform Resource Locator (URL). Internet entrepreneurs flocked to the web to develop its commercial potential, ultimately making HTML the predominant internet protocol. In 1993 the Mosaic browser added improved graphic design to the process, soon to be followed and superseded by Netscape Navigator and the Microsoft Internet Explorer.

In late 1994 the web was opened to commercial Internet Service Providers (ISPs). Among the thousands of ISP startups in 1995 were Amazon.com, eBay, and Craigslist, followed by Hotmail in 1996, with AOL, involved in online games and other services since the mid-1980s, offering a $19.95 a month access subscription rather than the hourly billing offered by others. Google Search, Yahoo!, and PayPal debuted in 1998.

The Napster Chronicles: The Disruption Begins

By 1999, young music-loving internet users, including college students with broadband access through their school email servers, as well as an assortment of programmers, hackers, gamers, and coding hobbyists were as aware as the record labels, if not more so, of the availability of free MP3 files on the internet. While the RIAA was pursuing action against offending websites, DRM-compliant tech companies were seeking the key to what they hoped could be a carefully monitored internet jukebox. Meanwhile, more and more songs were being added to the P2P stockpile of MP3 tracks.

The drama reached a crescendo in June 1999 when two teenage hackers, eighteen-year-old Northeastern University freshman dropout and self-taught coder Shawn Fanning, and nineteen-year-old Sean Parker, already a successful albeit small-scale internet entrepreneur, launched a new file-sharing service, which they named Napster after Fanning's web handle, a nickname that referred to his hair. The pair had met online several years earlier while surfing through hacker message boards.

Fanning wanted to find a more efficient way to share these already-compressed MP3 versions of CD tracks, which were way too many megabytes to be emailed, than what was currently in use by the P2P file-sharing community. He envisioned a program that would combine elements of instant messaging akin to the Internet Relay Chat (IRC) application that facilitated P2P text communication with file-sharing functions similar to the Microsoft Windows rapid search and filter program. After teaching himself both Windows programming and Unix server code, in the first half of 1999 Fanning wrote the code for an MP3 file-sharing program to serve as a conduit to find and connect through the Internet Protocol (IP) to other users' URLs to transmit files directly between them.

Fanning shared his enthusiasm with his w00w00 IRC computer security network. Fellow members Jordan Ritter organized the architecture for the Napster website, and Ali Aybar wrote its search engine software. The program also caught the attention of Parker, who was still living with his parents in Maryland. After extensively interviewing Parker for *Forbes* in 2011, Steve Bertoni wrote, "At 15 his hacking caught the attention of the FBI, earning him community service. At 16 he won the Virginia state computer science fair for developing an early Web crawler and was recruited by the CIA. Instead he interned for Mark Pincus' D.C. startup, Freeloader, and then UUNet, an early Internet service provider."[6] By June 1999, a year after he had graduated from high school, he had already made over $80,000. He joined Fanning as a partner with a $50,000 investment and they went online in June 1999. Napster immediately attracted a host of users.

After dropping out of Northeastern to develop the Napster code, Fanning stayed with his uncle John Fanning who ran the ChessNet and NetGames websites, and played professional poker. John had introduced Shawn to computers and programming at an early age. Seeing the potential in his nephew's vision, he incorporated the fledgling enterprise as Napster, Inc., with himself as CEO, owning 70 percent of the stock. He solicited $250,000 from a small Silicon Valley venture capital company, Valicert, Inc., whose CEO Yosi Amram was an investor in other Fanning ventures. Amram insisted they relocate to the Bay Area.

The younger Fanning, Parker, and Ritter moved in late summer and were joined by Aybar who was already working in Silicon Valley but soon moved to Napster as director of technology. Ritter continued supervision of structure and security issues. Boston venture capitalist Eileen Richardson invested in the company to become CEO and moved to California to join the team while John Fanning remained in Massachusetts. Former Sony executive Elizabeth Brooks was hired to direct marketing. She got Fanning extensive publicity, including the cover of *Time* magazine, creating national notoriety and empathy for the David vs. Goliath Napster story. She also coined the phrase "Thanks for sharing" that became a Napster slogan.

Fanning, Parker, and crew believed that Napster could serve the needs of both the public and industry concurrently. For music consumers it eliminated the need to buy an album to get just one track, provided access to a virtually unlimited selection of music, and bypassed the barriers to downloading CD files. For the record industry it could fulfill the demand for single tracks, serve as a promotional tool, and expose listeners to new acts and the latest releases. The major hurdle was how to monetize the Napster platform in a way to maintain their user base while satisfying the mercantile agenda of the record industry.

Having no experience in fundraising, corporate politics, or copyright, much less in creating a profitable business model, the young Fanning and Parker left those tasks to Richardson, Brooks, John Fanning, and their expanding circle of investors, advisors, and consultants. By the time they set up shop in San Mateo, California, in September 1999, they had forty thousand registered users with a few hundred of them connecting at any given time. Their numbers grew through the fall of 1999 and into 2000 to reach over 70 million users with an estimated 2.5 million connected simultaneously at peak user times. There is no precise record of how many billions of files were shared. The staff grew to over seventy people running hundreds of servers to keep up with user demand.

Although there were other P2P file-sharing sites, Napster's architecture was the most consumer friendly. Users had their song index and file transfer manager functions in a spreadsheet-style scroll that listed song title, artist, file size in MBs, kb/s bit rate, track time length, and user handle of the file owner. Tracks available from a specific user would only appear while that user was connected. The song files themselves were never posted on Napster itself. Rather, the scroll on Napster was a directory of user sites with P2P download capacity, directly linking ISP addresses to view one another's track listings. This was different from the websites previously prosecuted by the RIAA that actually stored files to be transmitted to consumers, often in exchange for the user transmitting other files back to the website.

While Fanning, Parker, and their team slaved tirelessly to keep up with the rocketing usage, John Fanning, Amram, and Richardson were soliciting additional investors and Brooks was building the Napster image and the promotional narrative that so captivated the public. Ron Conway, the principal investor in SV Angel LLP and an early investor in Ask Jeeves, PayPal, and Google, came on board in May 2000. He invested $200,000 after Napster won the 2000 Webby Award for best music technology from the San Francisco-based International Academy of Digital Arts and Sciences at their annual awards gala held on May 11, 2000. After getting to know Parker and Fanning, Conway eventually put in an estimated $2 million. VC firm Hummer Winblad Venture Partners put in $15 million and joined the board.

The Napster Chronicles: The Legal Battle

John Fanning had obtained an attorney's opinion stating that Napster was not infringing copyright as files were never physically on its site. Napster also posted an admonishment against sharing illegally obtained files and that copying and sharing by individuals via computer connection was exempt under the AHRA. On December 6, 1999, the RIAA sued in San Francisco in the US District Court for the Northern District of California, with Judge Marilyn Patel presiding. They claimed that Napster was participating in tributary copyright infringement under the 1997 No Electronic Theft (NET) Act, which expanded criminal liability when facilitating illegal exchange of copyrighted recordings "by the reproduction or distribution, including by electronic means, during any 180 day period, of 1 or more copies or phonorecords of 1 or more copyrighted works,"[7] even when not obtaining or expecting to obtain anything of value for participating in the infringement. Damages could reach $100,000 per infringement and treble if found willful, under US copyright law. Napster was granted a stay to remain in operation until the final hearing. On June 16, 2000, Napster brought in noted litigator David Boies five months before his historic involvement in Bush v. Gore. Boies had previous clients in technology disputes, including the government, in a case against Microsoft, and IBM in antitrust allegations. After reading both sides' arguments he gave Napster a fifty-fifty chance at victory.

Boies told ZDNet.com that the case "raises important questions of how the copyright laws are to be applied to this new medium. . . . It also raises important questions as to the extent to which Internet directories will remain free to permit individual users to use a directory to communicate and, in some cases, to share files without monitoring and regulating what those users do."[8] He added that the case also raises the question of whether an internet directory can be held liable for permitting users to engage in sharing, which lawyers for the recording industry called stealing, ". . . simply because the scale of the Internet greatly increases the extent of the sharing."[9]

Despite the suits filed by Metallica and Dr. Dre, there were Napster supporters, including Chuck D of Public Enemy, Dave Matthews, and Fred Durst of Limp Bizkit, whose summer tour was sponsored by Napster. Meanwhile the executive team now headed by Hummer Winblad partner/ attorney Hank Barry, who had replaced Richardson as CEO, continued to negotiate with the labels. Barry later recounted an early July 2000 meeting that he said included Sony Corp CEO Sir Howard Stringer, BMG's Thomas Middelhoff, and UMG's Edgar Bronfman Jr. Barry claimed that the labels agreed to negotiate and directed him to do so through Bronfman, but that Bronfman stonewalled him after Judge Patel ruled in the labels' favor on July 26, 2000, ordering Napster to remove offending users from their database.

Barry later told technology reporter Matt Hartley of Canada's *Globe and Mail*. "I assumed good faith on the part of the record companies, and that was a big mistake. While they were having nice cordial meetings with us and saying of course we must make a deal, they were making plans to have their own competitive services and indeed they were making plans to go out and sue 50,000 people that they ended up suing. So the idea that they were just the victims of this is hilarious and doesn't reflect in any way the really utterly bad faith nature of their approach to Napster."[10]

Bronfman, however, remembered discussions with Napster differently. In an August 2013 review of the VH1 documentary on Napster titled *Downloaded*, *LA Times* reporter and also author of the 2003 book *All the Rave: The Rise and*

Fall of Shawn Fanning's Napster, Joseph Menn wrote, "Later, secret settlement talks in the record labels' fatal lawsuit against Napster didn't collapse because of record label obstinacy. . . . Napster director John Hummer, whose venture firm kept John Fanning involved and put more than $13 million into the company, demanded that the labels buy the unlawful, revenue-deprived Napster for an astounding $2 billion, Universal Music's parent company CEO Edgar Bronfman told me. (Hummer this week recalled claiming that Napster would be worth 'more than a billion dollars' post-settlement.)"[11]

Napster appealed but lost again in February 2001 before a three-judge panel from the US Court of Appeals for the 9th Circuit. Judge Robert R. Beezer wrote that "a preliminary injunction against Napster's participation in copyright infringement is not only warranted but required."[12] Napster, however, was unable to remove copyrighted tracks as they were on users' computers, not on the Napster website. Nor were they able to discern which users had copyrighted tracks and which did not. Consequently, Napster shut down altogether in June 2001, just a month short of their second anniversary.

Fanning, Parker, and crew spent the next year trying to implement a fee-based subscription model. In October 2001 they entered into a loan-and-acquisition agreement with BMG but were unable to pique the interest of the other labels or additional investors. The ouster of Middelhoff at BMG in July 2002 killed that relationship. Napster went insolvent and sold off its remaining assets.

The Napster Chronicles: Napster RIP; The Postmortem

In April 2009 Shawn Fanning confided to Matt Hartley that he never really expected a deal with the labels. "I wasn't sitting and holding my breath that everything would be miraculously worked out and that a business or anything would be established with the industry. I knew that it was a pretty big change for them in terms of transitioning and authorizing digital distribution on the scale that would be necessary to maintain a quality service."[13]

In 2010 Sean Parker called it the education he never got at college. "I kind of refer to it as Napster University—it was a crash course in intellectual property law, corporate finance, entrepreneurship and law school. . . . Some of the e-mails I wrote when I was just a kid who didn't know what he was doing are apparently in [law school] textbooks."[14] He was referring to an email he sent on Napster's behalf used in the legal proceedings by the record industry as evidence of Napster's complicity in copyright infringement that referred to the files being exchanged by Napster users as being pirated music.

Napster's problems, as both Hartley and Joseph Menn asserted, stemmed from the people Fanning and Parker had brought in on the business side while they created the program that turned the music world upside down. Menn believed that the problems began with John Fanning. In a May 2003 online chat on the Forbes.com CEO Network, Menn expounded upon the dynamic between the two Fannings. "Shawn Fanning looked up to his Uncle John as a mentor, and more than that a father figure. John repaid his nephew's trust by keeping 70 percent of Napster's ownership for himself, by driving away seasoned investors who might have righted Napster's course, and by insisting that Napster was worth $1 billion despite having no revenue, let alone profit. John Fanning's track record . . . shows a history of failed or failing businesses, employees denied their due, multiple lawsuits, a tendency to mix personal and business affairs. . . . This is not the sort of man most people would pick to lead any business."[15]

John Fanning wound up with 12 percent of the company, all in preferred stock, while his nephew was left with only 6 percent, all of which was common stock. According to Menn, the elder Fanning also pocketed as much as $1 million out of the $15 to $20 million that had been invested. Hummer Winblad initially believed that they would be able to sell a part of the company to the record labels for a huge windfall due to the public clamor, the efficacy of the Napster design, and the lack of an alternative of their own. When the court ruled against Napster, however, they sold off the assets for just enough to recoup their investment, without remuneration to the younger Fanning, Parker, or their team.

In 2011, at the Le Web Conference in Paris, Parker ruefully reminisced about his days at Napster, "We failed with Napster to build a legal licensing model. As a result, we watched the industry we loved collapse. . . . The biggest failure we made there was hiring. We built the wrong team."[16] A different but perhaps more-to-the-point diagnosis came from Ron Conway, who had invested in what Fanning and Parker had created, not on what was pitched to him by the elder Fanning or Hummer Winblad. He continued to invest in all of both Fanning's and Parker's future endeavors, including Facebook. He told TechCrunch.com in a 2013 interview that the problem went beyond just the failure of the Napster business team. He saw it more as a shared but separate failing of two clashing business cultures, stating that "if people just left their ego at the door, I believe the problems would've been solved [long ago]," Conway said. "But everyone immediately went into macho mode."[17]

Apple Offers an Answer : Jobs on the Job

From the 1997 introduction of the MP3 player until the launch of the online iTunes Store in April 2003, the younger age groups solidified their preference for multi-artist playlists over solo artist albums through Napster and the P2P websites that succeeded it. The major label associated MusicNet and PressPlay offered legal alternatives but suffered from DRM restrictions, limited track selections, and other accessibility and convenience constraints. For immediate, cost-free access to MP3 tracks, consumers continued to use P2P sites, even if it meant risking copyright infringement, or copied them from a CD, whether their own or someone else's.

The iTunes Store debut in 2003 was not Apple's initial entry into digital music having introduced the iTunes app and iPod in 2001. Like Fanning and Parker, Apple cofounder/CEO Steve Jobs was a music fan, but already a billionaire. He had come back to Apple after an eleven-year hiatus to return the company to profitability. During his absence, Apple had fallen to under 5 percent of US home computer sales. Most of the others used Microsoft operating systems. Apple, however, was the favorite of the creative community in studios, both professional and at home, as well as for graphics and artwork. Jobs trimmed the product line, opened the online Apple Store, introduced the iMac, and returned Apple to the black, all in 1998. In 2001 Apple launched the Mac OSX operating system and opened its first retail stores. Within the next three years they did $1 billion in retail sales.

With Apple's control over its software, hardware, and both online and retail supply chains along with its fervently loyal, upper-income consumer base, Jobs saw an opportunity that could be highly profitable, not just in the sale of downloads, but even far more in the sale of Apple devices to access and listen to them. Having watched the failure of both Napster and MP3.com at dealing with the licensing demands of the content owners, the inability of the tech companies to create a user-friendly device, and then the ineptitude of the labels in licensing their own content for use in their own devices, Jobs envisioned an Apple-branded alternative that cured all the ills of the past and lifted all boats for the future. Apple would offer a superior user experience with hardware and software available from either its own retail or online stores and record product from all the major labels available for download from its website. Additionally, Apple players would store and play the users' already-amassed MP3 collections.

With this vision in hand, Jobs decided to pursue the record industry until they realized that Apple was the path to a profitable digital future that would make their product conveniently available to all consumers. He later told *Rolling Stone* that his pitch to the labels had been, "We're never going to stop the illegal downloading services, but our message is: Let's compete and win. . . . The truth is, it's really hard to talk to people about not stealing music when there's no legal alternative."[18]

Wanting to utilize only Apple software so the entire scope of his plan would be proprietary, Jobs purchased the SoundJam MP app from former Apple employees Jeff Robbin, Bill Kincaid, and Dave Heller. The app had been released previously through Casady & Greene, a software publisher that dealt primarily in Mac-compatible products. Jobs then brought the tech trio back to Apple to re-engineer the program to become an integral element of what appleinsder.com initially referred to as iMusic. They continued to refine the SoundJam app and contribute to the other elements of Jobs's master plan. Their original SoundJam app was taken off the market.

Apple Offers an Answer : Building the Blueprint

The first layer in the Jobs blueprint debuted with the introduction of iTunes Version 1.0 in January 2001, exclusively for Mac users as a free app downloaded from the Apple website. iTunes was the audio cornerstone for Jobs's digital hub concept whereby Mac technology would operate the digital delivery system for all intellectual property whether music, video, film, both spoken and written word, still imagery, or graphics. All were to be integrated through all possible consumer media platforms whether in the home, the car, or the workplace through computers, family entertainment centers, or portable devices. As the key music element of the digital hub, Apple touted iTunes as "the world's best and easiest to use jukebox software that lets users create and manage their own music library on their Mac."[19]

The tagline of "Rip. Mix. Burn." was used in iTunes' introductory television commercial. Users could import the data needed to make an MP3 copy from CD tracks, known as "ripping" in the digital vernacular, to be stored in their iTunes library. They could also transfer their already-existing cache of MP3s to iTunes. Then they could choose a selection of tracks, sequence or "mix" them to their liking, and then transfer them to a CD or cassette, referred to in computer parlance as burning. In the first week alone, 275,000 iTunes apps were downloaded.

Jobs's next step came nine months later in October 2001, when he introduced Apple's own portable MP3 device, the iPod. His sales pitch stated, "With iPod, Apple has invented a whole new category of digital music player that lets you put your entire music collection in your pocket and listen to it wherever you go. . . . With iPod, listening to music will never be the same again."[20] The initial iPod was Mac compatible only, had a 5 GB, 1.5" hard drive that Apple sourced from Toshiba to make the pocket-sized scaling possible. Working closely with Jobs, Apple's senior VP of industrial design Jony Ives, who had also designed the iMac, supervised the contemporary, sleek design of the iPod with its accompanying white earbuds. Members of his team told *Wired* magazine that his aesthetic design had been inspired by a vintage Braun transistor radio and a Bang & Olufsen telephone wheel-based user interface.

The initial iPod was higher in price than other MP3 devices, but superior in operability. The 5 GB iPod was $399 and a 10 GB model debuted at $499 with an approximately two thousand–song capacity. In July 2002 iTunes Version 2.0 accompanied the iPod 2nd Generation featuring a seamless integration of songs and playlists from computer to iPod through a FireWire connector along with equalizer and cross-fading control. iTunes Version 3.0 also added smart playlists, which could create and store curated track listings. Support for audiobooks was obtained through an exclusive license with Audible.com. Apple's SoundCheck automatically adjusted individual track volume levels when segueing from one to another. Apple then adjusted its pricing by lowering the iPod 3.0 5GB model by $100 to $299 and the 10GB version to $399. A 20GB iPod was added for $499.

Jobs now had his infrastructure in place with iTunes doing the ripping, the consumer doing the mixing, and then burning tracks onto an iPod. Both Mac and PC versions were available through both online and retail Apple Stores. Jobs then directed his efforts to the most necessary elements to fulfill his quest for a viable, legal, and profitable solution for the digital consumption of music by accessing content from the major labels.

In April 2002 Jobs approached AOL Time Warner's CEO Barry Schuler, who put him in contact with Paul Vidich, executive VP at WMG. Jobs told Vidich and his team that both of the recently released record industry digital delivery services—MusicNet, which they had co-ventured with BMG and EMI, and their Sony/Universal PressPlay rival—wouldn't succeed as neither provided 100 percent of the content in the marketplace, each had its own set of technical flaws, both were available only on computers and not available for portable devices, and neither was anywhere near as user friendly as Apple's iPod/iTunes tandem.

Jobs also charged that both were overpriced and that the mandated DRM restrictions further hampered their acceptance. He pointedly added that a large share of the records made in the past ten years had used Apple technology in recording, mixing, and/or mastering. Jimmy Iovine of Interscope/UMG joined in the discussions followed by then–WMG CEO Roger Ames, both of whom were sold on the efficacy of the iTunes interface and the consumer appeal of the iPod design. But roadblocks remained, including content licensing cost, pricing to consumer, Jobs's belief that DRM would hinder market success, and the hesitancy on the part of the labels to put all their content with an outside company in which they had no interest or control.

By the fall of 2002, it was becoming evident even to the record labels that PressPlay and MusicNet were not succeeding. Although Napster and MP3. com were gone, consumers continued P2P file-sharing through KaZaA, Gnutella, Aimster, Morpheus, Limewire, Pirate Bay, and other file-sharing websites. Left out of the major-label plans, Liquid Audio was faltering and in early 2003 sold its assets to Anderson Merchandisers, primary supplier to Walmart. Record sales had declined by 10 percent as a result of the recession following the dot.com bubble burst and 9/11. The AOL-Warner merger was having problems. The top investors in digital initiatives, Middelhoff at BMG and both Messier and Bronfman at Universal, had all been replaced.

Apple Offers an Answer : Disruption Goes Legit

Jobs's persistence paid off when all five majors agreed to license their catalogs to him, but not without compromise on both sides. The labels agreed to sell only single tracks unless an artist insisted on selling only in an album format. The parties agreed to a consumer price of 99¢ per track and $9.99 per album. Jobs agreed that initial sales would only be available to Mac users. This limited the initial roll-out to under 10 percent of computer owners, effectively making it a test market. Jobs further compromised by relenting on his view that DRM was a hindrance and offered to use FairPlay, a DRM system owned by Apple that was compatible only with Apple devices. FairPlay would restrict sharing to just three computers, all owned by the same user, while also limiting users' ability to burn any playlist to CD a maximum of seven times. But perhaps most important was that Apple agreed to guarantee a marketing budget deemed sufficient for creating a public demand, an element lacking in the PressPlay and MusicNet launches.

Apple also upgraded its digital file format from MP3 to the MP4 Advanced Audio Coding (AAC) file. AAC had been developed by a coalition including AT&T Bell Laboratories, Fraunhofer IIS, Dolby Laboratories, Sony Corporation, and Nokia to achieve a higher-quality sound at the same bit rate as an MP3. MPEG had officially approved AAC as an international standard in April 1997. While AAC had languished behind the ubiquitous MP3, its use by Apple prevented other companies' MP3-only players from competing with the iPod for iTunes downloads. Apple also made a free firmware upgrade available for Apple computers and all iPod players already in use that would transfer existing MP3 files and interface to the AAC format.

The iTunes Music Store debuted on April 28, 2003, with two hundred thousand tracks from all five major labels combined. iTunes sold more than a million downloads in the first week and by June a million new iPods had been sold. A million tracks yielded $990,000, with a split of 70 percent to the labels who paid the publishers, and 30 percent retained by Apple. A million iPods, however, delivered between $299 million and $499 million to Apple, depending on the mix of their various models. In October, the labels agreed to let Apple add Windows versions 2000 and XP compatibility to iTunes so it could be installed on PCs and downloaded to Windows-compatible iPods.

By the end of 2003 iTunes reached 30 million downloads. By the end of 2006 the cumulative total was approaching 2 billion, reaching that milestone on January 10, 2007. Just under $600 million of that total was retained by Apple while about $1.4 billion had gone to the record industry. About $182 million of that went to music publishers who accounted to their songwriters. At the same time, iPod sales were approaching 100 million units, reaching that benchmark in April 2007, for about $30 billion in cumulative sales since launch. Apple's $7.03 billion revenue for iPod sales in 2006 represented 36.4 percent of that year's $19.3 billion total revenue, with the company showing a 10.36 percent net margin of $2 billion. In 2001 and 2002, the two years prior to the launch of the iTunes Store, Apple revenues had been $5.4 and $5.7 billion with minimal net margin.

In 2004 Apple replaced the AAC standard file with their own proprietary version, dubbed Apple Lossless Audio Codec (ALAC), adding an additional level of separation from any rival device that could play AAC files. In addition to this competition-buffering function, ALAC could retain two to four times the information at the same bit rate as an AAC file when ripping a CD, retaining 40 percent to 60 percent of the information. This made it competitive with or better than the quality of Real Audio, Liquid Audio, or Microsoft's WAV audio files. Most important, the ALAC gave consumers greater fidelity and dynamic range on their portable devices.

ALAC also allowed Apple to add picture and then video capacity to the iPod with its QuickTime program on the way to making the mobile device a more complete digital hub. Over the next two years Apple introduced successive models, including the iPod Mini and iPod Nano, that increased storage capacity and battery life, decreased size, and added functions. In January 2005 the newly released iPod Shuffle became the least expensive flash memory–based device. The promotional material dubbed it "smaller and lighter than a pack of gum,"[21] with 512 MB of storage for about 120 songs at $99, with a $149 1 GB version for double the capacity. The name came from a new feature allowing the user to let the device select at random from the stored tracks, thus the name Shuffle. By the end of 2006 Apple had achieved market domination with 72 percent of total industrywide download sales to go with the 88.7 million iPods sold worldwide since its 2001 introduction.

Apple's concessions to the labels had been well worth the cost since its hardware would not have been as successful without access to the content. While only being a minor player in the computer field, they were on the way to becoming the market leader in portable devices and digital content commerce. The labels had established a consumer base for legal digital sales, somewhat curbed home piracy, and slowed the slide in their revenue.

By 2006 the implementation of Jobs's blueprint for domination of the digital music market had succeeded not only in billions in new revenue for Apple but also further reinforced the shift in consumer focus away from albums and back to single tracks. Consumer requirements of portability and copying capability had been achieved. They could now instantly purchase the latest track they had just listened to or heard about for 99¢ instead of going to a retail outlet to buy the album for $10 or more, or being forced to resort to illegal home duplication. Apple was now firmly entrenched as a leader in the retail music marketplace.

The Competition for the Consumer Leisure Dollar

In addition to its attempts to perpetuate the shelf life of the album format by stifling the growth of digital downloading with DRM and related restrictions, the record companies introduced several new products they envisioned as the next-generation sound carriers for the physical album format. These would-be successors included the 24-bit rate DVD-A and the SACD together with the Mini CD. The DVD-A was introduced in 2001 and the SACD debuted in 2003, each priced at well over $20 with high-end players not compatible with CDs nor with each other. The cost of re-mastering albums in full 24-bit studio master audio resolution limited the availability of catalog items. Combined, they shipped just under 5 million units by 2006, fewer than either cassettes or LPs over the same time period. Meanwhile the Mini CD never sold enough units to be tracked by the RIAA.

While consumer purchase of physical product continued to decline after 2001, both household income and entertainment spending were on an upward trajectory. In addition to spending their disposable dollars on other forms of entertainment, consumers were still spending money on music, but to a lesser degree on the album format, and single tracks were in severely limited availability other than through home duplication.

In 1996 the average avid music consumer preferred to experience music by listening to albums on home stereo units, seeing live music in clubs or small concert settings, and shopping in atmospherically appealing record stores. By 2006 this had shifted to listening to single tracks on portable devices through headphones, attending performances by their favorite artists in large venues that were as much a social networking event as a listening experience, and if still buying physical product, doing so by mail order or at big-box outlets, wherever they could get the best price.

In 1996 consumers spent $12.3 billion on physical product with digital sales still in the future. Another $1.1 billion as tracked by *Pollstar* went to concert tickets with additional spending of an estimated $2 billion on costs related to handling; the secondary ticketing market; parking, concessions, merchandise; and shows, tours, and venues of all sizes not monitored by *Pollstar*. Given the ratio between what consumers spent on print music and the NMPA's reported royalty receipts as outlined in earlier chapters, it's reasonable to believe that the print music total from retail and mail order combined, including public domain works, approached $2.7 billion in 1996. Adding together consumer spending on recorded music, printed copies, and the live performance experience for that year, the total came to an estimated $18 billion.

In 2006 consumer spending on physical and digital recorded music combined had declined from 1996's total by $2.4 billion to $9.88 billion. *Pollstar's* estimated concert ticket sales, however, had more than tripled to $3.6 billion with all other consumer spending on live music increasing in proportion. Some spending on print had shifted to online, possibly decreasing the total, but still about $2 billion, putting consumer spending on music for 2006 in the $24 billion range.

The secondary ticketing market also benefited from the commercialization of the internet. eBay, opened in 1995 as AuctionWeb, was one of the first online platforms to legally auction tickets. Over the ensuing decade brokers using a fee or commission model proliferated, including TicketsNow in 1999, with StubHub and LiquidSeats in 2000, Razorgator and The Ticket Reserve in 2001, and TicketExchange in 2005. While most were privately held, TicketExchange was a division of Ticketmaster, and StubHub had been a public company netting over $100 million in 2006 on 15 percent commissions. These Stub Hub commissions alone represented over $667 million in ticket costs to consumers, but only the face value of the ticket was included in any tour accounting both to the artists and in *Pollstar* and *Billboard* totals. At an estimated average 50 percent surcharge going to secondary market brokers, consumer spending on *Pollstar*-monitored tickets in 2006 rose by about $1.8 billion over face value.

While the money spent by consumers through the entire secondary market was hard to determine, an extensive research project by Arizona State professor of economics Stephen Happel titled "The Eight Principles of the Microeconomic and Regulatory Future of Ticket Scalping, Ticket Brokers, and Secondary Ticket Markets" estimated the worldwide total in 2006 including *Pollstar*-tracked music events and all other sports, theater, and shows not tracked by *Pollstar* to be between $10 and $12 billion. In a *Wall Street Journal* article in January 2008 on the eBay acquisition of StubHub, Ethan Smith wrote, "The size of the secondary ticket market is hard to judge, but estimates range from $2.5 billion to $5 billion a year in the US."[22]

By 2001 new mobile phone technology allowed consumers to replace generic tone signals with segments of recorded music for customized ringtones. The $2.49 average cost per ringtone included licensee fees for both publishing and master recording rights. Although the RIAA didn't list ringtones and ringbacks as a revenue line item until 2005, the PROs started tracking and paying publishers and songwriters for them in 2001. From 2001 to 2006 BMI processed over 500 million US ringtone sales. They pegged the US market at $68 million by 2003, growing to $600 million in 2006. The differing RIAA tally, however, cited $432.6 million in 2005 and $772.8 million in 2006, but included in this total were music videos and other full-length video downloads to mobile devices.

Retailers had experimented with and tested the kiosk concept, often at great cost, since the mid-1990s. Retailers envisioned this round of kiosks as a way to decrease inventory since back catalog items could be downloaded rather than racked as CDs. Kiosks were also envisioned by retailers as a source to replace the diminishing supply of singles. Initially tracks were burned from a hard drive whether instore, directly outside, or even in a different retail location that did not sell record products. Starbucks; Virgin Megastores; Musicmaker.com through selected Tower, Trans World, and Wherehouse stores; Liquid Audio; and Alliance all experimented with kiosks. The concept, however, never caught on with the public sufficiently to justify its cost. In the middle of the decade kiosks re-emerged, but this time with broadband digital downloads instead of burning to CD copies. Despite being less time-consuming, once again the kiosk experience failed to attract consumers.

Challenges Abound for a Piece of the Apple

The successful launch of the iTunes/iPod tandem triggered an avalanche of new music players. While Apple unveiled its proprietary ALAC codec and improved iPod at their 2004 MacWorld Conference and Expo, its rivals debuted their competing devices at the Consumer Electronics Show (CES) held every January in Las Vegas. Following Apple's lead were Sony, RealNetworks, Listen.com, SONICblue, Creative Labs, Samsung Electronics, Motorola, Netgear, Rockford Fosgate, RCA, Digital Networks North America, Creative Labs, Archos Electronics, Dell, and Gateway, both in combinations and separately, including smaller and less expensive devices, some with storage capacity up to 20 gigabytes.

They also anticipated what they termed an interoperable future where consumers' computers, portable devices, and televisions were all linked together. *Billboard*'s Antony Bruno observed from the 2005 CES, "Microsoft, Intel, Hewlett-Packard, Sony—touted the onset of the digital ecosystem and their respective roles in it. Driving this digital convergence, they said, is entertainment content."[23] Sony's Howard Stringer added, "Content and technology must learn to live together. All electronic devices, without content, are just sophisticated scrap metal."[24]

Sony was Apple's closest potential threat with its deep pockets, brand recognition, retail penetration, and access to content, but it chose to make its market push with a next-generation version of the CD MiniDisc. The new Hi-MD Walkman was announced at the 2004 CES and rolled out in May, playing interchangeable 3.25" one gigabyte discs that could hold over 650 songs and cost about $7 each disc with recordable players priced between $200 to $400. Concurrently Sony launched its Sony Connect webstore under the leadership of Jay Samit, former head of digital development at both EMI and Universal as well as a pioneer in developing content for both the LaserDisc and CD-ROM. Single tracks cost 99¢ with albums priced at $9.99 from a catalog of over five hundred thousand tracks from all five majors and selected independents.

At the same 2004 CES, RealNetworks revealed its own à la carte RealPlayer Music Store with a catalog of more than three hundred thousand tracks from major labels and independents. Like both Apple and Sony, tracks were 99¢; and like Sony, albums were $9.99. Although both Real and Apple used AAC files, their DRM encoding had compatibility issues with each other's portable devices. Real also entered into co-marketing campaigns with both Heineken beer and *Rolling Stone* magazine. Despite these heavily promoted efforts, by 2006 Apple had solidified its market dominance and its competitors could not draw consumers away from the peer group preference and stylish allure of the white earbuds, sleek design, and superior ALAC files supported by the efficacy of Apple's vertically integrated business model. Both Sony Connect and the RealPlayer stores would be shuttered in 2008.

By 2005 the new High Speed Downlink Packet Access (HSDPA) mobile phone technology, commonly referred to as 3G (third generation), had expanded mobile broadband to improve both web surfing and downloading of digital files in addition to its email, camera, GPS, mobile television, gaming, and video display functions. With this arsenal of options, the telephone industry entered the competition for the mobile music market, bolstered by already-existing billing systems. With their quick adoption of the smartphone, consumers had, by 2006, further distanced themselves from the repertoire restrictions and high prices imposed by the record business cartel for access to music.

In 2006 the Big Three mobility companies were Cellular (to be acquired by AT&T in 2007), Sprint, and Verizon. All were within a few points of one another at just above 25 percent of the cell phone market with T-Mobile trailing in fourth place at about 11.5 percent. They all considered mobile music an essential element of the new G3 market and they all had the financial resources to compete in the existing portable player market dominated by Apple.

Third-place Sprint debuted the first mobile music download store on October 31, 2005, with 250,000 tracks for consumers to browse, preview, and purchase at $2.49 per song, growing to a catalog of over 1.5 million by the end of 2006. Along with the store Sprint offered both Sanyo and Samsung phones starting at $199 with 16 MB and 32 MB memory cards, respectively, but each could be upgraded with a 16 GB card available from the Sprint Store that could hold over a thousand songs. Sprint claimed over 8 million downloads sold in their first year.

Second-ranked Verizon launched the VCast Music Store in early 2006. Prices for Samsung, LG, and UT Starcom VCast–enabled smartphones also started at under $200, utilizing Microsoft Windows Media Player 10 with memory cards that could hold over one thousand songs. Previously downloaded Windows Media Audio (WMA) files could be imported to the phones from other services. VCast initially had a $15 a month subscription fee, which it dropped in June 2006. Five hundred thousand tracks from all the majors for download to phones for $1.99 and to PCs for 99¢ were available at launch, increasing to over 1.5 million tracks by the end of 2006.

Cingular Wireless, then the largest US carrier, adopted the subscription model rather than the à la carte plans of Sprint and Verizon, unveiling its music offering in November 2006, combining on-demand services from Roxio's newly configured Napster, Yahoo!, and eMusic, along with programmed streaming from XM Satellite Radio for a $15 monthly fee. Their Samsung 3G flip phone was introduced at $50, cheaper than most other portable music players, including the $79 iPod Shuffle. Songs could also be added to the phone from consumers' accumulated library of WMA files, but not Apple's ALAC files.

American Idol Adds Interactivity to Music on Television

From its inception in 1981 MTV led the rollout of video cable channels with each focused on a specific blend of genre and/or age group. Bob Pittman and his cohorts had originally envisioned MTV to be a video version of the AOR format, but eventually moved closer to CHR. Its sister channel VH1 offered an AC sound. Pittman told *The New York Times* in 1985, "If you like MTV you won't like VH1. You'll find it much too slow, not enough on the cutting edge."[25] Other channels were BET for the black/urban audience and TNN and CMT for country. Pittman further explained that rather than follow the path of trying to make music fit into traditional television formatting, instead MTV utilized the non-linear and non-narrative new video clip format, which presented the audience with "the essence of what the music is as opposed to what television is."[26] He also explained why the rock-oriented MTV came first. "The rock audience instantly knew what to do. Now they will serve as role models for everyone else because MTV taught us how to use a new form."[27]

By 2000 MTV had started to cut back on music videos in favor of music-related lifestyle and game shows, which their research indicated would better hold the attention of their core fourteen-to-twenty-eight-demographic with greater peer group social interactivity than a continuous flow of video clips would do. Then in 2002 a new Fox Network music show featuring live performances by unknown artists swept across America to capture the number one primetime rating. Over the course of the 2002 summer replacement season, a set of twelve contestants who had survived an extensive auditioning process competed against one another on *American Idol* to win a record contract with RCA and management contract with show producer and Spice Girls' manager Simon Fuller's 19 Entertainment.

The show had its origin in the fall of 2001 when a Fuller-created show titled *Pop Idol* became a huge hit in the UK on independent channel ITV with veteran talent scout Simon Cowell serving as head judge. Co-producer/syndicator Freemantle Media, a division of Bertelsmann, immediately sold the concept to outlets around the world. Despite being rejected by the US networks until Fox CEO Rupert Murdoch's daughter convinced him to air the show, *American Idol* became *Pop Idol*'s most impactful spin-off. Cowell led the three-judge panel that included artist/choreographer Paula Abdul, producer Randy Jackson, and occasional guest judges on an eight-year run. Ryan Seacrest became the sole on-air host in the second season after sharing that role in the first year with comedian Brian Dunkleman.

The undeniable hit of the summer drew 33 million viewers for its finale. *Idol* became the most watched television program of the next seven years and was still on air with its nineteenth season entering 2020. The show retained Fuller's original format with live elimination rounds paring the competition down to the final two episodes with viewers joining the judges in voting via toll-free phone, with text and online voting added in subsequent years. The contestants were all in the same fourteen-to-twenty-eight age group as the targeted core audience. The audience participation factor meshed perfectly with the ongoing liberation of the public from the record industry's control over the music they heard by giving them a voice in deciding who should have a record deal.

19 Entertainment had options for management, publishing, and recording rights in all contestants' contracts. Performers from the 2002 through 2006 seasons who went on to greater success included Carrie Underwood, Kelly Clarkson, Clay Aiken, Ruben Studdard, Fantasia, Jennifer Hudson, Daughtry, Bo Bice, Kellie Pickler, Bucky Covington, and Katharine McPhee. Fourth-season winner Underwood has been the most successful contestant to date with over 70 million album sales worldwide and fourteen number one country singles, followed by first-season winner Kelly Clarkson with over 25 million album sales and three number one pop singles.

In February 2010, *The New York Times* published an article by Edward Wyatt on the earnings of *Idol* contestants. He concluded, "Including performance fees and merchandising royalties from the 'American Idol' tour, as well as other opportunities, winners have never failed to earn less than $1 million in the year or so after the contest."[28] Wyatt further stated that non-winners earned more than $100,000, with the ones who secured record contracts in the half million–dollar range.

Idol fans got to see the top-ten contestants the following summer on the *American Idol Tour*, which played sixty-five dates in 2006 with 10,101 attendees per show, grossed $35.81 million, and averaged $54.55 per ticket playing to a 94.3 percent venue capacity. In both 2005 and 2006 the live television show attracted over 30 million households per episode. For the 2006 season, two new weekly shows were introduced to further saturate the public with the *Idol* brand. *American Idol Rewind* was syndicated throughout the

US, featuring highlights of the week's show and other related activities and interviews. *American Idol Extra* aired on the Fox Reality cable channel also with *Idol*-related content.

Following the 2006 season CEO Jeff Zucker of rival NBC Universal told Bill Carter of *The New York Times*, "I think 'Idol' is the most impactful show in the history of television. . . . For perspective, at this point 'Idol' could lose half its audience and still rank among the top 10 shows on television. And no one dares predict when this phenomenon will fade."[29]

There had been successful talent shows in the past including Ted Mack's *The Original Amateur Hour* running from 1948 to 1970 and where Ann-Margret, Jose Feliciano, Irene Cara, and Tanya Tucker all debuted. *Star Search* was hosted by Ed McMahon between 1983 and 1995 and uncovered a bevy of artists who didn't win including Justin Timberlake, Britney Spears, and Christina Aguilera. The three were also members of the cast of *The All-New Mickey Mouse Club*, which aired on the Disney Channel between 1989 and 1995. Destiny's Child (then known as Girls Tyme), Alanis Morissette as Alanis Nadine, Aaliyah as Aaliyah Haughton, LeAnn Rimes, and Usher as Usher Raymond IV also first appeared on *Star Search*.

Arsenio Hall tried to revive *Star Search* for CBS in 2003 but couldn't compete with the *Idol* juggernaut. Other new shows in 2003 inspired by the success of *Idol* included *Nashville Star* on the USA Network, *Fame* on NBC, VH1's *Born to Diva*, and Showtime's *Interscope Presents the Next Episode*. P. Diddy's 2002 reworking of *Making the Band*, which he had previously hosted for boy band manager Lou Pearlman for three years, was brought back to MTV for a second run in 2003. Other shows in subsequent years included *Superstar USA* on WBTV in 2004, *Rock Star* on CBS in 2005, and *Celebrity Duets* on Fox in 2006.

The Widening Digital Divide

In 1996 the music then in distribution by the major labels dominated what the public heard on radio, saw in video clips, and bought at retail. Consumer interaction with the industry was limited to call-in requests to favorite radio stations and conversations with local record store clerks. The internet was still in its infancy, there were few smartphones, no texting, and fewer than 40 million people worldwide used email. Over the next decade a steady stream of digital innovation gradually expanded the options for both obtaining and listening to music. Consumer control over what they wanted to hear, and how, when, and where they chose to do so increased proportionately.

THE EVOLUTION OF PORTABLE PLAYING DEVICES

Pocket transistor radio circuitry

In 1950 consumers listened to recorded music at home on the radio or phonograph, on jukeboxes in clubs and soda shops, and for upper end consumers, custom-installed car radios operating on vacuum tubes.

Portable playing devices became possible when more efficient and miniaturized transistor circuitry replaced vacuum tubes for audio wave reception.

By the end of the '50s most cars had transistor radios in the dashboard. Music, news, and weather on the car radio were now a ubiquitous feature of American life. Simultaneously battery-operated transistor AM/FM radios including pocket-sized models extending portability into society as a whole.

This technology was also applied to record players including 45 rpm models for 7" singles adding track selection to portability.

Portable turntable

In 1965 8-track tape players coupled with AM/FM radio debuted in car

dashboards. Cassette players followed in the 70s and CD players in the 1980s.

In 1979 Sony introduced the Walkman, a portable cassette player with headphones but no speaker or recording function, that would sell almost 200 million units. Consumers copied their favorite tracks onto blank cassettes to create customized playlists.

Portable cassette player

Dual cassette "boombox" players with equalizers, woofers, tweeters, and mid-size speakers offered a portable home entertaining center for listening, recording, and playback.

After Napster transformed music consumption with P2P file sharing, Apple released the iPod digital player in 2001, and then opened the iTunes store in 2003 for legal and convenient downloading.

Boombox with dual cassette

In 2007 Apple introduced the iPhone, followed by Google's Android operating system in 2008 to jointly dominate the smartphone market.

In 2011 Spotify's U.S. debut launched the soon to be streaming tsunami. The entire catalog of recorded music was now legally accessible at will, on-demand anywhere a smartphone had connectivity by paying a minimal monthly fee.

Smart phone

Photo credit: iStock

Illustration 10.2 The Evolution of Portable Playing Devices

By 2006 over a billion people across the globe were using email and over 100 million consumers had bought smartphones. Consumers were using new digital media for direct contact with artists, bypassing the traditional path through the record labels. Although the celestial jukebox had not yet replaced the traditional brick-and-mortar structure of the record business, the consumer migration from buying albums to digitally sourcing music had caused record stores to tumble into crisis, sent the record companies into consolidation, and triggered a reduction in both work force and talent rosters across the industry.

Apple's iTunes market entry in 2003 had offered consumers an alternative, legal path to music with access and convenience superior to what the digital generation had previously experienced and without the possible legal consequences of home duplication. Smartphones posed even greater promise for the future when the price of legal downloads gave way to the low cost of subscriptions, and the volume of subscribers would create a profitable customer base for the industry. By the end of 2006, however, that shift had not yet occurred while the legacy of Napster persisted in the form of P2P file-sharing on what was purported to be a massive but undetermined scale.

Although there was no definitive data substantiating that the decrease in spending by the younger consumers was due to file-sharing, there was evidence of a likely connection. *The IFPI Annual Report* for 2006 cited a survey conducted in September 2006 showing that 76 percent of respondents between sixteen and twenty-four said that if they heard a track and liked it, they wanted immediate access to it. iTunes and the other e-tailers had fed that craving as consumers bought 586.4 million tracks and 27.6 million albums from them in 2006 for a total of $856 million. The industry, however, considered that number to be about 10 percent of what the value of illegal downloads through unlicensed P2P websites would have been had they been purchased legally.

The RIAA cited an August 2007 report by Stephen Siwek of the Institute for Policy Innovation claiming that "the U.S. economy loses $12.5 billion in total output annually as a consequence of music theft [and] . . . leads to the loss of 71,060 jobs to the U.S. economy. Music theft also leads to the loss of $2.7 billion in earnings annually in both the sound recording industry and in downstream retail industries."[30]

Although streaming—with its combination of access, convenience, and pricing at about $10 a month—had existed on a limited scale as a legally licensed source of music since at least 2002, it had lacked the necessary level of licensed content that Apple provided for downloading. Nonetheless, for the first time in the decades-long relationship between the public and the record labels, consumers were ahead of the industry in adapting to new technological innovation. For the first time, the labels had failed to control the development of a publicly acceptable next-generation sound carrier. Instead, a new cadre of digital interlopers stepped into the breach offering access and convenience to consumers while undermining the structure and economics of the record companies and their corporate parents.

Almost eighty years earlier, when technological advances in audio reproduction ushered in the age of talking pictures to replace silent movies, Al Jolson had proclaimed in his starring role in the first full-length, nationally distributed talking picture *The Jazz Singer*, "You ain't heard nothin' yet!"[31] His dramatic proclamation seemed as if he were peering into the crystal ball of the digital tomorrow rather than just expressing the wonders of the unfurling electronic age when transmission of now-antiquated monophonic analog sound was the wave of the future.

PART THREE
2007 TO 2019

11

The Game of Musical
Thrones: Riding the Digital Wave

Let the Games Resume

The year 2007 marked the tenth year of P2P file-sharing and the seventh year in the decline of the CD album format. That year 499.7 million CDs were shipped, down 120 million from 2006 for a 19.4 percent decrease, and just slightly more than half of the albums shipped in the boom years of 1999 and 2000. The vinyl, cassette, DVD-A, and SACD album formats barely topped 2 million units combined. Total 2007 RIAA-reported revenue value, however, was down just 9.4 percent from 2006 as the decline in album sales was partially mitigated by the surge in legal downloads and ringtones.

The year 2007 was also three years after the Big Five label groups became the Big Four following the consolidation of Sony and BMG. Under the guidance of Doug Morris, UMG had reigned atop the market share ratings since its own consolidation with PolyGram in 1999. The gap between UMG and the now-second place Sony-BMG widened in 2007 as UMG reached 31.9 percent while Sony-BMG dropped to 25 percent. Under the new Edgar Bronfman Jr. regime, WMG had grown to 20.3 percent, third in the rankings. EMI came in last at 9.4 percent. The Indie sector also topped EMI with a 13.5 percent market share. With falling overall industry revenue, budget management was more crucial than ever.

Then in late 2008 the national economic downturn devolved into the second recession of the decade, even more intense than the first, earning the sobriquet the Great Recession. The drop in overall consumer spending further deepened the divide between falling CD sales and increasing demand for downloaded tracks. Even though the highest-quality digital files were at best about 60 percent of the sonic caliber of CDs, the difference was hardly discernible for the consumers who listened on portable players, smartphones, home computers, or the car audio system through ear buds, headphones, or built-in speakers.

American Popular Music and Its Business in the Digital Age. Rick Sanjek, Oxford University Press. © Frederick Sanjek 2024.
DOI: 10.1093/oso/9780190653828.003.0011

MAJOR LABEL GROUP LEADERSHIP 2007-2019

THE "BIG FOUR" 2007-2012

UMG	EMI	WMG	Sony BMG
Doug Morris 2007-2011 ... Lucian Grainge 2011-2012	Elio Leoni-Sceti 2007-2010 ... Roger Faxon 2010-2011	Lyor Cohen 2007-2011 ... Stephen Cooper 2011-2012	Rolf Schmidt-Holtz 2007-2011 ... Doug Morris 2011-2012

CORPORATE OWNERSHIP / HEADQUARTERS / LEADERSHIP

UNIVERSAL VIVENDI France Jean-Bernard Levy 2007-2012 ... Jean-François Dubos 2012	EMI MUSIC UK Eric Nicoli 2007 ... Guy Hands 2007-2011 ... Citigroup 2011	WARNER MUSIC GROUP USA Edgar Bronfman, Jr. 2007-2011 ... Len Blavatnik 2011-2012	SONY CORP. / BERTELSMANN Japan / Germany 2007-2008 SONY CORP 2008-2012 ... Sir Howard Stringer 2007-2012

THE "BIG THREE" 2012-2019

UNIVERSAL MUSIC GROUP	WARNER MUSIC GROUP	SONY MUSIC ENT.
Lucian Grainge 2012-2019	Stephen Cooper 2011-2019	Doug Morris 2011-2017 ... Rob Stringer 2017-2019

CORPORATE OWNERSHIP / HEADQUARTERS / LEADERSHIP

UNIVERSAL VIVENDI France Jean-François Dubos 2012-2014 ... Arnaud de Puyfontaine 2014-2019	WARNER MUSIC GROUP USA Edgar Bronfman, Jr. 2004-2011 ... Len Blavatnik 2011-2019	SONY CORP. Japan 2012-2019 Sir Howard Stringer 2007-2012 ... Kazuo Hirai 2012-2018 ... Kenichiro Yoshida 2018-2019

AFFILIATED RECORD LABELS & KEY EXECUTIVES (AS OF 2019)

Republic Records Monty & Avery Lipman Interscope/Geffen/A&M John Janick Capitol Music Group Steve Barnett Def Jam Recordings Paul Rosenberg Motown Records Ethiopia Habtemariam UMG Nashville Mike Dungan Caroline Distribution Jacqueline Saturn	Atlantic Records Craig Kallman & Julie Greenwald Warner Records Aaron Bay-Shuck & Tom Corson Elektra Records Mike Easterlin & Gregg Nadel Warner Music Nashville John Esposito Alternative Distribution Alliance (ADA) David Orleans	Clive Davis, Chief Creative Officer, Sony Music Entertainment Columbia Records Ron Perry Epic Records Sylvia Rhone RCA Records Peter Edge Arista Records David Massey Sony Music Nashville Randy Goodman The Orchard Brad Nevin

Source: *Billboard*

Illustration 11.1 The "Big Four" Leadership, 2007–12

While downloadable digital files had been available for about ten years, the record industry still didn't have its own successful next-generation sound carrier or the copy-protection security it had been seeking for physical sales. Consumers were migrating to legal digital listening alternatives led by Sirius XM satellite radio, Pandora's interactive algorithm, and the downloaded tracks bought through iTunes. The labels had no financial stake in these new options, no control over what music was played or purchased, and with no physical manufacturing involved, they had no economic power in controlling shipments or pricing. Their only leverage was in licensing negotiations, but that advantage was tempered by the widespread access to illegal downloading.

CD sales in Sweden had been so devastated by P2P file-sharing that by 2008 the local Big Four label divisions were concerned about being shut down. UMG's Scandinavian CEO Per Sundin led the label groups and the Merlin alliance of independents in rolling the dice on the yet-to-be-launched streaming service Spotify, the brainchild of Swedish tech innovators Daniel Ek and Martin Lorentzon. Their strategy began with a free, ad-supported subscription providing legal, immediate, and on-demand computer access to the same library of tracks that the pirates offered, but eliminated both the P2P file-sharing process and any felonious ramifications. This freemium tier served as the carrot to entice consumers to an ad-free premium tier, which extended unlimited access to portable devices and smartphones for the equivalent of about $10 per month in the applicable currency. A 15 percent customer conversion rate from freemium to premium service would render the strategy sustainable, and a higher rate would make it profitable for both Spotify and the labels.

The labels, however, hedged their bets in the initial agreement by licensing only eight European territories including the UK, leaving the lucrative US market up for negotiation should Spotify prove successful. In 2011 Spotify raised an additional $100 million to facilitate their July US debut with a six-month unlimited freemium offering followed by the premium launch in January 2012. The Big Four, however, continued their consolidation of labels and services with budget, staff, and roster reductions to counter their revenue decline. Meanwhile, the sales of digital devices including smartphones, iPods, and tablets escalated, expanding the market for both downloads and streaming. In 2010 the balance between rising digital and faltering physical revenue stabilized at around $7 billion annually. In 2013 downloads joined physical product in declining sales, but the streaming revenue generated by Spotify and a handful of rivals filled that void to keep total revenue around the $7 billion mark through 2015.

In 2015 Apple Music and YouTube Music joined Spotify, Amazon Music, Pandora, iHeart Radio, and the partially artist-owned Tidal, headed by Jay Z, in the streaming marketplace. In 2016 streaming revenue grew $1.53 billion over its 2015 total, offsetting drops of $358 million in CD sales and $539 million in downloads, creating a $645 million uptick in 2016 RIAA-reported revenue to reach a total of $7.65 billion. After six years in the doldrums, the record industry was still afloat, revenue was rising, and the streaming tsunami was underway.

A Change in Ownership for EMI

London-based EMI was the first of the now Big Four label groups to react to the revenue downturn of 2006 and its anticipated continuation. After EMI suffered worldwide losses in 2006 of over $500 million, in May 2007 EMI chairman Eric Nicoli announced an offer by Terra Firma Capital Partners to purchase all stock for $4.89 billion. This would be the private equity firm's first foray into music. Its existing portfolio included property, hospitality, energy, and movie theaters. The forty-seven-year-old, Oxford-educated head of the company, Guy Hands, had worked for Goldman Sachs and the Japanese Nomura Principal Finance Group in leveraged buyouts before forming Terra Firma in 2002 with a $4 billion investment from Nomura. Then in 2004 he added another $4 billion from outside investors and $10 billion more in 2006. The acquisition of EMI became a target.

EMI shareholders clamored for action but feared that the WMG offer currently on the table would be delayed or scuttled again by regulatory scrutiny. EMI also feared a devaluation of the catalog as veterans Paul McCartney, The Rolling Stones, and Radiohead were leaving when their contracts expired. Terra Firma assured the EMI board that the purchase, rather than a merger, could conclude within ninety days since it was not subject to outside approval. The sale closed on August 22, 2007, when the needed 90 percent minimum of EMI shareholders accepted the offer. Nicoli had already ousted CEO/chairman Alain Levy with a $9 million buyout package. Nicoli himself was bought out a week later with a $3.23 million package supplemented by a pension and stock options.

After a four-month examination of EMI during which staffers were dismissed and artists dismayed by a lack of communication, Hands finally shared his long-term vision in January 2008 with staff and artists before a January 26, 2008, *Billboard* interview. In addition to the continuation of Nicoli's cost cutting, Hands planned a reorganization shifting from quasi-autonomous labels to a centralized system with three global divisions. The music division would coordinate A&R decisions for all labels, the administration division would manage all catalog, and the music services department would oversee marketing, sales, and licensing for all. He planned to eliminate over two thousand jobs and release hundreds of artists, but also pledged to invest another $500 million in the company.

Hands also supported Nicoli's decision to abandon DRM in favor of Apple's new DRM-free ALAC files. He told *Billboard*, "The label industry is still living effectively in the '90s. It hasn't understood what digitalization means, it hasn't understood what the consumer change has meant. . . . You need a very different approach to how you market, how you sell, how you use digital, and that change needs to happen to the industry as a whole."[1] Hands believed he could lead the industry across the digital divide by revamping operations to better accommodate the changes wrought by technology over the past ten years.

To helm his new executive team Hands hired forty-two-year-old, sixteen-year veteran of consumer goods company Reckitt Benckiser Elio Leoni-Sceti as CEO in June 2008. He also hired former Google VP of engineering/chief information officer thirty-eight-year-old Douglas Merrill as worldwide president of digital development. Although neither had experience with music, Hands believed their marketing and tech backgrounds would mesh with the experience of his new president of A&R forty-seven-year-old Nick Gatfield, who had just served for eight years as president of Island Records UK.

By the end of the third quarter of 2008, the plan seemed to be working. EMI posted pre-EBITDA earnings of $88 million for the previous six months, as opposed to a loss of $21 million for the same period in 2007. Cost control and a 37 percent rise in digital revenue from $110 to $152 million sparked the turnaround, but by the end of 2008, their album market share had declined from 9.4 percent in 2007 to 8.8 percent, still in last place. The only EMI artists in *Billboard*'s year-end Top 100 Albums and/or singles charts were Coldplay, Katy Perry, J. Holiday, Keith Urban, and Trace Adkins, a good nucleus, but not enough to compete in the Big Four.

BMG Exits from the Sony Venture

The combined entity of Sony and BMG had been formed to reduce distribution and other back-office costs. Savings, however, were negated to some degree as the Sony and BMG market shares in 2003 together had added up to 30.6 percent, but the Sony-BMG entity slid to 25 percent in 2007, compounded by declining overall industry sales. Attempting to stem the tide, in May 2008 Schmidt-Holtz once again shuffled the executive team, replacing RCA chairman/CEO Clive Davis with Barry Weiss, adding oversight of the RCA, J Records, LaFace, and Arista operations to Weiss's responsibilities at Jive. Davis assumed the newly created role of chief creative officer for the entire joint venture with expanded A&R responsibilities.

Five months later, in October 2008, Sony bought BMG out of their joint venture as the two companies differed on how music complemented their other core businesses. With Sony's base in electronics, Chairman Sir Howard Stringer envisioned future growth for music in synergy with mobile, gaming, and other home electronics areas, especially in the expanding markets throughout Asia. He told Mark Landler of *The New York Times* that digital technology made music "a less risky business. The advent of the cellphone as a conveyor of music globally takes away a lot of the risk."[2] Stringer further noted, "This acquisition will allow us to achieve a deeper and more robust integration between the wide ranging global assets of the music company and Sony's products, operating companies and affiliates. It enables us to offer a total entertainment experience to consumers."[3]

The Direct Media North America division—including the record, DVD, and book clubs—were sold to the Phoenix-based Najafi Companies private equity firm. Although BMG had asked Sony for more than $1.6 billion for its joint venture share, they eventually settled for a package of $600 million cash payment plus $300 million, which was half of the cash on hand. Bertelsmann, however, was not completely exiting the music business. As part of the separation settlement they would retain the rights to over eight thousand tracks by about two hundred artists, primarily Europe-based catalog acts including the Scorpions, Paolo Conte, Sylvie Vartan, Nena, Yves Montand, and Gilbert Becaud.

Later that month Bertelsmann announced the January 1, 2009, launch of BMG Rights Management, a partnership with private equity firm Kohlberg Kravis Roberts (KKR), to be located in Berlin and headed by former BMG Germany publishing CEO Hartwig Masuch, with satellite offices in Amsterdam, Madrid, Paris, Milan, and London. BMG Rights would pursue sync licenses from advertisers, film studios, broadcasters, and digital media companies while licensing the record distribution rights to the now-standalone Sony. Masuch portrayed BMG Rights' new role as "creating an attractive package of services for creative people and copyright holders."[4] Plans were also under way to relaunch a parallel BMG publishing arm later in the year.

Terra Firma on Shaky Ground

Like Thomas Middelhoff and the Messier-Bronfman team earlier in the decade, Guy Hands overestimated the speed of the industry's transition from physical to digital commerce and was likewise hindered by an unanticipated economic downturn. Sales for all labels were affected on a proportional level, but EMI felt the heat more than any other as it had a much higher debt-to-income ratio. An October 2008 *Billboard* article by Ed Christman analyzed how each label could handle an extended credit crisis. Both Sony and UMG were parts of larger, more diversified corporate entities with the ability to absorb the cost of adapting to the downturn in record sales, while EMI as well as WMG were standalone companies that didn't have the luxury of leaning on other divisions during a downturn. They did, however, have the two largest and most profitable publishing catalogs, which, if combined, would control over 50 percent of the market.

Christman further reported that as of June 30, 2008, WMG had $338 million in cash on its balance sheet. Its nine-month operating income before EBITDA had been $341 million, $25 million over the previous year. Its debt service in both 2007 and 2008 was about $200 million on $2.3 billion of debt. EMI, however, had an estimated $5 billion in debt and less than half of WMG's market share. EMI had only 47.1 million units reported through SoundScan in 2008 compared to WMG's 113.5 million, Sony's 135 million, and UMG's 150.6 million. Sales by independents were a total of 71.4 million units.

As the recession deepened, EMI was the first to react to the strain. Despite a catalog led by Beatles reissues, along with Katy Perry and Coldplay, the revamped EMI system yielded few new breakout artists. EMI was also still reeling from the 2005 loss of the Garth Brooks catalog. Despite a 22.8 percent improvement in 2009 pre-EBITDA earnings over 2008, the size of EMI's debt service made it impossible to meet Citibank's loan covenants without an infusion of $150 million in additional capital in early 2010. Hands dismissed Leoni-Sceti and his team in June 2010, adding the label group to publishing head Roger Faxon's responsibilities.

By 2010 Hands had somehow decided that Citigroup—especially his once close friend, golfing partner, and Citigroup's European head of investment banking David Wormsley—had misled him in determining EMI's value. Hands offered to put another $1.7 billion into EMI if Citigroup would forgive an equal amount of debt, which he believed Citigroup had already recovered from the US Troubled Asset Relief Program (TARP) bailout fund. Citigroup, however, would only consider an exchange of debt for equity.

Hands responded in October 2010 with a lawsuit seeking $8.3 billion in damages. Lead litigator David Boies argued that Hands was deceived into an exorbitant bid by Wormsley's false representation of a competing offer while he "secretly promised EMI to use his relationship with Guy Hands and Terra Firma to help EMI" up its price.[5] After three weeks of testimony the jury ruled in Citigroup's favor, with lead attorney Ted Wells addressing the court, "Rather than taking responsibility for making a mistake, he [Hands] turned around and filed this lawsuit. He made a bad business decision and is trying to shift responsibility to Citibank."[6]

Terra Firma had lost about $2.5 billion on the investment while Hands himself lost about $240 million, roughly two-thirds of his own net worth. His investors were questioning why Terra Firma put over a third of its capital into one investment. Wells stated the case in simple terms to the jury, succinctly summarizing the woes of the entire record industry. "Guy Hands couldn't fight technology. No one's buying records anymore." He further added on behalf of Citigroup, "We should not have loaned [Hands the money]. . . . We have to live with our own bad business decision, and so does he."[7]

Shuffling the Executive Deck

The year 2010 ended with the record industry's $7.02 billion RIAA-reported revenue value at its lowest point since 1990 and less than half of its peak in 1999. After Terra Firma's failed legal ploy with Citigroup, the other members of the Big Four, who had been circling the floundering EMI for years waiting for its board to finally accept an offer, all formulated plans to acquire all or just a part of what would be appropriated and auctioned by Citigroup. Also looking to participate in the bidding was expansion-oriented BMG Rights.

WMG was still in the hands of Edgar Bronfman Jr.'s investor group, including Thomas H. Lee and Bain Capital. Lyor Cohen was in his seventh year as head of the US creative department. WMG had been the first to have digital revenue exceed 50 percent of its total. WMG's SoundScan market share in 2010 was 19.9 percent. Bronfman's long-held yearning to add EMI's 9.7 percent share would put WMG close to equal footing with Sony and UMG, which had already been bolstered by their respective acquisitions of BMG and PolyGram. The combining of the EMI and Warner Chappell publishing holdings would put them in a clear-cut number one position in that sector.

Bronfman had tried twice before to link EMI with WMG, and many in the industry felt that his third time would be the charm. WMG's financial position, however, was his biggest obstacle. Without a larger corporate umbrella to cushion the cost, would the WMG board be willing to take on more debt in the face of an uncertain economy and declining record revenue? The answer was revealed in January 2011 when the WMG board hired Goldman Sachs to explore for potential buyers.

With the contracts of both Morris at UMG and Schmidt-Holtz at Sony due to expire March 31, each decided to reshape its executive team. Sony chose not to renew Schmidt-Holtz, the top-ranking BMG holdover. Barry Weiss was rumored to be in line to replace him based on his success at Jive and RCA, but Sony offered the top spot to Morris effective when his UMG contract expired. Despite an offered $10 million yearly salary to remain at UMG as just chairman with his CEO role filled by a new appointee, Morris agreed to replace Schmidt-Holtz in the chairman/CEO role at Sony. Morris was then succeeded as UMG CEO by Lucian Grainge, head of UMG International. At fifty-one, Grainge was twenty-one years younger than Morris.

Weiss then decided to make a switch of his own by joining UMG in April 2011 as chairman/CEO of New York–based Universal-Republic-Island-Def Jam, reporting to Grainge. Unlike Sony where the entire label group was in the same building in NYC, the other UMG division Interscope-Geffen-A&M under Jimmy Iovine was in Los Angeles along with Grainge's corporate headquarters. Weiss brought key members of his RCA/Jive team with him, including executive VP Peter Thea, a former entertainment attorney who had been with Weiss since 1999; and COO Ivan Gavan, who joined Weiss at Sony in 2007 after five years with EMI preceded by a twelve-year stint with Weiss at Jive. Weiss's new East Coast UMG division accounted for 11.2 percent of all SoundScan sales, the largest market share under a single executive at any of the Big Four, with Iovine in second with a 7.9 percent share.

Passing Weiss in reverse transit between UMG and Sony, Morris also brought along key executives. L.A. Reid assumed the CEO/chairman mantle at the Epic Records division. Longtime associate Mel Lewinter joined the Sony hierarchy as executive VP of label strategy. British expatriates CEO Rob Stringer and COO Steve Barnett were still on board at Columbia riding the enormous success of Adele. Chief creative officer Clive Davis weathered the transition, and with his fifty years in the business, was one of the few remaining record executives who predated Morris.

And Then There Were Three

Before the executive suite changes became official on April 1, 2011, Citigroup put the EMI sweepstakes into play by taking control of the label in February, triggered by Terra Firma's default on payments. With both EMI and WMG now up for bid, several possible scenarios were bandied about, but anything that resulted in just a Big Two or one company having more than a 50 percent interest in either the publishing or recorded music sector would probably not pass antimonopoly muster.

The first domino fell in May 2011 when the WMG board agreed to be purchased as a whole by Access Industries, a conglomerate controlled by Len Blavatnik, a WMG shareholder and former board director. Born in 1957 in Odessa when Ukraine was still part of the Soviet Union, Blavatnik attended college in Moscow. He then immigrated to America in 1978, earned an MA in computer science from Columbia, and then an MBA from Harvard. He received US citizenship in 1984 and opened Access in 1986. By 2011 he was worth at least $7.5 billion from investments in natural resources in Russia, and in petrochemicals during the 2008 economic crisis. Blavatnik held both US and UK citizenship and in 2015 was named the wealthiest person in the UK and Forbes's fiftieth wealthiest person in the world. He was knighted in the UK in 2017 for his extensive philanthropic work.

Access offered WMG shareholders a $3.3 billion all-cash buyout paying $8.25 per share, 34.4 percent above its last six-month average price. The deal closed in July 2011 with the company going private. Blavatnik contributed $1.1 billion of his own money with the balance in private bonds from Credit Suisse and UBS. He replaced Bronfman as CEO with restructuring specialist Stephen Cooper, whose previous stops included Krispy Kreme, Enron, MGM, and Hawaiian Telecom, but no experience in the music business. Cooper shared Blavatnik's view of music as a commodity, although a glamorous one, and favored tight budgetary control with salaries tied to productivity. Bronfman agreed to stay on as chairman to assist in the pursuit of finally uniting WMG with EMI. Lyor Cohen, who had built a close personal relationship with Blavatnik and had lobbied for the CEO position with Bronfman's backing, remained as head of worldwide recorded music operations, a position to which he had just been appointed.

After sifting through bids from over a half dozen suitors, in November 2011 Citigroup announced that it would be splitting up the EMI assets with the recorded music division going to UMG for $1.9 billion and the publishing group going for $2.2 billion to a consortium led by Sony/ATV. The two bids combined for more than WMG or any other combination of suitors offered. At a total of $4.1 billion, it was $200 million shy of what Citigroup had loaned to Terra Firma. *Billboard*'s Ed Christman opined, "If one considers the fees, interest and penalties it collected from EMI during the last four years, and whatever cash it reaped in the last year while it controlled the company, Citigroup may have taken out more than it put in."[8] Hands would try once again to recoup his losses coupled with penalties when he sued Citigroup in New York in 2016, but this time the action never made it to a jury as Hands withdrew the suit midway through the proceedings.

The realignment from Big Four to Big Three increased the 2012 UMG market share to 39.3 percent, with Sony at 29.1 percent, and WMG in third at 18.9 percent. The calculations included their indie label distribution divisions. To avoid duplication of services, UMG kept EMI's recently acquired Caroline distribution for independent labels and sold its smaller Fontana network to digital distributor Ingrooves. Already a minority owner in Ingrooves, UMG placed its digital administrations rights there, and in 2016 acquired the company. The remaining 12.7 percent of the 2012 retail market was controlled by a combination of truly independent distributors, but if their indie label clients were combined with the independently owned labels under distribution deals with Caroline, RED, and ADA, then 32.6 percent of the market was independent of ownership by the now Big Three, and growing.

Universal Music Group: An Even Bigger Number One

Lucian Grainge's ascendancy to UMG chairman on April 1, 2011, was not a surprise since corporate parent Vivendi had long been intent on retaining his services. While working under Morris as head of UMG International since 2005, he experienced the European launch and growth of both Spotify and Deezer, which prepared him for the US transition to a streaming future. He shared with Morris the strong belief that a diversified range of A&R talent was essential to maintaining the pool of artistic talent. Grainge was also keenly aware of the multiple options the public now had for consuming music. He told *Billboard* in February 2014, "Every morning when I wake up I realize the consumer has total choice. We don't have the divine right to expect consumers to buy our product. Yet after all is said and done, I believe the industry will return to the level of growth that we've hoped for and have been fighting for the last 10 years."[9]

By the end of 2013, Grainge had EMI integrated into the UMG system as the Capitol Records Group with separate A&R centers in the Capitol, Virgin, and Blue Note imprints along with the Caroline independent distribution system. Motown Records was moved from New York to Los Angeles and added to the Capitol Group. Newly installed Capitol chairman/CEO Steve Barnett had been hired away from Columbia. Barnett succeeded with British newcomer Sam Smith, Arcade Fire on indie Merge Records through Caroline, alternative pop veteran Beck, and legend Van Morrison doing a duet project under the direction of producer Don Was, president of Blue Note Records, who had replaced the retired Bruce Lundvall.

Grainge also put his imprimatur on the UMG hierarchy. He installed Boyd Muir, his CFO at UMG International, as CFO of the entire music group. Muir led the integration of EMI into the UMG fold, as well as the subsequent acquisitions of Terry Shand's Eagle Rock video company and Richard Branson's V2 Music Group. Grainge's executive inner circle was completed in 2013 with the hiring of Sony veteran Michele Anthony in the newly created position of executive VP of UMG as Grainge's interdepartmental ombudsman, parallel to the role she had filled at Sony during the Mottola regime. Veteran A&R executive VP Karen Kwak was moved to Grainge's office as the A&R conduit to the chairman for all UMG label heads.

In April 2014 Barry Weiss was allowed to resign from his executive post at UMG to develop his own label, but the planned venture never came to fruition. In early 2018 Weiss brought his RECORDS label he had in partnership with SONGS Music Publishing to Sony. The consolidated UMG label group he had helmed was disassembled into stand-alone labels each with its own A&R and marketing departments. Weiss's position and title were not refilled. Individual UMG label heads now also reported directly to Grainge's office. Steve Bartels, who had served as L.A. Reid's COO at Island/Def Jam, was upped to president.

In 2013 Grainge separated Island from Def Jam, leaving Bartels as CEO at Def Jam, and upping former Mercury president Dave Massey to CEO/president at Island. Republic Records returned to its autonomous status under the Lipman brothers team of chairman Monte and president/CEO Avery, with hits ranging from Drake to Ariana Grande to the Zac Brown Band. They also shared oversight of Taylor Swift's transition to pop megastar with Swift's UMG-distributed Big Machine label owned by Nashville-based Scott Borchetta. Republic then signed Swift directly when she parted ways with Borchetta in 2018 after a twelve-year association.

In May 2014, Jimmy Iovine's eighteen-year tenure at UMG came to an end when he and partner Dr. Dre sold their Beats streaming service to Apple for $3.2 billion and joined its executive team. Under Morris, UMG had invested $2.8 million in the MOG online subscription service in 2008, which was subsequently purchased by and incorporated within Beats as its own subscription service. As part of the Apple acquisition of Beats, UMG received about $448 million for its 14 percent share. Iovine was replaced by his understudy, John Janick, as chairman/CEO of Interscope-Geffen-A&M. Iovine had outbid

WMG for Janick's services in 2012 after WMG bought Janick's indie label Fueled by Ramen.

At the beginning of 2018, Paul Rosenberg, Eminem's manager and partner in Interscope-distributed Shady Records, was brought in by Grainge as Def Jam CEO to replace Steve Bartels, who had exited to join L.A. Reid's new Hitco independent venture. Despite being an attorney, Rosenberg had immense street cred from his years of working with Eminem, the biggest-selling rap artist of all time. At Shady he had also worked with 50 Cent on his first five albums and coproduced the Shade 45 channel on Sirius XM radio. While Bartels was an exemplar COO, Rosenberg apparently held a greater appeal to Grainge as an A&R-oriented CEO who could restore Def Jam to its historic position as a preeminent rap label.

The September 21, 2012, approval of UMG's purchase of EMI by the European Economic Community (EEC) and US Federal Trade Commission (FTC) included a mandated divestiture of approximately one-third of EMI's assets. WMG paid $765 million to UMG for the historic Parlophone catalog. The purchase included future releases by Coldplay, Radiohead (which was transferred to indie XL to be distributed in the US by WMG's ADA), and Pink Floyd, whose final album, *The Endless River*, was released in 2014 but on Columbia for the US, achieving gold but not platinum certification, but nonetheless selling over 2.5 million worldwide, split between Columbia and the now–WMG-owned Parlophone for the rest of the world.

WMG also acquired Chrysalis Records and both the EMI and Virgin Classics divisions, which were rolled into Warner Classics. The other Parlophone masters were assigned to WB Records. WMG was also obligated to carve out up to 30 percent of Parlophone to be eligible for purchase by independents to help maintain a competitive balance. Interested buyers had a window expiring at the end of February 2014 to inform WMG of the masters in which they were interested, and then until September 2017 to get artist permission and then close the purchase.

BMG Rights bought the Mute Records catalog containing Depeche Mode and Kraftwerk for an undisclosed amount, and the classic rock Sanctuary Music Group for about $70 million. Rap pioneer Tom Silverman secured the WMG half of the Tommy Boy Music albums produced during their 1995–2002 partnership. Management company Blue Raincoat Music in association with Chrysalis cofounder Chris Wright bought Chrysalis Records as well as the catalogs of Steve Harley & Cockney Rebel and Lucinda Williams.

Other prominent artists with albums moving to independent labels included Tom Waits, Howard Jones, Kim Wilde, Per Gessle and Marie Fredriksson of Roxette, Neil Finn, Jewel, Sérgio Mendes, the Lemonheads, the Groundhogs,

Patrice Rushen, Miriam Makeba, Ziggy Marley, Sugar Ray, Fat Joe, Thomas Dolby, Roy Ayers, Donovan, and Lulu. The common denominator was that most of these artists were active but no longer considered by the majors to have hit-single potential, and thus didn't fit into their marketing model.

Sony Music Entertainment: Two Out of Three Ain't Bad

From when Doug Morris ascended to chairman/CEO at Sony in April 2011 at the age of seventy-two until his retirement in April 2017, he proved to be almost everything the Sony corporate hierarchy had hoped for. With a steadying hand that swept out the final vestiges of the Sony-BMG cultural clash and reinvigorated both A&R talent and the artist roster, he also increased profit margins. His career had bridged the transition from the street-savvy instincts born of the 1960s singles era to the social media and analytics-driven awareness of the digital age. The only hope he didn't fulfill was for Sony to displace UMG from the number one spot, but that had been rendered virtually impossible by the UMG purchase of EMI.

Morris exhibited his trademark political mastery and personal charm to reinvigorate Sony including retaining rather that retiring his fellow septuagenarian Clive Davis, perhaps the only record man on par with Morris's mentor, Ahmet Ertegun. At UMG Morris had worked in lockstep with Edgar Bronfman Jr. in trying to launch a DRM-enabled digital distribution system, had been the first label group head to seek an ownership share from third parties exploiting his catalog, and had invested in the startup of digital pioneers Vevo, Spotify, and MOG. Morris also retained one overriding caveat from his record man roots, namely, success comes from hit singles. That core tenet was as applicable to the digital age as it had been in the analog era, especially with streaming poised to become the predominant source of recorded music revenue.

Morris continued to tinker with his A&R staff to ensure and improve product flow. In addition to appointing L.A. Reid to head Epic and Tom Corson at the RCA Group in 2011, in 2013 he added Sylvia Rhone at Epic. He also made a label deal with songwriter/producer Lukasz "Dr. Luke" Gottwald's Kemosabe Records that would tie him exclusively to Sony for the next three years. Dr. Luke had been the lead guitarist with the *Saturday Night Live* house band from 1997 through 2007 while becoming a successful songwriter and then producer for Kelly Clarkson, Katy Perry, Britney Spears, Nicki Minaj, Rihanna, Flo Rida, and Miley Cyrus at rival labels, and most recently with

Kesha for Sony. Morris also bought a share of Patrick Moxey's Ultra Music record and publishing EDM enterprise, installing Moxey as president of Sony's worldwide electronic music division.

Morris renewed his contract with Sony in early 2015 for two years for $17 million a year split between guarantee and attainable bonuses. In late 2016 he announced his retirement as of March 2017 from the CEO chair at the age of seventy-nine, passing control of the label group to Columbia's Rob Stringer. Morris had guided Sony to its best years, averaging just under a 29 percent market share compared to its under 27 percent during the seven previous years. He also increased the retained profit on that revenue. Morris stayed on in an emeritus role but resigned from that in 2018. As one of the last surviving record men of the 1960s, he wasn't quite ready to get out of the game and opened 12 Tone Records to be distributed by WMG.

Throughout Morris's more than fifty-five-year career, he selected his mentors and protégés with equal aplomb. His career was feted at his farewell celebration by many of his most accomplished colleagues from over his long career. Fellow former WMG executive and Rock and Roll Hall of Fame inductee Seymour Stein proclaimed, "Doug is certainly one of the greatest music execs of all-time. . . . He's truly done it all!"[10] Also adding their accolades were Jimmy Iovine now of Apple, Columbia's Rob Stringer, Craig Kallman from Atlantic, Sylvia Rhone who was with him at all three of his CEO tenures, L.A. Reid from both UMG and Epic, Tom Corson and Peter Edge from RCA, and the Lipman brothers from Republic Records. Rhone summarized the feelings shared by many. "Doug's most lasting legacy is that he has become the architect of so many people's dreams."[11]

Sony Music Entertainment: Rob Stringer Takes Command

Fifty-five-year-old Rob Stringer had been with Sony since the mid-1980s working his way up through A&R to head the UK division until he moved to New York in 2006 to take over the Columbia label. Although initially under the shadow of his twenty-year-older brother Sir Howard, who retired in 2012, Stringer had built his own network of allies and contacts with a lower-key, hands-on, and artist-oriented approach that had enabled him to succeed on his own merits. He told *Billboard*, "The question I get asked most is when is rock coming back? Can it just be the same as it was? Where's the protest music? There's tons of great music around. It's all there, it's just different. I don't ever look back."[12]

In addition to finding a replacement for himself at Columbia, Stringer was faced with two inherited sexual harassment cases involving two of his top producers as the Me Too movement was bubbling under the radar and about to explode a few months later. The more visible was the vitriolic suit between Dr. Luke and Kesha, whom Luke had signed to a production and publishing agreement in 2005 when she was eighteen. In 2009 they unleashed a string of seven top-ten singles on his Sony-distributed Kemosabe Records with "Tik Tok" and "We R Who We R" going number one and selling millions of singles and albums around the world. Their relationship deteriorated in 2013 after Kesha's second album *Warrior* failed to earn platinum status. Kesha complained that Luke had not allowed her enough creative input and in October 2014 she filed the first of a long string of lawsuits and countersuits centered around voiding her contract due to sexual assault, emotional abuse, and violation of California statutory business practices.

By August 2017 Sony had dissolved its agreement with Luke and taken over Kemosabe and Kesha's contract. Despite critical acclaim, two Grammy nominations, and a Grammy Awards show performance by Kesha of her single "Praying," neither chart nor sales success materialized. Going into 2020 the two former collaborators were still arguing in court, while Kesha had her fourth Kemosabe album scheduled for release and Luke had not yet replicated the success he enjoyed with her or other artists prior to his exclusive arrangement with Sony.

The other situation had deeper repercussions throughout the company but far less publicity. Just prior to Morris's retirement, a former Epic staffer notified the label of her claims of ongoing sexual harassment by L.A. Reid and inaction when notifying other Epic executives of the alleged situation. She threatened to sue unless the company settled. Stringer acted quickly and Reid departed Epic in early May with little comment from either. Reid had three Grammy Awards over his nearly thirty-year production career ranging from his days at his own LaFace Records label in partnership with Kenneth "Babyface" Edmonds through executive tenures at Arista and Def Jam prior to his six-year stint at Epic. Successes included TLC, Outcast, Toni Braxton, Justin Bieber, Kanye West, the Killers, Bon Jovi, Jennifer Lopez, Rihanna, and Avril Lavigne. At the time of his departure from Epic, his most recent projects were Meghan Trainor, Fifth Harmony, Future, Travis Scott, and DJ Khaled.

Reid's departure was somewhat tempered by the presence of Sylvia Rhone, who replaced him as Epic CEO/chairman. Reid soon joined forces with Clive Davis's longtime associate, former COO of BMG, and CEO of digital jukebox pioneer TouchTunes Charles Goldstuck, at HitCo Entertainment, with a reported $100 million in investment capital. In March 2018 HitCo signed its first artist in Big Boi, half of rap group Outkast, which Reid had signed to Arista; opened a fully staffed office in Los Angeles; and entered into a distribution agreement with independent EMPIRE Distribution of San Francisco.

The year 2017 ended with Sony's market share down from 2016's 28.3 percent to 27 percent, but due to the rise in total industry revenue driven by streaming, Sony's receipts were up by over $250 million. In January 2018 Stringer finally filled the vacant chairman/CEO position at Columbia with thirty-eight-year-old Ron Perry, part of the trio who had built independent publisher SONGS Music Publishing into a contemporary powerhouse. Stringer commented, "Ron is an immensely dynamic and forward thinking executive who excels at bringing the best out of artistic vision."[13] Perry exemplified the new generation of young executives with experience in social media and live performance, the new two-laned street of the modern music business. But like the record men of the past, these new A&R decision makers still understood that, as Perry stated to Billboard, songs "are the backbone of the business. . . . We have too many charts and metrics that only music industry professionals can understand. We need to simplify the process."[14]

In January 2018 Stringer had to fill another executive void when longtime RCA cochairman/COO Tom Corson left the label for a similar role at WB Records as half of the team hired to replace the departing Cameron Strang. Stringer looked within, tapping RCA executive VP John Fleckenstein and general manager/president of promotion Joe Riccitelli as RCA label group co-presidents who would report to the now-sole chairman/CEO Peter Edge. Fleckenstein had been with BMG and then Sony since 1998 before moving to RCA in 2014. Riccitelli had moved to Jive in 1999 after a five-year stint at Island, and then moved to RCA in 2011. They were responsible for all aspects of label operations except A&R, which remained Edge's domain. In May 2018 Edge upped RCA executive VP of A&R Keith Naftaly to president to report directly to him. Clive Davis had hired Naftaly away from radio in 1995 to join Arista and then J Records.

Warner Music Group: Number Three with an Asterisk*

The last time WMG finished as the number one major label group in SoundScan-tabulated sales had been in 1998—the last year of the Big Six. Then in 1999 the two usually cellar-dwelling MCA and Polygram were merged into UMG, propelling them collectively into the number one spot in the reconfigured Big Five. Suffering from lackluster leadership after the 1995 departure of Doug Morris, by 1999 WMG had spiraled down to number four with a 15.8 percent market share from its 1996 high of 21.1 percent. By 2003 WMG had rebounded to number two, but when Sony and BMG merged after several years of alternating between the number three and number four spots, the new joint venture vaulted over WMG to number two. Consequentially WMG dropped to a consistent number three in the Big Four era behind its two merged competitors, even though averaging over a 20 percent market share from 2007 through 2011. No other label group member of the pre-merger Big Six era other than WMG had ever enjoyed a 20 percent or more market share in SoundScan tabulations.

Had the three merger/acquisitions that transformed the Big Six into the Big Three never happened, WMG's 20 percent+ market share would have made it a perennial contender for number one in a Big Six. Thus the asterisk in the segment heading is for the wishful dreaming of those who would turn back time and reverse the conglomerate-led consolidation of the record industry. Further as to the justification of the asterisk, had WMG purchased EMI as Bronfman so fervently sought, the combination would have vaulted into a virtual three-way tie with its two already consolidated rivals.

Despite the limited experience in the record business of new owner Blavatnik and his CEO Cooper, WMG averaged an 18.7 percent share of SoundScan sales from 2012 to 2015 before rebounding to 21.4 percent in 2016 and 20.5 percent in 2017. Bronfman had departed at the end of 2011 leaving WMG with a wealth of A&R talent assembled by Lyor Cohen. Blavatnik wanted Cooper to utilize his turnaround skills in trimming costs, especially in executive compensation. This was quite the opposite of Bronfman, who liked to incentivize and reward his best executives with bonuses and stock options resulting in Cohen's $11 million pact, more than twice Cooper's contract and due to expire in late 2012. Cooper devised a senior management free cash flow plan that eliminated severance payments and bonuses, replacing them with dividends and a stake in any increased company value after a seven-year tenure.

The plan precipitated the departure of Cohen, with whom Cooper had often clashed, and his top associate Todd Moscowitz along with their salaries and easily attainable bonuses despite Cohen's close social relationship with Blavatnik. Cohen had a long history of mentoring and retaining top young executive talent. His departure left WMG with the executive teams of Julie Greenwald and Craig Kallman at Atlantic as co-chairmen and COO and CEO, respectively; chairman/CEO Cameron Strang of WB Records; and Electra Records president Jeff Castelaz. Cooper also eliminated Cohen's and Moskovitz's positions with the heads of the three record divisions now reporting directly to him. In December 2013 former Capitol president Dan McCarroll, who had managed the Parlophone catalog for EMI, was hired as president of WB Records to report to chairman/CEO Cameron Strang.

Finishing his fifth year at the WMG helm in 2016, Cooper realized it was time to reinstate the vacated Lyor Cohen position with someone who could also eventually fill Cooper's own CEO seat. He stayed within the stable of young A&R talent assembled by Cohen with the appointment of forty-four-year-old Max Lousada to the role in March 2017, effective as of October 1. Lousada had been with WMG UK since 2004, rising to president of Atlantic UK in 2009 and CEO/chairman of WMG UK since September 2013 with credit for Ed Sheeran's signing to the label. Lousada started reshaping the WMG management teams even before he assumed his new position. In July 2017 he named forty-seven-year-old Island Records executive VP of A&R Rani Hancock as president of WB Records division Sire Records as of August 1. Chairman Seymour Stein had founded Sire in 1967 with producer Richard Gottehrer and built it into an independent punk and avant-garde powerhouse with the Ramones and Talking Heads before selling the label to WMG in 1978. One of the last of the 1960s record men, seventy-five-year-old Stein remained as chairman emeritus and then retired a year later in July 2018.

The next move was to revamp the management at WB Records. Dan McCarroll exited in July 2017 and Cameron Strang resigned from the WMG board just a few days after Lousada announced his new executive team on October 3, 2017. Thirty-seven-year-old Interscope president of A&R Aaron Bay-Schuck was hired as the new WB Records label chairman and longtime RCA COO Tom Corson moved laterally to WB Records, effective January 1, 2018. Bay-Schuck and Corson would mirror the Greenwald-Kallman Atlantic team operating as an executive partnership, with Bay-Schuck handling creative direction and Corson overseeing operations, similar to the arrangement he had with Peter Edge at RCA. Lousada told *Billboard*'s Dan Rys, "They're a dynamic combination that will bring in a fresh, new era at one of the greatest record labels of all time."[15] Bay-Schuck had actually started at Atlantic UK in the mid-1990s where he worked with Bruno Mars, Flo Rida, and B.o.B. before moving to Interscope in 2014 to work with Selena Gomez, Imagine Dragons, Lady Gaga, Lana del Rey and OneRepublic, among others.

Strang was a thirty-two-year-old trial lawyer from Vancouver when he opened New West Records in 1998, which he built into an Americana powerhouse within a decade. Bronfman brought him to Warner Chappell in 2011 as CEO to reinvigorate the publishing company. WB Records and the Rhino back catalog division were added to his portfolio in 2012 and he was named to the WMG board of directors. While widely respected for his business skills, musical acumen, and management style, he didn't have the success with WB Records that he had achieved at Warner Chappell or with his own companies.

Finally Lousada separated Elektra from under the aegis of Atlantic, restoring the historic WMG label troika. The new Elektra executive team was led by co-presidents Mike Easterlin, previously head of Fueled by Ramen and Roadrunner, and Gregg Nadel, who had been running Elektra for the past two years. They would continue, however, to report to Kallman and Greenwald rather than directly to Lousada. Artists under their direction included Twenty One Pilots, Zac Brown Band, Paramore, Sturgill Simpson, Brandi Carlile, and Panic! at the Disco.

On the Outside Looking In(dependent)

While the major labels were consolidating, record sales declining, and streaming expanding, independent labels were thriving. Indies had always been a haven for new artists not yet, or perhaps never, ready for chart success with a major label, as well as for those whose chart run but not their careers had concluded. The independents also released back catalog, live recordings, soundtrack albums, multi-artist compilations, and box-sets as well as serviced genres that did not have corresponding radio formats. In 2017, 36.6 percent of Nielsen SoundScan tabulated sales and streams were credited to independent labels. Of these, 20.8 percent came from labels distributed by either Sony's RED, WMG's ADA, or UMG's Caroline. The other 15.8 percent comprised independent label-owned product handled by truly independent distributors.

While the majors dominated the top-three spots on the annual year-end *Billboard* Top 200 Album rankings throughout the first decade of the new millennium, a handful of independents consistently filled the rest of the top ten. Miami-based rap label Cash Money Records had been one of the most successful but was distributed directly through UMG's Republic Records and not through its Caroline subsidiary. Cash Money was owned by brothers and co-CEOs Bryan "Birdman" Williams and Ronald "Slim" Williams, who began as artists in 1991 before making Cash Money an outlet for other rappers in their native New Orleans. Their platinum success began with Lil Wayne in 1998 and extended through his first ten albums. Shortly after their initial success, the Williams brothers renegotiated their UMG agreement to a $30 million pressing and distribution deal on an 85 percent/15 percent split and retained ownership of all masters. In 2009 they signed rappers Nicki Minaj and Drake to Young Money Records which they then co-owned with Lil Wayne.

By the end of 2019 Drake had become *Billboard*'s most charted solo artist with close to 200 Hot 100 chart entries as well as the most number-one singles on the Hot Rap Songs, Hot R&B/Hip Hop Airplay, and Rhythmic Charts. All of his first five album and three of his six mixtapes were number one on the Top 200 album chart. Drake achieving that number of Hot 100 chart entries along with featured appearances on other artists' tracks was indicative of how much both rap and streaming had become major components of the pop charts. Nicki Minaj had a similar career trajectory but on a slightly smaller scale. Her first three albums were all multi-platinum with a fourth released in August 2018. She garnered 98 Hot 100 chart entries, yielding the most ever for female artists in any genre including seventeen top-ten singles, the most ever for a female rapper.

Nashville's Big Machine Label Group began its meteoric success with sixteen-year-old Taylor Swift's first album in October 2006. Over the next eight year her first four albums, all released in the country genre, sold over 25 million units worldwide. In October 2014 she released *1989* as a pop album with marketing assistance from Republic Records, which reached worldwide sales of over 10 million units. Despite Swift transferring her fan base to pop radio, Big Machine founder/president/CEO Scott Borchetta maintained his position on the country charts with newcomers Florida Georgia Line, the Eli Young Band, Thomas Rhett, Brett Young, Midland, and Carly Pearce. He also signed veterans Tim McGraw, Reba McEntire, Lady A, Sugarland, and Rascal Flats.

With her contract up in 2018, Swift was unable to come to terms with Big Machine on a new deal that would include transfer of her older masters to her ownership. Consequentially she signed directly with Republic rather than renew at Big Machine. Then in June 2019 *Billboard*'s Ed Christman reported that "Scooter Braun's Ithaca Holdings has agreed to acquire Scott Borchetta's Big Machine Label Group in a blockbuster deal backed by the Carlyle Group. Terms of the agreement were not disclosed, but a source told *Billboard* the deal topped $300 million and also includes the music publishing operation, Big Machine Music."[16]

The thirty-seven-year-old Braun already had relationships with rappers Drake; Future; and on-again, off-again with Kanye West; Ariana Grande for whom he organized the 2017 *One Love Manchester* benefit concert; long-time client Justin Bieber; Demi Lovato; Tori Kelly; and country acts Zac Brown Band and Dan + Shay. Big Machine would bring him a greatly expanded Nashville presence. The deal would in turn extend the fifty-five-year-old Borchetta's reach into the pop world. Ithaca was building a diversified hybrid content-owning company encompassing management, recording, publishing, and back-office artist services as a progenitor for the music company of the digital future.

Swift lambasted the deal on Tumblr. "When I left my masters in Scott's hands, I made peace with the fact that eventually he would sell them. Never in my worst nightmares did I imagine the buyer would be Scooter. He knew what he was doing; they both did. Controlling a woman who didn't want to be associated with them."[17] She also claimed to have no forewarning of the purchase even though her father was a minority shareholder in Big Machine. She continued about the future, "Thankfully, I am now signed to a label that believes I should own anything I create. . . . And hopefully, young artists or kids with musical dreams will read this and learn about how to better protect themselves in a negotiation. You deserve to own the art you make."[18]

The battle had begun with more to come. Swift fired the first salvo two months later in August 2019 on both *CBS Sunday Morning* and ABC's *Good Morning America* when she confirmed that she was planning to rerecord her Big Machine albums when restriction expired beginning in November 2020. In the December 2019 "Woman of the Decade" feature she told *Billboard* that despite the constant stream of sync license requests, because she controlled her publishing she had said no to all of them. "The reason I'm rerecording my music next year is because I do want my music to live on. I do want it to be in movies, I do want it to be in commercials. But I only want that if I own it. . . . It's going to be fun, because it'll feel like regaining a freedom and taking back what's mine."[19]

Building Independent Catalogs

After executive positions at Chrysalis, SBK/EMI, Rising Tide/Universal, and independent Artemis, Daniel Glass opened his own Glassnote Entertainment Group in 2007. In 2009 he licensed the US rights to the *Sigh No More* album by Mumford & Sons from their own UK-based Gentlemen of the Road label and won three 2011 Billboard Music Awards. Their second album *Babel* won the Grammy Award in 2013 for Album of the Year. Both albums sold around 3 million units in the US. Four other Glassnote albums have also been certified, *Wolfgang Amadeus Phoenix* by Phoenix, *Wilder Mind* by Mumford & Sons, and *Because the Internet* and *Awaken My Love!*, both by Childish Gambino.

Like many successful indies, Glassnote put an emphasize on touring and social media to create a fan base but recognized that even in the age of digital consumption, a hit single is essential for success. Glass told *Forbes*, "One thing streaming will teach you is that you need a hit to drive it. A lot of artists don't think about that, but it's hard to get your deep tracks heard without the hit. Without 'Born in the USA' and 'Dancing in the Dark,' a lot of those Bruce songs would have been lost. The hits led to album cuts and bootleg concerts, and eventually the live show."[20] Glass further explained how data revealing where acts were being streamed guided agents on where to book tour dates, and the use of social media for artists to stay in touch with their fan base kept fan interest high even when artists were off the road.

The Concord Music Group continued to expand since its 2004 success with Ray Charles led to a 2007 joint venture with Starbucks using its shops to augment traditional distribution outlets. Additional new albums by Paul McCartney, Joni Mitchell, James Taylor, and John Mellencamp soon followed. Subsequent acquisitions included the post-Beatles McCartney catalog and Rounder Records in 2010. Concord artists won eight Grammy Awards in 2013, the most for any label. In March 2013, MassMutual Financial Group, through its Wood Creek Capital Management, bought Concord. Wood Creek already owned the Bicycle Music Company and the back catalog of independent Wind-up Records.

In 2014 former WB Records chairman/CEO Tom Whalley joined Concord to take charge of new artist development. In 2015 the two companies were merged into Concord Bicycle Music, acquired the Welk Music Group including Americana/Folk labels Vanguard and Sugar Hill, bought the 1950s classic rock and R&B catalog of Vee-Jay Records, and took over the current Wind-up catalog. In 2018 they added the forty-six-year-old soundtrack and compilation specialist Varèse Sarabande and New York salsa pioneer Fania Records. The company as of 2019 had over twelve thousand albums, which have earned 388 RIAA gold or platinum certifications and accounted for 267 Grammy Awards.

In January 2017 BMG made its first foray back into Nashville since selling RCA to Sony. BMG Rights purchased the BBR Music Group (BBRMG) anchored by Broken Bow Records with platinum-selling Jason Aldean, Red Bow Records' Joe Nichols, Stoney Creek Records' Randy Houser, Wheelhouse Records' Trace Adkins, and music publishing division Magic Mustang Music. The majors bid against BMG to drive the final price to over $100 million, but the purchase gave BMG a ready-made Nashville presence while expanding international opportunities for the BBR roster. BMG CEO Hartwig Masuch told Billboard that BBRMG's "philosophy and commitment to its artists fit perfectly with the new BMG. The combination of BBR Music Group and BMG gives artists and songwriters in Nashville and beyond a new route to the worldwide market. We will be the alternative so many artists are looking for."[21]

Thirty Tigers was opened in 2002 by former Arista staffers David Macias and Deb Markland, who left the company in 2009, as a Nashville-based marketing, management, and distribution company steeped in Americana. Its website stated, "Thirty Tigers is a global music distribution, label services and management company based in Nashville, Tennessee with representation in Atlanta, New York, LA and London. Founded in 2001, Thirty Tigers has served as a label infrastructure for a vast client base including Jason Isbell and the 400 Unit, John Prine, Lucinda Williams, Patty Griffin, Trampled By Turtles, Sturgill Simpson, Metric, Lupe Fiasco, Alanis Morissette, The Smashing Pumpkins and many others. As part of our mission, Thirty Tigers strives to deliver Tenacity, Agility, Integrity, Love, and Service to all of our artists and clients."[22]

In 2013 Macias described the company zeitgeist to Jewly Hight of the *Nashville Scene*. "I'm definitely a proponent of the Duke Ellington school of music being in two camps: good and not. I'm interested in a lot of different types of music. As long as we can do a good job for the artist, and as long as we don't try to fool ourselves in thinking that we can bring utility to an artist when we really can't, then why shouldn't we try to bring them into the Thirty Tigers family? I mean, there's certain types of music that we understand better. We understand how the Americana world works. . . . But I don't want to limit us to any particular type of music."[23] In 2019 clients ranged from veterans Carlos Santana, Patti Griffin, Toby Keith, Lucinda Williams, Bruce Hornsby, and Delbert McClinton to current Americana mainstays Jason Isbell, Amanda Shires, the Milk Carton Kids, Trampled by Turtles, and Ryan Bingham.

Country Music: Still a World of Its Own

With its more than 2,100 radio stations in 2019, country music's record industry revenue was still dominated by radio play driving retail sales, which accounted for over 60 percent of the genre's revenue. This was diametrically opposite the industry as a whole with almost 80 percent of overall 2019 domestic revenue derived from streaming.

Taylor Swift had led country artists in utilizing social media to build her career into becoming the biggest-selling artist in the genre since Garth Brooks, but in October 2014 her fifth album *1989* switched her genre from country to pop. This move expanded her concert audiences from average receipts of $1.74 million per show to $2.94 million and increased her album sales from about 6 million units on the first four albums to over 10 million on *1989*. Other country artists followed Brooks's and Swift's platinum footsteps over the next several years. Florida Georgia Line, Jason Aldean, Kacey Musgraves, Thomas Rhett, Kane Brown, Sam Hunt, and Miranda Lambert also utilized social media to build their fan bases but remained in the country radio format. Nonetheless, the more ambitious and/or avant-garde did tracks with pop and rap collaborators to widen their audiences and increase their presence on the top streaming playlists that were not as genre specific as terrestrial radio.

Successful collaborations that found their way onto both pop streaming playlists and country airplay charts included Florida Georgia Line with Bebe Rexha on "Meant to Be" and with the Backstreet Boys on "God, Your Mama, and Me." "Say Something" and then "Tennessee Whiskey" both featured the pairing of Chris Stapleton and Justin Timberlake. "The Middle" combined Maren Morris with Zedd and Grey, and "The Champion" paired Carrie Underwood with Ludacris. The ubiquitous "Old Town Road" mixed Lil Nas X with Billy Ray Cyrus, Blake Shelton and Gwen Stefani duetted on "Nobody but You," Marshmello and Kane Brown did "One Thing Right," and Dan + Shay with Justin Bieber served up "10,000 Hours."

The three major labels maintained their stand-alone country divisions based in Nashville with autonomous promotion and marketing teams. The Capitol Nashville and UMG country divisions had been successfully merged under the direction of twelve-year Capitol incumbent Mike Dungan, making him the chairman/CEO of the newly created UMG Nashville.

In 2011 Sony chairman/CEO Joe Galante retired after thirty-eight years, spanning the Outlaw Movement of the mid-1970s, the BMG purchase of RCA, the Sony-BMG merger, and the Sony buyout of BMG. He was succeeded by Nashville Warner Chappell division GM Gary Overton, who was then replaced in 2015 by Randy Goodman. Goodman had worked for sixteen years under Galante at RCA before opening Lyric Street Records for Disney in 1997 where he guided the career of multi-platinum group Rascal Flatts for the label's thirteen-year existence.

Warner Nashville had been guided since 2009 by industry veteran and CEO/chairman John Esposito, who had worked in sales, marketing, and management at Warner, Island Def Jam, and PolyGram after a career in retail, which included COO for movies and music at the Wiz retail chain. Directly before moving to Nashville, he was president/CEO of WEA distribution, including oversight of worldwide digital distribution and the ADA independent distribution division.

Billboard's Top 50 Country artists for 2019 reflected the overall market share of the major label groups. In an analysis weighted by chart position, UMG-owned product led the field with 26.7 percent on eleven artists; followed by Sony with 18.8 percent on eight; and Warner at 15.5 percent also representing eight for a Big Three total of 60.6 percent on twenty-seven artists. Big Machine's 14.6 percent share on ten artists, however, was distributed by UMG not by its Caroline division. Curb's 4.6 percent covering two artists was distributed directly by WMG, while BMG Rights' Broken Bow labels' 11.4 percent on six artists was distributed through Warner's ADA. Thirty Tigers country wing Triple Tigers' 3.14 percent on two artists went through Sony-owned The Orchard, which had been merged with RED in 2017. That left Big Loud Records with three artists, who garnered a combined 5.7 percent market share as the only label to crack the 2019 Top 50 Country listing utilizing truly independent distribution.

The Big Three in 2019: A Rising Stream Lifts All Thrones

With the June 2015 launch of the Apple Music subscription service the streaming tsunami began in earnest. US streaming revenue more than quadrupled from $1.89 billion in 2014 to $8.88 billion in 2019. Conversely, combined 2019 physical and download sales were 40 percent of what they had been in 2014. Altogether annual RIAA revenue soared by over $4 billion between 2015 and 2019 to reach $11.13 billion, lifting the industry out of its six-year idle and prompting talk of prospective IPOs for both UMG and WMG.

In 2019 UMG once again led the major label groups in market share, extending its string to twenty-one years since the dawn of the Big Five era. Sony was second and WMG third in both domestic and international tallies. Global revenue reached an IFPI estimated total of $21.1 billion. Worldwide, streaming accounted for about 56 percent of the total. The higher percentage for streaming in the US marketplace reflected the greater penetration of smartphones and computers in the US while many developing territories still had large cassette markets plagued by high levels of tape piracy.

UMG held a 30 percent share of the global market at $6.4 billion in 2019. Sony had $4.17 billion for a 19.8 percent market share, while WMG was third at 18.2 percent on $3.92 billion. The remaining 32 percent of global revenue at approximately $7 billion went to a combination of independent labels and what was termed artist direct or DIY (for do-it-yourself) product.

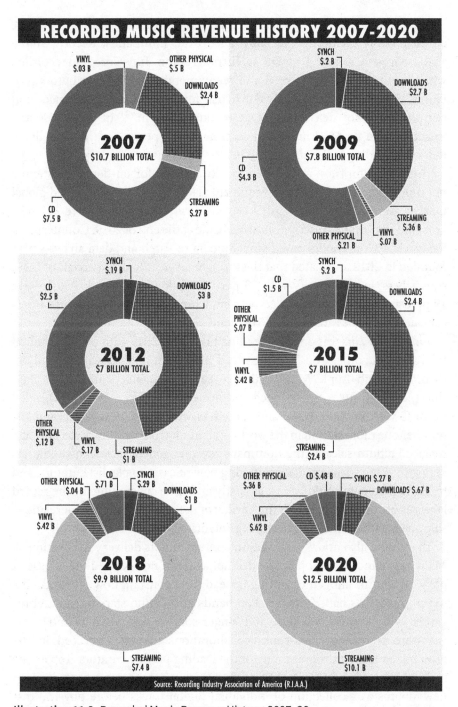

Illustration 11.2 Recorded Music Revenue History, 2007–20

These self-released projects collected royalties through online administrators including CD Baby, DistroKid, EmuBands, Record Union, Vydia, iGroove, Amuse, LANDR, ONErpm, Proton, TuneCore, and recordJet, which were Spotify's "preferred and recommended" artist distributors providing "instant access to Spotify For Artists for all their users [and] meet[ing] our standards for delivering music to our platform."[24] In 2019 DIY artists accounted for $873 million in revenue for 4.1 percent of the total global market according to the annual MiDiA Research market analysis.

This transition from acquisition to subscription for on-demand listening not only triggered a boost in revenue but also created a homogenized global market. According to IFPI's 2019 *Global Music Report* there were 341 million paid streaming subscriptions worldwide at the end of 2019. Counterpoint Research, a Hong Kong–based global media research and data analysis firm founded in 2012, estimated that the top-five services had 86 percent of these subscribers, led by Spotify with 35 percent, followed by Apple Music with 19 percent, Amazon Music at 15 percent, China's Tencent Music had 11 percent, and YouTube Music was at 6 percent.

Today's Top Hits was Spotify's leading playlist in 2019 with over 25 million followers. The other Top 20 lists ranged from 15 million down to 5 million each. Although Apple Music didn't reveal its audience statistics, its flagship playlist, *Beats 1*, was curated and hosted live by former radio D.J.s led by BBC veteran Zane Lowe and touted as worldwide, always on, and the number one radio station in the world. Accumulated single-track streams had replaced album sales as the dominant revenue generator. Meanwhile marketing through social media, promoting new releases to playlist curators, and tracking metadata could be just as costly and time consuming for the record labels as business had been in the heyday of the records-radio-retail relationship, even without the manufacturing and distribution costs.

There were also notable changes in content and its delivery to consumers. Many rap, dance, and pop artists deemphasized if not skipped the release of physical albums altogether, opting instead for a constant flow of tracks. The top pop playlists had Korean K-Pop bands and Latino stars in rotation together with rappers, rockers, and singer-songwriters. Even country artists were recording cross-genre collaborations to better succeed in the now-mixed format programming of the leading playlist curators. Top artists including Beyoncé, Jay Z, Drake, and Taylor Swift began to unexpectedly drop new albums as a collection of individual digital tracks before physical distribution to create demand for both album and concert ticket sales in what were termed guerrilla marketing campaigns. The simultaneous availability of fifteen to twenty different new tracks by a top artist was akin to shipping a million units in the CD era, under the supposition that concentrated listening in the new streaming paradigm would replicate the economic benefit of album sell-through at retail.

The Big Three in 2019: UMG Still in the Lead

In 2019 UMG's $6.1 billion in global revenue led the Big Three. Streaming accounted for 59 percent of that total at $3.6 billion, reflecting a lower share of revenue emanating from streaming in many territories outside of the US. UMG's physical sales brought in $1.1 billion for 18 percent of its revenue, downloads garnered $464 million for 7.6 percent, and licensing contributed $943 million for 15.4 percent, including revenue generated by its share of artist income under the 360° clause provisions of their recording agreements (more on 360° deals in chapter 14). UMG also led in the rate of growth with 2019 revenue increased 16.7 percent over 2018, compared to 11.4 percent for the industry as a whole.

Interscope's John Janick contributed about a third of UMG's chart success led by Billie Eilish, Lady Gaga, DaBaby, Maroon 5, and Imagine Dragons. Next up was Republic, still headed by brothers Monte and Avery Lipman and featuring Ariana Grande, Post Malone, the Jonas Brothers, and Taylor Swift. Just behind Republic was Steve Barnett at the Capitol Music Group, including the Caroline-distributed indie labels. Topping Capitol's roster were Lewis Capaldi, Halsey, Marshmello with Bastille, Sam Smith, Maggie Rogers, and Trippie Redd. Def Jam was in a rebuilding mode under Paul Rosenberg but still had mainstays Kanye West, Justin Bieber, and Rihanna. Island under Darcus Beese was also rebuilding, led by the rising Shawn Mendes.

Billboard's Power 100 listing for 2019 named Lucian Grainge as its executive of the decade stating that he "may well be the most powerful person in the music business, but we're honoring him for the role he played in helping the entire recorded music sector rebound to over $19 billion in sales in 2018."[25] HitsDailyDouble.com, the news service established in 2000 by prominent tip sheet *Hits Magazine*, launched in 1986, also praised Grainge's accomplishments in its "Rumor Mill" column. "He set the template for the entire industry amid the transition to digital and forged a global model for acquiring talent and bringing it to the marketplace via streaming. . . . UMG had four of the year's Top 5 albums . . . as well as seven of the Top 10 songs."[26]

The Big Three in 2019: The One Sony Still a Strong Second

Rob Stringer had big shoes to fill in replacing Doug Morris in 2017, but by July 2019 he had solidified his position sufficiently to be named chairman of the Sony Music Group, the new corporate identity for the combined record and publishing divisions. This integration, also referred to as the One Sony, had not been possible on a corporate basis until the buy-out of the Jackson estate interest in the Sony/ATV publishing joint venture (see chapter 13).

Sony's worldwide record revenue in 2019 reached $4.17 billion, a $255 million or 6.5 percent increase over 2018. Streaming accounted for 57.6 percent at $2.4 billion, physical sales were $803 million for 33.5 percent, downloads took in $321 million for 13.4 percent, with another $645 million in other revenue including licensing fees and 360° deal-related income. The Ron Perry–led Columbia was responsible for 7.3 percent out of Sony's 25.6 percent market share. His street-honed instincts led him to pick up Lil Nas X's country rap "Old Town Road" that had exploded on TikTok, and then to add country icon Billy Ray Cyrus to the track and video. "Old Town Road" spent a record-setting nineteen weeks at number one on the *Billboard* Hot 100 and was the most-streamed track in 2019, generating 2.35 billion streams. Coincidentally, Cyrus already had the record for longest run on the Billboard album chart at seventeen weeks for his *Some Gave All* album that contained his "Achy Breaky Heart" mega-hit. Lil Nas X won two Grammy awards out of six nominations and Perry was awarded with the inaugural *Billboard* Breakthrough Award.

The Peter Edge–led RCA contributed 5.3 percent of the Sony market share led by Khaled, Chris Brown, Pentatonix, P!nk, Miley Cyrus, and Justin Timberlake. Sylvia Rhone more than ably filled L.A. Reid's shoes at Los Angeles–based Epic, adding another 2.7 percent market share. She told *Billboard* that Epic artists "now occupy some very influential seats at the hip hop table. . . . We've empowered visionaries who continue to break new ground,"[27] including Travis Scott, DJ Khaled, Future, and 21 Savage. On the pop side, Rhone had Camila Cabello break through to stardom and Mariah Carey made a holiday comeback as "All I Want for Christmas Is You" reached number one on the *Billboard* Hot 100 twenty-five years after its initial release.

The Big Three in 2019: WMG-WEA Redux?

Stephen Cooper's choice of Max Lousada appeared prescient as his reworking of the executive team back into three label groups with multiple A&R staffs proved profitable as well as reminiscent of the Steve Ross pre–Time Warner era. WMG's fiscal 2019 ending in September was 11.7 percent over 2018, reaching $3.84 billion with 61 percent in the all-important Digital Revenue line item. Although still in third place in the Big Three, WMG had closed the revenue gap on Sony to just $260 million. Cooper's fiscal leadership netted a $258 million profit, improving Operating Income before Depreciation and Amortization (OIBDA) by 30 percent. Cooper told *Billboard*, "Our success comes from our belief in our artists, our songwriters and each other."[28] Lousada added, "To ignite passion from fans and then sustain that heat around the world requires local love and global collaboration. Our biggest successes, in any genre, come down to teamwork."[29]

Atlantic's Craig Kallman and Julie Greenwald received *Billboard*'s Clive Davis Visionary Award after leading all labels in current market share for the third straight year with 12.12 percent of the *Billboard* Top 200 albums. New artists Lizzo and A Boogie Wit da Hoodie each topped 1 million album equivalent units with Lizzo winning three Grammy Awards out of her eight nominations. In its first full year of independent operation out from under the Atlantic umbrella, Elektra, led by co-presidents Mike Easterlin and Gregg Nadel, scored with Tones and I, Panic! at the Disco, and Brandi Carlile.

Streaming into the Future

By 2007 the record industry had already started the transition to a digital marketplace, but in no way could the powers that be have anticipated what the consumption of music would look like in 2019 and beyond. Streaming had replaced acquisition with immediate and portable access through a verbal command to a virtual assistant interface on a smartphone. For a nominal monthly fee, consumers could hear almost any track ever recorded at any time in any location.

For the rightsholders, each track streamed by each consumer, if properly registered and tabulated, generated revenue for each artist, songwriter, record label, and publisher associated with that track just as each sale of each record had done. The most advanced tracking programs could now reduce royalty accounting from multiple calendar quarters to a matter of days, or in some instances, real-time delivery. For the record labels, the importance of retail bin placement and radio airplay had been replaced by the mining, identification, analysis, and exploitation of the gigabytes of information available from the streaming services.

In January 2019, director of the music business program at NYU Steinhardt School of Culture, Education, and Human Development, podcast host, and Musonomics founder Larry Miller published his study titled *Same Heart. New Beat. How Record Labels Amplify Talent in the Modern Music Marketplace.* After conducting interviews with over fifty top record executives, Miller summarized the current stream-dominated record business in stating that, "Labels are transitioning from B2B businesses to direct-to-consumer businesses focused on building direct relationships with fans."[30] Despite this switch in process, the weekly charts still served as the barometer of music consumption. The 2019 year-end *Billboard Top 100 Artists* list was still dominated by the major label groups. UMG labels had 54 artists on the chart, WMG followed with 25, and Sony contributed 17. The other four artists were with independent distributors.

Miller further noted, "On their own, artists and managers may find it nearly impossible to keep up with the crushing demand of the modern music marketplace, but record labels are purpose built for the current environment. In addition, the labels' promotional machines are equipped to push out a steady flow of singles, EPs, and albums and videos for all screen sizes and maximize the impact of each, while their social media teams enable artists to learn more about their fans while interacting directly with them."[31]

Consistent with Miller's observations, the industry was projected by most financial prognosticators to be on a path to return to and surpass the economic apex of the CD era, but despite the majors' clear-cut financial advantage, the indie share of 2019 global revenue grew to 40 percent. While all had been liberated to varying degrees from the cost of manufacturing and distribution, on their share of revenue now provided by streaming independents had especially benefited from equal access to on-demand listening and placement on consumer-generated playlists. Under the pre-streaming brick-and-mortar paradigm, this access would not have been as readily attainable. The major labels, however, could still create more revenue on individual projects by spending more money and mustering more resources in doing so.

While much had changed, much had also remained the same.

According to Nielsen's 2019 *Year-End Report*, US streaming consumption was divided at 36 percent for current product to 64 percent for catalog, which was still defined as tracks released more than eighteen months ago. In the brick-and-mortar era, sales revenue usually skewed more in favor of current releases. Both majors and independents benefited from this expanded access to catalog, but the majors still dominated in revenue derived from current releases. Regardless of the relative market shares, 2019 industry revenue was up about 57 percent over 2017. The digital waves of the streaming tsunami had indeed lifted all those still afloat.

12

Records, Radio, Retail, Streaming, and the Charts

Recession Rocks Record Sales

Over the decade prior to 2007, the retail marketplace had been affected by several interrelated trends that would intensify going forward. Underlying all was the shift in listening preference by young consumers for single tracks by different artists sequenced together rather than a single-artist album in its entirety. Increasing album prices coupled with diminished availability of singles at retail prompted these consumers to find their music elsewhere. As evidenced by the annual RIAA Consumer Profile reports, spending on records by the fourteen-to-eighteen age group decreased as the introduction of dual cassette decks and then the CD-R facilitated home duplication. Then the debut of the MP3 and launch of Napster provided a free and far more accessible supply of music that dwarfed anything retail outlets or physical copying could offer.

In 2007 over 25 percent of the 503 million physical album sales reported by the RIAA came through mail order whether from record club, infomercial, or e-tailer. Another 49.8 million albums were bought as digital downloads. There were also 819.4 million legally downloaded single tracks. Together these downloads accounted for 23.1 percent of all record purchases. Consumers also spent another $1.06 billion on telephone ringtones culled from single-record tracks, with another $234 million coming from streaming services.

Despite the increase in revenue from digital sources, overall revenue from recorded music had declined 27.3 percent from its 1999 peak to the 2007 total of $10.65 billion. Not only had the market contracted as a whole, but the brick-and-mortar share dropped from 96 percent to 75 percent. Furthermore, the new digital income streams were largely outside the purview of the traditional record-retail relationship. Wholesalers and store chains tried to capture part of the growing online market, but few had the needed expertise or resources.

Signs of what became the Great Recession began in December 2007. The crisis imploded in October 2008, and ran through June 2009 with a recovery

American Popular Music and Its Business in the Digital Age. Rick Sanjek, Oxford University Press. © Frederick Sanjek 2024.
DOI: 10.1093/oso/9780190653828.003.0012

TOP SELLING SOUNDSCAN ARTISTS & ALBUMS 2000-2009

R.I.A.A. revenue had dropped from 2000's $14.3 billion to $7.8 billion in 2009 as album sales fell from over a billion units to under 360 million. Digital tracks had replaced retail albums for acquisition of new music. The industry needed to find a way to monetize digital consumption to revitalize its revenue.

	TOP ARTISTS	TOTAL ALBUMS		TOP ALBUMS	TOTAL UNITS
1	Eminem	32.2 m	1	The Beatles / 1	11.5 m
2	The Beatles	30.2 m	2	'N Sync / No Strings Attached	11.1 m
3	Tim McGraw	24.8 m	3	Norah Jones / Come Away With Me	10.6 m
4	Toby Keith	24.5 m	4	Eminem / The Marshall Mathers LP	10.2 m
5	Britney Spears	23.0 m	5	Eminem / The Eminem Show	9.8 m
6	Kenny Chesney	22.0 m	6	Usher / Confessions	9.7 m
7	Linkin Park	21.4 m	7	Linkin Park / Hybrid Theory	9.7 m
8	Nelly	21.2 m	8	Creed / Human Clay	9.5 m
9	Creed	20.6 m	9	Britney Spears / Oops...I Did it Again	9.2 m
10	Jay-Z	20.4 m	10	Nelly / Country Grammar	8.5 m
11	Nickelback	19.8 m	11	50 Cent / Get Rich or Die Trying	7.9 m
12	Rascal Flatts	19.4 m	12	Soundtrack / O Brother Where Art Thou	7.5 m
13	Josh Groban	19.3 m	13	Evanescence / Fallen	7.3 m
14	Alan Jackson	18.9 m	14	Nickelback / All The Right Reasons	7.3 m
15	'N Sync	18.3 m	15	Santana / Supernatural	7.0 m
16	Dixie Chicks	18.2 m	16	Enya / A Day Without Rain	6.9 m
17	Johnny Cash	18.1 m	17	Carrie Underwood / Some Hearts	6.9 m
18	Kid Rock	17.6 m	18	Shaggy / Hot Shot	6.8 m
19	Metallica	17.4 m	19	Avail Lavigne / Let Go	6.7 m
20	Celine Dion	17.4 m	20	Limp Bizkit / Chocolate Starfish and the Hot Dog Flavored Water	6.7 m
21	George Strait	17.3 m	21	Nelly / Nellyville	6.5 m
22	Michael Jackson	17.3 m	22	Creed / Weathered	6.4 m
23	Norah Jones	17.1 m	23	Alicia Keys / Songs In A Minor	6.2 m
24	U2	16.8 m	24	Kelly Clarkson / Breakaway	6.1 m
25	Elvis Presley	16.5 m	25	Tim Mc Graw / Greatest Hits	6.0 m

TOP ARTISTS OF THE DECADE — **TOP ALBUMS OF THE DECADE**

Source: *Billboard* / R.I.A.A.

Illustration 12.1 Top 25 *Billboard* Hot 100 Artists & Top Pop Albums of the 2000s

that extended until the mid-2010s. Estimates of the decline in the average US household net worth ran between 17.3 percent and 24.4 percent. RIAA-reported revenue value registered at $7.01 billion for 2010, down 34.1 percent from 2007 and less than half of the peak revenue years of 1999–2000. Revenue value continued to hover around the $7 billion mark through 2015.

By 2012 CD sales had plummeted to $2.49 billion, just 18.8 percent of the CD's peak years. Cassette sales were no longer tracked by the RIAA. DVD-A and SACD combined for just $1.5 million in 2012 sales revenue. Music videos generated only $116 million, down from a high of $607 million in 2004. On a positive note, vinyl had made a comeback from a low of $26 million in 2006 to $165 million in 2012, a trend that would continue throughout the decade.

Meanwhile ringtones lost their luster as revenue tumbled from $1.06 billion in 2007 to $167 million in 2012. Subscription streaming remained static between 2007 and 2011, starting at $234 million before falling to $206 million and then recovering to $248 million. Ad-supported Streaming was introduced as a separate RIAA line item in 2011 at $114 million, driven by the US launch of the Spotify freemium tier. The 2012 debut of the Spotify premium service bumped paid subscription to $400 million for the year. Digital downloads including albums, singles, and videos grew from $1.34 billion in 2007 to $2.85 billion in 2012. Overall, the market was stabilized by growing digital consumption, but recovery was not yet on the horizon.

Billboard Rides the Rising Tide—Part 1: Digital Sales Enter the Charts

Subscriptions and advertising from the music business supplied the bulk of *Billboard*'s income. Maintaining as much of that revenue base as possible made it imperative that *Billboard*'s awareness of and adaptation to consumer listening trends and buying habits were now as crucial to its future as its news reporting. Shortly after the iTunes launch in July 2003, SoundScan added the measurement of digital sales data to its sales and airplay algorithm. In response to over 200 million digital tracks sold in 2004, *Billboard* introduced the Hot Digital Songs chart in 2005, later abridging it to just Digital Songs. Prior to this chart, tracks sold as downloads that did not have radio airplay or retail sales were not eligible for the Hot 100, but now Hot Digital Songs data would be included in formulating the Hot 100.

At the beginning of 2007, *Billboard*'s Dutch corporate parent Verenigde Nederlandse Uitgeverijen (VNU), which had acquired the trade magazine as part of the $220 million purchase of the BPI Communications media group, renamed itself The Nielsen Company. VNU had purchased the eighty-four-year-old Nielsen Media Research for $2.5 billion in 1999. Best known for its television ratings service, Nielsen was credited with creating the concept of market share and how to measure it through consumer impressions. The acquisition of BPI's SoundScan and BDS technology put Nielsen in a position to compete with Arbitron, the dominant market share barometer for the radio industry.

In July 2007, in anticipation of the further expansion of digital consumption of music, *Billboard* added subscription streaming as a component of the Hot 100 chart starting with information from the Yahoo! and AOL platforms. Director of charts Geoff Mayfield wrote, "Initially, *Billboard* expects those plays to account for about 5% of the chart's total points. . . . Meanwhile, this first recalibration since digital sales moved into the chart two years ago makes an adjustment to account for the vigorous growth that digital distribution has experienced in that span."[1]

Billboard, however, also faced the ramifications of the economic downturn as its advertising and subscription revenue fell in step with the decline in the revenue and marketing budgets of the labels. In March 2008 Nielsen senior VP Howard Appelbaum added *Billboard* president to his portfolio, joining editorial director Bill Werde, who had been hired away from *Rolling Stone* in 2005. Their mission was to further transform the bible of the music business into a contemporary blend of print and digital platforms, providing information in as close to a real-time availability as possible. They were also charged with expanding revenue by extending their client base to the much larger universe of music-loving, web-surfing consumers, as well as pursuit of co-branding opportunities.

Billboard's entry into the digital age had begun a decade earlier with the registration of the domain name billboard.com in November 1996, and the launch of the daily "Billboard Bulletin" email newsletter in February 1997. As the live performance sector grew from the late 1990s onward, *Billboard* increased touring coverage with its weekly BoxOffice reports and year-end touring charts and summaries compiled by Ray Waddell, editor of its 111-year-old sister publication *Amusement Business* (*AB*). When *AB* was shuttered in 2006, the nineteen-year holdover Waddell and his coverage shifted full time to *Billboard*.

In late June 2009, the revamped billboard.com emerged as a colorful interactive portal incorporating social media to exploit the vast reserve of *Billboard*'s content. Charts, tour dates, artists' pages, current chart songs available for both download and streaming, and individual playlist curation were comingled in a digital potpourri of the latest internet technology. Appelbaum enthusiastically effused, "Billboard.com delivers a truly exciting and immersive experience for both passionate and casual music fans. . . . We're going to fundamentally connect an advertiser's message with the consumers they're ultimately trying to reach."[2] Initial sponsors included Visa, SiriusXM, Sprint, and AT&T, as well as the record companies.

Billboard Rides the Rising Tide—Part 2: A Change in Ownership

In December 2009 e5 Media Holdings was formed by investment firms Pluribus Capital Management and Guggenheim Partners as the vehicle to buy *Billboard* from Nielsen. Also included in the purchase were *The Hollywood Reporter* (*THR*), *Mediaweek*, *Adweek*, and *Brandweek*, their associated trade shows, and the Clio Awards. The following year e5 was renamed Prometheus Global Media after Guggenheim bought out Pluribus. Nielsen retained SoundScan and BDS, and in 2015 acquired Arbitron to further solidify its position atop the media market share tracking sector.

In March 2010 *Conde Nast* editor Lisa Ryan Howard was hired as *Billboard*'s publisher. Later that month at the inaugural National Magazine Awards for Digital Media, billboard.com won the award for best design ahead of the websites for *New York Magazine*, *Life*, *National Geographic*, and *The Daily Beast*. There were tangible rewards as well. Google Analytics reported that *Billboard*'s year-over-year gains in March were 128 percent in monthly page views, 51 percent for unique visitors, and a 65 percent increase in average time spent. The *Billboard* team also transformed the print edition from a news-forward weekly summary to a feature- and analysis-driven gazette. Digital printing technology abetted the transition with more color photos, advanced graphics, feature sections, and new chart formats. Many charts other than the Billboard 200 albums and Hot 100 singles were truncated with readers directed to the website for the full listing. Some genre-specific charts would appear regularly online but with limited appearance in the print edition.

These charts and their underlying information, however, remained the essential link to and between *Billboard*'s record, radio, and retail subscription clients. Methodology was adjusted periodically to reflect the transition from a rapidly crumbling brick-and-mortar foundation into a more interactive, tech-driven digital future. The fifty-track Dance/Electronic Digital Songs chart was added in April 2010. In December 2010, the Billboard Social 50 was introduced to rank artists' social networking activity tabulated by measuring friends, fans, followers, likes, views, plays, and streams on social networks including YouTube, Vevo, Facebook, Twitter, Myspace, and iLike. Rihanna topped the first chart. Data was compiled by the New York–based music analytics firm Next Big Sound, which formed in 2008 as an outgrowth of a student research project at Northwestern University. In November 2012 SoundCloud and Instagram were added as chart contributors, followed by Vine and Tumblr in June 2015.

In July 2011 Howard brought in former recording artist Tommy Page as associate publisher. After scoring a number one *Billboard* single in 1990 with "I'll Be Your Everything" on Sire Records, Page spent four years at Warner Bros. records in promotion and A&R before getting a marketing degree from the NYU Stern School of Business. In March 2012 Howard moved on to *The New York Times* and Page stepped into the publisher post. Together Page and Werde further enhanced *Billboard*'s role as a multimedia content provider with another design makeover while maintaining its central position in the hit-driven relationship between records, radio, and retail.

Prince graced the cover of the January 26, 2013, issue accompanied by an interview conducted by senior correspondent Gail Mitchell. The new design employed more artistic photography, pithier headlines, and updated computerized graphics. Features dominated news with a more pronounced effort to direct subscribers to billboard.com. This issue also introduced the Dance/Electronic Songs chart, which listed the fifty most popular singles and tracks compiled from club play, singles sales, radio airplay, digital downloads, and online streaming. Lady Gaga's "Bad Romance" was its first chart topper.

In April 2013, Page himself moved on to VP of music partnerships at Pandora before finishing his tragically shortened career as senior VP of brand marketing for Cumulus. Werde recalled their initial encounter in a remembrance after Page's passing in 2017. "Lisa hired this crazily high energy guy I had never met before to drive advertising sales and partnerships for the magazine. And when Lisa eventually moved on, Tommy took over as publisher of Billboard and became my partner in crime. . . . Anyone who knew him or worked with him will tell you that if Tommy Page lacked for anything, it wasn't enthusiasm for the task at hand."[3]

Despite the valiant efforts of the *Billboard* team, apparently their results fell short of Guggenheim's expectations, leading to another management change in January 2014. Werde was shuffled out to a consulting role. He resurfaced in August 2017 as the director of the Bandier Program for Music Business and the Entertainment Industries at the S. I. Newhouse School of Public

Communications at Syracuse University. Namesake Martin Bandier had led the funding initiative for the program that opened in 2006.

Guggenheim split Prometheus into two divisions with John Amato, former head of *Backstage* magazine, running The Hollywood Reporter-Billboard Media Group. The other magazines together with the Clio Awards and *Film Expo* were placed in the separate *Adweek* Media Group. *THR*'s Janice Min added *Billboard* editorial responsibilities to her duties. *The Wrap*'s Sharon Waxman opined that Guggenheim envisioned that the new team might parley their media holdings into an entertainment news cable channel.

Billboard Rides the Rising Tide—Part 3: The Battle to Stay Current

In December 2015, Guggenheim agreed to sell the Media Group to board member Todd Boehly, who had advocated for the acquisition of both the magazines and the dick clark company (dcc). He also owned a share of the Los Angeles Dodgers. Boehly formed Eldridge Industries for the transaction and withdrew from an active role at Guggenheim. Min was shifted to a consultant role in March 2017 and was replaced at *Billboard* in September 2017 by thirty-year-old *Complex Media* blogger Ross Scarano.

In February 2018 Boehly shifted gears. With no takers for Eldridge's only profitable property dcc at the asking price of $1 billion, Boehly formed Valence Media to combine Eldridge with TV/film producer Media Rights Capital (MRC), another of his investments whose major asset was the *House of Cards* Netflix series. Boehly's MRC partners Modi Wiczyk and Asif Satchu were tapped to lead Valence and told *Variety*, "What we have as a foundation from day one is expertise and relationships across film, scripted TV, live events and digital media. That's a great base to build from."[4]

Combining the *House of Cards* and other MRC assets; the ongoing dcc productions *Dick Clark's New Year's Rockin' Eve*, the Golden Globe Awards, the American Music Awards, and the Academy of Country Music Awards; Clark's historic catalog of programming; and Media Group's magazine and trade show assets, Valence placed its value at $3 billion to serve as the anchor for additional acquisitions and in-house program development utilizing cross-platform marketing opportunities to scale ad buys across multiple properties. Wiczyk emphasized that *Billboard* and *THR* editorial independence would be maintained. "The integrity of editorial is of paramount importance and must be protected assiduously."[5]

In July 2018 *Billboard*'s Amato was dismissed amid accusations of suppressing coverage of the sexual abuse charges against Republic Records VP Charlie Walk. Also a judge on the Fox reality series *The Four: Battle for Stardom*, Walk left both positions in early February. Maxwell Tani of *The Daily Beast* reported on investigations into Amato's editorial bias in his friend Walk's favor putting his conduct under scrutiny as well. Reports circulated about a buyout for Amato and more widespread intra-company cultural problems. *The New York Times* published a report of a staff luncheon where "managers gave a PowerPoint presentation about corporate values, detailed the results of an employee survey and promised to improve the office culture. . . . The more than 100 employees gathered—from Billboard and sister publications like Spin and The Hollywood Reporter—asked pointed questions about executives' behavior and women's role at the company, and many walked away with a guarded sense of relief, according to four people who were at the meeting."[6]

MRC brought in Deanna Brown as managing director of the Media Group in August 2018 and promoted her to president in April 2019. Brown's thirty-year career included executive stints in both traditional and new media. Brown elevated *Billboard* news editor Hannah Karp to editorial director in September 2018. Before joining *Billboard* in April 2017 Karp led the music industry coverage at the *Wall Street Journal*. Brown commented, "Promoted from within, she both knows and is known to the industry, while her editorial vision aligns with the bigger business vision across platforms, genres and territory lines as well as print, digital and television live events and conferences. Also worth noting, Hannah is the first woman in the history of the publication to assume this role."[7]

Despite the economic turmoil and executive turnover, the *Billboard* brand remained the gold if not platinum standard for both industry news coverage and chart credibility. According to website activity tracking service ComScore, billboard.com was averaging 15.3 million visitors a month over the first half of 2018, more than the *Rolling Stone* site. Whatever news coverage that had been absent from or truncated in the print edition was available on a daily basis through the "Billboard Bulletin" or on billboard.com. *Billboard*'s 2018 media kit listed 20,568 print subscriptions with more than 18 million unique website visitors, 11.6 million unique mobile visitors, and more than 21 million social media followers for 2017. Subscriptions were about half of the more than forty thousand *Billboard* had in the 1990s, but the music business it covered had declined as well. And like that industry, potential for revenue growth was in the monetization of content in the digital domain.

From Bricks to Clicks: The Digital Metastasis at Retail

In 2007 the traditional brick-and-mortar retail business was still selling physical products, although declining sales had led to fewer outlets. The RIAA Consumer Profile indicated that retail shoppers were looking for better prices. 40.5% preferred the loss leader offerings at mass merchandisers, while only 6.2% still preferred locally owned independent stores.

According to an analysis by *Billboard*'s Ed Christman, 2007's top twenty retail and e-tail sales outlets combined for about 90 percent of all sales. The top five accounted for 58.4 percent and would increase that share to 65.8 percent in 2008. Three of the 2007 top five were mass merchandisers with Walmart in first place at 16.7 percent, consumer electronics giant Best Buy was third with 12 percent, and fellow big-box chain Target at fourth with 8.94 percent. Digital downloader iTunes was in second place with 12.7 percent but destined to replace Walmart in the lead in 2008 by growing to 17.8 percent. At fifth with 8.07 percent was one-stop Alliance, which combined retail racking at Kmart and Circuit City with its internet fulfillment division.

At the beginning of 2008, the bottom half of the top ten handled another 15.6 percent of the market. In sixth was online mass merchandiser Amazon with its blend of mail fulfillment and downloads. Book chain Borders was at seventh having just left its seven-year association with Amazon to open its own webstore. Record store chain Trans World was in eighth, handling physical units, downloads, and ringtones. Wireless carrier Verizon was ninth, selling ringtones and downloads. Rack jobber Handleman came in tenth, servicing the record bins at Best Buy, Kmart, and about 25 percent of the Walmart accounts. The other major rack jobber, Anderson Merchandisers, supplied the rest of the Walmart stores, its only music account but also a client for Anderson's books and videos.

The retailers rated eleventh through twentieth handled just 8.1 percent of total revenue, ranging from Baker & Taylor's 1.18 percent to a tie between T-Mobile and eMusic at .58 percent each. The outlets in between were a further reflection of changing music consumption habits. Baker & Taylor and Super D were traditional one-stops coupled with internet fulfillment divisions. Hastings and Virgin were chains that had expanded their product lines to DVDs, video games, and other music-related merchandise. RealNetworks' retooled Rhapsody, Roxio's reincarnation of Napster, and the download/streaming hybrid eMusic were all subscription services, while Sprint, AT&T, and T-Mobile were wireless carriers selling ringtones and downloads.

At the end of the first quarter of 2008, financial institutions were starting to feel the stress of a weakening economy. Combined with the now-seven-year trend in declining CD sales and their failure to capture a meaningful share of the new digital market, credit for traditional retailers tightened drastically. Handleman was the first to feel the crunch. The seventy-four-year-old rack jobber did over a billion dollars in 2007 billing, including its Crave videogame wholesaler, which accounted for 21.6 percent of the total intake. Like most of the publicly traded music distributors, Handleman operated on a re-volving credit basis with its inventory and receivables serving as collateral. Its $140 million loan agreement with main creditor Silver Point Finance neces-sitated the rack jobber to have $117.9 million in secured assets on hand as of January 31, 2008, but they were $8 million short.

Silver Point granted a stay until May 31, hoping to avoid default and liqui-dation. Handleman's problems were magnified by a $31.2 million loss for the nine-month period ending January 31, stemming from the high percentage of returns caused by soft sales in 4Q 2007. By March 31, its market capitalization had fallen to less than $5 million, its stock price was down to $.24 from a fifty-two-week high of $7.76, and its stock was subsequently delisted. Handleman sold its Walmart accounts and Canadian operation to Anderson. Dissolution was approved by shareholders in October. In addition to the psychological effect on the confidence of the retail sector, the Handleman closing also took a toll on the industry workforce. Over two thousand Handleman employees were let go, as well as the label and distributor staffers who serviced the rack jobber's account.

The spring 2008 credit crunch was followed by the fall market crisis. Electronics superstore Circuit City was the next casualty as it filed for Chapter 11 bankruptcy protection in November. The final numbers on fall sales led creditors to push the seven hundred-plus store chain into Chapter 7 and forced liquidation in February 2009. Although not a top-20 retail outlet for music product, its unsold inventory reintroduced top-line product as returns or discounted cutouts undermining prices throughout the entire supply chain.

The credit retrenchment also affected Borders Books, for which music was also a small share of total business, but still 3.2 percent of total CD sales in 2007 accounting for about $250 million in retail value. With its overall busi-ness in decline, Borders started a fruitless search for a buyer in 2008. After three years of growing losses and constant changes in its executive team, Borders filed for Chapter 11 protection in February 2011. An analysis by Josh Sanburn in *Time* magazine concluded that the 659-store chain had been severely overleveraged due to a rash of poor business decisions including excessive expansion just prior to the unexpected downturn; late entry into the e-book and mail fulfillment business after initially relegating them to Amazon; and overcommitment to shelf space for CDs just as the record business was turning over to digital sales. Creditors rejected an offer from Direct Brands, the Najafi Group company that had bought BMG Direct. In July 2012 Borders filed for Chapter 7 and went into liquidation.

Records and Radio Recover as Retail Decline Deepens

By the end of 2012, the recession had turned to recovery, but its aftermath had deeply affected the record industry with consolidation, budget trimming, and changes in consumer habits. RIAA-reported revenue was still around $7 billion, just under 50 percent of the peak year levels, and would stay there for the next three years. Revenue components, however, had shifted with 39.5 percent of 2012 revenue from physical sales, 43.1 percent from download sales, and 2.7 percent from sync license fees. The remaining 14.8 percent came from streaming sources including satellite radio, internet radio, and subscriptions, collectively surpassing $1 billion for the first time. On-demand access looked more and more like the future of music consumption. The mobile phone had become the leading portable playing device whether through earbuds, headsets, car speakers, or home audio systems, either plugged in or through a Bluetooth connection. Over 1.9 billion smartphones had been sold worldwide since its introduction in mid-decade, with over 680 million of them in 2012. Another 9.8 billion were sold from 2013 through 2019.

Over the same time the radio industry had recovered from its recession-induced 26 percent drop in revenue to settle around $17.5 billion from 2010 through to 2015, but still 18.6 percent below its all-time high in 2006. Unlike the record industry whose income came from selling direct to consumers, radio's revenue came from peddling time spots and sponsorships to third-party advertisers who wanted to market their products to radio's listeners. The value of spot ads was in direct proportion to audience size. If listeners switched to streaming for music, then radio's revenue dropped proportionally, whereas the record industry's income source just shifted along with its consumers as they moved from purchase to streaming. Radio's future revenue growth, or even just maintenance, was now threatened by these new digital sources.

Terrestrial radio, however, still had the advantage of being free to the consumer, longtime brand familiarity in local markets, and more than 90 percent market penetration in households and automobiles. To compete with the digital-only interlopers, the three largest station ownership groups—CBS, Cumulus, and Clear Channel's newly rebranded iHeartMedia—extended consumer access beyond computers to mobile phones with channel menus containing digital feeds of their larger stations conveying local news, weather, and advertising, along with content of national interest. This array of multiple audio channels was similar to and competitive with satellite radio but over the phone through a variety of platforms, with some including spot advertising.

The traditional retail sector, however, was the real casualty of digital disruption. In 2012 mass merchandisers accounted for almost 60 percent of declining brick-and-mortar sales, which were only 34.7 percent of what they had been in 2007. They still viewed music as a loss leader to lure consumers to stores to buy higher-priced items, but if the margins or the volume got too low, or if shelf space turned over too slowly, CDs could easily be replaced by more profitable items. These big-box stores were primarily concerned about the growing threat to their overall business by e-commerce discounters like Amazon.com.

Record store chains accounted for about 30 percent of the 2012 market for CDs and had diversified to include apparel, memorabilia, DVDs, games, and other music-related products to maintain cash flow. Independent record stores at $277 million were reduced to just 10 percent of the RIAA tally. They also turned to used CDs and the resurging demand for vinyl to prop up revenue.

Record Store Day Sparks the Vinyl Revival

The vinyl LP market rebounded from $22.9 million in 2007 to $160.7 million in 2012, and then more than tripled to $497.6 million in 2019, accounting for 43.3 percent of that year's physical sales revenue, mostly through independent record stores. Much of this growth was spurred on by the annual April Record Store Day that begun in 2008 with a second date added in 2010 on Black Friday after Thanksgiving. Special promotions and Record Store Day releases anchored store expansion from about seven hundred outlets in 2011 to over twenty-four hundred by 2019. This ad hoc network not only sold current product but also did a healthy business in recycling preowned LPs, rereleases on vinyl, and used CDs and cassettes. In addition to selling product in-store, they sold through website orders either directly themselves or through the ever-expanding Amazon.com mail order behemoth.

Record Store Day 2018 even caught the attention of *Fortune Magazine*, which listed the year's highlights as vinyl releases of Prince's *1999*; a collection of unreleased Jimi Hendrix tracks; a four-disc *Complete Clapton* collection; Ella Fitzgerald's *Ella Live at Zardi's*; The Flaming Lips' custom project for Dog Head Craft Brewery; David Bowie's 1967 debut album *David Bowie* and his 1978 *Welcome to the Blackout* live album; Taylor Swift's 2006 debut *Taylor Swift* with her *Fearless* Platinum Edition, and a hot-pink vinyl version of *1989*; along with Wu Tang Clan's 1993 debut album *Enter the Wu-Tang (36 Chambers)* for the first time on cassette.

Since its second year, Record Store Day has appointed a yearly ambassador as the featured spokes-artist for that year's campaign. From 2009 forward, the ambassadors have included Eagles of Death's Jesse "Boots Electric" Hughes, his bandmate Joshua Homme, Ozzy Osbourne, Iggy Pop, Jack White, Chuck D, Dave Grohl, Metallica, St. Vincent, and Run the Jewels. White Stripes, Raconteurs, and Dead Weather alumnus White has been a leading advocate for the vinyl revival. The Detroit native's Third Man Records Store in his adopted home of Nashville had a recording room and mastering/pressing equipment to make onsite recordings of live performances. He opened a second store in Detroit in 2015 and added a pressing plant there in February 2017.

White's passion for vinyl was evident in his 2013 ambassadorial statement, "We need to re-educate ourselves about human interaction and the difference between downloading a track on a computer and talking to other people in person and getting turned onto music that you can hold in your hands and share with others. The size, shape, smell, texture, and sound of a vinyl record; how do you explain to that teenager who doesn't know that it's a more beautiful musical experience than a mouse click? You put the record in their hands. You make them drop the needle on the platter. Then they'll know. . . . There is beauty and romance in the act of visiting a record shop and getting turned on to something new that could change the way they look at the world, other people, art, and ultimately, themselves. Let's wake each other up."[8]

The vinyl resurgence continued for the fourteenth consecutive year in 2019 with 18.84 million albums sold on Record Store Day, 19.1 percent over 2018's 15.8 million. The Beatles' *Abbey Road* led the top ten with 246,000 units with Billie Eilish's *When We All Fall Asleep, Where Do We Go?* as the only current entry in second place with 176,000 albums. Third through tenth included Queen's *Greatest Hits* and the *Bohemian Rhapsody* soundtrack, *Best of's* from the Beach Boys and Bob Marley, Pink Floyd's *The Dark Side of the Moon*,

Michael Jackson's *Thriller*, Fleetwood Mac's *Rumours*, and the soundtrack *Guardians of the Galaxy: Awesome Mix Vol. 1*.

The Ongoing Retail Pricing Squabble

By 2007, the long-simmering contention over pricing between the record labels and the retail sector extended into the digital domain. With the diminished demand for buying recorded music, the duel over nickels and dimes was more intense than ever. Analyzing data from the RIAA annual reports revealed that the actual average retail price for CDs had hovered around $14.91 since 2003, although top-selling artists had SRLPs as high as $19.99. The CD retailers contended that lower prices would attract more buyers, allowing volume to restore lost revenue. The labels countered that lowering prices would not reclaim digital defectors, so prices must be maintained or raised if volume continued to decline.

On the download front, in 2003 iTunes had set the bar at $.99 per track, or $9.99 for a full CD, which almost always had more than ten tracks, and sometimes fourteen or more to utilize the more than 74 available minutes for music. Steve Jobs believed that $10 was the price ceiling for albums to successfully compete for disposable income. The big-box stores concurred and were discounting retail prices to $10 or below. Financially depleted from trying to find their own legal alternatives to P2P file-sharing, the labels had agreed to 99¢ per track for the iTunes launch. Seventy percent was paid through to them, approximately the same as the ratio between wholesale and retail prices. The labels retained responsibility for mechanical royalties to publishers from out of their share. iTunes soared.

By 2007 Amazon and Walmart had settled into the second and third positions behind iTunes in the download derby, but the combined sales of all digital outlets could not counter the continuing downward descent of physical sales. Although iTunes had stood firm at 99¢ per track, Amazon and Walmart were experimenting with lower prices for back catalog tracks in an attempt to break iTunes' market dominance. Meanwhile the labels were clamoring for higher track prices to help make up for their losses. In April 2009, all three of the leading e-tailers introduced a variable pricing schedule that mirrored the labels' longtime album pricing policy with top line, mid-line, and budget-line categories. iTunes shifted from all tracks at 99¢ to pricing at $.69¢ for budget, $.99¢ for mid-line, and $1.29 for its top-line tier. Amazon switched to a similar spread. In keeping with its low-price modus operandi, Walmart undercut its rivals on all tier levels by a nickel.

Mass merchandisers had long sold top-line CDs, which had a wholesale cost above $10, for $10 and below as a loss leader to attract buyers for other far more expensive merchandise. In 2004 Walmart had tested a campaign with corrugated box displays placed on counters near cash registers outside of the record department. The boxes featured an agreed-upon selection of top-line CDs at $9.72 requiring a $7.50 wholesale price for Walmart to meet its normal 23 percent margin. Given that Walmart then accounted for about 22 percent of all CD sales, the labels reluctantly complied.

Then in March 2008, Walmart proposed a new five-level CD pricing tier with rounded prices, for instance, $10 rather than $9.72 for top-line product. Portable box displays holding 438 units would contain the top 15 to 20 current releases, each at $10. In the regular music racks other front-line titles would be advertised at $12, top catalog at $9, mid-line catalog at $7, and budget-line at $5. At the same time, Best Buy and Target moved both music and video racks to smaller and less visible positions in their stores and continued their loss leader pricing policies.

During the summer of 2009, Trans World, the largest remaining chain, conducted a retail pricing test in 54 of its 700 stores at $9.99 for all CDs to see if lower prices resulted in higher volume for greater profit. Sony, UMG, and EMI accepted the wholesale price of $7.50 while WMG didn't participate. Trans World chairman/CEO Bob Higgins proclaimed the test a success, having almost doubled sales at the participating locations and declared, "The results speak for themselves—when you offer the customer the right product at the right price, they will buy."[9] Nonetheless, CD sales overall continue to drop.

Charlie Anderson Weighs in on Future of Retail

In July 2010, Charlie Anderson, president/CEO of Anderson Merchandisers and sole supplier to Walmart, gave an exclusive interview to *Billboard*'s Ed Christman. Anderson warned that changes were eminent if CD sales continued to drop. "Walmart, Target and Best Buy are all managing [their music departments down] and reducing space. There will come a day when they say, 'It's just not worth it anymore.' And our projection is that it could happen at the end of three more years if nothing is done for the CD."[10] Anderson offered five suggestions he thought could possibly extend the life of physical product sales from his three-year estimate to as long as six years.

The first two involved price reductions to significantly under $10 with six to eight tracks rather than twelve to sixteen per disc, but with more frequent releases to create a more competitive playing field between downloads and physical sales. His third suggestion was even more controversial but in tune with consumer sentiment. "We believe that when you buy a CD, you should also have a [personal identification] number so you can receive a digital copy of what you just bought. Presently, you can [rip the CD] and put it on portable devices. You shouldn't have to do that. Music publishers will be a sticking point on that one. They are not going to like it, but that is what we are recommending."[11]

Number four was to change retail delivery of new CDs to coincide with release to radio and download stores, eliminating the time lag caused by shipping that put physical retailers at a disadvantage. His fifth suggestion was to go to a full-consignment sales policy with 100 percent penalty-free return rights. When asked what his suggestions would accomplish, Anderson replied, "If the industry adopts [those five things, it] would slow the decline and give us more time to find new revenue streams. We are not trying to perpetuate the CD forever. We are just trying to buy some time so that we can avoid a falling-off-the-cliff event for record labels."[12]

Judging from the subsequent annual RIAA reports, Anderson's message struck a chord as starting in 2010 the average CD price began to drop and reached $12.31 in 2013, down $2.60 from 2007's $14.91, a 17.4 percent drop in price. Over the same time period, however, RIAA CD shipments dropped by 325.9 million units to 173.8 million.

A monthly subscription fee for the right to listen on-demand rather than purchase a copy to do so, did precipitate the exit of some mass merchandisers from the distribution of recorded music, but it did not kill the record companies. They still owned the content and would accept payment for whatever and from whomever the public chose as the new avenue of consumption.

The Ever-Shifting Retail Landscape

2012 was a pivotal year in the ongoing displacement of physical sales by digital alternatives. For the first time revenue from downloads and streaming combined to exceed $4 billion, while physical sales fell below $3 billion for the first time since 1979. Also for the first time, in 2012 streaming revenue crossed the $1 billion threshold led by the Spotify launch while download sales peaked at just above $3 billion. In 2013 downloads joined CDs in a dual decline that would continue through the end of the decade. Streaming continued to escalate, countering the fall in sales to sustain the industry revenue idle at $7 billion+/-.

In June 2015 Apple Music launched its reconfigured and renamed Beats subscription service to compete with Spotify, but without a freemium tier. Its press release stated, "Starting with the music you already know – whether from the iTunes Store* or ripped CDs – your music now lives in one place alongside the Apple Music catalog with over 30 million songs. You can stream any song, album, or playlist you choose – or better yet, let Apple Music do the work for you. . . In addition to human curation, Siri* is also dedicated to helping you enjoy great music and have fun with Apple Music. Ask Siri to, 'Play me the best songs from 1994'. . . or 'What was the number one song in February 2011?'"[13]

In 2015 streaming revenue surged to $2.38 billion, just short of a tie with declining downloads at $2.41 billion. In 2016 streaming turned tsunami rising to $3.93 billion, exceeding 51 percent of total RIAA-reported revenue. In 2017 streaming grew to $5.7 billion for 64 percent of total revenue, and to $7.4 billion in 2018 for 75.8 percent, while both downloads and CDs continued their decline. In 2019 the RIAA revenue total reached $11.1 billion with streaming's $8.8 billion accounting for 79.5 percent. The record industry was well on the road to recovery. Goldman Sachs, Citigroup, and PricewaterhouseCoopers (PwC) all anticipated record sector revenue to more than double over the next decade as the access provided by streaming displaced the far more expensive, inconvenient, and time-consuming acquisition-and-accumulation model of the past century.

The survivors in the retail supply chain diversified their product lines to include non-music items including games, apps, and electronics supplies. Music had always been secondary for distributors Anderson and Baker & Taylor to their book and magazine divisions, which originated in 1828 for Baker & Taylor and 1917 for Anderson. One stops Alliance and Super D were doing far more retail volume in non-music items, while boosting their online divisions for mail-order fulfillment. At the local level, as much as two-thirds of the volume in independent stores came from merchandise other than current record releases. Legacy artists including AC/DC, Def Leppard, and Garth Brooks entered into exclusive distribution deals with mass merchandisers to guarantee shelf space, advertising, and in-store signage to support their tours.

The major label-owned indie distribution divisions reacted to the shrinking market by consolidating services and reducing their rosters. WMG's two subsidiaries—ADA and the Independent Label Group (ILG)—were merged, their staffs trimmed, and their back-office functions shifted to WMG. In 2012 they combined for a 3 percent market share from about 6 million album. Sony's RED indie distributor and its 3.7 percent market share were combined with recently purchased digital distributors Independent Online Distribution Alliance (IODA) and The Orchard for over 5 percent in combined market share. UMG sold its Fontana brand to independently operated Ingrooves to create a 1.5 percent combined market share. UMG retained a minority financial interest and continued to operate the former EMI Caroline indie distributor under the Capitol Records umbrella.

This consolidation trend extended into the distribution sector as well. Eleventh-ranked Irvine, California–based one-stop Super D acquired fifth-place Alliance in September 2013 to move ahead of Target into the fourth spot behind i-Tunes, Anderson, and Amazon. *Billboard* calculated the new entity to have about $450 million in CD sales with a 6.64 percent market share of total record industry revenue, and another $470 million primarily in DVD sales. Super D principals Bruce Ogilvie and Jeff Walker decided to continue operations under the Alliance name, moved management to the Alliance headquarters in Sunrise, Florida, and retained Alliance's newly opened even hundred thousand-square-foot warehouse fulfillment center in Shepherdsville, Kentucky.

In July 2016 Alliance purchased Anderson's CD sales division ANconnect, adding Walmart, Sam's Club, and Best Buy to their client list. This was six years to the month after Charlie Anderson's discourse on the life expectancy of CD sales. ANconnect's volume of $350 million was at about half of what it had been at the time of Anderson's prognostication. Combining this acquisition with existing business, Alliance was close to $1 billion in annual revenue. "We want to be the last guy standing,"[14] Ogilvie told *Billboard*'s Ed Christman in July 2018. Also in the plans were sales of pop culture merchandise. "Interestingly enough, there is not a one-stop wholesaler dealing in those goods," Walker added. "We want to have a wide selection of those products, just like we do for music."[15] Alliance envisioned a future serving all clients, from vinyl record shops to mass merchandisers, with all its music and related needs in one shipment, all on the same invoice. "We want to be the one-box solution,"[16] Ogilvie concluded.

Also in July 2018 Anderson's predicted demise of CD sales actually took a first step toward realization when Best Buy announced that it was phasing the CD out of its plans. Walmart and Target were still selling CDs, but in severely reduced rack space. Their sales were mainly country music and the latest releases by pop chart superstars like Adele, Taylor Swift, Ed Sheeran, Beyoncé, and Bruno Mars, for whom the major labels maintained a same-day release and delivery policy for both digital and physical configurations as well as marketing and advertising budgets to spend in support of retail sales.

To summarize the retail metamorphosis in album sales over this section's time period, in 2007, there were 501.8 million physical albums sold with over 99 percent of them in the CD format. In 2019, there were 47.5 million CDs sold and another 18.5 million vinyl discs for a total of 66 million physical units. Another 37.5 million albums were downloaded in 2019 compared to 49.8 million in 2007, a 25 percent drop. Unlike physical albums, however, downloaded album sales had continued to grow until they peaked at 118 million units in 2013 before the decline began.

Going into 2007, sales of physical singles in vinyl and CD formats had already been affected by digital technology. Between 2007 and 2019 physical singles continued their decline from 3.2 million in 2007 to under 400,000 in 2019. Downloaded singles in 2007 sold 819.4 million units, peaked at 1.4 billion in 2012 and then progressively dropped to 329.7 million in 2019.

From the retail point-of-purchase perspective, physical sales sloped steadily downward from 2007's $7.99 billion to $1.14 billion in 2019. These totals also included all mail order fulfillment through both record clubs and e-tailers. The difference between what the consumer paid for physical product and the wholesale price that was then paid to the labels dropped from a total of $2.64 billion in 2007 to $376 million in 2019. Consequentially, 86 percent of the 2007 brick-and-mortar record business had evaporated over the intervening years.

This dismantling of the retail sector clearly confirmed that the MP3 and its derivative file formats were indeed an example of Christensen's disruptive innovation thesis. As a result of the consumer-driven shift over the course of the 2000–2009 decade from accumulation of physical product to digital sources for at-will access, the record industry revenue declined by 50 percent. Over the 2010s, however, on-demand subscription services returned the industry to a revenue growth pattern, but longtime retail and wholesale partners were sacrificed in the process. Thanks to this consumer migration to digital access, in 2019 the record labels had rebounded to 76.4 percent of their all-time high-revenue mark with all analysts forecasting continued recovery and future growth to new revenue highs.

Digital Competition for Post-Recession Radio

Since the debut of radio in 1920, advertisers had paid to reach the desired demographic strata for their products. The SFX-Clear Channel roll-up of stations, performance venues, and outdoor advertising, however, offered the possibility of an even greater return on investment (ROI) through the multimedia synergy between these elements. Consumer spending on *Pollstar*-tracked concert attendance more than doubled from $1.75 billion in 2000 to $3.9 billion in 2007. Off-air revenue for radio grew as well. Cross-media ad buys had become a key marketing strategy for advertisers seeking further penetration into targeted listener groups ranging from the millennial and Gen-Z fans of Taylor Swift and Justin Bieber to baby boomers at U2 and Rolling Stones shows, and all age groups in between. In 2007 radio registered $21.3 billion in advertising revenue, just $359 million down from its all-time high in 2006, with $1.7 billion of that from the off-air category.

In 2008 the Great Recession hit radio as hard as it hit records and retail with an 8.6 percent drop in revenue to $19.5 billion, and then tumbled another 17.7 percent in 2009 to $16 billion, according to data from the Radio Advertising Bureau (RAB). About 75 percent of the drop came from loss of spot ads and 25 percent in off-air revenue. This advertising decline paralleled the reduction in consumer spending. In 2009 the RAB tracked revenue from stations' digital transmissions for the first time, adding $480 million to offset some of the spot ad losses. All revenue categories rebounded in 2010 to a collective total of $17.3 billion, a 7.9 percent recovery over 2009. Total revenues then slowly grew to $17.7 billion in 2017 before falling over the next two years to $14.5 billion in 2019.

The radio industry was aware of the impending threat to its revenue from new digital competitors, but prior to 2007 the consequences had been marginal. Then in 2007 the RIAA reported $36.2 million received from SoundExchange. These performance rights royalties were 10 percent of digital broadcasters' revenue to be paid to labels and performers under the provisions of the DMCA. Payments grew to $155.6 million in 2009. At the beginning of 2011 founding executive director John Simson left SoundExchange after a ten-year tenure to return to his legal practice. He had established SoundExchange as an industry institution and the only US collection society for artists' and labels' performance rights. Simson was replaced by Michael Huppe, who subsequently announced that as of 2012, SoundExchange's total historic royalty distribution had passed $1 billion. Then from 2013 through 2017 SoundExchange distributed another $4 billion. The artists' 50 percent went directly to them, not through the record labels. SoundExchange distributions topped $900 million for both 2018 and 2019.

The RIAA annual revenue report introduced a Subscription Streaming line item in 2004 at $149.2 million, which reached $201.3 million in 2007, and grew to $247.8 million in 2011, the year of Spotify's US debut. The launch prompted the introduction of On-Demand Streaming (Ad-Supported) as an additional RIAA line item at $113.8 million. In 2015, the year Apple Music launched, total streaming revenue topped $1.6 billion. In 2019 streaming revenue from premium and freemium combined was just under $8 billion with another $900,000 in SoundExchange receipts. The amount paid through to the labels by the streaming services was in the 60 percent range after publishing was deducted. The labels in turn cross-collateralized the artists' share with their other royalty sources to be paid out at the contractual royalty rate.

Smartphone sales boomed with the launch of the Apple iPhone in June 2007 and the T-Mobile G-1 in October 2008, extending the market for digital radio platforms beyond web browsers. Pandora, the most popular internet streaming service due to its Music Genome algorithm that introduced interactivity to shape playlists, became the first Apple store mobile phone music application (app). By the end of 2008 Pandora had over 20 million registered users and grew to over 80 million in 2012, propelled by the mobile phone market. Only about 1.8 million of those users, however, were fee-based accounts, generating $51.9 million in subscription revenue while its ad-based accounts supplied $375.2 million. Pandora's ad revenue then increased over the next five years to $1.02 billion in 2017.

In January 2007, competing satellite broadcasters, Sirius Satellite Radio and XM Satellite Radio, sought permission to merge since both were on tenuous financial ground, and claimed that their real competition was with digital radio, not with each other. Despite objections from the NAB, the FCC ruled in their favor over a year later. In January 2009 Liberty Media's John Malone came to the rescue with a $530 million loan in exchange for a 40 percent equity position to keep the newly christened SiriusXM Radio from bankruptcy. By the end of 2009 SiriusXM finally showed a profit, reaching over 20 million subscribers with $2.8 billion in revenue. This increase in subscriptions was closely tied to the resuscitation of the automobile market and a three-month free-trial subscription as part of the standard new-car package. By 2017, SiriusXM had $5.4 billion in revenue with over 36 million subscribers, representing about 12 percent of the 268 million registered vehicles in the US.

Radio Responds to the Digital Onslaught

With the introduction of smartphones that could transmit web radio platforms, and the survival of SiriusXM, the larger radio chains began to understand that digital technology was a threat to their listener base and thus their advertising revenue. As the smoke from the Great Recession cleared the air, annual radio revenue started to rebound but stalled around $17.5 billion from 2010 through 2014, $3.8 billion less than the 2007 level. The ad revenue of Pandora and other mobile app music providers experienced a growth pattern from 2007 through 2012 similar to SiriusXM.

The radio industry realized that action was needed before mobile technology became as disruptive an innovation for them as digital files had been a decade earlier for records and retail. The HD Radio Alliance initiated a study on how to split FM frequencies into multiple signals for simultaneous broadcasting of alternative programming. The larger station groups explored both simulcasting their terrestrial signals on their websites and the production of unique online programming. Podcasting, the transmission of digital files containing recorded blocks of audio content, was also gaining traction across the cyber community as an on-demand streaming parallel to the all-talk formats on both terrestrial and satellite radio.

Radio industry ownership hadn't changed much since the dust settled on the consolidations following Telecommunications Act of 1996. The top-ten station groups in 2008 took in 44.2 percent of total industry revenue. Clear Channel Communications, Inc. (CCC), was still the number one broadcasting group with $2.92 billion in 2008 revenue, 16.5 percent of the radio total. In July 2008, the Mays family sold CCC to private equity firms Thomas H. Lee Partners and Bain Capital (collectively Lee/Bain) in an $18.7 billion leveraged buyout. As part of the FCC approval process for the sale, CCC, now a division of CC Media Holdings, Inc., reduced their station count to 845 by selling the 448 that were outside of the top 100 markets as well as all their television properties.

CBS Radio was the second-largest group in 2008 with $1.59 billion in revenue, 9 percent of the industry total from 130 stations. The number three and four groups were Citadel Broadcasting and Cumulus Media with 4 percent and 205 stations, and 2.9 percent and 305 stations, respectively. Three more groups each had a 2 percent-plus share: Entercom had 112 stations, Cox Radio with 85, and Univision Communications at 72. Radio One, Bonneville International, and Emmis Communications rounded out the top ten with 52, 28, and 23 stations. There were another 40-plus station groups that had between 71 and 22 stations, but smaller revenue totals.

Both CCC and CBS decided to launch their own online freemium platforms to compete with Pandora and the mobile app versions of internet radio platforms. In May 2007 CBS spent $280 million on Last.fm, an internet radio website with 20 million users, operating on a proprietary data-sorting program that could both share and create user playlists. In April 2008 CBS entered into an arrangement for its stations to be transmitted on the AOL. Radio app. That same month CCC launched its own web platform, which it dubbed iHeartRadio with both entertainment and national news, both music videos and audio tracks on demand, and streaming transmission of over 750 CCC stations. In October 2008 the iHeartRadio iPhone app was unveiled with Blackberry and Android compatibility coming in 2009. CBS followed in 2010 with its own Play.it and Radio.com web platforms with corresponding apps utilizing the Last.fm technology.

Before CCC and CBS could fully promote these new initiatives or the smaller chains could develop their own platforms, the aftereffects of the October 2008 bank crisis and stock market crash moved their digital initiatives to the back burner. The radio consolidation of the late 1990s had created a heavily leveraged cash flow industry based on historic growth patterns. The Lee/Bain purchase had not anticipated the revenue drop that started just months after their June 2008 investment in CCC. When the radio advertising market stabilized two years later, it was at about 80 percent of the revenue level on which Lee/Bain had based their ROI projections. In June 2010, amid rumors of pending bankruptcy and pressure from its leading creditors, CCC president/CEO Mark Mays stepped down after a twenty-one-year tenure. Irving Azoff was added to the board and CCC initiated an executive search for a new CEO who could harness digital technology to guide the radio giant to profitability.

In October 2010, MTV cofounder and former Warner-AOL COO Bob Pittman, who earlier that year had invested in CCC, assumed the CEO mantle. At *Ad Age*'s April 2011 Digital Conference, Pittman noted that although just 3 percent of total radio listening came from digital platforms, capturing the potential of this market represented radio's best path to financial growth. He told the conference, "We have work to do. We actually have to make the digital revolution come to radio."[17] He cited the potential cross-platform ad opportunities between local radio and the iHeartRadio website and app where all CCC stations could now be found. He also likened local radio to a pre-internet social network. "When I was at AOL, we tried to spend a lot of time getting to local. . . . Not only is it targeted to specific audiences that hang together in a lot of characteristics, there is an emotional attachment to radio. Four in five listeners will be disappointed if their favorite station was no longer on the air. . . . It's the power of being local."[18]

Best Laid Plans . . . Often Go Awry

In February 2010, second-ranked CBS consolidated Play.it, Last.fm, and its other digital radio properties into its Radio.com platform, also available as a free mobile app offering two hundred CBS radio stations, AOL Radio, and Yahoo! Music. By 2012, however, it was evident that Radio.com had not gained enough traction to deliver a level of ad revenue sufficient to stay in competition with Pandora or iHeartRadio. The Play.it functions were scaled back leaving Radio.com strictly as a streaming audio platform. Meanwhile, CBS had been unloading stations that didn't have a CBS television affiliate in the market for cross promotional purposes. Finally deciding that radio couldn't produce the profit margins enjoyed by its other divisions, in February 2017 CBS agreed to merge its radio division with Entercom Communications, then the fourth-largest station group with $460 million in 2016 revenue from 125 stations. CBS had $1.22 billion in 2016 revenue from 117 stations.

In a tax-free transaction in which CBS shareholders retained 72 percent of the stock, Entercom took over management of the combined operations. After the perfunctory shifting of stations to meet FFC regulatory requirements, the reconfigured Entercom had 244 stations, including ones in all the top-ten markets, and in twenty-three of the top twenty-five. Management predicted $1.73 billion in revenue for 2017 that would approach $2 billion in 2021. Cost savings would be achieved by consolidating management services and staff reductions. Entercom president/CEO David Field expressed his optimism on the future in an interview with *Billboard*'s Cherie Hu. "We plan to make big investments in our brands, people, capabilities and innovation. We are also done apologizing about Radio, America's #1 Reach medium, which is massively undervalued and offers superior ROI to other media competitors."[19]

In December 2017 third-ranked station group Cumulus, which had acquired former rival Citadel in 2011 for $2.5 billion, filed for bankruptcy protection. The debt from the Citadel and subsequent 2013 Westwood One acquisitions had hampered investment for digital development. Over the next six months CEO Mary Berner worked on a reorganization plan that turned over a billion dollars of secured debt into equity. Then a sufficient number of the unsecured shareholders agreed to accept a reduced equity stake to avoid further loss. In June 2018, Cumulus exited bankruptcy with *Inside Radio* reporting that, "reducing its leverage now gives the company more financial flexibility to reinvest in the business. [Executive VP of Content and Programming Mike] McVay says he expects more resources will be freed up for digital initiatives, an area where the company is playing catch up with some of its peers."[20]

In March 2018, market leader iHeartMedia also filed a bankruptcy petition, but with problems on a much larger scale than Cumulus. Its 2008 leveraged buyout couldn't have been at a worse time with radio's revenue, growth pattern, and trailing cash flow history at all-time highs. It was still carrying close to $20 billion in debt with $6.2 billion in 2017 revenue, about $3.4 billion of that through the iHeartRadio division and the balance through its outdoor advertising wing, but only radio was subject to the bankruptcy filing. Despite iHeartRadio having half of all of terrestrial radio's digital traffic, that half amounted to only one-sixth the number of Pandora's active sessions. iHeartMedia hoped to restructure $10 billion of debt through the filing. Six months into the process, iHeartMedia acquired Stuff Media in September 2018 for $55 million. A ten-year pioneer in podcasts, one of Stuff's properties was the "How Stuff Works" library of content. The purchase was calculated to boost iHeartMedia's podcast division, complementing its talk formats, which were among its top revenue-producing radio products.

In 2017 media research analyst BIA/Kelsey reported $17.7 billion in total industry revenue, just slightly over the $17.5 billion average of the past five years, but network and local on-air revenue combined for a decline from $14.2 billion in 2016 to $13.9 billion, which was 78.5 percent of total income. The other 21.5 percent came from digital and off-air revenue, reflecting the shift in listening to digital platforms. The radio revenue in 2019 fell to $15.1 billion, a 17.2 percent drop from 2017, with on-air revenue falling further as digital alternatives continued to grow.

While revenue was down as a whole, the industry was hopeful about the future. Radio still had the largest market penetration. Over 90 percent of Americans listened to radio on a weekly basis, especially in cars during drive time. People who didn't spend money on music or new listening devices still listened to radio and bought the products advertised there. Both the larger station groups that had restructured their finances and the smaller chains that hadn't overextended themselves still viewed online/mobile listening to their signals as a promising avenue for revenue growth.

As Bob Pittman had articulated, the key to radio's success has always been its tie to the local community. Streaming services were national in scope and didn't have the local connections and related advertising opportunities enjoyed by radio. As long as these advertisers wanted to reach a specific demographic in a designated DMA through brand identification with a station's programming, radio still offered the best opportunity, especially during drive time hours, as evidenced by counting Home Depot, GEICO, JCPenney, McDonald's, Lowe's, AutoZone, Staples, Mattress Firm, Macy's, and the US Department of Transportation as radio's top-ten advertisers. At the end of 2019, radio was still an element of the national music charts, albeit on a far lesser scale than in the pre-streaming era, and still a cog in the success of the record industry and what remained of the brick-and-mortar retail business, especially in the country genre.

SiriusXM Expands with Pandora Acquisition

Radio's financial restructuring and plans for digital expansion didn't escape the watchful eye of John Malone, chairman and majority shareholder of Liberty Media, which owned 71 percent of SiriusXM. Nor did he miss the growth of premium streaming to over 300 million subscribers worldwide by the end of 2019. A 1963 Yale graduate, Malone was described by *Forbes* as a self-made billionaire with a "penchant for media deals and complicated corporate structures,"[21] whose fortune originated in the formative years of cable television.

SiriusXM entered 2018 with 36 million subscribers, $5.43 billion in 2017 revenue, and still had Howard Stern. Designed to compete with terrestrial radio, SiriusXM offered a commercial-free, voluminous, and diversified menu of channels, but lacked the on-demand interactivity of streaming. The automobile was its primary market, but new cars were now equipped with inputs for voice-activated portable devices to accommodate more technologically advanced alternatives.

In looking to reinvigorate before becoming a casualty of digital innovation, Malone invested $480 million in the financially struggling Pandora in 2017. In September 2018 SiriusXM announced its intent to acquire Pandora in an all-stock $3.5 billion tax-free transaction exchanging 1.44 SiriusXM shares for one of Pandora, subject to final approval by Pandora's shareholders. Upon completion of the deal in early 2019, SiriusXM became the largest digital audio company with $7.79 billion in 2019 revenue.

Analysts applauded the expected compatibility that would hopefully address each party's major weakness. Although SiriusXM had 36 million subscribers, at any given time roughly two-thirds of them were attached to new cars in a free three-month trial plan that had a high attrition rate. On the other hand, although the majority of Pandora's then-65 million active users had ad-based subscriptions, they were already acclimated to interactivity through its programming algorithm. SiriusXM CEO Jim Meyer told investors and analysts, "There is real money to be made in cross promotion of these platforms. . . . The addition of Pandora diversifies SiriusXM's revenue streams with the US's largest ad-supported audio offering, broadens our technical capabilities, and represents an exciting next step in our efforts to expand our reach out of the car even further."[22]

BTIG Research analyst Brandon Ross, who had predicted the SiriusXM-Pandora coupling, lauded the significance of accomplishing a major merger without acquiring additional debt while retaining liquid assets. Considering that Liberty Media already owned 34 percent of Live Nation and Malone's proclivity for consolidations, Ross told *Billboard*, "We believe Liberty . . . desires to not only collapse the [SiriusXM] share structure and take control of [SiriusXM's] cash flow but also to combine Sirius and Live Nation into a single music distribution company. We believe a Sirius/LN deal will come sooner rather than later."[23]

Only a dozen years after the dismantling of the CCC-SFX roll-up, Ross had in essence suggested that a resurrection of the Sillerman-Mays vision of interoperability might be more feasible this time around. Its first incarnation suffered from the inability to transform a collection of independent sole proprietors into a cohesive cadre attempting to integrate two separate although interlinked industries. The envisioned synergy might now work as the current set of executives was far more imbued in corporate culture while advances in data collection, mining, and exploitation were now far better understood and employed in all segments of the music industry.

In July 2019, the new SiriusXM-Pandora alignment signed Drake, the top-charting and most streamed artist of the past decade, to a multifaceted partnership for both content and curation covering both the satellite and streaming platforms. An agreement followed in December with U2. Artist-associated channels already on the SiriusXM menu included Willie's Roadhouse, Madonna's Madame X, Pitbull's Globalization, Phish Radio, The Garth Channel, The Beatles Channel, Tom Petty Radio, Pearl Jam Radio, and E Street Radio centered around Bruce Springsteen. Many pundits doubted this approach could overcome the Spotify and Apple technological advantage. SiriusXM, however, was banking that the combination of its artist channels and non-music content with Pandora's algorithm and new premium service would attract a sufficient share of both radio listeners and freemium consumers to maintain if not increase profitability.

From a competitive standpoint, SiriusXM's major streaming rival, now that it had added Pandora and upgraded its premium service, would appear to be Spotify. Each had both paid and ad-based tiers and were standalone content providers, while Apple Music and Amazon Music had only paid subscriptions whose streaming revenue was dwarfed by their corporate parent's other income sources. Despite all of its rivals' technological advantages, SiriusXM was on much better financial footing. *Billboard's* Glenn Peoples pointed out in December 2019 that "satellite radio is probably more profitable than the entire music streaming business. . . . Even with the cost of maintaining four satellites in geo synchronous orbit, SiriusXM comes out ahead . . . SiriusXM has enviable margins: Spotify keeps about

30% of its revenue and pays the rest to rights holders; after paying royalties and programming costs, SiriusXM keeps 70%."[24]

Digital Consumption Accelerates Chart Evolution

Billboard had always periodically updated its chart methodology to better assure that the weekly changes in chart position accurately represented the totality of music consumption. By the beginning of 2014 *Billboard* had not only introduced a series of charts for downloads and streaming but it had also added these data to the radio airplay used for the Hot 100 Singles chart. The Billboard 200 Album chart, however, still reflected sales only. Then in November 2014 *Billboard* announced that as of the December 13 issue, the Billboard 200 chart "will be the first to include on-demand streaming and digital track sales (as measured by Nielsen Entertainment) by way of a new algorithm. It is the most substantial methodology update since May 1991, when *Billboard* first used Nielsen's point-of-sale data—SoundScan—to measure album sales."[25] *Billboard* also announced that it would maintain a sales-only chart titled Top Album Sales.

Initially the Billboard 200 chart employed the IFPI multi-metric consumption formula, which equated ten digital track sales to one track-equivalent album (TEA) sale, and 1,500 streams of songs from an album to one stream-equivalent album (SEA) sale, with one stream being one consumer listening once to a track available through a subscription service. Then in May 2018 *Billboard* altered the formula again to better reflect the difference in revenue yield between paid and ad-based subscriptions. Going forward, on premium services 1,250 streams would equal one album. For freemium services, 3,750 streams would be equal to one album.

Concurrently, the metrics of the Hot 100 singles chart were revised to credit a premium stream with a full point value. Requested freemium streams would be credited with a 2/3 point value, and curated freemium streams would get a 1/2 point value. The *Billboard* chart staff further explained, "Those values are then applied to the chart's formula alongside all-genre radio airplay and digital song sales data. Streaming remains the most dominant factor on the chart, followed by radio airplay and digital sales in descending order of significance."[26] The importance of terrestrial radio had greatly decreased as it provided no direct revenue to the record labels as streaming did, and its historic role in driving consumers to buy albums had diminished in tandem with the decline in album sales.

THE TOP CHART SINGLES OF THE 2010-2019 DECADE

In 2010 chart position was determined by a combination of sales, radio, downloads, and streams, but by 2019 streaming dominated the charts just as it did label revenue.

	TITLE	ARTISTS	YEAR
1	Uptown Funk!	Mark Ronson feat. Bruno Mars	2015
2	Party Rock Anthem	LMFAO feat. Lauren Bennett & GoonRock	2011
3	Shape Of You	Ed Sheeran	2017
4	Closer	The Chainsmokers feat. Halsey	2016
5	Girls Like You	Maroon 5 feat. Cardi B	2018
6	We Found Love	Rihanna feat. Calvin Harris	2011
7	Old Town Road	Lil Nas X feat. Billy Ray Cyrus	2019
8	Somebody That I Used To Know	Gotye feat. Kimbra	2012
9	Despacito	Luis Fonsi & Daddy Yankee feat. Justin Bieber	2017
10	Rolling In The Deep	Adele	2011
11	Sunflower (Spider-Man: Into The Spider-Verse)	Post Malone & Swae Lee	2019
12	Without Me	Halsey	2019
13	Call Me Maybe	Carly Rae Jepsen	2012
14	Blurred Lines	Robin Thicke feat. T.I. + Pharrell	2013
15	Perfect	Ed Sheeran	2017
16	Sicko Mode	Travis Scott	2018
17	All About That Bass	Meghan Trainor	2014
18	Royals	Lorde	2013
19	God's Plan	Drake	2018
20	Moves Like Jagger	Maroon 5 feat. Christina Aguilera	2011
21	Happy	Pharrell Williams	2014
22	Just The Way You Are	Bruno Mars	2010
23	Rockstar	Post Malone feat. 21 Savage	2017
24	TiK ToK	Ke$ha	2010
25	See You Again	Wiz Khalifa feat. Charlie Puth	2015
26	Dark Horse	Katy Perry feat. Juicy J	2014
27	Thrift Shop	Macklemore & Ryan Lewis feat. Wanz	2013
28	One More Night	Maroon 5	2012
29	We Are Young	fun. feat. Janelle Monae	2012
30	That's What I Like	Bruno Mars	2017

Source: *Billboard*

Illustration 12.2 The Top Chart Singles of the 2010–19 Decade

On December 13, 2019, *Billboard* announced that as of the first chart of 2020, video streaming data from YouTube, Apple, Spotify, Tidal, and Vevo would be included in the Hot 200 album chart algorithm, completing the transition from a sales-centric metric to a more inclusive consumption barometer. Deanna Brown of *Billboard*'s parent MRC Partners pronounced, "As the steward of the definitive charts that uphold the industry's measurement of music consumption, our goal is to continually respond and accurately reflect the changing landscape of the music. Our decision to add YouTube and other video streaming data to our album charts reflects the continuing evolution of the music consumption market and the ways in which consumers connect to album-related content."[27]

Lyor Cohen, hired as global head of music at YouTube in December 2016, labeled the move a "very important moment in making the chart a more accurate representation of what people are listening to. Genres like Latin, hip-hop and electronic, which consistently dominate the YouTube charts, will now be properly recognized for their popularity. This is another great step in bringing YouTube and the industry together."[28]

Despite Cohen's encouraging words, YouTube was viewed by the labels as the most recalcitrant streaming service in paying its fair share for music. While the amount of the YouTube payout was on a relative par with Apple, Spotify, and Amazon, its 55 percent of the video music streaming total had one of the lowest average-per-stream rates due to its preponderance of freemium accounts. What's more, its safe harbor status under the DMCA shielded YouTube from liability when users posted content that hadn't been properly licensed. This left the infringed party to pursue the posting party on its own if the infringer didn't comply with a take-down notice issued by YouTube, the only action YouTube was required to take.

Nonetheless, YouTube represented the greatest streaming revenue potential for the music industry as it attempted to follow the Spotify model and convert a share of its massive core of freemium consumers to its fee-based service, YouTube Music Premium. Originally launched in 2014 as YouTube Music Key, YouTube Music Premium was transformed into YouTube Red, and finally into YouTube Music in 2018, which also corralled parent company Google's Google Play Music into its fold.

A week after announcing the inclusion of video streaming in chart determination, on December 18, 2019, Valence announced the acquisition of Nielsen Music, which included SoundScan, BDS, the in-development Music Connect, and a proprietary API analytics program. The newly branded MCR Data reunited *Billboard* and the Nielsen properties years after former owner VNU sold the various components to different buyers. Deanna Brown asserted that with the reunification "we're answering the request from the music industry for a more coordinated, powerful, agile and global suite of independent measurement products. . . . The new MRC Data division will leverage our scale and global, multimedia perspective to operate as a true accelerant for our music business colleagues and stakeholders."[29] This new international perspective was in step with the influence that *Beats 1* and Spotify's *Today's Top Hits* had on the industry in moving from territorial to worldwide marketing of top artists, opening the door for *Billboard's* December 2019 launch of the Global 100 chart it had announced that May, which would provide "a holistic view of the top songs and artists across the globe."[30]

Record Labels Recover, Retail Recedes, Radio Treads Water

Going into 2020 digital access through streaming had transformed the music business into a globally uniform marketplace where consumers the world over could simultaneously listen to the same live station presenting the most popular songs of the moment. Concurrently, each consumer also had 24/7 on-demand, immediate access to every version of any song ever recorded. According to the subscription services, there were also billions of available playlists from around the world, including curated, personalized, and user generated content (UGC), accompanied by millions of podcasts.

The labels had reacted to the more than one-third drop in industry revenue between 2007 and 2010 by trimming rosters and staffs, undergoing label mergers and consolidation, and initiating budget reductions to keep income and expense in balance. The July 2011 launch of Spotify lifted US streaming revenue to 9.2 percent of the overall total, up from 2.5 percent in 2007. In 2015, Jimmy Iovine and Dr. Dre's Beats subscription service transitioned into Apple Music to join Spotify, Amazon, and the other subscription services in the impending streaming tsunami. The RIAA reported $2.41 billion in 2015 streaming revenue for 34.3 percent of the $7.02 billion total. In 2016 RIAA-reported revenue grew out of its nearly $7 billion, six-year doldrum and from 2017 through 2019 the deluge was in full force. In 2019 streaming supplied 79.5 percent of the $11.1 billion record sector revenue total.

The historic roles played by radio and retail gave way to unlimited on-demand, at-will digital access to virtually all the music ever recorded. The celestial jukebox had arrived at $10 a month for unlimited access rather than the proverbial quarter in the slot for each listen. Whatever else streaming converts had previously spent on buying albums or tracks in excess of this monthly fee could now go to concert tickets, merchandise, or upgraded listening devices.

The record industry had survived the crisis triggered by the MP3 and was projected to soon surpass its 1999–2000 peak revenue. It took, however, twenty years and a collection of innovative interlopers from Napster's Fanning and Parker to iTunes' Jobs, and then on to Spotify's Ek and Lorentzon. Also of crucial importance to the industry's digital transformation were intuitive insiders Iovine, Grainge, Morris, Cohen, Bronfman, and Blavatnik, complemented by those who could span and command the gap between music and technology like Dr. Dre, Taylor Swift, Jay-Z, and Drake to preserve an industry that had seemed destined to self-implode.

Meanwhile, retail receded into the background as record chains folded with FYE, Sam Goody, and Rough Trade among the few still standing. Mass merchandisers reduced shelf space by racking just the chart toppers and legacy artist exclusives, if CDs were available at all. Music specialty stores diversified to include associated merchandise and magazines, sell previously owned CDs, and continued to enjoy the surge in vinyl. Radio revenue was down in 2019 by almost a third from its 2007 level. Stations retained the passive listeners who rarely spent money on music, as well as most of those who listened in the car, but lost the wealthiest of those to SiriusXM.

The cash flow funnel of the record business through which consumer and licensee dollars flowed into artists' pockets had survived a two-decade long overhaul as streams tallied on databases replaced albums scanned at retail counters. The labels, however, had not orchestrated this transformation, but rather played two decades of catch-up with both consumers and the tech interlopers leading them. Nonetheless, when they finally absorbed the message and experienced the results, the labels jumped into the fray wholeheartedly and did what they did best. They spent millions when and where they could, had the artists pay them back through royalty recoupment, and let the hits pay for the misses.

The trade journals, led by *Billboard*, *Pollstar*, *Variety*, *Hits*, *Rolling Stone*, and their digital age progeny including *Music Business Worldwide*, *Music and Copyright*, *MIDiA Research*, *Music Ally*, The *Lefsetz Letter*, *Hypebot*, and the many others along with their top-notch assemblage of editors, reporters, correspondents, chart departments, and data analysts had as always been way in the forefront of researching, reporting, and adapting to the changes wrought by digital innovation. They chronicled the emergence of streaming as the new normal of recorded music consumption and the transformation of live performance from intimate settings to arenas, festivals, and domed stadiums.

Although the majority of chart entries were still controlled by the now Big Three, the playing field had opened to allow independent labels and self-released DIY creators an ever-growing share of revenue. After two decades of uncertainty, the industry had righted itself and the marketplace had adjusted. The ever-replenishing ten-to-twenty-four-year-old demographic, however, now more than ever through their on-demand streaming choices, preprogrammed channel selections, and curation of UGC playlists, collectively decided which artists made it to the charts, how long they stayed there, and who would repeat the cycle with their next record.

13

Publishing and Copyright: The Digital Effect

The Rising Tide of Publishing Revenue

Unlike the record business with over 95 percent of 2007 RIAA-reported revenue derived from record product, only about 15 percent of publishing revenue was directly associated with record sales through mechanical license royalties, down from 25 percent in 1996. The rest of the 2007 publishing revenue came from the other rights granted under US copyright law, all of which had increased since 1996 due to licensing opportunities from digital technology.

Historically there had never been a summary of US publishing industry revenue, but by 2013 advances in metadata management enabled the NMPA to issue an industrywide appraisal of annual domestic revenue. The headline on a June 11, 2014, NMPA press release proclaimed "U.S. Music Publishing Industry Valued at $2.2 Billion." The text stated that "for the first time in history, NMPA can quantify the total industry revenue and value through information collected from NMPA's recent modernization program. The program requires music publishing members to provide revenue data and captures market share information. The total industry revenue is based on numbers reported to NMPA by its members for 2013."[1]

Fifty-two percent of the stated revenue was attributed to performing rights at $1.14 billion, 23 percent came from mechanical licenses totaling $506 million, 20 percent in sync licenses brought in $440 million, and 5 percent for $110 million was in the undefined "other" category. Members' revenue receipts were augmented by projected non-member revenue, copyright agencies' administration fees, songwriter share of domestic PRO royalties, and estimated SESAC profits.

Performing Rights

According to their annual reports, in 2007 ASCAP collected $863 million while BMI took in $840 million. SESAC was estimated at $75 million for a

American Popular Music and Its Business in the Digital Age. Rick Sanjek, Oxford University Press. © Frederick Sanjek 2024.
DOI: 10.1093/oso/9780190653828.003.0013

PRO total of $1.78 billion. In 2019 their reports listed ASCAP with S1.274 billion and BMI at $1.283 billion. A "Presale Report Analysis" prepared by Morningstar Credit Ratings for SESAC's refinancing bond sale listed SESAC's 2019 performing rights revenue at $254 million. Irving Azoff had opened GMR as a fourth PRO operational as of January 2017. Although its 2019 revenue was never publicly disclosed, *Billboard*'s Ed Christman estimated it at $90 million. Altogether these amounts came to about $2.9 billion for 2019, a 63 percent increase over 2007.

The 2019 NMPA report, however, listed the performing rights total at $1.945 billion, about $955 million less than the ASCAP and BMI totals combined with the estimated SESAC and GMR amounts. When asked about this discrepancy, NMPA CEO David Israelite explained in an email that incoming PRO royalties from foreign sources of approximately $710 million were not included in the NMPA PRO domestic revenue calculation. Most NMPA members had their foreign PRO earnings collected at source by their sub-publishers who then paid them directly after subtracting the sub-publishing commission. The NMPA did not consider the songwriters' share, which was the bulk of the incoming PRO foreign revenue, as publishing industry domestic revenue. This still left a difference of about $245 million.

Israelite listed the difference in the fiscal year periods and lag between receipt and payment of funds as possible factors. He further explained, "I grant that it is an imperfect exercise. It is the 'you don't know what you don't know.' I suspect we are missing quite a bit of very small DIY [do it yourself], although the aggregators like Song Trust do report."[2] This $245 million difference was about 11 percent of domestic PRO revenue, but given the nature of the data, which included currency exchange fluctuations, estimations, and the "you don't know what you don't know" factor, an 11 percent margin of error was no more imperfect than the results in any comprehensive survey that blended empirical data with estimated or incomplete amounts.

Mechanicals Shift from Sales to Streaming

HFA's year-end 2007 *SoundCheck* newsletter reported mechanical license collections for records, downloads, and ringtones for the first time, coming in at $393.6 million. Assuming that HFA represented about 80 percent of all mechanicals, then the industrywide total extrapolated to roughly $492 million. Meanwhile, 2007 RIAA-reported physical revenue, the usual estimation barometer for mechanical licenses, were down from 2006 by 9.9 percent, but ringtones were up 36.4 percent and downloads increased by

45 percent, resulting in an approximately $500 million total for the mechanical royalties from all three combined, in the same basic range as the HFA estimate.

With the migration of streaming services from computers to smartphones in its beginning stage (see chapter 15), mechanical licenses for streams were initiated in 2008 by the three-judge Copyright Royalty Board (CRB), established under the DMCA. The CRB set a base rate of 10.5 percent with adjustable conditions to allow for negotiations. Between 2007 and 2015 mechanical license revenue stabilized around $550 million as rising digital royalties balanced those from declining CD sales. In 2017 the CRB introduced a new minimum streaming rate to reach 15.1 percent by 2022 in five annual steps, but at the end of 2019 implementation was still pending appeals filed with the CRB by the streaming services.

By 2019 just under 20 percent of the RIAA revenue-based mechanical royalty calculation came from sales resulting in about $120 million in mechanical license revenue. Concurrently, Nielsen reported that there were 1.15 trillion individual on-demand streams tabulated in 2019, compared to 2015's 317 billion. This included premium subscription services; ad-supported on-demand services such as YouTube, Vevo, and the freemium Spotify tier; and streaming radio services including Pandora, SiriusXM, and iHeartRadio.

Calculating revenue from streaming mechanicals became further complicated since the minimum rates were subject to negotiation with varying outcomes. Rights management platforms MediaNet, RoyaltyExchange.com, and Songtrust.com all estimated the average payment at about $.006 per stream, which would put streaming mechanicals in 2019 at about $690 million. Combining this estimate with the $120 million for physical product put total mechanicals in the range of an estimated $810 million compared to the $689 million reported by the NMPA, putting the difference within range of Israelite's "you don't know what you don't know" maxim.

Sync Segment in Sync with Growing Video Production

The total for NMPA members' sync revenue grew from $440 million in its 2013 report to $844 million in 2019. In September 2019, Production Music Association (PMA) executive director Morgan McKnight told Emma Griffiths of synchtank.com, "Production music is a billion dollar a year global industry. . . . We estimate that production music generates $500 million a year in the U.S. alone. Production music is everywhere—blockbuster feature films, popular television shows, commercials for Fortune 500 brands, radio, news, sports broadcast."[3]

Production music libraries, however, were just one source of sync licenses. Library revenue came from both musical works and master recordings, as well as from PRO licenses. There were also MFN-governed publishing licenses matching the 2019 RIAA-reported $276 million in master recording sync licenses from use in film, television, commercials, and games. Songs adapted to new recordings used in visual media were also subject to sync licenses. There were also licenses issued by PMA members that were not NMPA members, and production libraries that weren't members of either trade group. Israelite's "you don't know what you don't know" precept was once again applicable. The 2019 US publishing sync license total may well have surpassed $1 billion, but without sufficient data, the exact amount remains an open question.

In the middle of the first decade of the twenty-first century the acquisition of production music libraries by the major publishers intensified. The UMPG purchase of BMG's publishing in 2007 included Killer Tracks, which then became the administrator for all UMPG production music. In 2019 Killer Tracks was rebranded as Universal Production Music with a catalog including Abbey Road Masters, Atmosphere Music, Chuck D Presents, ICON Trailer Music, Network Music, New York Beats, and Sonic Beat Records.

In 2008 Sony acquired Extreme Music as part of the Famous Music purchase. *Billboard*'s Susan Butler reported that as the leading contemporary library, Extreme accounted for more than 25 percent of Famous's NPS. Sony smartly retained Extreme founder Russell Emanuel. In 2014 Extreme opened the Bleeding Fingers joint venture with Hans Zimmer, a four-time Grammy winner, Oscar recipient for the *Lion King* score, and nominee for ten other films.

In 2007 Warner Chappell purchased twenty-six-year-old Non-Stop Music from cofounders Randy Thornton, Brian Hofheins, and Mike Dowdle to anchor their production music division. In 2010 they added Nashville-based 615 Music with owner and cofounder of the PMA Randy Wachtler joining their executive team. Other Warner Chappell library catalogs included CPM, Groove Addicts, V-The Production Library, and Full Tilt. Wachtler served as president/CEO from 2013 through 2017.

Sync revenue continued to expand as US box-office receipts and movie releases in 2019 were 17.5 percent over 2007 at $11.3 billion on 991 films. Cable revenue for 2019 almost doubled over 2007 to around $92 billion. After peaking in 2007 at $24 billion and then dipping with the recession, the home video market rebounded, but like the audio market, consumers shifted to the convenience of digital delivery alternatives. Sarah Whitten of CNBC.com reported in 2019 that DVD sales had declined by more than 87 percent since 2006, but "with the help of streaming services, the home video market has also been revived. In 2018, the U.S. market reached $23.2 billion."[4]

In 2007 video service providers YouTube, Google, Amazon Prime, and Netflix were in their formative stages and made little investment in new programming. By 2015, however, their collective revenue was at $7.1 billion, reached $18.8 billion in 2019, and was forecast to go to $42 billion by 2025. In 2019 Netflix and Amazon together spent $18.2 billion on content acquisition, up from $5.3 billion in 2015, which in turn increased sync license revenue.

Print Music

In 2019 almost all mainstream publishers' physical print rights were still licensed through distributors with the same previously outlined royalty rates. Licenses for digital delivery, however, were usually nonexclusive at a higher rate. The songwriter and any co-publisher share were paid in the next quarterly accounting or applied to any outstanding advances.

A NAMM study cited by *Billboard*'s Susan Butler listed members' 2006 retail print sales at $582 million. The 2015 NAMM financial report had 2014 at $515 million and 2015 at $505 million. These reports, however, tracked only NAMM member stores, excluding sales from digital, mail order, and non-NAMM retail outlet. The overall mail order market included selling, renting, and licensing orchestral, theatrical, band, choral, and religious scores and arrangements to educational, clerical, and community institutions and organizations. This product included current and catalog music, children's music, both classical and popular public domain works, and the distributors' own proprietary content.

In a 2019 article on the digital print segment, *Billboard* editor-at-large and *Rolling Stone* contributing editor Steve Knopper interviewed Kathleen Marsh, CEO of the leading online sheet music/tablature e-tailer Musicnotes.com, and president of the print industry trade association the Music Publishers Association (MPA). Marsh told Knopper that digital sources generated $240 million in 2018 global sales. Knopper further reported that overall digital business was expanding at a 7 percent yearly rate, and subscription sales based on a monthly fee for unlimited access were growing 50 percent annually, together projecting to about $270 million for 2019.

Adding It All Up

Since its debut in 2014, the NMPA survey has been accepted by the press, the investment community, and CISAC as the standard for evaluating US publishing revenue based on the premise that publisher royalties and licensing fees, adjusted by adding back in any deducted administrative expenses, and in the case of SESAC its profit, represented total music publishing revenue. In keeping with that premise, the NMPA used member royalty receipts as the base for its calculations.

Publishing revenue estimates for this book, however, including those calculated both before and after the 2014 unveiling of the NMPA survey, were based on a different methodology. Since NMPA membership revenue data was not publicly available for mechanical licenses prior to 2006 and not for the other revenue categories until the 2014 initial NMPA survey, other sources were researched and utilized.

This book's estimated mechanical royalties were initially calculated by applying the then-current statutory rate augmented by a range of rate-affecting conditions that were contractually applicable in varying degrees on a license-by-license basis. Then when the NMPA initiated its survey, the two methodologies were outlined and compared.

As sync licenses were and still are negotiated on a license-by-license basis between licensor and licensee, this revenue stream has long been publishing's least transparent revenue source. This book incorporated NMPA sync license data into its estimations as soon as they became available, but sync licenses were also issued by an unknown number of non-NMPA publishers, which were also considered in this book's estimates.

Performing rights, on the other hand, had always been the most transparent publishing royalty category. ASCAP annual reports had been available since before this book's time frame, and then BMI's reports were also referenced as soon as they became public in the mid-1990s. SESAC revenue was and is still estimated based on information from knowledgeable industry sources. The most obvious difference between the PRO estimates stemmed from the NMPA's decision not to include songwriter royalties sent to the domestic PROs from their foreign counterparts as a part of US publishing revenue, although the PROs and the songwriters themselves included these royalties in their reported income whether in financial reports or IRS filings.

The greatest discrepancy between the two methodologies, however, came in printed music, the oldest source of music publishing revenue. From the start of the book's narrative, printed music revenue has been estimated as what consumers spent at the point of purchase, not the royalties publishers received from their print distributors, which is how the NMPA total is calculated. This book has always considered the printed music distribution network to be a part of the music publishing sector just as the recorded music distribution infrastructure was included in the estimated valuation of the overall recorded music ecosystem.

Both the NMPA and this book's publishing revenue valuation methodologies were and are conceptually valid but based on different precepts. Understanding the nuances of the two models, however, has helped reconcile their differences and reinforce their compatibility since essentially both approaches reflect the growing stream of revenue and positive future for the publishing sector.

The Major Publishers: From Big Five to Big Three

The year 2007 opened with Martin Bandier's April 1 move from EMI to Sony/ATV, and the May sale of BMG publishing to UMPG for $2.19 billion. Bandier passed the EMI baton to CEO Roger Faxon, while twenty-year BMG veteran Nick Firth conveyed its assets to UMPG. Privately held Bertelsmann was eager to cash out of the slumping music business to focus on its more stable book, magazine, and administrative services holdings. Vivendi Universal hoped to elevate its publishing division from third to first place to mirror its record division.

Bandier told *The Hollywood Reporter*'s Chris Morris, "I was ready for my next challenge, as plain and simple as that. . . . One of the reasons to start this process (now) is to give myself a chance to explore all the opportunities that are available . . . I feel very positive that there's lots of people who'd be interested in speaking to me."[5] He subsequently accepted an offer to become CEO/chairman of fourth-place Sony/ATV replacing incumbent David Hockman. He retained New York–based Danny Strick as a co-president and added his former EMI VP Jody Gerson as co-president in Los Angeles.

Bandier began with the acquisition of the songs written by songwriter and rock-'n'-roll halls of fame inductees Jerry Leiber and Mike Stoller for $40 million. Longtime Leiber-Stoller president Randy Poe remained to oversee the catalog. In August the now-merged Sony/ATV bought Viacom's Famous Music catalog for $370 million, including its Hollywood and Tin Pan Alley classics amassed by Paramount Pictures since 1928 and acquired by Viacom in 1993. Also included were the works added under now-outgoing CEO/chairman Irwin Z. Robinson and COO/president Ira Jaffe, including Shakira, Akon, Eminem, and Busta Rhymes. Robinson's fifteen-year tenure at the helm of Famous had been preceded by twenty-four years at Screen Gems-Columbia Music.

Bandier's departure left Faxon to watch EMI sink deeper into uncertainty as the record division declined from a 9 percent market share in 2006 to 7 percent for 2007, once again generating rumors of a potential auction of assets. The Terra Firma purchase in August 2007 was 61 percent of what EMI had turned down from Edgar Bronfman Jr. just a few years earlier. In May 2010 Hands dismissed his executive team at the record company, adding its management to Faxon's portfolio. In February 2011 Citigroup seized EMI for loan default. In November 2011 the publishing assets were sold to a Sony/ATV-led group for $2.2 billion, reuniting Bandier with the EMI catalog, while UMG purchased the record division.

Sony/ATV itself acquired a 39.83 percent ownership share together with 100 percent of the administration. The other partners were the Abu Dhabi wealth fund Mubadala, Jynwel Capital of Hong Kong, four Blackstone/GSO investment funds, and David Geffen's Pub West. In April 2012, the EEC approved the transaction pending divestiture of Famous Music UK; Virgin Music in Europe, the UK, and the US; and administration for various songwriter-owned catalogs to the new BMG Rights Management. US regulatory approval was granted in June 2012 with the European final nod coming in May 2013.

Despite the turmoil, Faxon had kept EMI at the top of the *Billboard* publisher rankings, frustrating UMPG's hopes for ascendency. In 2012, the last year of its independent operation, EMI had 206 charted Hot 100 titles over the course of the year, just above UMPG's 200. Three through five were Sony/ATV, Warner Chappell, and Kobalt Music, followed by BMG Rights, Party Rock Music owned by pop duo LMFAO, Swedish songwriter/producer Max Martin's MXM Music AB, peermusic, and Where Da Kaz At Music owned by producer Lukasz "Dr. Luke" Gottwald.

The EMI acquisition vaulted Sony/ATV into the 2013 top spot with 303 charted singles. Although UMPG had more singles than in 2012, its 228 total fell further behind Sony/ATV. Warner Chappell was third with 173. The two largest independents then followed with Kobalt in fourth with 98 and BMG Rights in fifth with 72. Rounding out the top ten were Nashville songwriter-turned-entrepreneur Craig Wiseman's Big Loud Bucks, MXM Music, Pharrell Williams's The Waters of Nazareth Music, peermusic, and private equity newcomer Downtown Music.

Reorganizing the Executive Suites

From 2007 through 2010 UMPG had alternated with Sony/ATV in the second *Billboard* slot behind EMI. UMPG CEO David Renzer exited in April 2011 just a month after Doug Morris's departure. A year later Lucien Grainge shifted Zach Horowitz to chairman/CEO of UMPG. Although UMPG had barely trailed EMI in US publishing market share, it had been the top publisher on a global basis. With the EEC approval of Sony/ATV's EMI acquisition, UMPG's global status would drop to number two. Grainge still wanted to find a way into the US top spot.

Prior to WMG going up for sale in January 2011, Edgar Bronfman Jr. sought to rejuvenate Warner Chappell's creative team. At the suggestion of Lyor Cohen, Bronfman met with Grammy Award–winning New West Records owner Cameron Strang. By 2010 his publishing division roster included Bruno Mars and his writing team the Smeezingtons, the Kings of Leon, producer Brody Brown, Nashville hitmakers Ashley Gorley and Blair Daly, and Christian music star Matthew West. Two of the five Grammy nominations for 2010 Record of the Year were from his catalog. As Strang recounted to *Music Business Worldwide* (mbw.com) in 2015, "So Edgar came over and we talked for three or four hours in the back yard. At the end of it, he turned to me and said: 'I'd like to buy your business and I'd like you to run Warner/Chappell.'"[6]

In early January 2011 Strang replaced David Johnson as CEO. When the dust settled on the EMI auction, Strang offered EMI's Jon Platt the sole US presidency of Warner Chappell, a position that Sony/ATV couldn't match with two co-presidents already in place. Platt joined Warner Chappell in September 2012. In December 2012 Strang added the CEO/chairman position at Warner Bros. Records to his responsibilities following the departure of Cohen, elevating Platt to a higher level than initially anticipated.

Over the next year Platt revamped his creative team with senior VPs Ben Vaughn in Nashville and Jake Ottman in New York, extended its digital business initiatives, and expanded the sync licensing department. Joining the talent roster were Jay Z, Beyoncé, and the Roc Nation's publishing roster, lured away from EMI. Also coming on board were perennially award-winning Nashville writers Liz Rose and Lee Miller along with rock artists Slash and Dave Mustaine. Relationships were strengthened with Katy Perry, Michael Bublé, Led Zeppelin, Barry Gibb, and George Michael with revitalized exploitive services. Three out of the five 2013 Grammy song of the year nominees were Warner Chappell entries.

Back at UMPG, Grainge was still determined to move closer to if not ahead of Sony/ATV. Horowitz retired in July 2014 after a thirty-two-year tenure.

Concurrently, Jody Gerson had been renegotiating with Sony/ATV, seeking to remove "co-" from her title. After sitting at Bandier's right hand through two decades, Gerson felt she had earned the promotion. Bandier, however, wanted to retain her services but without altering his executive team. As Gerson later recounted in an interview with *Glamour*, she called Grainge who immediately asked, "Are you ready to be the global chairman of Universal Music Publishing? And I said yes."[7]

She joined UMPG on January 1, 2015, becoming the first woman to head a major music publishing company and one of publishing's three most powerful executives. She immediately filled the COO spot with Marc Cimino, then executive VP for business and legal affairs at Warner Bros. Records. She retained Evan Lamberg as president of UMPG North America and Kent Earls as executive VP/GM Nashville. In July 2015 eight-year UMPG veteran Jessica Rivera was promoted to executive VP/East Coast operations. In July 2016 David Gray was upped to executive VP/West Coast A&R. With her creative team in place Gerson took on Bandier and Platt head-on in competition for acquisitions, chart position, and market share.

The January 2018 Billboard Power 100 ranked Gerson at number eight, the top publisher spot three ahead of Platt and four ahead of Bandier. She also received *Billboard*'s 2018 Power 100 Clive Davis Visionary Award. Among her accomplishments were signing Bruce Springsteen to a global administration deal with his one-man Broadway show yielding immediate results; extending the UMPG administration deal with Disney Music Publishing to all of Europe; bringing rock innovator Jack White to UMPG; adding new chart toppers SZA, Quavo, and Lil Yachty; and inking legends Barry Gibb and Carly Simon for catalog administration.

Warner Chappell promoted Platt to CEO effective November 1, 2015, and chairman in May 2016, leaving Strang to focus solely on records. Platt had impressed Blavatnik and CEO Steven Cooper as he had the now-departed Bronfman. They believed Platt to be a generational leader capable of rivaling Bandier. Cooper commented: "His combination of artistic sensibility and commercial savvy is very rare; and is clearly why so many of the world's greatest songwriters want him as their partner and champion."[8]

Following Gerson's exodus, Bandier replaced her with Republic Records executive and former EMI senior VP Rick Krim in March 2015. Bandier renewed his own contract at the beginning of 2016 for three years. His next major task was to complete the buyout of the Jackson estate from Sony/ATV, which had been triggered in September 2015. In March 2016, the parties agreed to a $750 million purchase price. The estate's 10 percent share of EMI Music Publishing and Mijac Music, which contained Michael's own songs and other favorites he had acquired, would both continue to be administrated by Sony.

Jackson estate administrators John Branca and John McClain noted that the transaction "further validates Michael's foresight and genius in investing in music publishing. His ATV catalogue . . . was the cornerstone of the joint venture and, as evidenced by the value of this transaction, is considered one of the smartest investments in music history."[9] The estate had been rumored to be as much as $500 million in debt at the time of Jackson's death in 2009 but was now debt free and still held his songwriter, artist, Mijac catalog, and share of EMI royalties. The estate was estimated to have a $500 million valuation, producing $75 million in 2017 income.

In March 2017 Bandier promoted UK managing director/president of European creative Guy Moot to president, creative worldwide. Moot had worked for Bandier at SBK, EMI, and Sony/ATV. His signings had included Calvin Harris, Sia, Mark Ronson, Sean Paul, Amy Winehouse, Ed Sheeran, Arcade Fire, Lana Del Rey, Avicii, and Sam Smith. At the time of his appointment, Sony/ATV UK was on a roll with a fifty-two-week streak of UK number one singles.

Bandier had also empowered Moot to open a neighboring rights administration division in 2014, which signed a select group of artists including Lady Gaga, The Weeknd, Pharrell Williams, Mark Ronson, Nile Rodgers, and Sting. Neighboring rights governed the royalties due to artists, producers, and musicians related to the copyright in their sound recordings. These rights were not traditionally administrated by music publishers, but newcomers BMG and Kobalt were already doing so. Moot hired George Powell from the Phonographic Performance Ltd (PPL) agency, which had administrated these rights since the British Copyright Act of 1956. Given their decades-long relationship, the timing of his appointment, and the scope of his responsibilities, it appeared that Bandier was positioning Moot as an eventual successor.

Meanwhile, Back on the Charts . . .

In 2012, the final year of the Big Four, the yet-to-be-united Sony/ATV and EMI combined controlled 38.4 percent of the top 100 entries on the year-end *Billboard* Hot 100 chart summary. In 2013, the now-combined catalogs under the Sony/ATV banner dropped to 32.2 percent of the chart but still led the field. Second place UMPG jumped from 20.5 percent to 24.2 percent while Warner Chappell gained slightly from 18 percent to 18.4 percent for a Big Three total of 74.8 percent of the top 100 songs of 2013. The chart share for independents advanced from 22.4 percent to 25.2 percent.

Although the Hot 100 was the primary barometer for the interplay between US records, radio, and retail, it did not reflect the international responsibilities the Big Three CEOs had assumed. *Music & Copyright (M&C)* was a self-described "fortnightly research service covering global copyright and legal issues affecting the music industry."[10] For over a decade *M&C* had utilized publishers' financial statements to create an annual comparison of publishing sector revenue. For 2013 *M&C* credited Sony/ATV, including the EMI catalog, with a 29.4 percent share of the global market, with UMPG at 22.6 percent, and Warner Chappell at 13.2 percent, for a Big Three global market share of 65.2 percent. Meanwhile ratings and rankings from both global and domestic sources indicated a growing percentage of the independent segment going to Kobalt and BMG.

According to *M&C*, in 2019 Sony/ATV still led with $1.4 billion for 25 percent, UMPG placed second at $1.18 billion for 21 percent, and Warner Chappell came in third totaling $651 million on 11.6 percent. The Big Three had a total share of 57.6 percent. BMG took in $450 million for fourth at 8.4 percent, while Kobalt was fifth with $405 million for 7.6 percent. Together these five accounted for 73.6 percent of 2019 global publishing revenue. Even though the Big Three themselves were down in market share 7.5 percent between 2013 and 2019, the streaming tsunami caused a combined industry growth of 37.5 percent, making a larger profit on a smaller market share for all three. Revenue for the independents benefited from both market growth and the gain in the share lost by the Big Three.

By 2019 independents achieved significant growth in the year-end ranking with just over 40 percent of the top 100 songs. Kobalt moved into third place with 16.6 percent of the Hot 100, edging Warner Chappell into fourth at 14.5 percent. Kobalt's Hot 100 percentage was more than twice its overall global market share of 7.4 percent due to administrating a cadre of self-published songwriters who were active as artists and producers. They preferred Kobalt's metadata-driven accessibility over the far more traditional accounting systems of the Big Three. The more catalog-oriented BMG had an 8.4 percent global market share on $450 million in revenue with just 6.1 percent of the year-end Hot 100. Combined, the Big Three, Kobalt, and BMG controlled 86 percent of the Hot 100 chart's top 100 songs of 2019.

Sony Prepares for the Future

On April 1, 2018, Sony Corporation CFO Kenichiro Yoshida became president/CEO when incumbent Kazuo Hirai moved to become chairman. Hirai had succeeded Sir Howard Stringer in 2012 and left $12 billion in cash on the books as Yoshida assumed control. Even though Sony had bought the Jackson estate's share of Sony/ATV, the two were still partners in the EMI catalog with the consortium. On July 29, 2018, Mubadala et al. would be able to invoke a provision that gave Sony a two-month exclusive window to negotiate and agree upon a deal before the share was made available to other buyers.

Yoshida also had to decide what to do when Bandier's contract expired in March 2019: renew it, or if not, decide who would replace him; or if he renewed, who would be his eventual successor. By then Bandier would be over seventy-seven, well past the traditional Sony retirement age of sixty, but there were few publishers with Bandier's experience and skill set. The closest were considered to be those he had mentored, but Gerson and Platt had already been lured away by Sony's top competitors. EMI was now valued at $4.75 million, more than double the $2.2 billion 2012 purchase price. Yoshida needed to decide whether to sell and take the profit or invest further, betting that the music industry would continue on with its newly reignited growth trend.

In late May, Sony announced that it had a legally binding agreement to acquire the consortium's share, pending regulatory approval, for $2.1 billion, roughly doubling their investment, and assumption by Sony of $1.359 billion of debt. *Billboard*'s Christman calculated the sales multiple as being about 14.5 times the NPS. Sony quickly bought out the Jackson estate share for $287.5 million. There also was a management equity plan with a $190 million bonus for building the value of EMI over the past six years for Bandier and his senior executive team.

While waiting for regulatory approval of the purchase, which would finally come in mid-October, Yoshida contemplated Bandier's future. Then on September 13 Bandier was informed that Jon Platt would be his successor as of March 31, 2019. The next day, the news was all over the trade press and Warner Chappell confirmed that Platt was leaving as of December 31. Bandier addressed his staff in a September 17 memo: "Dear all, I want to let you know that I am planning to leave Sony/ATV at the end of my contract in March of next year . . . I can say without hesitation that my time here has been the absolute highlight of my career, and I am extremely proud of everything that we have achieved together."[11]

While Moot's resume certainly warranted consideration, Platt had already proven his bona fides at the worldwide CEO level. With Sony almost twice the size of Warner Chappell, and Bandier's shoes perhaps the biggest ever needing to be filled in the publishing sector, Yoshida went for the top possible candidate, no matter current affiliation or ultimate cost, and achieved his objective. Platt's attorney and industry deal-maker Joel Katz had quietly facilitated Platt's transition according to *Billboard*'s Melinda Newman. Katz subsequently told her, "The people at Warners are really good people and they understood the opportunity for Jon; and Jon, frankly, had the discussion with [Warner Music Group] at the highest of levels."[12]

Cooper in turn hired Moot in January 2019 to team as CEO/cochair with incumbent COO Carianne Marshall, who had "cochair" added to her title. Before joining Platt at Warner Chappell in 2018, Marshall had been a partner in independent publisher SONGS before its sale to Kobalt. This cochair/CEO-COO pairing mirrored the executive tandem structure WMG had built into its record division. Moot was also far more than a consolation prize. If Platt had not moved to Sony, Moot was the logical choice. His hiring at Warner Chappell put all of the Big Three in the hands of a Bandier protégé, perhaps the most complimentary element of what would be the legacy of a long and accomplished career.

The "Mini-Major" Independents: A New Rights Management Model

Founder and still CEO Willard Ahdritz opened Kobalt in 2000 as an administrative and royalty collection agent for independent songwriters and publishers rather than as a rightsholder. Ahdritz envisioned a transparent royalty system with a web portal where clients could track their royalties coupled with expedited accounting through automated bank transfer. Kobalt claimed its lower administration rates and systematic efficiency could result in up to 30 percent more in royalties that could otherwise be siphoned off in processing, absorbed in administrative costs, remain undetected, or be misidentified.

In July 2010 Ahdritz opened Kobalt Capital Limited (KCL) to accommodate clients who wanted to sell self-owned publishing rights in order to have money now rather that left to their estates. KCL would advise and administrate but not participate in investments. A year later KCL established Kobalt Music Copyrights (KMC) with $350 million in investment capital. Among its initial acquisitions were the publishing interests of Canadian management firm Nettwerk including songs by 10,000 Maniacs, Sinéad O'Connor, and country star Dierks Bentley.

In January 2012 Kobalt opened its Kobalt Label Services (KLS) with its acquisition of London-based digital distribution and marketing provider Artists Without a Label Limited (AWAL). Its over five thousand clients—including Radiohead, Arctic Monkeys, and Moby—would now be able to avail themselves of Kobalt's system modified to accommodate data from hundreds of digital platforms. AWAL put Kobalt in the center of the full-service rights administration competition. In 2014 Kobalt launched a music performance detection search system dubbed ProKlaim for tracking performances on YouTube, designed to be the next-generation innovation for royalty data management and accounting in the new age of subscription streaming. ProKlaim extended Kobalt's global detection from the traditional broadcasting and physical distribution sectors into all corners of new media.

In November 2017 KMC closed another round of investment for $600 million and immediately outbid fourteen other suitors with an estimated $160 million for the SONGS catalog. Developed by former EMI staffer Matt Pincus with Carianne Marshall and Ron Perry, all of whom participated in the proceeds, SONGS had been built without venture capital and signed co-publishing deals for life of copyright with contemporary songwriters before they had major success. Their roster included The Weeknd, Lourde, Diplo, Desiigner, and DJ Mustard. The addition of SONGS propelled Kobalt to the number two position behind Sony in the *Billboard* Hot 100 rankings for two quarters in 2018, and then occupied the third position ahead of Warner Chappell throughout 2019. The Kobalt publishing division collected $405 million for the fiscal year ending June 30, 2019, neighboring rights had $69.65 million in licenses, and AWAL handled $65.6 million in master rights revenue.

Former BMG senior executive Laurent Hubert joined Kobalt in 2016 and was named president in 2017. He described to *Music Business Worldwide* how he viewed Kobalt from the outside while still at BMG. "Kobalt came onto the market nearly 15 years ago with a vision and a mission—the notions of transparency, accountability and the idea that technology is a positive enabler in our business . . . Kobalt is a company that can enhance value for all copyrights, regardless of who owns them."[13]

After serving in executive positions with Virgin, Arisa, and Island, Lawrence Mestel opened Primary Wave Music in 2005 with the purchase of 50 percent of Kurt Cobain's share of the Nirvana publishing catalog from widow Courtney Love, and soon added a stake in Julian Lennon's share of his father's post-Beatles catalog. His blend of catalog management featuring in-house branding, digital marketing, TV and film development, talent management, and aggressive pursuit of syncs and endorsements has built a leading multiple rights administration and ownership firm for iconic catalogs. According to its website, Primary Wave controls all or part of over fifteen thousand songs with over seven hundred top 10 singles, and over three hundred number one hits.

In 2016 Smokey Robinson signed a $22 million catalog partnership deal with Primary Wave. In 2018 Mestel acquired 80 percent of Island founder Chris Blackwell's publishing rights to Blue Mountain Music for $50 million including the catalogs of Bob Marley, Toots & the Maytals, Marianne Faithfull, and the classic British rock band Free fronted by Paul Rodgers. At the time of the agreement with Blackwell Ben Sisario of *The New York Times* reported, "Unlike most publishers, Primary Wave sees itself as a branding house and an asset manager, exploiting song catalogs on behalf of investors that have contributed to an acquisition fund. The company, Mr. Mestel said, has about $400 million to invest in music on behalf of those investors, a group that includes BlackRock, the world's largest money manager."[14] Other Primary Wave acquisitions through 2019 included Steve Cropper, Alice Cooper, Kenny Loggins, Count Basie, Sly & the Family Stone, Culture Club with Boy George, Leon Russell, Paul Anka, producers Pete Waterman and Bob Ezrin, and the estates of Leon Russell and Whitney Houston.

In 2010 BMG continued its BMG Rights rebuild with the acquisition of Chrysalis Music for $168.6 million and Bug Music for another $300 million. Other acquisitions during that period included Stage Three Music, Cherry Lane Music Publishing, Crosstown Songs America, Adage IV, and Evergreen Copyrights. In 2012 BMG bought out investment partner KKR and expanded into master rights administration as well. They alternated in the *Billboard* year-end Hot 100 top ten publishers between fourth and fifth place with Kobalt Music after Sony/ATV acquired EMI. Still under the leadership of Hartwig Masuch, BMG's combined services generated $672 million in 2019.

By 2018 Concord Bicycle Music had joined the growing group of integrated rights management successes. The company was owned by Baring Asset Management, a division of Massachusetts Mutual Life Insurance Company, which had over $275 billion in managed assets through its private equity division Wood Creek Capital Management. In 2006 they acquired the thirty-two-year-old Bicycle Music publishing catalog from founder David Rosner. Norman Lear–led Concord Music was acquired in 2013. Bicycle and Concord merged in 2015 and shifted all record assets into Concord and publishing holdings into Bicycle.

Under the leadership of Jake Wisely at Bicycle and Wood Creek consultant Steve Salm at Concord, they targeted small catalogs containing songs ideal for sync exploitation along with corresponding master recordings when possible, similar to the BMG model. After the Bicycle-Concord consolidation, Wisely, now CEO of the publishing division and Salm, now chief business development officer, were given the green light by the chairman of the consolidated company, Steve Smith, for larger acquisitions.

In June 2017 Concord won the auction for Netherlands-based Imagem Music Group, which had been formed in 2008 to buy catalogs spun out of the UMPG purchase of the previous BMG publishing iteration as required by the EEC regulatory board. Imagem's 250,000 copyrights included works or shares thereof by Phil Collins, Mark Ronson, Daft Punk, and Pink Floyd; the classical giant Boosey & Hawkes; and the Rodgers & Hammerstein Organization. The acquisitions tripled Concord's catalog. *Billboard* estimated the deal to be in the $600 million range at approximately a 12 multiple, making it the largest purchase by an independent publisher and positioning Concord beside Kobalt and BMG as a mini-major rights management company.

While there was widespread speculation that Barings wanted to cash out, it had already turned down a $500 million offer from BMG prior to the Imagem purchase. Forty of the key executives in both publishing and recorded music divisions had themselves invested in equity positions. Managing director and board member Scott Pascucci told *Billboard*, "We're not a five-year private equity fund. . . . We have investors who like being in the music business. We make them money."[15]

Other Independents on the Rise

Downtown Music was opened in 2006 as a private equity–backed, full-service independent by twenty-six-year-old CEO Justin Kalifowitz after working at Spirit Music for five years. Downtown acquired both master recording and publishing rights to selected songs and catalogs, but also pursued current product, ranking number ten in the Billboard Top 100 for 2013. Downtown also owned Songtrust, an online, interactive royalty collection platform opened in 2011 for independent songwriters and publishers. While Downtown has about 100,000 songs in its catalog, Songtrust collected for over 2 million works as of the end of 2019 at a 15 percent administration fee.

Downtown had administration agreements with John Prine, Ryan Tedder, Benny Blanco, and Niall Horan, the John Lennon catalog, and Nashville independent Big Yellow Dog Music, which rated number ten in the 2015 Hot 100 Top Ten. With a songwriter roster including award-winning artists Meghan Trainor and Maren Morris, Big Yellow Dog, owned by leading artist business manager Kerry O'Neil and partner Carla Wallace, scored thirty-six number one chart songs, including shares of Trainor's worldwide hit "All About That Bass," and Lady Antebellum's "Need You Now."

Following the Chrysalis Music acquisition by BMG in 2010, former Chrysalis president Kenny MacPherson, along with colleagues Dave Ayers and Jamie Cerreta, founded Big Deal Music Group with an emphasis on current and emerging songwriters. They were joined by Mick Management's Michael McDonald and his Vinegar Hill/Propel Music publishing operation. Big Deal ranked eighth in 2016 and ninth in 2017 in the Hot 100 rankings. In late 2015 Big Deal acquired Nashville-based copyright administrator Words & Music, founded by Kim McCollum-Mele in 2002, to take over when its BMG administration deal expired at the end of the year. Big Deal operated out of Los Angeles with satellite offices in New York, Nashville, and London. Their writers included Ray LaMontagne, My Morning Jacket, St. Vincent, Dan Wilson, Teddy Geiger, Brad Tursi, Nick Lowe, Local Natives, Brett Beavers, and the Preservation Hall Jazz Band.

In 2011 New York–based Round Hill Music opened as another integrated rights management contender that by 2018 was vying for a spot in the yearly top ten ranking. A third-generation Wall Street investment banker, former indie rocker, and Berklee College of Music graduate, thirty-six-year-old chairman/CEO Joshua Gruss funded Round Hill with private financing. He hired former Sony/ATV president Richard Rowe as vice chairman and former Warner Chappell VP Neil Gillis as president. One of their first acquisitions was the US rights to six Beatles classics, "She Loves You," "From Me to You," "I Saw Her Standing There," "Misery," "There's a Place" and "I Wanna Be Your Man."

The first round of investment capital closed in July 2014 with $209 million, and the second round ended in December 2017 with $263 million. Round Hill acquired songs or shares thereof recorded by The Rolling Stones, Frank Sinatra, James Brown, Bruno Mars, Katie Perry, Bon Jovi, Aerosmith, NSYNC, Pat Benatar, The Four Tops, James Taylor, and Marvin Gaye, among many others. In November 2014 Round Hill expanded into Nashville with the acquisition of award-winning songwriter Craig Wiseman's Big Loud Shirt Industries. Wiseman's songwriter roster had thirty-two top ten records between them including number ones by Tim McGraw, Carrie Underwood, and George Strait. *Billboard* reported the price to be around $35 million, Round Hill's largest purchase to date.

Gruss then hired publishing and A&R veteran Mark Brown, who refurbished the historic Quadrafonic Studios for the Nashville headquarters. In November 2017 Round Hill formed a joint venture with New York/ Los Angeles–based sync licensing specialist Zync Music. Zync had processed over fifteen thousand licenses for nearly $100 million since its 2002 founding by co-CEOs Marisa Baldi and Sanne Hagelsten. In January 2018 Round Hill added Carlin Music, headed since 1989 by Freddy Bienstock's daughter Caroline, who also served as a board director for ASCAP, NMPA, and HFA prior to its purchase by SESAC. *Billboard* cited a price of $245 million at about a 16 multiple of NPS.

Two other full-service and long-established independents, peermusic and Walt Disney Music, made the Billboard Hot 100 top ten year-end ratings multiple times during this period. Big Loud Bucks ranked twice before its acquisition by Round Hill. Cherry Lane, Bug, Chrysalis, and Stage Three had all ranked in the top ten prior to their acquisition by BMG. SONGS was in the top ten rankings from 2014 through 2017. After that, their repertoire was included in the Kobalt total. Big Machine Records' publishing wing rated sixth for two quarters in 2019 and seventh in one other quarter. The other independent publishers in the year-end top ten list from 2007 through 2019 were primarily songwriter, producer, and/or artist-owned companies administrated by one of the Big Three or by a mini-major including Drake, Dr. Luke, Bruno Mars, Pharrell Williams, Max Martin, and Ed Sheeran.

Anthem and Hipgnosis Join the Fray

By late 2019 two other publishing companies had raised investment capital to acquire cash flow–producing music properties employing different strategies. Toronto-based Anthem Entertainment had been formed as ole Media Management in 2004 by former BMG Canada GM Robert Ott with $40 million in backing from the Ontario Teachers' Pension Plan. Ott assembled film and television production libraries and management of audiovisual sync and neighboring rights to generate cash flow to fund writer development and acquisitions.

By March 2017 ole's investment was valued at over $520 million. A less than projected ROI prompted the pension plan to seek a buyer with a minimum bid of $650 million calculated at a 11.4 multiple. With no acceptable offers, in May 2018 Ott was replaced by former PolyGram and WMG CFO Helen Murphy. She rebranded ole as Anthem Entertainment. In September 2019 Tim Wipperman joined Anthem as president of the Nashville office, bringing along his highly successful startup Rezonant Music, charged with increasing current catalog past the 50 percent of revenue level it had been under Ott. A twenty-nine-year Warner Chappell veteran, Wipperman had been named country music publisher of the year by each of the PROs more than ten times, and by 2018 three-year-old Rezonant had a share in twenty-one top 100 country chart singles.

Hipgnosis Songs opened in July 2018 as an investment trust fund on the London Stock Exchange. Founder and former artist manager Merck

Mercuriadis labeled Hipgnosis as a song management company selectively buying the rights to established songs and/or catalogs directly from songwriters. Trading in London under the SONG stock ticker symbol, Hipgnosis' first offering brought in $262 million. Fund managers and analysts at JP Morgan echoed the already published prognostications of Citigroup, PwC, and Goldman Sachs in believing that due to streaming the music industry would show revenue growth of 10 percent per annum through 2030. The Mercuriadis mantra of stable value and long-term sustainability was music to investors' ears and checkbooks, making Hipgnosis stock a strong play.

With the completion of additional funding rounds, by mid-December 2019 Hipgnosis had spent $684 million acquiring forty-two catalogs at what Mercuriadis termed a blended acquisition multiple of 12.84 percent, including thousands of top ten songs or shares thereof ranging from pop standards to current streaming chart toppers. The market cap value was roughly $855 million. Mercuriadis ebulliently effused, "This is an excellent NAV [net asset value] result. . . and supports our thesis that songs are a new asset class to be taken as seriously as gold and oil. Our results are not only positive news for Hipgnosis and our shareholders but for all songwriters."[16]

BMI and ASCAP Reach Parity and Change Leadership

In 2009 total US PRO revenue passed $2 billion for the first time with ASCAP and BMI close to parity, and SESAC estimated at a little over $100 million. Radio contributed about 33 percent of the domestic total, television and cable combined for about 49 percent, and 3 percent was generated by new digital media. General licensing provided the bulk of the remaining 15 percent. Except for the license fees for the top three hundred *Pollstar* tours, which had their own live performance distribution pool, the general licensing collections were added to the radio distribution. In 2011 the PROs all set up their own interactive programs—BMI Live, ASCAP OnStage, and SESAC Live Performance—for singer/songwriters to log the set lists from their own performances on smaller tours and club performances for inclusion with the *Pollstar* data in the live performance distribution.

When ASCAP and BMI's radio licenses expired at the end of 2009, the economic downturn had reduced radio revenue to $14.3 billion from a peak of over $20 billion in 2006. The Radio Music License Committee (RMLC) believed that the industrywide flat-fee basis had become disadvantageous to smaller market stations and wanted a return to the percentage formulation used in previous contracts. ASCAP agreed in January 2012, followed by BMI in June, to run through 2016 with a 1.73 percent base rate with certain defined deductions, streamlined reporting requirements, and digital revenues included at the same rate eliminating the more costly webcasting license rate.

Most significantly, however, radio now regarded ASCAP and BMI to be on a par, as tacitly acknowledged by these new agreements. The longstanding, contentious acrimony that had lingered since the 1940 ASCAP radio boycott had finally seemed to abate with a new generation of PRO leadership. Award-winning songwriter Paul Williams replaced Marilyn Bergman as president and chairman of the board in 2009. John Lofrumento retired in 2014 after seventeen of his thirty-three years at ASCAP as CEO, having bridged the gap between the last survivors of the pre-BMI era and the advent of the digital age. He was succeeded in January 2015 by Elizabeth Matthews, then forty-six, who had joined ASCAP in 2013 as EVP and general counsel, positions she previously held at Viacom Media Networks, formerly MTV Networks, since 1998.

In September 2013 Michael O'Neill, then fifty-one, was named CEO of BMI, and then president in June 2014, succeeding Del R. Bryant. A Rutgers MBA, O'Neill had joined BMI's licensing department in 1995 from CBS-TV Network affiliate relations. In 1998 he became VP of sales and administration for media licensing. During Bryant's ten-year term, O'Neill gradually assumed more administrative responsibilities. In 2006 he was appointed senior VP, licensing, and in 2010 repertoire was added to his portfolio.

SESAC Changes Hands . . . Twice

In January 2013 venture capital firm Rizvi Traverse Management bought 75 percent of SESAC for $600 million. Formed in 2004 by Suhail Rizvi and John Giampetroni, Rizvi Traverse's investments had included talent agency ICM and *Twilight* movie series producer Summit Entertainment. According to *Billboard*'s Ed Christman, in 2010 the Swid-Gershon-Smith SESAC ownership team had sold 36 percent to asset management firm Och-Ziff for $146.7 million. As part of the Rizvi Traverse transaction Swid et al. bought out Och-Ziff for $216 million and retired another $140 million in debt, netting $244 million from the sale on top of the $176 million in dividends they paid to themselves between 2010 and 2012. They also retained a 25 percent ownership share. While the industry was stunned by the price, the sale documents gave a closer look at SESAC's financial dealings. In the prior three years, SESAC had paid out only $167 million in royalties from their $356 million in licensing collections, only 46.9 percent of the total. The $167 million was only

3.3 percent of the total distribution by all three PROs combined, although SESAC took in 5.9 percent of total revenue.

The SESAC financials utilized earnings before interest, taxes, depreciation, and amortization (EBITDA) as the valuation methodology measuring net profits as a percentage of gross revenue after deducting operating expenses and before considering the acronymized line items. EBITDA was popularized by John Malone while building his Liberty Media empire and used extensively during the dot-com bubble. SESAC's EBITDA had a compound annual five-year growth rate of 13 percent through the economic turndown and its recovery. Unlike ASCAP and BMI with their consent decrees and rate courts, SESAC could sue infringers under the highly punitive provisions of US copyright law as its recourse to unsuccessful negotiations.

SESAC COO Pat Collins, who had replaced Bill Velez in 2004 after nine years as senior VP for licensing and twenty-four years in licensing at ASCAP before that, became CEO of performing rights. Allen & Co. executive and SESAC board member John Josephson was named CEO/chairman. In July 2014 SESAC added sync license administrator Rumblefish and in September 2015 SESAC acquired HFA from the NMPA for $20 million. HFA's mechanical licensing collections had fallen with the decrease in record sales. HFA's value was in its database and metadata along with its 11.5 percent commissions from the $150 million in annual gross licensing revenue, about half of what it had been in 2010.

In January 2017, *Billboard*'s Christman reported, "Blackstone's Core Equity Partners fund acquired SESAC in what might well be a $1 billion deal. That's the rumored price tag floating around the industry."[17] *Moody's Investors Service* reported SESAC's 2016 annual revenue to be about $248 million, with EBITDA somewhere between 30 percent and 35 percent of revenue, or between $74.4 million and $86.8 million. At the average of those figures, a $1 billion price tag was a 12.4 multiple. Christman added that seller Rizvi Traverse had bought the company for a 13.7 multiple. Blackstone had noted SESAC's ten years of annual growth, diversified portfolio of licensing sources, lack of regulation by consent decree and rate court, and predicted future growth for the industry as a whole. Blackstone invested in what looked like, on an EBIDTA basis, both a profitable history and a promising future.

In July 2017 SESAC and the RMLC received their first ever arbitration ruling, which covered radio licenses for January 2016 through December 2018. SESAC had sought more than 10 percent of PRO collections from radio revenue, but the arbiters ruled on a lower rate of .2557 percent of radio revenue compared to the 1.73 percent base rate ASCAP and BMI were each receiving. This was about 60 percent of what had been paid under the interim rate with make-up credits due to settle the difference. CEO Josephson put a positive spin on the ruling in stating to *Variety*'s Paula Parisi, "While it's true that the aggregate amount of money we will receive has gone down, there is one very significant element of the award that must be considered: we now have an independently adjudicated rate that implies a value for rates of music in radio at approximately 50 percent above the current ASCAP rate."[18]

Former ASCAP economist Barry Massarsky, whose clients have included Sony, Universal, the RIAA, and SoundExchange, distilled the contention over the value of music between radio and the PROs to its bare essence in telling Parisi that US radio station programming is "about 78% music, yet it accounts for only about four percent of their budget. . . . Compare that to what Turner or HBO or anyone else spends on [television] programming, it's more like 30%-40% of operating costs."[19] This observation was certainly not lost on ASCAP, BMI, Blackstone, or Irving Azoff.

Despite the July 2017 arbitration ruling, SESAC's pre-EBIDTA valuation still looked good to the investment community. SESAC was able to refinance its capitalization in September 2019 with $530 million in secured corporate bonds replacing the debt Blackstone had utilized, along with $30 million in revolving credit. *Billboard*'s Christman reported, "In a first for the music industry, the deal was structured as a whole business securitization, which means that all of the company's income streams and assets—including its licenses to music users and its contracts with songwriters—are backing the bonds."[20] Christman also ascertained from credit reports, that in 2018 SESAC produced $79.8 million in earnings before EBITDA, on $274.8 million in revenue, out of which $254.4 million were performing rights collections. The reports also revealed that general licensing provided 42.4 percent of SESAC's total with television at 23.5 percent, digital at 16.3 percent, and radio at only 10.2 percent. Foreign revenue supplied 6.8 percent.

Azoff Alters the Balance

In 2013 Irving Azoff launched GMR as a part of his Azoff/MSG Entertainment joint venture with Madison Square Garden's (MSG) James Dolan. Attorney and former ASCAP executive VP Randy Grimmett joined as CEO/partner. They believed that a select roster of one hundred top songwriters could attain a balance between market share and overhead to deliver a 30 percent higher payout than the established PROs. Licensing agreements were targeted to commence in January 2017, giving them time to solidify their songwriter agreements, establish new GMR-affiliated publishing companies, and negotiate terms with licensees. The projected roster included the Eagles, Jay-Z, Beyoncé, Pharrell Williams, Florida Georgia Line, Christina Aguilera, Bruno Mars, Alicia Keyes, Bruce Springsteen, Drake, Metallica, John Meyer, Harry Styles, Ryan Tedder, and the estates of John Lennon and George Gershwin.

Prior to GMR, the RMLC had considered ASCAP and BMI to be basically at parity, controlling about 97 percent of the market with SESAC representing the remainder. Now GMR was seeking $42 million from radio for 2017, about a 12 percent share of PRO radio royalties. The RMLC, however, maintained that GMR was in the 5 percent to 7 percent range, leading to a federal antitrust lawsuit in the US District Court for the Eastern District of Pennsylvania in which the RMLC charged GMR with creating an artificial monopoly to extort higher rates from stations. GMR followed with a countersuit filed in the US District Court of Central California claiming the RMLC to be an illegal cartel. In the meanwhile, GMR demanded an interim license at $2.5 million per month with a carve-out for license settlements done with several large radio groups, including iHeart and Entercom. In August 2018, the California court stayed the GMR case under a first-to-file ruling putting jurisdiction in Pennsylvania. GMR continued to appeal while operating under the interim licenses. In April 2019, the Pennsylvania court ruled to consolidate the two cases in California. The initial interim licenses were renewed again.

At the end of 2019, the case was scheduled to be back to court in 2020. The Department of Justice (DOJ) filed a brief on December 5 suggesting that the RMLC was operating as a "buyer's cartel . . . that can be equally destructive of competition as a sellers' cartel."[21] Azoff proclaimed, "Today is a great day for artists, who have been bullied by the RMLC since the dawn of the modern radio industry. We believe the days of this brazen, long-running cartel are now numbered."[22] On the other hand, Ed Christman reported that the RMLC had long refuted the GMR and DOJ contentions by claiming that GMR had leveraged a competitive vacuum created by the ASCAP and BMI consent decrees to create "an untenable and illegal situation wherein RMLC's members are forced to either pay overly priced licensee fees to GMR or face copyright infringement claims."[23]

ASCAP and BMI Adapt to the Changing Market

With both SESAC and GMR aggressively seeking to impinge upon the market dominance and balance achieved by the two larger PROs, ASCAP's and BMI's common threats and current needs now took precedent over their historic competition. Their consent decrees had been imposed upon them in 1941, before the market penetration of television, much less the debut of digital media. The last modification for BMI came in 1994 with the DOJ agreeing to a BMI rate court to replace arbitration for licensing disputes; and in 2001 for ASCAP, clarifying their rate court judge's role and refining licensing categories. These consent decrees did not allow ASCAP or BMI to use the higher royalty rate SoundExchange paid to artists and labels for performance rights in court as comparative evidence of value.

This issue came to the fore in 2012 as several music publishers—including Sony/ATV, Universal, and BMG Rights—notified ASCAP and BMI of their intent to exercise their contractual right to direct license their performing rights to Pandora. Because publishers were not parties to the consent decrees, they could use the SoundExchange rate as a negotiating tool. The publishers proceeded with varying results, but then the rate court ruled that partial withdrawal of a catalog was not allowable. Pandora, however, agreed to pay higher rates to the larger Sony/ATV and Universal catalogs at more than twice the PRO rates, with BMG and other smaller publishers closer to the PRO rates. Meanwhile the rate courts raised the base rate for both ASCAP and BMI from 1.73 percent to 2.5 percent using the rates achieved by the publishers' direct licenses, some of which the PROs administered, as a comparison.

Concerned about further attempts at partial withdrawal, ASCAP and BMI each petitioned the DOJ to review the consent decrees for amendment and possible sunsetting. Although it declined to make any change, the DOJ proposed a switch from the existing practice of fractional licensing by which each PRO included only its share of co-licensed songs in its own blanket license, to 100 percent licensing whereby one PRO could license 100 percent of co-licensed songs and be responsible for payments to all participants. Neither ASCAP's nor BMI's systems were structured to accommodate such a proposal.

In 2016, the rate courts ruled against the DOJ proposal. At about the same time, Pandora decided that to remain competitive it needed to create a more interactive premium tier and softened its posture with the PROs and publishers to avoid antagonism in any future negotiations. Direct licenses were concluded with the majors thus rendering the rate court ruling against partial withdrawal inconsequential as when disputes are resolved, they are no longer under the jurisdiction of the rate court.

The Music Modernization Act of 2018

In 2013 House Judiciary Committee chairman Bob Goodlatte (R-VA) signaled his willingness to consider an overhaul of parts of US copyright law. He encouraged the music industry to introduce pieces of legislation that could be bundled in an omnibus bill. Four and a half years later, in October 2018, the Orrin G. Hatch-Bob Goodlatte Music Modernization Act (MMA) became law, consolidating three existing proposed bills into one.

The Songwriter Equity Act became Title I of the MMA, creating a blanket license system for disbursing mechanical royalties from DSPs for streamed transmissions separately and directly to both songwriters and publishers. Title II adapted the record labels' Fair Play Fair Pay Act, which had proposed the establishment of performance rights royalties for sound recordings from radio transmissions, but opposition from the NAB continued to block it. Rather than lose the entire bill, the labels settled for royalties on digital transmissions only, leaving terrestrial radio without them. Title II adapted the Classics Protection and Access Act, aka the CLASSICS Act, to grant copyright protection and digital revenue for sound recordings created prior to 1972, rights that had not previously existed in the US. Also included as Title III was the Allocation for Music Producers Act, which added royalties for music producers, mixers, and engineers as part of performance rights for digital transmissions.

Ever since Spotify's 2011 agreement with HFA to distribute their mechanical royalties to US publishers, payment of these royalties to many independents had been contentious if ever paid at all. Title I of the MMA also created the nonprofit Mechanical Licensing Collective (MLC) to introduce and administrate the blanket license process. The Copyright Office was authorized to accept applicants and select one to operate the new agency. The MMA also empowered the PROs to use SoundExchange rates as comparative evidence in future rate court hearings.

After settling lawsuits with both the NMPA and a class-action case by several disgruntled songwriters, Spotify and its fellow DSPs agreed to support the MMA since they still faced the threat of infringement liability involving as much as 20 percent of past US mechanical streaming royalty obligations. Spotify agreed to a $43.45 million fund to settle any class-action claims, setting January 1, 2018, as the filing deadline. Protesting that the fund was insufficient, Bob Gaudio of Four Seasons fame and independent publishing administrator Bluewater Music both filed their own suits. Immediately before the deadline, Wixen Music also filed its own $1.5 billion action. All were eventually settled on a confidential basis before the implementation of the MMA.

With two different applicants in the final running, in June 2019 the Copyright Office chose the Mechanical Licensing Collective, Inc. (MLCI) over the rival American Mechanical Licensing Collective (AMLC). Endorsed by the NMPA, NSAI, Songwriters of North America (SONA), and the

DIGITAL TECHNOLOGY CREATED NEW INCOME STREAMS

Streaming services, websites featuring music, and satellite radio were new revenue sources for both songs and recordings. As digital consumption expanded, consumers shifted away from record sales, terrestrial radio, and MP3 downloads. By 2019 digital sources were providing 80% of label revenue and about 25% of publishing income.

Performing Rights

PRO collections from domestic digital licenses were over $500 million in 2019. Paid via **PROs** direct to both publishers and songwriters.

Performance Rights

Collections from licenses for digital transmissions produced over $900 million in 2019. Paid via **SoundExchange** direct to both master recording owners and artists.

SONGWRITER
COMPOSERS
LYRICISTS

RECORDING
ARTISTS
PRODUCERS

WRITER SHARE   **ARTIST SHARE**

PUBLISHERS
INCLUDING
CO-PUBLISHERS

MASTER
RECORDING
OWNERS

Digital Mechanical Licenses

As of January 1, 2021 paid through the Mechanical Licensing Collective (MLC). Before that paid through HFA, MRI, other administrators, or direct to copyright owner.

Digital Label & Artist Royalties

Streaming services paid to labels which then paid artists at their contractual royalty rates ranging from 16% of wholesale for new artist to as much as 25% for superstars.

SUBSCRIPTION STREAMING SERVICES AND OTHER DIGITAL TRANSMITTERS
On-demand services such as Spotify and Apple Music paid about 70% of revenue in rights fees. Publishing received 10.5% through 2018 after which a five-year schedule of increases to 15.35% was implemented. The balance went to the master recording owners. Less interactive transmitters such as Pandora and SiriusXM paid at lower rates.

Source: BMI / SoundExchange / MLC / All You Need To Know About the Music Business

Illustration 13.1 Digital Technology Created New Income Streams

Association of Independent Music Publishers (AIMP), the MCLI had a much larger base of support. The MLCI now became the MLC, with ABKCO Music COO Alisa Coleman named board chair. James Duffett-Smith of Amazon was named by the Digital Media Association (DiMA) to chair the Digital Licensing Coordinator (DLC) team to work on behalf of the DSPs in cooperation with the MLC. By January 1, 2021, when the MMA royalty calculation and distribution process would commence, DiMA members would provide the MLC with $33.5 million for start-up costs and an initial annual assessment of $28.5 million, as outlined in a November 2019 agreement.

Coleman and Duffett-Smith released a joint statement, "Today's agreement between the MLC and the DLC represents a landmark achievement for every facet of the music industry. . . . We will now continue our work together to finalize the operations and other requirements under the law as we prepare to help songwriters get the royalties they are owed."[24] The NMPA's David Israelite added, "The deal struck with the biggest streaming companies in the world to fund the collective's start up and future operational costs is an important step forward for our industry. The collective Is an unprecedented agency serving both songwriters and streaming services so that the entire system works better."[25]

The NSAI's executive director, Bart Herbison, whose songwriter board had become a regular presence on the ground in Washington over the past two and a half decades lobbying for crucial copyright issues, summarized the progress. "For the first time in history songwriters sit on the board and committees of a mechanical licensing entity. And for the first time the digital distributors of music pay the cost to administer such licensing oversight. As part of the MMA judges are now randomly selected for any ASCAP or BMI rate court proceeding as well as allowing market-based evidence into the proceedings, which definitely benefits the songwriter royalty rate arguments."[26]

ASCAP and BMI Merge Databases and Seek to Sunset Consent Decrees

In December 2016, ASCAP concluded a five-year license with the RMLC through 2021 under basically the same terms of their previous agreement. BMI, however, sought an increase, claiming that it had lost less market share to GMR than ASCAP, and that the RMLC knew this prior to finalizing the ASCAP agreement. The dispute went to the BMI rate court, which extended current terms on an interim license basis. In late 2018, BMI sued GMR to provide the rate court with information relative to the substantiation of BMI's

PERFORMING RIGHTS VS. PERFORMANCE RIGHTS

PERFORMING RIGHTS provides a royalty stream to songwriters and publishers from radio, television, cable, digital media, and other businesses that use music, whether live or recorded, to make or enhance their profit. Historically, ASCAP, BMI, SESAC, and since its founding in 2013, Global Music Rights (GMR) have provided 50%[+/-] of total publishing revenue.

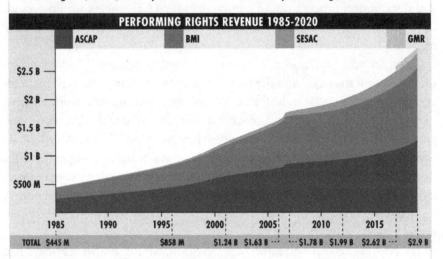

Established in the U.S. in 1998 by the Digital Millennium Copyright Act, PERFORMANCE RIGHTS provide a royalty stream for artists and master recording owners parallel to performing rights royalties, but only for digital transmissions, exempting terrestrial radio from these payments. SoundExchange was established in 2003 as the administrative agency for them.

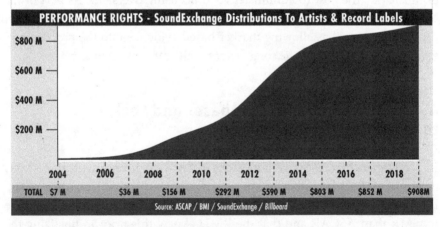

Source: ASCAP / BMI / SoundExchange / *Billboard*

Illustration 13.2 Performing Rights vs. Performance Rights

claim that the number of ASCAP's defections left BMI with a larger comparative market share, and thus deserved a higher rate. The case was still pending at the end of 2019.

Despite still competing for market share, in late 2015 ASCAP and BMI started the development of a joint repertoire database with the goal of creating an accurate, comprehensive resource for the proper crediting of and payment for music performances in all media worldwide. When their plans were publicly revealed in July 2017, the two PROs were criticized by the rest of the industry for acting surreptitiously. It was soon revealed, however, that the RIAA and NMPA had jointly engaged in the same pursuit, but their even more clandestine quest yielded no anticipated date of completion. Although ASCAP and BMI had initially targeted late 2018 for the debut, completion was still pending by the end of 2019. They stated that after successful consolidation of catalog metadata, they intended to approach SESAC and GMR about joining them to create a 100 percent inclusive index of all commercially exploited songs and other musical compositions.

Neither the NMPA nor the RIAA made royalty payments or gathered financial information pertinent to royalties on specific songs or records. This data remained in the administrative systems of their individual members. As their respective sectors' primary trade associations, their annual financial reports were from a macro rather than micro perspective. On the other hand, the PROs were linked on a worldwide basis through assigned IPI/CAE digital identification numbers for publishers and songwriters, and ISWC numbers for musical works, to serve as the conduits to transmit and receive specific financial and performance accountings. Nonetheless, they all united in crafting and passing Title I of the MMA to standardize mechanical licensing for digital transmissions parallel to SoundExchange for artist/label performance rights and the PROs for writer/publisher performing rights. This was a step forward, but not yet the final piece needed for a truly worldwide, comprehensive metadata network.

The passage of the MMA and anticipation of their joint database prompted ASCAP and BMI to once again ask the DOJ to revisit their consent decrees seeking a possible sunset to allow market determination of future royalty rates. The two PROs proposed that any new decree would maintain public access to repertoire; include a streamlined process when negotiating licenses; retain the rate court for disputes; incorporate the MMA market share comparisons; retain direct license carve-outs, and preserve the blanket license as the primary format along with adjustable fee and per program alternatives.

The DOJ antitrust subdivision assistant attorney general Makan Delrahim favored elimination of outdated consent decrees and asked for industrywide comments on the ASCAP-BMI proposal. At the August 2019 Park City, Utah, *Music Licensing in the 21st Century* symposium organized by the Orrin G. Hatch Foundation, Delrahim stated he had received 850 comments to review and expected to have a decision in 2020 for presentation to ASCAP, BMI, and their respective rate courts for approval. NAB president and former Oregon senator Gordon Smith as well as ASCAP's Elizabeth Matthews and BMI's Mike O'Neill also addressed the conference.

The NAB favored the retention of the consent decrees. "So if radio can't play music or can do so at the peril of their balance sheet, then who is going to do the local news?" Smith rhetorically queried, evoking empathy for local stations, but also, perhaps inadvertently, emphasizing the key role music played in their programming and hence its value to them.[27] Matthews told the confab that the performing rights landscape had changed drastically since the consent decrees were initiated in 1941. Independent radio stations had given way to corporate giants, which she described as "savvy smart tech driven companies that are all lawyered up and incredibly unregulated. . . . A songwriter today in 2019 is more government regulated than Facebook, which is kind of crazy."[28] O'Neill added, "We believe a free market is the best way for music creators to be rewarded for their hard work and creativity. . . . BMI is not looking to increase our power but to increase competition."[29]

Infringement Litigation

In December 2008, the RIAA announced that it had stopped the pursuit of individual consumers for illegal file-sharing. Out of the estimated thirty-five thousand legal actions, only two went to trial with both ending in large judgments. Others were settled with fines of up to several thousand dollars. While the RIAA claimed that the public awareness generated had lessened the need for legal action, others opined that the decline in industry revenue and thus funding for the lawsuits was more of a factor. With illegal duplication problems far more rampant internationally, both the RIAA and the NMPA left the battle in the hands of IFPI and CISAC.

Although the licensing of samples had become standard procedure, both substantive and nuisance plagiarism claims persisted. While many were settled quietly and confidentially, the ones involving major stars generated major headlines. A 2007 suit against Avril Lavigne's "Girlfriend," cowritten with Dr. Luke, was launched by the writers of the Rubinos' 1979 power pop cult hit "I Wanna Be Your Boyfriend." After over a year on the legal docket and the plaintiffs' posting of both songs on YouTube seeking public response by asking, "Avril Lavigne Vs. The Rubinos: You Decide,"[30] the parties agreed to an undisclosed settlement. *MTV News* suggested that Lavigne's camp had offered a settlement to avoid the cost of a lengthy litigation.

A 2011 suit filed against Lady Gaga's "Judas" charged that it infringed Rebecca Francescatti's 1999 album track "Juda," because the same bass player performed on both records and thus established access, one of the major criteria needed to win a plagiarism suit. The case was tossed out in 2014 when the judge ruled that a shared musician was not a valid connection, nor was there a sufficient similarity between the two songs, the other major benchmark.

In July 2014, Katy Perry became the target when Christian rap group Flame claimed that her pop-rap hybrid "Dark Horse" was identical to their 2008 Grammy and Dove Award nominated "Joyful Noise." Capitol Records, producer Dr. Luke, cowriter Max Martin, and guest rapper Juicy J were also named as defendants. The suit also charged that "Joyful Noise" had been "irreparably tarnished by its association with the witchcraft, paganism, black magic, and Illuminati imagery evoked by the same music in *Dark Horse*."[31] Again the case was dismissed by the judge as Flame failed to demonstrate sufficient similarity.

In 2017 Taylor Swift also experienced a plagiarism allegation against her 2014 worldwide number one single "Shake It Off," brought by Sean Hall and Nathan Butler, who wrote the 2001 single "Playas Gon' Play" for the group 3WL. Although the 3WL record reached number eighty-one on the *Billboard* Hot 100, providing potential access, the duo didn't provide sufficient evidence to established similarity and this case was also dismissed.

Results, however, could also go the other way. In 2016, Ed Sheeran was served with a $20 million lawsuit over similarities between his worldwide hit "Photograph," and *X-Factor* 2010 winner Matt Cardle's single "Amazing." Songwriters Martin Harrington and Thomas Leonard cited evidence from a musicologist's identification of thirty-nine identical notes in the melody. In April 2017, the suit was privately settled, with no admission of guilt on behalf of Sheeran. The "Amazing" writers received a 35 percent royalty share. Boston Conservatory at Berklee musicologist Dr. Joe Bennett told *The Guardian* that despite the obvious similarity, this was more likely "an example of cryptomnesia—inadvertent plagiarism—when you mistake a memory for a new idea, which can accidentally slip through in the songwriting process."[32]

A similar case had been resolved the previous year between the 1989 Tom Petty classic "I Won't Back Down" and Sam Smith's Grammy Award winner "Stay with Me." When the similarity was brought to their attention a month before the 2015 awards ceremony, Smith and his two cowriters immediately granted a 25 percent interest to Petty and his cowriter Jeff Lynne. A Smith spokesman told *The Guardian* that Smith and his cowriters had not previously heard "I Won't Back Down," but after hearing it, acknowledged the similarity. Petty added, "All my years of songwriting have shown me these things can happen. . . . The word lawsuit was never even said and was never my intention. And no more was to be said about it. How it got out to the press is beyond Sam or myself. . . . A musical accident, no more no less. In these times we live in this is hardly news."[33]

Perhaps the most consequential and certainly most publicized plagiarism litigation came with the decision against Pharrell Williams and Robin Thicke for the 2013 worldwide mega-hit "Blurred Lines" for plagiarizing Marvin Gaye's 1977 number one hit "Got to Give It Up." In 2015, a Los Angeles jury ordered Williams and Thicke to pay the Gaye estate more than $5.3 million in damages and a 50 percent interest in the song. This decision took much of the industry, especially Williams and Thicke, by surprise, as there was no similar lyrical, melodic, or chord elements, just similarities in style and feel, which the defendants admitted as intentional, arguing that style and feel were not protected under the copyright in a musical composition. California's Ninth Circuit Court of Appeals ruled two-to-one to uphold the jury verdict.

Dissenting judge Jacqueline Nguyen, however, differed. She stated, "The majority allows the Gayes to accomplish what no one has before: copyright a musical style." She further pointed out the inherent irony in the decision. "The Gayes, no doubt, are pleased by this outcome. They shouldn't be. They own copyrights in many musical works, each of which (including 'Got to Give It Up') now potentially infringes the copyright of any famous song that preceded it."[34]

"Blurred Lines" had indeed blurred the lines for future copyright infringement, leaving the creative community in turmoil over the specter of lawsuits from the artists who had inspired their careers. Many in the legal community, however, considered the ruling a result of procedural circumstances that would not create case precedent for future infringement claims.

14

The Creators: A Bigger Piece of a Bigger Pie

Artist Revenue: Records Down; Box Office Up

In 2007 the decline in record sales affected even those at the top of the charts. SoundScan's ten top-selling albums registered 24.8 million units, including downloads, compared to the top ten in 1999, which scanned 54.7 million albums. RIAA sales revenue was down by over 25 percent in 2007 from its 1999 peak and would fall further to under 50 percent by 2010. Many albums that reached the Billboard 200 chart never sold enough to recoup their initial expenses. More than ever, cash advances had become the operable currency between artists and their labels as recoupment of recording and marketing costs had become rare.

For artists who toured extensively, however, royalty losses were balanced by gains on the road. In 2007 *Pollstar*'s major US concert revenue totaled $3.9 billion, more than twice 1999's $1.7 billion. In estimating how much artists retained from box-office totals for major concert tours, *Billboard*'s Top Money Makers annual list used 34 percent of the box office as the assumed average artist net after all expenses. Applying this supposition to 2007, the estimated take home from $3.9 billion was about $1.3 billion, an increase of $722 million over 1999's $578 million.

There were thousands of other artists, however, who played theaters, clubs, armories, cruise ships, resorts, casinos, community arts centers, lounges, bars, private parties, outdoor events, and even played shows in the top concert facilities who didn't make the trade journals' listings, but they still made a living as performers. *Billboard*'s Ray Waddell quantified what he believed to be the scope of the worldwide industry in his 2015 year-end summary, "Live Music's $20 Billion Year." He gave credit to the healthy economy, plethora of popular artists, power of new media marketing, and "a general consumer trend toward

American Popular Music and Its Business in the Digital Age. Rick Sanjek, Oxford University Press. © Frederick Sanjek 2024.
DOI: 10.1093/oso/9780190653828.003.0014

the purchase of experiences as opposed to possessions . . . " for creating " . . . an estimated $20 billion global juggernaut in the digital age."[1]

Meanwhile, financial analysts were evaluating the music industry for clients interested in publicly traded entertainment companies, IPOs, or private equity offerings. Goldman Sachs estimated the 2015 live performance industry at $25 billion and predicted a rise to $39 billion by 2030. Citigroup's analysis pegged 2018 global ticket sales at $20 billion. Also in 2018, PwC estimated total music ticket sales at about $21 billion and predicted the market would reach $24 billion by 2022 with another $7 billion in merchandise and sponsorship revenue.

Live Nation controlled about 60 percent of the major concert events tracked by *Pollstar*. Live Nation's 2019 SEC Form 10-K cited its global concert revenue as $9.4 billion, up from $3.1 billion in 2007. The Form 10-K further stated that Live Nation "promoted shows or tours for over 5,000 artists globally" and "we had nearly 110 managers providing services to more than 500 artists,"[2] well in excess of the several hundred artists that made the *Pollstar* and *Billboard* year-end lists. AEG and the other smaller promoters were privately owned and didn't reveal financial information. It was generally believed, however, that AEG had at least half of the balance of tours with the rest handled by local and regional promoters. In 2019 overall, *Pollstar* tabulated over $11 billion in its major concert tour survey.

For the 2019 tally, only one of the *Pollstar* Top 200 North American Tours averaged less than $100,000 in gate receipts per show and only twenty averaged less than $200,000. The 200th-ranked tour grossed $4.2 million on twenty-six shows for an average nightly box office of $161,000 while playing to an average audience of 3,173 with an estimated $1.4 million take home after all expenses, calculating to over $53,000 per show.

The Top 40 Moneymakers

From 2006 through 2009 *Billboard*'s Top 40 Money Makers list was based on worldwide box-office grosses and US record sales, but from 2010 forward *Billboard* updated its criteria to the following: "Our rankings take into consideration how much each artist earned from a wide range of income sources. . . . We're looking here at closely estimated take-home pay. Net, not gross. The categories: touring; sales of physical albums, digital albums and digital tracks; tethered music downloads; on-demand music streams; noninteractive streams; and video streams."[3]

Lady Gaga topped 2010 on the strength of her first album and tour with pretax take-home at $30.6 million including a $23.8 million net from her $70.4 million tour gross, along with nearly 12 million downloads and 2.6 million streams. Bon Jovi was a close second with $30.4 million. Four acts in the top ten earned over 90 percent of their take-home from tour earnings, led by Roger Waters in third place on the beginning leg of his three-year *The Wall Live Tour*. Dave Matthews was in fourth, the Eagles in eighth, and Paul McCartney at tenth.

Teen pop star Justin Bieber was fifth, then-still-country phenom Taylor Swift was sixth, Canadian crooner Michael Bublé was seventh, and ninth-place hip hop/pop quartet the Black-Eyed Peas had more diversified blends of revenue sources. *Billboard*, however, acknowledged that the methodology lacked verifiable totals on merchandise sales, sponsorships, sync deals, international touring, PRO royalties, and DVD and ringtone sales because "there just isn't enough of that kind of data available across the whole board."[4]

While the sale of tour-related merchandise, that is, T-shirts, caps, jackets, and so forth, were not included in the Money Makers rankings, these items provided another source of artist revenue coming directly from consumers. Money Makers noted that for the 2007 top-ranked *Police Reunion Tour*, "a conservative estimate of tour merchandise revenue, the lion's share of which goes to the band, is in the $40 million range."[5] That $40 million was the equivalent of an additional 16.9 percent of the concert ticket gross. Merchandise sales also extended into post-tour retail and mail order sales.

Between 2007 and 2019 merchandise sales escalated dramatically. The Licensing Industry Merchandisers' Association (LIMA) estimated merchandise to be around $3.6 billion in 2019, equal to about a third of the box-office gross. With major concert tours requiring designated trucks and crew, merchandise companies offered advances to handle manufacturing, sales, and logistics. There were a variety of economic models available. Terms varied according to size of the advance, volume of turnover, and scope of responsibilities. Artist net ranged between 25 percent and 40 percent of sales receipts. By 2019, the major labels had their own in-house divisions to compete with the independent purveyors for exclusive merchandise contracts.

The 360° Contract Paradigm

Under the premise that they spent the bulk of the money developing artists' brands to generate ticket sales, merchandise purchases, and radio play, the labels sought to insinuate themselves into these income streams to offset the loss of record sales. Starting early in the first decade of the new millennium multiple rights provisions were added to contracts whereby labels participated in an artists' concert box office, merchandise sales, and publishing revenue to help recover their investment. These contracts became known as 360° deals as they could encompass the total range of artist revenue. Which rights were included, at what percentage, and for what amount of front money, were all negotiable depending on the relative bargaining power between artist and label.

A 2002 contract renewal between EMI and Robbie Williams, then EMI's biggest-selling international solo act, with a $157 million advance was often identified as the progenitor of the 360° deal. The parties formed a joint venture whereby EMI received 25 percent of Williams's net income from his other entertainment sources. While the term "360°" was not yet used, it eventually became the favorite sobriquet for multiple rights, even if such branded deals were 90° or 180° short of 360°. The first use of 360° in *Billboard* appeared in a September 9, 2004, report by Ed Christman on the annual NARM convention. In his keynote speech, Clive Davis eschewed "360-degree label deals" akin to Williams's. "I wouldn't do that," Davis stated. "You have to justify the investment on the investment itself."[6]

In 2005 the release of the Nashville-based pop band Paramore by the ADA-distributed Fueled by Ramen label is often credited as the first 360° deal with a new artist to yield platinum sales results. Sixteen-year-old vocalist Hayley Williams already had a solo deal with Atlantic, but she preferred being an alt-rock act cowriting with her bandmates. Attorney Jim Zumwalt and her management team were leery of letting Williams switch direction without a serious financial commitment from Atlantic. To accommodate the move, Zumwalt and Atlantic business affairs EVP Michael Kushner sculpted what would become the template for the 360° deals of the future.

The reconfigured agreement covered four albums over five years with a 70-percent-to-the-label and 30-percent-to-the-artist split of net revenue on all versions of recorded music including physical, downloads, videos, and streams devoid of the myriad deductions in pre-360° contracts, as well as giving the label a share of merchandise and box office. Atlantic agreed to pay for an opening spot on the multiple-band *Vans Warped Tour* and guaranteed another $250,000 support/marketing budget for a worldwide tour. Although considered the 360° model, the contract was actually a 270° arrangement. Zumwalt negotiated separate co-publishing agreements for each band member with Warner Chappell independent of the record agreement. The 70-30 split was also a departure from what would become the more prevalent model of a percentage of wholesale price, but similar in the simplification of the royalty calculation process. Paramore garnered four platinum albums and over 15 million downloaded tracks over the next six years.

According to its 2008 SEC Form 10-K, WMG had Artist Services and Expanded Rights (AS/ER) clauses in one-third of its contracts worldwide, expanding to half in 2009. AS/ER encompassed both the label's 360° percentage and revenue from label divisions that actually managed their artists' merchandise, ecommerce, VIP ticketing, and/or fan club operations through ancillary agreements. The 2012 10-K read, "As of September 30, 2012, we had expanded-rights deals in place with more than 75% of our active global Recorded Music roster."[7] AS/ER revenue was 10.7 percent of the WMG total. The 2019 10-K attributed a 16.4 percent share to these rights, up from 11.6 percent in 2018, crediting the growth to its 2018 purchase of EMP Merchandising.

Because UMG was a part of Universal Vivendi (UV), a public company registered in France, its finances were part of its UV annual Financial Report and Audited Consolidated Financial Statements filed there. Merchandising Contracts and Artist Services first appeared as a revenue line item in 2007 at €61 million. In 2008 the line item was retitled Artist Services and Merchandising listing €173 million and grew to €247 million in 2012, listed as Merchandising and Others. It was 5.4 percent of UV's 2012 recorded music division revenue. The percentage averaged 6.65 percent from 2013 through 2018 and finished 2019 at 6.8 percent. The third major label group, Sony Music Entertainment, was a part of the Sony Corporation registered in Japan. Its annual SEC Form 20-F did not separate 360°-related or artist services revenue from overall record division revenue.

The 360° Calculus

In presenting a 360° agreement, the dangled carrot was a simplified royalty computation process based on the labels' actual receipts, with a higher rate based on actual wholesale rather than using an obfuscated rate based on SRLP. The stick was more of a bludgeon as this was the primary way labels would structure new or restructured artist contracts. The rewards went both ways with more front money and tour support for artists while the 360° elements gave the labels additional avenues for recoupment. Nonetheless there still were items to negotiate including advances, budgets, sales-based royalty rate increases, and the specifics of the 360° provisions. Artists' management also knew that with success, they could renegotiate as they would then have a stick of their own in the delivery of the next album.

In the 2015 printing (9th edition) of *All You Need to Know About the Music Business*, Don Passman added an analysis of 360° deal royalty calculation methodology to his discourse on pre-360° agreements from earlier editions. He wrote that by 2015 record companies usually shared "the artist's net income from non-record sources, with the majority falling in the 15% to 30% range. . . . It varies a lot with bargaining power and from company to company. It can also vary by category, e.g., 20% for publishing but 30% on merchandising."[8]

As Passman noted, most pre-360° royalty rates were based on SRLP with 25 percent deductions for packaging and 15 percent for free goods/discounts, generally lowering the actual royalty base to 63.75 percent of the royalty rate stated in the contract. Thus a 12 percent rate was reduced to 7.65 percent, a 15 percent rate to 9.6 percent, and a superstar 20 percent rate to 12.75 percent. In most cases, producer royalties were about 25 percent and included within the artist rate but were not subject to recoupable costs other than recording, and after recoupment, retroactively paid from the first record sold. Passman also observed that by 2015 most artist deals signed since the middle of the first decade of the new millennium were 360° deals based on wholesale price, also called Published Price to Dealer (PPD), which was about 70 percent of the SRLP. Rates ranged from 13 percent to 16 percent for new artists, 15 percent to 18 percent for mid-level artists, and 18 percent to 20 percent or more for superstars.

To compare calculation methods, a post-deduction 9.6 percent rate of a 15 percent rate in a pre-360° deal applied to $1 million in SRLP yielded $96,000. Applying an 18 percent of PPD rate from a 360° deal with no deductions to the PPD for the same $1 million in SRLP computed to about $126,000, a 31.3 percent higher return. The rise in royalties, however, was counterbalanced by the label's share of 360° revenue in differing degrees for each artist. Under both formulas, all otherwise payable royalties were applied against recoupable costs before anything was paid out.

While each artist's royalty account was calculated separately, overall A&R costs greatly exceeded royalty obligation. The 2019 WMG Form 10-K cited A&R costs at $1.57 billion, which was 41 percent of the $3.84 billion revenue total. Because the $629 million in AS/ER income was not subject to royalties, the remaining $3.12 billion in revenue worked out to $562 million in royalties at an average 18 percent of PPD. At that rate, $1.02 billion was left as unrecouped A&R expenses. There was also an undefined share of the $827 million in marketing expenses listed in the 10-K that were also recoupable from royalties, further lessening the artists' actual payout.

The three major label groups' financial reports were under different governances and hence varied in structural details and reporting obligations. While WMG's line items for AS/ER and third-party licensing income combined for 24.4 percent of total recorded music revenue, UMG's License and Other, and Merchandise and Other line items covered parallel revenue sources to AS/ER, accounting for 22.2 percent of combined recorded music and merchandise revenue. Comparable financial details were not publicly available from Sony.

360° Becomes Status Quo, but Some Things Remain the Same

The 360° deals proved to be a godsend for the labels. While US recorded music retail value as reported by the RIAA stalled at $7 billion from 2010 through 2015, major concert revenue as compiled by *Pollstar* grew 62.4 percent from $4.25 billion in 2010 to $6.9 billion in 2015 with merchandise expanding in tandem. The labels benefited proportionally through their 360° imposed levy. Then the bonanza grew even greater as *Pollstar* yearly totals expanded to $10.8 billion in 2018 and then even higher in 2019 with merchandise revenue growth tagging along.

Although 360° was a pithy epithet ideal for trade paper headlines, *Billboard*'s senior editorial analyst Glenn Peoples felt it was somewhat of a misnomer. "Most deals are about 270, maximum, not 360 degrees. . . . In theory a 360-deal encompasses all revenue that an artist brings in, and hence the name, '360 degrees'. . . . Usually in my writing I call it 'multi-rights.' "[9]

Of the rights covered by the 360° umbrella, record rights were the initial quadrant. If most deals were indeed 270° maximum, as Peoples contended, it's likely that touring and merchandise were the second and third quadrants since the labels were often already participating in publishing revenue in some way. First was the decades-old practice of including publishing rights as part of the record deal, which evolved in the 1970s into co-publishing relationships. Whether full publishing or co-publishing, all PRO, mechanical print, and sync income were administered by the label's associated publishing division. The second alternative was a stand-alone co-publishing agreement with the label's publishing affiliate similar to what Paramore had with WMG's Warner Chappell Music.

Third was the controlled composition clause, which was virtually ubiquitous in all contracts by the late 1970s, in effect rebating at least 25 percent of mechanical license payments back to the label. After 2006 when the mechanical rate settled at 9.1¢, if an artist failed to secure the 75 percent reduced rate for tracks under five minutes, $22,750 was charged per track as a recoupable cost on an album that sold a million units. The controlled composition clause did not apply to digital sales.

The 360° scenario as outlined thus far has been from a macro perspective, but the industry conducted business on a micro level with each artist agreement a customized entity unto itself with its own accounting ledger. By 2019 Edgar Bronfman Jr. and Lyor Cohen, who had led the charge for the 360° prototype, were seven years removed from the major label inner circle of power. Their advocacy for this paradigm, however, had provided the gift that kept on giving, and provided a cushion for the labels should their artist partners demand a larger slice of the pie.

Nonetheless, one thing had not changed. Any leverage for artists in contract renegotiations was still in direct proportion to their current success. In effect, the old adage "a hit record cures all ills" was more applicable than ever, as the current level of success during negotiations directly affected the de facto currency of the music business, which was still cash advances. When large enough to keep the focus away from the fine details, these advances could even maintain the 360° deal balance tipped to the label's advantage for recoupment while keeping the artists and their teams happy with cash in hand rather than waiting for the next accounting period.

The Digital Royalty Rate Debate

In most pre-360° contracts, revenue from third-party licenses, including when other labels manufactured or distributed, was split 50-50 between label and artist. At first the labels treated downloads as sales, paying royalties at the same rates applicable to CDs. Questions soon emerged as to whether downloads as well as streams were not sales, but rather third-party licenses subject to the 50-50 royalty split. The royalty rates in 360° deals, however, were all consolidated into one rate to specifically include digital sources at the same rate as physical sales.

Nonetheless, many artists with pre-360° contracts and/or their financial and legal advisors took note of the 50-50 split for performance rights royalties set by the CRB, examined their old contracts, and questioned the application of retail sales rates to digital revenue. They were further fortified by Steve Jobs's reference to the relationship between iTunes and the labels as a license in his February 2007 "Thoughts on Music" open letter to the music industry. iTunes sold its 10 billionth download on February 24, 2010. With iTunes at 70 percent of the download business, this calculated to over 14 billion total downloads, with prices ranging from $.59 to $1.29. Assuming a $1 average with 70 percent paid to the labels, and after subtracting the 9.1¢ publishing mechanical payment, the 50-50 split would be about 30¢ each. Application of the top retail royalty rate would yield at most 10¢. Theoretically, if all downloads to date were to be adjusted retroactively to the higher rate, the difference could be in the hundreds of millions if not over a billion dollars.

One of the first cases involving this digital royalty divide to receive widespread publicity went to court in 2009 with Eminem's original producers F.B.T. Productions LLC, represented by music litigator Richard Busch, against the Jimmy Iovine/Dr. Dre Aftermath Records imprint co-owned and distributed by Interscope. F.B.T. was owned by brothers Mark and Jeff Bass who had co-production credits on just over half of the tracks on Eminem's first three albums, which sold over a combined 60 million units. After losing in the initial filing and in a subsequent jury trial, the US Court of Appeals for the Ninth Circuit ruled in July 2010 that F.B.T. and Eminem combined were owed 50 percent of the net revenues from downloads and ringtones. In March 2011, the Supreme Court declined to hear the case, leaving the appeals decision as the final adjudication.

This ruling set off a spate of legal actions by artists including Pink Floyd, Cheap Trick, Kenny Rogers, Sister Sledge, Rob Zombie, and a class-action suit filed by the estate of Rick James, Chuck D of Public Enemy, and twelve other artists against UMG. In April 2015 Hugh McIntyre reported in *Forbes* that the James et al. case was settled for $11.5 million and was open to all artists signed to a UMG label prior to 2004. He further added that Sony and WMG had previously settled class-action suits of their own. Nonetheless, new filings would arise occasionally. In 2017 the Carpenters filed against A&M, then owned by UMG, for $2 million. The complaint was settled and withdrawn.

In January 2018 two lawsuits for underpaid royalties received press attention, but the royalties in question were from streaming revenue rather than downloads. In 2014 Richard Busch filed suit on behalf of *American Idol* producer 19 Entertainment and its artists against 19's record distributor Sony. The suit sought at least $10 million in damages, but in 2018 the parties notified the court that a settlement was pending, and the proceedings were discontinued. The second lawsuit was by Enrique Iglesias against Interscope and was still pending as of the end of 2019. It claimed that "up until approximately 2016, Interscope properly recognized and credited Iglesias's streaming royalties at fifty percent. However, upon receiving a directive from UMG, Interscope, without consulting or otherwise notifying Iglesias, began crediting streams at the incorrect, lower record royalty rate."[10]

Billboard Unveils "The Power 100"

The *Billboard* annual feature, The Power 100 debuted in the February 4, 2012, issue. Bolstered by fifteen top industry journalists, the editorial team initiated a comparative ranking of power players, creating a year-end scorecard for industry power politics. Editor Bill Werde wryly wrote in his introduction to the list, "I like to call it the issue that will make one person love us and everyone else stop taking our calls."[11] Werde also observed that "power is always shifting. Just a few years ago, at least seven or eight of the top spots on this list would have gone to label executives. Today that number stands at four, and some would argue that's generous."[12] Those four were Lucian Grainge at number three, Doug Morris at number five, Len Blavatnik at number eight, and Jimmy Iovine at number ten.

Irving Azoff, then of Live Nation with touring, ticketing, and management divisions, led the top ten with Red Light Management owner Coran Capshaw at number two. The only publisher was Martin Bandier at number four. Michael Rapino of Live Nation was number six, CAA's Rob Light came in at number seven, and Tim Leiweke of the Anschutz Entertainment Group (AEG) at number nine. Summing up the perspective gained and hopefully conveyed in initiating the list, Werde opined, "Irving Azoff and Coran Capshaw clearly have the juice, because ultimately, it's the artists who have the real power."[13] Azoff concurred in stating, "The worst thing one can do is think the power is yours, and not the artist's."[14] Altogether there were nineteen on the list from record labels, eight from radio, and two from retail. The other seventy-one came from the live performance, digital, management, publishing, legal, branding, sponsorship, investment, and media segments other than radio.

For the rest of the decade Lucien Grange and Michael Rapino swapped the number one spot back and forth. Azoff, Capshaw, Light, and Leiweke remained constants while Spotify's Daniel Ek and Jimmy Iovine, after joining Apple, surged up the list as the streaming tsunami washed over the industry. Jody Gerson and John Platt reached top-ten status as their mentor Martin Bandier exited the publishing sector. Both retail and digital sales slipped out of the listing other than for Amazon, which was also a streaming power. Pandora and SiriusXM replaced terrestrial radio except

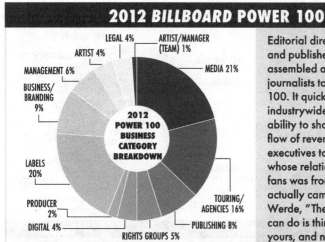

2012 *BILLBOARD* POWER 100

LEGAL 4%
ARTIST 4%
ARTIST/MANAGER (TEAM) 1%
MANAGEMENT 6%
MEDIA 21%
BUSINESS/BRANDING 9%
2012 POWER 100 BUSINESS CATEGORY BREAKDOWN
LABELS 20%
PRODUCER 2%
DIGITAL 4%
TOURING/AGENCIES 16%
PUBLISHING 8%
RIGHTS GROUPS 5%

Editorial director Bill Werde and publisher Tommy Page assembled a team of top journalists to create the Power 100. It quickly became an industrywide "must read". The ability to shape and direct the flow of revenue linked these executives to the top artists whose relationship with their fans was from where the power actually came. Irving Azoff, told Werde, "The worst thing one can do is think the power is yours, and not the artist's."

POWER 100 DESIGNEE, POSITION, COMPANY		CATEGORY
1	Irving Azoff, chairman, Live Nation	Touring/Agencies
2	Coran Capshaw, founder, Red Light Management	Management
3	Lucian Grainge, chairman/CEO, UMG	Labels
4	Martin Bandier, chairman/CEO, Sony/ATV Music	Publishing
5	Doug Morris, CEO, Sony Music Entertainment	Labels
6	Michael Rapino, CEO, Live Nation	Touring/Agencies
7	Rob Light, CAA, managing partner	Touring/Agencies
8	Len Blavatnik, owner, WMG	Labels
9	Tim Leiweke, president/CEO, AEG	Touring/Agencies
10	Jimmy Iovine, chairman, Interscope Geffen A&M Records	Labels
11	Eddy Cue, senior VP & Robert Kondrk, senior director, Apple	Digital
12	John Hogan, president/CEO, Clear Channel	Media
13	Jay-Z & Beyonce	Artists
14	Lyor Cohen, chairman/CEO recorded music, WMG	Labels
15	Randy Phillips, president/CEO, AEG Live	Touring/Agencies
16	Emmanuel Seuge, global marketing, Coke	Business/Branding
17	Frank Cooper, chief consumer marketing officer, Pepsi	Business/Branding
18	Barry Weiss, chairman/CEO, Universal Republic & Island Def Jam	Labels
19	Rob Stringer & Steve Barnett, co-chairman/CEO & COO, Columbia	Labels
20	Arthur Fogel, chairman global touring, Live Nation	Touring/Agencies

Source: *Billboard*

Illustration 14.1 2012 *Billboard* Power 100

2019 *BILLBOARD* POWER 100

As the sectors most directly connected with the largest source of artist revenue, touring/agencies along with management grew from 2012's 23% to 37%.

Media fell from 2012's 21% to 8% as streaming displaced radio in both revenue and influence. The labels grew to 27% from 20%, also a result of the rapid rise in streaming.

RIGHTS GROUPS 4%
BUSINESS/BRANDING 4%
MULTISECTOR 4%
MANAGEMENT 13%
MEDIA 8%

2019
POWER 100
BUSINESS
CATEGORY
BREAKDOWN

TOURING/AGENCIES 24%
LABELS 27%
LEGAL 3%
DIGITAL 8%
PUBLISHING 5%

POWER 100 DESIGNEE, POSITION, COMPANY		CATEGORY
1	Lucian Grainge, chairman/CEO, UMG	Labels
2	Michael Rapino, president/CEO, Live Nation	Touring/Agencies
3	Daniel Ek, CEO, & executive team, Spotify	Digital
4	Irving Azoff, chairman/CEO, the Azoff Company, Jeffrey Azoff, partner, Full Stop Management	Multisector
5	Rob Stringer, CEO, Sony Music Entertainment	Labels
6	Steve Cooper, CEO & Max Lousada, CEO recorded music, WMG	Labels
7	Oliver Schusser, VP, & Apple Music executive team, Apple	Digital
8	Jon Platt, incoming chairman/CEO, Sony/ATV Music	Publishing
9	Craig Kallman, chairman/CEO, & Julie Greenwald, chairman/COO, & executive team, Atlantic Records	Labels
10	Boyd Muir, Michele Anthony & executive team at UMG	Labels
11	Monte Lipman & Avery Lipman, co-founders, Republic Records	Labels
12	Coran Capshaw, founder, Red Light Management	Management
13	Steve Boom, VP, & Ryan Redington, director, Amazon Music	Digital
14	Jody Gerson, global chairman/CEO, UMPG	Publishing
15	John Janick, chairman/CEO & exec. team, Interscope Geffen A&M	Labels
16	Scooter Braun, founder, SB Projects	Management
17	Martin Bandier, outgoing chairman/CEO, Sony/ATV Music	Publishing
18	Steve Barnett & executive team, Capitol Music Group	Labels
19	Guy Oseary, co-founder/principal, Maverick Management	Management
20	Jay Marciano, COO, AEG & AEG Presents executive team	Touring/Agencies

Source: *Billboard*

Illustration 14.2 2019 *Billboard* Power 100

for Bob Pittman, reflecting iHeart's successful diversification into the digital radio realm.

Free from Clear Channel, Live Nation Does Its Own 360°

Considered the weak link in the CCE roll-up and separated out to allow the radio division to be the centerpiece of a leveraged buyout, Live Nation emerged as the stronger survivor of the disengagement. Michael Rapino took the necessary steps to strengthen internally and led the live performance sector in its upsurge during the post-recession recovery. In 2007 Live Nation's worldwide revenue tally was $4.3 billion and it owned and/or operated 155 facilities with about forty-seven hundred full-time employees. Its 2007 SEC Form 10-K annual report described its strategy as "to connect the artist to the fan. We believe that this focus will enable us to increase shareholder value by developing new ancillary revenue streams . . . through the live music experience."[15] Live Nation's database became as invaluable in driving revenue in the emerging age of consumer analytics with information on "over 580 million fans across all of our concerts and ticketing platforms in 46 countries during 2019."[16]

In September 2007 Rapino acquired the remaining share of Michael Cohl's CPI for $123 million in stock and $10 million cash, turning Cohl into Live Nation's largest shareholder. Cohl became chairman of the new Live Nation Artists (LNA) division formed to sign and manage additional rights from artists whose concerts were already promoted by Live Nation. The next month LNA signed Madonna to a ten-year $120 million agreement, including 1.2 million Live Nation shares and moving her from WMG to Interscope. Merchandising, fan club, website, all film and video projects, and associated sponsorship agreements were included in the agreement, but publishing was not. Next LNA added Jay-Z in a ten-year $150 million deal that created Roc-Nation, a joint venture full-service entertainment company operated by Jay-Z. Roc-Nation earnings combined with Jay-Z's artist career propelled him onto *Forbes* 2019 rankings as its first billionaire rapper, separate and apart from the $400 million net worth of his wife, Beyoncé.

Shortly after these signings, the economy started to soften in advance of the September 2008 meltdown. Cohl planned more signings, but with a 44 percent drop in Live Nation share value Rapino urged him to slow down. Nonetheless, Cohl entered into agreements with U2, Shakira, Nickelback, and the Jonas Brothers, triggering a contentious rift with Rapino despite a nearly twenty-year relationship. Cohl departed with a $9.85 million contract buyout that allowed him to continue as the promoter for The Rolling Stones and Barbra Streisand.

The Live Nation-Ticketmaster Merger

Rapino wanted to bring Live Nation's ticketing in-house when its contract with Ticketmaster expired at the end of 2008 to gain exclusive control over the corresponding customer data. He believed that Live Nation's network of facilities would also attract other clients away from Ticketmaster to his new ticketing operation. While running Live Nation in Europe Rapino had worked with German-based CTS Eventim and turned to them to help develop Live Nation Ticketing.

Meanwhile, in 2007 Ticketmaster's parent company, Barry Diller's InterActiveCorp (IAC), acquired a share of Irving Azoff and Howard Kaufman's Front Line Management Group, which had been formed in 2005 as a roll-up of independent management firms financed by T. H. Lee and Bain Capital along with WMG. Next IAC bought online secondary market broker TicketsNow to supplement its already-existing but underperforming TicketExchange division. It also added several smaller ticketing services, the SLO Ltd VIP ticket packaging service, and then introduced its Paperless Ticket™ program to help counter rival ticket brokering.

IAC then split into five separate NASDAQ listings. The now freestanding Ticketmaster Entertainment, Inc., bought out Lee and Bain's share of Front Line, and brought in MSG's James Dolan to help buy out WMG's 30 percent for $123 million. Azoff was named CEO and the Azoff Family Trust received about 4.5 percent of the new company's value in restricted stock. Diller remained as board chairman. Ticketmaster now had its own array of diversified assets to compete with Rapino's expansion plans. Live Nation, however, found that even with Eventim's experience in Europe, it was unable to meet the deadline needed to exit from its Ticketmaster contract and had to renew.

In January 2009, Diller and Azoff proposed an even better opportunity in a merger with the publicly traded Live Nation, which was saddled with debt and low on net profit. A year later the deal was finalized as an all-stock transaction creating Live Nation Entertainment, Inc. Several binding terms and measures were imposed by regulators to protect competitive conditions in the marketplace including an option for Ticketmaster's pre-merger client AEG to license the Ticketmaster system for up to five years while developing its own proprietary program.

In February 2011 Azoff became chairman, replacing John Malone of Liberty Media, Live Nation's largest shareholder. Liberty invested another $76 million to increase its position to 25 percent. It also bought out MSG's and Azoff's remaining shares of Front Line with $56.5 million in cash and $59.7 million in stock. Rapino remained as CEO/president and Liberty CEO Greg Maffei was appointed chairman of a newly formed executive committee. Less than two years later at the end of 2012, Azoff resigned to attend to his other business interests.

Liberty bought Azoff's shares to further increase its position. Azoff left with a three-year non-compete clause for management, except for the Eagles, Van Halen, Christina Aguilera, and Steely Dan who all departed with him. Frontline's remaining team of associated but independent managers was left intact, led by Kaufman's HK Management with Jimmy Buffett and Stevie Nicks, Ken Levitan of Vector Management with Kings of Leon and Kid Rock, Clint Higham of Morris Management with Kenny Chesney, Peter Rudge of London-based Octagon Music, Clarence Spalding of Spalding Entertainment with Brooks and Dunn, and over 100 other executive and associate managers representing over 250 acts.

With Azoff gone Rapino became even more visible as the voice and visionary behind what was now the largest entity in the music industry. The 2012 revenue of $5.8 billion included $3.9 billion from concerts, $1.4 billion from ticketing fees on $9.15 billion in ticketing, $400 million on the Artist Nation management division from commissions on artist revenue, and $247 million on sponsorships and advertising. There were 14,962 US events with 32 million in attendance, and another 7,000 events outside the US selling 16.8 million seats. Their proprietary database of consumer information had grown to 119.6 million customers.

Over the next six years major acquisitions included EDM promoter Insomniac Events for its collection of venues, festivals, and record label; the Voodoo Music & Arts Experience music festival in New Orleans; the Maverick Group management company led by Madonna's manager Guy Oseary; Austin-based C3 Presents, which controlled the Austin City Limits and Lollapalooza festivals; the Governors Ball Music Festival in New York; Knoxville-based AC Entertainment which coproduced the Bonnaroo Festival; the Bottlerock Napa Valley Music Festival; and Emporium Presents, which produced hundreds of club and theater events.

In 2019 Live Nation took in $11.5 billion with $9.4 billion from almost forty thousand events, which had over 98 million attendees. Rapino had also diversified the venue inventory to accommodate artists from first release to superstardom. Between owned, leased, operated, and exclusive booking rights, Live Nation controlled 273 facilities worldwide along with a mix of parking, concession, sponsorship, and merchandise rights. Included were fifty-nine amphitheaters, sixteen arenas, ninety-one theaters, forty-nine clubs, eighteen restaurants and music halls, thirty-eight festival sites, and two stadiums. Although most of the ticket revenue went to the artists, Live Nation netted $232 million on $1.53 billion in ticket-handling revenue. The sponsorship and advertising division made a $316 million operating margin on $590 million in revenue.

AEG Still Led the Competition in an Expanding Market

While Live Nation was a publicly traded company, most of its competitors were privately held entities that rarely divulged financial information. Nonetheless, the box-office totals from both *Billboard* and *Pollstar* indicated that AEG was the second-largest anchored by the AEG Live, Concerts West, and Golden Voice divisions, along with Messina Touring Group and Marshall Arts co-ventures, but was only about a quarter of Live Nation's size in revenue. AEG also owned the spring Coachella Festival, the highest-grossing domestic outdoor event, as well as its fall country music counterpart Stagecoach. AEG's primary business, however, was still centered around ownership of sports teams and facilities with music intended to fill in the open dates, and still led by Tim Leiweke.

AEG's Randy Phillips was at the center of the industry's biggest story in 2009 when Michael Jackson died three weeks before the start of his fifty-day *This Is It* residency at the AEG-managed O2 Arena in London, intended to be the first leg of his worldwide farewell tour. With a huge amount already spent, AEG faced losing both investment and anticipated profit. Jackson, however, had meticulously documented ninety hours of rehearsal footage, which Phillips quickly edited into the *Michael Jackson's This Is It* film. Debuting in October 2009, just five months after Jackson's death, the film did over $250 million in theatrical box office and more than $60 million in home video in the year after its release.

In September 2012 owner Philip Anschutz tasked Leiweke with selling AEG at a price based on winning its bid to build the stadium for a new Los Angeles NFL team as part of Anschutz's LA Live construction project anchored by Staples Center. By March 2013 it had become apparent that AEG wouldn't win the stadium bid and thus no one would meet Anschutz's price. Leiweke left after seventeen years as CEO and Anschutz assumed a more active role. In November 2013 Phillips also exited with COO Jay Marciano replacing him.

James Dolan made his own move into the LA arena market in 2012 buying the Inglewood Forum as a West Coast bookend to MSG and started a total renovation. MSG also hosted a December 2012 live telethon to raise proceeds for Hurricane Sandy victims featuring Bruce Springsteen, Roger Waters, Bon Jovi, Kanye West, Billy Joel, and The Rolling Stones. In October 2013 Dolan joined the now-independent Azoff in opening Azoff MSG Entertainment as a potpourri of music-related enterprises and services including the new GMR PRO. MSG contributed $125 million to the partnership and up to $50 million of revolving credit loans. In January 2014 the Forum reopened with six shows by the Eagles.

In November 2015 Azoff and Tim Leiweke formed the Oak View Group (OVG) to develop and manage sports/music facilities starting with the new Key Arena in Seattle, followed by arenas in Long Island, New York, Austin, Texas, and Palm Springs, California. In 2016 OVG formed the Arena Alliance to promote the common interests of independent arenas in twenty-four of the top thirty US markets. In October 2018 Azoff bought MSG out of their partnership for $125 million but continued to advise Dolan on new properties in both Las Vegas and London. Going forward he operated as the Azoff Company. His son Jeffrey joined him as a partner in their Full Stop management company that included The Eagles and Harry Styles on its roster.

Robert F. X. Sillerman, the originator of the roll-up that became Live Nation, reentered the live performance arena in 2012, resurrecting the SFX brand with a plan for a roll-up of electronic dance music (EDM) companies. The term "EDM" was coined as a collective brand for the differing dance styles created in the post-disco era including house, techno, trance, drum and bass, and dubstep. Top EDM D.J.s became highly paid club stars, advancing to concerts, festivals, and records including production and dance mixes for pop acts wanting to expand into EDM.

With Europe, Asia, and South America ahead of the US in large-scale development of EDM, Sillerman saw a ground-floor opportunity. First, he acquired festival promoter James "Disco Donnie" Estopinal Jr.'s Disco Donnie Presents with Estopinal becoming a partner in SFX, and then lined up another eight companies for a $350 million cash and stock combination to create a diversified EDM consortium. This time, however, Sillerman decided to stage an IPO claiming a market value of $1 billion rather than sell the aggregated SFX to an established entertainment conglomerate and take his profit. Over the next two years Sillerman once again proved to be better at selling a vision than managing one as SFX stock collapsed.

In February 2016 SFX declared bankruptcy. Axar Capital and German insurance giant Allianz bought the assets and brought in Randy Phillips to rebrand SFX as LifeStyle. The company was still the largest promoter of EDM music festivals, with plans to expand into a wider array of genres. After selling some assets, including its 40 percent stake in the Rock in Rio festival to Live Nation, LifeStyle showed $20 million in pre-EBITDA earnings in both 2017 and 2018, after losses of $30 million in 2016.

In September 2019 Phillips resigned and returned to artist management, commenting to *Billboard*'s Dave Brooks that he was brought on "as a gun slinger to clean it up, get it functional and prepare it for sale . . . and I fulfilled my mission."[17] Two months later Sillerman passed away after a long battle with cancer in the midst of both bankruptcy and a fraud indictment; a sad finish for the man whose vision shaped much of what the music industry had become.

Live Performance Surges: Oak View Acquires *Pollstar*

The industry metrics collected by the trade periodicals have always been skewed toward the top end of the business that provides the bulk of the magazines' revenue. Current news, contact information, industry trends, record reviews, box-office totals of the top-earning performers, printed directories, and market analysis reports have always been their primary revenue sources. What had changed over the years, however, was that consumer data, especially buying habits, locations, and contact information, had become perhaps the most valuable asset in the trade periodical information arsenal. For over a century the *Boxscore* tallies from *Billboard* and *Amusement Business* (*AB*) had been the primary public source for live performance data. By 2019, however, *Billboard*'s annual Year in Music report had long been condensed to top twenty-five lists for events, tours, and promoters along with top-ten ratings for stadiums, festivals, and amphitheaters comparing gross revenue, total attendees, and number of shows.

Pollstar was founded in 1981 by Gary Smith and Gary Bongiovanni, and by 2007 had worked its way into a competitive position with *Billboard* for live performance information. Since then the *Pollstar* database had become the concert industry's primary barometer for comparative data. Its annual Business Analysis featured the Top 200 North American Tours and the Top

100 Worldwide Tours rankings, including the attendance, ticket price, dollar gross, and other pertinent statistics.

At the end of November 2016 Ray Waddell left *Billboard* after a thirty-year tenure to become OVG's president of media and conferences. In addition to his journalistic duties, Waddell had also built the annual Touring Conference and Awards into a major event and would assume parallel functions for OVG. Immediately after Waddell's arrival, OVG announced the purchase of *Venues Today*, *Pollstar*'s major competition in catering to the concert industry. Six months later OVG also completed the purchase of *Pollstar* along with its trade convention division with Smith staying on board as executive advisor and Bongiovanni preparing for his retirement in 2018. Waddell also added *Billboard* veterans Andy Gensler as executive editor of media and conferences for the magazines and trade shows, and Bob Allen as box-office liaison to co-ordinate data and information across all OVG platforms.

Gensler's 2017 Pollstar Year End Report reflected OVG's shift of the magazine away from its decades long, data forward orientation to the more industry-inclusive editorial style developed in Waddell and Gensler's tenures at *Billboard*. With punchier headlines, confident touting of its year-end reports and analysis, and extensive quoting of industry leaders, OVG was making its bid to solidify its journalistic preeminence and insider position in the live performance and trade show arena.

In 2018 *Venues Today* was relaunched by its founder and former *AB* staffer Linda Deckard as *Venues Now* after which she retired. In his "Letter from the Publisher" in the 2019 *Pollstar* Business Analysis, Waddell described *Pollstar* and *VenuesNow* as dedicated to the coverage of the live music industry. "That is the role of *Pollstar* and *VenuesNow*, the Voice Of Live speaking not exactly to you, but more correctly speaking from you. In a very real sense, with our stories and quotes and news and even box office data, we are you."[18]

Pollstar's Tours Top $10 Billion

By 2018 *Pollstar* and *VenuesNow* surpassed *Billboard* in their comprehensive coverage of the concert business, catering to its base of subscribers, advertisers, sponsors, and event attendees. *Billboard*, however, still was nonpareil as the overall industry's source for daily news and analysis through the "Billboard Bulletin," billboard.com, and its print edition covering the music industry as a whole.

In 2018 the box-office data collected by *Pollstar* registered its highest ever total at $10.4 billion from more than forty-four thousand events selling over

152.1 million tickets. The Top 100 Worldwide Tours and Top 200 North American Tours were still *Pollstar*'s two primary listings. When merged together with duplicate listings eliminated, there were 213 tours that grossed $6.66 billion, 64 percent of *Pollstar*'s total tally. This was not, however, a complete picture of the live performance ecosystem. The $3.94 billion balance came from 2018 tours or single engagements, inputted into *Pollstar*'s database, that took in less than $4.9 million, which was the lowest tour total on the merged list.

Eleven acts grossed more than $100 million, led by Ed Sheeran's $432.4 million, Taylor Swift in second with $345.1 million, and the Jay-Z/Beyoncé tour at $254.1 million. Jay-Z generated another $24.2 million on his solo tour. The other eight over $100 million in descending order were P!nk, Bruno Mars, the Eagles, Justin Timberlake, Roger Waters, U2, The Rolling Stones, and Kenny Chesney. Another twenty-three tours grossed between $50 million and $97.8 million.

The highest-priced tickets were for *Springsteen on Broadway* at a $508.93 average and several Vegas residencies in the $200 range. The top road tours were the Eagles at $172.13, Andrea Bocelli at $164.65, and Sir Paul McCartney at $155.74 neck-and-neck with The Rolling Stones at $155.26. P!nk, Bruno Mars, Justin Timberlake, U2, Phil Collins, Billy Joel, Sir Elton John, and Cher were all clustered around $130.00.

The 2019 *Pollstar* year-end Business Analysis did not include a box-office total, instead emphasizing that it was "a year that saw new records set in gross revenue both globally and North America based on sales from the Top 100 tours."[19] From 2010 to 2019 box-office receipts grew 72.1 percent, average attendance per show increased 38.9 percent from 9,585 to 13,397, and average ticket price went up from $70.33 to $96.17 for a 37.7 percent increase. The 2019 Top 100 Worldwide Tours grossed $5.6 billion, a 72.4 percent increase over 2010's $3.22 billion.

CAA and WME Still the Top Agencies

In *Pollstar*'s Top 30 Artists of the Decade ranking, the listed agency for five of the top ten artists was also the promoter. Live Nation represented number one ranked U2, taking in $1.04 billion on five tours, as well as Roger Waters at number ten with $702 million on two tours. AEG-affiliated promoters were the credited agency with Concerts West representing The Rolling Stones, who had moved away from Michael Cohl after two decades together, at number two with $929 million on five tours; Messina Touring shepherded Taylor Swift to number four for $900 million from five tours; and Marshall Arts guided Sir Paul McCartney through five tours to number seven with a gross of $814 million.

There were four more artists in the top thirty with their promoter listed as the agent of record, P!nk through Marshall Arts at number sixteen, Jay-Z and Live Nation at number seventeen, Madonna with Live Nation at number twenty-five, and Beaver Productions with Michael Bublé at number twenty-eight. Of the other twenty-one artists, CAA represented eight and WME had four, leaving Paradigm Talent with three, AGI with two, and the Howard Rose Agency and United Talent one each. The other two, Celine Dion and Dutch classical sensation André Rieu, had their own companies listed as their agencies.

The demographic range for these acts was spread fairly evenly with nine legacy artists from the 1960s or 1970s in U2, The Stones, McCartney, Springsteen, Waters, Elton John, the Eagles, Billy Joel, and Fleetwood Mac. Another twelve including Bon Jovi, Beyoncé, Coldplay, Metallica, Guns N' Roses, Jay-Z, Kenny Chesney, Justin Timberlake, Celine Dion, André Rieu, Madonna, and Trans-Siberian Orchestra, began their careers in the 1980s or 1990s. The other nine who emerged after 2000 were Sheeran, Swift, One Direction, P!nk, Lady Gaga, Bieber, Bruno Mars, Bublé, and Luke Bryan. Although last on this list, Bryan still grossed $425.5 million at the box office over the decade.

Foregoing the services of a booking agent to save the 10 percent commission may have played well for the artists who felt Live Nation or AEG provided sufficient ancillary revenue opportunities, but most artists depended on their agencies for these services, indicative of how effectively their agents worked for them. Co-branding sponsorships, product endorsements, and television and film appearances were best attained through the larger, diversified agencies who were part of what was dubbed The Major Seven by *The Hollywood Reporter*.

CAA was regarded as the leader of the pack. In January 2019 *Billboard*'s Melinda Newman reported on the thirty-fifth anniversary of both CAA's music division and its managing director Rob Light's tenure there. CAA had 190 music division clients who ranked as headliners, including legacy artists Bob Dylan, Eric Clapton, and James Taylor, to current pop stars Lady Gaga, Cardi B, and the Chainsmokers. Newman added, "Light points out that the agency has signed over 90 acts before their first record came out. Many of those have gone on to become superstars themselves, including Maroon 5,

Lorde, Katy Perry, One Direction, Radiohead, Urban, Underwood and Grande."[20]

While the music revenue continued to grow, benefiting both artists and agents, CAA executive management branched out into other areas including sports, product branding, and multimedia matchmaking. This expansion had been financed by TPG Capital, which acquired 35 percent of CAA for $165 million in 2010, and then another 18 percent in 2014 for $225 million. CAA's estimated value grew from $700 million in 2010 to almost $2 billion in 2015. Three of the Young Turks who took over the agency in 1995 were still in top positions with Richard Lovett as president and Kevin Huvane and Bryan Lourd as managing partners. Rumors circulated of a future IPO as their exit strategy. In June 2015 Lovett told *The Hollywood Reporter*'s Kim Masters, who had coined the Young Turks sobriquet twenty years earlier, "We have no need to go public. Is it an option? Of course."[21]

WMA strengthened its second-place position after its 2009 merger with the TV/film-oriented Endeavor Talent Agency to form William Morris Endeavor (WME). Shortly thereafter Endeavor's Ari Emanuel and Patrick Whitesell took over from retiring WMA veteran Jim Wiatt. In 2012, tech sector investor Silver Lake acquired 31 percent of WME and another 20 percent in 2015 for undisclosed sums. WME then acquired the much larger IMG sports media conglomerate for a reported $2.4 billion, unveiling the new WME-IMG corporate identity. In 2017 WME-IMG utilized another private equity infusion to acquire Ultimate Fighting Championship for $4 billion, lifting the WME-IMG value to over $7 billion.

Although the overall company rebranded as Endeavor, the music division retained the WME acronym. In the year of the IMG acquisition, documents revealed that the music division had generated $88 million in commissions, accounting for 24.1 percent of the total WME revenue of $365 million, matching the film/commercial division's earnings. WME's top touring acts in 2019 included Garth Brooks, Justin Timberlake, Dead & Company, Eric Church, Trans-Siberian Orchestra, the Backstreet Boys, Florida Georgia Line, Mumford & Sons, John Mayer, Thomas Rhett, Luke Bryan, Zac Brown Band, and Luis Miguel.

In May 2019 Endeavor filed for an IPO expecting a market cap of around $8 billion but postponed as reaction indicated that $6.5 billion was more likely. *Variety* reported that many agents at WME had expected a generous payday from a share of the long-anticipated IPO. "There's sure to be some frustration expressed now that there's a delay in monetizing those shares. WME's rivals were quick to note that the industry powerhouse may be vulnerable to having high-performing agents recruited away by competitors. . . . Endeavor may have to pay out some retroactive bonuses to calm the waters."[22] Nonetheless there was still strong internal support for Emanuel and Whitesell. One senior WME agent told *Variety*, "Nobody is betting against Ari. It was just a bad moment [for an IPO]."[23]

In November 2019 Anousha Sakoui of the *Los Angeles Times* reported that "some of Hollywood's top talent agents and executives at Creative Artists Agency . . . are in line for a nearly $400-million payday as the agency seeks a $1.15-billion loan to help buy back employee shares."[24] Paul Bond of *The Hollywood Reporter* added, "The move represents a potential liquidity event for top earners at the agency in a similar fashion as an IPO might have, since the company has no plans to go public in the wake of rival Endeavor's failed attempt to do so."[25] A successful capital raise would provide Lovett, Huvane, and Lourd, who collectively controlled a majority of agent-owned shares, with their golden parachute after twenty-five years at the top of the agency power pyramid whether they banked it and stayed or moved on, leaving CAA in the hands of an even younger generation of Turks.

The Rest of the Pack

In 2019 Paradigm represented nineteen and one split tours for third place behind WME and CAA. Chairman/CEO Sam Gores had opened the agency in 1992 in Beverly Hills after fifteen years of experience as a film agent. Paradigm added Monterey Peninsula Artists in 2005, Little Big Man in 2006, the EDM AM Only agency in 2013, and a 50 percent share of UK contemporary pop agency Coda Music in 2015, buying the other half four years later. In 2019 former Little Big Man owner Marty Diamond was named president. Paradigm acts included Ed Sheeran (for US), Coldplay, Dave Matthews Band, Imagine Dragons, Halsey, The Lumineers, Bon Iver, and Janelle Monáe.

United Talent Agency (UTA) was in fourth in the Major Seven with ten tours in 2019 led by number six the Jonas Brothers and number seventeen Post Malone along with Guns N' Roses, Muse, Chicago, and a strong cast of comedians. UTA had been formed in 1991 by the merger of the Hollywood-based Bauer-Benedek and Leading Artists agencies to focus on film, television, and comedy acts. New York–based N. S. Bienstock, which specialized in newscasters, was added in 2014. In 2015 UTA acquired contemporary music oriented The Agency Group, whose founder Neil Warnock became head of the UTA music division. Clients included Lenny Kravitz, Marshmello, Mariah Carey, Toby Keith, DJ Khaled, Paramore, and the Black Keys.

Of the other agencies, ICM had five tours for fifth place led by Bob Seger & The Silver Bullet Band in the number three spot, grossing $97 million. Sixth-place APA with its large roster of esoteric artists that regularly played clubs, colleges, theaters, and art centers had three tours, Frankie Valli & The Four Seasons, the co-headlining tour for Mexican pop acts Camila and Sin Bandera, and soul legend Mary K. Blige. The Gersh Agency was the final member of the Major Seven but had virtually no presence in pop music.

New York–based and music-driven AGI also scored three and one split tours in the Top 200 with Billy Joel in eleventh place, Metallica at twenty-ninth in North America but fourth worldwide, and Def Leppard in seventieth place. In 2012 founder Dennis Arfa sold controlling share of AGI to Ron Burkle's Yucaipa investment firm, and brought in veteran agent Martha Vlasic from IMC as the new AGI president. Her clients included Neil Young, Elvis Costello, Regina Spektor, Cage The Elephant, Iggy & the Stooges, Moby, and Ben Folds to add to AGI's incumbent clients including Mötley Crüe, Megadeth, and Linkin Park. Two boutique music agencies also scored with two artists each in the Top 200 North American Tours. The Howard Rose Agency represented Sir Elton John and Jimmy Buffett, while the Cara Lewis Group scored with rap artists Travis Scott and Khalid.

Despite the corporate preoccupation with other fields of entertainment and financial machinations, CAA and WME maintained their standing in the yearly *Pollstar* Agency of the Year and Bobby Brooks Agent of the Year nominations from 2007 through 2019. CAA was named the top agency eight out of the thirteen years, with WME garnering the top spot in 2014. Paradigm had four nods in 2015, 2017, 2018, and 2019. CAA also led in Brooks award nominees with twenty-eight over the time frame, but no CAA agent achieved the honor. WME had twenty-three nominees, with the award going to Marc Geiger in 2009 and John Huie in 2013.

Although Paradigm had only fourteen agents nominated over the thirteen years, they took in seven Brooks awards with Chip Hooper in 2007, 2012, 2014, and 2015; Jonathan Levine in 2011; and Mary Diamond in 2018 and 2019. Outside of these three agencies, the Brooks award went to Steve Martin of APA in 2008, Frank Riley of singer/songwriter-oriented High Road Touring in 2010, Sam Hunt of Windish in 2016 (a year before it was merged into Paradigm), and Cara Lewis in 2017.

On the Road Again . . . Bigger and Better Than Ever

Between them, CAA and WME booked just over half of the Pollstar Top 200 North American tours in 2019. WME handled fifty-two and one split tours, while CAA booked forty-nine and one split. Five of the top-twenty tours, however, bypassed an agency with their promoters serving as the agency of record. The AEG Concerts West division was number one with The Rolling Stones while AEG stablemate Marshall Arts had P!nk coming in third, Sir Paul McCartney ranking eighteenth, and Cher in the twentieth spot. Independent Beaver Productions was at number seventeen with Michael Bublé. The year 2019 was a quiet one for Live Nation doubling as agent of record with only Madonna at number seventy-seven, playing just thirty-six shows in six locations.

Prior to 2007 only eight tours had topped $200 million on a global basis over the course of the entire tour whether it ran for just one year or over multiple years. Then from 2007 through the end of 2019 another twenty-eight tours exceeded the $200 million level. On The Stones' final 2007 leg of their *A Bigger Bang Tour* they extended their box-office record to $558.3 million on a total of 144 shows with 4.68 million attendees. Still with Michael Cohl, tickets ranged from $350 for platinum to $100 for general admission and $50 for side seating before the additional charges and secondary market markups. The stage was eighty-four-feet tall with a video screen of live shots and multimedia effects including their infamous red tongue logo, and curved lighting panels to each side with computer-generated graphics and customized lighting effects. Rear balconies accommodated four hundred VIPs, and a catwalk extended out into the stadium along which the bandstand area of the stage was propelled.

On June 30, 2009, U2 launched its own record-breaking *360° Tour*, which grossed over $736 million in its two-year run playing to 7.27 million fans averaging 66,110 per show, all records still standing as of the end of 2018. The centerpiece of the tour was the two hundred–ton, arachnid-shaped staging ensemble nicknamed The Claw, which Dylan Jones described in his *From The Ground Up: U2 360 Tour Official Photobook*: "Suspended over the centre of the stage was a vast cylindrical video screen composed of 888 individual panels and containing a total of 500,000 pixels. A cable pulley system enabled it to expand and contract like a giant Slinky."[26]

The pulleys extended to 151 feet above the 89-foot-tall, 213-foot-wide, and 161-foot-deep Claw, whose stage supported 250 tons of equipment and speakers. One hundred twenty trucks moved three duplicates continually ahead of one another with a total crew of three hundred and a daily cost of $750,000. Jones added, "It was not only the biggest ever staged by a rock band, not only the most technologically innovative and the most expensive, it also featured the largest stage and the loudest sound system ever assembled for a rock 'n' roll tour. It made Pink Floyd's *The Wall* look like a village fete."[27]

The other tours that exceeded $200 million featured eleven pop legacy acts, seven from the 1980s, three who found fame in the 1990s, and another six artists who were products of the twenty-first century. The only country act was Garth Brooks with his wife, Trisha Yearwood. Guns N' Roses and Coldplay broke the $500 million barrier, while Waters, AC/DC, and Madonna topped the $400 million mark. Brooks & Yearwood, The Police, Springsteen (twice), Taylor Swift, Madonna, and Joel all exceeded $300 million.

Then a twenty-eight-year-old redheaded, bespectacled singer/songwriter spent 2017 through 2019 selling out large venues around the world. Accompanied by just his guitar and a customized Chewie Monsta foot pedal rig combined with an Ableton MIDI program on a laptop to supply his backing tracks, Ed Sheeran had mastered the ability to mesmerize an entire arena, amphitheater, or stadium as easily as he did a small club, prompting all to sing along to his infectious choruses no matter the size of the venue. His two-and-a-half-year ÷ *Tour* set new records for total box-office receipts and tickets with $776.2 million and 8.8 million attendees on 260 shows, which averaged almost thirty-four thousand per show. Not bad for someone who was playing pubs and house parties just ten years prior.

The Recording Academy and Diversity Politics: The Incident

The February 2007 Grammy Awards drew 20.05 million households, the highest rating since 1991. Each year the Academy selected the talent for the twenty or so performances to strike a balance between genre diversity and entertainment value that could hold the attention of both the national-television and live-venue audiences for over three hours. There were additional pressures from CBS to satisfy its sponsors, and from the labels with each vying for its share of the performers and presenters. In 2007 there were fifteen song segments, with four of them in medley form, involving twenty-five artists with nine of them female and sixteen male. This same general format and talent blend continued through the next decade.

The 2008 economic downturn caused thirty-second time buys to slip from $557,300 in 2007 to $426,000 for 2010 and the television audience fell back under 20 million. In 2010 Beyoncé, Taylor Swift, the Black Eyed Peas, Lady Gaga with Sir Elton John, Eminem, Bon Jovi, and Lady Antebellum

ABOUT THE RECORDING ACADEMY®

MISSION

To recognize excellence in the recording arts and sciences, cultivate the well-being of the music community, and ensure that music remains an indelible part of our culture.

PURPOSE

As the leading community of music professionals, the Academy works every day to:

ADVOCATE - Fight for the rights of all music creators and ensure pro-music policy at the national, state, and local levels.

CELEBRATE - Bestow the GRAMMY® Award – the single most coveted accolade in music – and recognize the contributions of all creators throughout the year.

EDUCATE - Inspire the next generation of music creators and professionals by providing opportunity, enrichment, and mentorship.

SERVE - Purposely participate in service, to respect our shared love of music and prioritize community above self. The Academy is a community that cares.

GOVERNANCE - The Academy's main headquarters and administration are in Santa Monica CA under the governance of a board of trustees elected by the membership. Recording Academy® information and updates can be found at www.grammy.com.

VOTING MEMBERSHIP

Performers, songwriters, producers, engineers, instrumentalists, and other creators currently working in the recording industry are eligible for Voting Membership. Over 12,000 Voting Members determine GRAMMY® winners each year. Proof of a primary career focus in music, plus at least twelve commercially distributed, verifiable credits in a single creative profession, all subject to peer review.

PROFESSIONAL MEMBERSHIP

For music businesspeople whose full-time, primary business activity directly supports music creators such as music executives, creator representatives, industry writers, and music educators who are not Voting Members.

Source: RecordingAcademy.com

Illustration 14.3 About the Recording Academy®

performed along with a tribute to the recently deceased Michael Jackson. Ratings rebooted to 25.8 million households.

With the streaming tsunami looming on the horizon, younger consumers driving the market, and inspiration from the improved ratings, the Academy decided to fine-tune the show. Awards for 2011 were reduced from 109 to 78. Best male and female performance awards in the pop, R&B, rock, and country fields were consolidated into gender-free categories. From 2010 through to 2017 the audience averaged 28.5 million, peaking in 2012 at 39.9 million. Thirty-second time buys exceeded $1 million from 2015 forward.

Going into the 2018 awards, however, a combustible set of conditions coalesced around the gender inequity issue sparked by the Me Too Movement. On the show itself, there were only two females out of twenty nominees for the four major awards and the only female Album of the Year nominee, Lorde, was not invited to perform on the show. That week the USC Annenberg School for Communication and Journalism released a report citing a male predominance worse than four to one in the overall industry, and the recent Charlie Walk sexual abuse exposé had just rocked the industry. Academy head Neil Portnow ignited a furor with a poorly worded, post-show statement that was perceived as tone deaf. Unfortunately for the Grammy Awards and the Academy as a whole, the incident became the symbolic punching bag for the usually unspoken truth about the position of women in the business.

When questioned about Lorde, longtime producer Ken Ehrlich offered a partial mea culpa. "These shows are always a matter of choices. . . . She had a great album . . . but there's no way we can really deal with everybody. Sometimes people get left out that shouldn't, but on the other hand, we did the best we can to make sure that it's a representative and balanced show."[28]

Portnow, however, attempted a commentary on the state of the entire industry, which began with a call for "women who have the creativity in their hearts and souls, who want to be musicians, who want to be engineers, producers, and want to be part of the industry on the executive level. . . . [They need] to step up because I think they would be welcome. I don't have personal experience of those kinds of brick walls that you face but I think it's upon us— us as an industry—to make the welcome mat very obvious."[29] The reaction from women in the industry as well as many male supporters of gender equity subsequently intensified. Whether the word choice of "step up" and "it's us as an industry," with "us" interpreted as the cabal of older white men who controlled the industry, was an unfortunate gaffe or a revelatory slip, the damage had been done and change was imminent.

The Recording Academy and Diversity Politics: The Blowback

P!nk, one of the few female performers on the show, tweeted the next day, "Women in music don't need to "step up"—women have been stepping since the beginning of time. Stepping up, and also stepping aside. Women OWNED music this year. They've been KILLING IT. And every year before this."[30]

Two days later a letter from twenty-one female industry executives added, "We step up every single day and have been doing so for a long time. The fact that you don't realize this means it's time for you to step down. . . . Your comments are another slap in the face to women, whether intended or not, whether taken out of context, or not. Needless to say, if you are not part of the solution, then you must accept that YOU are part of the problem. Time's up, Neil."[31] The same day a Care2 petition was started seeking Portnow's ouster, eventually gathering over thirty thousand signatures. #GrammysSoMale and #TimesUp hashtags were circulating. The next day a petition by male industry executives made the rounds.

Much of this response called for the Academy to correct its gender imbalance as if this would affect the disparities outlined in the USC report. As to what the Academy could control, from 2011 through 2018 there had been 304 performers on the show, of whom 35 percent were female, 62 percent male, and 3 percent mixed gender. Although a better ratio than the industry as a whole, it was still not a true reflection of society. Recognizing that although the Academy might not be the root of the problem, but a part of it nonetheless, plans were announced to form a Diversity and Inclusion Task Force to examine the "barriers and biases affecting women and other underrepresented voices in the music industry and, specifically, the Recording Academy."[32]

At the end of the tumultuous week, former *Billboard* editorial director Bill Werde wrote in a thought-provoking guest commentary, "With all the change that has begun to happen—the marginalized finding voice, platform and power—one thing that hasn't generally changed is the leadership of the music business. At the Recording Academy, and all across the music industry, the power structure is not only still overwhelmingly white and male, but the same white men who were in charge 10, 15, 20 years ago. I know many of these folks personally, and many of them are great humans with a track record for elevating and promoting women and people of color.

"But they are going to have to prove that they are now up for very different leadership challenges. Even if your track record is great, how's your consciousness? How's your organizational culture? Your policies and implementation of them? Where is the money you are spending on your commitment to real change, and where is that real change? How close are you to 51 percent (or more) of your most senior team being women? How do you know that a woman feels she has a safe path to report harassment or abuse? Would you get great responses on these questions if you anonymously surveyed the women in your company?"[33]

Billboard.com senior editor/R&B/hip hop and former Academy trustee Gail Mitchell commented in *Billboard*, "The Recording Academy can only work with the content it's given, accepting entries online from its members and registered media companies, including record labels. As such, arriving at an effective solution to gender, racial or other imbalances at the award show also starts with label and A&R executives hiring and signing more female executives, artists, songwriters, producers and engineers."[34]

The Recording Academy and Diversity Politics: Seeking a Solution

In May, Academy task force chairperson, respected litigator, and former Obama assistant Tina Tchen announced the eighteen-member panel comprising fifteen females and three males. There were three multiple-Grammy winners, three previous nominees, three label executives, and six CEOs from other music industry sectors. At the Academy's annual board meeting the number of nominees in the four major categories was increased from five to eight to provide a wider choice and greater inclusivity.

Following the board meetings, Portnow announced that he would not seek renewal of his contract when it expired in June 2019. Highlights of his tenure included the 2016 ten-year $600 million television agreement with CBS; the Grammy Museum in Los Angeles with branches in Newark, Mississippi, and Nashville; MusiCares fundraising totals of $8.5 million in 2017 and $7 million in 2018 bringing distributions to over $60 million since its 1989 inception; creating the annual Music Educator Award in 2014; initiating the Grammy on the Hill Lobbying Day; and developing the online voting process for the Grammy Awards.

The search was on to find a successor while implementing the task force suggestions. By September, the nominations review committees had been elevated to 51 percent female from 28 percent in 2017, while members of color rose to 48 percent from 37 percent. The eight national governance committees moved to 48 percent female from 20 percent, while people of color went to 38 percent from 30 percent. The voting membership blend, however, was only 21 percent female. Fifty-five percent identified as white with 28 percent as people of color, while 17 percent declined to define their racial identity. In October the Academy invited nine hundred qualified women and/or people of color under the age of thirty-nine to join as voting members by November 15 in order to be eligible to vote for the upcoming awards.

Announced in early December, thirteen of the thirty-two nominees in the four major categories were female, nine were male, and ten were mixed gender. In the twenty-three pop nominations, ten were female, eight male, and five mixed. In producer of the year, which had been grouped with the major categories in the USC study and Times Up petition, Linda Perry was nominated in this virtually all-male category. Lauryn Hill had been the last female nominee in 1999 when she won five Grammy Awards, but not the one for producer. The other awards, while not as visible to the public or as significant in stimulating record sales, were still dominantly male. Did the large number of females nominated in the major categories indicate a democratizing trend in the industry, or just a reflection of that year's marketplace?

Whatever the answer, Academy leadership seemed to be doing what it could in the pursuit of gender equity as evident by the performers scheduled for the February 2019 show. Fifty-six percent of the thirty-nine performers were female, 41 percent male, with one mixed-gender duet. The show closed with four all-female performance slots culminating with Fantasia, Andra Day, and Yolanda Adams paying tribute to the late Aretha Franklin with a rousing rendition of "(You Make Me Feel Like) A Natural Woman." The winners in the general categories were split in gender with Kacey Musgraves for Album of the Year, Dua Lipa for Best New Artist, and Childish Gambino taking Record of the Year and Song of the Year for "Only in America." Best Pop Performances went to Lady Gaga for Solo and Duo/Group with Bradley Cooper. Ariana Grande received the nod for Best Pop Album Performance.

At the May 2019 trustees meeting Deborah Dugan was announced as Portnow's replacement, to begin August 1. Attorney Dugan had just served for eight years as CEO of Bono's AIDS awareness charity following executive positions at Disney Publishing, EMI/Capitol, and SBK Records. An anonymous Academy insider told *Variety*'s Jem Aswad, "Look at everything she's done—the music industry, the corporate, Wall Street, the pro bono legal work, she's educated and I don't know anyone who'd have a bad thing to say about her. I think she's exactly what the Academy needs."[35]

Dugan herself voiced her excitement. "I'm honored, humbled, and ready. The goal of the Recording Academy is to support, encourage, and advocate for those within the music community. I will listen to and champion all of those individuals, and lead this iconic organization into the future."[36] Dugan dug in, the diversity committee released its report with eighteen recommendations, and the Grammy nominations were announced in November 2019 with fourteen female artists, thirteen male, and five mixed-gender nominees in the four main categories. In the twenty pop category nominees, eleven were female, seven were male, and two mixed. Newcomers led overall, as Lizzo received eight nominations, while Billie Eilish and Lil Nas X had six each.

The Rising Tide of Artist Revenue

Pollstar-tabulated box-office receipts for the top 2019 tours totaled over $11 billion, almost three times 2007's $3.9 billion. Estimated collective take home calculated at $3.7 billion compared to $1.3 billion in 2007. Revenue from an estimated 25 percent net on $3.6 billion in merchandise sales accounted for about $900 million more, four times the net return in 2007. Publishing overall had grown by at least 60 percent.

Billboard's 2019 Top 40 Money Makers netted an estimated $950 million, almost double 2007's $492 million. The top-ten earners were The Rolling Stones with $65 million in take home, followed by Ariana Grande, the Jonas Brothers, Queen, Post Malone, P!nk, Elton John, Kiss, Billy Joel, and Justin Timberlake in descending order from $44.3 million for Grande down to $25.9 million for Timberlake. Panic! at the Disco came in at number forty with $15.4 million. Despite scoring heavily in sales and streaming, Taylor Swift, Drake, and Ed Sheeran who were number one, number three, and number five, respectively, in 2018, were absent from the 2019 list due to reduced tour schedules.

The 2019 list reflected a wide array of genre diversity with fourteen pop, fourteen rock, eight country, three R&B/hip hop, and one Latin artist. Age demographics covered six decades with five acts that began in the 1960s, six in the 1970s, three in the 1980s, seven in the 1990s, eight between 2000 and 2009, and eleven after 2010. When it came to gender, however, there were only eight female artists for 20 percent of the total, reflecting the gender imbalance throughout the industry as a whole.

While artist revenue from concerts, merchandise, and publishing were on a steady upward pattern as the economy recovered from the 2008 downturn, record royalties mirrored the labels' decline into a six-year stall at $7 billion from 2010 through 2015. In 2016 RIAA-reported revenue finally started to rise, reaching $11.1 billion in 2019. In 2007 87.3 percent of revenue had come from physical and download sales, but by 2019 they contributed only 18.5 percent. Concurrently, streaming revenues grew from 2.5 percent in 2007 to 79.5 percent in 2019.

By 2019 almost all label contracts contained 360° provisions with royalty rates between 16 percent and 20 percent of wholesale receipts, and sometimes higher for superstars, and still subject to recoupment from advances, recording costs, and other agreed-upon expenditures. Some independent labels paid as high as 50 percent of net revenue. Even after deducting the labels' share of 360° revenues, as a whole artists were doing considerably better than in 2007. The totally independent DIYers netted the balance of incoming revenue after distribution, collection, nonproprietary publishing, and any manufacturing costs.

The Streaming Economy of Scale

In the pre-streaming era, the use of "million" had long been associated with RIAA platinum certifications, or a millionaire award for a million logged radio performances under the BMI airplay survey. As applied to streaming, however, the use of "million" was on a totally different economy of scale. One stream entailed one device receiving one transmitted track played once in real time, whether on-demand or as part of a playlist. Total streams tracked by Nielsen in 2019 surpassed 1.1 trillion. Although one million streams sounded like a lot, there were 1.1 million sets of one million in 1.1 trillion.

In a June 2019 industry data aggregator, soundcharts.com reported on a study by artist rights blog *The Trichordist* analyzing the rates paid by different DSPs to a mid-sized indie label with over 1.5 billion streams in 2019. Spotify averaged $.0035 per stream over its three tiers, while Apple Music, with only a premium tier, paid $.0068. The same study had YouTube's ad-based tier "which for this label accounts for 51% of streams but only 6% of revenue, at a per-stream rate of $0.00022."[37] *The Trichordist* also reported that for the same label YouTube's Red premium tier delivered $.01.09 per stream. General consensus across the industry was that the average payment on 1 million streams in 2019 was in the $6,000 range.

The approximately 70 percent share of streaming service revenue paid to rightsholders, including the publishing share, originated with Spotify's initial 2008 label licensing agreements. This rate mirrored what Steve Jobs had negotiated for iTunes downloads, which itself replicated the then-approximate ratio between wholesale and retail prices for physical sales. According to RIAA data, 85.4 percent of 2019 streaming value came from 60.4 million paid subscriptions. Ad-based tiers accounted for over 45 percent of total streams, but generated only the other 14.6 percent of streaming revenue. In 2019 the higher priced services with CD or Hi-Res quality files, paid per-stream rates as high as 1.1¢. Ad-based tiers and services paid lower rates with some under .1¢, corroborating the study done by *The Trichordist*.

Advanced metadata technology enabled Nielsen to track and account for over a trillion individual streams as they were listened to across the globe at the average rate of over 125 million streams per hour. They were instantly sorted and transported for payment through their ISRC and ISWC identifiers to reach the proper royalty recipients as long as those recipients had registered their works with their collection representatives. Streaming had replaced the generations-old brick-and-mortar distribution network with immediate, totally mobile access to an even wider and more diverse audience. Even with the major labels' economic advantage, indies had captured 40 percent of consumer listening time. Combining this increased market share, worldwide growth in subscriptions, and more services with CD or Hi-Res quality at higher monthly rates, the economic future for artists everywhere was looking better all the time.

15

The Consumer: Leading the Digital Transition

The State of Music Consumption in 2007

The year 2007 marked a milestone in the transformation of music consumption from physical sales to digital delivery. It was the first year that consumers spent over $1 billion on both downloads at $1.31 billion, and ringtones at $1.1 billion. Concurrently, spending on physical product declined by $1.88 billion from 2006 to 2007 as CD sales plummeted by 120 million units from 619.7 million to 499.7 million. It was also the year that Apple launched the iPhone to emerge as the leader in the migration of streaming access from desktop to portable devices.

Between 1973 and the start of 2007, about $268 billion in consumer spending had passed through the cash registers of the retail supply chain or accounting ledgers of the record clubs. From 45 rpm and LP discs through 8-track and cassette tape cartridges, then to CDs and DVDs, and most recently digital downloads, consumers embraced the newest sound carrier alternative, often rebuilding their personal music libraries in the new format. The MP3 digital file, however, was the first new sound carrier not presented by the record industry in tandem with new playing devices from the electronics industry.

The younger age groups were the most computer savvy, and as such found access to this new sound carrier through Napster and other file-sharing platforms. The record industry attempted to block what it could not control, but electronics companies filled the demand for portable players anyway. Midway through Napster's two-year run, RIAA-reported revenue reached its peak, and then entered a slow decline as purchases of physical product by younger consumers decreased in favor of file-sharing. It wasn't until the debut of iTunes in April 2003 that the major labels agreed in earnest to license their catalogs to a company in which they had no control.

The $7.48 billion consumers spent on albums in 2007 was down from 1999's all-time high by 86 percent. Legal downloads and ringtones, however, lessened

American Popular Music and Its Business in the Digital Age. Rick Sanjek, Oxford University Press. © Frederick Sanjek 2024.
DOI: 10.1093/oso/9780190653828.003.0015

the impact, boosting the 2007 total consumer expenditure on recorded music to $10.65 billion, but this was $3.9 billion less in 2007 than in 1999, also the year Napster had debuted. Consumers were listening to as much if not more music, but the industry monopoly over the supply chain had been disrupted.

Even the most intransigent elements of the record business recognized that eleven-to-twenty-six-year-old Millennials favored single tracks over albums, allowing them to create their own multi-artist playlists. Of the 883 million legal download purchases in 2007, 819 million were single tracks, 50 million were albums containing at least another 500 million tracks, and 14 million were music videos. The digital transformation of music consumption, however, was still in its infancy as 83.9 percent of 2007 consumer spending on recorded music was in physical sales, while downloads, including videos and ringtones, generated 14 percent. Streaming was still a minor factor with about 1.8 million consumers with paid subscriptions at an average yearly cost of $130 each.

In 2007 terrestrial radio was still consumers' primary source for new music. Over 92 percent of the population had free access to radio as its revenue base was totally ad-supported. The major radio formats were still tightly programmed and limited to the records supplied by the labels coupled with previously acquired catalog items. Radio revenue had been over $21 billion since 2004, indicating that manufacturers and service providers who wanted to co-brand with music still believed in the efficacy of radio as an advertising tool.

The triangular accord formed between radio, record companies, and the retail supply chain in the days of Top 40 radio had adapted to the introduction of FM radio, survived the Sony Walkman, thrived with the debut of the CD, and even grew in profit during the home duplication epidemic until file-sharing began its disruption. The radio industry hierarchy, however, was aware of the impending competition from satellite radio for its upper-income, in-car listeners. They were also attuned to the even greater threat in streaming as Pandora's interactive algorithm sparked the migration to the smartphone as a source for music with rudimentary consumer interactivity.

2007 Consumer Profile

Since the iTunes store launched in 2003, digital files were legally available at 99¢ each for on-demand, at-will access on computers and portable players. The same tracks were still available through Napster's successors, but the P2P process needed a higher degree of digital dexterity, had a lower sonic quality, was considered home piracy by the record industry, and risked possible legal action. Nonetheless, home duplication was still a problem for the record industry.

A poll of consumers conducted in 2007 by Entertainment Media Research (EMR) of the UK indicated that 43 percent of respondents admitted to illegal downloading, up from 36 percent in 2006 while concern about prosecution dropped to 33 percent from 42 percent. The poll also revealed that social network sites were influencing music consumption habits. EMR CEO Russell Hart told the UK's *Telegraph*, "Social networks are fundamentally changing the way we discover, purchase and use music. The dynamics of democratization, word of mouth recommendation and instant purchase challenge the established order and offer huge opportunities to forward-thinking businesses."[1] A 2008 IFPI global poll corroborated the EMR findings, estimating that 40 billion tracks were shared that year through unauthorized P2P connections, compared to 2.3 billion downloaded legally.

As for those who obtained recorded music legally, the 2007 RIAA Consumer Profile report indicated that 82.6 percent still favored buying physical product. Three quarters of them preferred to shop at retail, divided 50-50 between record stores and big-box outlets. The remaining CD buyers were divided evenly between record clubs and a myriad of online sources led by Amazon. On-demand listening on portable devices was limited to tracks from consumers' CD libraries that were copied, ripped, and burned into digital files; downloaded tracks which could then be copied to those devices; and/or digital files obtained through P2P file-sharing whether legal or illicit.

Although radio still dominated listening in 2007 when away from the home entertainment center, there were several emerging offerings that ranged from already formatted internet radio stations for passive listeners, to more interactive options with choice of genre, mood, or even specific tracks. Streaming subscription services eMusic, last.FM, Rhapsody, and Pandora were only available on computers or some smartphones. Still struggling through their merger approval process, satellite radio providers Sirius and XM were primarily in-car alternatives to terrestrial radio with a wider selection of niche-formatted channels, but no opportunity for specific song selection.

On January 10, 2007, iTunes sold its 2 billionth track and then 4 billionth in January 2008. Estimating that if iTunes accounted for about 70 percent of the download business, then overall track purchases to date were in the range of 5.7 billion, the monetary equivalent of over a half billion albums in the four and a half years since the 2003 iTunes launch. This was a good start but nowhere near the purported number of illegal downloads or a full replacement for the revenue shortage caused by declining physical sales.

Evolution of the Mobile Phone: From Analog to Digital

By 2007 over 75 percent of Americans owned mobile phones, but the vast majority of them were first-generation (1G) cellular models operating on analog technology at below 2.4 kilobits per second (Kbps). Battery life was limited, and call dropouts frequent. The second-generation (2G) cellular offering emerged in the late 1990s transmitting digitally encrypted signals at speeds up to 50 Kbps for networks employing Code Division Multiple Access (CDMA) developed by Qualcomm. Networks utilizing Global System for Mobile Communications (GSM) networks, simultaneously but separately developed in both the US and Europe, could transmit at up to one megabit per second (Mbps). Phones utilizing 2G supported short message service (SMS) texting, international roaming, conference call, call hold, and real-time electronic billing.

The 2G 1996 Nokia 900 Communicator was the first mobile phone with a QWERTY keyboard. In 2002 Nokia introduced a limited mobile phone internet service. Also in 2002 the Sony Ericsson P800 offered a touchscreen operated with either fingers or stylus while Sanyo and Nokia introduced the first mobile phone cameras. In 2003 the Palm One Treo and Research In Motion (RIM)'s BlackBerry smartphones launched third-generation (3G) networks with speed capable of up to 3.1 Mbps, opening the door for full internet connectivity and global roaming. In 2006 over 990 million mobile phones were sold worldwide, but less than 10 percent were 3G smartphones. Nokia led the overall market with 34.8 percent of sales, followed by Motorola with 21.1 percent, and Samsung with 11.8 percent.

Steve Jobs introduced the future of the mobile phone at the January 2007 Macworld convention by announcing the June launch of Apple's iPhone to be sold exclusively through AT&T's Cingular Wireless division. "iPhone is a revolutionary and magical product that is literally five years ahead of any other mobile phone,"[2] Jobs proclaimed. In secret development for the previous two years, the iPhone was Apple's initial foray into the mobile phone market, combining the latest 2G refinements with the music functions of the iPod, all run by Apple's new iPhone Operating System (iOS) that synchronized with the mac OS computer operating system for data exchange.

The iPhone placed a miniaturized computer in consumers' pockets with search engine, email, phone, video streaming, camera, texting, and downloading capabilities integrated with the functions of the iPod. The physical keyboard, small touchscreen, and writing stylus available from the competition were replaced by a keyboard embedded within a capacitive touchscreen covering the surface of the 4.5″ by 2.4″ and .46″ thick device. Jobs explained at the introductory presentation, "We are all born with the ultimate pointing device—our fingers—and iPhone uses them to create the most revolutionary user interface since the mouse."[3] Its uncluttered menu of options and direct-to-computer data connectivity made it a far more user-friendly combination of phone, personal data assistant (PDA), and music player all in one slim and stylish, Jony Ive–designed alternative to carrying three separate devices. Jobs correctly anticipated that the iPhone would catapult the smartphone from business convenience to public necessity.

The iPhone operated on a quad-band GSM network with both Bluetooth and Wi-Fi as well as a USB port for a wired connection to Apple computers running Mac OSX, or to either Windows 2000 or XP for PC users. The 4GB listed at $499 and the 8GB at $599 came with Ive's newly designed successor to the iPod's iconic white earbuds. These white pendent earphones had a squeeze-activated capsule in the line to the right earpiece housing a microphone, volume controls, and a single button capable of managing a wide array of tasks. With its multigenerational peer group appeal, Jobs proclaimed it to be truly revolutionary. Then due to negative consumer reaction over the cost, the price for the 8GB model was lowered in September to $399 with rebates to earlier buyers. The 4GB was dropped due to overwhelming consumer preference for the 8GB.

Evolution of the Mobile Phone: Android Takes a Bite at the Apple

In June 2008 Apple announced the release of the iPhone 3GS, upping RAM capacity to 16 GB while adding 3G speed and Global Positional System (GPS), along with automated-brightness and screen-orientation sensors. The headphone jack was adjusted to allow non-Apple headsets. Apple concurrently stocked its App Store with third-party apps. Sales of the 2G speed iPhone were curtailed, and the 7 million sold to date were offered an upgrade to 3G. The 3GS became available through AT&T with a two-year service plan. AT&T contributed half the cost of the phone, then a common practice in the mobile phone business, lowering consumer out-of-pocket expense to a minimum of $199.

Apple's sudden domination of the smartphone market, however, was about to be challenged. While Jobs was clandestinely planning both the iPhone and iPhone 3GS launches, other companies were also working on capacitive touchscreen functions. Sony Ericsson, Nokia, Samsung, Microsoft, and RIM, which was about to reidentify as BlackBerry, all tried to augment their physical keyboards with small touchscreens. In 2005, just after the 3G debut, Google had purchased a small tech development company named Android that was very quietly working on an open source Linux kernel-based operating system. The Andy Rubin–led Android team moved to Google with the purchase. *AndroidAuthority.com*, an independent blog dedicated to all aspects of Android since 2007, quoted Rubin as saying the purpose of Android was to allow "smarter mobile devices that are more aware of its owner's location and preferences."[4]

The success of the iPhone made it obvious to the rest of the mobile industry that a full-size touchscreen with fingertip operability rather than stylus and/or physical keyboard was the future of the smartphone. Google helped organize the Open Handset Alliance™, which debuted in November 2007. Alliance members pooled their resources to develop competition for Apple before it established a stranglehold on the smartphone sector just it had done with the iPod. Pursuing an open source rather than developing a proprietary operating system would not only speed the process but also create clients for Google's other products.

The Alliance website proclaimed, "The Open Handset Alliance is a group of 84 technology and mobile companies who have come together to accelerate innovation in mobile and offer consumers a richer, less expensive, and better mobile experience. Together we have developed Android™, the first complete, open, and free mobile platform. We are committed to commercially deploy handsets and services using the Android Platform. . . . All parts of the mobile ecosystem are represented in the Alliance. Members include mobile operators, handset manufacturers, semiconductor companies, software companies, and commercialization companies."[5]

In June 2008, the same month as the iPhone 3GS launch, T-Mobile announced the first Android 1.0-operated smartphone dubbed the G1 for T-Mobile's first-generation model, not for 1G speed. The G1 had 3G speed. First shipped in October 2008, the G1 had a full-surface touchscreen that slid out revealing a physical keyboard underneath. While the touchscreen interface was not as functionally intuitive as the iPhone and had far fewer apps, it did feature Google Maps, YouTube, a pre-Chrome browser, and Google's search engine. Nokia, Samsung, Motorola, and Sony-Ericsson quickly followed.

It took several years, however, for the Alliance members to totally abandon the physical keyboard and stylus options. Compared to the slimmer, sleeker design and navigational ease of the iPhone, a physical keyboard proved ponderous and a stylus superfluous, and perhaps even more important, out of fashion with the social media influencers of the digital culture. The Android overtook the iPhone in market share by 2011, propelled by an over four-to-one ratio of PC owners over MAC users and hence greater familiarity with Google applications. In 2013 Apple sold just 151 million iPhones out of the 970 million worldwide smartphone total. Almost all of the non-Apple smartphones were Android-operated with the exception of Blackberry and five other contenders all vying for a distant third place listed in June 2014 by ZDnet.com as Sailfish, Firefox, Ubanti Touch, Samsung's Tizen, and Microsoft's Windows Phone. For most active music consumers, smartphones had replaced digital MP3-playing devices just as the CD and its player had replaced the cassette a generation earlier.

Evolution of the Mobile Phone: The Smartphone Takes over as a Music Device

The Great Recession triggered a drastic downturn that extended from October 2008 into 2010. The consumption of music suffered along with all other economic sectors. Consumer spending on CDs fell by 54 percent from 2007's $7.99 billion to 2010's $3.66 billion.

Consumer purchase of downloads had grown from 2004 through 2008, then stabilized from 2008 through 2010, fluctuating within 1 percent of $2.68 billion. The purchase of ringtones, which had peaked at $1.1 billion in 2007, started to slide in 2008 to under $100 million by 2013, and then down to $24.9 million in 2019 primarily due to the ringtone-generating function available on smartphones. Downloads, however, more than doubled between 2007 and 2013. Revenue-wise, this growth countered the ringtone drop as well as the decline in physical sales to maintain the annual consumer expenditure on recorded music around the $7 billion level from 2010 through 2015.

The migration to smartphones also negatively affected the sales of digital file-playing devices including the iPod, which had about 75 percent of the US market. Annual iPod sales peaked in 2008 at 59 million units and then fell to 26 million units in 2013 with the rest of the player market declining accordingly. In 2014, Apple stopped reporting iPod sales in their annual revenue recap. In 2017 the Nano and the Shuffle were discontinued totally, leaving the iPod Touch as the only model still available. The iTunes Store, however, was available to consumers on all smartphones. Although iTunes was still the market leader in download sales going into 2019, Apple announced its close as of the end of the year with download purchases and file storage transferred to Apple Music. In 2019 US consumers paid $856 million for downloads of albums, individual tracks, music videos, and ringtones combined, just 7.7 percent of total recorded music spending compared to 79.5 percent for streaming.

Although moving consumers from iPod to iPhone was part of Steve Jobs's blueprint to retain Apple's digital dominance, he didn't believe in streaming as a viable option for music consumption. Both PressPlay and MusicNet had subscription streaming as key components, but they were poorly conceived, inadequately supplied with content, and thus failed to attract customers. Jobs blamed the concept rather than the execution. In 2015 at the launch of the Apple Music subscription service, Thomas Ricker recalled in *The Verge* what Jobs had said at the launch of iTunes in 2003, "We think subscriptions are the wrong path. . . . We think people want to buy their music on the internet by buying downloads just like they bought LPs, just like they bought cassettes, just like they bought CDs. . . . When you own your music it never goes away. When you own your music you have a broad set of personal use rights—you can listen to it however you want."[6]

Streaming, however, was not the sole reason for the demise of PressPlay and MusicNet as there was a plethora of other problems that plagued them. Former MusicNet CEO Alan McGlade wrote in a *Forbes* guest column in 2013, "Steve Jobs was contemptuous of subscription services from the start. . . . Surely he could have claimed that subscription services weren't yet user friendly; broadband speeds were still marginal for streaming and there were all sorts of limitations with portable music devices (an issue the iPhone ultimately solved). But he was firm in his stance. He said that people weren't willing to have their music disappear if they stopped paying fees."[7]

Although a consummate innovator and avid music consumer, Jobs conflated the act of acquisition with the experience of listening. Historically, each advance in sound carrier technology had been the newest, best option for on-demand listening when live performance was unavailable. The music consumer had always adapted to better reproduction and improved access even if more expensive, as substantiated by the success of CDs despite costing twice as much as cassettes or LPs. Subscription streaming, however, was dramatically less expensive, more efficient, and an instantaneous path to an even more extensive catalog of music. Contrary to Jobs's position regarding the pitfalls of streaming, the music was never taken away. Access could be interrupted but could always be restored with the resumption of the monthly fee or willingness to endure commercials. A physical or digital library that was lost or damaged had a far higher replacement cost than just paying between $4.99 and $19.99 per month for reconnection.

Despite's Jobs's misgivings, streaming would become the unintended beneficiary of the smartphone's success. Prior to the iPhone, music consumers from baby boomers to millennials had become accustomed to creating their own track lists through home duplication as an alternative to the restricted and repetitive rotation on radio. Although download technology had freed consumers to select their own music, the process was limited by the availability of their two most precious commodities, money to purchase CDs or downloads, and time to transfer them to the portable device. Even illegal P2P file-sharing took time. Furthermore, prior to the smartphone, subscription services required wired computer connectivity and were limited in repertoire.

The introduction of 3G speed to mobile phones, as McGlade noted, rectified that problem. Ad-free services eliminated the cost for immediate access to a vast number of tracks while pre–Hi Res premium services capped the cost at the equivalent of buying one CD or downloading ten tracks per month. If a consumer listened to streaming one hour a day, that would equate to over five hundred streams a month. Streaming also eliminated the time otherwise needed to copy, rip, and burn each track, whether purchased or pirated, in order to add it to a mobile device. The smartphone's speed, portability, and superior functionality provided the catalyst needed to revive the relationship between the record industry and file-sharing Gen X'ers and millennials. Contrary to Jobs's belief that ownership was essential to on-demand listening, these consumers were far more prone to paying the minimal cost for the convenience of unfettered access than spending time and money in purchasing and maintaining a music library.

The record labels and Apple, as the largest digital supplier to the consumer, had expected downloads to be the replacement for physical sales, but once the market bottomed out from the 2008 recession, consumer resurgence in spending shifted to live performance while illicit file-sharing remained unabated. A new cadre of investors and innovators, however, envisioned streaming as the future of the record industry. The major questions were how long would it take and how many subscribers were needed to achieve and maintain the necessary critical mass to re-establish the profitability of the record industry while falling within the convenience and cost parameters of the public.

The legal framework for streaming was already incorporated within copyright law through the DMCA but had to be contractually and financially refined. Unlike at the advent of downloading, streaming innovators were united in their intent on copyright compliance; the record labels were resolved not to sabotage a second chance for their economic recovery; and thanks to the growing sway of social media and its influencers, the public was prepared to adopt and adapt to a new form of delivery built on convenience and immediacy at an acceptable price.

Pandora's Algorithm: Interactivity with a Thumbs Up!

Already the internet radio leader, Pandora quickly became the first streaming service to transition to the smartphone. Will Glaser, Jon Kraft, and Tim Westergren founded Pandora in 2000 as a B2B service for music stores under the corporate umbrella of Savage Beast Technologies. Their patented Music Genome Project created a unique digital profile for each track entered into their repertoire, compiled by a team of trained music analysts based on evaluating up to four hundred distinct characteristics for each song. By 2001 the venture was out of funding. Glaser and Kraft left Westergren alone to carry on with a volunteer staff.

In 2002 Larry Marcus of Walden Venture Capital joined Westergren to recapitalize and rebrand as internet radio platform Pandora. Their Genome's proprietary algorithm utilized interactive listener prompts of Thumbs Up, Thumbs Down, Skip, or Drop to tailor personalized playlists. Listeners could also tune in to existing playlists created by other users structured around specific characterizations rather than compile their own. In 2006 Pandora was named by *Time* magazine as one of the nine coolest new entertainment, arts, and media websites along with YouTube and Wolfgang's Vault, the repository of Bill Graham's library of memorabilia. Pandora was also touted by the *San Francisco Chronicle* as the best place to discover new music, *PC World* named it one of the 100 Best Products of 2007, and *Fortune* pronounced it as the most efficient way to discover new music.

Accolades and internet success were followed in 2008 by Pandora becoming both the first free and the first third-party music app in the Apple Store. It also gained placement on wireless networks and smartphones for AT&T, Windows Mobile, Motorola, and BlackBerry. By the end of 2008 Pandora had 20 million registered users between the phone and web radio, which grew to over 125 million by the end of 2011. Pandora cited 47 million of them as active listeners in its January 2012 annual report. Web ratings service Triton Digital credited Pandora with a 69 percent share of the listeners of the top twenty internet radio providers. Although not a fully on-demand streaming platform, Pandora provided an intermediary step for music consumers between the traditional records-radio-retail model and the yet-to-come celestial jukebox.

Pandora stated in its 2012 annual report, "Through personalization and interaction, we've redefined radio and disrupted one of the largest consumer media categories—where 80 percent of all music listening happens. . . . Where users can interact with radio by creating their own stations, following their friends' stations, and personalizing their radio listening experience. . . . We've rethought how we can help our listeners discover music from their musical mentors and friends by helping them easily identify musical influencers and effortlessly follow them."[8] Other Pandora features included access to lyrics, biographies, and photos; links to buy albums from Amazon or tracks from iTunes; and connectivity through Facebook and other social media platforms to share playlists and personalized stations.

In its fiscal 2012, which ended January 31, 2012, Pandora had $274.3 million in revenue, up from $14.3 million in 2008. Of that, 86 percent— $235.9 million—came from advertising on its freemium accounts, while only $34.4 million came from the Pandora One premium subscription fees at $36 annually, or $3.99 if billed monthly. Pandora claimed to generate 8.2 billion listening hours in 2011, which was equal to a 5.6 percent share of the RAB's US terrestrial radio listening audience. The RAB estimated 2011 on-air spot revenue at $15.9 billion; 5.6 percent of that came to $875 million. Pandora's $240 million in ad revenue was only 27.4 percent of that amount, making it an earnings underachiever with ample room for revenue growth on both its rate card and premium service subscriber base. Pandora's royalty payments for fiscal 2012 were 54.2 percent of revenue, but the company ran a pre-EBITDA loss of $16 million.

The Competition Heats Up

Pandora also outlined in the 2012 report that there was no lack of competitors for either of its subscription tiers. "We compete for listeners with broadcast radio providers, including terrestrial radio providers such as Clear Channel and CBS and satellite radio providers such as SiriusXM. . . . We also compete directly with other emerging non-interactive online radio providers such as CBS's Last.fm, Clear Channel's iHeartRadio and Slacker Personal Radio. . . . We face competition from providers of interactive on-demand audio content and prerecorded entertainment, such as Apple's iTunes Music Store, RDIO, Rhapsody, Spotify and Amazon that allow listeners to select the audio content that they stream or purchase."[9]

Despite the promising future of digital broadcasting, collectively Pandora and the rest of the top twenty internet radio platforms were under 10 percent of total Triton-tabulated consumer listening hours in 2011, leaving the other 90 percent-plus to terrestrial radio. About 30 percent of all stations, which included public radio, featured non-music formats exclusively or predominantly, including talk, news, sports, and religious. Most of the stations that programmed music were part of the record-radio-retail alliance that focused on selling ads for radio and CDs at retail. In local markets listeners could access fifteen to fifty stations depending on the market size, usually with competing stations in the top-rated formats. Larger markets typically had fifteen or more different formats while the smallest markets had ten or fewer. Most of radio's audience were passive listeners using radio for local information and background music while driving or at work.

The consumers who opted for Pandora's freemium service enjoyed the same no-cost benefit they derived from terrestrial radio but with the added capacity to help shape their own playlists. The greater popularity of this ad-based tier over the premium service was much to the dismay of the record labels who received less revenue per subscriber from freemium than from premium. While Pandora's algorithm introduced interactivity to the music consumers, its $4.99 monthly ad-free tier was too limited to compete, despite its lower cost, with the impending tide of ad-free, on-demand, at-will access offered by subscription streaming at $9.99 per month that was about to inundate the digital ether.

Coming out of the economic downturn in 2010, Clear Channel rebranded itself for the mobile market as iHeartRadio, while CBS combined Last.fm and Play.it into Radio.com. They couldn't, however, match Pandora's unique algorithm despite their deeper financial resources. Even the mobile versions of established internet web stations RDIO, Slacker, and Rhapsody failed to grow sufficiently in market share to compete with Pandora's algorithm driven technology. While Apple's iTunes and Amazon Music had great penetration in the digital market, they were still focused on sales and wouldn't debut their streaming services until 2014 for Amazon and 2015 for Apple. In 2011 purchase of downloads had reached 41.9 percent of consumer spending on recorded music but streaming providing only another 9.4 percent, with physical sales, retail, or mail order still ahead of downloads at 48.7 percent.

SiriusXM's 150-channel satellite feed was a blend of music, talk, sports, and news providing dozens of niche music and superstar-branded formats in addition to the standard chart-oriented genres. Although listeners received a greater variety of content than terrestrial radio offered, SiriusXM didn't have the interactivity of Pandora beyond choice of channel, much less what true streaming access offered. It did have, however, great diversity in music genre formats, audio feeds from the cable news and sports channels, and of course

Howard Stern. An average fee of $9.89 per month made it a viable alternative for upper-income consumers listening in the car. In 2011 SiriusXM had 21.9 million premium subscribers with $2.6 billion in revenue.

SiriusXM also had freemium-tier revenue in 2011 of about $400 million from advertising on its non-music channels, including its audio feeds from cable television with space to fill where the ads had been, sale of listening devices, and royalties from its Canadian division. SiriusXM's addition of subscribers was largely a product of three-month trials for buyers of new automobiles who then picked up the option for a yearly subscription. The $3 billion in 2011 total revenue had grown from $640 million in 2006. Much of the growth had been due to Sirius' premerger signing of Stern, along with whom came his daily audience of over 1 million listeners. While not a major competitor for radio's advertising revenue, SiriusXM's presence in the car made it relevant in the premium subscription market.

Spotify's Streaming Solution

As the US came out of the recession, the major question for the music industry was how to re-engage the consumer with the record business in a way that would be economically acceptable to the public and generate enough revenue to be sustainable for the industry. The answer finally came with the launch of Stockholm-based Spotify in 2008, although it took another three years for its 2011 US debut. While the US record business in 2010 was down 50 percent from its peak years, Sweden had declined by 2007 to just one-third of what it had been prior to file-sharing.

As part of a mid-1990s digital education initiative, the Swedish government financed both computers and broadband access for schools and students. Sweden's teenagers were digitally prepared for the P2P file-sharing craze. The government also decided not to prosecute them for illegal downloads. Even though Napster was shut down in 2001, other file-sharing websites took its place. Sweden-based The Pirate Bay opened in 2003 to become one of the more prominent and persistent. With the Swedish record industry at its nadir in 2007, twenty-four-year-old Daniel Ek started knocking on their doors.

Born and raised in Stockholm, Ek had been introduced at age five to both a guitar and a Commodore VIC-20 computer. They became his two main passions. At fourteen he started a web design company a staff of twenty-five employees before he left high school. He dropped out of college after six weeks to continue with his business pursuits. In 2005 he sold his Advertigo online tracking program and other patents for $2 million to Stockholm-based web advertising agency Tradedoubler. Ek had forged a relationship with thirty-seven-year-old Tradedoubler CEO Martin Lorentzon, who had just personally netted $70 million taking the company public on the Stockholm NASDAQ. Both were seeking an inspirational business opportunity and had complementary skill sets; Ek with his digital design talents and Lorentzon with his e-commerce entrepreneurial experience that had been honed in Silicon Valley in the 1990s with pre-Google search engine Alta Vista.

Lorentzon put €1 million in the new company and resigned from his CEO position at Tradedoubler. As two passionate music fans, they decided to find a solution for the failing record business and needed to choose a brand name. Ek replied to a query about the origin of the Spotify name on quorum.com in December 2010. "Martin and I were sitting in different rooms shouting ideas back and forth of company names. . . . Out of the blue Martin shouted a name that I misheard as Spotify. I immediately googled the name and realized there were no Google hits for the word at all. A few minutes later we registered the domain names and off we went. We were a bit embarrassed to admit that's how the name came up so our after-construction was to say that Spotify stems from SPOT and IDENTIFY."[10]

With Lorentzon a web-savvy marketeer and Ek a problem-solving program creator, they brought a fresh perspective to their chosen task. In a 2010 interview Ek told the *Daily Telegraph* that after watching the evolution of KaZaA, Bit Torrent, The Pirate Bay, and the other successors to Napster, "I realised that you can never legislate away from piracy. Laws can definitely help, but it doesn't take away the problem. The only way to solve the problem was to create a service that was better than piracy and at the same time compensates the music industry."[11]

In 2013 Ek told Dorian Lynskey of *The Observer* that he and Lorentzon had always been sure that the problems of the record business were solvable. "There was this paradox. People were listening to more music than ever in history and yet the music industry was doing worse and worse. So the demand for content was there but it was [now] a different business model." Lynskey added, "Ek's theory was that people were willing to do the right thing but only if it was just as rewarding, and much less hassle, than doing the wrong thing. He says that Spotify subscribers don't pay for content—they can get that for free through piracy—they pay for convenience."[12]

Spotify's plan began with an ad-based freemium level that was faster and easier to navigate than pirate sites, and had legal access to major label current and back catalog product. Spotify, however, would only stream and not sell downloads. Once a critical mass of users was established, Spotify would launch its enhanced, two-tiered premium alternative. They were confident that a sufficient number of users would pay for the improved access and convenience for the company to reach profitability. The first tier was Spotify Unlimited at $4.99 per month with ad-free, unlimited streaming for mobile devices. Spotify Premium at $9.99 added access to all curated playlists, and the opportunity for subscribers to post their own. A Napster-like hybrid P2P architecture connected registered Premium users to share licensed files and playlists stored on Spotify's database. The emphasis was on speed, access, and scalability at a negligible cost that also eliminated potential infringement liability. Taking a cue from Apple, they employed a simple and user-friendly interface with contemporary design.

After striking out with the majors on worldwide licenses, Ek approached their pirate-riddled Swedish divisions to use Scandinavia as a test market. He loaded a demo model with copies of their songs, just as Jobs had done with iTunes. Also like the position Jobs eventually acceded to, Spotify was willing to accept DRM because it wouldn't impede functionality or inconvenience subscribers. Also like Jobs, Spotify would pay about 70 percent of revenue to rights holders. But unlike Jobs, Spotify offered the labels an equity position for a cash investment to all of the Big Four label groups and indie label association Merlin.

The European Launch

The first on board was Per Sundin, who had recently moved from heading Sony in Sweden to UMG managing director of Scandinavia. The Pirate Bay was in court, about to be shut down with its founders sentenced to jail since Sweden was finally enforcing the EU anti-piracy measures. Looking back in 2013, Sundin told *The Observer*'s Lynskey about the opportunity Spotify offered. "It was the perfect storm. It wasn't just that it was now illegal. People discovered Spotify and realized it was actually better than piracy."[13] The other majors and Merlin soon followed, with apparently all sufficiently impressed with the demo model. The combined investment of €8.8 million yielded 18 percent ownership, with Sony receiving 6 percent of the company stock; Universal got 5 percent; Warner landed 4 percent; and EMI got 2 percent. Merlin received 1 percent on behalf of its largest labels. Ek with 23.3 percent and Lorentzon with 28.6 percent retained 51.9 percent of the company with the balance in the hands of other investors. Ek and Lorentzon, however, controlled over 80 percent of the voting shares.

With licenses in place, Spotify launched in October 2008 as an invitation-only free service in Scandinavia, Spain, the UK, and France. In February

2009, the freemium version was opened to the general public. In August 2009, Sundin stated, "In five months from the launch Spotify became our largest digital source of income and so passed by iTunes."[14] That same month, Ek received a 1,765-word email dated August 25 from Napster cofounder Sean Parker in response to viewing Spotify's demo. After Napster Parker helped Facebook transform from a college project to a social media behemoth as its president in the middle of the first decade of the new millennium and was still a major shareholder and advisor to Facebook founder and CEO Mark Zuckerberg.

"Ever since Napster I've dreamt of building a product similar to Spotify," Parker wrote to Ek. "You guys nailed the core experience: it's at least as good as Napster for search and listening, and everything else can be built from there. . . . Direct integration with Facebook is a good idea too but this should happen via an exclusive partnership . . . (I can help you with this on many levels. . . . Zuck and I have been talking about what this partnership should look like . . . as I mentioned we've already passed on iTunes, LaLa, etc.). . . . In order to create the next revolution in digital music I believe that you must both meet and exceed the bar set by Napster a decade ago. You guys have finally done it. . . . Let me know how I can be helpful to you with Facebook, platform, viral optimization, investment, etc. I'm eager to participate in all of these ways and more. . . . You should consider me both a fan and supporter of yours!"[15]

In January 2010 Rob Wells, senior VP digital for UMG International, told Emma Barnett of *The Telegraph* that Spotify was performing as Ek had predicted. "Spotify pays the labels from a mixture of the money it generates from advertising revenues and subscriptions. That to me equates to a sustainable business model."[16] He added that results thus far indicated that Spotify only needed to convert 10 percent to 12 percent of its freemium users to premium accounts in order to generate enough revenue to fulfill their contractual obligations with the labels. Then in February 2010 Parker spearheaded a $15 million investment in Spotify by the Peter Thiel–led angel investment firm Founders Fund where Parker was a partner. Parker also received a seat on the Spotify board, bringing his knowledge, experience, and contacts to the table.

In May 2010 Spotify reached its critical mass of consumers with Sweden leading the way and launched the two-tier premium combination. By October 2010 Spotify was the largest source of label revenue in Sweden, ahead of all other retailers, both physical and digital. Sony Music Sweden's director of digital sales Jacob Herbst told Musically.com, "Looking at the past few months. . . . We already have several artists who receive 80 percent of their revenues from Spotify. An artist who draws in half a million kronor [then $75,000] can get

200,000 to 300,000 from Spotify."[17] At that time, Spotify had already paid €30 million to rightsholders from its European territories. After passing 1 million premium subscriptions by March 2011, Spotify completed licensing negotiations for the US launch, triggering another $100 million in investment capital, and finalized its integration relationship with Facebook.

Spotify in the USA

Facebook co-promoted Spotify's July 2011 US launch along with other sponsors Coca-Cola, Chevrolet, Motorola, Reebok, Sonos, and News Corp's iPad news feed *The Daily* in the same three-tiered staggered rollout employed in Europe. Spotify's opening gambit that over 15 percent of freemium subscribers would then want to upgrade their listening experience for just $9.99 a month proved to be a winning strategy. In March 2012 Spotify announced that it had reached 10 million active users with 3 million of them on paid subscriptions, a 30 percent conversion rate of freemium users migrating to premium, twice what was deemed necessary for sustained success.

Although overall consumer spending on recorded music remained static, hovering around $7 billion through 2015, CDs fell from 47.4 percent of the total in 2011 to 28.8 percent in 2015, and downloads declined from 40.1 percent to 34 percent while streaming, led by Spotify, grew from 9.2 percent to 34.3 percent to balance the decline in sales and downloads. This trend paralleled smartphone growth as consumer habits for social media engagement, access to entertainment, and management of personal finances were all shifting from the computer on their desks to the one in their pockets.

In April 2018 Spotify went public on the New York Stock Exchange (NYSE) with a market cap just under $30 billion. The subscriber base had grown to 180 million with 83 million of them on premium for a 46.1 percent conversion rate. The ROI on the labels' €8.8 million ante, at the time worth approximately $15.8 million, for 18 percent of Spotify would partially if not totally counter the losses from their other digital investments. Shortly after Spotify went public, WMG liquidated its shares for $500 million, pledging to distribute 25 percent to its artists. Sony sold half of its stock for about $750 million with a payout plan based on artists' regular royalty rates. Merlin also sold its shares, netting over $100 million to be distributed among the labels that participated in the initial investment. Universal had no plans to sell its stock, including the EMI share that it now owned, but when Spotify went public, the value was over $1 billion.

Apple Enters the Streaming Derby

Apple Music's streaming service had its roots in Jimmy Iovine's desire to successfully merge tech with music after meeting the Apple executive team following the Napster disruption. He subsequently became one of iTunes' leading advocates within the upper echelon of the record business. He told Burt Helm, in a May 2014 Slate.com feature, "Steve Jobs was the first to marry technology directly with popular culture. I thought, Wow, technology is the new artist."[18] Iovine, however, believed streaming, not downloading, was the proper path contrary to Jobs's insistence that consumers needed to own their music. After the iTunes launch, his Interscope artist, producer, and good friend Dr. Dre expressed his disappointment in the quality of the iPod ear buds. Iovine further recalled to Helm, "Apple was selling $400 iPods with $1 earbuds. Dre told me, 'Man, it's one thing that people steal my music. It's another thing to destroy the feeling of what I've worked on.'" Iovine continued, "They're making a beautiful white object with all the music in the world in it. . . . I'm going to make a beautiful black object that will play it back. Dre and I decided to market this product just like it was Tupac or U2 or Guns N' Roses.'"[19]

Starting in 2006 with Dre's specs for how to achieve the appropriate audio fidelity when listening to digital files through headphones, especially on the bass end, they enlisted a series of designers, manufacturers, and investors to build Beats by Dr. Dre into a business worth over $1 billion a year. By 2014, Beats had refined its product and marketing to dominate the premium headphone market with an almost 70 percent share. Beats' $300 headphones employed fashionable design, product placement, and celebrity endorsers including LeBron James, Lady Gaga, and Justin Bieber to successfully propel premium headphones into the apparel and merchandise markets.

In July 2012 Beats acquired the five-year-old MOG streaming platform, shut it down in January 2014, and quickly redesigned and reopened as Beats Music. By then, three years after Jobs's death, Apple was ready to jettison his long-held opposition to streaming and embraced Iovine and Dre as the ideal team to effectuate the integration of streaming into the existing Apple infrastructure. In May 2014 Apple acquired Beats in a $3 billion stock/cash transaction along with management contracts for its principals. In June 2015 the Beats platform shut down and with some tweaking from the Apple tech team, relaunched as Apple Music to contend with Spotify, Amazon Music, Pandora, and the rest of the field, but with no freemium tier. The iTunes track archive was included within the new structure along with the Beats 1 worldwide radio station, and other playlist curation features and options.

To counter Spotify's four-year lead to market that had amassed 77 million active users and 22 million paying subscribers, Apple offered to convert its list of 400 million customer credit card accounts to the new streaming service that would preserve all the best features of iTunes including downloading and retention of its customer's library of accumulated tracks. The timing was perfect as streaming was about to lift the music industry out of its six-year $7 billion doldrums. Iovine told *Wired Magazine*'s Jason Tranz in a cover interview just after the sale of Beats, "Apple got the best people in pop culture. Whether it succeeds or not, it's the beginning of what the future should look like."[20]

Iovine left Apple Music in August 2018. *Billboard*'s Lars Brandle reported, "It is believed his departure is timed to his Apple shares fully vesting, sources tell *Billboard*."[21] It was also at the time his Apple contract expired as well as shortly after his sixty-fifth birthday. The fifty-three-year-old Dre remained and continued to update and enlarge the Beats line of audio products, incorporating technical innovation developed by Apple's corps of engineers. By the end of 2019 Apple Music had 50 million premium subscribers and $2.8 billion in 2019 revenue. Beats' headphones did around $1.5 billion including sales as an alternative to the compact Apple earbuds. Although Spotify was still ahead in subscribers, Apple's consumer hardware and software sales cushioned its transition into the streaming market.

At the end of 2019, the retired Iovine told Ben Sisario of *The New York Times* why he built up Beats only to sell to Apple. Iovine explained that he first realized the power of digital technology twenty years prior during the Napster disruption and that adaptation to new technology was necessary for survival. "I realized that the record business at that moment, the way it was responding to Napster, was not cool . . . putting up a moat, like that was going to do something. So I said, 'Oh, I'm at the wrong party.' And I met a bunch of people in tech. I met Steve Jobs and Eddy Cue from Apple. And I said, 'Oh, *this* is where the party is.'"[22]

Pandora Loses Ground

By the end of 2017, the final year before its acquisition by SiriusXM, Pandora's income had topped $1 billion for the second year in a row. Of that revenue, 21.5 percent came from the 5.48 million paid subscribers, who were only 7.3 percent of its 74.7 million active users. Pandora was still losing money as well as losing ground not only to Spotify but now also to Apple, Amazon, and the gaggle of other streaming services. In an attempt to compete, in April 2017 Pandora introduced its premium subscription service, which combined on-demand requests with their algorithm-driven playlists for an improved level of consumer interactivity. Pandora's ad-supported tier, however, remained the choice of the vast majority of its user base.

According to its 2017 financials, Pandora paid 57.8 percent of its revenue in licensing costs to rightsholders. Although slightly lower that its streaming rivals' 70 percent licensing obligation, Pandora had the ongoing cost of its Music Genome Project song-by-song analysis that was central to its programming methodology, an expense its rivals didn't have. Meanwhile, terrestrial radio, a major rival for its ad-based tier, paid under 10 percent of its revenue, including the recently launched GMR, to publishers and songwriters in PRO licensing fees and nothing to labels and artists.

By the end of 2018 the streaming sector as a whole had provided the balance between an acceptable cost for unlimited on-demand access to both current and catalog music, and a revenue source for the labels to fund the creation and mass distribution of new music to an ever-expanding consumer base. In Pandora's case, however, not enough of their existing users upgraded, or new ones joined in, to Pandora Plus or Pandora Premium to reach profitability. This did not, however, deter SiriusXM in its acquisition plans, still believing that the coupling of Pandora's interactivity and now premium tier with the SiriusXM economic and programming model would strengthen existing business and make them both competitive in the overall streaming marketplace.

The Secondary Ticketing Market: The Cost of Convenience

Concurrent with the decline in consumer spending on recorded music that began after 1999, *Pollstar*-tabulated spending on major concert tickets increased by $2.2 billion, going from $1.7 billion in 1999 to $3.9 billion in 2007, and then almost tripled to over $11 billion in 2019. With the shift from physical acquisition to digital access, consumers were able to get the tracks they wanted without buying albums, freeing them to shift the balance of what they had previously spent on albums to tickets for live music instead. Then when streaming came into vogue, even more of what the public spent on recorded music in the past was applied to live performance.

There was a major difference, however, between the supply of recorded music and availability of concert tickets. As more records could always be pressed to fill demand, and the supply of digital music was endless, the only limitation was how much consumers could spend. Supply of tickets, however, was capped at the number of seats in a facility and by the number of shows performed on a tour. When demand exceeded supply, that is, 150,000 people couldn't fit in a 60,000-seat stadium, the marketplace found ways to extract a higher price from the consumers who did attend the shows. Items that weren't mentioned until getting either a credit card receipt or statement included ticketing service, facility, and processing surcharges; delivery, shipping, e-ticket convenience, or will-call pickup costs when applicable; as well as credit card fees. These costs could add an additional 25 percent or more for the top tours above the ticket's face value. Facilities then also charged for parking and sold concessions and merchandise.

The face value of tickets from *Pollstar*'s Top 100 North American Tours grew from an average of $25.81 per ticket in 1996, to $62.07 in 2007, and to $94.83 in 2019, with the related costs expanding proportionally. This growth was a product of supply and demand with demand dictating the choice of venues, ticket pricing, and length of tours, which enabled bigger and more expensive productions that in turn further energized demand. As important, the opening of the internet to commercial enterprise had enabled the secondary ticketing market to become as sophisticated, if not more so, than the primary market. It was also crucial, however, for them to maintain consumer confidence in their service to sustain repeat business.

By 2007 ticket buyers were already accustomed to convenience charges in the primary market, rising ticket prices, and the competition for tickets created by increased demand. Peer group social network pressure to be there for millennials, and the baby boomer penchant to not miss what could be their lifelong favorite's last waltz or farewell tour further fueled demand. These consumers often bought the best seats to the top tours for several times the ticket face value through the secondary market. Not all shows, however, were sellouts. Some early buyers, driven by a change of plans, needed to sell tickets at the last minute. Some fans even bought tickets with the intention to resell for a profit. For those willing to wait and take a risk, there were almost always tickets available at the last minute, but no guarantee that supply would meet demand or anything would be available at a reasonable price. Altogether, however, the yearly cost of tickets on the secondary market was estimated to be as much as another 50 percent or more above the aggregated box-office total.

The leading internet ticket brokers came from the tech sector applying their coding skills to creating automated internet programs called Ticket Bots, a term derived from robot. A 2016 report by New York State attorney general Eric Schneiderman explained, "A Ticket Bot is software that automates ticket buying on platforms such as ticketmaster.com. Automation lets the Bot (1) perform each transaction at lightning speed, and (2) perform hundreds or thousands of transactions simultaneously. As a result, in the first moments after tickets to a top show go on sale, Bots crowd out human purchasers and can snap up most of the good seats."[23]

The industry as a whole expressed unhappiness that the secondary market was profiting to such a large extent, particularly the artists and their agents who did not share, at least publicly, in this revenue stream. They were hesitant, however, to raise ticket face price too high in fear of negatively affecting demand. In January 2008 Ticketmaster announced it would buy the second-largest legal broker, TicketsNow, for $265 million. Founded in 1999 TicketsNow had resold 1.7 million tickets in 2007, compared to over 5 million by market leader StubHub, according to *Billboard*'s Ray Waddell. Ticketmaster combined TicketsNow with its already-existing TicketExchange resale platform setting the stage to also become a major player in the secondary market.

In February 2009 Ticketmaster's involvement in this area was addressed at the congressional hearings for approval of its merger with Live Nation during the testimony of newly appointed CEO Irving Azoff, a longtime and highly vocal critic of the resale market when he was an artist manager. Bruce Springsteen had just publicly raised a ruckus over his fans being redirected by Ticketmaster to the more expensive TicketsNow. Reuters reported that when "pressed on whether Ticketmaster would sell TicketsNow, Azoff demurred at first, but finally said that for the right price, 'I would certainly vote to do that.'"[24]

The merger was approved later that year, but a year afterward when Azoff exited Ticketmaster and went back to artist management, TicketsNow was still a part of Ticketmaster. Four years later, in 2016, Azoff was just as critical as ever of the secondary-market profiteers. Commenting on entering a new VIP ticket venture, Azoff stated, "It's my answer to what's broken in the system, which is what I call 'the StubHub factor.' You have lots of people with no skin in the game escaping with lots of money."[25]

The Empire State Strikes Back at the Secondary Market

Ticketmaster had long enjoyed a near monopoly on ticket sales, but its power intensified after the union with Live Nation, just as Azoff, Michael Rapino, Barry Diller, and John Malone had envisioned when the mega-merger was first suggested. The new Live Nation Entertainment was a vertically integrated enterprise designed to synergistically maximize revenue at each level. According to its 2019 IRS Form 10-K, "Ticketmaster provides ticket sales, ticket resale services and marketing and distribution globally through www.ticketmaster.com and www.livenation.com and our other websites, mobile apps, numerous retail outlets and call centers, selling over 485 million tickets in 2019 through our systems. Ticketmaster serves nearly 11,500 clients worldwide across multiple event categories, providing ticketing services for leading arenas, stadiums, festival and concert promoters, professional sports franchises and leagues, college sports teams, performing arts venues, museums and theaters."[26]

Concurrently, the Live Nation concert promotion division connected "nearly 98 million fans to more than 40,000 events for over 5,000 artists in 2019."[27] The entire conglomerate's actions, however, were not always in sync with the policies espoused in its annual reports, compounded by the extent that its reach dominated in all directions. This made it an easy target upon which to pin the ills of the industry, whether justified or not. As a public company whose first obligation was to its shareholders, Live Nation trod the line between maximizing profit and customer service while placating any complaints from artists, fans, or the press. At the end of 2019 Live Nation had increased revenue over 2018 by 7 percent to $11.55 billion, operating income by 19.2 percent to $328 million, and had control of around 50 percent of the secondary market.

In a position of that magnitude, sometimes things went awry when opportunities arose to make a clandestine profit outside of normal business practices, such as the aforementioned incident with Springsteen. Whether the result of an overly aggressive inner-company initiative, an employee acting independently, actions by an artist's management team, or something totally outside of its purview, Live Nation condemned the incident when appropriate, abided by the results of any legal action, and outlined them no matter the outcome, with full disclosure in its annual Form 10-K, while all along conducting business as usual.

Schneiderman's report covered 2012 through 2015, examining why and how tickets for the top Live Nation and AEG shows were going to certain ticket brokers before being available to the public, including some who were unlicensed and/or illegally using ticket bots. The report further found that "on average, only about 46% of tickets are reserved for the public." The rest were allocated 16 percent as "Holds" for "industry insiders, such as artists, agents, venues, promoters, marketing departments, record labels, and sponsors," and "Pre-Sales" for "non-public groups before they go on sale to the general public."[28]

The pre-sales category included credit card holders, fan clubs, and group promotions by the marketing teams of the show venues, promoters, and artists, or a combination thereof. All of the tickets that were dispersed through these groups were susceptible to being surreptitiously diverted to bots controlled by the targets of Schneiderman's probe, which also included anyone involved with them from the legitimate side of the process. Tickets for charitable, civic, and clerical events were also subject to manipulation by bots. Schneiderman observed, "Even those who intend their events to be free, like Pope Francis, find their good intent defeated by those who resell tickets for hundreds or even thousands of dollars."[29]

The New York Attorney General's report provided the data needed to support the passage of the Better Online Ticket Sales Act, or the BOTS Act of 2016, signed by President Obama in December, which placed bots under the jurisdiction of the Federal Trade Commission. New York Senator and bill sponsor Chuck Schumer declared, "With this soon-to-be-new law that will eliminate 'bots' and slap hackers with a hefty fine, we can now ensure those who want to attend shows in the future will not have to pay outrageous, unfair prices."[30] Ticketmaster concurred with an official statement that read, "On behalf of artists, venues, teams, and especially fans, Ticketmaster is pleased that the BOTS Act is now a federal law. Ticketmaster worked closely with legislators to develop the BOTS Act and we believe its passage is a critical step in raising awareness and regulating the unauthorized use of Bots."[31]

Despite the BOTS Act and prior legislation in several states including New York, California, and Tennessee that outlawed bots, the secondary market continued to grow under legitimate resellers led by eBay's StubHub and Ticketmaster's own TicketExchange and TicketsNow. Although artists, the press, the public, and even Ticketmaster itself were all often critical of the ticketing ecosystem, the convenience for ticket buyers and their surety of getting specific seats seemed to outweigh whatever dissatisfaction there was as the public continued to buy the best tickets from wherever they could.

Many pundits, however, suggested that the real way to gain control over the ticket pricing quandary was for the primary market to initially list the best seats at the level the public was willing to pay through the secondary market, but many artists were worried about what that would do to their image and relationship with their fans. Others called for the breakup of Live Nation's divisions into separate entities. Nonetheless ticket prices steadily increased, especially for the top artists, as had the total gross for the *Pollstar* top tour rankings. Ticketmaster initiated a paperless ticketing program, but that had its own set of logistical problems. Then at the prodding of artists, Ticketmaster tested a verified fan program in 2016 with Dead & Company, and had a full launch in 2017 with Ed Sheeran, followed by Taylor Swift, Springsteen on Broadway, and *Hamilton*. Results were mixed as a few more fans got good seats at face value, but neither the reforms of the BOTS Act nor specialized ticketing alternatives slowed down the higher-priced secondary market for the majority of ticket buyers.

Digital technology had introduced a high level of customer convenience, abetted the consolidation of the industry, and more likely than not, would continue to be utilized in new ways to support the industry as currently constituted, rather than radically change it in any way. Nonetheless, Live Nation and the other top power brokers would initiate and support improvements in consumer comforts and convenience, as long as they didn't negatively alter the bottom line or control at the top of the live performance hierarchy.

The Consumer in 2019

The year 2019 was the twentieth anniversary of the launch of Napster, sixteen years after the opening of the iTunes store, twelve years past the unveiling of the iPhone, eight years following the Spotify US debut, and only four years since Beats became Apple Music. The college freshmen of 1999 who were born in the first year of the millennial generation turned thirty-eight in 2019 and were now out in the workforce with many raising families of their own.

The consumption of music had changed drastically over the time period. File-sharing and the economic effects of the 2001 recession facilitated the conversion from listening to single-artist albums to compiling multi-artist playlists. The iTunes/iPod combination enabled the rise of digital technology as a legal source for access to new music followed by the ascendency of subscription streaming led by Spotify. Apple's subsequent switch from acquisition of downloaded files to on-demand, at-will access through Apple Music opened the final floodgate for the streaming tsunami to storm through.

Although it was a cadre of tech-savvy innovators and risk-taking investors who blazed this new path of access to music, it was the first time that consumers were ahead of the industry in embracing a new sound carrier. The decades-old process of acquiring music through the record-retail-radio relationship had morphed into one efficient on-demand, at-will experience totally at the control of the consumer by vocal or touch-type command, a near perfect panacea for the immediate gratification tendencies of those born and raised in the digital age.

This new direction in music consumption also affected the Gen X'ers and baby boomers who were respectively thirty-nine to fifty-four and fifty-five to seventy-three in 2019, as well as the even older 1950s Teens. They quickly

CONSUMER SPENDING ON MUSIC IN 2019

After the debut of the iPhone in 2007 and Android in 2008, there were 112 million smartphones in the U.S. when Spotify launched in 2011, 228 million in 2015 when Apple Music debuted, and 299 million by 2019.

Prior to streaming, buying records had long been the best substitute for in-concert performance. Streaming, however, offered greater access and convenience at a fraction of the cost, along with a wider range of non-interactive listening options than radio.

By 2019 over 75% of consumer spending for recorded music came from paid subscriptions. Concurrently, ad-based streaming produced licensing revenue as advertisers followed listeners, precipitating a drop in annual radio revenue by over 45% since 2007. Nonetheless, radio still filled local needs for programming and advertising.

Live performance propelled consumer spending from 2006's estimated $24.1 billion to 2019's $46.2 billion, clearly establishing the major venue concert experience as the leading choice for the upper economic echelon of music fans.

Between 1995 and 2019, live performance and its associated costs grew from $3.2 billion for 17.7% of total consumer spending on music to 80.9% at $37.4 billion. Print fell from 14.8% to 4.4% while staying at relatively the same in dollar value.

Between 2006 and 2019, spending on recorded music declined from $9.9 billion to $6.8 billion, while label licensing increased from $1.2 billion to $4.3 billion, boosting industry revenue to $11.1 billion and forecast to grow even further over the ensuing years.

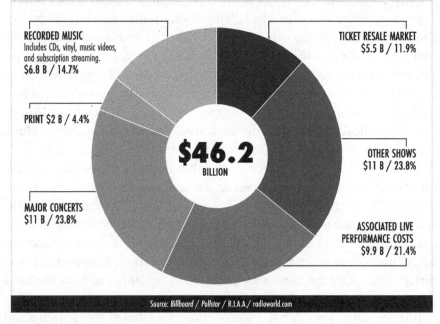

RECORDED MUSIC
Includes CDs, vinyl, music videos, and subscription streaming.
$6.8 B / 14.7%

PRINT $2 B / 4.4%

MAJOR CONCERTS
$11 B / 23.8%

TICKET RESALE MARKET
$5.5 B / 11.9%

OTHER SHOWS
$11 B / 23.8%

ASSOCIATED LIVE PERFORMANCE COSTS
$9.9 B / 21.4%

$46.2 BILLION

Source: Billboard / Pollstar / R.I.A.A./ radioworld.com

Illustration 15.1 Consumer Spending on Music in 2019

learned that they could also enjoy their favorite songs whether by The Beatles, Aretha, Otis Redding, Streisand, Elton John or any other legendary artist with a verbal command to the virtual assistant on their newly acquired smartphones. Nielsen, reunited with *Billboard* under the MRC Data banner, credited current music releases as only 36 percent of all streams in 2019, while catalog selections, defined as over eighteen months old, were at 64 percent. According to the MusicWatch information service helmed by veteran data analyst Russ Crupnick, which now provided the RIAA with its annual consumer profile report, 38 percent of music-streaming consumers in 2019 were in the over-forty-five age groups. In comparison, 24 percent were between thirteen and twenty-four, while the twenty-five to forty-four age cohort also had 38 percent.

MusicWatch further reported in its Annual Music Study that during 2019 there were 116 million US music buyers over age thirteen who purchased subscriptions, CDs, digital downloads, and/or new vinyl. These 116 million represented approximately 42 percent of the thirteen-plus population. Eighty million, or just over two-thirds of them, were premium streaming subscriptions. Nielsen added that "more than half (53%) of consumers use free, ad-supported streaming audio services,"[32] many of whom did so in the car when streaming wasn't readily available or when they needed to check local weather, traffic, or news.

Streaming, however, didn't take up all their listening time. Although consumers with an internet connection spent 39 percent of their listening hours via streaming, MusicWatch also related that radio was second with 19 percent closely followed by home music collections at 18 percent. Satellite radio had 7 percent, and the remaining 17 percent grouped in a catch-all "other" category. In addition to virtual assistants on their smartphones, 104 million music consumers also had smart speaker systems that responded to verbal commands or through wireless connectivity.

Combining the $11.1 billion in 2019 consumer and licensee spending with the more than $11 billion they spent in the top-end major concert sector tracked by *Pollstar*, the merchandise sales cited by LIMA at $3.6 billion, and the $1 billion-plus in retail sales of printed or downloaded sheet music and tablature, there was already over $26 billion in consumer spending on music compared to about $15 billion in 2007. These totals did not include the ticket handling and secondary market costs, live performances not tracked by *Pollstar*, and non-retail print sales that took total music consumer spending over an estimated $40 billion.

Radio's decrease in ad revenue from over $21 billion in 2007 to roughly $14 billion in 2019 reflected the listener migration to streaming, but radio still remained the consumer's top source for music in the car. MRC Data rated radio in 2019 as the most used format for 44 percent of US music listeners, particularly those who didn't have streaming access. News, talk, and sports topped the radio formats with a combined 13.8 percent of MRC-measured audience share. AC was first among the music formats at 8.1 percent, followed in descending market share by country, CHR, classic hits, classic rock, hot AC, and urban AC at 4.7 percent. Together these formats, most of which were skewed toward an older demographic, took up 55.7 percent of radio listening.

Despite the revenue rebound for recorded music led by streaming, music piracy in 2019 still persisted on a widespread scale. The more sophisticated and digitally advanced BitTorrent file-sharing protocol that was introduced in 2001 applied rip, burn, and copy techniques directly to online platforms. Andy Chatterley, who had launched piracy-tracking service MUSO in 2009, reported in *Music Business Worldwide* that 33.6 percent of all music-related online piracy visits worldwide in July 2019 came through unlicensed streaming sites, and 31.3 percent were unauthorized rip-and-burn visits to legitimate services.

Chatterley further reported that catalog was victimized along with current releases. His tracking in July 2019 revealed that Ed Sheeran's then-current *Divide* release exceeded 612,000 ripped album downloads worldwide. Kanye West's *The Life of Pablo* (2016) measured at 280,000, while Lady Gaga's *The Fame Monster* (2009) totaled over 202,000. For legacy artist catalog albums, Pink Floyd's *Dark Side of the Moon* was ripped for 131,000 units, and *Sgt. Pepper's Lonely Hearts Club Band* was lifted over 182,000 times.

Chatterley considered these hijackers more likely to be fans looking for specific content rather than casual browsers. He also noted that with only 10 percent of the world's 3.5 billion internet users having paid music subscriptions, there was an enormous potential for additional legal subscribers, and "piracy is an obvious place to find them. . . . Anti-piracy and content protection technologies are as crucial as they have ever been in stemming the illegal distribution of content but coupled with a data-led understanding of what, how and why people illegally download music they can garner significant insights and create value, growth and revenue."[33]

Streaming into the Future

Streaming had affected not only how the public consumed recorded music but also the sectors of the music business that supplied it to them. Freemium tiers

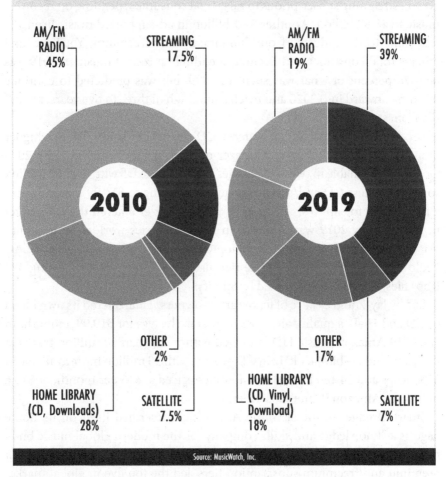

COMPARISON OF 2010 & 2019 MUSIC LISTENING HOURS

Prior to the late 1990s, consumer access to recorded music had been limited to radio, jukeboxes, or home libraries for on-demand listening.

Following the Napster-led proliferation of illegal downloading from 1999 to 2001, legal access to digital music expanded with portable MP3 players and the debut of iTunes in 2003. Leading streaming services included eMusic, Rhapsody, Last.fm, and Pandora. Both iPhone and Android offered streaming and downloading in one device.

The 2019 Music-Watch's Annual Music Study reported that 116 million consumers paid for music, 80 million of whom had paid subscriptions. Another 124 million listened through ad-supported services.

The study also compared 2019 listening habits with 2010, the year prior to Spotify's U.S. launch when Pandora's ad-supported tier dominated streaming.

AM/FM RADIO 45%   STREAMING 17.5%

AM/FM RADIO 19%   STREAMING 39%

2010

2019

OTHER 2%

OTHER 17%

HOME LIBRARY (CD, Downloads) 28%   SATELLITE 7.5%

HOME LIBRARY (CD, Vinyl, Download) 18%   SATELLITE 7%

Source: MusicWatch, Inc.

Illustration 15.2 Comparison of 2010 and 2019 Music-Listening Hours

mirrored radio with its ad-supported transmission, but with some degree of interactivity. The $21.7 billion spent in 2006 on radio spots fell to $14.5 billion in 2019 as many advertisers switched from radio to ad-based streaming services. Radio advertisers were left with all-talk formats, listening in the car, and consumers who didn't spend money on music but nonetheless listened to it.

Premium streaming with monthly fees ranging from $4.99 to $19.99 had replaced the need to accumulate a CD library, providing far more content, all immediately available rather than having to be accumulated over an extended period of time. Consumer retail spending had shrunk from a high of over $14.5 billion in 1999, then all on physical product, to $2.02 billion in 2019 on physical and downloaded productcombined. They spent another $6.76 billion on streaming subscriptions to raise total consumer spending on recorded music to $8.82 billion. Another $2.1 billion in ad-supported music licensing fees came to the industry from Pandora, Spotify freemium, YouTube, and others. Total consumer and licensee spending on record music in 2019 was only 76 percent of what was spent in 1999, but was predicted to continue trending upward into 2020 and reach a new high in three to five years, primarily from streaming.

Several subscription services offered CD-quality or Hi-Res files at a higher monthly fee. Both Qobuz and Deezer opened in France in 2007. By 2019 Qobuz was available in twelve countries including the US with over 50 million songs in lossless CD and/or Hi-Res quality, starting at $14.99 a month with a family plan for up to six persons at $24.99. Deezer entered the US market in 2016 and by 2019 was available in most countries worldwide at similar pricing. Deezer offered over 50 million CD-quality 16-bit, 1411 Kbps FLAC audio files, and had a lower price tier also with family plans featuring 320 Kbps files, the same file size used by Spotify.

Led by Jay-Z and a cadre of fellow artist-owners, Tidal offered its own blend of CD and Hi-Res quality along with artist exclusives for $19.99 a month. In late 2019 Amazon Music HD launched with more than 50 million tracks at 850 Kbps and 16-bit/44.1 kHz in CD quality, with 10 million more available in 3730 Kbps and 24-bit/192 kHz Hi-Res files priced at $15 per month, or $13 a month for Amazon Prime subscribers.

Stuart Dredge, editor of *Music Ally*, which described itself on its home page as a "knowledge and skills company for the modern global music business,"[34] did a 2019 year-end survey of DSP market share. Spotify, with both premium and freemium subscription tiers, led the top five in global market share at 35 percent with 124 million premium subscribers out of 291 million users. Apple Music followed at 19 percent with about 70 million paying users. Amazon Music came in third at 15 percent with about 55 million premium customers. In fourth, China's Tencent Music had 11 percent, with 35.5 million paying customers out of 661 million total monthly users. Rounding out the top five, YouTube Music was at 6 percent with only 20 million paying subscribers, but YouTube revealed in May 2018 that it had "more than 1 billion music fans come to YouTube each month to be part of music culture and discover new music."[35]

All but Spotify were parts of larger entities where music brought attention and attracted consumers parallel to the loss-leader role CDs had played two decades earlier at big-box retailers and mega-stores. In his weekly *Rolling Stone* column at the end of August 2019 questioning "Who Will Own Spotify in Five Years?" *Music Business Worldwide* founder and publisher Tim Ingham questioned whether Spotify would ever turn a profit on its own, despite its lead in market share, while paying 70 percent of its revenue to rightsholders. Or like Pandora, would Spotify be absorbed by a larger, more diversified conglomerate to fill a synergistic slot in its Venn diagram of corporate divisions? Ingham listed "five other huge businesses that, with some strategic reasoning, could make a play to own Spotify over the next five years,"[36] identifying the five as Netflix, Facebook, AT&T, Samsung, and Tencent.

Jimmy Iovine offered his own observations on the sustainability of stand-alone DSPs in his December 2019 interview in *The New York Times*. When Ben Sisario asked what's the major problem facing the streaming music business, Iovine replied, "Margin. It doesn't scale. At Netflix, the more subscribers you have, the less your costs are. In streaming music, the costs follow you. And the streaming music services are utilities—they're all the same. . . . What happens when something is commoditized is that it becomes a war of price. If you can get the exact same thing next door cheaper, somebody is going to enter this game and just lower the price."[37]

Considering Spotify's status as a nondiversified, standalone business model, whether it would be acquired or merged due to its debt-to-earnings ratio akin to the SiriusXM absorption of Pandora, or persevere and thrive from an upswing in subscriptions is still to be determined. Either way consumers had a plethora of what Iovine had termed utilities from which to get their daily supply of on-demand music. Should a larger share of consumers decide to opt for higher fidelity from CD or Hi-Res files delivered through 5G bandwidth and the next generation of cellphones, it might cost them another $5 to $10 a month, a meager price for the upper-economic echelon of music consumers.

If past is indeed prologue and consumers react similarly to when LPs and 45s succeeded 78s, CDs supplanted both cassettes and vinyl, and streaming access displaced physical sound carrier sales, then lossless CD-quality and Hi-Res files should indeed replace compressed MP3 variations in conjunction with improvements in both smart speakers and headphones. If 50 million premium subscribers, or about 15 percent of the worldwide total, decide to opt for CD or Hi-Res quality by moving up from $10 per month to $15, that would be a $250 million per-month increase, or $3 billion annually, with 70 percent of that going to rightsholders. To tap into that potential market as their better-financed competitors were already doing, Spotify would have to make a big investment in system upgrades or find a merger partner who could fund such an initiative.

Music consumers were still the bedrock of the industry whether enjoying the instant delivery of a favorite song anytime anywhere in solitude on a cellphone, in small groups on smart speakers, or on a more traditional home entertainment system. They also shared in the euphoria of the in-person social networks of tens of thousands at a live event that they transmitted even further to millions more across social media platforms with selfies, self-recorded smartphone audio, and camera clips reinforcing their peer-group standing.

Despite the two decades of predictions and conclusions that digital technology would destroy the record business, the now digital-centric industry was the strongest it had been since the intrusion of the MP3 triggered those predictions two decades earlier. Consumers had greater access to on-demand listening than ever before imagined. The investment world predicted industry growth over the next decade that could as much as double its 1999 $14.6 billion peak. The experience of listening to music had become more personal, while at the same time truly universal, moment by moment, note by note, and stream by stream.

Epilogue: 2020—Into the Future

On the Eve of Disruption

The year 2020 began as one of optimism. The longest bull run in stock market history had begun in 2009 and propelled the Dow Jones index to an all-time high on February 12, 2020. The four-year upward trend in both live and recorded music revenue appeared to be the harbinger of things to come. Glowing forecasts issued by Citigroup, PricewaterhouseCoopers, and Goldman Sachs had contributed to venture capital infusions into all sectors of the industry, predicting that both recorded music and live performance revenue would almost double over the next decade.

Daily operations continued as usual. There were concerts, new record releases, and plans made for the rest of the year and beyond. Data was tabulated and sorted, tracks were streamed and downloaded, CDs and LPs were purchased, and studios churned out new recordings. The charts came out weekly as they always had, with new tracks rising as older ones receded, all moving on their own unique trajectories. Overall, 2020 was anticipated to be a year of industrywide highs.

Then with hardly a warning a new disruptive force beyond the collective imagination of the entire industry arrived in the form of the COVID-19 virus. As January's whispers transformed into February's misgivings, and then into March's declaration of pandemic, the fear of a resulting economic downturn replaced the expectation of a continuing boom. How COVID-19 would affect each sector of the industry became the central issue of both immediate agenda and long-term planning. What had appeared to be another year of growth turned into an ongoing succession of uncertainties, and not just for the music industry but for the entire nation.

COVID-19 Closes the Concert Circuit

The live performance sector was the first to react to the looming pandemic, affecting all from club to Coachella, lounge owners to concert promoters, roadies to rock stars, and everybody and everything in between. By the first week of March, confirmed cases were escalating. On March 5 San Francisco's Ultra Music Festival shut down followed the next day by the cancellation of Austin's South by Southwest. A few days later Coachella rescheduled to October. Early on March 12 Live Nation called all tours home, postponing all shows until at least April when it would re-evaluate. Although there were no immediate layoffs, staffers were told to stay home and work remotely. AEG and the major talent agencies joined in for an industrywide postponement of all major concerts through at least March.

With all tours still on hold, in mid-April Live Nation initiated a salary reduction plan for senior executives, including Michael Rapino, who canceled his compensation for the duration of the crisis. A hiring freeze, reduction in all expenses, rent renegotiations, staff furloughs, and careful monitoring of all discretionary spending also went into effect. Live Nation also obtained a $120 million increase in its revolving credit line and set up the Crew Aid charity for laid-off tour workers, while Rapino made a personal purchase of $1 million in Live Nation stock to demonstrate his confidence in an eventual recovery. AEG initiated similar across-the-board reductions while trying to avoid layoffs.

From the very beginning of the shutdown, policies were formed on the hope to be back on the road by fall, but it become apparent to all that returning to a fall schedule was not feasible. Industry attention turned to the second half of 2021 or even 2022 as a possible target for a return to touring. Many promoters tried to reschedule rather than cancel the postponed tours to avoid refunding ticket purchases. In May Live Nation boosted its financial position with $1.2 billion in debt funding with repayment due in 2027 at 6.5 percent interest per annum to help cushion the effects of the pandemic should it extend into 2021 or beyond. Because most other promoters including AEG were privately held, their financial plans were not made public. Booking agencies initiated parallel rounds of cost reduction in all departments as film and television productions were also suspended.

In May Goldman Sachs issued an addendum to its Music in the Air equity report titled "The Show Must Go On" forecasting a 25 percent decline in overall music industry revenue in 2020 due to the closure of live performances, with a rebound in 2021. The addendum further projected that in 2020 streaming revenue would rise by 18 percent, CD/LP sales by 3 percent, and publishing income by 3.5 percent to maintain the overall industry revenue decline at the projected 25 percent. The addendum further predicted that 79 percent of fans would resume attendance at live events four months after the lifting of COVID-19 restrictions, and the industry as a whole would eventually rebound to match or top their pre–COVID-19 estimates.

Box Office 2020: The Year that Could Have Been and the Year that Was

Immediately after the March shutdown, a flurry of artists including Keith Urban, John Legend, and producer David Foster with his wife Katharine McPhee along with many other artists attempted to boost public spirits by staging home-based events on social media platforms and websites. On March 23 Garth Brooks and Trisha Yearwood drew 3.4 million viewers to their home studio feed on Facebook causing intermittent crashes on the platform due to the magnitude of the traffic.

Looking back at 2020 in *Pollstar*'s year-end analysis, *Boxoffice* liaison Bob Allen wrote, "Using the first quarter's growth percentages for the Top 100 tours, we estimated in the Q1 analysis in March that grosses . . . might have produced the first $12 billion year"[1] for all the major tours and venues tracked by *Pollstar*. Despite the promising start, at year's end total gate receipts were down 78 percent from pre-pandemic expectations.

In considering what could have been, *Pollstar*'s executive editor, Andy Gensler, hypothesized, "If one were to add the multiplier effect of each ticket . . . it doesn't take much calculus to arrive at a full economic impact of greater than $30 billion."[2] That estimate included events outside of the tours and venues that reported to *Pollstar* as well as related ticketing costs; sponsorships; merchandise sales; concessions; and transportation when going to festivals, residencies, or other cities for tour dates. Also to be considered were the secondary ticketing market resale markups.

In the second half of 2020 a consistent 25 percent or so of respondents to MRC/Nielsen polling replied that they had seen a livestreamed concert in the past two weeks. By the end of the year, livestreaming transmissions over social media and pay-per-view platforms reached $610 million, culminating on New Year's Eve in competition with the annual network offerings. Justin Bieber staged his first show since 2017 sponsored by T-Mobile, Kiss streamed from Dubai accompanied by $1 million of pyrotechnics, and BTS celebrated from Seoul with guests Halsey and Lauv. In recognition of this innovation, *Pollstar*'s 2020 year-end rankings included new categories for Top 100 Livestreams and Top 100 Livestreamers.

Transmitted from the Grand Ole Opry stage before an empty house with over 30.3 million viewers spread over twenty-eight shows, Circle Opry Live was *Pollstar*'s top livestreamer. The series was accessible through Circle TV's facebook.com/AllAccess YouTube channels featuring a revolving lineup of Opry members. Thirteen of its shows drew over a million viewers each, led by Reba McEntire and Vince Gill attracting 2.6 million on July 2, and Carrie Underwood with Brad Paisley on September 5 drawing 2.3 million.

Verzuz Presents, second in the *Pollstar* listing, staged nine shows with a total audience of 15.5 million on the Instagram.com/verzuztv channel. Conceived and produced by Swizz Beatz and Timbaland, each show was a battle between two artists alternating performances with viewer voting. Their top shows were Gladys Knight versus Patti LaBelle with 3.7 million views and DMX against Snoop Dogg, drawing 3.4 million through Instagram and Facebook.

The other top-ten livestreamers were Norah Jones, the Camping World Concert Series, Sofi Tukker, Deana Martin, Save Our Stages, Josh Daniels' Quarantine Sessions, Lucas Hoge, and Bandsintown Live Outskirts. The July 29 through August 1 Wacken World Wide metal festival in Germany was the top livestream event with 11 million watching on its own channel. Second was producer/DJ David Guetta's May 30 United at Home COVID-19 relief fundraiser in New York seen by 7.7 million on Facebook and YouTube. The band Dropkick Murphys came in third on May 29 from an empty Fenway Park for their Streaming Out of Fenway with 5.9 million viewers as Guest Bruce Springsteen joined them remotely for two songs. Altogether there were thirty-four shows with over a million views each from thirteen different producers.

In her January 2021 *Billboard* article "As Livestreaming Goes Mainstream, It Could Be Survival of the Biggest," Tatiana Cirisano reported that going into 2021 livestreaming had the potential to rival live performance in economic potential due to its "unlimited global audience capacity and lower costs than physical touring . . . but with at least 30 companies now competing for artists and audiences' attention, don't expect them all to stick around."[3] Included in the livestream mix were several industry veterans. Scooter Braun and Bonnaroo cofounder Rick Farman of Superfly Presents invested in four-year-old Wave to fund expansion. Former Pandora CEO Tim Westergren opened Sessions to livestream new independent acts. Former Sony executive Thomas Hesse launched Dreamstage. In July AEG veteran John Petrocelli's pay-per-view Bulldog Digital Media, operational since 2012, introduced an opening live teaser before going to online ticketing. Regarding a suddenly full field of competition, Petrocelli observed, "I don't know how all of these companies will survive. . . . Even though livestreaming is so popular now, there are few people who understand how to properly code and make the audio sound correct"[4] in Cirisano's August *Billboard* article *If You Stream It, Will They Come?*

In May tech giant Salesforce veteran Mary Kay Huse launched Indianapolis-based Mandolin with scheduled livestreams from both the Ryman Auditorium in Nashville and various City Winery locations. To fill another niche, in October Huse raised $5 million from investors including Salesforce CEO Marc Benioff to open Parties, which featured chats in private settings during the events, along with customized merchandise sales and specialized catering for watch parties. Companies with need-filling niche services like Parties were confident of their place in a growing sector where major entertainment companies were more likely to acquire or sub-contract new technology than create it. Huse told Cirisano, "I see now as the time that the music industry is going to go through a digital revolution."[5]

Several promoters tried to fill consumer longing for in-person attendance with both live and remote concerts at drive-in movie theaters and other locations with large parking lots. Nederlander CEO Alex Hodges told *Pollstar* in its year-end review that "two and a half months in, we went from over 191 concerts, and 92 special events confirmed to nothing . . . we pivoted quickly and will end this year presenting over 50 drive-ins. As of today, we have hosted 12,000 cars, grossing over $3 million" compared to $58.5 million in 2019 tickets sales. "Although our drive-in model has proven successful for us . . . it is not financially sustainable and is just a stop-gap solution."[6]

Shawn Gee, president of Live Nation Urban, summed up the future for the live performance sector telling Gensler, "I don't have the answer to when the live industry will be back. . . . That will be driven by science and governance, and we will follow all rules and protocols until that time presents itself. However, my answer to HOW the industry will come back is stronger than ever."[7] Despite the circumstances, Gee had reason to be optimistic on a corporate level. Although Live Nation showed a loss of $1.72 billion after all expenses, its stock price closed 2020 at $74.57 a share, slightly higher than its January opening at $72.00, and almost twice its price on March 12 when Rapino bought $1 million worth to substantiate his confidence in the company.

That livestream revenue, however, and its accompanying technological advances had been noticed by Live Nation, YouTube, Amazon, Facebook, and other consumer-oriented behemoths that were closing in on acquisitions or reexamining where they were already positioned to profit from livestreaming. Live Nation's Rapino told *Billboard*'s Cirisano, "Livestreaming is a great complement to our core business and gives any show an unlimited capacity."[8]

Billboard's Glenn Peoples further reported that Rapino addressed the blending of livestreaming with live performance in a company earnings call. He suggested that in some cases, livestreaming could complement in-person shows in addition to being a product on its own. "We think we have a unique advantage because we have the 30,00 [*sic*] physical shows" which could offer the online concert as a value-added VIP option "or possibly you can come to the show and you want some[times] to look at other camera angles on your phone."[9]

The primary goal, however, remained the return to a full slate of concert tours as soon as possible without threatening the health of consumers, performers, or support personnel. Livestreaming would be integrated into the mix as additional revenue. Goldman Sachs stated in "The Show Must Go On," "In the near term, we believe that artists will likely experiment with new ways of connecting with their fans and monetizing their music such as livestreaming. Longer term we believe consumers will be eager to get back to concerts and festivals. . . . We expect the growth of live streaming to be more complementary than cannibalistic to the industry."[10]

Postponed until Further Notice

As spring became summer and the virus surged, the general consensus was that all would work out in the end, but no prediction was offered for how or when. While businesses could shift to working remotely, and consumers still had access to music through radio, smartphone, and home entertainment centers, touring artists had their lives and plans totally disrupted by this sudden shutdown. Net revenue from gate receipts normally accounted for the largest share of artist income.

Even though touring revenue was postponed along with the shows, the artists were still contractually obligated for expenses that were guaranteed or paid in advance but not covered by insurance. *Billboard*'s Ed Christman wrote that 2020's forty top earners' revenue "fell tenfold, from $779 million in 2019 to $79 million and accounted for just 20% of artists' collective 2020 take-home pay. In previous years, it has made up 75% to 80% of the top 40 Money Makers' income."[11]

Leading the 2020 *Billboard* moneymaker list was Taylor Swift, who netted an estimated $23.8 million with no concert dates but a Grammy-winning album of the year in *folklore*. Post Malone was right behind her at $23.2 million, but with $12.4 million from touring prior to closure. Third was Celine Dion with almost all of her $17.5 million from her Las Vegas residency that shuttered before March. The Eagles were in fourth with $16.3 million, $11.4 million of which came from pre-pandemic shows. At fifth was newcomer Billie Eilish with only $1 million of her $14.7 million from touring. Together these five collected 67.2 percent of the tour earnings from the top-forty list. Their

2019 & 2020 *BILLBOARD* TOP 20 MONEY MAKERS
take-home net (in millions)

All 2020 major tours shut down in mid-March due to COVID leaving year-end touring revenue at only 11.4% of the 2019 total. **Touring Net** calculated as 34% of the box office total. **Royalties** were comprised of artists' net revenue from sales, streams, and publishing.

2019				2020			
ARTIST	**TOTAL**	**TOURING NET**	**ROYALTIES**	**ARTIST**	**TOTAL**	**TOURING NET**	**ROYALTIES**
Rolling Stones	$65.0	$60.5	$4.5	Taylor Swift	$23.8	N/A	$23.8
Ariana Grande	$44.3	$27.3	$17.0	Post Malone	$23.2	$12.4	$10.8
Elton John	$43.3	$39.5	$3.8	Céline Dion	$17.5	$17.0	$0.5
Jonas Brothers	$40.9	$39.5	$1.4	Eagles	$16.3	$11.4	$4.9
Queen	$35.2	$14.4	$20.8	Billie Eilish	$14.7	$1.0	$13.7
Post Malone	$34.2	$18.4	$15.8	Drake	$14.2	N/A	$14.2
Pink	$30.5	$26.0	$4.5	Queen	$13.2	N/A	$13.2
Kiss	$26.7	$25.8	$0.9	The Beatles	$12.9	N/A	$12.9
Billy Joel	$26.1	$23.0	$3.1	NBA YoungBoy	$11.9	$0.1	$11.8
Justin Timberlake	$25.9	$23.7	$2.2	Lil Baby	$11.7	$0.3	$11.4
Eric Church	$25.9	$22.8	$3.1	The Weeknd	$10.4	N/A	$10.4
Cher	$25.2	$24.5	$0.7	Aventura	$10.2	$8.8	$1.4
Paul McCartney	$23.9	$21.6	$2.3	AC/DC	$10.1	N/A	$10.1
Trans-Siberian Orchestra	$25.2	$24.6	$0.6	Eminem	$9.7	N/A	$9.7
Céline Dion	$21.9	$20.4	$1.5	Lil Uzi Vert	$9.5	N/A	$9.5
Dead & Company	$21.9	$19.8	$2.1	Luke Combs	$9.2	$1.0	$8.2
George Strait	$21.3	$17.8	$3.5	DaBaby	$9.1	$0.3	$8.8
Lady Gaga	$21.1	$3.5	$17.6	Metallica	$9.0	N/A	$9.0
Backstreet Boys	$21.1	$2.1	$19.0	BTS	$8.9	N/A	$8.9
Michael Bublé	$21.0	$3.0	$18.0	Pink Floyd	$8.8	N/A	$8.8
TOTALS in millions	**$600.6**	**$458.2**	**$142.4**	**TOTALS** in millions	**$254.3**	**$52.3**	**$202.0**

Source: *Billboard* Money Makers

Illustration E.1 2019 and 2020 *Billboard* Top 20 Money Makers

combined revenue from all sources, however, netted only $95.5 million compared to $228.7 million for 2019's top five.

Help, however, was on the way. As part of the March 2020 $2.3 trillion Coronavirus Aid, Relief, and Economic Security Act (CARES), music touring and production companies were eligible for loans under the Paycheck Protection Program (PPP), a large share of which would be forgivable if dispersed according to program guidelines. The application process began on April 1. Among those cited in the press as utilizing the PPP funds to help pay their employees included Guns N' Roses, the Eagles, Pearl Jam, Green Day, the Chainsmokers, Cheap Trick, Imagine Dragons, Jason Isbell, Lil Jon, Nickelback, Papa Roach, Pentatonix, Rascal Flatts, Chris Stapleton, Weezer, and Wiz Khalifa. Promoters Live Nation and Louis Messina; booking agency APA; indie labels Third Man Records, Sub Pop, Stones Throw, and Reckless; and publisher/recorded music catalog owner ABKCO were among the others receiving funds.

In December 2020 Congress passed and the president signed the $15 billion Shuttered Venue Operators Grant (SVOG) specifically for the live performance sector to bring additional relief in 2021. Promotors, venue owners, and agencies worked with their clients as well as for themselves to get a share of the relief dollars for which they were eligible under PPP and SVOG. With the announcements on the efficacy of the newly developed COVID-19 vaccines at the end of 2020, hope rose for a return to touring in the second half of 2021.

Taylor's Year at the Top

Never before had *Billboard*'s top-ranked money maker attained that height without going on the road, but milestones were nothing new to Taylor Swift. The conflict between Swift and Scooter Braun continued into 2020. In April Big Machine released a new album of eight live performances taken from a 2008 radio broadcast. Notified by her fans immediately upon its release, Swift thanked them via Instagram for "making me aware that my former label is putting out an 'album' of live performances of mine tonight. . . . I'm always honest with you guys about this stuff so I just wanted to tell you that this release is not approved by me."[12]

Swift's command of social media interaction with her fanbase worked its magic so that unlike any of her other releases, the live album neither charted nor received any appreciable airplay. The next month Swift released some live tracks of her own choosing and ownership. She was also planning to record her own version of her Big Machine album *Fearless (Taylor's Version)* for an early 2021 release when her rerecording restriction expired. Meanwhile, she decided to deny publishing sync licenses for her Big Machine tracks, preventing the label from licensing any sync usages since permission from both label and publisher was necessary.

Then in July Swift dropped (the industry term used for an unannounced release) her album *folklore*. From a marketing standpoint, the release was a departure from her usual carefully orchestrated prerelease promotional campaign, and from a musical standpoint, a more intimate, singer-songwriter presentation. Her fans embraced the album; critics hailed it; and chart, streaming, and sales success followed. She received six Grammy Award nominations, reaffirming her position in the pantheon of top pop performers, winning Album of the Year. She was honored as *Billboard*'s Woman of the Decade for her five number one albums and five number one singles on the *Billboard* charts, her touring success, and two *Billboard* Woman of the Year Awards. She was also lauded for her commitment to a list of causes including advocacy for the rights of creators, music education, literacy initiatives, cancer research, disaster relief, and women's rights.

In November, Braun's Ithaca Holdings sold Swift's master recordings to Shamrock Capital, an investment fund founded by the late Roy Disney, nephew of Walt and a longtime Disney executive, for his heirs' inheritance holdings. The price was purported to be more than $300 million, about what Ithaca paid for the entire Big Machine catalog, leaving Braun with the rest of the company assets including master recordings by Florida Georgia Line, Tim McGraw, Carly Pearce, Lady A, Midland, and Thomas Rhett, as well as Big Machine's publishing assets. Swift reaffirmed that she would still rerecord the six albums she did for Big Machine, and when they came out, these new "Taylor's Version" tracks and publishing would be available together from her for sync usages.

Despite COVID-19, Recorded Music Revenue Continues to Climb

The live performance sector may have been the first to react to COVID-19, but the rest of the industry was not far behind. Labels and publishers sent their staffs home to work remotely for the balance of the crisis. Internal and external in-person meetings easily transferred to remote operations utilizing conferencing apps, combined with shared document storage programs, or on direct link to their own computer systems. Despite the shift to remote, there were no immediate staff and salary cuts as revenue from streaming continued to grow to more than counter the ongoing decline in retail and downloads.

RIAA-reported revenue rose in 2020 by $1.02 billion over 2019 to $12.2 billion, a 9.2 percent increase, extraordinary in a year that experienced a stock market crash, absorbed 9 million lost jobs, and ended with many still mired in quarantine awaiting their turn for a newly developed vaccine. Streaming contributed 82.5 percent of RIAA revenue, up from 79.5 percent in 2019. MCR/Nielsen-measured streams were at almost 1.3 trillion, up 17 percent from 2019. At $619.6 million, vinyl was 29.2 percent over 2019's total for 54.4 percent of physical product, while CDs were down 23.4 percent and downloads fell by 18 percent. Revenue in 2020 from 360°-related sources also decreased for record labels with the moratorium on touring.

Although the RIAA annual report and the top *Billboard* charts were still focused on the US, most of the online newsletters, blogs, and information aggregators had adopted a global perspective, most notably when estimating market share. Music & Copyright (M&C) attributed 68.3 percent of 2020 global recorded music revenue to the majors with UMG at 32.1 percent, Sony with 20.6 percent, and 15.6 percent to WMG. Independents had the remaining 31.7 percent, just a step behind UMG but well ahead of Sony and WMG.

MIDiA Research's Mark Mulligan combined the same data with his own survey of independent labels' repertoire and revenue to differentiate between what the Big Three owned and what they distributed for others. Mulligan's analysis, *Streaming Forward—Digital Media Association Annual Music Report—A MIDIA Research Report*, showed that about $2.1 billion of the $15.1 billion attributed to the Big Three came from the independent product they distributed. Thus, on an ownership rather than distribution basis, independents owned about 43 percent of the music consumed worldwide. Mulligan further concluded that the independent ownership of the total market, major label and independent distribution combined, was both larger and growing faster than generally assumed.

The Demographics and Data of Streaming in 2020

The RIAA annual report still tabulated US totals of both dollars and units for sound carriers as provided by its member labels. The report, however, still listed industrywide totals without revealing the individual artist or label specifics. Nonetheless, market share remained a key competitive issue between RIAA members, and they looked to other sources for additional

RECORD BUSINESS TOPS $12 BILLION IN 2020 WITH OVER $10 BILLION FROM STREAMING

BILLBOARD'S TOP TEN ALBUMS IN 2020

ARTIST	ALBUM TITLE	TEA (album equivalency)	ALBUM SALES	TRACK SALES	AUDIO STREAMS	VIDEO STREAMS
Lil Baby	My Turn	2.63 M	40 K	366 K	3.2 B	718 M
Taylor Swift	folklore	2.21 M	1.28 M	281 K	1.1 B	52 M
Pop Smoke	Shoot For The Stars Aim For The Moon	2.20 M	106 K	270 K	2.7 B	372 M
The Weeknd	After Hours	2.03 M	480 K	785 K	1.9 B	176 M
Juice Wrld	Legends Never Die	1.99 M	301 K	200 K	2.4 B	249 M
Post Malone	Hollywood's Bleeding	1.90 M	117 K	642 K	2.3 B	217 M
Lil Uzi Vert	Eternal Atake	1.86 M	28 K	95 K	2.6 B	176 M
Roddy Ricch	Please Excuse Me For Being Antisocial	1.79 M	26 K	289 K	2.4 B	311 M
Harry Styles	Fine Line	1.52 M	420 K	517 K	1.4 B	100 M
Luke Combs	What You See Is What You Get	1.48 M	184 K	810 K	1.5 B	133 M

NOTE: In calculating TEA, 10 tracks, 1,250 premium or 3,750 freemium streams equal one album

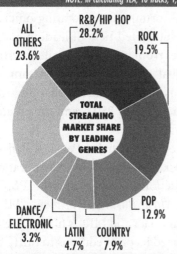

ALL OTHERS 23.6%
R&B/HIP HOP 28.2%
ROCK 19.5%
POP 12.9%
COUNTRY 7.9%
LATIN 4.7%
DANCE/ELECTRONIC 3.2%

TOTAL STREAMING MARKET SHARE BY LEADING GENRES

55.9 million RIAA-reported album and 4.2 million track sales combined with 1.3 trillion streams tabulated by Nielsen to produce an 11% rise in revenue over 2019.

2020's top ten albums and tracks from them accounted for about 6% of total sales, but their combined streams were less than .2% of the Nielsen total.

Overall, catalog tracks, defined as older than 18 months, with 63.3% of all streams topped current releases with just 36.7%. This ratio included all genres.

Streaming offered greater access and convenience than buying records at a fraction of the cost, along with a wider range of non-interactive listening options than radio.

Source: MRC Data / Billboard / R.I.A.A.

Illustration E.2 Record Business Tops $12B in 2020 with over $10B from Streaming

information, especially the recently formed MRC Data roll-up of news sources, trade journals, and market share data aggregators.

The MRC Data/*Billboard* Year-End Report U.S. 2020, listed the ratio of current releases at 36.7 percent of all streams, while attributing 63.3 percent to catalog tracks. This ratio was a reversal from 1999 when current releases as tabulated by SoundScan accounted for 66.4 percent of all revenue with catalog producing just 33.6 percent. Audio streams had expanded to 79 percent of total album consumption (TAC) value, with video streams supplying another 5.2 percent. The influence of purchased sound carriers in chart position was further reduced with downloads at 7.2 percent of TAC, while sales of CDs and vinyl combined accounted for 8.5 percent.

The four top MCR-listed genres dominated music consumption with 68.5 percent of TAC. R&B/hip hop had 28.2 percent, with 19.5 percent for rock, pop at 12.9 percent, and country came in at 7.9 percent. These statistics combined both current releases and catalog tracks in each genre. The other genres listed on the report's TAC chart were Latin at 4.7 percent, and dance/electronic with 3.2 percent, followed by Christian/gospel, world music, children, jazz, and classical all between 1 percent and 1.9 percent.

On September 14, 2020, after more than a year in development, *Billboard* introduced two new charts to join its weekly U.S. Hot 100 singles and *Billboard* 200 album charts: the *Billboard* Global 200 and the *Billboard* Global 200 Excluding the US. International editor Alexei Barrionuevo explained, "The chart rankings will be based on a weighted formula incorporating official-only streams on both subscription and ad-supported tiers of leading audio and video music services, plus download sales from top music retailers across the globe."[13] In calculating the *Billboard* Global 200, 200 premium streams or 900 ad-supported streams were equivalent to one track sale whether physical or download. For the *Billboard* Global Excluding U.S., 250 premium streams or 1,125 ad-supported streams equaled one track sale.

A week later MRC announced a joint venture with Jay Penske's Penske Media Corporation (PMC) to create Penske Media Rights Corporation (PMRC). PMRC would manage MRC's trade journals together with PMC's *Variety*, *Rolling Stone*, and recent acquisition *Music Business Worldwide*. MRC Data would manage and exploit all proprietary data and MRC's film and television properties. *Billboard* had already reduced its print editions to thirty by 2019 and then to nineteen in 2020, although the weekly charts and feature articles were still available through digital subscription and news from the daily billboardbulletin.com. Whether a new hand on the wheel would sustain the current balance between traditional print distribution of the older version of industry news and the rising tide of digital dissemination, or would it steer music journalism through the same transformation that music content had just experienced was still to be determined going into 2021 and beyond.

. Right on the heels of the *Billboard* global charts and subsequent PMRC announcements, in early October Spotify introduced its own weekly charts including a U.S. Weekly Album Chart, a Global Weekly Album Chart, a U.S. Weekly Song Chart, and a Global Weekly Song Chart. Music Business Worldwide Founder/Publisher Tim Ingham, since 2018 a part of the growing Penske media empire, commented, "For some time, Spotify's daily charts have been an essential measure of music industry success. . . . That being said, Spotify's chart obviously only covers the popularity of music on one service (erm, Spotify), rather than a range of platforms and/or retailers."[14]

The RIAA year-end report listed 75.5 million US paid subscribers for $7.01 billion in premium streaming revenue, a 25 percent increase over 2019, with another $723.6 million in limited-tier subscription revenue and $1.394 billion in ad-supported streaming. From an international perspective, however, the IFPI's Global Music Report for 2020 stated there were 443 million paid streaming subscribers worldwide at the end of 2020, up 102 million over 2019's 341 million, a 29.9 percent increase. Spotify and Apple led the market with about one-third and one-sixth, respectively. Chinese conglomerate Tencent and Amazon Music were just behind with about 13 percent each, and the recently consolidated Google music services now under the YouTube Music umbrella had grown to about 8 percent.

The Big Three: Planning for the Post-Covid Future

According to the Vivendi Financial Report for the Year 2019, UMG entered into a December 31, 2019, agreement with a consortium led by Chinese media giant Tencent Music Entertainment "for 10% of UMG's share capital, based on an enterprise value of €30 billion [then equal to $33.6 billion] for 100% of UMG's share capital. . . . The Consortium has the option to acquire, on the same price basis, an additional amount of up to 10% of UMG's share capital"[15] to be exercised by January 15, 2021, and concluded within the first half of 2020.

Tencent, founded in 1998 in Shenzhen, a special economic zone adjacent to Hong Kong, was listed on the Hong Kong exchange in 2004, and then on the New York Stock Exchange in 2018. Tencent described its Vision & Mission as "Value for Users, Tech for Good. . . . User value is our guiding principle, we strive to incorporate social responsibility into our products and services; promote technology innovation and cultural vitality; help industries digitally upgrade; collaborate for the sustainable development of society."[16]

Best known outside of China for its video games and social media, in July 2020 Tencent briefly surpassed Facebook with a market capitalization of $664.5 billion, making it for a short time the most valuable company in the world. Other milestones achieved during 2020 included business communications platform WeCom, servicing more than 5.5 million companies and 130 million monthly active users; video conferencing service Tencent Meeting/VooV, available in more than one hundred territories; and over 400 million daily active users of the app bundle Weixin Mini Programs. In 2019 Tencent Video passed 100 million subscribers, and daily transactions on Tencent's mobile payment services went over 1 billion in 2018.

In early February WMG announced plans for its own IPO, but was delayed until late May. The offering was 77 million shares of Class A common stock at $25 per share with a $12.7 billion value, including shares sold by WMG parent Access Industries, and shares it held for the WMG executives who participated in the company's Senior Management Free Cash Flow Plan, which it had initiated in 2012.

Meanwhile, Sony approached April 1, 2020, the beginning of its fiscal year, more cautiously than UMG and WMG who were already one quarter and two quarters into their 2020 fiscal years, respectively. Ed Christman reported in the May 13 *Billboard Bulletin* that "Sony didn't forecast its fiscal guidance for music's sales and operating income for 2020, as it usually does at year end. Instead, it will probably do so at the end of the fiscal second quarter after its operations have had more experience in dealing with the economic recession caused by the pandemic."[17] The filing also suggested that its music revenue would be down somewhere between 25 percent and 40 percent due to falling sales of physical product in markets not as heavily digitized as the US.

Nonetheless, in the very early days of the pandemic, Sony Publishing formed a partnership with BeatStars, which often referred to itself as the leading place to buy & sell beats. A beat is a rhythmic pattern underlining a track that can range from a simple cadence to a complete arrangement. Founded by Abe Batshon in 2008, BeatStars featured beats self-posted by their creators for sale or licensing. Little Nas X bought a beat posted by YoungKio for $30 for the instrumental bed to his worldwide hit "New Town Road." After its debut on TikTok, Columbia's Ron Perry picked it up for distribution, added Billy Ray Cyrus, and gave YoungKio a coproduction credit. The partnership with Sony offered global administration and pitching services for a 20 percent fee to BeatStars clients. The ever–forward-thinking publishing CEO Jon Platt told Music Biz Nation, "BeatStars has successfully created a new lane, fostering the collective talent of emerging songwriters and producers online, and we look forward to furthering this effort with Sony/ATV's best-in-class service."[18]

COVID-19 Cannot Stop the Growth of Publishing Revenue

COVID-19 had a minimal effect on publishing other than employees' relocation to home offices, but falling revenue in areas that dealt with retail sales and live performances slowed what would otherwise have been a robust year in revenue growth. Retail sales of printed music dropped 14 percent below the 2019 level. Mail order sales of sheet music and scores used in productions at schools and arts centers were also affected due to cancellation of performances as part of COVID-19 protocol. CD mechanicals fell by 23.4 percent, but vinyl was up by 29.2 percent.

PRO general licensing was down in 2020 by 30 percent at ASCAP and 23 percent at BMI due to the shutdown of concert touring and decline in the retail and hospitality segments. Fees from digital licensing sources, however, rose by 16 percent at BMI while audio streaming revenue grew by 28 percent at ASCAP to counter the general licensing losses. Their combined revenue increased by 3.2 percent over 2019, but there would have been a greater boost had there been no pandemic. BMI stated in a press release that even though "revenue performance surpassed last year's results, BMI estimates it absorbed a $60 million negative impact to its revenues due to the COVID-19 effect across multiple businesses."[19] Assuming that SESAC and GMR collections stayed at their 2019 estimated levels, then total PRO revenue was close to the $3 billion threshold from $2.9 billion in 2019 despite the effect of COVID-19.

The annual NMPA accounting of their membership's 2020 revenue cited a 9.6 percent increase over 2019. CEO David Israelite listed a 13 percent increase in sync license fees, and a 19.5 percent gain in mechanicals, but the "other" licensing area fell by 17.1 percent. Israelite pointed out during the meeting that the overall growth "speaks to the strength of not only the diversification of our income streams, but also because of how songs perform even in a bad economy."[20]

Hipgnosis Leads the Charge in Rights Acquisition

Israelite was not alone in noticing the strength of the publishing sector. Led by the aggressive approach of Hipgnosis since its founding in 2018, the competition for catalogs intensified. According to the Hipgnosis September 2020 semi-annual report, since inception it had acquired 117 catalogs, containing over 57,836 songs valued at £1.18 billion with an average multiple of 14.76 times net publisher share. Of those songs, 44,545 had been added since the advent of the pandemic, including the $323 million purchase of the Kobalt Capital first fund catalog established in 2011, in the largest publishing transaction since 2017. Hipgnosis, however, had limited infrastructure to administer and exploit its growing collection of catalogs. In September 2020 Hipgnosis acquired the Big Deal Music Group led by Kenny MacPherson in a cash and stock transaction. In addition to its 4,440 songs, Big Deal came with staff and structure to become the administrative and creative wings of the Hipgnosis Songs Group with MacPherson as CEO, reporting to founder Merck Mercuriadis.

In an article for the *Guardian*, Dorian Lynskey interviewed Mark Ronson whose "Uptown Funk" was Hipgnosis' third-most streamed song with 1.26 billion streams that had generated somewhere between $5 million and $8 million in streaming mechanicals. Ronson told Lynskey, "The number one rule in music always used to be: never sell your publishing. But Merck has upended that entire way of thought." Lynskey also interviewed Mercuriadis himself, who described many legacy artists as "at a point in their life when they may never go back on tour again and are dotting the Is and crossing the Ts on their estate planning."[21] By the end of 2020, a diverse list of artists including Nile Rodgers, the Four Seasons, Chrissie Hynde, L.A. Reid, Barry Manilow, Devo, Nikki Sixx, Shakira, Dave Stewart, RZA, members of Blondie, Air Supply, Fleetwood Mac, Journey, Disturbed, Blink 182, Goo Goo Dolls, and the estates of Ray Charles and Rick James had sold some combination of their rights to Hipgnosis or one of its competitors.

In early December the largest-to-date purchase of a single songwriter's collected works was announced by UMPG when it bought Bob Dylan's six hundred–plus song catalog. While terms were not disclosed, *Billboard*'s Ed Christman reported, "The price is thought to be between $375 million and $400 million, based on the $11 million to $14 million Dylan's catalog generates every year, according to sources familiar with the business."[22] The transaction included both the songwriter and publisher shares with a multiple somewhere between 25 and 30.

Not all publishing veterans shared Mercuriadis's vision of songs as commodities. After over forty years of administering rights for clients from Tom Petty to Sturgill Simpson, Wixen Music Publishing founder Randall Wixen commented on the growing trend in a December 2020 communique to prominent industry blogger Bob Lefsetz of the *Lefsetz Letter* fame, "Bob, we have been the back-office administrators for a number of catalog investment vehicles. We've seen firsthand how many of them operate. It's easy to tout how great your marketing department is if you're getting a ton of licenses by giving quotes on your newly purchased assets at a third of what they're worth. . . . I don't know a single person that has sold their catalog that hasn't eventually regretted it. I always try and talk clients out of selling, and when they ignore me I feel more comfortable in making them an offer. . . . As a person who has built a career out of protecting creators, it just kills me to see people selling their lives' work in this manner."[23]

Metadata Management: CISAC Appoints New ISWC Administrator

In September 2020 CISAC announced the transfer of the worldwide ISWC network into the hands of Spanish Point Technologies, a member of the Microsoft Partner Network with a Gold Competency rating. *Microsoftcustomers.com* explained that Spanish Point ". . . builds solutions for CMOs [collective management organizations] in the music industry to help them accurately invoice for royalties and distribute payments fairly to artists and publishers."[24] The ISWC system needed an update to accommodate the demands of the new streaming paradigm for instantaneous data transfer. Spanish Point CEO Donal Culen stated in the CISAC press release, "Our Matching Engine uses the latest cloud and AI technology to help creators worldwide get paid quicker and with great accuracy."[25]

Since the introduction of the ISWC system in the late 1990s, codes had been assigned to 52 million songs by CMOs in seventy-nine countries. With annual streaming consumption having surpassed 1 trillion individual streams by 2019, existing infrastructure was no longer capable of handling the load of data, which was in excess of 120 million streams per hour globally, all of which needed to be tabulated and accounted for.

"The upgrade of the ISWC could not come at a timelier moment for songwriters and composers, who are now depending more than ever on digital income for their livelihoods," CISAC president Björn Ulvaeus observed in the press release. Ulvaeus was also ABBA's cofounder and a cowriter of "Dancing Queen," which was assigned the first ISWC #000000001 when the system was introduced. "ISWC is one of the most important identifiers in the music industry. . . . It will track music works better and faster and help put more money more quickly into creators' pockets."[26]

The major music publishers concurred. Sony/ATV senior director Alex Batterbee added, "The new ISWC system will lead to significantly faster creation of codes and increased sharing of codes between the different stakeholders. That is good for creators and good for the whole digital market."[27] Spotify senior director of licensing Victoria Campoamor, indicated that the DSPs were on board as well: "We applaud CISAC's much-needed and long-awaited modernization of ISWC. We hope to see dissemination of this very important work identifier across the whole ecosystem."[28]

Metadata Management: ASCAP and BMI Launch Shared Database

On December 20, after five years in development, the joint ASCAP-BMI database SONGVIEW debuted. Their press release described SONGVIEW technology as allowing "ASCAP and BMI to seamlessly display an agreed-upon view of detailed, aggregated and reconciled ownership data for performing rights for more than 20 million musical works in their combined repertoires, including a breakdown of shares by ASCAP and BMI. The information is accessible, free to the public, on both ASCAP's and BMI's websites."[29] BMI's executive VP/distribution Alison Smith and ASCAP's executive VP/digital officer Nick Lehman led SOUNDVIEW's development.

Each website contained three different search options. First was the default SONGVIEW database, which contained all works, with a green checkmark on song screens for which both societies verified the percentage splits. Then each had two customized listings, the first with each society's wholly or partially controlled works excluding the works wholly controlled by the other. The other option had just the songs 100 percent controlled by that PRO. SONGVIEW could be searched by title, performer, writer/composer, publisher, ISWC, or catalog number.

ISRCs were not included because the PROs were not responsible for royalties to the artists or the owners of sound recordings. Each song screen, however, contained a field where publishers or songwriters could list the performers who had recorded the song. This practice had originated in pre-digital days when songwriters were often not listed on records and having the artist's name could be useful in crediting the performance to the correct song. There were, for instance, over twelve thousand entries on SOUNDVIEW with "Hold On" as the song title or its first two words. At least ten of them had been award-winning chart songs created by different songwriters. In 1990 Wilson Phillips and En Vogue both had records titled "Hold On" but with different songwriters, and coincidentally both had been on the Billboard Hot 100 at the same time and were both in the year-end top ten. Situations like this had spurred the initial adoption of the ISWC system.

BMI's Mike O'Neill commented, "When two companies that are fierce competitors come together on a project this ambitious to address a need identified by the marketplace, it says a lot about how important greater data transparency is to both of our organizations."[30] ASCAP's Elizabeth Matthews added, "We have built a convenient new digital tool for anyone who licenses music."[31]

Metadata Management: The MLC Prepares for Launch

In January 2020 the MLC named WMG head of US legal shared services Kris Ahrend as CEO and tasked him to open an office in Nashville with a projected staff of over one hundred. Before his six-year stint at WMG, Ahrend worked in business and legal affairs for eight years with Rhino and five years at Sony/BMG. MLC chair Alisa Coleman stated in the press release, "The unique combination of his experience with license administration, his tenure as a business and legal affairs executive in the music industry, and his most recent involvement in leading the design and operation of a large client service organization makes him well-suited to operate the MLC. He has spent his career making sure artists and songwriters get paid, and the Board is thrilled to have found someone whose passion and expertise align so well with the mission of the MLC."[32]

The MLC had previously announced in November 2019 that "former Digital Data Exchange (DDEX) chair Richard Thompson will serve as the nonprofit's Chief Information Officer responsible for overseeing the development and launch of the MLC's revolutionary data platform to distribute royalties payable to songwriters and copyright owners."[33] Thompson had been serving in an interim capacity since February 2019 while developing the NMPA/NSAI-backed MLC proposal. Thompson had spent seventeen years as chief technology officer (CTO) at Kobalt before his two-year stint as chair of DDEX, a not-for-profit, membership organization that included the major publishers and leading independents focused on development and support of new methods of digital data exchange.

At the same time the MLC had announced that HFA and blockchain technology company ConsenSys had "received unanimous approval from the MLC Board to become the primary vendors responsible for managing the matching of digital uses to musical works, distributing mechanical royalties, and onboarding songwriters, composers, lyricists, and music publishers and their catalogs to the database."[34] Global branding consultant Prophet and DDEX were to design and create the portal interface.

The three major publishers and independents BMG, Kobalt, peermusic, ABKCO, Pulse Music Group, Big Machine Music, and Concord Music were named voting members of the MLC board of directors, as were songwriters Kara DioGuardi, Oak Fielder, Kevin Kadish, and Tim Nichols. Danielle Aguirre of the NMPA, Bart Herbison of the NSAI, and a spot reserved for the DLC appointee held nonvoting membership. The board also established three advisory committees: the Unclaimed Royalties Oversight Committee and the Dispute Resolution Committee were evenly divided between publishers and songwriters, while the Operations Advisory Committee had six publisher members and six DiMA members.

Several independent publishers and songwriters questioned the choice of HFA due to its decade-long relationship with Spotify. Attorney Richard Busch filed a legal action in June 2019 on behalf of publisher Eight Mile Style, which had a share of 243 songs by Eminem including the number one chart topper and Oscar winning "Lose Yourself," accusing Spotify and HFA together of infringement. Resolution was still pending going into 2021. HFA, however, had gone through several ownership changes since its initial agreement with Spotify and had reinforced both its systems and standing in the publishing community.

Despite past problems with independent publishers' songs, the HFA database had the most complete collection of back catalog mechanical license metadata. It had administered licenses for around 80 percent of record releases going back to the introduction of computerized royalty systems. The HFA database included ISRC#s, publisher splits, contact information, and its own internal identifiers. Its transformation into the foundation for the new MLC portal utilizing ConsenSys technology involved the addition and integration of all these identifying codes, all of which would also appear on the public search engine and monthly royalty statements.

Just like its HFA predecessor, however, as well as the PROs and SoundExchange, the task of registering new works rested with the rightsholders. While the future of MLC looked bright to all, especially for dealing with persistent problems associated with unidentified streaming royalties, it was especially beneficial to the DSPs as the MMA had greatly reduced potential infringement liabilities for them.

Having waged a decades-long campaign for proper performance identification and payment, the NSAI's Herbison observed on the anticipated launch of the MLC, "The songwriter board and committee members ensure an unprecedented level of transparency in the MLC processes including making the entire database publicly available. It was a Herculean effort, but they also ensured that songwriter priorities were a part of how unclaimed funds are collected and distributed, how disputes are resolved, and are an integral part of the overall MLC governance structure."[35]

Metadata Management: ISRC Infrastructure to SoundExchange

The recorded music sector also made several advances in centralized metadata management to tighten the accuracy and connectivity of the network of ISRC identification numbers. In July 2020 the RIAA announced, "In order to address the issue of 'authority' in the ISRC system, i.e., whether an ISRC is 'officially' assigned to a particular sound recording, SoundExchange has been designated as the authoritative source of this information for the US market. Recognizing an authorative source of this ISRC data has become important as the music ecosystem evolves and new legislation and regulation is implemented."[36]

The announcement further recommended that any holders of previously assigned US ISRC numbers check on the SoundExchange database to be sure their numbers had been registered there. The SoundExchange database had been opened to the public in 2016 and was chosen at that time by IFPI to serve as the search engine for assigned ISRC numbers for its own ifpi.org website.

Strife Shakes the Recording Academy . . . Again

COVID-19 wasn't the first unexpected disruption of 2020. Just two weeks into January the issue of gender inequity that rocked the 2018 Grammy Awards took center stage again, looking as if it would be the major story of the year. Ten days before the January 26 telecast, the Academy placed CEO Deborah Dugan on paid administrative leave just over five months into her tenure. Board chair Harvey Mason Jr. assumed her responsibilities on an interim, unsalaried basis.

In a January 20 posting on the Academy website, Mason wrote, "In November of 2019, the Executive Committee became aware of abusive work environment complaints alleged against Ms. Dugan and in December 2019, a letter was sent from an attorney representing a staff member that included additional detailed and serious allegations of a 'toxic and intolerable' and 'abusive and bullying' environment created by Ms. Dugan towards the staff. Given these concerning reports, the Executive Committee launched an immediate and independent investigation.

"After we received the employee complaints against Ms. Dugan, she then (for the first time) made allegations against the Academy. In response, we started a separate investigation into Ms. Dugan's allegations. Ms. Dugan's attorney then informed the Executive Committee that if Ms. Dugan was paid millions of dollars, she would "withdraw" her allegations and resign from her role as CEO. . . . Following that communication from Ms. Dugan's attorney, Ms. Dugan was placed on administrative leave as we complete both of these ongoing investigations."[37]

The next day Dugan filed a "Charge of Discrimination" against the Academy with the Equal Employment Opportunity Commission (EEOC) citing "egregious conflicts of interest, improper self-dealing by Board members and voting irregularities with respect to nominations for Grammy Awards, all made possible by the 'boys' club' mentality and approach to governance at the Academy."[38] Dugan also made claims of sexual misconduct by two high-ranking Academy officials, one that involved her during her interview process. The other stemmed from past, already reviewed and dismissed accusations that did not involve her and preceded her contact with the Academy. Both allegations were strongly denied.

Her EEOC filing further read, "After Ms. Dugan wrote her December 22, 2019 email, she put the Academy on notice that she intended to bring claims against the Academy. On January 16, 2020, after the Academy backed out of a resolution that had nearly been reached in principle to resolve Ms. Dugan's legal claims, Mr. Mason conveyed the Board's new unacceptable offer of settlement. Mr. Mason also told Ms. Dugan that she had only one hour to accept the Academy's proposal. When Ms. Dugan failed to do so, the Board immediately put her on administrative leave. The leave had nothing to do with any accusations made against Ms. Dugan. It was retaliation, pure and simple."[39]

That same day four longtime female trustees and members of the executive committee—-current vice chair Tammy Hurt, chair emeritus Christine Albert, trustee and former chair Leslie Ann Jones, and trustee Terry Jones—also weighed in, commenting, "The Academy is keenly sensitive to any and all allegations of harassment or abuse, and we support the independent investigations that have been launched. . . . We have collectively volunteered many years of service guiding and supporting this organization. . . . We would not have taken precious time away from our families and careers if we felt that it was a 'boys' club.' We are leaders of this organization and fully committed to transformational change both within the Academy and within our industry at large."[40]

Then just three days before the telecast, the Academy's Task Force on Diversity and Inclusion issued a statement of their own. Explaining that they had submitted their report in December recommending eighteen systemic changes needed to improve diversity and inclusion and were reconvening in 90 days to review the progress, they nonetheless wanted to speak up at this time in their own voice. "While we understand there are ongoing investigations about the issues raised over the last week, our experience and research tells us that if the Academy leadership, its staff, and the nominating committees that govern the Awards were more diverse and inclusive, there would be better processes for resolving problems and more trust in the Academy as a whole. Those seeking to make such reforms need to be supported, not impeded."[41]

The task force statement concluded, "Change is hard. It won't be easy to make these changes. But we are deeply disappointed at the level of commitment by some of the Academy's leadership in effecting the kind of real and constructive change presented in our report. We are confident that they can do better. Music has historically catalyzed and galvanized mass social change. And so it must again. Now."[42]

Despite the turmoil of the previous ten days, Music's Biggest Night went on as scheduled. Billie Eilish won all four general category awards, the first such quadfecta since Christopher Cross in 1981. Alicia Keys reprised her role as host, with the eighteen presenters comprising eight females, seven males, and three mixed-gender groups. Women garnered all five Best Pop Solo Performance slots and four out of five for Best Pop Album. Were the Academy's approximately twelve thousand voting members and the show's producers taking the lead in sensitivity to gender equity or were the awards just a true reflection of the best eligible recordings, or somewhere in between?

On February 12, 2020, *Billboard*'s Paul Grein interviewed Mason and Academy VP of membership and industry relations Laura Segura Mueller, who told Grein that seventeen of the eighteen task force recommendations had already been endorsed by the trustees; the campaign to increase female membership "added 563 female members in our first year, so we're well on track" and that a "diverse slate hiring requirement" would be implemented, and that "at least 50 percent of the candidates for every position" would be female, non-white, and/or age thirty-nine or under. Mason added, "I know we're not perfect. I know there's work to be done."[43]

On March 2, the Academy executive committee notified its voting members that Dugan's termination was official, and the search would begin for a new CEO. The reasons listed in the letter included the timing and content of her campaign in the media, which the Academy described as an attempt to derail the Grammy Awards show, her public charges that the awards system was both rigged and corrupt, the time and cost of the investigations of both the charges made by her and against her, and her management deficiencies and failures. Eve Barlow of Vulture.com reported that academy chair emeritus Christine Albert commented, "It was not one thing that led to this action but rather the large number of incidents that demonstrated poor judgment, both before and after Ms. Dugan went on administrative leave. There was just no way she could continue to serve this organization."[44]

Dugan issued her own statement, "I was recruited and hired by the Recording Academy to make positive change; unfortunately, I was not able to do that as its CEO. . . . Is anyone surprised that its purported investigations did not include interviewing me or addressing the greater claims of conflicts of interest and voting irregularities?. . . So, instead of trying to reform the corrupt institution from within, I will continue to work to hold accountable those who continue to self-deal, taint the Grammy voting process and discriminate against women and people of color. Artists deserve better. To me, this is the real meaning of 'stepping up.'"[45]

On April 30, the Academy announced the hiring of Valeisha Butterfield Jones as its chief diversity and inclusion officer. She had most recently served in a similar capacity for Google after stints with Women in Entertainment Empowerment Network (WEEN), HBO, and the Obama administration. With her hiring and the approval by the trustees of the task force recommendations, the Academy had survived a tumultuous year that to some degree had scarred almost all involved but was on the path toward fulfilling the mandate that had been set in motion after the 2018 post-awards "step up" incident. Whether, when, and to what degree the Academy would itself further step up to lead the industry toward greater diversity would be in the hands of its next CEO. At the end of 2020 the Academy was waiting for the results of both a search for that CEO and the conclusion of the Dugan arbitration proceedings.

COVID and the Music Consumer

The end of 2020 arrived with live music still on hiatus. Plans for 2021 were hopeful, but sketchy. *Rolling Stone*'s Jon Blistein and Ethan Millman conducted interviews with infectious disease experts and touring professionals for their December 22 feature titled "When Will Live Music Return?" Most agreed that the efficacy of the just-announced vaccines, adherence to safety protocols, and the rate of vaccination would be major factors since a premature return could cause a serious setback. Also of consequence was establishing a sufficient time to properly plan and execute a comprehensive comeback plan. Blistein and

Millman concluded that "in many ways, the live music industry is at the same limbo place it was at the start of the pandemic—when the industry was confident that shows would be back by fall 2020, only to have its plans wrecked again and again."[46]

Although consumers could no longer attend live performances, all their other listening options were still available, including physical purchase through mail order. Many who were at work, at school, commuting, enjoying meals, seeing movies, attending sporting events, or indulging in other social activities in years past were now at home. According to calculations by Sherin Shibu of *PC Magazine*, US consumer time on smartphones in 2020, which included web browsing, streaming, and social media in addition to calling and texting, was up 45 percent over 2019. Premium audio subscriptions as tabulated by the RIAA rose by 25 percent. Seventy-eight percent of US households had streaming video access, while video game companies sold $76.13 billion in games, equipment, apps, and programs, up $14.9 billion over 2019.

With no clear sign of the resumption of live performance, social media platforms became even more crucial for introducing the latest music through peer group interaction. Streaming with its likes, thumbs up, and on-demand requests had already replaced station call-ins and listener surveys. Record label marketing campaigns were repurposed to boost artist identity online, in print, and through social media influencers. The curators of the dozens if not hundreds of top playlists with worldwide audiences had replaced both radio programmers and retail account managers as the targets of label promotion efforts.

Just as radio's reporting stations had influenced secondary markets in previous decades, promotional efforts toward the top curators trickled down to influence the next level of playlists, including the ones customized for friends, family, and personal enjoyment, but nonetheless available to all others who might find them. Every stream listened to, whether on-demand, from a curated channel, or from a consumer playlist, was tabulated with the relevant data available from the DSPs to the trade journals for chart positions, and to the rightsholders through their collection agencies for royalty distribution.

YouTube and Spotify Strive to Define the New Normal

Since Lyor Cohen's appointment as YouTube global head of music in the fall of 2016, his mission was to transform the antagonism between YouTube and the labels into a mutually beneficial partnership. His goal was to turn YouTube into the largest supplier of paid subscription revenue on a global basis while maintaining his share of the freemium segment, or, to borrow from his former colleague Jimmy Iovine, become the dominant utility. In 2020 Cohen's strategy yielded results as YouTube's 2020 royalties grew from 2019's $3 billion to $4 billion, compared to Spotify's $5 billion, which Cohen hoped to surpass in the next year or two.

As always, MIDiA Research's Mark Mulligan analyzed the marketplace with a global perspective pointing out that Google, including YouTube, had led the market in growth rate at 60 percent, followed by Tencent at 40 percent, Amazon at 27 percent, and Apple by just 12 percent. He added, "Google's YouTube Music has been the standout story of the music subscriber market for the last couple of years, resonating both in many emerging markets and with younger audiences across the globe. The early signs are that YouTube Music is becoming to Gen Z what Spotify was to Millennials half a decade ago."[47]

Meanwhile, Spotify finally registered its first profitable quarter in 2019 but reverted to an operational loss in 2020 despite a rise in revenue. The pandemic-induced increase in average hours per user endangered the carefully calibrated balance Daniel Ek had constructed between revenue, royalties, and expenses more than a decade earlier. The major danger was determining the point at which more per-user streams, which generated more royalty obligations, would threaten corporate stability or cause a decrease in payment per stream to rightsholders? Jimmy Iovine's observation, "What's the streaming business's problem on the horizon? Margin. It doesn't scale," was more pertinent than ever.[48]

In anticipation of this quandary, Spotify and its rival music-intensive DSPs pursued an increase in podcast inventory, the streaming parallel to the talk radio format. Podcasters sold sponsorships and spot ads in a revenue-sharing arrangement with DSPs. Under this relationship, licenses for any music in podcasts were the podcaster's responsibility and thus not part of the DSP's royalty calculations. A higher percentage of non-royalty-bearing hours could counter the increase of user-hours per subscription to maintain the DSPs' revenue/royalty balance. The Interactive Advertising Bureau (IAB) reported $842 million in podcast ad revenue for 2020, a 19 percent increase over 2019, and predicted over $1 billion in 2021, and over $2 billion by 2023.

Spotify had been acquiring podcast content for several years but accelerated in 2020, led by a multiyear exclusive license for the eleven-year-old *The Joe Rogan Experience* library of existing and ongoing podcasts reported by CNBC to be worth over $100 million. Spotify also announced the addition of video podcasts, or vodcasts, including the more recent Rogan episodes, which they could stream as either a vodcast or audio-only podcast. Podcasts could also be downloaded to a mobile device for time-shifted offline listening. Other Spotify signees included Kim Kardasian, DC Comics, Michelle Obama, and Prince Harry and Meghan, Duchess of Sussex.

The TikTok Phenomenon

TikTok was introduced in August 2018 as an adaptation of the already-existing Musical.ly app, which featured fifteen-second videos created by users lip-syncing and/or dancing to existing music tracks. Chinese tech innovator and Tencent rival ByteDance had purchased Musical.ly for close to $1 billion in 2017, shut it down, and incorporated its technology into its already-operating China-based app Douyin, and the newly created TikTok for the rest of the world. Like other social media platforms, TikTok employed proprietary algorithms to mine and monetize the data related to its users' tastes and preferences.

As TikTok gained traction and then national attention in 2019 with the viral-propelled success of "Old Town Road," there were politically generated accusations of TikTok supplying consumer information to China. ByteDance insisted that TikTok's servers operated independently, were located in the US and Singapore, and had no exchange of consumer data with ByteDance. Nonetheless the Trump administration tried to force a sale of TikTok's US division to a domestic owner or force it to shut down. Bobby Allyn of NPR.org reported that on December 7, 2020, DC District Judge Carl Nichols "was the second judge to rule against the president's ban. . . . Despite talks aimed at safeguarding U.S. user data being hashed out in a separate process, Commerce Secretary Wilbur Ross continued to push for TikTok to be blacklisted in the U.S." Allyn then cited Judge Nichols's ruling, stating that "the Secretary did not consider any alternatives before effectively banning TikTok from the United States, nor did the Secretary articulate any justification (rational or otherwise) for failing to consider any such alternatives."[49]

In 2020 the approximately 68 million US Gen Z'ers ranged in age from eight to twenty-three. They were the first age group to have access to smartphones before entering their teens. Along with the younger millennials, they were the top targets for marketing new acts. Terry Collins's April 2021 USA Today analysis of a Pew Research survey on the COVID-19–related differences in digital consumption trends between different age groupings asked, "Have Social Platforms Reached Their Peak?" Collins observed, "The striking short-form viral videos and images of Instagram, Snapchat, and TikTok continue to climb in popularity with Gen Z."[50]

Collins also cited University of Buffalo associate communication professor Helen Wang, in describing Gen Z's affinity for these more interactive platforms. "They grew up immersed in rich media and they are naturally equipped with better digital media literacy skills to navigate across different platforms competently and nimbly. . . . So even though they might have started on these social media for fun, these social media channels can also be part of their digital toolbox and help with other purposes when needed."[51]

The skills described by Professor Wang became a major factor in TikTok's meteoric rise to reach $1.9 billion in revenue in 2020, a 457 percent increase over 2019's $350 million. According to research conducted by Rebecca Bellan for *Forbes*, TikTok led all social media apps with 82 million downloads to new users' smartphones in 2020. As described by Bellan, "The app makes it easy to create or binge-watch micro-entertainment, short vids dripping with pep and Moxy and serving up Gen Z realness. Videos often take the form of challenges that run the gamut of dance challenges . . . to multi-generational explorations of music. Tutorials and life hacks also tend to go viral, and users often joke that they learn more from TikTok than they do from school."[52] Trailing TikTok in new user accounts were Instagram with 57.5 million downloaded apps, Snapchat at 43 million, Facebook with 42 million, and Twitter at 25 million.

After millions of selfies and countless home videos taken with their smartphone cameras over the past dozen years, millennials and Gen Z'ers easily mastered the editing and production apps that accompanied TikTok's launch. Millions of them, along with the more digitally dexterous of the older age groupings, flocked to this participatory form of music consumption. TikTok clips still had the fifteen-second time limit that it had inherited from Musical.ly, but allowed up to four to be uploaded in tandem as a unified production with a one-minute limit, which was then extended to three minutes at the end of 2020.

The record labels, however, had their own set of tech-savvy millennials who recognized TikTok's marketing potential. They sponsored competitive dance contests created by a suddenly popular cadre of TikTok influencers who challenged consumers to create and post their own video versions. Also popular was TikTok's Duet function, which allowed users "to build on another user's video on TikTok by recording your own video alongside the original as it plays. It's a creative format for interacting with others' videos, building on existing stories, and creating new and unique content in collaboration with creators across the platform."[53]

Billboard deputy editor Andrew Unterberger queried "Can TikTok Rival MTV's Heyday For Gen-Z?" in a December 2020 column, suggesting that when music fans of the 1980s recall the top hits of the era such as Men at

Work's "Down Under," The Police's "Every Breath You Take," or Michael Jackson's "Billie Jean" they "almost certainly recall images of each song's music video, made unavoidable through heavy airplay on MTV. If you're a teenage music fan doing the same with 2020 No. 1s (Megan Thee Stallion and Beyoncé's 'Savage,' Doja Cat and Nicki Minaj's 'Say So,' 24kGoldn and iann dior's 'Mood'), you'd probably remember similar images. But rather than the artists' own videos, they'd be of viral dance challenges born on TikTok."[54]

Corey Sheridan, TikTok's head of music partnerships and content operations, told Unterberger that while MTV had the market to itself for a dozen years with no real competition, "TikTok has competition, will have competition, and its competition doesn't just come from its competitors, but from whatever we can't forecast that will be the new TikTok. . . . I hope a few years from now we can look back and say, 'This is the TikTok generation.'"[55]

At about the same time that Musical.ly morphed into TikTok, Facebook launched its new virtual reality (VR) headset Oculus Quest, which would become another competitor for the digital attention of Gen Z'ers. The Oculus was a self-contained portable gaming console encased within a set of enlarged opaque goggles with built-in speakers and attached hand controls. It quickly became a favorite for playing Epic Games' *Fortnite: Battle Royale*, which grew to over 350 million users worldwide by mid-2020 who competed in and then watched the ensuing series of tournaments that narrowed down to a single grand champion.

In June 2020 *Fortnite* added a radio to the cars used within the game featuring a curated playlist of top current hits titled Party Royale that included Justin Bieber, Ed Sheeran, Ariana Grande, Drake, Carly B, Bad Bunny, Marshmello, J. Belvin, and Post Malone. Three more stations were added in August: Beat Box had a hip hop slant, Power Play was Top 100 chart pop, while Radio Yonder was dance-oriented. All stations also appeared as playlists on DSPs. An improved Oculus Quest 2 with a better supply chain plan debuted in October and quickly became the top console in the VR market, selling over a million units through the end of the year generating $5.2 billion in 2020 sales, while gearing up for an even larger 2021.

Gazing at the Future through a Digital Crystal Ball

On December 31, 2020, the ball in Times Square dropped as usual with over fifty artists performing to millions of viewers over separate NBC, ABC, Fox, Univision, and CNN telecasts. But instead of the usual live audience of over a million holiday revelers, only the production crews and special guests were in attendance, appropriately masked and socially distanced, an emblematic conclusion to a disconcerting year for the live performance industry.

The worldwide shutdown had felt like the flipping of a massive circuit breaker, but with 2021 about to unfurl, the concert industry remained poised to turn the lights back on when they achieved the necessary level of vaccination and safety protocols to stack the odds against a premature reboot. As early as July 22 Goldman Sachs had revisited its May "The Show Must Go On" equity report to reflect the reality of when a return to touring was reasonable. "This will also lead to some events originally scheduled for 2021 being shifted to 2022, for which we estimate 40% growth implying a return to 94% of 2019 levels."[56]

Rolling Stone's Samantha Hissong reported in December that AEG CEO Jay Marciano hoped for a fall 2021 return, but not if audience capacity was limited through social distancing. He told Hissong, "We built an industry based upon selling out. . . . If all you're going to sell is 50 percent of tickets, nobody's making any money. Selling 85 percent of tickets is roughly the break-even." He also favored a national reopening rather than in regional stages. "It doesn't do us any good to have five states open and ten states closed. We really need the country to open at once."[57]

Meanwhile the record and publishing sectors had adjusted to the inconveniences of the pandemic and performed throughout 2020 according to, if not above, expectations. The personnel turmoil at the Recording Academy seemed to take a back seat once the pandemic hit. The Academy joined the rest of the industry in remote operations, but Harvey Mason Jr. and his staff continued to implement the suggestions from the task force in the pursuit of a step-up on the scale of accountability in its diversity policy.

The Grammy nominations announced at year's end reflected the Academy's stated efforts to lead in that pursuit whether the industry followed along or not. Beyoncé led the field with nine nominations; Taylor Swift and Dua Lipa garnered six each as did male nominee Roddy Ricch; Brittany Howard received five; and Phoebe Bridgers, Billie Eilish, and Megan Thee Stallion had four each, as did John Beasley, Justin Bieber, DaBaby, and David Frost. Record and Album of the Year nominations were both split between four females and four males. The eight Song of the Year nominations went to five females, two males, and a mixed-gender duo. Collectively these songs were written by a total of twenty-one males and twelve females. The Best New Artist nominees—Ingrid Andress, Phoebe Bridgers, Chika, Noah Cyrus, D Smoke, Doja Cat, Kaytranada, and Megan Thee Stallion—diversified in genre spanning rap, country, dance, indie rock, and indie pop, with six females out of the eight candidates. Producer of the Year nominees, however, were once again all male.

The rise in 2020 of TikTok and Oculus-*Fortnite* for discovering new music were not products of the pandemic, having been introduced before COVID-19. Although having Gen Z'ers at home helped feed their popularity, their market penetration was expected to continue when touring resumed and schools reopened. The use of demographically targeted music to attract young gamers had been going on for several decades through both the licensing of back catalog and custom recording.

By using current releases, however, both TikTok and *Fortnite* came to the attention of the label promotion departments. After the success of Lil Nas X with "Old Town Road," TikTok joined the pool of sources that influenced DSP playlists, shaped radio station rotations, and inspired on-demand streaming requests. They were in effect twenty-first-century parallels to FM radio in the 1960s and MTV in the 1980s. Songs played on *Fortnite*'s radio stations caught the attention of teens and young adults that in past generations would have been listening to Top 40 on actual car radios.

The technology fine-tuned as a part of livestreaming had raised home entertainment to new heights. Once concert venues reopened, livestreaming could add an opportunity for those who could not afford the time or cost involved in attending concerts, but nonetheless wanted to experience the inherent energy of being there. For these fans, a small gathering in a home theater with large-screen television, immersive or 5.1 surround sound delivered in Hi-Res twenty-four-bit audio files, and video produced on large-format digital cinema cameras might well be ideal for a one-degree-of-separation alternative.

Combining an Oculus-type VR experience with multiple-camera switching access as suggested by Michael Rapino could well be the next step in merging extended reality (XR) with the livestream experience. Livestreaming might also help alleviate the supply-and-demand issues associated with the number of tickets limited by the number of seats in a limited number of venues. Livestreaming could offer worldwide, real-time market penetration for a greater number of viewers at a more affordable cost to generate a large amount of ancillary revenue.

TikTok, video gaming, livestreaming, and other digital developments over the course of 2020 offered expanded revenue opportunities. Consequentially the record labels and publishers had extended their web of licensing into these new areas on a global basis, hoping to drive revenue and royalties to higher levels. This growth, both already achieved and anticipated for the future, pleased the investment community, further validating the UMG and WMG IPOs as well as the catalog roll-ups of Hipgnosis, BMG, Round Hill, Primary Wave, Reservoir, and the other rights aggregators.

By the time this book reaches readers' hands, the economic issues that accompanied the pandemic will most likely be resolved, or be on the way to resolution, and the technological advances that emerged either implemented, expanded, altered, or abandoned, with even more led by the rapidly developing artificial intelligence (AI) already on the horizon. All this will be decided by how they fit into the future flow of consumer spending and licensing fees that pass through the hands of the music industry into the pockets of the creative community. At the onset of 2021, however, vaccinations were just beginning, the protocol for resuming live performance was still in development, and a full touring schedule was still a year or more away.

The genres that had increased market share and chart position during the transition from sales to streams reflected the globalization of the entire industry. K-pop emerged as a worldwide phenomenon on the scale of the boy bands of the late 1990s. Spanish-speaking artists with diverse styles long grouped together in the eponymous Latin category now flourished in the worldwide market on an equal footing with rock, rap, R&B, and EDM. Hit-making producers and songwriters from the Swedish pop scene had become omnipresent on the global charts. Singer-songwriters and legacy legends as well as indie bands found it much easier to reach their audiences through streaming than they had been able to do during the waning days of the brick-and-mortar retail infrastructure. The country genre widened its lyrical content, edging a little more toward pop to better blend into the new world of global playlists. The rising tide of streaming had truly worked its magic, lifting all involved to higher revenue levels.

If past, however, is indeed prologue, then the weekly charts and year-end summaries will remain the barometers of music consumption with careers depending upon the readings. With over 6 billion smartphones in the world but less than a 10 percent market penetration for subscription music services at the end of 2020, streaming will continue to expand in audience and revenue. New digital technologies, both those already implemented and those only imagined, will widen existing revenue and generate additional revenue streams to flow through the financial, administrative, and marketing engine of the music industry.

Even a year or more of empty stages could not silence the creative flow or diminish consumer enthusiasm. The basic, organic relationship between a unique performance, whether live or replicated for on-demand access, and the emotion it stirs, will continue to be the foundation of a thriving music business far into the future.

Acronyms

1G	First Generation
2G	Second Generation
3G	Third Generation
5G	Fifth Generation
A&R	Artist and Repertoire
AAC	MP4 Advanced Audio Coding digital file
AB	*Amusement Business*
ABC	American Broadcasting Company
ABC	Associated Booking Corporation
AARC	Alliance of Artists and Recording Companies
AC	Adult Contemporary
ACPA	Anti-Cybersquatting Consumer Protection Act
ADA	Alternative Distribution Alliance
AEC	Alliance Entertainment Corporation
AEG	Anschutz Entertainment Group
AFM	American Federation of Musicians
AFTRA	American Federation of Television and Radio Artists
AGI	Artists Group International
AHRA	Audio Home Recording Act of 1992
AI	Artificial Intelligence
AIMP	Association of Independent Music Publishers
ALAC	Apple Lossless Audio Codec
AMEX	American Express
AMRA	American Mechanical Rights Association
AOR	Album-oriented Radio
APA	Agency for the Performing Arts
API	Application Programming Interface
APM	Associated Production Music
AS/ER	Artist Services and Expanded Rights
ASCAP	American Society of Composers, Authors and Publishers
ATI	American Talent International
AWAL	Artists Without a Label Limited
B2B	Business to Business
BDS	Broadcast Data Systems
BET	Black Entertainment Television
BIN	*Billboard* Information Network
BMG	Bertelsmann Music Group
BMI	Broadcast Music, Inc.
BPI	Billboard Publications, Inc.

BUMA/STEMRA	*Vereniging Buma/Stichting Stemra* (Buma Association/Stemra Foundation)—Holland
CAA	Creative Artists Agency
CAE	Compositeur Auteur Editeùr
CARES	Coronavirus Aid, Relief, and Economic Security Act
CARP	Copyright Arbitration Royalty Panel
CBBS	Computerized Bulletin Board System
CBS	Columbia Broadcasting System
CCC	Clear Channel Communications
CCE	Clear Channel Entertainment
CD	Compact Disc
CDC	Control Data Corporation
CDMA	Code Division Multiple Access
CEMA	Capitol, EMI, Manhattan, and Angel
CES	Consumer Electronics Show
CHR	Contemporary Hit Radio
CIS	Common Information System
CISAC	*Confédération Internationale des Sociétés d'Auteurs et Compositeurs* (International Confederation of Societies of Authors and Composers)
CMA	Country Music Association
CMC	Cable Music Channel
CMA	Creative Management Associates
CMHOF	Country Music Hall of Fame and Museum
CMT	Country Music Television
CMO	Collective Management Organization
CMPA	Church Music Publisher's Association
CPI	Consumer Price Index
CPI	Concert Productions International
CRT	Cathode Ray Tube
DARPA	Defense Advanced Research Projects Agency
DART	Digital Audio Recording Technologies Fund
DAT	Digital Audiotape
DBMS	Database Management System
dcc	dick clark company
DiMA	Digital Media Association
DIY	Do It Yourself
DLC	Digital Licensing Coordinator
DMA	Designated Market Areas
DMCA	Digital Millennium Copyright Act
DOCSIS	Data Over Cable Service Interface Specification
DOJ	Department of Justice
DPRA	Digital Performance Right in Sound Recordings Act of 1995
DRM	Digital Rights Management
DSP	Digital Service Provider

DVD	Digital Video Disc
DVD-A	Digital Video Disc-Audio
EBITDA	Earnings Before Interest, Taxes, Depreciation, and Amortization
EDM	Electronic Dance Music
EEC	European Economic Community
EEOC	Equal Employment Opportunity Commission
EMD	EMI Music Distribution
EMMS	Electronic Music Management System
FCC	Federal Communications Commission
FLAC	Free Lossless Audio Codec
FRC	Federal Radio Commission
FTC	Federal Trade Commission
FTDA	Federal Trademark Dilution Act
FTP	File Transfer Protocol
GAC	General Artist Corporation
GATT	General Agreement on Tariffs and Trade
GB	Gigabyte
GEMA	*Gesellschaft für Musikalische Aufführungs- und Mechanische Vervielfältigungsrechte* (Society For Musical Performing and Mechanical Reproduction Rights)—Germany
GMR	Global Music Rights
GPS	Global Positioning System
GSM	Global System for Mobile Communications
GTA	General Talent Agency
HBO	Home Box Office
HFA	Harry Fox Agency
HOB	House of Blues
HSDPA	High Speed Downlink Packet Access
HTTP	Hypertext Transfer Protocol
HTML	Hypertext Markup Language
IAB	Interactive Advertising Bureau
IAC	InterActiveCorp
ICANN	Internet Corporation for Assigned Names and Numbers
ICM	International Creative Management
IDS	Integrated Database System
IEC	International Electronical Commission
IFA	International Famous Agency
IFPI	International Federation of the Phonographic Industry
ILG	Independent Label Group
ILS	Independent Label Services
iOS	iPhone Operating System
IP	Intellectual Property
IP	Internet Protocol
IPI/CAE	Interested Parties Information/*Compositeur Auteur Editeur* (Composer Author Publisher)

IPO	Independent Promoters Organization
IPO	Initial Public Offering
IRC	Internet Relay Chat
ISO	International Organization for Standardization
ISP	Internet Service Provider
ISRC	International Standard Recording Code
ISWC	International Standard Musical Work Code
ITG	International Talent Group
KBPS	Kilobits Per Second
KCL	Kobalt Capital Ltd
kHz	Kilohertz
KLS	Kobalt Label Services
KMC	Kobalt Music Copyrights
LIMA	Licensing Industry Merchandisers' Association
LNA	Live Nation Artists
LOC	Library of Congress
M&C	Music & Copyright
MAP	Minimum Advertised Price
MB	Megabyte
MBPS	Megabit Per Second
MBW.com	MusicBusinessWide.com
MCA	Music Corporation of America
MCPS	Mechanical Copyright Protection Society
MFN	Most Favored Nations
MIDEM	*Marché International du Disque et de l'Édition Musicale* (International Record and Music Publishing Market)—France
MIT	Massachusetts Institute of Technology
MLC	Mechanical Licensing Collective
MMA	Music Modernization Act
MOR	Middle of the Road
MPA	Music Publishers Association
MP3	MPEG Audio Layer-3
MPEG	Moving Picture Experts Group
MRC	Media Rights Capital
MSG	Madison Square Garden
MSGE	Madison Square Garden Entertainment
MTV	Music Television
MUSIC	Music United for Strong Internet Copyright
MTI	Music Theater International
NAB	National Association of Broadcasters
NAIRD	National Association of Independent Record Distributors
NAMM	National Association of Music Manufacturers
NARAS	National Academy of Recording Arts and Sciences (The Recording Academy)
NARM	National Association of Recording Merchandisers

NASDAQ	National Association of Securities Dealers Automated Quotations
NAV	Net Asset Value
NBC	National Broadcasting Company
NET Act	No Electronic Theft Act
NMPA	National Music Publishers' Association
NPS	Net Publishing Share
NSAI	Nashville Songwriters Association International
NTIA	National Telecommunications and Information Administration
NYSE	New York Stock Exchange
OCILLA	Online Copyright Infringement Liability Limitation Act
OIBDA	Operating Income before Depreciation and Amortization
OVG	Oak View Group
P&D	Pressing & Distribution
P2P	Peer to Peer
PA	Public Address
PC	Personal Computer
PDA	Personal Data Assistant
PMA	Production Music Association
PMC	Penske Media Corporation
PMRC	Parents Music Resource Center
PMRC	Penske Media Rights Corporation
PPD	Published Price to Dealer
PPL	Phonographic Performance Ltd
PPP	Payroll Protection Program
PRO	Performing Rights Organization
PRS	(British) Performing Right Society
PwC	PricewaterhouseCoopers
QBC	Queen Booking Corp.
R&B	Rhythm & Blues
RAB	Radio Advertising Bureau
RAC	Recording Artists Coalition
RAM	Random Access Memory
RCA	Radio Corporation of America
RED	Relativity Entertainment Distribution
RFID	Radio Frequency Identification
RIAA	Recording Industry Association of America
RIM	Research In Motion
RLG	RCA Label Group
RMLC	Radio Music License Committee
ROI	Return On Investment
RPM	Revolutions Per Minute
RNS	Rabid Neurosis
SACD	Super Audio CD
SACEM	*Société des Auteurs, Compositeurs et Éditeurs de Musique* (Society of Authors, Composers and Music Publishers) (France)

SCMS	Serial Copy Management System
SDMI	Secure Digital Music Initiative
SESAC	Society of European Stage Authors and Composers
SGA	Songwriters Guild of America
SHOF	Songwriters Hall of Fame
SHVIA	Satellite Home Viewer Improvement Act of 1999
SIAE	*Società Italiana degli Autori ed Editori* (Italian Society of Authors and Publishers) (Italy)
SMS	Short Message Service
SRF	Sound Recordings Fund
SRLP	Suggested Retail List Price
STIM	*Svenska Tonsättares Internationella Musikbyrå* (Swedish Performing Rights Society)—Sweden
SUISA	Swiss Cooperative Society for Music Authors and Publishers—Switzerland
SVOG	Shuttered Venue Operators Grant
SWSA	Small Webcaster Settlement Act of 2002
TAC	Total Album Consumption
TARP	Troubled Asset Relief Program
TCP/IP	Transmission Control Protocol and the Internet Protocol
THR	The Hollywood Reporter
TNA	The Next Adventure
TNN	The Nashville Network
TRIPS	Trade-Related Aspects of Intellectual Property Rights
TRS	Ticket Reservation Systems
UCC	Universal Copyright Coalition
UMG	Universal Music Group
UMPG	Universal Music Publishing Group
URAA	Uruguay Round Agreements Act
URL	Uniform Resource Locator
USB	Universal Serial Bus
UTA	United Talent Agency
VH-1	Video Hits One
VNU	*Verenigde Nederlandse Uitgeverijen* (United Dutch Publishers)—Holland
WBP	Warner Bros. Publications
WCI	Warner Communications, Inc.
WEA	Warner Elektra Atlantic
WIPO	World Intellectual Property Organization
WMA	William Morris Agency
WMA	Windows Media Audio
WME	William Morris Endeavor
WMG	Warner Music Group
WTO	World Trade Organization
WWW	World Wide Web

Notes

Prologue: Part One

1. The Dolphin Music Group, "The Condon Collection," promotional brochure circa 1990.
2. The Dolphin Music Group, "The Condon Collection."
3. Russell Sanjek, *American Popular Music and Its Business*, vol. 3, *The First Four Hundred Years* (New York: Oxford University Press, 1988), 39.
4. Burt A. Folkart, "Singer Snooky Lanson; Starred on 'Hit Parade,'" *Los Angeles Times*, July 4, 1990, *Singer Snooky Lanson; Starred on "Hit Parade." Los Angeles Times (latimes.com)*.
5. Russell Sanjek, "Americans Are Making More Music and Listening to More Music than Ever Before in History," BMI ad in *Billboard*, January 25, 1964, 25.

Prologue: Part Two

1. Alan Cross, "Where Did the Phrase 'Sex, Drugs and Rock 'n' Roll' Actually Come From?" ajournalofrockthings.com, April 6, 2016, Alan Cross, *Where Did the Phrase "Sex, Drugs and Rock'n'Roll" Actually Come From? (ajournalofmusicalthings.com)*.

Chapter 1

1. Mark Lander, "The Media Business; Big Severance Deal Seen at Warner Music," *New York Times*, July 7, 1995, The Media Business; Big Severance Deal Seen at Warner Music, *The New York Times* (nytimes.com).
2. Fred Goodman, "The Rolling Stone Interview: Walter Yetnikoff," *Rolling Stone*, December 15, 1988, The Rolling Stone Interview: Walter Yetnikoff.
3. Rafly Giland, "The Rise & Fall of Milli Vanilli: The Duo Who's Never Really Sung," thethings.com, April 7, 2020, The Rise & Fall of Milli Vanilli: The Duo Who's Never Really Sung (thethings.com).
4. Michael Cieply and Steve Hochman, "Azoff Resigns as Head of MCA Music Unit to Form Own Firm," *Los Angeles Times*, September 6, 1989, Azoff Resigns as Head of MCA Music Unit to Form Own Firm, *Los Angeles Times* (latimes.com).
5. Irv Lichtman, "Three Partners Bank on Music Publishing," *Billboard*, December 20, 1986, 4.
6. Alan Citron, "Q&A with Joe Smith: He Brought Us Jimi, Bonnie and the Dead, Gratefully," *Los Angeles Times*, March 31, 1993, Q&A with Joe Smith: He Brought Us Jimi, Bonnie and the Dead, Gratefully, Los Angeles Times (latimes.com).

Chapter 2

1. Billboard Staff, "Billboard's Guide to Record Co. Promotion," *Billboard*, July 12, 1986, 68.

2. Walter Yetnikoff and David Ritz, *Howling at the Moon: The Odyssey of a Monstrous Music Mogul in an Age of Excess* (London: Abacus, 2005), 112–13.

3. Yetnikoff Ritz, *Howling at the Moon*, 113.

4. Irv Lichtman and Sam Sutherland, "Capitol, MCA Drop Indies; RIAA Subpoenaed," *Billboard*, March 8, 1986, 1.

5. Lichtman and Sutherland, "Capitol, MCA Drop Indies," 1.

6. Lichtman and Sutherland, "Capitol, MCA Drop Indies," 1.

7. Fred Goodman, "Labels Adjust for Post-Indie Era," *Billboard*, July 12, 1986, 1.

8. Goodman, "Labels Adjust for Post-Indie Era," 1.

9. Chuck Philips, "EMI Hires Controversial Promoter," *Los Angeles Times*, March 4, 1993, EMI Hires Controversial Promoter: Records: Alfred DiSipio Quit the Business After the Payola Scandals of the Mid-'80s. Now He's Caused a Stir by Resurfacing as a Consultant, *Los Angeles Times* (latimes.com).

10. Fred Goodman, "Azoff Takes No Prisoners: Blasts Industry at NARM Convention," *Billboard*, March 22, 1986, 1.

11. Goodman, "Azoff Takes No Prisoners," 1.

12. Goodman, "Azoff Takes No Prisoners," 1.

13. George Anastasia, "Godfather of Rock and Roll," *Jersey Man Magazine*, July, 1, 2022, Godfather of Rock and Roll, *Jersey Man Magazine*.

14. Chuck Philips, "Rock 'n' Roll Revolutionaries: SoundScan's Mike Shalett and Mike Fine," *Los Angeles Times*, December 8, 1991, Rock 'n' Roll Revolutionaries: SoundScan's Mike Shalett and Mike Fine Have Shaken Up the Record Industry with a Radical Concept: Accurate Sales Figures, *Los Angeles Times* (latimes.com).

15. Marc Ferris, "IN BUSINESS; On the Charts," *New York Times*, July 8, 2001, IN BUSINESS; On the Charts, *The New York Times* (nytimes.com).

16. Ferris, "IN BUSINESS; On the Charts," IN BUSINESS; On the Charts, *The New York Times* (nytimes.com).

17. Kees Immink, "How We Made the Compact Disc," *Nature Electronics*, April 17, 1918, How We Made the Compact Disc (researchgate.net).

18. Ed Christman, "Metromedia Deal Makes a Fruitful Alliance for Bianco," *Billboard*, December 12, 1995, 90.

Chapter 3

1. Don Passman, *All You Need to Know About the Music Business*, 10th ed. (New York: Simon & Schuster, 2019), 264–65.

2. Irv Lichtman, "Annual NMPA Meeting Hears Good News; Harry Fox Revenues Hit Record High," *Billboard*, June 29, 1985, 4.

3. Irv Lichtman, "Worldwide Pub Revenues Hit $3 Bil in 1989," *Billboard*, October 6, 1990, 4.

4. Lichtman, "Worldwide Pub Revenues Hit $3 Bil In 1989," 4.

5. Lichtman, "Worldwide Pub Revenues Hit $3 Bil In 1989," 4.

6. Frank DiCostanzo, "Print Music Strikes Profitable Chord: For Record Stores, It's a Growth Area," *Billboard*, September 24, 1994, 64.

7. The Retail Print Music Dealers Association, "The Voice of the American Print Music Industry: Resources," printmusic.org/resources. As of September 1, 2021, Resources: Retail Print Music Dealers Association.

8. Russell Sanjek, *American Popular Music and Its Business*, vol. 3, *The First Four Hundred Years* (New York: Oxford University Press, 1988), 619.

9. Kembrew McLeod and Peter DiCola, *Creative License: Digital Sampling and the Law* (Durham, NC: Duke University Press, 2011), 166.

Chapter 4

1. Paul Virello, "Frank Barsalona, Pioneering Rock Agent Dies at 74," *The New York Times*, November 28, 2012, Frank Barsalona, Rock 'n' Roll Concert Promoter, Dies at 74, The New York Times (nytimes.com)

2. David McGee, "Bruce Springsteen Reclaims the Future," *Rolling Stone*, August 11, 1977, Bruce Springsteen Reclaims the Future (rollingstone.com).

3. Jordan Runtagh, "Farm Aid Grows: How John Mellencamp Is Continuing the 31-Year Crusade for Family Farmers," *People*, September 16, 2016, Farm Aid Grows: How John Mellencamp Is Continuing the 31-Year Crusade for Family Farmers (yahoo.com).

4. Chris Willman, "Why Are the Eagles So Hated? An Explainer on the Immensely Popular Yet Divisive Rock Band," *Billboard*, January 20, 2016, Why Are the Eagles So Hated? An Explainer on the Immensely Popular Yet Divisive Rock Band, *Billboard*.

5. Ray Waddell, "Making 'History': The Eagles' Legacy as the Billion-Dollar Road Band," Billboard, January 26, 2016, Making 'History': The Eagles' Legacy as the Billion-Dollar Road Band, Billboard

6. Waddell, "Making 'History,'" Making 'History': The Eagles' Legacy as the Billion-Dollar Road Band, Billboard.

7. Rich Cohen, "Tour De Force: The Rolling Stones Rake It in and Rock the House," *Rolling Stone*, November 3, 1994, Tour De Force: The Rolling Stones Rake It in and Rock the House.

Chapter 5

1. Bloomberg Business News, "Microsoft Co-founder Paul Allen Buys Control of Ticketmaster," *Bloomberg News*, November 23, 1993. Microsoft Co-Founder Paul Allen Buys Control of Ticketmaster (chicagotribune.com).

2. Eric Boehlert, "Billboard Concert Crossroads: Pearl Jam Maps Tour Minus Ticketmaster," *Billboard*, April 15, 1995, 1.

3. Boehlert, "Billboard Concert Crossroads: Pearl Jam Maps Tour Minus Ticketmaster," 1.

4. Kerry Segrave, *Ticket Scalping: An American History, 1850–2005* (Jefferson, NC: McFarland & Company, 2007), 215.

5. Segrave, *Ticket Scalping*, 215.

6. Segrave, *Ticket Scalping*, 216.

7. Segrave, *Ticket Scalping*, 216.

8. Segrave, *Ticket Scalping*, 216.

9. Raina Douris, "The First 100 Videos Played on MTV," npr.com, July 30, 2021, The First 100 Videos Played on MTV, NPR.

10. Fred Goodman, "Azoff Takes No Prisoners: Blasts Industry at NARM Convention," *Billboard*, March 22, 1986, 82.

11. Kory Grow, "PMRC's 'Filthy 15': Where Are They Now?" *Rolling Stone*, September 17, 2015, PMRC's 'Filthy 15': Where Are They Now? rollingstone.com).

12. Jon Wiederhorn, "Sex, Violence, Cursing: Explicit Lyrics Stickers Get Explicit," *MTV News*, June 3, 2002, Sex, Violence, Cursing: Explicit Lyrics Stickers Get Explicit, MTV.com.

13. *The New York Times*, "Tipper Gore Widens War on Rock," January 4, 1988, Tipper Gore Widens War on Rock, *The New York Times* (nytimes.com).

14. *The New York Times*, "Tipper Gore Widens War on Rock."

15. *The New York Times*, "Tipper Gore Widens War on Rock."

16. Chilton Research Services, "1995 Consumer Profile Report," *Recording Industry Association of America*, RIAA 1998 Consumer Statistics (vision-multimedia.qc.ca)

17. Clayton M. Christensen and Joseph Bowers, "Disruptive Technologies: Catching the Wave," *Harvard Business Journal*, January–February 1995, Disruptive Technologies: Catching the Wave (hbr.org).

Chapter 6

1. Jeff Clark-Meads, "EMI Music to Stand Alone: 'Maxi' Offer Could Spur Sale," *Billboard*, March 2, 1996, 1.

2. Sally Pook and George Trefgarne, "Undignified Ending to Reign of the Queen of Rock and Roll," *The Telegraph*, October 25, 2001, Undignified Ending to Reign of the Queen of Rock and Roll (telegraph.co.uk).

3. Chris Morris, Ed Christman, Don Jeffries, Jeff Clark-Meads, and Adam White, "EMD's Bach Replaced by U.K. Executive," *Billboard*, July 5, 1997, 1.

4. Morris, Christman, Jeffries, Clark-Meads, White, "EMD's Bach Replaced by U.K. Executive," 1.

5. *Billboard*, "The Road to 'Unigram': A Chronology of Significant Events," December 19, 1998, 75.

6. Don Jeffrey, "A New Universal Emerges as a Global Force: Morris' Team Puts Plans into Action," *Billboard*, December 19, 1998, 75.

7. Andrew Pollack, "Warner Music Group Gets New Chief," *New York Times*, August 17, 1999, Warner Music Group Gets New Chief: The New York Times (nytimes.com).

8. Seth Sutel, "AOL Buys Time Warner for $162 Billion," *ABCNews*, January 10, 2000, AOL Buys Time Warner for $162 Billion (journaltimes.com).

9. Wolfgang Spahr, "Middelhoff: 'How to React to Napster,'" *Billboard*, September 2, 2000, 1.

10. Mike Bielenberg, "The Single Richest Man the Music Business Has Ever Produced," *MusicRevolution.com*, November 6, 2015, The Single Richest Man the Music Business Has Ever Produced, Blog.musicrevolution.com Blogs.

11. Mark Coatney, "Person of the Week: Jean-Marie Messier," *Time*, July 5, 2002, Person of the Week: Jean-Marie Messier, TIME.

12. Jamey Keaten and Franklin Paul, "Vivendi Toasts Seagram," *CNNMoney*, June 20,2000, Vivendi to Buy Seagram, Deal Creates World's No. 2 Media Company (cnn.com).

13. Tim Arrango, "How the AOL-Time Warner Merger Went So Wrong," *New York Times*, January 10, 2010, How the AOL-Time Warner Merger Went So Wrong, The New York Times (nytimes.com).

14. Rita Gunther McGrath, "15 Years Later, Lessons from the Failed AOL-Time Warner Merger," *Fortune*, January 10, 2015, 15 Years Later, Lessons from the Failed AOL-Time Warner Merger, *Fortune*.

15. Paul Bond, "Gerald Levin Apologizes for AOL-TW Merger," *The Hollywood Reporter*, January 4, 2010, Gerald Levin Apologizes for AOL-TW Merger, The Hollywood Reporter.

16. Rumor Mill, "Lisa Ellis Gets EVP Stripes," *Hits*, December 7, 2006, LLisa Ellis Gets EVP Stripes, HITS Daily Double.

Chapter 7

1. Sony.com, "High-Resolution Audio vs. CDs vs. MP3s," website as of August 19, 2020, *Sony Sound Quality Comparison of Hi-Res Audio vs. CD vs. MP3*.

2. Robert G. Woletz, "POP MUSIC; Technology Gives the Charts a Fresh Spin," *New York Times*, January 26, 1992, POP MUSIC; Technology Gives the Charts a Fresh Spin, *The New York Times (nytimes.com)*.

3. Ed Christman, "Clubs Scale Back Freebies, Employees," *Billboard*, April 14, 2001, 3.

4. Brett Atwood, "Web Music Sales Expected to Soar," *Billboard*, June 21, 1997, 6.

5. Hilary Rosen, "Commentary: Net Community Must Respect Music Biz," *Billboard*, July 5, 1997, 4.

6. Robert Conlin, "Faucet Opened: Liquid Audio Adds New Distribution, Releases," *E-Commerce*, September 3, 1999, Faucet Opened: Liquid Audio Adds New Distribution, Releases (ecommercetimes.com).

7. Conlin, "Faucet Opened."

8. Ed Christman, "Sony Distribution to Raise MAP By $1," *Billboard*, March 22, 1997, 3.

9. Sdmi.org, The Secure Digital Music Initiative (SDMI) Website, as of May 18, 2001, *SDMI, Home (archive.org)*.

10. Leonardo Chiariglione, "Riding the Media Bits: Opening Content Protection," public email from Chiarigleone.org, November 9, 2001. *Opening Content Protection, Riding the Media Bits (chiariglione.org)*.

11. Don Jeffrey, "Label Execs Assess Results of Digital-Delivery Music Test, *Billboard*, February 19, 2000, 3.

12. Brian Garrity, "Distant Profits or 'Pipe Dreams'?" *Billboard*, November 24, 2001, 1.

13. Penelope Patsuris, "Other Labels Must Follow EMI's Lead," *Forbes*, October 2, 2001, Other Labels Must Follow EMI's Lead (forbes.com).

14. Garrity, "Distant Profits or 'Pipe Dreams'?" 1.

15. Garrity, "Distant Profits or 'Pipe Dreams'?" 1.

16. Brian Garrity, "Digital Services Need to Offer More Hit Music," *Billboard*, May 4, 2002, 48.

17. Garrity, "Digital Services Need to Offer More Hit Music," 48.

18. Garrity, "Digital Services Need to Offer More Hit Music," 48.

19. Stephen Witt, *How Music Got Free: The End of an Industry, the Turn of the Century, and the Patient Zero of Piracy* (New York: Viking Press 2015), 252.

20. 104th Cong Rec., "Public Law 104-104-Telecommunications Act of 1996," February 8, 1996, *Public Law 104-104-Telecommunications Act of 1996" (govinfo.gov)*.

21. Radio Advertising Bureau, "Annual Revenue (in Billions) 1945–2014."

22. Gary Graff, "The Year Radio Woke Up," *Billboard*, December 23, 2006, 26.

23. Graff, "The Year Radio Woke Up," 26.

24. Anastasia Tsioulcas, "The Life and Death of Tower Records, Revisited," NPR, October 20, 2015, *The Life and Death of Tower Records, Revisited, NPR, The Record.*
25. Tsioulcas, "The Life and Death of Tower Records, Revisited."
26. Brian Garrity, "The Music Industry Big 10," *Billboard*, December 23, 2006, 11.

Chapter 8

1. Phil Gallo, "BMI Swan Song Cued Up for Topper Preston," *Variety*, April 4, 2104, BMI Swan Song Cued Up for Topper Preston (variety.com).
2. Susan Butler, "Harry Fox Agency Synching Up? Mechanical Rights Agency Eyes New Opportunities" *Billboard*, August 18, 2007, 20.
3. Susan Butler, "Top Publishing Exec Splits EMI: Bandier's Departure Sure to Mark a Cultural Shift," *Billboard*, November 11, 2006, 8.
4. "Our Company: Meet Kobalt," https://www.kobaltmusic.com/who-we-are/, accessed September 1, 2022, Who We Are, Kobalt Music.
5. Kevin Gray, "Kobalt Changed the Rules of the Music Industry Using Data—and Saved It," *Wired.com*, May 1, 2015, https://www.wired.co.uk/article/kobalt-how-data-saved-music.,
6. Phil Gallo, "EverGreen Grows Global: Kick Off Worldwide Publishing Company," *Variety*, January 22, 2006, EverGreen Grows Global (variety.com).
7. "Inside WIPO: What Is WIPO," WIPO.int/about.wipo, accessed September 1, 2020, WIPO Lex.
8. Digital Millennium Copyright Act, October 28, 1998, The Digital Millennium Copyright Act of 1998.
9. No Electric Theft Act, December 16, 1997, PLAW-105publ147.pdf (govinfo.gov).
10. Peter H. Lewis, "Judge Rejects Computer-Crime Indictment," *New York Times*, December 31, 1994, *Judge Rejects Computer-Crime Indictment, The New York Times* (nytimes.com).
11. *Cybersquatting and Consumer Protection: Ensuring Domain Name Integrity: Hearing on S. 1255,1st Session before the Comm. on the Judiciary United States Senate*, 106th Cong. (1999), Cybersquatting and Consumer Protection: Ensuring Domain Name Integrity (govinfo.gov).
12. Cybersquatting and Consumer Protection.
13. WIPO Arbitration and Mediation Center, "Administrative Panel Decision, Madonna Ciccone, p/k/a Madonna v. Dan Parisi and 'Madonna.com,'" October 12, 2000, *WIPO Domain Name Decision: D2000-0847.*
14. Bill Holland, "Steps Taken Toward Reversal of New Law," *Billboard*, July 29, 2000, 1.
15. Holland, "Steps Taken Toward Reversal of New Law."
16. Benny Evangelista, "Napster Runs Out of Lives: Judge Rules Against Sale," *San Francisco Chronicle*, September 4, 2002, *Napster Runs out of Lives—Judge Rules Against Sale (sfgate.com).*
17. Letter from Hilary Rosen, to Michael Robertson, "RIAA Sues MP3.com," *CMJ New Music Report*, February 7, 2000, CMJ New Music Report, Google Books.
18. Eileen Fitzpatrick, "RIAA Suit vs. MP3.com Raises 'Fair Use' Issues," *Billboard*, February 5, 2000, 10.
19. Eileen Fitzpatrick, "MP3.com Suit Questions Actions of the RIAA," *Billboard*, February 19, 2000, 1.
20. Fitzpatrick, "MP3.com Suit Questions Actions of the RIAA," 1.

21. Eileen Fitzpatrick, "RIAA Suit vs. MP3com Raises 'Fair Use' Issues," 10.

22. Eileen Fitzpatrick, "RIAA Suit vs. MP3com Raises 'Fair Use' Issues," 10.

23. Phillip R. Bagley, *Extension of Programming Language Concepts*, Air Force Office of Aerospace Research (Gaithersburg, MD: National Bureau of Standards, Institute for Applied Technology, 1968), AD0680815.pdf (dtic.mil).

24. Jeff Clark-Meads, "Cannes Accord Welcomed: Deal a Relief for U.S. Publishers," *Billboard*, February 8, 1997, 4.

25. Jeff Clark-Meads, "Global Confab to Unite Copyright Execs: Goal Is to Iron Out Int'l Performance Royalty Issues," *Billboard*, April 19, 1997, 8.

26. Clark-Meads, "Cannes Accord Welcomed," 4.

27. Jeff Clark-Meads, "CISAC Congress Sees Bodies Form Group to Move on CIS," *Billboard*, September 19, 1998, 8.

28. Marilyn A. Gillen, "Rights Societies Make Web Plan," *Billboard*, October 7, 2000, 1.

29. "50 Years of Protecting Intellectual Property Rights: Suisa Mechanlizenz," *Billboard*, November 6, 1976, C-48.

30. Lars Brandle, "Paris-based Publishers' Society CISAC Has Launched a Database of Musical Works That Will Connect Its 209 Member Societies," *Billboard Newsline: The International Week in Brief*, February 14, 2004, 54.

31. Brandle, "Paris-based Publishers' Society CISAC Has Launched a Database of Musical Works That Will Connect Its 209 Member Societies," 54.

Chapter 9

1. Don Passman, *All You Need To Know About the Music Business*" (New York: Simon & Schuster, 2019), 78.

2. Passman, *All You Need to Know About the Music Business*, 78.

3. Chuck Taylor and Melinda Newman, "SFX Buys Promoter Delsener/Slater," *Billboard*, October 26, 1996, 90.

4. Melinda Newman, "Indie Concert Promo Biz Reshaped by SFX's Rise," *Billboard*, September 4, 1999, 105.

5. Newman, "Indie Concert Promo Biz Reshaped by SFX's Rise," 105.

6. Ray Waddell, "SFX, Clear Channel Re-sculpting Music-Biz Landscape: Is New Entity Savvy Strategist or Scary Octopus?" *Billboard*, August 12, 2000, 78.

7. Waddell, "SFX, Clear Channel Re-sculpting Music Biz Landscape," 78.

8. Waddell, "SFX, Clear Channel Re-sculpting Music Biz Landscape," 78.

9. Ray Waddell, "The Concert Master: Michael Rapino Sets Out to Reshape the Future for Clear Channel," *Billboard*, May 7, 2005, 25.

10. Ray Waddell, "Clear Channel to Spin Off Concert Biz," *Billboard*, May 14, 2005, 21.

11. Ray Waddell, "Concerts West Deal Boosts AEG," *Billboard*, December 26, 2000, 1.

12. Waddell, "Concerts West Deal Boosts AEG," 1.

13. Charles Duhigg, "House of Blues Sold to Live Nation," *Los Angeles Times*, July 6, 2006. House of Blues Sold to Live Nation, Los Angeles Times (latimes.com).

14. Duhigg, "House of Blues Sold to Live Nation."

15. Duhigg, "House of Blues Sold to Live Nation."

16. Bob Allen, "The Year in Touring: How The Charts Are Compiled," *Billboard*, December 29, 2001, YT-4.

17. Melinda Newman, "I Pull Rabbits Out of Hats:' CAA's Rob Light on the Talent Agency's Magic Touch," *Billboard*, January 12, 2019, CAA's Rob Light on the Talent Agency's Magic Touch, *Billboard*.

18. Melinda Newman, "NARAS Enters a Post-Greene Era," *Billboard*, May 11, 2002, 8.

Chapter 10

1. Andrew Hampp, "Clear Channel's Pittman, 'We Have to Make the Digital Revolution Come to Radio,'" *Ad Age*, April 7, 2011, Clear Channel's Pittman: 'We Have to Make the Digital Revolution Come to Radio,'" Ad Age.

2. Bob Dylan, vocalist, "Subterranean Homesick Blues," by Bob Dylan, recorded January 14, 1965, track 1 on *Bringing It All Back Home*, Columbia Records, 43242, WebVoyage Record View 1 (loc.gov).

3. Mike Hennessey, "Piracy: Counting the Real Cost, *Billboard*, January 24, 1987, 1.

4. Audio Home Recording Act of 1992 (AHRA), Pub. L. No. 102-563, S. 1623, 102nd Cong, STATUTE-106-Pg4237.pdf (govinfo.gov).

5. Audio Home Recording Act of 1992 (AHRA).

6. Steven Bertoni, "Sean Parker: Agent of Disruption," *Forbes*, September 21, 2011, Sean Parker: Agent of Disruption (forbes.com).

7. No Electronic Theft Act (NET)," Pub. L. No. 105-147, 111 Stat. 2678 (1997), BILLS-105hr2265enr.pdf (govinfo.gov).

8. Margaret Kane, "David Boies Hired to Defend Napster," *ZDNet.com*, June 16, 2000, Napster Hires DOJ Lawyer Boies, ZDNET.

9. Kane, "David Boies Hired to Defend Napster."

10. Matt Hartley, "Thank you, Napster," *The Globe and Mail*, April 22, 2009, Napster Was Ill-managed as Much as It Was Illicit, Reuters.

11. Joseph Menn, "Napster Was Ill-managed as Much as It Was Illicit," *Reuters*, August 1, 2013. Napster was ill-managed as much as it was illicit | Reuters

12. Matt Richtel, "The Napster Decision: The Overview; Appellate Judges Back Limitations on Copying Music," *New York Times*, February 13, 2001, The Napster Decision: The Overview; Appellate Judges Back Limitations on Copying Music, *The New York Times* (nytimes.com).

13. Hartley, "Thank you, Napster."

14. Steven Bertoni, "Sean Parker: Agent of Disruption," *Forbes*, September 21, 2011, Sean Parker: Agent of Disruption (forbes.com).

15. Joseph Menn, "Napster's Rise and Fall—and Its Future," *Forbes.com*, May 28, 2003, Napster's Rise and Fall—and Its Future (forbes.com).

16. Erick Schonfeld, "Sean Parker and Shervin Pishevar at Le Web, 'If You Don't Fail, You Haven't Tried Hard Enough,'" *Techcrunch.com*, December 11, 2011, Music, TechCrunch .

17. Darrell Etherington, "Ron Conway Talks Napster and the Sharing Economy Problem that "Never Got Solved," *TechCrunch.com*, April 30, 2013. Ron Conway Talks Napster and the Sharing Economy Problem that "Never Got Solved," TechCrunch .

18. Jeff Goodell, "Steve Jobs: Rolling Stone's 2003 Interview," *Rolling Stone*, October 6, 2011, Steve Jobs: Rolling Stone's 2003 Interview.

19. Apple, "Apple Introduces iTunes: World's Best and Easiest to Use Jukebox Software," news release, January 9, 2001, Apple Introduces iTunes—World's Best and Easiest to Use Jukebox Software, Apple.

20. Apple, "Apple Presents iPod," news release, October 23, 2001, Apple Presents iPod, Apple.
21. Apple, "Apple Introduces iPod Shuffle, First iPod Under $100," news release, January 11, 2005, Apple Introduces iPod Shuffle, Apple.
22. Ethan Smith, "Ticketmaster Buys Major Reseller," *Wall Street Journal*, January 15, 2008, Ticketmaster Buys Major Reseller, WSJ.
23. Antony Bruno, "Content Reigns at CES: Interoperability Sought for All Things Digital," *Billboard*, January 22, 2005, 1.
24. Bruno, "Content Reigns at CES," 1.
25. Sally Bedell Smith, "Robert Pittman Begins a New Music Channel," *New York Times*, January 2, 1985, Robert Pittman Begins a New Music Channel, The New York Times (Nytimes.Com).
26. Smith, "Robert Pittman Begins a New Music Channel."
27. Smith, "Robert Pittman Begins a New Music Channel."
28. Edward Wyatt, "'Idol' Winners: Not Just Fame but Big Bucks," *New York Times*, February 23, 2010, "American Idol" Winners Collect Big Bucks as Well as Fame, *The New York Times* (nytimes.com).
29. Bill Carter, "For Fox's Rivals, 'American Idol' Remains a 'Schoolyard Bully,'" *New York Times*, February 20, 2007, American Idol-Ratings-Television, *The New York Times* (nytimes.com).
30. Stephen E. Siwek, "The U.S. Music Industries: Jobs & Benefits," *Recording Industry Association of America*, April 2018, US-Music-Industries-Jobs-Benefits-Siwek-Economists-Inc-April-2018-1-2.pdf (riaa.com).
31. Michael Freedland, "You Ain't Heard Nothin' Yet: The Moment Al Jolson Sounded the Birth of the Talkies," *The Guardian.com*, October 7, 2017, *You Ain't Heard Nothin' Yet: The Moment Al Jolson Sounded the Birth of the Talkies, The Guardian.*

Chapter 11

1. Mark Sutherland, "Hands on Deck: Venture Capitalist Unveils His Vision for Turning Around EMI," *Billboard*, January 26, 2008, 22.
2. Mark Landler, "Sony and Bertelsmann End Their Partnership in Music," *New York Times*, August 5, 2008, Sony and Bertelsmann End Their Partnership in Music, *The New York Times* (nytimes.com).
3. Sony-BMG, "Music Company to Become Wholly Owned Subsidiary of Sony Corporation of America," news release, August 3, 2008, Sony Completes Acquisition of Bertelsmann's 50% Stake in Sony BMG, Sony Music.
4. Wolfgang Spahr, "Starting Over: Bertelsmann Launches Music Rights Management Unit," *Billboard*, November 8, 2008, 16.
5. Daily Express Reporter, "Hands Starts Citi Lawsuit over EMI Bid," *Daily Express*, October 19, 2010, *Express.co.uk*.
6. Peter Lattman, "Citigroup Is Cleared of Fraud in EMI Sale, a Setback for British Financier Guy Hands," *New York Times*, November 5, 2010, Citigroup Is Cleared of Fraud in EMI Sale, a Setback for British Financier Guy Hands, Web Log, NYTimes.com.
7. Lattman, "Citigroup Is Cleared of Fraud in EMI Sale."
8. Ed Christman, "Hello Goodbye: EMI Divvied Up," *Billboard*, November 26, 2011, 7.
9. Yinka Adegoke, "Lucian Grainge," *Billboard*, February 1, 2014, 8.

10. Ed Christman, "A Sendoff to Sony Music Chief Exec Doug Morris: 'Doug-isms' & Lessons Learned from Iovine, Lipman & Others," *Billboard*, March 24, 2017, A Sendoff to Sony Music Chief Exec Doug Morris, *Billboard*.

11. Christman, "A Sendoff to Sony Music Chief Exec Doug Morris."

12. Billboard Staff, "Power 100—No. 5: Rob Stringer," *Billboard*, January 25, 2018, Power 100—No. 5: Rob Stringer, *Billboard*.

13. Dan Rys, "Ron Perry Officially Named Chairman/CEO of Columbia Records," *Billboard*, January 2, 2018, Ron Perry Officially Named Chairman/CEO of Columbia Records, *Billboard*.

14. Billboard Staff, "Power 100: Ron Perry, No. 28," *Billboard*, January 25, 2018, Power 100: Ron Perry, No. 28, *Billboard*.

15. Dan Rys, "Aaron Bay-Schuck and Tom Corson Will Take Over Warner Bros. Records, Cameron Strang to Step Down," *Billboard*, October 3, 2017, Warner Bros. Records Changes Leadership: Bay-Schuck, Corson, *Billboard*.

16. Ed Christman, "Scooter Braun Acquires Scott Borchetta's Big Machine Label Group, Taylor Swift Catalog for Over $300 Million," *Billboard*, June 30, 2019, Scooter Braun Acquires Big Machine Label, Billboard.

17. Taylor Swift (taylorswift), "For years I asked and pleaded for a chance," *Tumblr*, June 30, 2019, Taylor Swift, For years I asked, pleaded for a chance (tumblr.com).

18. Swift, "For years I asked and pleaded for a chance."

19. Jason Lipshutz, "Billboard Woman of the Decade Taylor Swift: 'I Do Want My Music to Live On,'" *Billboard*, December 11, 2019, Taylor Swift: Billboard's Woman of the Decade Cover Story, *Billboard*.

20. Danny Ross, "Meet the Music Exec Taking Bands from the Fringes to the Grammys," *Forbes*, May 23, 2018, Meet the Music Exec Taking Bands from the Fringes to the Grammys (forbes.com).

21. Marc Schneider and Ed Christman, "BMG Acquires Nashville Indie BBR Music Group, Home of Broken Bow Records and Jason Aldean," *Billboard*, January 30, 2017, BMG Acquires Nashville Indie BBR Music Group, Home of Broken Bow Records and Jason Aldean, *Billboard*.

22. Thirty Tigers, "About Us: We Provide a Home for Individual Artists," news release, September 1, 2022, About Thirty Tigers.

23. Jewly Hight, "David Macias on the Singular Thinking behind His Singular Company, Thirty Tigers," *Nashville Scene*, December 19, 2013, David Macias on the Singular Thinking behind His Singular Company, Thirty Tigers, nashvillescene.com.

24. "Spotify for Artists: Provider Directory," *Spotify.com*, September 1, 2022, Provider Directory, Spotify for Artists.

25. *Billboard* Staff, "Billboard's 2019 Power 100 List Revealed," *Billboard*, February 7, 2019, .

26. I. B. Bad, "Near Truths: Year-End Wrap-Up, Part 1," *Hits Rumor Mill*, December 10, 2019, Near Truths: Year-End Wrap-Up, Part 1: HITS Daily Double.

27. Billboard Power 100 List 2020, "Label Groups: Sony Music Entertainment," *Billboard*, January 23, 2020, Billboard's 2020 Power List, *Billboard*.

28. *Billboard* Staff "The 2020 Billboard Power List Revealed," *Billboard*, January 23, 2020, Billboard's 2020 Power List, *Billboard*.

29. Billboard Staff, "The 2020 Billboard Power List Revealed."

30. Larry S. Miller, Same Heart. New Beat: How Record Labels Amplify Talent in the Modern Music Marketplace," *Musonomics*, January 2019, New Report Illustrates How Modern Record Labels Remade Themselves in the Streaming Era, (musonomics.com).
31. Miller, "Same Heart. New Beat."

Chapter 12

1. Geoff Mayfield, "Billboard Hot 100 to Include Digital Streams," *Billboard*, August 4, 2007, 43.
2. Billboard Staff, "A New Experience: Billboard.com Relaunches with Interactive Charts, Social Media," *Billboard*, August 1, 2009, 6.
3. Bill Werde (@BillWerde), "#RIP Tommy Page," *Twitter*, March 4, 2017, #RIP Tommy Page [Bill Werde], Hypebot.
4. Andrew Wallenstein, "Media Rights Capital, Dick Clark Prods., THR-Billboard Form Combined Company," *Variety*, February 1, 2018, Media Rights Capital, Dick Clark Prods., THR-Billboard Combine Company (variety.com).
5. Wallenstein, "Media Rights Capital, Dick Clark Prods., THR-Billboard Form Combined Company."
6. Ben Sisario, "After Top Executive Leaves, Billboard Confronts Its Internal Culture," *New York Times*, July 31, 2018, A New Editor, and a New Start, for Troubled Billboard Magazine, *The New York Times* (nytimes.com).
7. Billboard Staff, "Hannah Karp Named Editorial Director of Billboard Media Group," *Billboard*, December 6, 2018, Hannah Karp Named Editorial Director of Billboard Media Group, *Billboard*.
8. Jack White, "Ambassador History," *Recordstoreday.com*, February 2013, Ambassador History Record Store Day.
9. Ed Christman, "Rock Steady: Despite Challenges, Trans World Looks Sound for Now," *Billboard*, October 3, 2009, 6.
10. Ed Christman, "Charlie Anderson: The Head of the Largest US Rackjobber Lays out Five Steps He Thinks Labels Must Take to Shore Up CD Sales," *Billboard*, July 17, 2010, 9.
11. Christman, "Charlie Anderson."
12. Christman, "Charlie Anderson."
13. Apple.com, "Introducing Apple Music: All The Ways You Love Music. All in One Place," news release, *Apple.com/newsroom*, June 8, 2015, Introducing Apple Music—All The Ways You Love Music. All in One Place., Apple.
14. Ed Christman, "Meet the Company Preparing to Be the Last CD Distributor Standing," *Billboard*, August 24, 2018, Meet the Company Preparing to Be the Last CD Distributor Standing, Billboard.
15. Christman, "Meet the Company Preparing to Be the Last CD Distributor Standing."
16. Christman, "Meet the Company Preparing to Be the Last CD Distributor Standing."
17. Andrew Hampp, "Clear Channel's Pittman: 'We Have to Make the Digital Revolution Come to Radio,'" *Ad Age*, April 7, 2011, Clear Channel's Pittman: "We Have to Make the Digital Revolution Come to Radio," *Ad Age*.
18. Hampp, "Clear Channel's Pittman."

19. Cherie Hu, "Entercom Finalizes Merger with CBS Radio, Becoming No. 2 Radio Operator in US," *Billboard*, November 17, 2017, Entercom Finalizes Merger with CBS Radio, Becoming No. 2 Radio Operator in US, *Billboard*.

20. "Bankruptcy Exit Is Game-Changer Inside Cumulus, Too," *Insideradio.com*, June 6, 2018, Bankruptcy Exit Is Game-Changer Inside Cumulus, Too, insideradio.com.

21. "New Worth: #67 John Malone," *Forbes*, November 13, 2018, Forbes 400 Dominated by Media Moguls: Rupert Murdoch, Oprah & More, Observer.

22. Marc Schneider, "SiriusXM to Acquire Pandora in $3.5 Billion Deal," *Billboard*, September 24, 2018, SiriusXM to Acquire Pandora in $3.5 Billion Deal, *Billboard*.

23. Marc Schneider, "Analyst: After Pandora Deal, SiriusXM Should Pursue Live Nation," *Billboard*, September 25, 2018, Analyst: After Pandora Deal, SiriusXM Should Pursue Live Nation, *Billboard*.

24. Glenn Peoples, "Will the SiriusXM-Pandora Merger Pay Off? Drake and U2 Are Aboard, but Rocky Waters May Lie Ahead," *Billboard*, December 13, 2019, Will the SiriusXM-Pandora Merger Pay Off? Drake and U2 Are Aboard, but Rocky Waters May Lie Ahead, *Billboard*.

25. *Billboard* Staff, "Billboard 200 Makeover: Album Chart to Incorporate Streams & Track Sales," *Billboard*, November 29, 2014, Billboard 200 Makeover: Album Chart to Incorporate Streams & Track Sales, *Billboard*.

26. *Billboard* Staff, "Billboard Finalizes Changes to How Streams Are Weighted for Billboard Hot 100 & Billboard 200," *Billboard*, May 1, 2018, Billboard Updates Streams Weighting for Hot 100 & 200, *Billboard*.

27. *Billboard* Staff, "Billboard 200 to Include Official Video Plays from YouTube, Streaming Services," *Billboard*, December 13, 2019, Billboard 200 to Include Official Video Plays from YouTube, Streaming Services, *Billboard*.

28. *Billboard* Staff, "Billboard 200 to Include Official Video Plays from YouTube, Streaming Services."

29. Colin Stutz, "Billboard Parent Company Valence Media Acquires Nielsen Music," *Billboard*, December 18, 2019, Billboard Parent Company Valence Media Acquires Nielsen Music, Billboard.

30. Stutz, "Billboard Parent Company Valence Media Acquires Nielsen Music."

Chapter 13

1. National Music Publishers Association, "U.S. Music Publishing Industry Valued at $2.2 Billion, NMPA Estimates More than Half of Value Lost Due to Govt Regs," News Release, June 11, 2014, U.S. Music Publishing Industry Valued at $2.2 Billion, NMPA Estimates More than Half of Value Lost Due to Govt Regs, National Music Publishers' Association.

2. David Israelite, email to author, November 30, 2020.

3. Emma Griffiths, "Production Music Association's Morgan McKnight on This Year's Conference and Trends in This Billion Dollar Sector," *Synchtank*, September 9, 2019, Production Music Association's Morgan McKnight on The Sector (synchtank.com).

4. Sarah Whitten, "The Death of the DVD: Why Sales Dropped More than 86% in 13 Years," *CNBC.com*, November 8, 2019, *The Ddeath of the DVD: Why Sales Dropped More Than 86% in 13 Years (cnbc.com)*.

5. Chris Morris, "Bandier Quits as EMI Publishing Co-CEO," *The Hollywood Reporter*, October 31, 2006, Bandier Quits as EMI Publishing Co-CEO, *The Hollywood Reporter*.

6. Tim Ingham, "Warner Bros Records Boss Cameron Strang: 7 Lessons from My Career," *musicbusinessworldwide.com*, May 12, 2015, Warner Bros Records Boss Cameron Strang: 7 Lessons from my Career, Music Business Worldwide .

7. Tim Ingham, Jody Gerson: Why I Quit Sony/ATV—and Stopped Being the 'Loyal Good Girl,'" *Music Business Worldwide*, November 22, 2017, Jody Gerson: Why I Quit Sony/ATV—and Stopped Being the "Loyal Good Girl," Music Business Worldwide.

8. Ed Christman, "Jon Platt Named CEO of Warner/Chappell," *Billboard*, December 6, 2015, Jon Platt Named CEO of Warner/Chappell, *Billboard*.

9. Ed Christman, "Sony to Buy Out Michael Jackson Estate's Half of Sony/ATV Music Publishing," *Billboard*, March 14, 2016, Sony to Buy Out Michael Jackson Estate's Half of Sony/ATV Music Publishing, Billboard.

10. "About Music & Copyright," https://musicandcopyright.wordpress.com/about/, accessed December 1, 2020, About Music & Copyright, Music & Copyright's Blog (wordpress.com).

11. Ed Christman, "Martin Bandier Will Step Down from Sony/ATV in March 2019: Read His Farewell Memo to Staff," *Billboard*, September 17, 2018, Martin Bandier to Step Down from Sony/ATV in March 2019, *Billboard*.

12. Melinda Newman, "A-List Lawyer Joel Katz Talks James Brown, Negotiating for Jon Platt and Why Labels Are Adding Moral Clauses for Execs," *Billboard*, February 15, 2019, Lawyer Joel Katz: Music Industry Insights, *Billboard*.

13. Tim Ingham, "Should You Go into Business with Kobalt?" *Music Business Worldwide*, November 8, 2016, Should you go into business with Kobalt?, Music Business Worldwide.

14. Ben Sisario, "Buying a Piece of Bob Marley's Song Catalog, and His Enduring Legacy," *New York Times*, January 13, 2018, Buying a Piece of Bob Marley's Song Catalog, and His Enduring Legacy, *The New York Times* (nytimes.com).

15. Melinda Newman, "Not Just Jazz: Inside Concord Music's Buying Spree," *Billboard*, September 15, 2017, Inside Concord Music's Buying Spree, *Billboard*.

16. Tim Ingham, "Merck Mercuriadis' Hipgnosis Songs Fund Is Already Worth over $850m," *Music Business Worldwide*, November 26, 2019, Merck Mercuriadis' Hipgnosis Songs Fund Is Already Worth over $850m, *Music Business Worldwide*.

17. Ed Christman, "Was Blackstone's SESAC Acquisition a $1 Billion Deal?" *Billboard*, January 6, 2017, *Was Blackstone's SESAC Acquisition a $1 Billion Deal?, Billboard*.

18. Paula Parisi, "SESAC, Radio Music Licensing Committee Both Claim Victory in Price War," *Variety*, July 31, 2017, SESAC, Radio Music Licensing Committee Claim Victory in Price War, *Variety* (variety.com).

19. Parisi, "SESAC, Radio Music Licensing Committee Both Claim Victory in Price War."

20. Ed Christman, "SESAC Completes Capital Structure Refinancing, Raising $560 Million," *Billboard*, September 25, 2019, SESAC Completes Capital Structure Refinancing, Raising $560 Million, *Billboard*.

21. United States Department of Justice, "Statement of Interest," Global Music Rights, LLC, Plaintiff, v. Radio Music License Committee, Inc. et al., Defendants, December 5, 2019, Statement of Interest of the United States: Global Music Rights, LLC v. Radio Music License Committee, Inc., et al. (justice.gov).

22. *Business Wire* "U.S. Department of Justice Sides with Global Music Rights," news release, December 6, 2019, *U.S. Department of Justice Sides with Global Music Rights, Business Wire*.

23. Ed Christman, "Battle over Radio Royalties Goes West: What's at Stake as RMLC & GMR Head to Court," *Billboard*, April 12, 2019, Battle over Radio Royalties Goes West: What's at Stake as RMLC & GMR Head to Court, *Billboard*.

24. LB Cantrell, "Mechanical Licensing Collective, Digital Licensee Coordinator Reach Agreement," *MusicRow*, November 14, 2019, Mechanical Licensing Collective, Digital Licensee Coordinator Reach Agreement, MusicRow.com.

25. Cantrell, "Mechanical Licensing Collective, Digital Licensee Coordinator Reach Agreement."

26. Bart Herbison, email to author, January 20, 2022.

27. Christman, "ASCAP & BMI Consent Decrees Review Expected to Conclude This Year While Both Sides Argue Worst-Case Scenarios."

28. Christman, "ASCAP & BMI Consent Decrees Review Expected to Conclude This Year While Both Sides Argue Worst-Case Scenarios."

29. Christman, "ASCAP & BMI Consent Decrees Review Expected to Conclude This Year While Both Sides Argue Worst-Case Scenarios."

30. James Montgomery, "Avril Lavigne Responds to Lawsuit, Says She's Been 'Falsely Accused,'" *MTV News*, July 9, 2007, Avril Lavigne Responds to Lawsuit, Says She's Been "Falsely Accused," MTV.

31. Robert Patrick, "St. Louis Christian Hip-hop Singers Sue Katy Perry over 'Dark Horse,'" *St. Louis Post-Dispatch*, July 1, 2014, St. Louis Christian Hip-hop Singers Sue Katy Perry over "Dark Horse" (stltoday.com).

32. Hannah Ellis-Petersen, "Ed Sheeran May Regret Photograph that Led to $20m Copyright Case," *The Guardian*, April 11, 2017, Tom Petty on Sam Smith Song Similarity: "Nothing More than a Musical Accident," *The Guardian*.

33. Guardian Music, "Tom Petty on Sam Smith Song Similarity: 'Nothing More than a Musical Accident,'" *The Guardian*, January 29, 2015, Tom Petty on Sam Smith Song Similarity: "Nothing More than a Musical Accident," *The Guardian*.

34. Adrienne Gibbs, "Marvin Gaye's Family Wins 'Blurred Lines' Appeal; Pharrell, Robin Thicke Must Pay," *Forbes*, March 21, 2018, Marvin Gaye's Family Wins "Blurred Lines" Appeal; Pharrell, Robin Thicke Must Pay (forbes.com).

Chapter 14

1. Ray Waddell, "Live Music's $20 Billion Year," *Billboard*, December 11, 2015, Live Music's $20B Year: Grateful Dead, Taylor Swift, Billboard.

2. Live Nation Entertainment, Inc., "U.S. Security and Exchange Commission 2019 Form 10-K," for Fiscal Year Ending December 31, 2019, lyv-20201231 (livenationentertainment.com).

3. Ed Christman, Gordon Murray, Geoff Peoples, and Bob Allen, "Money Makers 2011: The Lesson? Touring Pays," *Billboard*, February 19, 2011, march-31-2022-billboard-bulletin.pdf.

4. Christman, Murray, Peoples, and Allen, "Money Makers."

5. Gordon Murray, "Money Makers 2008, 1: The Police," *Billboard*, February 2, 2008 27.

6. Ed Christman, "From Davis to Solomon, NARM a Success," *Billboard*, September 11, 2004, 34.

7. Warner Music Group Corp, "U.S. Securities and Exchange Commission Form 10-K for the Fiscal Year Ending September 30, 2012," Annual Reports, Live Nation Entertainment (LYV).

8. Don Passman, *All You Need to Know About the Music Business*, 9th ed. (New York: Simon & Schuster, 2015), 103.

9. Tom Cole, "You Ask, We Answer: What Exactly Is a 360 Deal? *NPR.com*, November 24, 2010, You Ask, We Answer: What Exactly Is a 360 Deal?, NPR.

10. Eriq Gardner, "Enrique Iglesias Sues Universal Music over Streaming Royalties," *The Hollywood Reporter*, January 24, 2018, Enrique Iglesias Sues Universal Music over Streaming Royalties, *The Hollywood Reporter*.

11. Bill Werde, ed., "A Letter from the Editor," *Billboard*, February 4, 2012, 5.

12. Werde, "A Letter from the Editor."

13. Werde, "A Letter from the Editor."

14. Werde, "A Letter from the Editor."

15. Live Nation, Inc., "U.S. Securities and Exchange Commission Form 10-K for the Fiscal Year Ending December 31, 2007, Form 10-K for the Fiscal Year Ended December 31, 2007 (livenationentertainment.com).

16. Live Nation, Inc., "U.S. Securities and Exchange Commission Form 10-K for the Fiscal Year Ending December 31, 2007.

17. Dave Brooks, "Randy Phillips Steps Down as CEO of LiveStyle, Shifts Focus to Managing Boy Band Why Don't We: Exclusive," *Billboard*, September 5, 2019, Randy Phillips Steps Down as CEO of LiveStyle, *Billboard*.

18. Ray Waddell, "*Pollstar* Letter from the President," *Pollstar*, December 16, 2019, 4,128_121619letter_804.pdf (pollstar.com).

19. Andy Gensler, "2019 Business Analysis: The State of the Concert Business: F**kin' Perfect!" *Pollstar*, December 16, 2019, 2019 Business Analysis: The State of the Concert Business Is "F**kin' Perfect," *Pollstar*.

20. Melinda Newman, "'I Pull Rabbits Out of Hats': CAA's Rob Light on the Talent Agency's Magic Touch," *Billboard*, January 12, 2019, CAA's Rob Light on the Talent Agency's Magic Touch *Billboard*.

21. Kim Masters and Stephen Galloway, "Now, It's Personal: The Epic, Inside Drama Behind the New Hollywood Agency Wars," *The Hollywood Reporter*, June 3, 2015, Now, It's Personal: The Epic, Inside Drama Behind the New Hollywood Agency Wars, *The Hollywood Reporter*.

22. Cynthia Littleton and Gene Maddaus, "Endeavor Pulls IPO Amid Investor Concerns, Market Instability," *Variety*, September 26, 2019, Endeavor Pulls IPO Amid Investor Concerns, Market Instability (variety.com).

23. Littleton and Maddaus, "Endeavor Pulls IPO Amid Investor Concerns, Market Instability."

24. Anousha Sakoui, "CAA's Top Agents in Line for a Nearly $400-Million Payday," *Los Angeles Times*, November 13, 2019, CAA's Top Agents in Line for a Nearly $400-million Payday, *Los Angeles Times* (latimes.com).

25. Paul Bond, "CAA to Raise $393 Million to Buy Equity from Employees," *Hollywood Reporter*, November 13, 2019, CAA to Raise $393 Million to Buy Equity from Employees, *The Hollywood Reporter*.

26. Dylan Jones, "The Biggest Rock Tour in History: Behind U2's Gigantic £450 Million Live Performances," *The Mail on Sunday*, October 6, 2012, U2's £450 Million Tour: Behind the Group's Gigantic 360 Degrees Concerts, *Daily Mail Online*

27. Jones, "The Biggest Rock Tour in History."

28. Gil Kaufman, "Recording Academy CEO Neil Portnow Responds to 'Step Up' Backlash: 'I Wasn't as Articulate as I Should Have Been,'" *Billboard*, January 30, 2018, Recording Academy CEO Responds to "Step Up" Backlash, *Billboard*.

29. Gil Kaufman, "Petition Asking Recording Academy Chief to Step Down Nears 10,000 Signatures," *Billboard*, January 31, 2018, Petition Asking Recording Academy Chief to Step Down Nears 10,000 Signatures, *The Hollywood Reporter*.

30. Kaufman, "Recording Academy CEO Neil Portnow Responds to 'Step Up' Backlash."

31. Patrick Shanley, "Recording Academy Chief Asked to Step Down by Female Executives," *The Hollywood Reporter*, February 1, 2018, Recording Academy CEO Responds to "Step Up" Backlash, *Billboard*.

32. Tim McPhate, "Recording Academy Names Diversity and Inclusion Task Force Members," Grammy.com, May 9, 2018, Recording Academy Names Diversity And Inclusion Task Force Members. *GRAMMY.com*.

33. Bill Werde, "On the Grammys, the Music Industry & Progress," *Billboard.com*, February 6, 2018, Werde: On the Grammys, the Music Industry & Progress, Billboard.

34. Gail Mitchell, "Why Recording Academy Trustees and Staff Are Standing by Their Leader Neil Portnow," *The Hollywood Reporter*, February 13, 2018, Why Recording Academy Trustees and Staff Are Standing by Neil Portnow, *The Hollywood Reporter*.

35. Jem Aswad, "It's Official: Deborah Dugan Named President-CEO of Recording Academy," *Variety*, May 8, 2019, It's Official: Deborah Dugan Named President/CEO of Recording Academy (variety.com).

36. Aswad, "It's Official."

37. Soundcharts Team, "What Music Streaming Services Pay Per Stream (And Why It Actually Doesn't Matter)," *Soundcharts Blog*, June 29, 2019, Streaming Payouts [2020]: What Spotify, Apple, & Others Pay (soundcharts.com).

Chapter 15

1. Tom Ryan, "Illegal Music Downloads Continue to Rise," *retailwire.com*, July 31, 2007, Social Sites Grow as Do Illegal Downloads (telegraph.co.uk).

2. Apple, "Apple Reinvents the Phone with iPhone," news release, January 9, 2007, Apple Reinvents the Phone with iPhone, Apple.

3. Apple, "Apple Reinvents the Phone with iPhone."

4. Bijay Pokharel, "The History of Android OS: Its Name, Origin and More," *abijita.com*, May 27, 1918, The History of Android OS: Its Name, Origin and More (abijita.com).

5. Open Handset Alliance, "Overview: FAQ," *Openhandsetalliance.com* Website, July 2011, Alliance FAQ | Open Handset Alliance.

6. Thomas Ricker, "First Click: Remember when Steve Jobs said even Jesus couldn't sell music subscriptions?" *The Verge*, June 8, 2015, First Click: Remember When Steve Jobs Said Even Jesus Couldn't Sell Music Subscriptions?, The Verge.

7. Alan McGlade, "Steve Jobs Was Wrong—Consumers Want to Rent Their Music, Not Own It," *Forbes*, March 25, 2013, Steve Jobs Was Wrong—Consumers Want to Rent Their Music, Not Own It (forbes.com).

8. Pandora, "Form 10-K-Annual Report for Fiscal Year 2012," January 31, 2012, Form 10-K (sec.gov)

9. Pandora, "Form 10-K-Annual Report for Fiscal Year 2012."

10. Daniel Ek, "How Did Spotify Get Its Name?" *Quorum.com*, December 31, 2010, How Did Spotify Get Its Name?, Quora.

11. Rupert Neate, "Daniel Ek Profile:- 'Spotify Will Be Worth Tens of Billions," *The Telegraph*, February 17, 2010, Daniel Ek Profile: "Spotify Will Be Worth Tens of Billions" (telegraph.co.uk).

12. Dorian Lynskey, "Is Daniel Ek, Spotify Founder, Going to Save the Music Industry . . . or Destroy It?" *The Observer*, November 10, 2013, Is Daniel Ek, Spotify Founder, Going to Save the Music Industry . . . or Destroy it? *The Guardian*.

13. Lynskey, "Is Daniel Ek, Spotify Founder, Going to Save the Music Industry . . . or Destroy It?"

14. Emma Barnett, "Spotify to Make 'Significant' Revenue for UK Record Labels 'within Six Months,'" *The Telegraph*, August 25, 2009, Spotify to Make "significant" Revenue for UK Record Labels "Within Six Months" (telegraph.co.uk).

15. Sean Parker, "Sean Parker's Email to Spotify's Daniel Ek," *genius.com*, August 25, 2009, Sean Parker, Sean Parker's Email to Spotify's Daniel Ek, Genius.

16. Emma Barnett, "Spotify Now Makes Record Labels Money," *The Telegraph*, January 21, 2010, Spotify Now Makes Record Labels Money (telegraph.co.uk).

17. Music Ally, "Spotify Reveals," *Musically.com*, October 28, 2010, Spotify Reveals, Music Ally.

18. Burt Helm, "How Dr. Dre's Headphones Company Became a Billion-Dollar Business," Slate.com, April 25, 2014, Beats by Dre: How the Headphones Company Became a Billion-dollar Business. (*slate.com*).

19. Burt Helm, "How Dr. Dre's Headphones Company Became a Billion-Dollar Business."

20. Jason Tanz, "Relentless: Apple Music's Jimmy Iovine and Dr. Dre Have a Plan to Teach the Next Generation of Creators How to Lead," *wired.com*, August 18, 2015, Can Jimmy Iovine and Dr. Dre Save the Music Industry?, WIRED.

21. Lars Brandle, "Jimmy Iovine to Leave Apple Music in August," *Billboard*, January 1, 2018, Jimmy Iovine Leaving Apple Music in August, Billboard.

22. Ben Sisario, "Jimmy Iovine Knows Music and Tech. Here's Why He's Worried," *New York Times*, December 30, 2019, Jimmy Iovine Knows Music and Tech. Here's Why He's Worried, *The New York Times* (nytimes.com).

23. Eric Schneiderman, "Obstructed View: What's Blocking New Yorkers from Getting Tickets," Office of the New York State Attorney General, January 28, 2016, Obstructed View: Eric T. Schneiderman New York State AΣorney General, New York State Attorney General (readkong.com).

24. Reuters Staff, "Ticketmaster CEO Amenable to Sale of TicketsNow," *Reuters*, February 26, 2009, Ticketmaster CEO Amenable to Sale of TicketsNow, Reuters.

25. Robert Levine, "The New Pioneers: Irving Azoff on His Plan to Deal with the 'StubHub Factor'—'You Have Lots of People Escaping with Lots of Money,'" *Billboard*, August 11, 2016, Irving Azoff on Dealing with the "StubHub Factor," Billboard.

26. Live Nation Entertainment Inc., 2019 Security and Exchange Commission Form K-10, February 20, 2020, lyv-20191231 (livenationentertainment.com).

27. Schneiderman, "Obstructed View."

28. Schneiderman, "Obstructed View."

29. Ben Sisario, "Congress Moves to Curb Ticket Scalping, Banning Bots Used Online," *New York Times*, December 8, 2016, Congress Moves to Curb Ticket Scalping, Banning Bots Used Online, *The New York Times* (nytimes.com).

30. Ben Sisario, "Congress Moves to Curb Ticket Scalping, Banning Bots Used Online."

31. Sisario, "Congress Moves to Curb Ticket Scalping, Banning Bots Used Online."

32. "Ad-Supported Audio Presents a Compelling Opportunity," Neilsen.com/insights, February 2020, Ad-Supported Audio Presents a Compelling Opportunity, Nielsen.

33. Music Business Worldwide, "The Music Industry Shouldn't Kid Itself: Piracy Was Never Killed by Streaming . . . but It Might Be More Valuable Than You Think," *Music Business Worldwide*, November 11, 2019, The Music Industry Shouldn't Kid Itself: Piracy Was Never Killed by Streaming . . . but It Might Bbe More Valuable than You Think, *Music Business Worldwide*.

34. Music Ally website home page, *musically.com*, accessed January 15, 2024. Music Ally Is a Knowledge Company.

35. Stuart Dredge, "How Many Users Do Spotify, Apple Music and Other Big Music Streaming Services Have?" *Music Ally*, February 19, 2020, How Many Users Do Spotify, Apple Music and Sstreaming Services Have? (musically.com).

36. Tim Ingham, "Who Will Own Spotify in Five Years?" *Rolling Stone*, August 28, 2019, Spotify: Who Will Own the Streaming Music Service in 5 Years? (rollingstone.com).

37. Ben Sisario, "Jimmy Iovine Knows Music and Tech. Here's Why He's Worried," *New York Times*, December 30, 2019, Jimmy Iovine Knows Music and Tech. Here's Why He's Worried, *The New York Times* (nytimes.com).

Epilogue

1. Bob Allen, "2020 Business Analysis: What Might Have Been Vs. What Was," *Pollstar*, December 11, 2020, 2020 Business Analysis: What Might Have Been Vs. What Was, *Pollstar News*.

2. Andy Gensler, "2020*—A Year Forever Qualified," *Pollstar*, December 11, 2020, 2020*—A Year Forever Qualified, Pollstar News.

3. Tatiana Cirisano, "As Livestreaming Goes Mainstream, It Could Be Survival of the Biggest," *Billboard*, January 29, 2021, Livestreaming Competition Grows With Live Nation Entry, *Billboard*.

4. Tatiana Cirisano, "If You Stream It, Will They Come? Inside the Livestream Boom," *Billboard*, August 31, 2020, Inside the Livestream Boom, *Billboard*.

5. Cirisano, "If You Stream It, Will They Come?"

6. Gensler, "2020*—A Year Forever Qualified."

7. Gensler, "2020*—A Year Forever Qualified."

8. Cirisano, "As Livestreaming Goes Mainstream, It Could Be Survival of the Biggest."

9. Glenn Peoples, "US Livestreams Earned $610M in 2020: Study," *Billboard*, March 11, 2021, Livestream Revenue Hit $610M in US in 2020, *Billboard*.

10. Goldman Sachs Equity Report, *The Show Must Go On*, May 14, 2020, Portrait (goldmansachs.com).

11. Ed Christman, "Billboard's U.S. Money Makers: The Top Paid Musicians of 2020," *Billboard*, July 19, 2021, Highest Paid U.S. Money Makers in Music: 2020 Rankings, *Billboard*.

12. Hugh McIntyre, "Taylor Swift Fights Back Against Her Former Label with Her Latest Single Releases," *Forbes*, May 20, 2020, Taylor Swift Fights Back Against Her Former Label With Her Latest Single Releases (forbes.com).

13. Alexei Barrionuevo, "How Billboard Formulated the New Global Charts," *Billboard*, September 15, 2020, How Billboard Formulated the Global Charts, Billboard.

14. Tim Ingham, "Spotify Gets Serious About Its Charts, Launching Weekly Top 50 Lists for Albums and Songs,"*Music Business Worldwide*, October 5, 2020, Spotify Gets Serious about Its Ccharts, Launching Weekly Top 50 Lists for Albums and Songs, Music Business Worldwide.

15. Vivendi, "Financial Report and Audited Consolidated Financial Statements for the Year Ended December 31, 2019," February 13, 2020, 20200213_VIV_Financial-Report-and-Consolidated-Financial-Statements-FY-2019.pdf (vivendi.com).

16. Tencent, "About Us," March 1, 2022, Tencent 腾讯.

17. Ed Christman, "Sony's Music Operations Post Nearly 40% Gain in Operating Income as Streaming Revenue Surges," *Billboard*, May 13, 2020, Sony's Music Operations Post Nearly 40% Gain in Operating Income as Streaming Revenue Surges, *Billboard*.

18. MBN Staff, "Sony/ATV and BeatStars Strike Deal to Provide Publishing Services to Composers," *Music Biz Nation*, April 14, 2020, Sony/ATV and BeatStars Strike Deal to Provide Publishing Services to Composers, Music Biz Nation.

19. BMI, "BMI Announces Record Revenue of $1.311 Billion," news release, September 9, 2020, BMI Announces Record Revenue Of $1.311 Billion (prnewswire.com).

20. Ed Christman, "Music Publishing Revenue Topped $4B in 2020, Says NMPA," *Billboard Bulletin*, June 15, 2021, Music Publishing Revenue Topped $4B in 2020: NMPA, *Billboard.*/

21. Dorian Lynskey, "'Record Companies Have Me on a Dartboard': The Man Making Millions Buying Classic Hits," *The Guardian*, February 27, 2021, "Record Companies Have Me on a Dartboard": The Man Making Millions Buying Classic Hits, *The Guardian*.

22. Ed Christman, "Bob Dylan's Next Big Deals: What's Still in Play After Landmark Publishing Sale," *Billboard*, December 15, 2020, How Bob Dylan Brought His Song Catalog Back Home by 1990, *Billboard*.

23. Randall Wixen, "Randall Wixen on Selling Your Publishing," *The Lefsetz Letter*, December 10, 2020, Lefsetz Letter » Blog Archive » Randall Wixen on Selling Your Publishing, https://redef.com/author/5fd2d4a3253b9a0779ba4a5a.

24. Spanish Point Technologies, "CISAC Selects Spanish Point and Our Innovative Matching Engine to Build the Next Generation ISWC System," news release, February 4, 2019, CISAC Selects Spanish Point and Our Innovative Matching Engine to Build the Next Generation ISWC System, Spanish Point Technologies Ltd.

25. CISAC.org/Newsroom, "New Improved Music Identifier Will Help Creators in the All-important Digital Market," news release, September 24, 2020, New improved music identifier will help creators in the all-important digital market | CISAC.

26. CISAC.org/Newsroom, "New Improved Music Identifier Will Help Creators in the All-Important Digital Market."

27. CISAC.org/Newsroom, "New Improved Music Identifier Will Help Creators in the All-Important Digital Market."

28. CISAC.org/Newsroom, "New Improved Music Identifier Will Help Creators in the All-Important Digital Market."

29. ASCAP, "ASCAP and BMI Launch SONGVIEW, a Comprehensive Data Resource for Music Users," news release, December 21, 2020, New Improved Music Identifier Will Help Creators in the All-important Digital Market, CISAC.

30. "ASCAP and BMI Launch SONGVIEW, a Comprehensive Data Resource for Music Users."

31. "ASCAP and BMI Launch SONGVIEW, a Comprehensive Data Resource for Music Users."

32. The MLC, "The Mechanical Licensing Collective Announces Kris Ahrend as CEO," news release, January 15, 2020, The Mechanical Licensing Collective Announces Kris Ahrend as CEO, Mechanical Licensing Collective (themlc.com).

33. The MLC, "The MLC Announces Key Leadership Post and Selects Experienced Partners to Develop First-of-Its-Kind Data Portal," November 26, 2019, The MLC Announces Key Leadership Post and Selects Experienced Partners to Develop First-of-Its-Kind Data Portal, Mechanical Licensing Collective.

34. The MLC, "The MLC Announces Key Leadership Post and Selects Experienced Partners to Develop First-of-Its-Kind Data Portal."

35. Bart Herbison, "Quotation on Mechanical Licensing Collective," *Nashville Songwriters Association International*, January 21, 2022, Bart Herbison, Mechanical Licensing Collective (themlc.com).

36. RIAA, "Designation of SoundExchange as Authoritative Source of ISRC Data in the United States," news release, July 22, 2020, designation-of-soundexchange-technical-document.pdf (usisrc.org).

37. Harvey Mason Jr., "An Important Message from Harvey Mason, Jr., Chair of the Board and Interim President-CEO," Grammy.com, January 20, 2020, An Important Message From Harvey Mason, Jr., Chair of the Board and Interim President/CEO, *GRAMMY.com*.

38. Deborah Dugan, "Charge of Discrimination," EEOC Los Angeles Office Filing, January 20, 2020, filed-eeoc-supplement-wm.pdf (deadline.com).

39. Dugan, "Charge of Discrimination."

40. Tammy Hurt, Christine Albert, Chair Emeritus, Terry Jones, "Statement from the Women on the Executive Committee of the Recording Academy," *Variety*, January 22, 2020, Recording Academy Women Defend Board, Deny 'Boys Club' in Letter (variety.com).

41. Chris Eggertsen, "Recording Academy Diversity Task Force Issues Blistering Statement in Wake of Deborah Dugan Allegations,"*Billboard*, January 23, 2020, Recording Academy Diversity Task Force Update, *Billboard*.

42. Chris Eggertsen, "Recording Academy Diversity Task Force Issues Blistering Statement in Wake of Deborah Dugan Allegations."

43. Paul Grein, "Months After Recording Academy's Diversity and Inclusion Report, What's Next?" *Billboard*, February 12, 2020, Recording Academy Diversity and Inclusion Task Force, *Billboard*.

44. Eve Barlow, "All Hell Has Broken Loose Within the Grammys," *Vulture.com*, March 3, 2020, Grammys Scandal with CEO Deborah Dugan, Explained (vulture.com).

45. Barlow, "All Hell Has Broken Loose Within the Grammys."

46. Jon Blistein and Ethan Millman, "When Will Live Music Return?" *Rolling Stone*, December 22, 2020, *Covid-19 Wiped Out a Year of Concerts. When Will Live Music Return? (rollingstone.com)*.

47. Mark Mulligan, "Global Music Subscriber Market Shares Q1 2021," *MIDiA Research*, September 9, 2021, Global Music Subscriber Market Shares Q1 2021 (midiaresearch.com).

48. Ben Sisario, "Jimmy Iovine Knows Music and Tech. Here's Why He's Worried," *New York Times*, December 30, 2019, Jimmy Iovine Knows Music and Tech. Here's Why He's Worried, *The New York Times* (nytimes.com).

49. Bobby Allyn, "U.S. Judge Halts Trump's TikTok Ban, the 2nd Court to Fully Block the Action," *npr.org*, December 7, 2020, U.S. Judge Halts Trump's TikTok Ban, the 2nd Court to Fully Block the Action, NPR.

50. Terry Collins, "Have Social Platforms Reached Their Peak? Pew Research Survey Shows Little User Growth Since Last Year," *USA Today*, April 7, 2021, Pew Survey: Gen Z Gravitates to Instagram, Snapchat and TikTok (usatoday.com).

51. Collins, "Have Social Platforms Reached Their Peak?"

52. Rebecca Bellan, "The Top Social Media Apps of 2020, According to Apptopia," *Forbes*, December 3, 2020, The Top Social Media Apps of 2020, According to Apptopia (forbes.com).

53. "Feature Highlight: New Layouts for Duet," September 30, 2020, Feature Highlight: New Layouts for Duet, TikTok Newsroom.

54. Andrew Unterberger, "Can TikTok Rival MTV's Heyday For Gen-Z?" *Billboard*, December 21, 2020, TikTok's Music Industry Impact: Is It the New MTV? *Billboard*.

55. Unterberger, "Can TikTok Rival MTV's Heyday For Gen-Z?"

56. Goldman Sachs Equity Report, "The Show Must Go On," May 14, 2020, Portrait (goldmansachs.com).

57. Samantha Hissong, "New Venues, High-Tech Concerts: AEG's Plan to Come Out of Covid Stronger than Ever," *Rolling Stone*, December 9, 2020, New Venues, High-Tech Concerts: AEG's Plan to Come Out of Covid (rollingstone.com).

Bibliography

Websites

AnnualReports.com
ASCAP.com
BLS.gov, "Bureau of Labor Statistics Archive by Date"
BMI.com
BroadwayLeague.com, "Research & Statistics," 1985–2020
Businessofapps.com
CISAC.org
Copyright.gov
FCC.gov
GlobalMusicRights.com
Grammy.com
HarryFox.com
IAB.com
IFPI.org
Licensinginternational.org, formerly Licensing Industry Merchandisers Association (LIMA)
LOC.gov
Motionpictures.org
Nashvillesongwriters.com
Nashvillesongwritersfoundation.com
Net-informations.com
Newzoo.com
Nielsen.com
Pewresearch.com
PrimaryWave.com
RAB.com
RIAA.com
SESAC.com
SoundExchange.com
Spotify.com
Statista.com
Techterms.com
TheMLC.com
Tritondigital.com
vgsales.fandom.com

Books

Brabec, Jeff, and Todd Brabec. *Music Money and Success: The Insider's Guide to Making Money in the Music Business*. 8th ed. New York: Schirmer Trade Books, 2018.

Carlin, Richard. *Godfather of the Music Business: Morris Levy (American Made Music Series)*. Oxford: University Press of Mississippi, 2016.

Chapple, Steve, and Reebee Garofalo. *Rock 'n' Roll Is Here to Pay—The History and Politics of the Music Industry*. Chicago: Nelson-Hall, 1977.

Christensen, Clayton M. *The Innovator's Dilemma*. Boston: Harvard Business Review Press, 1997.

Cornyn, Stan, with Paul Scanlon. *Exploding: The Highs, Hits, Hype, Heroes, and Hustlers of the Warner Music Group*. New York: Harper Collins, 2002.

Dannen, Fredric. *Hit Men: Power Brokers and Fast Money Inside the Music Business*. New York: Vintage Books, 1991.

Duncan, James H., Jr. with assistance by Ty and Peggy Johnson. *An American Radio Trilogy, 1975–2004*. Tesuque, NM: Duncan American Radio, 2004.

Hull, Geoffrey P., Thomas William Hutchison, and Richard Strasser. *The Music Business and Recording Industry: Delivering Music in the 21st Century*. Milton Park, UK: Taylor & Francis, 2011.

Mulligan, Mark. *Awakenings: The Music Industry in the Digital Age*. Scotts Valley, CA: CreateSpace Independent Publishing Platform, 2015.

Passman, Donald S. *All You Need to Know About the Music Business*. New York: Simon & Schuster. 3rd ed. 1997; 6th ed. 2006; 9th ed. 2015; 10th ed. 2019.

Sanjek, Russell. *American Popular Music and Its Business: The First Four Hundred Years*. Vol. 1, *The Beginning to 1790*. New York: Oxford University Press, 1988.

Sanjck, Russell. *American Popular Music and Its Business: The First Four Hundred Years*. Vol. 2, *From 1790 to 1909*. New York: Oxford University Press, 1988.

Sanjek, Russell. *American Popular Music and Its Business: The First Four Hundred Years*. Vol. 3, *From 1900 to 1984*. New York: Oxford University Press, 1988.

Sanjek, Russell. *From Print to Plastic: Publishing and Promoting America's Popular Music, 1900–1980*. Institute for Studies in American Music (I.S.A.M.) Monographs, no. 20. New York: Brooklyn College of the City University of New York, 1984.

Sanjek, Russell. "The War on Rock." *Down Beat Music '72*. Chicago: Maher Publications, 1972.

Sanjek, Russell, and David Sanjek. *American Popular Music Business in the 20th Century*. New York: Oxford University Press, 1991.

Sanjek, Russell, updated by David Sanjek. *Pennies from Heaven: The American Popular Music Business in the Twentieth Century*. New York: Da Capo Press, 1996.

Segrave, Kerry. *Ticket Scalping: An American History 1850–2005*. Jefferson, NC: McFarland & Company, 2007.

Waddell, Ray D., Rich Barnet, and Jake Berry. *This Business of Concert Promotion and Touring: A Practical Guide to Creating, Selling, Organizing, and Staging Concerts*. New York: Billboard Books, 2007.

Witt, Stephen. *How Music Got Free: The End of an Industry, the Turn of the Century, and the Patient Zero of Piracy*. New York: Penguin, 2015.

Yetnikoff, Walter, and David Ritz. *Howling at the Moon: The Odyssey of a Monstrous Music Mogul in an Age of Excess*. New York: Broadway Books, 2004.

Periodicals, Websites, and Blogs with Pertinent Articles

The A Register

Gordon, Steve. "The Billion Dollar Ringtones War, Civil Strife as Labels Fight Publishers." January 8, 2007.

Apple.com

"Apple Launches iTunes Plus." News release. May 30, 2007.

"Apple Reinvents the Phone with iPhone." News release. January 9, 2007.

"Apple Unveils New iPods—5GB, 10GB and 20GB Versions for Mac and Windows." News release. July 17, 2002.

"Changes Coming to the iTunes Store." News release. January 6, 2009.

"Introducing Apple Music—All the Ways You Love Music. All in One Place." News release. June 8, 2015.

"iTunes Plus Now Offers over Two Million Tracks at Just 99 Cents." News release. October 17, 2007.

Jobs, Steve. "Thoughts on Music." February 6, 2007.

ASCAP.com

"ASCAP Surmounts Pandemic Challenges to Collect $1.327 Billion in Revenue in 2020." News release. March 9, 2021.

Asbury Park Press

Jordan, Chris. "Dropkick Murphys, Bruce Springsteen Fenway Livestream: Greetings from the Irish Riviera." May 27, 2020.

bankmycell.com

"How Many Smartphones Are in the World." News release. June 1, 2020.

BEA.com

Soloveichik, Rachel. "Music Originals as Capital Assets." Bureau of Economic Analysis. June 2013.

biakelsey.com

BIA Advertising Services. "BIA Revises Local Radio Advertising Estimates Down to $12.8 B in 2020 Due to Pandemic; Transition to Digital Accelerating." June 25, 2020.

107th Congress of the United States

"Small Webcaster Settlement Act of 2002." December 4, 2002.

ABCNews.com

Deliso, Meredith. "VNU Changes Name to the Nielsen Co." January 18, 2007.

Rowell, Erica D. "Court Rules Against Napster." February 2, 2001.

AdWeek IQ New

Sacharow, Anya. "Music Boulevard to Sell Downloadable Singles." July 14, 1997.

ampthemag.com

Brooks, Dave. "Ray Waddell Is Leaving Billboard." November 30, 2016.

Androidauthority.com

Android Authority. "About Us." November 11, 2020.

Callahan, John. "The History of Android OS—Its Name, Origin and More." July 3, 2018.

apmmusic.com

KPM. "The Benchmark for High Quality Production Music." December 15, 2020.

appleinsider.com

Jade, Kasper. "Apple Acquires SoundJam, Programmer for iMusic." January 8, 2001.

Ars Technica

Anderson, Nate. "Making Money Selling Music without DRM: The Rise of eMusic." May 22, 2006.

Cheng, Jacqui. "iTunes through the Ages." November 23, 2012.

Associated Press

Ho, David. "Royalty Relief for Internet Radio." October 7, 2002.

Moody, Nekesa Mumbi. "Clive Davis Replaced by Barry Weiss as BMG Head." April 18, 2008.

Newswire. "Record Company Mogul Morris Levy Faced Prison for Conspiracy Conviction." May 22, 1990.

The Atlantic

LaFrance, Adrienne. "The First-Ever Banner Ad on the Web." April 21, 2017.

BBC.com.news
BBC Newsbeat. "How Spotify Came to Be Worth Billions." March 1, 2018.

Bedtracks.com
Cliffen, Jason. "A Brief History of Music Libraries." May 30, 2017.

Billboard
Atwood, Brett. "Nordic Bows Sales of Digitally Sent Music," 6. April 26, 1997.
Bessman, Jim. "ASCAP Distributes Record Sum in Royalties,"3. February 16, 2002.
Billboard Brand Partnership Staff. "Billboard Media Kit 2018." February 2018.
Billboard Staff. "BMG Direct Takes over Columbia House." May 17, 2005. BMG Direct Takes Over Columbia House.
Billboard Staff. "Dutch Conglomerate VNU to Purchase BPI Communications," 3. January 29, 1994.
Billboard Staff. "Tunes, Amazon, Wal-Mart Unveil New Pricing," 8. April 18, 2009.
Billboard Staff. "Vivendi Universal Acquires MP3.com." May 31, 2001. Vivendi Universal Acquires MP3.com.
Boehlert, Eric. "The Ticketmaster Saga: How David Became the Goliath of the Industry," 1. July 9, 1994.
Brandle, Lars, and Ray Waddell. "Sillerman Shopping Again: Entrepreneur Buys Fuller's 'Idol' Company," 1. April 2, 2005.
Brandle, Lars. "EMI Completes Acquisition of Jobete Catalog." March 31, 2004. EMI Completes Acquisition of Jobete Catalog.
Brandle, Lars. "AEG Buys Chunk of Marshall Arts." October 17, 2006. AEG Buys Chunk of Marshall Arts.
Brooks, Dave. "A Conscious Uncoupling: What's Next After the MSG-Azoff Split?" October 12, 2018. *Billboard.*
Brooks, Dave. "After Success His Entire Career, Robert Sillerman's Final Years Were Marked by Pain, Loss and Deception." November 27, 2019. Robert Sillerman Obituary: Music Industry Loss, *Billboard.*
Bruno, Antony. "Radio Waves: Clear Channel, CBS Expand Online," 14. May 24, 2008.
Bruno, Antony. "Digital Sector Still Evolving," 40. December 24, 2005.
Bruno, Antony. "Double-Time Growth: Second Life and Social Networks Explode onto the Scene," 40. December 23, 2006.
Bruno, Antony. "How Long Can Apple Stay on Top? Market Leader Faces Growing Competition," 30. August 27, 2005.
Bruno, Antony. "Evolutionary Road: More Digital Music Advances Will Perfect Biz Models, Not Blow Them Up," 8. December 12, 2009.
Bruno, Antony. "Outfitting the iPhone: New Ways to Access Music Via Apple's App Store," 8. July 26, 2008.
Bruno, Antony. "Telephone Tunes: Cingular, Verizon and Sprint Tested the Waters of Subscription and a la Carte Services," 20. December 23, 2006.
Bruno, Antony. "Verizon Launches Mobile Music Store New Service Undercuts Sprint Price Point," 8. January 1, 2006.
Butler, Susan. "Guitar Tabs Publishers Disagree on Best Biz Model,"19. September 1, 2007.
Butler, Susan. "Top Publishing Exec Splits: EMI Bandier's Departure Sure to Mark a Cultural Shift," 8. November 11, 2006.
Callahan, Jean. "WB's Cornyn Tells Tribunal of Cost Fears,"4. July 12, 1980.
Chicago Bureau. "New Post for Ross," 6. August 11, 1962.
Christman, Ed. "Warner Rocks Its Indie World in a Shifting Market, WMG Marries Indie Distribs and Labels Under One Roof," 5. August 4, 2012.

Christman, Ed, and Glenn Peoples. "Wait, What? The Copyright Royalty Board, Webcasting Rates and Paying Artists, Explained." December 16, 2015. Wait, What? The Copyright Royalty Board, Webcasting Rates and Paying Artists, Explained.

Christman, Ed, and Leila Cobo. "How Billboard's 2018 Money Makers Were Determined." July 20, 2018. Highest-Paid Musicians: How Billboard's 2018 Money Makers Were Determined, *Billboard*.

Christman, Ed. "Alliance, Trinity Seal Merger Deal; Wholesaler Back on Acquisition," 93. December 18, 1993.

Christman, Ed. "An Industry Reshaped: Sales of EMI and WMG, Leadership Changes Make for a Tumultuous Year," 16. December 17, 2011.

Christman, Ed. "BMI Rate-Court Judge Rules Against DOJ Dept. of Justice's '100 Percent' Licensing Decision." September 16, 2016. BMI Rate-Court Judge Rules Against Dept. of Justice's '100 Percent' Licensing Decision, *Billboard*.

Christman, Ed. "BMI, Department of Justice Square Off in Appeals Court over Latest Consent Decree Ruling." December 1, 2017. BMI, Department of Justice Square Off in Court Over Latest Consent Decree Ruling, *Billboard*.

Christman, Ed. "CD-Burning Kiosks Look Promising for Retail Use, but Profits Could Be Elusive," 27. May 21, 2005.

Christman, Ed. "Chain Reaction: What's Next for EMI, Universal and Sony after the WMG Auction," 5. May 21, 2011.

Christman, Ed. "Concord Bicycle Music Acquires Imagem in $600 Million Deal, Sources Say." June 2, 2017. Concord Bicycle Music Acquires Imagem in $600 Million Deal, Sources Say, *Billboard*.

Christman, Ed. "EMI's Challenge: Contracts, Deadlines, New Hires on the Road to Restructuring," 10. April 26, 2008.

Christman, Ed. "Fate of Singles: Who Can Kill or Save Them and Why," 5. March 16, 2002.

Christman, Ed. "Handleman Accounts for Most Music," 120. May 13, 1993.

Christman, Ed. "Indies No. 1 in Total Album Market Share for First Time: WEA Is No. 1 in Current Share," 60. January 18, 1997.

Christman, Ed. "Kill the Jewel Box: A Mistake from the Start, Landfill Forever," 26. June 23, 2007.

Christman, Ed. "Labels Prep Madison Project," 1. December 26, 1998.

Christman, Ed. "Lyor Cohen's Move to YouTube: Good or Bad for the Music Industry?" October 3, 2016. Lyor Cohen to YouTube: Good or Bad for the Music Industry? *Billboard*.

Christman, Ed. "Match Point EMI's Fate Could Sway Warner's Next Move," 5. February 5, 2011.

Christman, Ed. "Merchants Are Optimistic About Singles Price Hikes," 8. June 24, 2000.Christmas, Ed. "Music Reports Launches New Tool to Begin Solving 'The Database Problem.'" March 17, 2016. Music Reports Launches New Tool to Begin Solving "The Database Problem," *Billboard*.

Christman, Ed. "NMPA Claims Victory: CRB Raises Payout Rate from Music Subscription Services." January 27, 2018. Copyright Royalty Board Raises Payout Rate from Music Subscription Services, *Billboard*.

Christman, Ed. "Numbers Look Up for U.S. Biz: Album Sales Reverse Skid in '04," 5. January 15, 2005.

Christman, Ed. "Out of Business Shuttered Stores and CD Sales' Downward Slide," 25. March 3, 2007.

Christman, Ed. "Pandora Appeals BMI Rate Court Ruling." October 21, 2015. Pandora Appeals BMI Rate Court Ruling, *Billboard*.

Christman, Ed. "Pandora Signs Mutually Beneficial Licensing Deals with ASCAP, BMI." December 22, 2015. Pandora Signs Mutually Beneficial Licensing Deals with ASCAP, BMI, *Billboard*.

Christman, Ed. "Suitors at the Door: Prospective Buyers Ready Their Bids on EMI and UMG Label Assets," 6. January 19, 2013.

Christman, Ed. "Retail Tracks: Longbox Saga Goes On," 42. August 1, 1992.

Christman, Ed. "Rizvi Traverse Invests in SESAC," 13. January 26, 2013.

Christman, Ed. "Round Hill Finalizes $245M Acquisition of Carlin America, Home to Elvis Presley & AC/DC Catalogs." January 1, 2018. Round Hill Finalizes $245M Carlin America Deal, *Billboard*.

Christman, Ed. "Slugging It Out: Apple, Wal-Mart Flip-Flop at the Peak of Our Top 20 Retailers List," 12. May 10, 2008.

Christman, Ed. "Sony Agrees to Buy Additional 60 Percent Stake in EMI Music Publishing, Now to Own 90 Percent." May 21, 2018. Sony Agrees to Buy Additional 60 Percent Stake in EMI Music Publishing, Now to Own 90 Percent, *Billboard*.

Christman, Ed. "Sony Completes Acquisition of Michael Jackson Estate's Share of EMI Music Publishing." July 31, 2018. Sony Completes Acquisition of Michael Jackson Estate's Share of EMI Music Publishing, *Billboard*.

Christman, Ed. "SoundExchange Releases Most Recent Finance Data." December 23, 2016. SoundExchange Releases Most Recent Finance Data, *Billboard*.

Christman, Ed. "Taking Stock: Even Discounting Digital Distribution, Market Numbers Show . . ." a Tough Physical Retail Year," 6. January 13, 2007.

Christman, Ed. "The Long Goodbye Once-Mighty Record Clubs Fade Away," 12. August 16, 2008.

Christman, Ed. "UMG Tops Album Share for Fifth Year," 38. January 17, 2004.

Christman, Ed. "UMG's Lead Grows as Top U.S. Distributor," 20. January 21, 2006.

Christman, Ed. "UMVD Marks 3rd Straight Year as Leader Iin Total, Current Album Share," 51. January 21, 2002.

Christman, Ed. "UMVD No. 1 Iin Market Share for Albums, Singles In 2000," 70. January 26, 2001.

Christman, Ed. "UMVD Takes $18.98 Leap Merchants Worry that Other Labels Will Follow," 5. August 28, 1999.

Christman, Ed. "UMVD Share Tops Sony, BMG," 35. January 22, 2005.

Christman, Ed. "Universal Is '99's Top Distributor in Several Markets in 1999," 57. January 22, 2000.

Christman, Ed. "Warner Resets for 21st Century: The Universal Approach," 4. November 17, 2012.

Christman, Ed. "WEA #1 in '97 Album Market Share Despite Decline," 76. January 24, 1998.

Christman, Ed. "WEA Holds Off Sony to Retain Crown as Top Album Distributor," 75. January 23, 1999.

Christman, Ed. "WEA Remains Top U.S. Music Distributor in '95: Indies Closing Gap on No. 1," 55. January 20, 1996.

Christman, Ed. "Weathering the Storm: Can the Major Labels Handle Their Debt?" 7. October 18, 2008.

Christman, Ed. "Will Industry Let CD Fade with a Bang or Whimper?" 21. January 14, 2006.

Christman, Ed. "Winding Down Handleman: What to Expect from the Rackjobber's Liquidation," 22. June 21, 2008.

Christman, Ed. "1995 Figures Show Industry Imbalance: Small Number of Albums Take Bulk of Year's Sales," 6. June 15, 1996.

Christman, Ed. "Clubs Scale Back Freebies, Employees," 3. April 14, 2001.

Christman, Ed. "Executive's Vision Has Shaped the Wal-Mart Chain into a Major Music Destination," 16. August 5, 2006.

Christman, Ed. "Have Sales Finally Hit Bottom?" 1. January 17, 2004.

Christman, Ed. "Wal-Mart Stirs Pricing Pot," 12. March 8, 2008.

Christman, Ed. "Warner Eyes Indie Biz with 'Incubator' Labels," 1. September 11, 2004.

Conniff, Tamara. "The Year in New Media: Battles Raged in 2000, but Cooperation Is the Theme for 2001," 78. January 20, 2001.

DiMartino, Dave. "Decalogue—The '80's," D-8. December 23, 1989.

DiMartino, Dave. "Exec in Direct Line to Succession Menon Details Fifield Role at EMI Music," 4. May 14, 1988.

Dupler, Steven. "Decision Said to Be Likely This Week, Warner Amex Listening to Buyout Offers," 8. May 25, 1985.

Dupler, Steven. "Freston New MTV Net CEO Title Comes with Exit of Roganti," 8. August 22, 1987.

Ellis, Michael. "Commentary: How to Revive Singles Market," 1. April 14, 2001.

Fitzpatrick, Eileen. "Kiosk Commerce: Brick-and-Mortar Retailers Take Digital Distribution Under Their Wings. . . with In-Store Kiosks," 76. July 29, 2000.

Fitzpatrick, Eileen. "Labels, MP3.com May Soon Settle, Then Collaborate," 12. June 17, 2000.

Flick, Larry. "Indie Promoters Form Association," 1. August 21, 1999.

Garrity, Brian, and Ed Christman. "A Forum for Views on Singles, CD Prices, Internet," 79. March 23, 2002.

Garrity, Brian, and Ed Christman. "NARM Debates Burning Issues, Piracy Is Prime Topic at Convention," 1. March 23, 2002.

Garrity, Brian. "BMG Direct Buys Rival: Columbia House Addition Makes for Combined 16M Subscribers," 10. May 21, 2005.

Garrity, Brian. "Clubs Seek Better Access to Hits," 5. October 4, 2003.

Garrity, Brian. "EMI Pub, Sony BMG Forge Digital Licensing Pact," 3. December 25, 2004.

Garrity, Brian. "Licensing Competition Emerging," 54. January 26, 2002.

Garrity, Brian. "Music Companies Feel Dotcom Meltdown," 1. January 13, 2001.

Garrity, Brian. "New Media: Online Music Went Legit in 2001," 58. December 29, 2001.

Garrity, Brian. "RealNetworks Bows Subscription Service," 61. December 15, 2001.

Garrity, Brian. "The MP3 Question: MySpace Turns Up the Format's Volume, but Are Majors Tuning In?" 12. September 16, 2006.

Garrity, Brian. "UMG Takes Its Cut," 11. December 23, 2006.

Garrity, Brian. "Wal-Mart formally Launched Its Online Download Store," 10. April 3, 2004.

Garrity, Brian. "Web Stocks Face Wild Ride on Street," 1. September 25, 1999.

Garrity, Brian. "Web Cos. Positioned for Growth '99's: IPU Frenzy Lifted Start-Ups, Majors Seen Tapping Mkt. in 2000," 1. January 8, 2000.

Gett, Steve. "Managers Are in the Thick of It—1986 Brings More Responsibilities," 5. December 27, 1986.

Gett, Steve. "Rascoff, Zysblat Merge into New Artist Management Co.," 88. May 28, 1988.

Gillen, Marilyn A. "Major Labels See Benefits in Licensed Song Streaming." June 24, 2000.

Gillen, Marilyn A. "The Future of Downloadable Music New Playback Devices, Alliances Unveiled at CES Confab." January 22, 2000.

Goodman, Fred. "Can Music Exec Lyor Cohen Bridge the Divide Between YouTube and the Music Industry." March 2, 1917.

Goodman, Fred. "RIAA: Warnings Yes but Ratings No." August 17, 1985.Grein, Paul. "Billboard Charts of the Future," 24. Special Edition. December 15, 1984.

Haring, Bruce. "Stones Tour Fulfills ''Gross' Promise," 82. January 13, 1990.

Hay, Carla. "Programming: Top Dogs, Fallen 'Idols' in TV's 2003," 68. December 27, 2003.

Hay, Carla. "Proper Role of Music TV Debated in U.S.," 1. February 17, 2001.

Hennessey, Mike. "Welk Deal Helps P'Gram Build Pub Unit," 5. October 10, 1988.

Holland, Bill. "Ticketmaster Is Under Fire; House Hearings Begin," 1. July 9, 1994.

Holland, Bill. "Artists & Lawyers Decry Contract Clause," 1. October 6, 2001.

Holland, Bill. "Ruling on Copyright Extension Leaves Foes with Little Recourse," 1. January 25, 2001.

Holland, Bill. "Senate to Probe Payola," 1. April 12, 1986.

Holland, Bill. "Work-for-Hire Rollback Legislation Ready," 5. September 2, 2000.

Holland, Bill. "Year-End Topics at Congress Include Internet, Bootlegs," 9. December 23, 1995.

Holland, Bill. "Coalition Sets Anti-Piracy Ad Campaign," 4. October 5, 2002.

Hu, Cherie. "Entercom Finalizes Merger with CBS Radio, Becoming No. 2 Radio Operator in US." November 17, 2017. Entercom Finalizes Merger with CBS Radio, Becoming No. 2 Radio Operator in US, *Billboard*.

Hunter, Nigel. "PolyGram Acquires Welk Catalogs: Purchase Price Believed to Be $25 Mil," 5. October 8, 1988.

Israelite, Larry, "Home Computing Scenarios for Success," 90th-46. December 15, 1984.

Jeffrey, Don, and Ed Christman. "Retail Reacts to 'Madison' Project," 1. February 20, 1999.

Jeffrey, Don. "An Analysis of Consumer Purchasing Trends," 55. May 3, 1997.

Jeffrey, Don. "Downloading Songs Subject of RIAA Suit Action Intended to Stem Flow of Internet Piracy," 3. June 21, 1997.

Jeffrey, Don. "Grammys Stay at CBS, Move to N.Y.'s Garden," 8. November 2, 1996.

Jeffrey, Don. "Jamieson Named RCA Records President After 7-Month Search," 3. April 8, 1995.

Knopper, Steven. "As Podcast Industry Grows, Licensing Music Can Get Complicated—and Pricey." September 12, 2019. As Podcast Industry Grows, Licensing Music Can Get Complicated—and Expensive, *Billboard*.

Knopper, Steven. "Sheet Happens: One of Music's Oldest Businesses Is Growing in the Digital Age." June 2, 2019. Sheet Happens: One of Music's Oldest Businesses Is Growing in the Digital Age, *Billboard*.

Koranteng, Juliana. "MP3 Debate Emerges at Conference," 69. June 3, 2000.

Lander, Howard. "A Letter from the Publisher: Billboard Debuts Piece Counts on Two Music Sales Charts," 1. May 25, 1991.

LeGrand, Emmanuel. "At MIDEM, Newfound Taste for Online Music," 5. February 7, 2004.

Levine, Robert. "Between Rock and a Database: Streaming Services, Artists and Music Publishers Are Colliding." March 11, 2016. Between Rock and a Database: Streaming Services, Artists and Music Publishers Are Colliding, *Billboard*.

Levine, Robert. "Citi's Music Industry Report, Dissected: What the Financial Giant Gets Right and (Very) Wrong." August 13, 2018. Citi's Music Industry Report, Dissected: What the Financial Giant Gets Right and (Very) Wrong, *Billboard*.

Levine, Robert. "Is the Record Business Really Back?" November 12, 2016. Is the Record Business Really Back? How Streaming Is (And Isn't) Turning a Profit, *Billboard*.

Levine, Robert. "Lyor Cohen: Warner's Label Chief Speaks Out on 360 Deals. . . .," 17. January 1, 2009.

Levine, Robert. "On Eve of 'Blurred Lines' Appeal Hearing, Richard Busch Is the Music Industry's Most Feared Lawyer." October 5, 2017. "Blurred Lines" Appeal Hearing, *Billboard*.

Levine, Robert. "SFX Emerges from Bankruptcy with a New Name, LiveStyle, and New Leader in Randy Phillips." December 7, 2016. SFX Emerges from Bankruptcy with a New Name, LiveStyle, and New Leader in Randy Phillips, *Billboard*.

Levine, Robert. "Taylor Swift Is the Latest Superstar to Use Ticketmaster's Verified Fan Program—but Does It Work?" August 25, 2017. Taylor Swift Is Using Ticketmaster's Verified Fan Program — But Does It Work? *Billboard*.

Lichtman, Irv. "Japan Hops to 2nd in NMPA Survey; Replaces Germany in '94 Collections Study," 34. July 20, 1996.

Lichtman, Irv. "'50s-'80s Hits Are in the Spirit: Former BMI Executive's Firm Deals for Oldies." 44. October 12, 1996.

Lichtman, Irv. "1995 Receipts, Distribs Break ASCAP Records," 6. February 24, 1996.

Lichtman, Irv. "95 Global Publishing Revenue Grew Modestly," 94. August 2, 1997.

Lichtman, Irv. "Annual NMPA Meeting Hears Good News—Harry Fox Revenues Hit Record High," 4. June 29, 1985.

Lichtman, Irv. "ASCAP Reaches New High in '96 for Distributions," 8. February 22, 1997.

Lichtman, Irv. "Global Pub Royalties Hit $4.71 Bil in 1992," 9. July 30, 1994.

Lichtman, Irv. "Global Publishing Report: Figures Show Modest Growth," 1. July 31, 1999.

Lichtman, Irv. "Global Revival Follows DJM Purchase Polygram Bows Publishing Unit," 6. November 15, 1986.

Lichtman, Irv. "Importer Sued on Issue of Mechanicals," 1. June 22, 1985.

Lichtman, Irv. "Inside Track—Print Deal—CCP Belwin," 74. April 30, 1988.

Lichtman, Irv. "Inside Track—Thank$," 90. June 17, 1889.

Lichtman, Irv. "NMPA: Mechanical Income Booming Upbeat News on Digital Future, Too," 6. July 22, 1995.

Lichtman, Irv. "Print Firms Are Optimistic Despite Economy's Woes," 1. January 16, 1982.

Lichtman, Irv. "Pub Meet Sings Aa Triumphant Note: Digital Royalty Bill Has Senate Sponsors," 5. August 3, 1991.

Lichtman, Irv. "Publishing Spotlight: Selling Fine Print Music," 62. June 3, 1995.

Lichtman, Irv. "Sony Music Enters Deal with Michael Jackson, ATV Catalog," 10. November 18, 1995.

Lichtman, Irv. "WB Publications Agrees to Buy CPP-Belwin: Purchase of Competitor Would Make Firm No. 2 in U.S.," 6. May 7, 1994.

Lichtman, Irv. "World's Third-Largest Pub. Co. Likely from Merger of MCA, PolyGram Operations," 3. June 13, 1998.

Lichtman, Irv. "Worldwide Pub Revenues Hit $3 Bil In 1989," 1. October 6, 1990.

Los Angeles Bureau. "It's Set: Merger of CMA, IFA," 14. November 16, 1974.

Mayfield, Geoff. "Totally '90's: Diary of a Decade," YE-16. December 25, 1999.

Morris, Chris, and Melinda Newman. "Reaction Mixed to A&M's Indie Promo Cutback," 9. December 27, 1997.

Morris, Chris. "Azoff Exits AEG," 8. August 2, 2003.

Morris, Chris. "Isgro Trial Testimony Bares Payoffs but Judge Warns of Possible Dismissal," 1. September 8, 1990.

Music Week Staff. "Where Are They Now? Ex - MCA 10 Percenters Scurrying Here & There," 6. September 1, 1962.

Newman, Melinda. "NARAS Enters a Post-Greene Era," 8. May 11, 2002.

Newman, Melinda. "The Guy Who Made Concert Tees Cool Looks Back on 40 Years of Retail Hits." May 22, 2017. Dell Furano: The Guy Who Made Concert Tees Cool on 40 Years of Retail Hits, *Billboard*.

Olsen, Catherine Applefeld. "The Spice of Life: Spice Girls and Idols Rack Up Boxscore Success," 48. May 24, 2008.

Orshoski, Wes. "MP3.com Could Face Additional Lawsuits," 10. December 2, 2000.

Peoples, Glenn, and Ed Christman. "The Pandora-Sony/ATV Deal: What It Means, Who Wins." November 13, 2015. The Pandora-Sony/ATV Deal: What It Means, Who Wins, *Billboard*.

Peoples, Glenn. "Apple, Labels Close in on Pricing," 8. March 21, 2015.

Peoples, Glenn. "Apple: Changing Web Radio in 2013," 42. December 22, 2012.

Peoples, Glenn. "D.C. Sets New Webcasting Rates: Free Streams Up, Paid Streams Down (with an Asterisk)," 42. December 16, 2016. D.C. Sets New Webcasting Rates: Free Streams Up, Paid Streams Down (with an Asterisk), *Billboard*.

Peoples, Glenn. "A New Kind of Freedom: Spotify, Mog, Radio: Subscription Services Ride Freemium to New Heights," 30. December 17, 2011.

Peoples, Glenn. "Proving Ground: The U.S. Launch of Spotify Is a Key Test of the Viability of Subscription Services," 5. July 23, 2011.Peoples, Glenn. "What Happens When Spotify Gets

Behind an Artist? A Case Study of Hozier and Major Lazer." August 7, 2015. Hozier, Major Lazer See Big Gains from Spotify Support, *Billboard*.

Pietroluongo, Silvio. "Charting Demand: How Billboard Recaps New Social Charts and Much More," 61. December 22, 2012.

Pietroluongo, Silvio. "How We Chart the Year," 82. December 20, 2008.

Reece, Doug. "Online Label GoodNoise to Buy Two MP3 Firms," 8. October 24, 1998.

Reece, Doug. "RIAA Files Suit over MP3 Player," 8. October 24, 1998.

Rosen, Craig. "Questions Arise at MCA as Morris Succeeds Teller," 6. December 2, 1995.

Rys, Dan. "Guy Moot, Carianne Marshall Set as Warner/Chappell's New Leadership Team." January 9, 2019. Guy Moot, Carianne Marshall Set as Warner/Chappell's New Leadership Team, *Billboard*.

Rys, Dan. "Jay Z, Live Nation Sign New 10-Year, $200 Million Touring Deal." May 11, 2017. Jay Z, Live Nation Officially Sign New 10-Year Touring Deal, Billboard.

Rys, Dan. "Jon Platt Exiting Warner/Chappell Music for Top Role Aat Sony/ATV." September 14, 2018. Jon Platt Exiting Warner/Chappell Music For Top Role At Sony/ATV, Billboard.

Rys, Dan. "President Obama Signs Anti-Scalping Bill into Law." December 15, 2016. President Obama Signs Anti-Scalping Bill into Law, Billboard.

Saxe, Frank. "MusicNet Proposal Raises Questions of Fairness," 1. April 14, 2001.

Schneider, Marc, and Andrew Flanagan. "Apple's Streaming Service: Everything We Know So Far." April 21, 2015. Apple's Streaming Service: Everything We Know So Far, *Billboard*.

Schneider, Marc. "Merlin Divests Fully from Spotify, Shares Proceeds with Members." May 15, 2018. Merlin Divests Fully from Spotify, Shares Proceeds with Members, *Billboard*.

Sexton, Paul. "Concerts at the Kremlin: A Profile of ICM/Fair Warning/Agency," 53. February 13, 1993.

Silverman, Tom. "Commentary: Preserving Diversity in the Music Biz," 6. May 18, 1996.

Spahr, Wolfgang. "Middelhoff: 'How to React to Napster,'" 1. September 2, 2000.

Stark, Phyllis. "Garth, Capitol Part Ways," 66. June 18, 2005.

Stine, G. Harry. "Retailing in the Electronic Age," 90th-22. December 15, 1984.

Sukin, Michael. "Billboard Op Ed—The Menace in Parallel Imports," 10. February 2, 1985.

Sutherland, Mark. "Showdown at the EMI Corral: Inside Guy Hands' London Meeting . . . with Artist Managers," 22. January 26, 2008.

Sutherland, Sam. "MCA Reveals Pisello Deals, Internal Report Details Payments," 6. May 25, 1985.

Talent Section Staff. "Open New Agency in Carmel," 24. January 25, 1975.

Talent Section Staff. "Three Talent Agencies in Merger to Form Triad," 30. August 18, 1984.

Traiman, Steve, and Matthew Benz. "Virgin and Trans World Incorporate Internet Kiosks," 67. November 3, 2001.

Traiman, Steve. "Expanded Monitoring, Collection & Disbursement Systems Are Rapidly Changing the Face and Pace of Publishing," 50. *Billboard Spotlight on Music Publishing*, June 13, 1998.

Traiman, Steve. "Off-Price Millions: The Secret in the Vault," 50. April 13, 1996.

Traiman, Steve. "Publishing Uses Technology for New Services, Protections,"69. August 14, 1999.

Tucker, Ken, with additional reporting by Antony Bruno. "Clearer Channels: Radio Stations Begin to Untangle the Web," 38. December 20, 2008.

Verna, Paul, and Ed Christman. "BMG Unwraps CD Package Rebate: Offer Is 17-cent Across the Board Discount," 10. August 22, 1992.

Verna, Paul. "Global Publishing Revenues Up Only 0.3% in 1996," 3. July 25, 1998.

Verna, Paul. "Sony, Philips at Work on Successor to CD," 1. June 21, 1997.

Waddell, Ray. "AEG Live Gets Ticketing and Fuse TV to Compete with Live Nation," 6. March 8, 2008.

Waddell, Ray. "As Album Sales Dwindle, Merch Is on the March as the Industry's Reliable Revenue Generator," 24. July 26, 2008.

Waddell, Ray. "Austin Fest Expands Its Boundaries," 21. May 14, 2005.

Waddell, Ray. "Azoff Exits Live Nation," 4. January 12, 2013.

Waddell, Ray. "Booking 'Quality Before Quantity': The Booking King from Queens, Dennis Arfa Marks Two Decades at the Top of His Game," 28. April 22, 2006.

Waddell, Ray. "CC Better Without Concerts? Report Suggests Sale of Live-Entertainment Division," 8. October 25, 2003.

Waddell, Ray. "CCE Curbs Exec Exodus," 9. November 15, 2003.

Waddell, Ray. "Clear Channel Is Taking Its Concert Biz Public," 32. November 26, 2005.

Waddell, Ray. "Clear Channel's Impact: Unclear; "Rivals Debate Role of Touring/Radio Giant in Shaping Concert Landscape," 1. February 15, 2003.

Waddell, Ray. "Concerns Raised over SFX/Clear Channel Deal," 1. March 11, 2000.

Waddell, Ray. "Concert Industry Marks Big Year," 1. January 8, 2000.

Waddell, Ray. "Entertainment Trends Debated, AMC Confab Panel," 17. October 12, 2002.

Waddell, Ray. "Executive Picture Now Clear at Clear Channel," 8. August 14, 2004.

Waddell, Ray. "For Messina, a New Day Dawns on Long Career," 15. July 5, 2003.

Waddell, Ray. "From Pandora's Box to Voodoo Lounge: Michael Cohl." November 13, 2004.

Waddell, Ray. "FXM Acquisition Creates Industry Buzz," 28. November 25, 2000.

Waddell, Ray. "Hot Seats: What Ticketmaster's Acquisition of TicketsNow Means for the Biz," 12. January 26, 2008.

Waddell, Ray. "Inside the Music Industry—and Congress'—Fight Against Ticket Bots." June 23, 2016. Music Stars Fight to Make "Ticket Bots" Software Illegal, *Billboard*.

Waddell, Ray. "Paradigm Acquires Little Big Man." August 21, 2006. Paradigm Acquires Little Big Man, *Billboard*.

Waddell, Ray. "Paradigm Shifts with MPA Buy," 6. November 13, 2004.

Waddell, Ray. "Randy Phillips Aims for Touring Industry 'Devolution,'" 8. March 2, 2002.

Waddell, Ray. "Rise of the Super-Manager: As Labels Stumble, Managers Become the Industry's Force to Be Reckoned With," 10. December 20, 2008.

Waddell, Ray. "SFX Adds More Venues to Its Growing Slate," 12. February 13, 1999.

Waddell, Ray. "SFX Claims Top Promoter Title Via PACE Purchase," 6. January 10, 1998.

Waddell, Ray. "SFX Rapidly Becoming Entertainment Goliath," 1. May 16, 1998.

Waddell, Ray. "SFX, Ticketmaster Strike Long-Term Deal," 3. November 28, 1998.

Waddell, Ray. "Stones Roll to No. 1: Tally of the Year's Top 25 Tours Tracks a Record-Setting Year," YE-92. December 23, 2006.

Waddell, Ray. "Survival of the Fittest Indie Promoters," 24. May 19, 2001.

Waddell, Ray. "Ten Years After Consolidation Swept Concert Promoters, the Dominance of Live Nation and AEG Defines the Industry," 27. October 4, 2008.

Waddell, Ray. "Tix $$ Raise Fan Ire: Concert Industry Frets, but No Price Cuts Seen," 1. January 10, 2004.

Waddell, Ray. "Who Needs Tickets: eBay's Acquisition of StubHub Brings More Juice to Secondary Biz," 18. February 3, 2007.

Waddell, Ray. "House of Blues Buys Universal Concerts," 8. August 7, 1999.

Waddell, Ray. "SFX Buys Three Concert Promoters: Move Marks a Major Consolidation of the Industry," 98. December 27, 1997.

Walsh, Christopher. "JDS Capital Buys DreamWorks Publishing Assets." November 11, 2004. JDS Capital Buys DreamWorks Publishing Assets, *Billboard*.

Werde, Bill. "Welcome to the New Billboard," 4. January 26, 2013.

Williams, Jean. "MCA Studies Its Independent Promoters' Expenditures," 1. November 15, 1980.

Billboard Annual Feature
Billboard Staff. "The Year in Music. 1985–2020.

*Billboard.com*Aniftos, Rania. "The 25 Best Musical TikTok Trends of 2020." December 18, 2020. The 25 Best Musical TikTok Trends of 2020, *Billboard.*

Billboard Chart Beat Staff. "Billboard 200 Makeover: Album Chart to Incorporate Streams & Track Sales." November 19, 2014. Billboard 200 Makeover: Album Chart to Incorporate Streams & Track Sales, *Billboard.*

Billboard Staff. "ASCAP, BMI Launch RapidCue," 6. August 25, 2007.*Billboard* Staff. "Billboard Charts to Adjust Streaming Weighting in 2018." October 19, 2017. Billboard Charts to Adjust Streaming Weighting in 2018, *Billboard.*

Billboard Staff. "Billboard's Genre Album Charts Will Now Incorporate Streams & Track Sales." January 26, 2017. Billboard's Genre Album Charts to Incorporate Streams & Track Sales, *Billboard.*

Billboard Staff. "Hot 100 News: Billboard and Nielsen Add YouTube Video Streaming to Platforms." February 20, 2013. Hot 100 News: Billboard and Nielsen Add YouTube Video Streaming to Platforms, *Billboard.*

Billboard Staff. "Michele Anthony Named Universal Music EVP, U.S. Recorded Music." September 26, 2013. Michele Anthony Named Universal Music EVP, U.S. Recorded Music (Exclusive), *Billboard.*

Brooks, Dave. "AEG to Make Significant Layoffs and Furlough Employees, Staff Memo Says." June 8, 2020. AEG to Make Significant Layoffs and Furlough Employees, Staff Memo Says, *Billboard.*

Brooks, Dave. "Five Things to Know About Competition in Ticketing, Eight Years After Live Nation-Ticketmaster Merger." April 2, 2018. Live Nation-Ticketmaster Merger: Five Facts on Ticketing Competition, *Billboard.*

Caulfield, Keith. "26% of All Physical Albums Sold in 2019 in U.S. Were Vinyl, Led by The Beatles." January 9, 2020. 26% of All Physical Albums Sold in 2019 in U.S. Were Vinyl, Led by The Beatles, *Billboard.*

Chart Staff. "Billboard Finalizes Changes to How Streams Are Weighted for Billboard Hot 100 & Billboard 2000." May 1, 2018. Billboard Updates Streams Weighting for Hot 100 & 200, *Billboard.*

Christman, Ed. "Alliance Entertainment in Talks to Acquire Anderson—Move Would Make Company Biggest Physical Wholesaler in U.S." May 15, 2016. Alliance Entertainment in Talks to Acquire Anderson, *Billboard.*

Christman, Ed. "Best Buy to Pull CDs, Target Threatens to Pay Labels for CDs Only When Customers Buy Them." February 2, 2018. Best Buy Pulling CDs, Target to Only Pay Labels for CDs When Bought, Billboard.

Christman, Ed. "Blavatnik Gets His Prize," 10. February 23, 2013.

Christman, Ed. "CD Sales Are Not Dying, but They Are Heading Towards Niche Status Like Vinyl." September 26, 2018. CD Sales Are Not Dying, but They Are Heading Towards Niche Status Like Vinyl: Analysis, *Billboard.*

Christman, Ed. "Copyright Royalty Board? Statutory, Mechanical Performance? A Primer for the World of Music Licensing." August 18, 2016. Music Licensing: A Primer on Pricing, *Billboard.*

Christman, Ed. "Exit Ramp: Wholesalers Poised to Fill Void Left by Handleman's Departure," 6. June 14, 2008.

Christman, Ed. "Inside the Music Publishing World's Epic Struggle to Build a Single Song Database." August 2, 2017. Inside the Music Publishing World's Epic Struggle to Build a Single Song Database, *Billboard.*

Christman, Ed. "Irving Azoff's Global Music Rights Offers Temporary License to Radio Stations." December 24, 2016. Irving Azoff's Global Music Rights Offers Temporary License to Radio Stations, *Billboard*.

Christman, Ed. "John Janick to Succeed Jimmy Iovine as Chairman, CEO of Interscope Geffen A&M." May 28, 2014. John Janick to Succeed Jimmy Iovine as Chairman, CEO of Interscope Geffen A&M, *Billboard*.

Christman, Ed. "New BMI Radio Royalties Revealed Following RMLC Settlement." April 15, 2020. BMI Radio Royalties Revealed Following RMLC Settlement, Billboard.

Christman, Ed. "Nielsen 360 Study Finds Consumers Love Streaming Music, but Radio Still Strong." November 15, 2017. Nielsen 360 Study Finds Consumers Love Streaming Music, but Radio Still Strong, *Billboard*.

Christman, Ed. "Questions Answered on Rizvi Traverse's SESAC Investment." January 22, 2013. Questions Answered on Rizvi Traverse's SESAC Investment, *Billboard*.

Christman, Ed. "Sony Music Completes Orchard Buy-Out." March 18, 2015. Sony Music Completes Orchard Buy-Out, *Billboard*.

Christman, Ed. "Super D Acquires Alliance Entertainment, Creating Second Largest US Music Wholesaler." September 4, 2013, Super D Acquires Alliance Entertainment, Creating Second Largest US Music Wholesaler (Sources), *Billboard*.

Christman, Ed. "Taylor Swift's Catalog Could Have Doubled in Value Since Scooter Braun's Purchase." February 28, 2020. Taylor Swift's Catalog Could Have Doubled in Value Since Scooter Braun's Purchase, *Billboard*.

Christman, Ed. "Top-Dollar Tunes: A Timeline of 21st Century Song Catalog Deals." November 20, 2020. 21st Century Song Catalog Deals: A Timeline, *Billboard*.

Christman, Ed. "Universal Music Group's Profit Margins Grew in 2020, Despite Pandemic." March 3, 2021. march-03-2021-billboard-bulletin-1614816272.pdf.

Christman, Ed. "Why Warner Music Is Going Public Now & How No One Saw It Coming" February 13, 2020. Warner Music Is Going Public: Why Now & How No One Saw It Coming, *Billboard*.

Christman, Ed. "Who Owns That Song? ASCAP & BMI's New Joint Data Platform Will Tell You." December 21, 2020. Who Owns That Song? ASCAP & BMI's New Joint Platform Will Tell You, *Billboard*.

Christman, Ed. "SESAC Buys the Harry Fox Agency." July 7, 2015. SESAC Buys the Harry Fox Agency, *Billboard*.

Cirisano, Tatiana. "If You Stream It, Will They Come? Inside the Livestream Boom." August 31, 2020. Inside the Livestream Boom, *Billboard*.

Eggertsen, Chris. "Music Streaming and Sales Rebound—Will Concerts Follow Suit? Five Key Insights from New Nielsen Music/MRC Data COVID-19 Report." July 7, 2020. Music Streaming & Sales Rebound—Will Concerts Follow Suit? Nielsen Music/MRC Data Study, *Billboard*.

Flanagan, Andrew. "It's Official: Jay Z's Historic Tidal Launches with 16 Artist Stakeholders." March 30, 2015. It's Official: Jay Z's Historic Tidal Launches with 16 Artist Stakeholders, *Billboard*.

Flanagan, Andrew. "A Look Back at Spotify's U.S. Launch for Clues to Apple Music's Future." June 30, 2015. A Look Back at Spotify's U.S. Launch for Clues to Apple Music's Future, *Billboard*.

Halperin, Shirley. "How Universal Music Group's New Top-Level Troika Brings Peace (For Now)." April 4, 2014. *Billboard*.

Hayden, Erik. "CAA Announces 'Significant' Layoffs Amid COVID-19 Pandemic." July 28, 2020. CAA Announces "Significant" Layoffs Amid COVID-19 Pandemic, *Billboard*.

Knopper, Steven. "As Podcast Industry Grows, Licensing Music Can Get Complicated—and Pricey." September 12, 2019. As Podcast Industry Grows, Licensing Music Can Get Complicated—and Expensive, *Billboard*.

Knopper, Steven. "Why the Music Industry Should be Watching Liberty Media CEO Greg Maffei's 2020 Moves." January 10, 2020. Why Liberty Media CEO Greg Maffei Is One to Watch in 2020, *Billboard*.

Marks, Craig. "Classic Power Squad: MTV Founders Reunite, Reflect on 'Life Changing' Channel." February 9, 2017.

Medved, Matt. "Ultra Music Founder Patrick Moxey on Dance Music Going Mainstream." October 16, 2015. Ultra Music Founder Patrick Moxey on Dance Music Going Mainstream and OMI's Global Success, *Billboard*.

Newman, Melinda. "Why the Music Publishing Market Is Still Booming—and How Long the Party Will Last." November 29, 2020. Inside the Music Publishing Market Boom (and How Long It Will Last), *Billboard*.

Peoples, Glenn. "How 'Playola' Is Infiltrating Streaming Services: Pay for Play Is 'Definitely Happening'." 15. August 19, 2015Peoples, Glenn. "Live Nation Raising Another $1.2B to Weather Uncertain Year," 15. May 14, 2020. Live Nation Raising Another $1.2 Billion to Weather Uncertain Year, *Billboard*.

Peoples, Glenn. "Recording Industry 2015: More Music Consumption and Less Money, That's Digital Deflation." January 7, 2016. Recording Industry 2015: More Music Consumption and Less Money, That's Digital Deflation, *Billboard*.

Pham, Alex. "NMPA Targets Unlicensed Lyric Sites, Rap Genius Among 50 Sent Take-Down Notices." November 11, 2013. NMPA Targets Unlicensed Lyric Sites, Rap Genius Among 50 Sent Take-Down Notices, *Billboard*.

Rys, Dan. "A Brief History of the Ownership of the Beatles Catalog." January 20, 2017. A Brief History of the Ownership of the Beatles Catalog, *Billboard*.

Rys, Dan. "Lyor Cohen Named YouTube's Global Head of Music." September 28, 2016. Lyor Cohen Named YouTube's Global Head of Music, *Billboard*.

Rys, Dan. "Why YouTube and the Music Biz Are Getting Along Better Than Ever." February 13, 2020. Why YouTube and the Music Biz Are Getting Along Better Than Ever, *Billboard*.

Schneider, Mark. "Spotify Increases Paid User Base to 124M, Reports $7.44B Revenue in 2019." February 5, 2020. Spotify Increases Paid User Base to 124M, Reports $7.44B Revenue in 2019.

Sun, Rebecca. "Endeavor to Cut Pay Companywide Amid Pandemic." April 1, 2020. Endeavor to Cut Pay Companywide Amid Pandemic, *Billboard*.

Waddell, Ray. "Veteran Marsha Vlasic to Bring Deep Client Roster to Artist Group International." September 9, 2014. Exclusive: Veteran Marsha Vlasic to Bring Deep Client Roster to Artist Group International, *Billboard*.

Billboard Bulletin

Atwood, Brett. "The History of the Music Industry's First-Ever Digital Single, 20 Years After Its Release." September 13, 2017. The History of the Music Industry's First-Ever Digital Single for Sale, 20 Years After Its Release, *Billboard*.

Brooks, Dave. "Need Tickets? Get in Line, as Emails Reveal How Brokers Get First Crack at Tix for Big Arena Shows." December 14, 2018. Brokers Get First Crack at Tix for Big Arena Shows, *Billboard*.

Brooks, Dave. "The Price Is Right: Touring Sector Sees Growth by Finding What Fans Are Willing to Pay." December 18, 2018. The Price Is Right: Touring Sector Sees Growth by Finding What Fans Are Willing to Pay, *Billboard*.

Brooks, Dave. "Two Years After Emerging from SFX Bankruptcy, LiveStyle Is Growing Again (and Profitable)." December 14, 2018. LiveStyle Is Growing Again (and Profitable),

Billboard.Christman, Ed. "Apple Music, Spotify Battle Heats Up Again as Race for US Subscribers Gets Closer." February 5, 2018. Apple Music, Spotify Battle Heats Up Again as Race for US Subscribers Gets Closer, *Billboard*.

Christman, Ed. "Competing Publishing Industry Wishes, Concerns Give DOJ Plenty to Ponder. . . in Consent Decree Review." November 20, 2019. Competing Publishing Industry Wishes, Concerns Give DOJ Plenty to Ponder in Consent Decree Review, *Billboard*.

Christman, Ed. "How the SiriusXM-Pandora Deal Would Impact the Music Business." September 27, 2018. How the SiriusXM-Pandora Deal Would Impact the Music Business.

Christman, Ed. "Sony Completes Acquisition of EMI Music Publishing Despite Indie Objections." November 14, 2018. Sony Completes Acquisition of EMI Music Publishing Despite Indie Publisher Objections, *Billboard*.

Christman, Ed. "Warner Music's IPO Arrives with Roughly $12.5 Billion Valuation." May 26, 2020. Warner Music Group Launches Initial Public Offering, *Billboard*.

Giardina, Carolyn. "CES: Consumer Tech Industry Could Reach $398 Billion in 2019, CTA Projects." January 7, 2019. CES: Consumer Tech Industry Could Reach $398 Billion in 2019, CTA Projects, *Billboard*.

Hu, Cherie. "Anatomy of a Sample: The Legal Complexities Behind Hip Hop's Creative Backbone." September 24, 2018. Anatomy of a Sample: The Legal Complexities Behind Hip-Hop's Creative Backbone, *Billboard*.

Hu, Cherie. "Car Wars: Spotify Faces Stiff Competition as Music Streaming's Battle to Conquer the Road Heats Up." April 11, 2018. Spotify Faces Stiff Competition as Music Streaming's Battle to Conquer the Car Heats Up, *Billboard*.

Peoples, Glenn. "Consumers Now Favor Streaming Services for Music Discovery over All Other Sources." September 30, 2020. Consumers Favor Streaming for Music Discovery Over All Other Sources, *Billboard*.

Peoples, Glenn. "Music's 3Q Earnings Preview: 7 Key Points to Watch." October 19, 2020. Music's Third-Quarter Earnings Preview: Seven Key Points to Watch, *Billboard*.

Rys, Dan. "Nielsen Releases In-Depth Statistics on Live Music Behavior: 52 Percent of Americans Attend Shows." November 15, 2018. Nielsen Stats on Live Music Behavior, *Billboard*.

Rys, Dan. "Recording Academy Chief Neil Portnow to Step Down Next Year." May 31, 2018. Recording Academy Chief Neil Portnow to Step Down Next Year, *Billboard*.

Rys, Dan. "Troy Carter Explains How Spotify's Free Tier Upgrade Can Fuel Company's Growth." April 25, 2018. Troy Carter Explains How Spotify's Free Tier Upgrade Can Fuel Company's Growth, *Billboard*.

Werde, Bill. "Move the Grammys to Atlanta." January 27, 2018. Grammys 2018: Move the Awards to Atlanta, *Billboard*.

BitTorrent.org

Cohen, Bram. "The BitTorrent Protocol Specification." February 4, 2017, bep_0003.rst_post (bittorrent.org).

bizjournals.com

Temple, James. "Listen.com Acquires TuneTo.com." April 5, 2001, Gavin-2001-04-13.pdf (worldradiohistory.com), 9.

blog.songtradr.com

Songtradr. "What Are ISWC/ISRC Codes and How Do I Get Them?" September 6, 2016. What Are ISWC/ISRC Codes and How Do I Get Them? The Songtradr Blog.

Bloomberg Businessweek

Elgin, Ben. "Google Buys Android for Its Mobile Arsenal." August 17, 2005. Google Buys Android for Its Mobile Arsenal (tech-insider.org).

BMI.com

BMI.com News. "BMI, ASCAP Announce Launch of RapidCue Online Cue-Sheet Technology." August 14, 2007. BMI, ASCAP Announce Launch of RapidCue Online Cue-Sheet Technology, BMI.com.

BMI.com News. "Bob Israel Living 'An American Dream' in Studio." April 17, 2001. Bob Israel Living "An American Dream" in Studio, News, BMI.com.

Brighthub.com

Smith, M. S. "The History of File Sharing: Where Did It Begin?" May 23, 2011.

Brittannica.com

Gregersen, Eric. "Bit Torrent." January 6, 2012.

broadcastingcable.com

Eggerton, John. "ASCAP, BMI Propose Interim, Time-Limited Consent Decrees to DOJ." March 1, 2019. ASCAP, BMI Propose Interim, Time-Limited Consent Decrees to DOJ, Next TV.

broadcastlawblog.com

Oxenford, David. "Background on the GMR/RMLC Dispute—5 Questions on the Basics of the Controversy." January 12, 2017. Background on the GMR/RMLC Dispute—5 Questions on the Basics of the Controversy, Broadcast Law Blog.

Oxenford, David. "Details of the ASCAP Settlement with the Radio Industry—What Will Your Station Pay?" January 30, 2012. Details of the ASCAP Settlement with the Radio Industry—What Will Your Station Pay? Broadcast Law Blog.

burntorange.com

Daniel, Cody. "The University of Texas, Oak View Group Agree to Build 'World-Class' On-Campus Arena." December 20, 2018.

Business 2.0 Magazine

Keegan, Paul. "Is the Music Store Over?" March 1, 2004.

businessinsider.com

Saint, Nick. "Spotify Picks Up Substantial Investment from Founders Fund." February 24, 2010.

Stuart, Matthew, and Clancy Morgan. "How Columbia House Sold 12 CDs for as Little as a Penny." January 2, 2019.

BusinessofApps.com

Iqbal, Mansoor. "Spotify Usage and Revenue Statistics (2019)." May 10, 2019.

Businesswire

Ole. "ole Announces Sale of CEO Stake to Ontario Teachers', Robert Ott to Continue as CEO." News release. May 17, 2018.

PolyGram. "PolyGram Acquires 50% of Def Jam." News release. November 16, 1994.

Technavio Research Staff. "Secondary Ticket Market to Grow by $6.96 bn in 2020." November 4, 2020.

canalys.com

Canalys Staff. "64 Million Smart Phones Shipped Worldwide in 2006." February 12, 2007.

CBC Investigates

Seglins, Dave, Rachel Houlihan, and Laura Clementson. "'A Public Relations Nightmare': Ticketmaster Recruits Pros for Secret Scalper Program." September 19, 2018.

CBS News

CBS San Francisco News Staff. "Congress Cracks Down on 'Bots' That Buy Up Concert Tickets." December 7, 2016.

Pires, Lisa. "Billboard Introduces Social 50 Music Chart." December 2, 2010.

CelebrityAccess.com

Le Blanc, Larry. "Industry Profile: Michael Cohl." Part 1, March 6, 2013; Part 2, March 13, 2013.

CGA.CT.gov
Watson, Judy. "Ticket Scalping Laws in Other States." October 7, 2003.

Chalmers.com
Plaza, Anna. "Martin Lorentzon—Founder of Spotify." September 9, 2015.

chicagoreader.com
Raymer, Miles. "Drake Charts a Course for Pop." November 17, 2011.

citi.com/citigps
Citi GPS: Global Perspectives & Solutions. "Putting the Band Back Together: Remastering the World of Music." August 2018.

Cleveland Plain Dealer
Cooley, Patrick. "Belkin Productions at 50: Jules and Mike Belkin Look Back on 5 Decades of Cleveland Rock (Vintage Photos)." February 4, 2016.

cnbc.com
Bursztynsky, Jessica. "Spotify Made Huge Investments in Podcasts—Here's How It Plans to Make Them Pay Off," December 19, 2020.
Guzman, Zack. "The Surreptitious Rise of the Online Scalper." December 17, 2015.
Kharpal, Arjun. "China's Tencent Is Now Bigger than Facebook After Adding Around $200 Billion to Its Value This Year." July 29, 2020.

cnet.com
Abrar Al-Heeti, Abrar. "TikTok Is Reportedly Experimenting with 3-Minute Videos." December 2, 2020.
Fried, Ian, and Paul Festa. "Jobs Unveils New iPods and iMac." July 17, 2002.
Hamashige, Hope. "MP3.com Founder Michael Robertson Discusses His Revolutionary Company." February 28, 2000.
Hu, Jim. "Web, Music Giants March to Different Tunes." January 2, 2002.
Kawamoto, Dawn. "Sprint Dials into Music." December 8, 2005.
Krigel, Beth Lipton. "MP3.com IPO Prices over Top of Range." July 20, 1999.
News Staff. "RealNetworks Launches Hot IPO." November 27, 1997.
News Staff, "CDnow Goes Public with a Bang." February 10, 1998.
News Staff. "Steve Jobs: A Timeline." October 5, 2011.
Pendlebury, Ty, and Xiomara Blanco. "Best Music Streaming Service for 2020: Spotify, Apple Music, Amazon and More." April 6, 2020.

CNN Money
Hamashige, Hope. "MP3.com Founder Michael Robertson Discusses His Revolutionary Company." February 28, 2000.

Collectors Weekly
Marks, Ben. "If You're Too Young to Remember the Magic of Tower Records, Here's What You Missed." April 13, 2016.

Computer World
Williams, Martyn. "Apple's iTunes Store Served Its 10 Billionth Music Download, According to the Company." February 24, 2010.

consensus.net
Consensys. "About Us." January 14, 2022.

copyright.gov
US Copyright Office. "Digital Millennium Copyright Act—Copyright Office Summary." December 1998.
US Copyright Office. "The Music Modernization Act—Frequently Asked Questions." December 1, 2020.

The Copyright Alliance
Hart, Terry. "A Brief History of Webcaster Royalties," November 28, 2012.

counterpointresearch.com
Kumar, Abhilash. "Global Online Music Streaming Grew 32% Y-O-Y to 350 M Subscriptions." April 3, 2020.

Crain's Detroit Business
Kaffer, Nancy. "Handleman Liquidation Leaves Questions for Shareholders." October 5, 2008.
cyber.harvard.edu/archived_content/events/netmusic
Harvard Law School. "Signal or Noise: The Future of Music on the Net." February 25, 2000.

The Daily Beast
Tani, Maxwell. "Billboard Chief Squashed Sexual-Harassment Stories About His Record Exec Pal," May 4, 2018.

dailywireless.com
Churchill, Sam. "T-Mobile: $10B in 3 Years." January 15, 2008.

david.weakley.org
Weakly, David E. "MP3 Summit Two: 1999." June 19, 1999.
Weakly, David E. "1998 MP3 Summit Report." June 9, 1998.

ddex.net.about
Digital Data Exchange Website. "A Not-for-Profit, Membership Organisation." December 1, 2020.

deadline.com
Fleming, Mike, Jr. "TPG Spends $225 Million in Deal that Ups Stake in CAA to 53%." October 20, 2014.

Deadline Hollywood
Lieberman, David. "Philip Anschutz Decides to Hang on to AEG; Tim Leiweke Leaving as CEO." March 14, 2013.
deployedresources.com
Deployed Resources Team. "The Rising Trends of Music Festivals." June 13, 2018.

DeWolfeMusic.com
De Wolfe Music. "110 Years of De Wolfe Music." December 15, 2020.

digitalmusicnews.com
Price, Jeff. "The US Gov't Is Forcing Streaming Services to Pay Songwriters 43.8% More." January 28, 2018.
Resnikoff, Paul. "A Comprehensive Comparison of Performance Rights Organizations in the US." February 20, 2018.
Sanchez, Daniel. "Irving Azoff's GMR Faces a Serious Legal Setback Against U.S. Radio Stations." August 16, 2018.
Sanchez, Daniel. "War Erupts over Whose Global Music Rights Database Is Better." August 4, 2017.

dima.org
Mulligan, Mark. "Streaming Forward—Digital Media Association Annual Music Report—A MIDIA Research Report." March 2018.
Mulligan, Mark. "Streaming Forward—Digital Media Association Annual Music Report—A MIDIA Research Report." 2020.

E-Commerce Times
Conlin, Robert. "Cox Plays $45 Million MP3.com Tune." June 9, 1999.

EFF.com

Electric Frontier Foundation. "RIAA vs. The People." September 30, 2008.

Entertainment and Sports Law Journal 3(2)
Fuhr, Joseph. "The Antitrust Implications of Minimum Advertised Pricing." 2016.

Entertainment Weekly
Browne, David. "A Case in Omaha Reopens the Explicit Content Debate." May 22, 1992.

exploration.io
Christman, Ed. "What Is Music Reports?" July 20, 2018.

fastcompany.com
Lidsky, David. "The Definitive Timeline of Spotify's Critic-Defying Journey to Rule Music." August 6, 2018.

The Financial Times
Edgecliffe-Johnson, Andrew, and David Gelles. "The Man Who Made Music Videos Pay," November 21, 2011.

foley.com
Foley, Caitlyn M. "The Coronavirus Aid, Relief, and Economic Security Act ("CARES Act") Is Enacted into Law." March 27, 2020.

Forbes
Aydar, Ali. "What Was It Like to Work at the Old Napster?" July 3, 2012.
Desmond, Maurna. "Clear Channel Deal Finally Closed." May 4, 2008.
Frommer, Dan. "Cingular Tunes In." November 2, 2006.
Greenburg, Zack O'Malley. "Buying The Beatles: Inside Michael Jackson's Best Business Bet." June 2, 2014.
Greenburg, Zack O'Malley. "Dr. Dre's $3 Billion Monster: The Secret History of Beats." March 8, 2018.
Hu, Cherie. "Is Now Really the Best Time to Invest in Music Royalties?" January 4, 2018.
Hunckler, Matt. "MusicSpoke Looks to Disrupt $1 Billion Sheet Music Industry with Marketplace for Artist-Owned Scores." October 25, 2017.
Laurson, Jens F., and George A. Pieler. "The Tower That Fell." November 15, 2006.
Lunny, Oisin. "Battle for $15.19 Billion Secondary Ticket Market Heats Up with First Europe-Wide Anti Touting Law." June 24, 2019.
Mitchell, Julian. "Meet the CEO Spearheading a $2B Global Music Market." February 8, 2017.
Press, Gil. "A Very Short History of the Internet and the Web." February 2, 2015.
Rosenblatt, Bill. "Vinyl Is Bigger than We Thought. Much Bigger." September 18, 2018.
Trainer, David. "It Sounds Like Spotify Is in Trouble." October 13, 2020.

Fortune
Nieva, Richard. "Ashes to Ashes, Peer to Peer: An Oral History of Napster." September 5, 2013.

Segarra, Lisa Marie. "Here Are Some of the Best Releases from Record Store Day's 2018 List." April 21, 2018.

Foundation for Economic Education (FEE.com)
Bilodeau, Charles. "Pearl Jam vs. Ticketmaster: A Holy War on Reality." May 1, 1995.

futureofmusic.org
Future of Music Coalition and Fractured Atlas. "Too Big to Fail? Live Nation + Ticketmaster One Year Later." April 18, 2011.

gamerant.com

The Gavin Report
Beran, David, and Jennie Ruggles. "This is Radio Web." September 13, 1996.
Parks, William. "All Fortnite Radio Stations and Songs." August 5, 2020.

Goldman Sachs & Co.

Goldman Sachs Equity Research Report. "Music in the Air: The Show Must Go On." May 14, 2020.

Goldman Sachs Equity Research Report. "Music in the Air: Stairway to Heaven." October 4, 2018.

Grammy.com

"The Recording Academy® Continues Evolution of Grammy® Awards Process." News release. April 6, 2011.

Weatherby, Taylor. "Taylor Swift's Road to 'Folklore': How the Superstar Evolved from 'Diaristic' Country Tunes to Her Most Progressive Music Yet." March 10, 2021.

The Guardian

Swash, Rossie, "Online Piracy: 95% of Music Downloads Are Illegal," January 16, 2009.

halleonard.com

"Corporate History and Profile." September 27, 2020.

Harrison (AR) Daily Times

Dezort, Jeff. "Rock and Roll's 50th Anniversary Celebrated at Hall of Fame." October 5, 2004.

Harvard Business Review

Christensen, Clayton M., and Joseph L. Bowers. "Disruptive Technologies: Catching the Wave." January–February 1995.

Silverman, David. "Why the Recording Industry Really Stopped Suing Its Customers." December 22, 2008.

hdradio.com, Xperi.com

"Multicasting Definition." 2020.

hfapress@harryfox.com

"HFA Administers Publishing for Spotify's Highly-Anticipated U.S. Launch." News release. July 18, 2011.

highsnobiety.com

Hall, Jake. "The Evolution of Tour Merch." October 18, 2018.

history.com

Andrews, Evan. "Who Invented the Internet?" December 18, 2012.

historyofinformation.com

"The First Music CDs Pressed in the United States." September 1984.

History-of-rock.com

Peneny, D. K. "American Society Composers and Publishers (ASCAP)." March 1, 1998.

Peneny, D. K. "Broadcaster Music Inc. (BMI)." March 1, 1998.

hitsdailydouble.com

Hits News Staff. "Ringtone Market Heading Downstream, BMI Stats Show." March 27, 2007.

Pollack, Marc. "Slater Clears the Way: Veteran Promoter Sells Metropolitan to Clear Channel." December 9, 2002.

The Hollywood Reporter

Associated Press. "Ticketmaster Takes Stake in Front Line." October 23, 2008.

Butler, Susan. "ASCAP, BMI Launch RapidCue for PROs." August 15, 2007.Christman, Ed. "Steve Jobs Remembered by Edgar Bronfman Jr. Martin Bandier and Other Executives." October 6, 2011. Steve Jobs Remembered by Edgar Bronfman Jr., Martin Bandier and Other Executives. *The Hollywood Reporter.*

Coleman, Jonny. "Critic's Notebook: Unpacking the Politics of the 2019 Grammy Changes." February 27, 2018.

Cullins, Ashley. "Global Music Rights Takes Fire at Radio 'Cartel.'" December 6, 2016.

Gardner. Eriq. "BMI Demands Licensing Documents from Irving Azoff-Led Competitor." September 12, 2018.

Gardner, Eriq. "Irving Azoff Song Licensing Outfit Gains Edge in Antitrust Battle with Radio Stations." November 30, 2017.

Gardner, Eriq. "Kesha's Amended Lawsuit Against Dr. Luke Rejected by Judge." March 21, 2017.

The Hollywood Reporter Staff. "How Do APA, CAA, Gersh, ICM Partners, Paradigm, UTA and WME | IMG stack up? THR Breaks It Down." June 4, 2015.

Szalai, Georg. "Liberty Media Moves Live Nation Stake from Formula One to SiriusXM." April 23, 2020. Liberty Media Moves Live Nation Stake from Formula One to SiriusXM, *The Hollywood Reporter.*

Szalai, Georg. "Warner Music Group Names Cameron Strang CEO of Warner/Chappell." January 4, 2011.

Vlessing. Etan. "Irving Azoff Takes Full Control of MSG Joint Venture." October 8, 2018.

Vlessing. Etan. "Warner Music Group Sells Spotify Stake for $504M." August 7, 2018.

huffingtonpost.com

Bhasin, Kim. "Why Fancy Headphones Got So Incredibly Popular." May 29, 2014.

Kusek, David. "Musicians May Be Owed Billions in Unpaid Digital Music Royalties." April 8, 2011.

hyperbot.com

Chartmetric. "20 Most Popular Playlists on Spotify." November 12, 2020.

iab.com

Internet Advertising Bureau. "U.S. Podcast Advertising Revenue Study: Full-Year 2020 Results & 2021–2023 Growth Projections." May 2021.

IFPI.org

International Federation of the Phonographic Industry. "Global Music Report 2006: Annual State of the Industry." April 2006. 2006, *IFPI* (yumpu.com).

International Federation of the Phonographic Industry. "Global Music Report 2017: Annual State of the Industry." April 25, 2017. State of the Industry—Global Music Report Shop, *IFPI.*

International Federation of the Phonographic Industry. "Global Music Report 2018: Annual State of the Industry." April 24, 2018. IFPI Global Music Report 2018, *IFPI.*

International Federation of the Phonographic Industry. "Global Music Report 2019: Annual State of the Industry." September 24, 2019. Global_Music_Report-the_Industry_in_2019-en.pdf (ifpi.org).

International Federation of the Phonographic Industry. "IFPI Piracy Report 2000." 2021. GMR2021_STATE_OF_THE_INDUSTRY.pdf (ifpi.org).

International Federation of the Phonographic Industry. "Music Consumer Insight Report 2018." October 9, 2018. 091018_Music-Consumer-Insight-Report-2018.pdf (ifpi.org).

imore.com

Hackett, Stephen. "The Advent and Evolution of Apple's Digital Hub." May 27, 2015.

Inc.com

Clifford, Stephanie. "Pandora's Long Strange Trip." October 1, 2007.

indystar.com

Lindquist, David. "Indianapolis Company Mandolin Emerges as an Industry Leader in Livestream Concerts." November 2, 2020.

inews.co.uk

Finnis, Alex. "Taylor Swift Masters: The Controversy Around Scooter Braun Selling the Rights to Her Old Music Explained." November 17, 2020.

insider.com

Haasch, Palmer. "TikTok Took over This Week's Billboard Hot 100 Singles Chart, Showing How the App Is Becoming Part of the Music Industry." April 13, 2020.

insideradio.com

Inside Radio Staff. "The Inside Story on How Cumulus Ended Up in Bankruptcy Court." December 14, 2017.

Inside Radio Staff. "The 'New Entercom': $1.94 Billion in Revenue by 2021." April 14, 2017.

Inside Radio Staff. "RMLC Seeks a Reset as BMI Fine-Tunes Its Radio Rate Proposal." January 7, 2019.

"New Licensing Deal Keeps Hold on Radio's Royalty Rates to SESAC." News release. August 24, 2020.

International Directory of Company Histories

"The Arbitron Company History." FundingUniverse.com, 2001.

Gale, Thomas. "Handleman Company." 2006.

"William Morris Agency, Inc. History." FundingUniverse.com. From *International Directory of Company Histories*, vol. 23. Detroit: St. James Press, 1998.

investors.wmg.com/news-releases

Warner Music Group. "Alfred Publishing to Purchase Warner Bros. Publications." News release. December 16, 2004.

isotope.com

Pangburn, DJ. "A Brief History of Pitch Correction in Music." October 29, 2018.

Journal of Law and Commerce

Happel, Stephen. "The Eight Principles of the Microeconomic and Regulatory Future of Ticket Scalping, Ticket Brokers, and Secondary Ticket Markets." jlc.law.pitt.edu/ojs/jlc. May 1, 2010.

JumpPhilly.com

Horst, Tyler. "Larry Magid: The Scene Builder." August 19, 2016.

kobaltmusic.com

"Kobalt Capital Closes Second Music Royalties Fund with $600 Million in Investment Capacity." News release. November 6, 2017.

Lefsetz Letter

Lefsetz, Bob. "A Public Relations Nightmare: Ticketmaster Recruits Pros for Secret Scalper Program." September 19, 2018.

Leonard Audio Institute

John Burnett. "Professional Live Music: History." June 6, 2009.

lexology.com/blogs

Ackerman LLP. "BMI Redux: BMI Seeks to Move to 'Clarify' the DOJ Position on Partial Licenses." August 15, 2016.

Ackerman LLP. "DOJ Rejects Modifications of ASCAP, BMI Consent Decrees." August 9, 2016.

Lifewire.com

Costello, Sam. "This Is the Number of iPods Sold All-Time." May 17, 2018.

Live Nation Entertainment LLC

Lavigne-Delville, Melissa, and Amanda Fraga. "The Power of Live: Global Live Music Fan Study." September 2018.

LOC.org

Congressional Resource Service Report for Congress. "The Work Made for Hire and Copyright Correction Act of 2000." January 2, 2001.

Long Island Pulse

Heffernan, Lisa. "Ron Delsener Celebrates 50 Years in the Biz." June 28, 2015.

Los Angeles Times

Bates, James. "Polygram to Buy Motown in Deal Worth $325 Million." August 4, 1993. Polygram to Buy Motown in Deal Worth $325 Million: Music: Purchase Is Expected to Make a Global Entertainment Firm of Revived Motown, Which Sold in 1988 for $61 Million, *Los Angeles Times* (latimes.com).

Battaglio, Stephen. "CBS Extends Its Deal to Air the Grammy Awards through 2026." June 15, 2016.

Bernheimer, Martin. "What Little Ears You Have, Grammy!" March 9, 1986. What Little Ears You Have, Grammy! *Los Angeles Times* (latimes.com). What Little Ears You Have, Grammy! *Los Angeles Times* (latimes.com).Cieply, Michael. "Inside *the* Agency: How Hollywood Works: Creative Artists Agency and the Men Who Run It." July 2, 1989. Inside <i> the </i> Agency : How Hollywood works: Creative Artists Agency and the men who run it - Los Angeles Times (latimes.com).

Cieply, Michael, and Leslie Helm. "Matsushita to Buy MCA—$6.5 Billion." November 27, 1990.

Citron, Alan. "Talent Agencies Find Galaxies Beyond Stars." September 17, 1991. Talent Agencies Find Galaxies Beyond Stars: Entertainment: The Top Firms Are Assuming Roles Ranging from Merchandising Consultant to Merchant Banker, in Addition to Influencing Trends in Movies, Television and Music, *Los Angeles Times* (latimes.com).

Citron, Alan. "13 InterTalent Agents Move to Positions at ICM." 13. October 23, 1992. InterTalent Agents Move to Positions at ICM, *Los Angeles Times* (latimes.com).

Delugach, Al, and William K. Knoedelseder Jr. "Four Indicted in Payola Probe of Record Industry." February 27, 1988. Four Indicted in Payola Probe of Record Industry, *Los Angeles Times* (latimes.com).

Duhigg, Charles. "Hitmakers Implicated in 'Pay for Play' Plans." December 4, 2005.

Duhigg, Charles. "Two Top Sony BMG Executives Step Down." June 2, 2006. Two Top Sony BMG Executives Step Down, *Los Angeles Times* (latimes.com).

Easton, Nina J. "Sony OKs Paying Up to $500 Million to Get 2 Producers." November 17, 1989. Sony OKs Paying Up to $500 Million to Get 2 Producers, *Los Angeles Times* (latimes.com).

Eller, Claudia. "Inheriting CAA Mantle Will Put Young Turks to the Test." August 23, 1995. Inheriting CAA Mantle Will Put Young Turks to the Test, *Los Angeles Times* (latimes.com).

Eller, Claudia. "So, Now What?: Ovitz Decision Stirs Things Up at CAA and Rival Agencies." June 6, 1995. So, Now What?: Ovitz Decision Stirs Things Up at CAA and Rival Agencies, *Los Angeles Times* (latimes.com).

Fritz, Ben. "Hollywood Reporter, Billboard Sold." December 10, 2009. Hollywood Reporter, Billboard Sold, *Los Angeles Times* (latimes.com).

Goldstein, Patrick, and Paul Grein. "Keeping a Scorecard on Winners, Losers in Record Industry Wars." December 17, 1989. Hollywood Reporter, Billboard sold, *Los Angeles Times* (latimes.com).

Goldstein, Patrick. "CBS' Battle of the Bosses: Springsteen vs. Yetnikoff." September 2, 1990. CBS' Battle of the Bosses: Springsteen vs. Yetnikoff, *Los Angeles Times* (latimes.com).

Kennedy, Gerrick D. "L.A. Reid's Exit from Epic Tied to Harassment Allegations." May 15, 2017.

Knoedelseder, William K., Jr. "Morris Levy Gets 10-Year Sentence: Roulette Records Chief Fined $200,000." October 29, 1988.

Knoedelseder, William K., Jr. "Morris Levy: Big Clout in Record Industry." July 20, 1986.

Knoedelseder, William K., Jr. "Record Promoter's Suit Against MCA, Warner Dismissed." August 23, 1988.

Knoedelseder, William K., Jr. "The Rap on RCA Records: The Original U.S. Record Company Is Back in Groove." September 18, 1988.

Lewis, Randy. "Grammy Awards 2018: How the Recording Academy Has Evolved Toward Relevance." January 28, 2018.

Mcdermott, Terry. "NWA: Straight Outta Compton." April 14, 2002.

Ng, David. "Talent Agencies Are Reshaping Their Roles in Hollywood. Not Everyone Is Happy About That." April 6, 2018.

Pascrell, Rep. Bill. "Everyone's Worst Fears About the Live Nation-Ticketmaster Merger Have Come True," Op-Ed, May 17, 2018.

Peltz, Jennifer. "Kesha Made a False Claim About Producer Dr. Luke, according to Judge," February 7, 2020.

Pham, Alex. "'Big Jon' Platt, a Music-Publishing Power, Joins Warner/Chappell." September 10, 2012.

Philips, Chuck. "4 Music Companies Wooing Interscope." December 1, 1995.

Philips, Chuck. "Judge Dismisses Payola Charges Against Record Promoter Isgro." March 26, 1996.

Richter, Paul, and William K. Knoedelseder, Jr. "Sony Buys CBS Record Division for $2 Billion." November 19, 1987.

Sanchez, Jesse. "Rhino Records, EMI Buy Roulette's Labels." June 2, 1989.

Verrier, Richard. "UTA Buys the Agency Group." August 20, 2015.

Weinstein, Henry. "U.S. Indicts 3 on Music 'Payola,' Fraud Charges." December 1, 1989.

lowendmac.com

LEM Staff. "History of the Compact Disc," May 1, 2014.

macrumors.com

Hardwick, Tim. "Beats 1 Is 'the Biggest Radio Station in the World,' Says Apple Music." March 27, 2017.

macworld.com

Macworld Staff. "iTunes Store and DRM-free Music: What You Need to Know." January 7, 2009.

McElhearn, Kirk. "15 Years of iTunes: A Look at Apple's Media App and Its Influence on an Industry." January 9, 2016.

makeuseof.com

Price, Dan. "The 7 Best Music Streaming Services for Audiophiles." May 22, 2020.

Manatt.com/insights

Bromley, Jordan. "U.S. Music Streaming Royalties Explained a/k/a $$$ from Spotify and Apple?" October 12, 2016.

marketwatch.com

Witkowski, Wallace. "Videogames Are a Bigger Industry than Movies and North American Sports Combined, Thanks to the Pandemic." January 2, 2021.

medium.com

Jim, Jonathan. "Why Apple's Beats Acquisition Keeps Improving with Age." April 21, 2020.

midiaresearch.com

Mulligan, Mark. "The Music Industry's Next Five Growth Drivers." May 22, 2020.

Mulligan, Mark. "Recorded Music Revenues Hit $23.1 Billion in 2020, with Artists Direct the Winners—Again." March 15, 2021.

Milwaukee Journal Sentinel

Romell, Rick. "Hal Leonard Buys Sheet Music Plus." February 27, 2017.

money.cnn.com

Disis, Jill. "What Happened to Pandora?" March 29, 2018.

Moody's Investors Service

Fisher, Gregory A., and John Diaz. "Moody's Rating of SESAC." April 1, 2014.

Morningstar Credit Ratings LLC

Morningstar Pre-Sale Report. "SESAC Finance, LLC, Series 2019–1." July 19, 2019.

MP3newsletter.com

Menta, Richard. "MusicNet and Duet: Downloads Expire After 30 Days." May 17, 2001.

MTV News

Marsh, Dave. "MTV News Special Report: Dave Marsh on the Pearl Jam/Ticketmaster Mess." May 11, 1995.

Music Law Blog

Oxenford, David. "Music Rights Suit by Radio Music License Committee Against GMR Moved to California Courts—No End in Sight?" April 4, 2019.

musically.com

Dredge, Stuart. "Analysis: The Music Industry Enters 2020 on a Wave of Growth—and Optimism." January 3, 2020.

Dredge, Stuart. "How Many Users Do Spotify, Apple Music and Other Streaming Services Have?" July 28, 2020.

Forde, Eamonn. "Report: There Were 358m Music Subscribers by the End of 2019." April 6, 2020.

musicandcopyright.wordpress.com

Music and Copyright. "Global Recorded-Music and Music Publishing Market Share Results for 2018." May 8, 2019.

Music and Copyright. "UMG and SME Put the Market Share Squeeze on WMG and the Independent Sector." April 21, 2021.

MusicBizAcademy.com

Knab, Christopher. "Music Distributors: How to Attract Them and How to Work with Them." February 2008.

musicbusinessresearch.wordpress.com

Tschmuck, Peter. "The Global Music Publishing Market—An Analysis." January 31, 2016.

musicbusinessworldwide.com

Crupnick, Russ. "The Music Industry Is Still Obsessed with Charts—but Is It Always Looking at the Right Data." May 27, 2020.

Ingham, Tim. "Apple Music Just Made a Lot of Claims About What It Pays Artists. Let's Take a Closer Look." April 19, 2021.

Ingham, Tim. "David Crosby Forced to Sell His Song Catalog: 'It's My Only Option . . . Streaming Stole My Record Money.'" December 7, 2020.

Ingham, Tim. "Here's Exactly How Many Shares the Major Labels and Merlin Bought in Spotify—and What Those Stakes Are Worth Now." May 14, 2018.

Ingham, Tim. "Hipgnosis Songs Fund Is Now Worth $1.7bn . . . and Is on Course to Generate $120m-Plus This Year." December 4, 2020.

Ingham, Tim. "How Many Artists Are Generating $50k+ a Year on Spotify? Over 13,000." March 18, 2021.

Ingham, Tim. "Is Len Blavatnik About to Complete the Shrewdest Deal in the History of the Record Business?" May 26, 2020.

Ingham, Tim. "Nearly a Third of People in the Us Are Using Music Streaming Subscriptions." August 28, 2020.

Ingham, Tim. "Scooter Braun Joins $30m Investment in Avatar-Based Virtual Concert Startup Wave." June 10, 2020.

Ingham, Tim. "Sony Music Revenues Soared Above $4.5bn in 2020, After Huge Final Quarter of the Year," February 3, 2021.

Ingham, Tim. "Universal: We Will Share Spotify Money with Artists When We Sell Our Stock in Streaming Platform." March 5, 2018.

Ingham, Tim. "Warner IPO Saw Group of Senior Execs Share $593m Result from Long-Term Incentive Plan." October 19, 2020.

Ingham, Tim. "Fueled by Ramen: The Next Generation." December 17, 2015.

Music Business Worldwide Staff. "Kobalt Acquires AWAL, Launches Label Services Division." January 23, 2012.

Music Business Worldwide Staff. "Sony/ATV Unveils Neighbouring Rights Division." May 12, 2014.

Stassen, Murray. "BMG Eliminates 'Poisonous' Controlled Composition Clauses from Its US Record Contracts." October 8, 2020.

Stassen, Murray. "Lyor Cohen: YouTube Music Is 'The Fastest Growing Subscription Service Out There.'" June 3, 2021.

musicgateway.com/blog/how-to

D'Agostino, Julyo. "Does TikTok Pay You for Your Music?" July 31, 2020.

musicindustryblog.wordpress.com

Mulligan, Mark. "Kobalt Is Now a Next Generation Major Label in the Making." March 7, 2019.

musicrow.com

Hollabaugh, Lorie. "Reservoir Acquires Shapiro Bernstein, Including 16,000 Copyrights." May 18, 2020.

Nashville Post

Richard Lawson. "Hilley's Successor Announced at Sony/ATV." December 20, 2005.

National Public Radio (NPR.com)

Cole, Tom. "You Ask, We Answer: 'Parental Advisory' Labels—the Criteria and the History." *The Record Music Newsletter*. October 29, 2010.

Flanagan, Andrew. "New Music Law Expedites a $1.6 Billion Lawsuit Against Spotify." January 5, 2018.

Flanagan, Andrew. "Spotify Cops to Its Problems and Reveals the Massive Ambitions of Its Founder." March 2, 2018.

Stephen Witt. "Spotify Is, for Now, the World's Most Valuable Music Company." April 4, 2018.

New York Daily News

Smith, Candace. "Where Are They Now? Past Stars of 'The All New Mickey Mouse Club.'" December 21, 2015.

The New Yorker

Seabrook, John. "The Price of the Ticket: What Does It Take to Get to See Your Favorite Band?" August 10, 2009.

Bruck, Connie. "The Man Who Owns L.A.—A Secretive Mogul's Entertainment Kingdom." January 16, 2012.

New York Post

Arango, Tim. "It's 'Sony-Nara' as Mottola Jumps." January 10, 2003.

Gallivan, Joseph. "Napster Gets $15m & New CEO from VC in Tune-up." May 23, 2000.

New York Times

Associated Press. "Sony BMG Tentatively Settles Suits on Spyware." December 30, 2005.

Bloomberg News. "RealNetworks to Acquire Listen.com, a Music Site." April 22, 2003.

Blumenthal, Ralph. "U.S. Ends Ticketmaster Investigation." July 6, 1995.

Bray, Chad. "Guy Hands Abandons Legal Battle with Citigroup over EMI." June 10, 2016.

Cohen, Finn. "De La Soul's Legacy Is Trapped in Digital Limbo." August 9, 2016.

Cohen, Roger. "The Creator of Time Warner, Steven J. Ross, Is Dead at 65." December 21, 1992.

Coscarelli, Joe. "Kesha Again Blocked from Breaking Contracts with Dr. Luke." May 29, 2018.

Creswell, Julie. "Turning Music into Dollars at Sony/ATV." August 22, 2009.

De La Merced, Michael J. "A Media Veteran Joins Clear Channel." November 14, 2010.

De La Merced, Michael J., and Ben Sisario. "Warner Music Is Sold, Ending a Long Auction." May 6, 2011.

Delkic, Melina. "Covering Beyoncé and the Surprise Album Drop." July 1, 2018.

Elliott, Stuart. "Clear Channel in $3 Billion Deal to Acquire SFX Entertainment." March 1, 2000.

Fabrikant, Geraldine. "Polygram in Motown Agreement." September 24, 1991.

Fabrikant, Geraldine. "Seagram Puts the Finishing Touches on Its $5.7 Billion Acquisition of MCA." April 10, 1995.

Fabrikant, Geraldine. "Viacom Board Agrees to Split of Company." June 15, 2005.

Fabrikant, Geraldine. "Westinghouse Sets Deal to Buy 10 Radio Stations." April 8, 1989.

Ferris, Marc. "In Business; on the Charts." July 8, 2001.

Fisher, Lawrence M. "Company News; Microsoft Co-Founder in Ticketmaster Deal." November 23, 1993.

Flynn, Laurie. "Price Wars on Personal Computers Are Already Heating Up Sales for Holiday Season." December 4, 1995.

Gilpin, Kenneth N. "Polygram Records Names President." October 18, 1985.

Harmetz, Aljean. "Big Gains for Video Cassettes." August 21, 1985.

Hiltzik, Michael A. "Viacom to Buy MTV and Showtime in Deal Worth $667.5 Million." August 27, 1985. Viacom to Buy MTV and Showtime in Deal Worth $667.5 Million, *Los Angeles Times* (latimes.com).

Holson, Laura M. "Liquid Audio Gets a Buyer for Its Assets." January 24, 2003. *The New York Times* (nytimes.com).

Labaton, Stephen. "5 Music Companies Settle Federal Case on CD Price-Fixing." May 11, 2000, 5 Music Companies Settle Federal Case on CD Price-Fixing, *The New York Times* (nytimes. com).

Leeds, Jeff. "Clear Channel to Spin Off Its Entertainment Division." April 30, 2005. Clear Channel to Spin Off Its Entertainment Division, *The New York Times* (nytimes.com).

Leeds, Jeff. "Labels Win Suit Against Song Sharer." October 5, 2007. Labels Win Suit Against Song Sharer, *The New York Times* (nytimes.com).

Lewis, Peter. "Business Technology; Peering Out a 'Real Time' Window." February 8, 1995. Business Technology; Peering Out a 'Real Time' Window, *The New York Times* (nytimes.com).

Lewis, Peter. "Judge Rejects Computer-Crime Indictment." December 31, 1994. Judge Rejects Computer-Crime Indictment, *The New York Times* (nytimes.com).

New York Times Staff. "MP3.com Loses Copyright Case." September 6, 2000. MP3.com Loses Copyright Case, *The New York Times* (nytimes.com).

O'Brien, Timothy L. "What Happened to the Fortune Michael Jackson Made?" May 14, 2006. What Happened to the Fortune Michael Jackson Made? *The New York Times* (nytimes.com).

Pareles, Jon. "CBS Records to Buy Tree, Ending an Era in Nashville." January 4, 1989. The MEDIA BUSINESS; CBS Records to Buy Tree, Ending an Era in Nashville, *The New York Times* (nytimes.com).

Pareles, Jon. "Issue and Debate; Royalties on Recorders and Blank Audio Tapes." November 21, 1985. "Issue and Debate; Royalties on Recorders and Blank Audio Tapes."

Richtel, Matt. "Napster Has a New Interim Chief and Gets a $15 Million Investment." May 23, 2000. Napster Has a New Interim Chief and Gets a $15 Million Investment, *The New York Times* (nytimes.com).

Rosen, Ellen. "Student's Start-Up Draws Attention and $13 Million." May 26, 2005. *The New York Times* (nytimes.com).

Rosenbloom, Stephanie. "Circuit City Seeks Bankruptcy Protection." November 10, 2008. Circuit City Seeks Bankruptcy Protection, *The New York Times* (nytimes.com).

Saba, Jennifer. "Blackstone's Latest Move Has the Look of a Hit." January 5, 2017. *The New York Times* (nytimes.com).

Safronova, Valeriya. "Maestros of the Concert Merchandise Movement." July 25, 2017. Maestros of the Concert Merchandise Movement, *The New York Times* (nytimes.com).

Shapiro, Eben. "Blockbuster Agrees to Buy Music Store Chain." October 20, 1992. Company News; Blockbuster Agrees to Buy Music Store Chain, *The New York Times* (nytimes.com).

Sisario, Ben. "Boutique Music Publisher Invests in Six Early Beatles Songs." January 11, 2012. Boutique Music Publisher Invests in Six Early Beatles Songs, *The New York Times* (nytimes.com).

Sisario, Ben. "EMI Is Sold for $4.1 Billion in Combined Deals . . . , Consolidating the Music Industry." November 11, 2011. *The New York Times* (nytimes.com).

Sisario, Ben. "First Royalty Rates Set for Digital Music." October 2, 2008. First Royalty Rates Set for Digital Music, *The New York Times* (nytimes.com).

Sisario, Ben. "iHeartMedia, U.S.'s Largest Radio Broadcaster, Files for Bankruptcy." March 15, 2018. IHeartMedia, U.S.'s Largest Radio Broadcaster, Files for Bankruptcy, *The New York Times* (nytimes.com).

Sisario, Ben. "Lyor Cohen Resigns from Warner Music." September 24, 2012. *The New York Times* (nytimes.com).

Sisario, Ben. "Paul McCartney's Tip to Michael Jackson Pays Off." March 15, 2016. https://www.nytimes.com/2016/03/16/business/media/paul-mccartneys-tip-to-michael-jackson-pays-off.html. Paul McCartney's Tip to Michael Jackson Pays Off—*The New York Times* (nytimes.com).

Sisario, Ben. "The Music Industry's Math Changes, But the Outcome Doesn't: Drake Is No. 1." July 9, 2018. *The New York Times* (nytimes.com).

Sisario, Ben. "Music Publishing Deal Driven by Shift from Sales to Streaming." July 5, 2015. Music Publishing Deal Driven by Shift from Sales to Streaming, *The New York Times* (nytimes.com).

Sisario, Ben. "A New Spotify Initiative Makes the Big Record Labels Nervous." September 6, 2018. A New Spotify Initiative Makes the Big Record Labels Nervous, *The New York Times* (nytimes.com).

Sisario, Ben. "New Venture Seeks Higher Royalties for Songwriters." October 29, 2014. New Venture Seeks Higher Royalties for Songwriters, *The New York Times* (nytimes.com).

Sisario, Ben. "Paul McCartney's Tip to Michael Jackson Pays Off." March 15, 2016. *The New York Times* (nytimes.com).

Sisario, Ben, and Graham Bowley. "Live Nation Rules Music Ticketing, Some Say with Threats." April 1, 2018. *Live Nation Rules Music Ticketing, Some Say with Threats, The New York Times* (nytimes.com).

Smith, Ben. "The Media Equation—How TikTok Reads Your Mind." December 5, 2021. How TikTok Reads Your Mind, *The New York Times* (nytimes.com).

Sorkin, Andrew Ross. "Soundscan Makes Business of Counting Hits." August 11, 1997. Soundscan Makes Business of Counting Hits, *The New York Times* (nytimes.com).

Stevenson, Richard W. "Geffen Records Sold to MCA for Stock Worth $550 Million." March 14, 1990. Geffen Records Sold to MCA for Stock Worth $550 Million, *The New York Times* (nytimes.com).

Strauss, Neil. "A Major Merger Shakes Up the World of Rock." December 21, 1998. A Major Merger Shakes Up the World of Rock, *The New York Times* (nytimes.com).

Strauss, Neil. "Rolling Stones Live on Internet: Both a Big Deal and a Little Deal." November 22, 1994. Rolling Stones Live on Internet: Both a Big Deal and a Little Deal, *The New York Times* (nytimes.com).

Tsang, Amie, and Edmund Lee. "SiriusXM to Buy Pandora for $3.5 Billion. . . in Bid to Expand Reach." September 24, 2018. SiriusXM to Buy Pandora for $3.5 Billion in Bid to Expand Reach, *The New York Times* (nytimes.com).

Uncredited. "Tipper Gore Widens War on Rock." January 4, 1988. Tipper Gore Widens War on Rock, *The New York Times* (nytimes.com).

Vitello, Paul. "Frank Barsalona, Pioneering Rock Agent, Dies at 74." November 28, 2012. Frank Barsalona, Rock 'n' Roll Concert Promoter, Dies at 74, *The New York Times* (nytimes.com).

Wiggins, Phillip. "Turner Will Sell Cable Music Channel to MTV." November 29, 1984. Turner Will Sell Cable Music Channel to MTV, *The New York Times* (nytimes.com).

Woletz, Robert G. "Pop Music: Technology Gives the Charts a Fresh Spin." January 26, 1992. Pop Music; Technology Gives the Charts a Fresh Spin, *The New York Times* (nytimes.com).

Zipern, Andrew. "Technology Briefing: Software: Alliance Will Acquire Liquid Audio." June 14, 2002. Technology Briefing | Software: Liquid Audio Ends Merger Plans, *The New York Times* (nytimes.com).

newrepublic.com

Dayen, David. "The Ticket Monopoly Is Worse Than Ever (Thanks, Obama)." May 15, 2018.

Newzoo.com

Takahashi, Dean. "Smartphone Users Will Top 3 Billion in 2018, Hit 3.8 Billion by 2021." September 11, 2018.

Nielsen Company

Nielsen.com/insights. "Ad-Supported Audio Presents a Compelling Opportunity." February 2020.

Nielsen Music. "2018 U.S. Music 360." 2018.

Nielsen Music. "2019 Nielsen Music/MRC Data Year-End Report." 2020.

NMPA.com/MP3.com

News Views Press Release. "Music Publishers and Mp3.Com Reach Landmark Agreement." October 18, 2000.

notc.com

Who's Who at Famous Artists Agency. "Interview with Jerry Ade." n.d. 1990.

O'Reilly and Associates

Niederst, Jennifer. "Web Design in a Nutshell (Second Edition)." September 2001.

Paste Magazine

Blau, Max. "4 Ways Steve Jobs and Apple Changed the Music Industry." October 11, 2011.

pcmag.com

Shibu, Sherin. "Which Generation Is Most Dependent on Smartphones? Hint: They're Young." November 20, 2020.

pcmag.org

Greenwood, Will. "Augmented Reality (AR) vs. Virtual Reality (VR): What's the Difference?" March 31, 2021.

"Oculus and PlayStation VR Jockey Atop the Virtual Reality Market." October 4, 2019.

Segan, Sascha. "3G vs. 4G: What's the Difference?" February 10, 2015.

PCWorld.com

Montalbano, Elizabeth. "Microsoft, RealNetworks Settle for $761 Million." October 11, 2005.

Tynan, Dan. "The 25 Worst Tech Products of All Time," May 26, 2006.

Pew Research Center

Fox, Susannah, and Lee Rainie. "The Web at 25 in the U.S." February 27, 2014.

Pew Research Staff. "Americans Going Online . . . Explosive Growth, Uncertain Destinations." October 16, 1995.

Philips.com

"The History of the CD: The 'Jewel Case.'" philips.com/a-w/research/technologies/cd/jewel-case.

playlistresearch.com

Cosper, Alex. "History of Record Labels and the Music Industry." 2009.

Pollstar

Gensler, Andy. "How Ed Sheeran's 2018 Divide Tour Set the All-Time Touring Record." December 17, 2018.

"*Pollstar* Awards." 1996–2019.

Pollstar Newsletter Staff. "Venues Today to Re-Boot as VenuesNow; Knapp and Muret Join." December 12, 2017.

Pollstar Staff. "The Impact 50: 2019 Honorees." May 17, 2019.

"*Pollstar* Year End Business Analysis." 2001–20.

"*Pollstar* Year in Review." 2001–20.

popcrush.com

Russell, Erica. "Pop Stars Who Were Slapped with Music Lawsuits." April 11, 2018.

presstelegram.com

"The Carpenters, the Famous Singing Duo from Downey, Settles Lawsuit over Royalties." September 1, 2017.

Prezi.com

Erickson, Mariah. "History of the World Wide Web." September 30, 2017.

provideocoalition.com

Tépper, Allan. "Understanding 24-bit vs 16-bit Audio Production & Distribution." March 30, 2015.

pulseaudio.com

Fereydouni, Habil. "The Complete History of Headphones." October 15, 2015.

RadioInk.com

Radio Ink Staff. "How Much Ad Revenue Will Radio Get This Year?" July 9, 2019.

Radio Music Licensing Committee

Christian, Ed. "RMLC Letter to Stations Defining GMR Terms." January 9, 2017.

radioworld.com

McLane, Paul. "Broadcast Radio Ads Tank While Digital Holds Up." June 25, 2020.

McLane, Paul. "On-Air Radio Revenue Tanked ~ 24% in 2020." May 14, 2021.

Stine, Randy J. "Are Higher Music Licensing Costs Cued Up?" March 1, 2018.

Recording Academy Press Release

MusiCares Foundation. "MusiCares Foundation Acquires Musicians' Assistance Program." September 21, 2004.

Recording Industry Association of America

Peter Hart Research (1999–2004) and The Taylor Research & Consulting Group, Inc. (2004–2008). "2008 Consumer Profile." 1999–2008.

Stoner, Robert, and Jessica Dutra. "The U.S. Music Industries Jobs Benefits 2020 Report." Prepared for Recording Industry Association of America (R.I.A.A.)." February 2021.

Taylor Nelson Sofres Intersearch (Chilton Research Services). "Annual Consumer Profile." RIAA.com. 1989–98.

Referenceforbusiness.com

"History of International Creative Management, Inc." n.d. 2000.

The Register

Smith, Tony. "MP3.com Settles with Paul McCartney, NMPA, Agrees to Pay $30 Million for Rights." October 19, 2000.

research.philips.com/newscenter

Philips Research Archive. "Beethoven's Ninth Symphony of Greater Importance than Technology." January 29, 2008.

retailwire.com

Ryan, Tom. "Illegal Music Downloads Continue to Rise." July 31, 2007.

Reuters

Technology Staff. "Sirius XM Posts Profit, Its First Since Merger." February 25, 2010.

rhino.com

Cornyn, Stan. "Stay Tuned by Stan Cornyn: 7 Arts Buys Atlantic, Too." May 23, 2013.

Cornyn, Stan. "Stay Tuned by Stan Cornyn: Steve Ross Gets Agreeable." May 30, 2013.

Rolling Stone

Boehlert, Eric. "Pearl Jam: Taking on Ticketmaster." December 28, 1995.

Browne, David. "Inside Music's Merch Gold Rush." February 6, 2018.

Dansby, Andrew. "Clark Sues Greene over Jackson. . . ." December 20, 2001.

Goodman, Fred. "The Rolling Stone Interview: Walter Yetnikoff." December 15, 1988.

Grow, Korn. "PMRC's 'Filthy 15': Where Are They Now?" September 17, 2015.

Ingham, Tim. "The Three Biggest Myths Deluding the Modern Music Business." January 26, 2021.

Knopper, Steven. "The End of Owning Music: How CDs and Downloads Died." June 14, 2018.

Knopper, Steven. "iTunes' 10th Anniversary: How Steve Jobs Turned the Industry Upside Down." April 26, 2013.

Knopper, Steven. "Steve Jobs' Music Vision: How the Apple CEO Transformed an Industry." October 7, 2011.

Kreps, Daniel. "Charlie Walk, Republic 'Agree to Part Ways' After Sexual Misconduct Investigation." March 28, 2018.

Kreps, Daniel. "12 for One CD Deals No More: BMG Music Service Ends in June." March 10, 2009.

Leight, Elias. "What Will Billboard's New Streaming Rules Really Mean?" November 29, 2017.

Parker, Lyndsey. "Losing to Win: Remembering the Real Stars of 'Star Search.'" April 18, 2014.

Perpetua, Matthew. "Bids for EMI Much Lower than Expected." October 17, 2011.

Rolling Stone Staff. "Rolling Stone and Music Business Worldwide Enter Comprehensive New Deal." February 11, 2020.

Runtagh, Jordan. "Songs on Trial: 10 Landmark Music Copyright Cases." June 8, 2018.

Salon.com

Boehlert, Eric. "Payola City: In the Wild World of Urban Radio, Money Buys Hits—and Nobody Asks Questions." July 25, 2001.

San Francisco Chronicle

Evangelista, Berry. "Industry Starting to Endorse Net Music/Listen.com to Offer Songs from All Five Major Labels." July 1, 2002.

siriusxm.com

"SiriusXM Reports Fourth Quarter and Full Year 2020 Results." News release. February 2, 2021.

slate.com

Dayal, Geeta. "Is De La Soul's Long Fight to Release Its Music Digitally Finally Over—or Just Beginning?" February 25, 2012.

Hamilton, Jack. "Columbia House Offered Eight CDs for a Penny, but Its Life Lessons Were Priceless." August 12, 2015. Columbia House Bankrupt: Mail-order CD Club's Owner Finally Going Out of Business (slate.com).

Schwedel, Heather. "A Guide to TikTok for Anyone Who Isn't a Teen." September 4, 2018. A Guide to the App TikTok for Anyone Who Isn't a Teen (slate.com).

SonyUSA.com

Sony Connect. "Sony Connect Online Music Store Launches Today, Offering Music Fans More than 500,000 Legal Downloads from Major and Independent Record Labels Around the Globe." News release. May 4, 2004.

SoundExchange.com

SoundExchange. "SoundExchange Executive Director, John Simson to Leave by Year's End." News release. July 2, 2010.

South Florida Sun Sentinel
Weaver, Jay. "Melodic Merger." October 5, 1994.

Sports Business Journal
Mickle, Tripp. "WME Outlines Plan for IMG." April 14, 2014.

spotify.com
"Discover the Releases Rocking the World with Spotify's Weekly Music Charts." News release. October 5, 2020.

Statista.com/statistic
Statista Research Department. "Retail Sales of Printed Music in the U.S. 2005–2020." May 31, 2021.

StreamingMedia.com
Graves, Matt. "Listen.com Launches Rhapsody Digital Music Subscription Service." December 3, 2001.

The Sun Sentinel
Stieghorst, Tom. "SFX Pays $105m for Cellar Door." April 14, 1998.

synchtank.com
Alexander, Bryan. "'We're All in This Together': Garth Brooks, Trisha Yearwood Home Concert Crashes Facebook Live." March 23, 2020.
Forde, Eamonn. "A Metadata with Destiny: The Next Steps for Digital Music Information." December 7, 2020.
Forde, Eamonn. "That Was the Year That Was: Music Publishing In 2018." December 11, 2018.
Forde, Eamonn. "2020 X 20: The Themes That Defined a Blockbuster Year in Music Publishing Deals." December 18, 2020.
McFarland, Cestjon. "Could Sync Revenues Be About to Explode?" June 16, 2020.

techcrunch.com
Etherington, Darrell. "Charting the iTunes Store's Path to 25 Billion Songs Sold, 49 Billion Apps Downloaded and Beyond." February 6, 2013.
Perez, Sarah. "Spotify Settles the $1.6B Copyright Lawsuit Filed by Music Publisher Wixen." December 20, 2018.
Schonfeld, Erick. "Ticketmaster Buys Online Scalper TicketsNow for $265 Million." January 15, 2008.

Tedium.com
Smith, Ernie. "Lessons from the Music Industry's Initial Consumer-Hostile Reaction to the Napster Saga." January 30, 2018.

The Telegraph
Barnett, Emma. "Steve Jobs 'Single-handedly' Created the Digital Music Market." October 6, 2011.

Telegraph.co.uk
White, Dominic. "Nicoli Leaves EMI with a £1.65m Payoff." August 30, 2007.

thebalancecareers.com
McDonald, Heather. "Who Votes for the Grammy Awards? A Look Behind the Scenes of the Grammy Voting Process." November 12, 2018.

themusicnetwork.com
Murphy, Sam. "Why the Surprise Album Drop Is Falling in Popularity." September 29, 2019.

Wilson, Zanda. "How TikTok Became the New Music Tipsheet for Radio Programmers." May 11, 2020.

thenextweb.com
Ghoshal, Abhimanyu. "A Nostalgic Look Back at Digital Music Piracy in the 2000s." December 28, 2018.

TheRegister.com
Smith, Tony. "Ten Years Old: The World's First MP3 Player." March 10, 2008.

theticketingbusiness.com
The Ticketing Business Staff. "Live Nation Artist Management Division Soaring Despite Resale Link." February 28, 2017.

Ticketmaster.com
Ticketmaster. "Ticketmaster Historic Timeline." N.d. 2010.

Tiktok
TikTok. "The Year on TikTok." December 2, 2020.

Time
Greenfeld, Karl Taro. "Meet the Napster." October 2, 2000.
Gregory, Sean. "How Liquidators Profit from Circuit City's Loss." January 22, 2009.
Haire, Meaghan. "A Brief History of the Walkman." July 1, 2009.
Pickert, Kate. "A Brief History of Ticketmaster." February 11, 2009.
Sanburn, Josh. "5 Reasons Borders Went Out of Business (and What Will Take Its Place)." July 19, 2011.
White, Martha C. "Best Buy Is Done Selling CDs, but These Stores Haven't Abandoned Them (Yet)." July 3, 2018.

Ultimateclassicrock.com
Wawzenek, Bryan. "25 Years Ago: The SoundScan Era Rocks the Music Industry." May 25, 2016.
UniversalProductionMusic.com
Universal Music Production Music. "Our History." December 14, 2020.
University of North Dakota Law School
Johnson, Eric E. "The Record Industry Fails to Stop the MP3 Player." 2008.

Uproxx.com
Reiff, Corbin. "How Frank Barsalona Created the Modern Rock Concert and Got Himself into the Hall of Fame." January 30, 2017.

Urban Dictionary
Highway to Hell. "Rap/Hip-hop." October 5, 2009.

USA Today
Gundersen, Edna. "For Jackson, Scandal Could Spell Financial Ruin." November 24, 2003.
White, Jaquetta. "Touring Musicians Get New Road to Performance Royalties." April 12, 2013.
USC Gould School of LA
Music Copyright Infringement Resource. "Cases 1990–2017." 2017.

Uswitch.com
Uswitch. "History of Mobile Phones and the First Mobile Phone." February 21, 2019.

Variety
Aswad, Jem. "Grammy Awards Eliminate 'Secret' Nominating Committees." April 30, 2021. Grammy Awards Eliminate "Secret" Nominating Committees (variety.com).
Aswad, Jem. "Guns N' Roses, Eagles, Pearl Jam Took PPP Loans for Canceled Tours." July 7, 2020. Guns N' Roses, Eagles, Pearl Jam Took PPP Loans for Canceled Tours (yahoo.com).

Aswad, Jem. "Live Nation CEO Michael Rapino Gives Up Salary, Top Execs Take Pay Cuts as Company Tightens Belt." April 13, 2020. "Live Nation CEO Michael Rapino Gives Up Salary, Top Execs Take Pay Cuts as Company Tightens Belt." April 13, 2020. Google Search.

Aswad, Jem. "Oak View Group Acquires Pollstar." July 12, 2017. Oak View Group Acquires Pollstar (variety.com).

Aswad, Jem. "Recording Academy Invites 900 Women and Minorities to Join, Based on Task Force Findings." October 4, 2018. Recording Academy Invites 900 Women and Minorities to Join (variety.com).

Aswad, Jem. "Spotify to Launch HiFi Option Later This Year, Paid Out $5 Billion in Royalties in 2020." February 22, 2021. Aswad, Jem. "Spotify to Launch HiFi Option Later This Year, Paid Out $5 Billion in Royalties in 2020." February 22, 2021. Google Search.

Aswad, Jem. "Warner Music Group Sells Its Entire Stake in Spotify." August 7, 2018. Warner Music Group Sells Entire Stake in Spotify (variety.com).

Aswad, Jem. "Warner Music Valued at Nearly $15 Billion After IPO." June 3, 2020. "Warner Music Valued at Nearly $15 Billion After IPO." June 3, 2020. Google Search.

Aswad, Jem. "Warner to Launch Elektra Music Group as Standalone Company." June 18, 2018.

DiMartino, Dave. "Live Nation Leads the Charge in Concert Business' Booming Revenue." February 8, 2017. Live Nation Leads a Boom in the Concert Business (variety.com).

Halperin, Shirley. "Scooter Braun Sells Taylor Swift's Big Machine Masters for Big Payday." November 16, 2020. Scooter Braun Sells Taylor Swift's Big Machine Masters for Big Payday (variety.com).

Halperin, Shirley, and Jen Aswad. "Doug Morris to Exit Sony Music at the End of March." February 24, 2018. Doug Morris to Exit Sony Music at the End of March (variety.com).

Israelite, David. "5 Real Ways YouTube Can Fix Its Problems with the Music Industry." August 25, 2017. Ways YouTube Can Fix Its Problem with the Music Industry (Guest Post) (variety.com).

Maddaus, Gene. "DOJ Sides with Irving Azoff Against Radio Stations." December 6, 2019. DOJ Sides with Irving Azoff Against Radio Stations (variety.com).

Maddaus, Gene. "UFC Sale Revives Talk of WME-IMG IPO." July 19, 2016. UFC Sale Spurs WME/IMG IPO Talk (variety.com).

Maddaus, Gene. "WME-IMG to Receive $1.1 Billion Cash Infusion." August 2, 2017. WME-IMG to Receive $1.1 Billion Cash Infusion (variety.com).

Morris, Chris. "INgrooves Acquires Fontana Distribution." March 2, 2012. INgrooves Acquires Fontana Distribution (variety.com).

Parisi, Paula. "Production Music Is a Billion-Dollar Business." September 18, 2017. Production Music Is a Billion-Dollar Business: Trade Group Study (variety.com).

Sandler, Adam. "EMI Acquires Windswept." July 29, 1999. EMI Acquires Windswept (variety.com).

Sandler, Adam. "SFX Nabs Top Promoters—Deal Creates One of Industry's Largest Outfits." December 14, 1997. SFX Nabs Top Promoters (variety.com).

Spangler, Todd. "iHeartMedia to Buy *HowStuffWorks* Podcasting Parent for $55 Million." September 13, 2018. iHeartMedia Acquires HowStuffWorks Podcast Parent for $55 Million (variety.com).

Spangler, Todd. "Spotify Debuts 'Vodcasts': Launches First Set of Video Podcasts." July 21, 2020. Spotify Launches First Video Podcasts Worldwide (variety.com).

Steinberg, Brian. "CBS Gears Up for Million-Dollar Ads at the Grammys." January 26, 2018. CBS Gears Up for Million-Dollar Ads at the Grammys (variety.com).

Variety Staff. "Dan McCarroll, Former President of Warner Bros. Records, Joins Amazon." February 20, 2018. Dan McCarroll, Former President of Warner Bros. Records, Joins Amazon (variety.com).

Variety Staff. "Killer Tracks Rebrands as Universal Production Music." September 12, 2019. Killer Tracks Rebrands as Universal Production Music (variety.com).

Variety Staff. "Realsongs Big in Pub Business, Warren Created Company to House Her 800-plus Songs." January 20, 2000. Realsongs Big in Pub Business (variety.com).

Venues Today

Deckard, Linda. "Oak View Group Acquires Pollstar." July 12, 2017.

Verizon Wireless Archives

Verizon Wireless. "Music for All: The Next Evolution of V CAST Music from Verizon Wireless." News release. July 31, 2006.

Wall Street Journal

Schuker, Lauren A. E. "Hollywood's CAA Sells Stake to TPG." October 4, 2010.

Steele, Anne. "Apple Music Reveals How Much It Pays When You Stream a Song." April 16, 2021.

Stynes, Tess. "Live Nation Buys Artist Agency." February 7, 2011.

Walmart

"Garth Brooks: The Lost Sessions CD Released." News release. January 6, 2006.

Warner Chappell PM

Warner Chappell Production Music. "Our Story." December 14, 2020.

Washington Post

Harrington, Richard. "A Concert Promoter Out to Steal the Show?" August 28, 1998. A Concert Promoter Out to Steal the Show? *The Washington Post*.

Harrington, Richard. "RIP: The CD Longbox." April 7, 1993. RIP: The CD Longbox. *The Washington Post*.

Yahr, Emily. "New Year's Eve Countdown Specials 2021: Where to Watch and Who Has the Best Celebrity Guests." December 31, 2020. New Year's Eve Countdown Specials 2021: Where to Watch Online and on TV, Best Celebrity Performers, *The Washington Post*.

whatisthebusinessmodelof.com

whatisthebusinessmodelof.com Staff. "Fortnite Business Model: How Fortnite Makes Money." February 1, 2022. Fortnite Business Model: How Fortnite Makes Money (whatisthebusinessmodelof.com).

whatisthebusinessmodelof.com Staff. "TikTok Business Model Case Study." November 12, 2021. TikTok Business Model: How TikTok Makes Money (whatisthebusinessmodelof.com).

Wired

Chen, Brian X. "Apple Opens iTunes Store." April 28, 2003.

Gray, Kevin. "Kobalt Changed the Rules of the Music Industry Using Data—and Saved It." May 1, 2015.

Jossi, Frank. "Internet Creates a Radio Star." March 1, 1996.

Kravets, David. "Copyright Lawsuits Plummet in Aftermath of RIAA Campaign." May 18, 2010.

Long, Tony. "Now Hear This . . . the iPod Arrives." October 23, 2008.

Reuters Business. "CDNow: Now Is the Time." March 18, 1999.

Sorrel, Charlie. "Gallery of Gadgets Which Inspired Modern Day Tech." May 13, 2011.

Sorrel, Charlie. "Spotify Launches in the U.S. at Last." July 14, 2011.

Sullivan, Jennifer. "Grammy Gives MP3 the Boot." February 19, 1999.

Van Buskirk, Eliot. "Sweet: Pandora's Streaming Radio App for iPhone." July 10, 2008.

Wired.com Security. "Feds Crack 'Rabid Neurosis' Pre-Release Piracy Group." September 9, 2009.

wmg.com

"Warner-Chappell Music Acquires Renowned Production Company 615 Music." News release. December 10, 2010.

"Warner Music Group Corp. Announces Pricing of Initial Public Offering." News release. June 2, 2020.

The Wrap

Charlton, Jordan. "Guggenheim Media Spins Off Money-Losing Hollywood Reporter, Billboard to Company President Todd Boehly." December 17, 2015.

Ellefson, Lindsey. "Variety Parent Penske Media to Take Over Hollywood Reporter, Billboard in Joint Venture With MRC." September 23, 2020.

Waxman, Sharon. "Inside Guggenheim's Plans for THR, Billboard—a Cable Channel (Exclusive)." January 14, 2014.

ZDNet.com

Gomes, Lee. "Napster Investors Stand to Prosper." November 2, 2000. Napster Investors Stand to Prosper. ZDNET.

Index

For the benefit of digital users, indexed terms that span two pages (e.g., 52–53) may, on occasion, appear on only one of those pages.